HENRY VII'S NEW MEN A
OF TUDOR EN

Henry VII's New Men and the Making of Tudor England

STEVEN GUNN

OXFORD
UNIVERSITY PRESS

OXFORD

UNIVERSITY PRESS

Great Clarendon Street, Oxford, OX2 6DP,
United Kingdom

Oxford University Press is a department of the University of Oxford.
It furthers the University's objective of excellence in research, scholarship,
and education by publishing worldwide. Oxford is a registered trade mark of
Oxford University Press in the UK and in certain other countries

© Steven Gunn 2016

The moral rights of the author have been asserted

First Edition published in 2016

Impression: 1

Published in the United States of America by Oxford University Press
198 Madison Avenue, New York, NY 10016, United States of America

British Library Cataloguing in Publication Data
Data available

Library of Congress Control Number: 2016933518

ISBN 978–0–19–965983–8

Printed in Great Britain by
Clays Ltd, St Ives plc

For my daughters, Sarah and Eleanor

Acknowledgements

This book has been an unconscionable time in the making. It originated in the project I proposed to pursue when applying for junior research fellowships in 1985, it was trailed in a footnote in my first book in 1988, and parts of it have been appearing in articles since 1990. Conceived five hundred years after Henry VII's accession, it has taken seven years longer to write than he did to reign. I have incurred many debts of gratitude along the way.

I have benefited from many discussions with the small but international band of scholars who study Henry, notably Paul Cavill, Margaret Condon, Sean Cunningham, John Currin, Ralph Griffiths, David Grummitt, Sam Harper, Mark Horowitz, Michael K. Jones, Tom Penn, and James Ross. For references to sources and other advice I am grateful to George Bernard, Tom Carter, Kirsten Claiden-Yardley, James Clark, Alasdair Hawkyard, Anita Hewerdine, Richard Hoyle, Michael C. E. Jones, James McComish, Malcolm Mercer, Stuart Minson, Robert Peberdy, Tracey Sowerby, Tim Thornton, Ann Weikel, and Margaret Yates. Susan Brigden, Nicholas Orme, and John Watts read drafts of some chapters and provided helpful comments and John in particular has shared thought-provoking discussion about the end of the Middle Ages over many years. Ian Archer, Alex Gajda, and Martin Ingram, together with all the participants in our Early Modern Britain seminar, have generated intellectual stimulation and support. My tutorial colleagues at Merton, Philip Waller, Robert Gildea, Karl Gerth, Matthew Grimley, and Micah Muscolino, have been models in their different ways both of good historical practice and of collegial friendship. Cliff Davies has been a constant source of encouragement and ideas since he first commented, as my doctoral supervisor, on my plans for a post-doctoral project. Rhys Robinson, always a generous guide to the history of Tudor Wales, kindly bequeathed to me his impressive collection of books on Tudor history.

I am grateful to Major Richard Coke and Dr Jacques Beauroy for their help with the Weasenham Hall muniments, to Professor Sir John Baker for help with those of St Catharine's College, Cambridge, and to the staffs of the many archives and libraries in which I have worked for their patient assistance. Jill Gascoigne transcribed Edmund Dudley's accounts for me and David Ashton searched some king's bench files. I am grateful to His Grace the duke of Rutland for access to the Belvoir Castle archives, to His Grace the duke of Northumberland for access to those at Alnwick Castle, to the Marquess of Bath for access to those at Longleat and to the Dean and Canons of Windsor for access to those at Windsor. Sir Robert Worcester kindly showed me his home at Allington Castle and shared with me his work on its history.

I have been fortunate to spend my academic life to date in only two institutions, Merton College, Oxford, and the University of Newcastle upon Tyne, and both have supported my research generously, as did the Huntington Library with a visiting research fellowship in 1996. Many schools and Historical Association groups provided hospitality for trips to archives in return for lectures. At Oxford University Press, Robert Faber, Cathryn Steele, Stephanie Ireland, Rupert Cousens, Ela Kotkowska, and several anonymous readers have each contributed in different valuable ways to shaping this book. My wife has provided cheerful encouragement and loving support throughout its long gestation, as have my parents and parents-in-law. My daughters, to whom the book is dedicated, have grown up with it. I hope it has not distracted me too much from the more important and pleasurable matter of spending time with them.

In quotations from primary documents I have modernized spelling at the suggestion of one of the publisher's readers. There is a loss of fidelity in this, but also a gain in immediacy; and I hope that making this explicit will allay suspicion that I have employed sleight of hand to make the new men speak to us more directly. Perhaps I deceive myself in thinking that their careers carry sufficient fascination to make such trickery unnecessary.

Contents

NEW MEN

SERVICE

POWER

WEALTH

SURVIVAL

List of figures

List of genealogical tables

List of abbreviations

AC	*Archaeologia Cantiana*
Addl. Ch.	Additional Charter
Addl. MS	Additional manuscript
ADN	Archives Départementales du Nord, Lille
App.	Appendix
AHPV	*The Anglica Historia of Polydore Vergil AD 1485–1537*, ed. D. Hay, CS, 3rd ser. 74 (London, 1950)
BCL	Birmingham Central Library
BI	Borthwick Institute, York
BIHR	*Bulletin of the Institute of Historical Research*
BLARS	Bedfordshire and Luton Archives and Records Service
CA	College of Arms
CBS	Centre for Buckinghamshire Studies
CAD	*A Descriptive Catalogue of Ancient Deeds in the Public Record Office,* 6 vols (London, 1890–1915)
CCA	Canterbury Cathedral Archives
CCR*	*Calendar of Close Rolls*
CEPR*	*Calendar of Entries in the Papal Registers relating to Great Britain and Ireland*, ed. W. H. Bliss et al., 19 vols to date (London and Dublin, 1893–)
CFR	*Calendar of the Fine Rolls preserved in the Public Record Office, Henry VII* (London, 1962)
CIPM	*Calendar of Inquisitions Post Mortem, Henry VII*, 3 vols (London, 1898–1955).*
CP	G. E. Cokayne, *The Complete Peerage*, ed. V. Gibbs et al., 13 vols (London, 1910–59)
CPR	*Calendar of Patent Rolls*
CS	Camden Society
CSPM	*Calendar of State Papers and Manuscripts in the Archives and Collections of Milan 1385–1618*, ed. A. B. Hinds (London, 1912)
CSPS	*Calendar of Letters, Despatches, and State Papers, relating to the Negotiations between England and Spain, Preserved in the Archives at Simancas and Elsewhere*, ed. G. Bergenroth et al., 13 vols (London, 1862–1954)
CSPV	*Calendar of State Papers and Manuscripts, Relating to English Affairs, Existing in the Archives and Collections of Venice and other Libraries of Northern Italy, 1534–1554*, ed. R. Brown (London, 1873)
CYS	Canterbury and York Society
d	penny
DCRO	Duchy of Cornwall Record Office
EETS	Early English Text Society
ESRO	East Sussex Record Office
ERO	Essex Record Office
EHR	*English Historical Review*

fo./fos.	folio/s
HJ	*Historical Journal*
HKW	H. M. Colvin (ed.), *The History of the King's Works*, 6 vols (London, 1963–82)
HL	Huntington Library, San Marino, CA
HMC	Historical Manuscripts Commission
HMC Rutland	*The Manuscripts of His Grace, the Duke of Rutland, G.C.B., preserved at Belvoir Castle*, 4 vols, HMC 24 (London, 1888–1908)
HR	*Historical Research*
HS	Harleian Society
JRL	John Rylands Library, Manchester
KHLC	Kent History and Library Centre, Maidstone
KUL	Keele University Library
LA	Lincolnshire Archives
LJ	*Journals of the House of Lords*, 10 vols (London, 1846 edn)
LJRO	Lichfield Joint Record Office
LMA	London Metropolitan Archives
*LP**	*Letters and Papers, Foreign and Domestic, of the Reign of Henry VIII*, ed. J. S. Brewer et al., 23 vols in 38 (London, 1862–1932)
LPL	Lambeth Palace Library
LPRH	*Letters and Papers illustrative of the Reigns of Richard III and Henry VII*, ed. J. Gairdner, 2 vols, Rolls Ser. 24 (London, 1861–3)
Materials	*Materials for a History of the Reign of Henry VII*, ed. W. Campbell, 2 vols, Rolls Ser. 60 (London, 1873–7)
Memorials	*Memorials of King Henry VII*, ed. J. Gairdner, Rolls Ser. 10 (London, 1858)
NA	*Norfolk Archaeology*
NRO	Norfolk Record Office
NRA	National Register of Archives ('NRA report' indicates documents I have not seen in the original)
n.s.	new series
NUL	Nottingham University Library
ODNB	*Oxford Dictionary of National Biography*, ed. H. C. G. Matthew, B. Harrison, 60 vols (Oxford, 2004)
OHC	Oxfordshire History Centre
OHS	Oxford Historical Society
ORS	Oxfordshire Record Society
o.s.	old series
PML	Pierpoint Morgan Library, New York
PRO	The National Archives: Public Record Office
PROME	*The Parliament Rolls of Medieval England, 1275–1504*, ed. C. Given-Wilson (Woodbridge and London, 2005)
RCHM	Royal Commission on Historical Monuments
REED	*Records of Early English Drama*
RS	Record Society
s	shilling
SCC	*Select Cases in the Council of Henry VII*, ed. C. G. Bayne, W. H. Dunham, SS 75 (London, 1958)

ser.	series
SHC	Surrey History Centre
SROB	Suffolk Record Office, Bury St Edmunds
SROI	Suffolk Record Office, Ipswich
SS	Selden Society
StP	*State Papers, King Henry the Eighth*, 5 vols in 11 (London, 1830–52)
TBPV	*Three Books of Polydore Vergil's English History, Comprising the Reigns of Henry VI, Edward IV, and Richard III*, ed. H. Ellis, CS o.s. 29 (London, 1844)
TEAS	*Transactions of the Essex Archaeological Society*
TRHS	Transactions of the Royal Historical Society
TRP*	*Tudor Royal Proclamations*, ed. P. L. Hughes, J. F. Larkin, 3 vols (New Haven CT and London, 1964)
VCH	*Victoria County History*
VE	*Valor Ecclesiasticus*, ed. H. Caley, 6 vols (London, 1810–33)
WAM	Westminster Abbey Muniments
WSHC	Wiltshire and Swindon History Centre
WSRO	West Sussex Record Office
YAS	Yorkshire Archaeological Society
YASRS	Yorkshire Archaeological Society Record Series

* References in these sources are usually made to document number, rather than to pages.

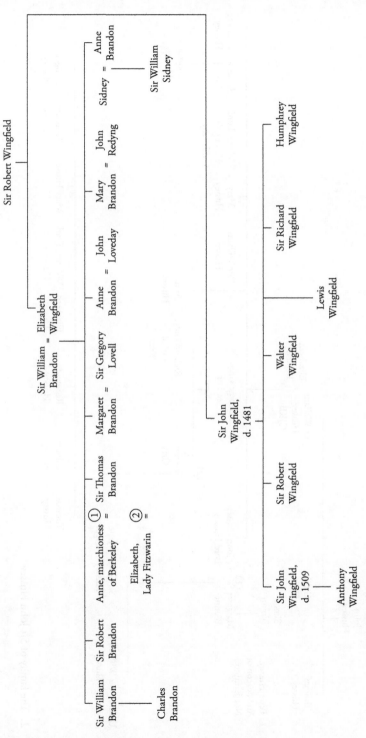

1. The family of Sir Thomas Brandon

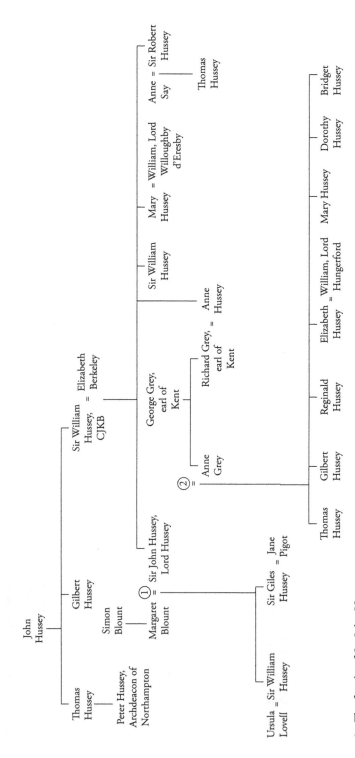

2. The family of Sir John Hussey

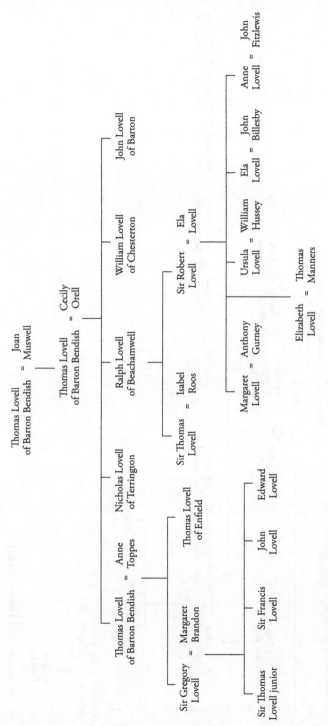

3. The family of Sir Thomas Lovell

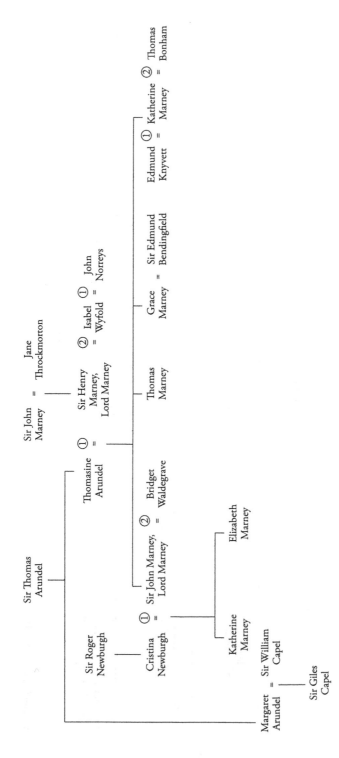

4. The family of Sir Henry Marney

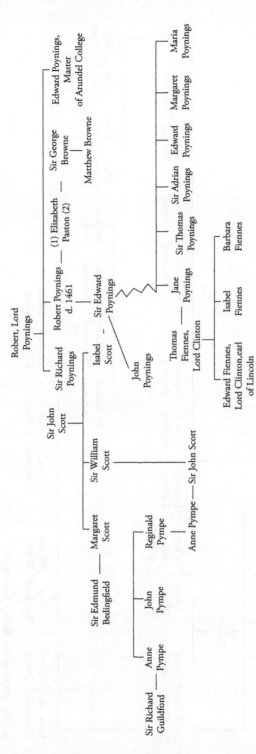

5. The family of Sir Edward Poynings

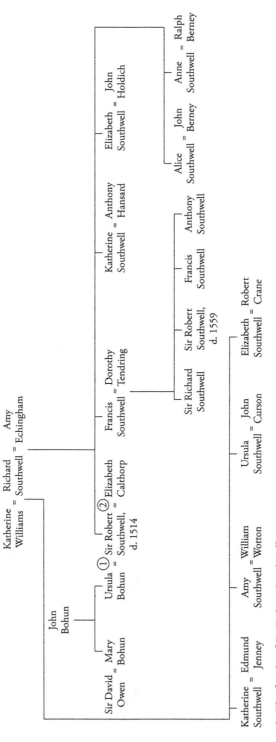

6. The family of Sir Robert Southwell

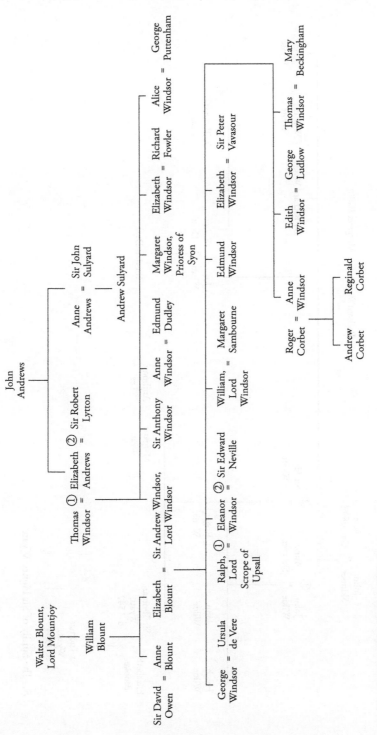

7. The family of Sir Andrew Windsor

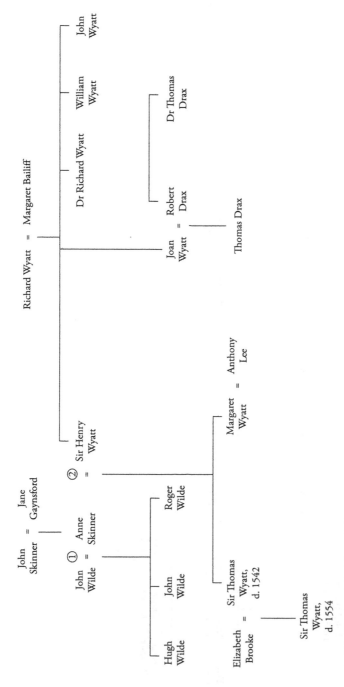

8. The family of Sir Henry Wyatt

NEW MEN

1

Caitiffs and villains of simple birth

In summer 1497 Perkin Warbeck prepared to invade England from Scotland, claiming the throne on the basis that he was Richard, duke of York, one of the long-lost Princes in the Tower. To prepare the way, he issued a bitter indictment of his rival, King Henry VII. His charges ran from judicial murder and extortionate taxation to breach of the church's liberties; but prominent among them was that Henry, 'putting apart all well disposed nobles', had 'none in favour and trust about his person' but 'caitiffs and villains of simple birth', men who had been 'the principal finders, occasioners and counsellors of the misrule and mischief now reigning in England'.[1]

The accusation was unoriginal. In 1450 Jack Cade's rebels had denounced the 'mean persons of lower nature exalted and made chief of privy counsel'. In 1460 the commons of Kent blamed the 'false brought up of nought ... persons daily and nightly about his highness' for the failings of Henry VI's government. In 1536 the Pilgrims of Grace would say much the same about the ministers of Henry VIII.[2] But in 1497 the charge hit home. Warbeck named names, nineteen of them. A few were bishops, like the successive royal secretaries, Richard Fox and Oliver King. A few were courtiers and captains, like the king's bastard relatives, Charles Somerset and David Owen, or the commanders Warbeck had lately faced across the Scottish border, Richard Cholmondely, Thomas Garth, and William Tyler. Most, however, came from the distinctive group of lawyers and administrators at the heart of Henry VII's regime: Bray, Lovell, Risley, Litton, Guildford, Empson, Hobart, Cutt, Hussey, and Wyatt, as they appeared, in rough order of political prominence, in Warbeck's damning litany.

The charge made sense to contemporaries. A London chronicle noted matter-of-factly that Bray and Lovell, blamed for high taxes, were among those the rebels of 1497 'intended to have removed from the king'. Between them these men served Henry in a bewildering array of offices, fiscal, legal, and domestic. They held posts in the exchequer, the chamber, the duchy of Lancaster, and the royal mint; as the king's legal counsel; in the household, the wardrobe, and the jewel house. But there was more to it than that, as Warbeck knew. These were men close to the king, trusted, influential, so much

---

[1] *The Reign of Henry VII from Original Sources*, ed. A. F. Pollard, 3 vols (London, 1913–14), i. 150–5.
[2] *The Politics of Fifteenth-Century England: John Vale's Book*, ed. M. L. Kekewich et al. (Stroud, 1995), 204, 210; A. Fletcher, D. N. J. MacCulloch, *Tudor Rebellions* (4th edn, London, 1997), 131.

so that, as it was said of a later recruit to the group, Edmund Dudley, 'he had such authority that the chief lords of England were glad to be in his favour'.[3]

KING HENRY

In 1497 Henry had been king for twelve years. He had won the throne on 22 August 1485, killing Richard III at the battle of Bosworth. Few would have bet on his success either before or after that fateful day.[4] When he was born in 1457 his father was already dead, and the first blows had lately been struck in what would prove to be thirty years of intermittent civil war. He had too much royal blood to avoid high politics, but scant enough to claim the throne. His father, Edmund Tudor, earl of Richmond, was half-brother to the Lancastrian king Henry VI, but through their mother, Catherine of Valois, daughter of Charles VI of France, rather than through the English royal line. His mother, Margaret Beaufort, was great-great-granddaughter of King Edward III, but through the legitimized Beaufort descendants of John of Gaunt by his mistress, rather than the main Lancastrian lineage. He would have come nowhere near the crown were it not for the royal blood-letting of the Wars of the Roses.

Historians have, naturally, debated why one of the strongest monarchies in Christendom, able under Edward III and Henry V to conquer swathes of France and to impose justice, taxation, and royal power over the church more effectively than most other regimes of the time, should have collapsed in the mid-fifteenth century. Naturally, they have disagreed. Some stress adverse circumstances: deep economic depression; defeat after defeat in France until only Calais remained English; the elaboration of 'bastard feudal' ties between great noblemen and their followers that escalated disputes up and down the social scale and gave ambitious magnates the means to corrupt royal government and confront the king. Others stress dynastic rivalry and the righting of wrongs: the Lancastrians had taken power in 1399 by deposing Richard II, a controversial but indisputably rightful king, and the Yorkists, bearers of two blood-lines of descent from Edward III, might credibly claim to have more right to rule than their cousins. Others again stress the awful incapacity of Henry VI in a system dependent on the active exercise of an independent royal will at the heart of government. King from the age of eight months, he survived his minority but never grew into the demands of adult kingship. Unable to lead in war, resolve disputes, or distribute reward with the deftness needed to allay rather than inflame factionalism, he ruled disastrously.

All three explanations are right in their way. Henry's failings made the worst of the circumstances and the dynastic rivalry presented a drastic but appealing

---

[3] *The Great Chronicle of London*, ed. A. H. Thomas, I. D. Thornley (London, 1938), 278, 348.
[4] For what follows, see S. J. Gunn, 'Henry VII', *ODNB*; S. Cunningham, *Henry VII* (London, 2007); C. Carpenter, *The Wars of the Roses: Politics and the Constitution in England, c.1437–1509* (Cambridge, 1997).

solution, his replacement in 1461 by Edward of York as Edward IV. Diehard Lancastrians and disaffected Yorkists combined to restore Henry VI in 1470, but in 1471 Edward returned from exile and re-established his rule on a firmer basis. Meanwhile, Henry Tudor was growing up, first under the control of a trusted Yorkist lord, William Herbert; in 1470–1, mostly with his uncle, Jasper Tudor, earl of Pembroke; and then in long exile at the court of the duke of Brittany. It was Edward IV's sudden death in 1483 and the renewed rupture in the Yorkist regime, as Richard III, Edward's brother, pushed aside Edward V, Edward's son, that gave Henry his chance. One revolt against Richard failed, but the survivors joined Henry in exile, where he promised them that he would marry Elizabeth of York, Edward IV's daughter, if they could place him on the throne. Borrowing money to hire French troops, writing ahead to stir up support, hoping to inspire Welsh loyalties with Henry's Tudor ancestry, they sailed for Pembrokeshire. A long campaign, a nerve-wracking wait for supporters to break cover, hard fighting at Bosworth and last-minute defections from Richard's forces brought victory. But stability was hard to find.

Henry duly married Elizabeth, and in 1486 they had a son, Arthur; but Yorkist resistance persisted. In 1486 there were risings in Yorkshire and the Midlands led by Viscount Lovell and Humphrey Stafford. In 1487 a major invasion brought Lambert Simnel, who had been crowned Edward VI in Dublin on the pretence that he was Edward, earl of Warwick, nephew of Edward IV and Richard III, to Nottinghamshire, where Henry defeated him at Stoke. In 1489 Henry's taxes prompted revolt in Yorkshire, and in 1497 the same happened in the south-west, generating the uproar on which Warbeck, the latest Yorkist claimant, was seeking to capitalize when he issued his manifesto against Henry and his new men. In 1497 Henry survived again, beating the rebels at Blackheath and marching into the South-West, where Warbeck was captured. But rest continued to elude him. In hunting out Warbeck's supporters he had had to destroy two of his leading household officers, Sir William Stanley and John, Lord Fitzwalter. Amid wars and complex diplomatic realignments in France, Italy, and the Netherlands, English interests, strategic and commercial, had to be asserted without stimulating foreign support for pretenders. More Yorkist challengers arose, and between 1500 and 1503 death robbed him of two sons, Arthur and Edmund, and of his wife, Elizabeth of York. Henry's rule became brooding and suspicious as he manipulated the political nation into submission to his authority and compliance with the succession of his remaining son, the future Henry VIII.

Repeated crises and a slide towards tyranny, then, were characteristics of Henry's rule, but they were not the whole story. Henry and those around him saw that recovery from civil war would not be achieved merely by the repression of opposition and the elimination of rival claims to the crown. Good governance was required: effective justice, fiscal prudence, national defence, fitting royal magnificence, and the promotion of the common weal. More controversial or painful change might be needed to entrench good governance: perhaps a re-balancing of the local power of great noblemen and that of lesser men more beholden to the king, or a centralization of justice at the cost of local autonomy, or an elaboration of the king's means to tap his subjects' wealth, or a lessening of the church's independence from crown control. All these Henry and his advisers worked towards in different ways and at various times in the reign, sometimes building on initiatives taken by Edward IV or even earlier kings. It may be that their vigour sometimes stoked unrest or built support for challengers to his rule. But in the long run their efforts made his government of England and that of his successors more ambitious and more powerful than any that had gone before.

THE STORY SO FAR

Historians have long recognized that Henry's advisers were different from those of earlier English kings. Francis Bacon, writing in the 1620s, crisply anticipated modern debate on the peculiarities, strengths, and weaknesses of Henry's kingship by arguing that

> He kept a strait hand on his nobility, and chose rather to advance clergymen and lawyers, which were more obsequious to him but had less interest in the people; which made for his absoluteness, but not for his safety.[5]

By 1917, when Gladys Temperley wrote her biography of the king, the language of historical analysis had changed, but the basic picture had not. Henry chose 'middle-class ministers' from a 'new official class', 'men of comparatively obscure birth, who owed everything to the king and had no traditions of aristocratic independence behind them'. Like Bacon, she noted the role of churchmen among them, men who 'obtained the dignity necessary for their exalted office by holding high ecclesiastical rank', but she was more struck by the laymen who paved the way for the 'new nobility' of the sixteenth century.[6] In 1950, S. T. Bindoff could summarize nearly four centuries of consensus. True, Henry took counsel from men of talent who had risen through both royal service and the church hierarchy, and this gave his regime 'a medieval air'. Richard Fox or John Morton roughly fitted the pattern of earlier political bishops of commoner stock, William Wykeham, Simon Sudbury, or Henry Chichele. More novel were the lowly born laymen:

> In place of the great nobles who had previously dominated the council, Henry drew his leading counsellors from men of lower rank and smaller fortune...Henry's dependence upon these 'new men', who in turn were wholly dependent upon him for their position and prospects, has long since become a commonplace in the appraisal of his government.[7]

Like many commonplaces, it perhaps seemed too obvious to warrant further investigation, though S. B. Chrimes in his standard biography of Henry noted how the importance and versatility of Bray, Guildford, Lovell, and Risley among the

[5] Francis Bacon, *The History of the Reign of King Henry VII and Selected Works*, ed. B. Vickers (Cambridge, 1998), 201.
[6] G. Temperley, *Henry VII* (London, 1917), 248.
[7] S. T. Bindoff, *Tudor England* (Harmondsworth, 1950), 59–60.

inner ring of councillors merited 'a far more detailed study than has yet been accorded to them'.[8] Only three scholars in the twentieth century sought to explore in depth what the new men did and how they did it, and my debt to their work will be evident. D. M. Brodie led the way with an article on Edmund Dudley. She characterized him as one of the 'strong, vigorous personalities' who took charge of England's destiny in the 'formative period' of the 'modern state'; she carefully set the ideas of his treatise, the *Tree of Commonwealth*, of which she subsequently produced an edition, in the context of his career and of Henry VII's policies.[9] Margaret Condon followed. First in a brief but sweeping study of the change in England's ruling elites in the course of Henry's reign, then in an exhaustive examination of Sir Reynold Bray's fortune, she showed how the new men fitted into Henry's regime and how the mightiest of them made his power pay.[10] Then Mark Horowitz, first in a study of Sir Richard Empson's career, then in detailed analyses of Empson's and Dudley's exactions in London and beyond, showed how Empson's slower rise through royal service took him to the influential position from which, by the end of the reign, he and Dudley enforced the king's claims over his subjects to the point of injustice.[11]

Bray was the first and greatest of the new men. He was the second son of a surgeon—a blood-letter and bone-setter, not a university graduate in medicine, though by the 1540s some claimed he had been Henry VI's physician—from Bedwardine in Worcestershire. For twenty years he served as an estate officer for Henry VII's mother, Lady Margaret Beaufort, and her successive husbands. A leading role in the conspiracies of 1483–5 that brought Henry to the throne won him the confidence both of the new king and of his fellow-conspirators, men who rose to high office in Henry's regime such as John Morton and Sir Giles Daubeney. His skills in estate management and financial supervision were immediately called into play as chancellor of the duchy of Lancaster and he even served as a stopgap lord treasurer for four months in 1486. As the reign went on, he accumulated a wide range of other offices and established himself as the coordinator of the king's financial policies and of the enforcement of the king's rights through the council learned in the law. His surviving correspondence, patchy though it is, confirms the range of his contacts and the depth of his influence. His death in 1503 necessitated significant restructuring in the fiscal side of government.[12]

---

[8] S. B. Chrimes, *Henry VII* (London, 1972), 109–10.

[9] D. M. Brodie, 'Edmund Dudley: Minister of Henry VII', *TRHS* 4th ser. 15 (1932), 133–61; Edmund Dudley, *The Tree of Commonwealth*, ed. D. M. Brodie (Cambridge, 1948).

[10] M. M. Condon, 'Ruling Elites in the reign of Henry VII', in C. D. Ross (ed.), *Patronage, Pedigree and Power in Later Medieval England* (Gloucester, 1979), 109–42; M. M. Condon, 'From Caitiff and Villain to *Pater Patriae*: Reynold Bray and the Profits of Office', in M. A. Hicks (ed.), *Profit, Piety and the Professions in later Medieval England* (Gloucester, 1990), 136–68.

[11] M. R. Horowitz, 'Richard Empson, Minister of Henry VII', *BIHR* 55 (1982), 35–49; M. R. Horowitz, '"Agree with the King": Henry VII, Edmund Dudley and the Strange Case of Thomas Sunnyff', *HR* 79 (2005), 325–66; M. R. Horowitz, 'Policy and Prosecution in the reign of Henry VII', *HR* 82 (2009), 412–58; M. R. Horowitz, '"Contrary to the Liberties of this City": Henry VII, English Towns and the Economics of Law and Order', *HR* 85 (2012), 32–56.

[12] M. M. Condon, 'Bray, Sir Reynold [Reginald]', *ODNB*; O. Barron, 'The Brays of Shere', *The Ancestor*, 6 (1903), 2–3; John Leland, *The Itinerary of John Leland in or about the Years 1535–1543*, ed. L. T. Smith, 5 vols (London, 1906–10), v. 229; WAM 16016–80.

Among the beneficiaries of that reorganization were Empson and Dudley. Empson's father was a minor property-owner in Towcester, in Northamptonshire, rich enough to pay for his son's legal education, but not much more. The training paid off when Richard secured appointment as attorney-general to the duchy of Lancaster in 1478. Fortunately, as it turned out, he was sacked by Richard III, and thus available for re-appointment under Henry VII, when he soon attached himself to Bray. Steadily he bought up lands, collected local offices and worked his way up through the duchy hierarchy to the pinnacle of the chancellorship. From there he led the council learned in the law as Bray had done, ferreting out offences by the landed classes and taking bonds for payment of the resulting fines.[13]

Alongside Empson worked Dudley, a younger and more flamboyant figure.[14] He was of higher descent than most of the new men, his grandfather a baron, his uncle bishop of Durham. But his father was a younger son, who had married a minor heiress for her half-share in four manors in Hampshire and the Isle of Wight and made a career in the service of the Fitzalan earls of Arundel. In the 1490s, Edmund was a rising Gray's Inn lawyer. He was marked out both by his sharp readings on the statutes, including the first known reading on *quo warranto*, the procedure by which the crown challenged private jurisdictions, and by his compelling contributions to the debates on other readings.[15] From 1496 to 1502, he administered justice in the London courts as under-sheriff and in 1503 he was about to take the next step up the legal ladder with appointment as a serjeant-at-law, normally the prelude to nomination as a judge, when he changed course. Early in 1504 he presided as speaker of the commons over the testy debates of Henry's last parliament; from October 1504 he was retained as a full-time royal councillor with a fee of £66 13s 4d, probably more lucrative than his landed inheritance; and by July 1506 he was president of the king's council.[16] Already in September 1504 he had begun to make entries in the account books that would be the lasting proof of his efficiency in extracting money from his subjects for the king.

In less than four years Dudley collected some £219,316 6s 11d in cash and bonds for future payment, equivalent to nearly two years' worth of royal income from more regular sources such as the crown lands and the customs.[17] He raised this money on a remarkable range of pretexts, including the sale of offices and wardships, fines on clergymen for the confirmation of their estates or escapes from their prisons, and pardons for a galaxy of offences. In the process, he upset almost every influential constituency in Henry VII's England, from noblemen through bishops to the London merchants he pursued for customs evasion. When the king died in the night of 21–2 April 1509, he and Empson were rapidly arrested,

---

[13] Horowitz, 'Empson', 35–49; M. M. Condon, 'Empson, Sir Richard ', *ODNB*.

[14] S. J. Gunn, 'Dudley, Edmund', *ODNB*; Dudley, *Tree*, 1–11; N. Saul, 'The Cuckoo in the Nest: A Dallingridge Tomb in the Fitzalan Chapel at Arundel', *Sussex Archaeological Collections* 147 (2009), 128–32.

[15] *Readings and Moots at the Inns of Court*, ed. S. E. Thorne and J. H. Baker, 2 vols, SS 71, 105 (London, 1952, 1989), ii. pp. lxix, lxxxi–lxxxv, c–cii; *John Spelman's Reading on Quo Warranto*, ed. J. H. Baker, SS 113 (London, 1997), xviii.

[16] *CIPM*, iii. 489; PRO, SC6/HenVIII/6217.   [17] HL, MS El. 1518.

charged with rather improbable treasons against the new regime, and conveniently blamed for all their late master's extortions. It did them little good either that it had been Henry who had designed the exploitative policy of which they were the agents or that, as Dudley pointed out in a petition he wrote from the Tower, some of the largest fines they had negotiated were not even intended to be paid, but to hang over the heads of leading subjects to compel their loyalty, Henry wishing to keep 'many persons in his danger at his pleasure'.[18] Empson and Dudley were cast as the archetypal low-born men on the make, contrasted even with Bray who was unpopular and 'plain and rough in speech' but at least a dependable patron, whereas they—Dudley the star lawyer in particular—were smooth-talking deceivers, men who could 'speak pleasantly and do overthwartly'.[19] They were tried, convicted, and left to stew in prison. In August 1510, after the king's progress exposed him to a new wave of grumbling about their depredations, they met their end on the block.[20]

A WIDER CIRCLE

Bray, Empson, and Dudley tell us a lot about the functions and fortunes of Henry's new men. Yet to know the new men properly, we must get beyond this triumvirate. None of them survived beyond 1509, so we cannot use them to see whether the group's influence outlasted their master's death. Bray, and even more so Empson, were closely bound up with the duchy of Lancaster, and Dudley's career floated rather free of fiscal and legal institutions, so there are many parts of Henry's governmental machinery into which they cannot take us. None of them had major military or diplomatic responsibilities or much of a role at court. Bray had deeper roots in the service of Henry's family than any other councillor; Empson, with his years of work for the Yorkists, rose more slowly than anyone else; Dudley rose faster than anyone else, and more disruptively. There are signs, too, that Empson's and Dudley's political bonds with one another were strong—just as they had each apparently been promoted by Bray—but that they were less close to others who fared better in 1509. Indeed, that isolation may help to explain why it was they who were selected for sacrifice.[21]

Sir Thomas Lovell's career is a useful corrective. Born around 1449, he was perhaps a decade younger than Bray, of an age with Empson and a dozen years older than Dudley. His father, Ralph, was an aggressive younger son from a minor Norfolk gentry family. Thomas's grandfather and uncle were lords of Barton Bendish, but his father got his hands on the manor of Beachamwell only by marrying a widow, allegedly by force, matching her daughter with a 'knave' and then buying out her title, exploiting her condition as 'a simple person and a very idiot

18 'The Petition of Edmund Dudley', ed. C. J. Harrison, *EHR* 87 (1972), 86.
19 *Great Chronicle*, 325–6.
20 E. Hall, *Hall's Chronicle* (London, 1809 edn), 515.
21 S. J. Gunn, 'The Accession of Henry VIII', *HR* 64 (1991), 284–7.

from time of her birth till the time of her decease'.[22] Thomas arrived at Lincoln's Inn in 1464. He was a less brilliant scholar than Dudley, but probably a better networker. In 1483, he was one among many East Anglian lawyers with a practice in local land transactions and a small role in local government, but in the turmoil of 1483–5 he proved himself invaluable to Thomas Grey, marquess of Dorset, the highest-ranking Yorkist aristocrat to join Henry's cause.[23] Named speaker of the commons in the parliament of 1485—when the burgesses of Colchester, reporting back to their constituents, could identify him only as 'a gentleman of Lincoln's Inn'—he soon began to accumulate posts of responsibility in the new regime.[24]

From the start he was versatile. At court, he was an esquire for the king's body by October 1485, possibly helping Henry to dress and undress, and by 1503 he had risen to be treasurer of the household.[25] In the financial administration he became, within months of Henry's accession, both chancellor of the exchequer and treasurer of the king's chamber; he went on to serve from 1513 as master of the wards.[26] He fought at Stoke and Blackheath.[27] Year by year he accumulated local offices on the crown estates from his native Norfolk through the Midlands and even into Yorkshire, all regions in which he also held land once the king put into his hands the estates of his incapable brother-in-law Lord Roos. And unlike his more notorious colleagues, he sailed through the crisis of 1509. He was one of the half-dozen most active attenders in Henry VIII's council until his death in 1524, rich and full of honours.[28]

Lovell was far from unique. Sir Henry Wyatt had humbler roots, in Yorkshire and Surrey, but a more sensational claim on Henry VII's gratitude for his role in the conspiracies of 1483–5. His family later claimed that his devotion to Henry's cause saw him imprisoned one or more times in the Tower of London or in Scotland, tortured with the barnacles used by blacksmiths to grasp the noses of restive horses, and kept alive only by a cat which caught pigeons for him to eat. He, too, held financial offices, clerk, then master of the king's jewel house, comptroller of the mint, and eventually, from 1523 to 1528, treasurer of the chamber. He does not seem to have had as much legal training as most of his colleagues, though he was a member of Lincoln's Inn by 1509. But he doubled up between 1488 and 1497 as an ambassador to Scotland, royal commissioner in Ireland, and military governor of Carlisle.[29]

[22] G. L. Harrison, 'A Few Notes on the Lovells of East Harling', *NA* 18 (1912), 46–7; *Paston Letters and Papers of the Fifteenth Century*, ed. N. Davis, 2 vols (Oxford, 1971–6), i. 558–9; PRO, C1/590/31–4.

[23] *TBPV*, 199; *PROME*, vi. 246.

[24] *The Red Paper Book of Colchester*, ed. W. G. Benham (Colchester, 1902), 62.

[25] *CPR 1485–94*, 23; *A Collection of Ordinances and Regulations for the Government of the Royal Household* (London, 1790), 109–16, 118; PRO, E101/415/3.

[26] *CPR 1485–94*, 18; *LP* I, ii. 2222(12).

[27] W. A. Shaw, *The Knights of England*, 2 vols (London, 1906), ii. 24, 28.

[28] W. H. Dunham, 'The Members of Henry VIII's Whole Council, 1509–1527', *EHR* 59 (1944), 207–10.

[29] S. Brigden, *Thomas Wyatt: The Heart's Forest* (London, 2012), 65–70; Dudley, *Tree*, 3n; *The Records of the Honourable Society of Lincoln's Inn: Admissions from AD 1420 to AD 1799* (London, 1896), 33; A. Conway, *Henry VII's Relations with Scotland and Ireland, 1485–1498* (Cambridge, 1932), 7–115; BL, Addl. MS 62135, fos. 456r, 465r–467r.

Sir Robert Southwell's career was shorter, terminated by his death in 1514, and more specialized in financial affairs, but still wide in its reach. He was another Lincoln's Inn lawyer sprung from the Norfolk gentry, his father, Richard, a servant of the Mowbray and Howard dukes of Norfolk who sat as MP for Yarmouth in 1455 and married an heiress who brought him the family seat at Woodrising.[30] Robert made his way up through the crown lands administration in the 1490s with a series of receiverships and special commissions until by 1503 he and Roger Layburne, bishop of Carlisle, were acting as general surveyors of all the royal lands. Meanwhile, he had time to oversee the arrangements for Katherine of Aragon's reception in 1501 and take charge of the import duties on wines as chief butler of England from 1504. His appointment as an extraordinary auditor of the exchequer in 1510 and endowment with additional powers by a special act of parliament in 1512 made him a central figure in the preservation of Henry VII's flexible financial machinery amidst the reaction at the start of his son's reign.[31]

Others combined courtly and financial duties with more of an accent on the court. Sir Andrew Windsor and Sir John Hussey were among the youngest of the new men, born in the mid-1460s. Windsor, educated at the Middle Temple, had the longest pedigree of any, stretching back to Walter Fitzother, constable of Windsor Castle and lord of Stanwell, Middlesex, in Domesday Book. But his family had not been distinguished in recent generations, and his father, a Middlesex justice of the peace who married a minor Suffolk heiress, had died in 1485 after backing Richard III. Andrew was lucky in his step-father, Sir Robert Litton, a long-serving exchequer official and royal councillor who passed on to him the keepership of the king's great wardrobe at his death in 1505. For a time he was also lucky in his brother-in-law, Edmund Dudley, though the connection proved in 1509 the first of many tests through which Windsor's career would pass, more or less serenely, to the award of a peerage in 1529 and a peaceful death in 1543, still keeper of the great wardrobe and the last of Henry's new men.[32]

Hussey had an even better head start, as the son and heir of Sir William Hussey, attorney-general in the 1470s and chief justice of king's bench from 1481 to 1495, a judge of unusual political prominence, and the creator of an impressive landed estate centred on Sleaford in Lincolnshire. Early in Henry's reign, John entered the service of the king's mother, a powerful patron and a major landowner in the area where his father was buying up lands. From then on his career combined offices on the crown lands, at first held in partnership with his father's friend Bray, with fiscal posts such as the mastership of the wards, established in the reorganization

[30] *Lincoln's Inn Admissions*, 23; J. C. Wedgwood, *History of Parliament: Biographies of the Members of the Commons House, 1439–1509* (London, 1936), 783–4; *The Household Books of John Howard, duke of Norfolk, 1462–71, 1481–1483*, ed. A. Crawford (Stroud, 1992), p. lv; F. Blomefield, *An Essay towards a Topographical History of the County of Norfolk*, 11 vols (London, 1805–10), x. 274.

[31] W. C. Richardson, *Tudor Chamber Administration, 1485–1547* (Baton Rouge LA, 1952), 459–62; *LPRH*, i. 406; B. P. Wolffe, *The Crown Lands, 1461–1536* (London, 1970), 71–9.

[32] Wedgwood, *Commons*, 11, 565–6, 954–5; S. T. Bindoff, *History of Parliament: The House of Commons 1509–1558*, 3 vols (London, 1982), iii. 633–6; A. Collins, *Historical Collections of the Noble Family of Windsor* (London, 1754), 1–47.

following Bray's death, and the chief butlership, held from 1521, and more courtly positions, comptroller of the king's household in 1507–9 and chamberlain of Princess Mary's from 1533. He, too, was promoted to a peerage in 1529, but fumbled in his response to the Lincolnshire rising of 1536, incurred the king's suspicion, and was executed in the following July.[33]

Further towards the courtly end of the spectrum, and more substantial in their diplomatic and military responsibilities, were Sir Edward Poynings and Sir Thomas Brandon. Poynings had distinguished ancestry, but, like Dudley, he came from a junior line. Worse, his father, Robert Poynings of Maidstone, Kent, a younger son of Robert, Lord Poynings (1382–1446), having fought to reclaim some of the family lands from the Percy earls of Northumberland, to whom they had passed by marriage, was killed at the second battle of St Albans in 1461, when Edward was one year old or perhaps even younger. His uncle, a clergyman and master of Arundel College, did what he could to help his mother cling on to some of Robert's estates as the Percies and others scrambled for them, but without much success. More promising were the links to the Yorkist household establishment created by his mother's re-marriage in 1466. Sir George Browne, one of Edward IV's most intimate courtiers, became his step-father and endowed his mother with a comfortable jointure. At Browne's arrangement, Sir John Scott, comptroller of Edward's household, became Poynings's father-in-law, though the modest sums Scott paid Browne for the marriage suggest the thinness of Poynings's prospects. Scott was also knight marshal of Calais and had been on embassy four times to the Burgundian court, where Charles the Bold gave him the gilt standing cup with a greyhound in the bottom bequeathed to Poynings's mother in 1487.[34]

In the long run these connections would equip Poynings for his career. In the short run they led him into rebellion alongside Browne in 1483 and flight to Flanders, then Brittany, to join Henry. His military skills shone among the exiles, who made him 'chief captain of the army' and one of the leaders of their hasty escape from Brittany into France before the successful invasion of 1485.[35] From then on he pursued a glittering course in which military responsibilities alternated with diplomatic and courtly: command at Sluis in 1492, at Calais in 1493, in Ireland in 1494–6, in Guelders in 1511, at Tournai in 1513–15; five embassies to the Habsburg court in the Netherlands between 1493 and 1516; the comptrollership from 1509, then the treasurership of the household; and a leading role in the

[33] Norman Doe, 'Hussey [Huse], Sir William', *ODNB*; E. W. Ives, *The Common Lawyers of Pre-Reformation England. Thomas Kebell: A Case Study* (Cambridge, 1983), 230, 245–6, 260–2, 310, 374–6, 378, 466; Bindoff, *Commons*, ii. 423–4; M. K. Jones and M. G. Underwood, *The King's Mother: Lady Margaret Beaufort, Countess of Richmond and Derby* (Cambridge, 1992), 80, 132.

[34] R. E. Horrox, *Richard III: A Study of Service* (Cambridge, 1989), 252; J. R. Scott, *Memorials of the Family of Scott of Scot's-Hall* (London, 1876), 108, 117, 126; Wedgwood, *Commons*, 750–2; R. Jeffs, 'The Poynings–Percy Dispute: an Example of the Interplay of Open Strife and Legal Action in the Fifteenth Century', *BIHR* 34 (1961), 148–64; *CIPM*, i. 434, 436–7; C. Richmond, *The Paston Family in the Fifteenth Century: Fastolf's Will* (Cambridge, 1996), 103n.

[35] *TBPV*, 200, 208; M. Jones, '"For My Lord of Richmond, a *pourpoint* ... and a palfrey": Brief Remarks on the Financial Evidence for Henry Tudor's Exile in Brittany 1471–1484', *The Ricardian* 13 (2003), 293.

Field of Cloth of Gold where, some suspected, the French slipped him a slow poison that accounted for his death in the following year, before the king could carry out his declared intention of creating him a baron.[36]

Brandon had connections in the Yorkist court, like Poynings, but also, like Southwell, in the East Anglian following of the Mowbray dukes of Norfolk. He was the third son of Sir William Brandon, an influential Mowbray counsellor who kept his place in the royal household and the administration of Suffolk after the death of the last Mowbray duke in 1476. With his elder brother William, master of the henchmen at Edward IV's court, who had taken part in the 1483 rebellion, Thomas fled to join Tudor's exiles on a stolen ship in November 1484. He soon marked himself out by an act of derring-do, leading a party of thirty men to break into the fortress of Hammes in the Calais Pale and reinforce the garrison, which had declared against Richard. His brother was killed at Bosworth, his father died in 1491, and his mother left him one Suffolk manor at her death in 1497. His military career continued after 1485, at sea in 1487, in France in 1492, and at Blackheath in 1497. Diplomatic missions took him to Germany in 1503 and to the south coast in 1506, to welcome the shipwrecked Philip the Fair, archduke of the Netherlands, and take him to meet Henry. But it was at court, where he jousted, hunted, and hawked and, from at least 1501, presided over the royal stables as master of the horse, that most of his duties lay. All seemed set fair for his court career to continue into the new reign when he fell ill and died in January 1510.[37]

As Brandon lay dying, Sir Henry Marney's career was just taking off. Its course suggests a final variation in the fates of Henry's new men. Born in the mid-1450s to a knightly Essex family, Marney had seen younger men than himself climb high in Henry VII's later years. But he could afford to bide his time, for he had a stake in what later generations would call the reversionary interest. As a leading member of Prince Henry's household he shot to prominence in 1509, appointed captain of the guard, chief steward of the duchy of Cornwall, and chancellor of the duchy of Lancaster; a peerage followed in 1523.[38]

Between them, Brandon, Hussey, Lovell, Marney, Poynings, Southwell, Windsor, and Wyatt will dominate this book. The right evidence survives for us to investigate different features of their individual careers—Lovell's local power, Poynings's military campaigns, Wyatt's land purchases, Hussey's dilemmas in the troubled 1530s—and thereby to obtain a panoramic view of the new men's role in Henry VII's government and beyond. But their experience can be set in context by occasional consideration of a further selection of their colleagues. Sir Richard Guildford and Sir James Hobart, for example, had much in common with those we have already examined. Guildford was a Yorkist household

---

[36] Bindoff, *Commons*, iii. 146–7; Hall, *Chronicle*, 632; *LP* III, i. 223.

[37] Wedgwood, *Commons*, 102–3; R. Virgoe, 'Sir John Risley (1443–1512), Courtier and Councillor', *NA* 38 (1981–3), 143; PRO, E404/75/3/16, PROB11/11/9; *TBPV*, 200, 213, 225; S. J. Gunn, 'Brandon, Sir Thomas', *ODNB*.

[38] Wedgwood, *Commons*, 575–6.

man from Kent, about Lovell's age, son of Edward IV's comptroller of the household. He rebelled in 1483, came back from exile with Henry, and rose to be master of the ordnance, one of the leading councillors of the 1490s and, by 1494, comptroller himself. Hobart, born in Suffolk, was a contemporary of Lovell's at Lincoln's Inn and a colleague of Southwell's in the service of the Mowbray and Howard families. Named attorney-general in 1486, he was a trenchant enforcer of the king's rights in collaboration with Bray, Empson, and Dudley. Yet unlike those we have examined so far, Guildford's and Hobart's careers ended in controversy long before Henry VII's death, Guildford leaving a spell of imprisonment for a fatal pilgrimage to Jerusalem in 1506 and Hobart resigning his office and paying a large fine in 1507, then surviving till 1517. We shall have to examine why.[39]

The list could go on. Sir John Mordaunt, chancellor of the duchy between Bray and Empson, said in his youth to have followed Warwick the Kingmaker, and Sir John Cutt, who began as Bray's bailiff and rose to receiver-general of the duchy and under-treasurer of the exchequer, amplify our knowledge of the duchy of Lancaster connection and add Bedfordshire and Cambridgeshire to the counties where the new men made their mark.[40] Sir Thomas Englefield, a Middle Temple lawyer from Berkshire, made his main contribution to Henry's regime in the Welsh Marches, serving on Prince Arthur's council, before returning to an active role in central government after 1509.[41] Sir John Risley was another Yorkist courtier who served Henry in war and diplomacy; William Cope another household administrator, this time cofferer, who started as one of Bray's clerks, founded a gentry family, and built a house to match, a brick castle at Hanwell in Oxfordshire; John Heron, a conspirator from 1485, who emerged from an apprenticeship under Lovell to coordinate crown finances as treasurer of the chamber until his death in 1521; Thomas Lucas, another East Anglian lawyer, who sued out the king's rights as king's solicitor from 1497; John Ernley, an associate of Dudley from Gray's Inn and Sussex, who succeeded Hobart as attorney-general; Sir Robert Sheffield, a Lincolnshire lawyer and long-serving recorder of London who joined the council by 1508.[42] And the further one looks, the more the new men surprise by their versatility. Richard Sutton was not just another council lawyer, an Inner Temple man from Cheshire, but also the co-founder of Brasenose College, Oxford, who took up residence at Syon Abbey and oversaw the printing of devotional texts.[43] Edward Belknap was not just another fiscal enforcer, successively surveyor of the king's prerogative, general

[39] S. Cunningham, 'Guildford, Sir Richard', *ODNB*; E. W. Ives, 'Hobart, Sir James', *ODNB*.
[40] H. Summerson, 'Mordaunt, Sir John', *ODNB*; *Bedfordshire Wills proved in the Prerogative Court of Canterbury 1383–1548*, ed. M. McGregor, Bedfordshire Historical RS 58 (Bedford, 1979), 68; R. Somerville, *A History of the Duchy of Lancaster, I, 1265–1603* (London, 1953), 263, 401.
[41] Bindoff, *Commons*, ii. 103–4.
[42] Virgoe, 'Risley', 140–8; PRO, E36/285; *The Reports of Sir John Spelman*, ed. J. H. Baker, 2 vols, SS 93–4 (London, 1976–7), ii. 392; Richardson, *Tudor Chamber Administration*, 115–16, 484–5; Christopher Whittick, 'Ernley, Sir John', *ODNB*; Bindoff, *Commons*, iii. 304–5.
[43] J. G. Clark, 'Sutton, Sir Richard', *ODNB*.

surveyor of crown lands, chief butler, and master of wards, but also the man who fought his way through the rebel army at the battle of Blackheath in 1497 to capture Michael Joseph an Gof, the blacksmith leader of the Cornish revolt.[44] The new men were everywhere in Henry VII's regime and brought to its service a galaxy of talents.

[44] Richardson, *Tudor Chamber Administration*, 198–214, 288–90; HL, MS STT Personal box 1(4).

2

Principles and talents

To know Henry's new men properly we need to know a wider circle than just Bray, Empson, and Dudley. To know them in the round, we must also get beyond Warbeck's fulminations to understand the principles that drove them and the talents they brought to the king's service.

MEDWALL AND DUDLEY

One contemporary who helps us to see matters from the new men's point of view is Henry Medwall. His play, *Fulgens and Lucrece,* was probably written in the 1490s for performance in the household of Henry's chancellor Cardinal Morton and was printed in 1512. It dramatized a story from Buonaccorso da Montemagno's humanist treatise on true nobility, which had been translated into English and published by William Caxton in 1481. Lucres, daughter of Fulgens, must choose between two suitors. Publius Cornelius is blue-blooded and wealthy, but a wastrel. Gaius Flaminius is very different:

> Borne of a poor stock, as men doth say.
> But for all that, many a fair day
> Through his great wisdom and virtuous behaviour
> He ruled the common weal to his great honour.

He is not just a technocrat and moralist, but also, like Belknap, an effective warrior:

> One time with study my time I spend
> To eschew idleness, the causer of sin
> Another time my country manly I defend.

He is devoted to God and charitable to his neighbours, and his efforts lead him not only to rise 'unto great honour from low degree' but also to gain 'moderate riches'.[1] His temperance and avoidance of vice are even more strongly stressed in Medwall's text than they had been in his sources.[2] No wonder he gets the girl. Medwall's

[1] *The Plays of Henry Medwall*, ed. A. H. Nelson (Cambridge, 1980), 31–89; quotations from ll. 94–7, 679–81, 687, 696.
[2] R. Lexton, 'Henry Medwall's *Fulgens and Lucrece* and the Question of Nobility under Henry VII', in L. Clark (ed.), *Rule, Redemption and Representations in Late Medieval England and France* (Woodbridge, 2008), 168–71.

setting was Roman, his ideas Italian, but his keywords were English—common weal, country, study, honour, riches—and his characters recognizable. If Warbeck's manifesto distilled the hostile image of the new men, Medwall captured their view of themselves.

Only rarely can we catch them spelling out their ideas and values in person. The priceless exception is Dudley's *Tree of Commonwealth*. Dudley wrote from his prison in the Tower in 1509, analysing the duties and temptations of each group in society and counselling the new king as how best to 'revive the common wealth' by his 'study and policy'.[3] His device was a rather ponderous metaphor of society as a tree, held up by the roots of love of God, justice, fidelity, concord, and peace, and bearing the fruits of honouring God, honourable dignity, worldly prosperity, tranquillity, and good example. We may fear he got rather carried away when he pursued his analogy to investigate the peel or slices of each fruit that should be handed round to various people, the dangerous cores that might poison them, and the healthy sauce with which each should be consumed. But in practice it was in these elaborations of his argument that his most interesting attitudes were revealed.

Much of his advice was worthy but predictable. Subjects should obey their prince and princes protect their subjects, good churchmen should be promoted rather than bad, noblemen should defend the realm, diplomatic agreements should be carefully contracted and faithfully observed, counsel should be taken from 'good and wise men', idleness should be discouraged, we should remember that death comes to us all. Each individual should 'be content to do his duty in the office, room, or condition that he is set in', and the inferior should not 'pretend or counterfeit the state of his better' or 'usurp . . . to take his superior's part'. Yet he was quick to stress that 'it is not honourable blood and great possession, or rich apparel, that maketh a man honourable, himself being of unhonourable conditions': Gaius Flaminius, predictably, was more his type than Publius Cornelius. He pointed out to the nobility and gentry that their sons were so lacking in education, 'the learning of virtue and cunning', that 'the children of poor men and mean folk' were promoted over their heads. And it was the king's prerogative to bestow such promotion: none should presume to help themselves to the fruit of honourable dignity, 'but must have it by deliverance of his sovereign terrestrial'. The nobility in particular, while it was 'tolerable' for them to desire worldly dignity 'when they are meet therefor', should 'not presume to take it of their own authority for then it will surely choke them'. Nor should clergymen be distracted from their spiritual cure by holding 'temporal office'; certainly, they should not pursue it, though, he admitted, they might accept it if the king offered. The universities where the clergy studied should be protected, but particularly for the study of theology, as opposed to the Roman law usually studied by clerical politicians. That seemed to leave educated, and if needs be, upwardly mobile laymen to hold power under the king.[4]

Dudley envisaged a strong moral role for the king, not just discouraging sin among the laity but exhorting and equipping the clergy to live up to their calling,

---

[3] Edmund Dudley, *The Tree of Commonwealth*, ed. D. M. Brodie (Cambridge, 1948), 22, 50.
[4] Dudley, *Tree*, 24–7, 31, 40–1, 45–6, 53–4, 56–7, 62, 65–8, 82–4.

a subject on which he was not slow to elaborate. Moral dealing was also seen as political, social, and economic cement, for fidelity to one's undertakings promoted the 'friendship and confidence' that underpinned trade, legislation, and political relationships and legitimated the landed prosperity of the social elite. Yet this moralized vision did not deny social problems that demanded practical remedies of the sort broached by legislation or projected legislation in Henry's reign. Vagabonds needed to be set to work, tenants should not be oppressed, the lower orders should not waste their resources in unlawful games or excessive litigation. Economic intervention by government might also be necessary, especially to ensure the quality of English products and thus protect their position on foreign markets, a matter on which the king and his council should take the advice of 'wise and expert men'. A prime reason for the maintenance of peace with other countries was the need for healthy trade.[5]

Obedience to 'our sovereign lord the king' ran right through Dudley's vision of society. Yet this was not out of reverence for the mystique of royal succession. Henry VII's claim was notionally Lancastrian, yet Dudley described the Lancastrian Henry IV as 'another having no title' for whom Richard II's subjects abandoned him. Henry VII's regime was in practice much bolstered by Yorkist loyalty to the line of Edward IV transmitted through his daughter Elizabeth of York, yet Dudley speculated that Edward's sons were taken away as a providential punishment for his excessive indulgence of his 'fleshly appetite'. Dudley, perhaps under the influence of Cicero, conceptualized his duty as lying more to 'the prosperous estate of my natural country' than to any dynasty. That duty, however, involved the avoidance of discord, conspiracy, and rebellion, with all their destructive consequences, and therefore in practice dictated the maintenance of the Tudor regime. The tranquillity secured by good government was of supreme benefit to the common people, for it enabled craftsmen, workers, and husbandmen 'to apply diligently with true labours and honest diligence and busyness'. But to enjoy its blessings they must turn their backs on 'lewd enterprise' which might be prompted by discontent at rents, or taxes, or 'disdain to be in . . . obedience or subjection to your superiors or betters'; they must conduct themselves like 'politic and discreet commoners'.[6]

Justice was a key function of government, to be driven by the king in person though worked out through his chancellor, judges, sheriffs, and 'other general and special commissioners in every county and shire'. It was important that those appointed to such offices be 'such as will deal indifferently between the subjects', but also that they 'let not for fear or displeasure of any of his own servants or counsellors to do true justice nor for fear of any great persons in his realm', such that justice might be executed 'as well against the noblest as other'. Dudley was

    [5] Dudley, *Tree*, 24–6, 32–3, 37–40, 42–4, 46, 48–50, 54, 62–6; S. J. Gunn, 'Edmund Dudley and the Church', *Journal of Ecclesiastical History* 51 (2000), 509–26; P. R. Cavill, *The English Parliaments of Henry VII, 1485–1504* (Oxford, 2009), 82, 90–1, 167, 181–2.
    [6] Dudley, *Tree* 22, 29, 33, 40, 55, 87, 96; D. R. Starkey, 'England', in R. Porter and M. Teich (eds), *The Renaissance in National Context* (Cambridge, 1992), 152.

concerned about the tensions evident in Henry's reign between common law and ecclesiastical law, clergy and laity, declaring that 'any manner of grudge' between the king's 'subjects of the spiritualty and his subjects of the temporality for privilege or liberties' might be 'established and reformed' only by the king. But he harped above all on the need to impose justice on the powerful. Maintenance, the support of offenders to deflect prosecution, 'done most commonly by men of great power and authority', should be punished by the prince. Justice should be done 'as well to the poor as to the rich', and the poor should be defended by the prince so that 'they be not oppressed by great men'. It was above all crucial for the king to do effective justice between 'the nobles of his realm', because if they were suffered 'to revenge their own quarrels, old or new, by force or by violence' then 'beware the prince in a while': here was the lesson of Henry VI's reign, when failure to regulate noble feuding had led on to civil war.[7]

Dudley was also aware of the fiscal bases of royal power. He thought that the 'due order and course of his laws' was 'the most honourable and sure way for the prince to have his right of his subjects'. But he was also very clear that it was the duty of good subjects to 'be ready and diligent to the uttermost of their powers, with body and goods, in the rescue of him and of his realm, and to yield and pay to him truly all rights, revenues and casualties, without fraud or coven'. He was well aware of the 'large profits and customs' the king could gather from vigorous trade. Money raised should be spent in appropriate ways, such that, for example, the king should 'keep his honourable household in plenteous manner'. A ruler should be warned that 'right great treasure is soon spent in a sharp war', but also take note that other princes will deal with him more seriously if 'in time of peace he make good and sure preparation for war'.[8] All this fitted well with Henry's pursuit of increased income from customs and lands, more effective direct taxation, and measured expenditure on royal magnificence, while amity with his neighbours was balanced by naval rearmament and the licensed retaining of troops.

Some of Dudley's comments seemed pointedly to reject the emphases of Henry VII's regime. He countered the idea that the king's 'surety standeth much in plenty of treasure' with the argument that 'the profit of every christian prince dependeth in the grace of God which is won by mercy and liberality', and added to his account of Henry III's 'insatiable' extortion of his subjects the coda that the only fault of 'some other of time late' was a similar 'appetite'. Criticism of the pursuit of the king's rights by the 'imprisonment or sinister vexation' of individuals also looks like a repudiation of practices with which Dudley himself had been associated. Personal confession came nearer still with the warning that a prince might have councillors who 'in his own causes will do further than conscience requireth, and further than himself would should be done, oftentimes to win a special thank of the king, and sometimes for their proper advantage and sometimes for avenging of their own quarrels, grudges or malice'. Practices he criticized in the church— simony and nepotism, in particular—were those he himself had practised on his

---

[7] Dudley, *Tree*, 34–6, 41, 54, 102.   [8] Dudley, *Tree*, 36, 42, 50.

own behalf or the king's. Personal experience or observation of his upstart colleagues may have inspired his warning against the pride in success that left men

> so loath to know and remember from whence we came that we in no wise will be known of our grandfather or grandmother, or else we will be loath to meddle with any man that knoweth them, and peradventure even so by our fathers and mothers, and other of our near kin.[9]

Under sentence of death, Dudley wrote in reflective, even penitential mode, ending his treatise with the insistence that all the fruits of the tree of commonwealth must be consumed with the sauce of fear of God, and their poisonous cores neutralized by the supreme fruit of the honour of God, as men sought their true reward in heaven.[10] Yet many of his prescriptions for good government were exactly those pursued by Henry VII and his councillors. Many of the phrases he used were those characteristic of the regime's public communication. He desired rule by 'great study, wisdom and policy', where Henry had vaunted two years earlier his achievement of a marriage alliance with the Habsburgs by his 'great labour, study and policy'.[11] Archbishop Warham three years before that had opened parliament with a long speech on the supreme necessity for justice.[12] Common weal, reformation, policy, peace, tranquillity or quietness, indifferent justice, punishment of wrongs, and remedies for idleness coursed through the statutes of the 1495 and 1504 parliaments and the royal proclamations of the reign as they did through Dudley's text.[13] Many of the priorities, prejudices, and doubts he expressed can be traced elsewhere in the lives and more fleeting writings of his fellow new men.

CROWN AND KING

The new men's commitment to Henry's regime was strengthened by a number of overlapping considerations. They shared Dudley's sense that the common weal might best be served by adherence to the principles of what Lovell called 'good governance and rule' and the submission of problems to 'reformation'.[14] Just as Dudley thought that pity was worthy but should not be given 'all times to all them that needeth it lest justice would cease', and just as a proclamation of 1502 stated that illegal retaining to the 'subversion of all good policies' should be met with 'convenable remedy', so Lovell thought that those who were minded 'of their wilful disposition to subvert . . . good rule' merited 'condign punishment'.[15] The proper

---

[9] Dudley, *Tree*, 28, 36–7, 81; Gunn, 'Edmund Dudley and the Church', 516–25.

[10] Dudley, *Tree*, 92–107.

[11] Dudley, *Tree*, 103; *The Reign of Henry VII from Original Sources*, ed. A. F. Pollard, 3 vols (London, 1913–14), i. 303.

[12] *PROME*, vi. 520.

[13] 11 Henry VII cc. 2–5, 7, 9, 11, 12, 21, 24–6; 19 Henry VII cc. 5, 7, 10, 12–14, 16, 17–18, 32; *TRP*, i. 5, 14–15, 17–20, 23, 27–8, 30, 32–3, 37, 39, 42–50, 56–8, 60, 62–3, 70, 74.

[14] PRO, SP1/8, fo. 159v (*LP* I, ii. 3087); *Records of the Borough of Nottingham*, ed. W. H. Stevenson, 9 vols (Nottingham, 1882–1936), iii. 341, 402.

[15] Dudley, *Tree*, 61; *TRP*, i. 55–56; *Records of the Borough of Nottingham*, iii. 343.

framework for justice, punishment, and indeed most of government was the English common law, which most of them had spent years studying and practising.

It was a law that protected the rights of subject against subject, while also promoting the rights of the crown over the kingdom. It allowed for testing and extension of the king's rights, an extension which was running fast from the 1470s as lawyers debated the king's prerogatives over those who held land from him and saw how they could be deployed to strengthen his fiscal and political power. But it also prescribed due forms in which royal power should be exercised and, as often as not, appropriate agents for that exercise in the persons of the lawyers in crown service. Hobart and Mordaunt, for example, were leading counsel for the crown in test cases on wardship and uses, while Hussey and Lovell served as masters of the wards.[16] Henry VII's ministers were prepared to defend not only the principles of the law, but also the processes through which it enforced the king's power. In 1514, the duke of Buckingham sued the crown for the return of a manor found not to be his by an inquisition of 1505. He argued, with characteristic tactlessness, that this had happened 'in the time of King Henry VII, when no one could have justice'. The inquisition's finding, countered Lovell in open court, 'was as true as gospel'.[17]

The principles of good order were not the sole property of the lawyers, but might be disseminated through education to the general benefit. The ordinances of the Nottingham free school Lovell helped to found in 1512 explained that 'by learning the public weal commonly is governed', and Lovell pursued this through his own household, paying not only a writing master to teach ten young gentlemen being brought up with him, but also a schoolmaster for the townsfolk of Enfield.[18] Mordaunt, too, promoted education, requiring one of his chantry chaplains to teach grammar free of charge to all comers in his home village of Turvey, while Marney and Wyatt left money for relatives or godsons 'to find them to school'.[19] Bray's widow endowed the post of grammar master at Jesus College Cambridge, again to teach not just the college choristers, but anyone else who came.[20] This was just as Dudley would have wanted: he thought there should be more 'good and substantial scholars of grammar' teaching in towns, religious houses, colleges, bishops' households and the 'houses of men of honour of the temporality', and in his will he instructed the priest singing for his first wife's soul to teach the local choirboys.[21]

With these attachments to what we might call the state and good citizenship went a fierce personal devotion to the king, tested in the struggle to win and keep the throne. Poynings, the rebellion in Kent and his step-father's subsequent execution

---

[16] W. Ives, *The Common Lawyers of Pre-Reformation England. Thomas Kebell: A Case Study* (Cambridge, 1983), 222–62; M. McGlynn, *The Royal Prerogative and the Learning of the Inns of Court* (Cambridge, 2003), 15–159.

[17] *Reports of Cases by John Caryll*, ed. J. H. Baker, 2 vols, SS 115–16 (London, 1999–2000), ii. 652.

[18] *Records of the Borough of Nottingham*, iii. 453; *LP* IV, i. 366.

[19] *Bedfordshire Wills proved in the Prerogative Court of Canterbury 1383–1548*, ed. M. McGregor, Bedfordshire Historical RS 58 (Bedford, 1979), 68; 'Ancient Wills', ed. H. W. King, *TEAS* 4 (1869), 153–4; PRO, PROB11/26/7.

[20] A. Gray and F. Brittain, *A History of Jesus College Cambridge* (London, 1979), 30.

[21] Dudley, *Tree*, 62; *LP* I, i. 559.

fresh in his mind, would have been there with Guildford in Rennes Cathedral at Christmas 1483, when Henry promised to marry Elizabeth of York; there, now with Brandon and Risley, too, on the beach near Milford Haven where Henry landed in 1485; there in the slaughter at Bosworth.[22] Belknap, Hussey, Lovell, Marney, and Mordaunt joined them at Stoke, more still at Blackheath.[23] Cutt, Lovell, and Mordaunt, in some cases years after Henry's death, specified in their wills that their chantry priests were to pray for the soul of the ruler Cutt called 'the most famous king of most blessed memory'; and when Lovell died his probate inventory recorded only one painting in any of his houses, a portrait of Henry VII.[24]

Here perhaps Dudley, a schoolboy or at best a law student in the stirring 1480s, was different. His bond with the king was more that of a shared fascination with the pos-sibilities of power. It was symbolized by the notes he made in his accounts in December 1507 and February 1508 that he had returned to the king 'his great book called Jura Regalia which I had of his highness' and 'the great book of recognisances which I had once of his deliverance', and by his assertion after his fall that he knew the late king's 'inward mind' regarding the debts his subjects owed him.[25] He seemed to recognize, too, that Lovell and Bishop Fox, veterans of 1485, had a rather different relationship from his own with 'their old and loving master King Henry the 7th of noble memory deceased', who 'had as much confidence and trust' in them 'as in any living man'.[26]

If law provided most of the language for commitment to the crown, chivalry did the same for service to the king. Nearly all the new men received the accolade of knighthood at the king's own hands, forging the special bond between a man of honour and the superior who had initiated him into the way of the knight. Their heraldic mottoes made crisp pledges: Poynings's 'loyaulté n'a peur' combined dependability with courage; Marney vowed he would 'loyaulement servir'; Wyatt's 'oublier ne puis' was more ambiguous, but presumably referred to his sufferings in his master's cause; while Lovell's 'Dieu soit loué' might evoke praise for divine promotion of his master as well as of Lovell himself.[27] Among the new men the chivalrous cast of mind was most evident in their engagement with the order of the garter. Poynings, who had first been nominated as early as 1488, was chosen a knight by 1499; Lovell, Bray, and Guildford between 1500 and 1503; Brandon in 1507; and Marney in 1510. Those who were not chosen by the king were some-times nominated for consideration when the knights met in chapter: Windsor, perhaps frustratingly, fourteen times between 1523 and 1541, sometimes by just one knight and sometimes by as many as ten; Hussey, a less convincing exponent of chivalrous values, only once, in 1525, and only by one nominator. Those elected

[22] M. Bennett, *The Battle of Bosworth* (Stroud, 1985), 61–2, 86.

[23] *AHPV*, 23.

[24] H. W. King, 'The Descent of the Manor of Horham, and of the Family of Cutts', *TEAS* 4 (1869), 34; *Bedfordshire Wills*, 68; PRO, PROB11/23/27, PROB2/199, m. 5.

[25] HL, MS El. 1518, fos. 54r, 56r.

[26] 'The Petition of Edmund Dudley', ed. C. J. Harrison, *EHR* 87 (1972), 86–7.

[27] 'Thomas Wall's Book of Crests', *The Ancestor* 11 (1904), 183, 187; S. Brigden, *Thomas Wyatt; The Heart's Forest* (London, 2012), 67; W. Robinson, *The History and Antiquities of Enfield, in the County of Middlesex*, 2 vols (London, 1823), i. 134.

attended with dedication. Poynings missed only three out of fourteen annual chapters between 1499 and 1519, apparently on each occasion because he was out of the country. Lovell was often excused attendance by Henry VII, who presumably needed him for more urgent business, but came into his own after 1509, missing only one chapter out of eleven between then and his serious illness in May 1523, and taking part in several Windsor feasts. Marney attended seven out of eight chapters between 1514 and 1523, and in the one year he missed the chapter he attended the feast.[28]

The visual language of the order and of chivalrous culture more generally was important to them. Lovell's head was surrounded by the garter in the bronze portrait medallion, attributed to Pietro Torrigiani, he commissioned for his house at East Harling, as were the arms he put on his seals, on the gatehouse at Lincoln's Inn and in the windows at Enfield parish church.[29] Marney's tomb showed the garter eight times around his arms in the side panels and once strapped around the armoured leg of his effigy.[30] Poynings had St George on horseback carved in stone over the entrance to his house at Westenhanger and painted in the stained glass of his chapel in the parish church.[31] In his houses at Holywell and Elsings by Enfield, Lovell had tapestries of St George and the Nine Worthies.[32] Among his best clothes Bray had 'a gown of crimson with the hood lined with white sarcenet of the order of Saint George' and 'a mantle of blue velvet lined with white sarcenet with a garter of gold'.[33] Poynings even took his robes on embassy with him, so that in Brussels, on St George's day 1516, he and the sixteen-year-old Charles, king of Castile, who had just sworn formally to observe the treaty Poynings had come to negotiate, could dine in their garter regalia.[34] The new men's heraldic identities were proudly bound up with the king's and the order's in the choir at St George's Chapel, Windsor, built between 1506 and 1508 under a contract made by Lovell, Daubeney, and the earl of Shrewsbury, where the badges of all the current knights were displayed on the roof bosses among the roses and portcullises: Poynings's crowned key, Brandon's lion's head, Lovell's falcon's wing.[35] That work led on from Bray's own sumptuous contribution to St George's, the completion of the nave, sprinkled with his hemp-bray badge.[36]

[28] *The Register of the Most Noble Order of the Garter*, ed. J. Anstis, 2 vols (London, 1724), i. 231–422; *LP* III, ii. 3024.
[29] D. R. Starkey (ed.), *Henry VIII: A European Court in England* (London, 1991), 33; BL, Addl. Ch. 8404; *An Inventory of the Historical Monuments in London*, 5 vols, RCHM (London, 1924–30), ii. 45; *HMC Rutland*, iv. 265.
[30] *An Inventory of the Historical Monuments in Essex*, 4 vols, RCHM (London, 1916–23), iii. 159.
[31] E. Hasted, *The History and Topographical Survey of the County of Kent*, 12 vols (Wakefield, 1972 edn), viii. 65; T. S. Frampton, 'St Mary's, Westenhanger (church destroyed). Rectors and Patrons', *AC* 31 (1915), 83.
[32] PRO, PROB2/199, mm. 6, 9.   [33] PRO, E154/2/10, fos. 1–2.
[34] *Inventaire-sommaire des archives départementales antérieures à 1790: Nord*, ed. C. Dehaisnes et al., 10 vols (Lille, 1863–1906), vii. 256–7; *LP* II, i. 1818, 1822.
[35] C. J. P. Cave and H. S. London, 'The Roof-Bosses in St George's Chapel, Windsor', *Archaeologia* 95 (1953), 107–21; Bodl. MS Ashmole 1125, fos. 11r–12r.
[36] T. Tatton-Brown, 'The Constructional Sequence and Topography of the Chapel and College Buildings at St George's', in C. Richmond and E. Scarff (eds), *St George's Chapel, Windsor, in the Late Middle Ages* (Windsor, 2001), 18–23.

Their commitment extended beyond Henry to his family, a commitment made personal in the rituals of the royal life-cycle. Thomas Brandon guarded the font at Arthur's christening and served him at dinner on the eve of his knighting.[37] Five years later, he was one of Prince Henry's two esquires when he, in turn, was knighted.[38] Bray's and Lovell's attachment to Arthur was made luminously visible in the windows they commissioned for Great Malvern Priory, showing him together with his parents and the donors.[39] The devotion extended to Henry VIII as king. Dudley doubtless had an eye to the possibility of pardon when he prayed that 'our saviour Jesu Christ safely guide' Henry 'with the long continuance of virtue and honour, for he is the prince that shall revive the common wealth within this his realm'.[40] But Poynings, too, prayed Jesus 'to preserve your most noble and royal estate' and Wyatt protested his 'old love faith and truth to my said sovereign lord', 'for a more faithful and loving prince was there never in England'.[41] This loyalty reached down the generations to heirs as yet unborn. Dudley promised Henry as the fruit of chaste living 'plenty of fair issue which shall succeed him in honour and virtue'.[42] As his own death approached, Wyatt told Henry that he prayed that 'ere I die I might see of you some young master', for he would have 'more glad heart to go hence with such comfort'.[43] Hussey rather tactlessly wrote in a book he gave to Henry VIII's daughter Mary 'Jesus keep and send the king a prince. John Huse, the king's true servant'.[44] He did not live to see his prayer fulfilled, though he did have the more awkward pleasure of carrying the canopy over Mary's supplanter Princess Elizabeth at her christening.[45]

A double attachment to crown and king made treason anathema to them. Wyatt thanked God that the treasons around Anne Boleyn had been revealed and wished 'the false traitors to be punished according to justice to the example of other'.[46] Dudley's and Hussey's horror of treason was such that neither could comprehend how they had been tried and convicted for it. From the Tower Dudley protested that 'I never offended in treason or thing like to it to my knowledge as my sinful soul be saved'.[47] In the same predicament two decades later, Hussey petitioned the king to pay his debts from his confiscated property, insisting that 'I never offended His Grace in will deed or thought in any treason by the death that I shall die and

---

[37] *The Herald's Memoir 1486–1490: Court Ceremony, Royal Progress and Rebellion*, ed. E. Cavell (Donington, 2009), 102, 177.

[38] J. Anstis, *Observations Introductory to an Historical Essay upon the Knighthood of the Bath* (London, 1725), 44.

[39] F. Hepburn, 'The Portraiture of Prince Arthur and Katherine of Aragon', in S. Gunn and L. Monckton (eds), *Arthur Tudor, Prince of Wales: Life, Death and Commemoration* (Woodbridge, 2009), 32.

[40] Dudley, *Tree*, 22.

[41] PRO, SP1/8, fo. 139, SP1/103, fo. 251 (*LP* I, ii. 3025, X. 819).

[42] Dudley, *Tree*, 30.   [43] PRO, SP1/113, fo. 195 (*LP* XI. 1492).

[44] *A Descriptive Catalogue of the Western Manuscripts in the Library of Queens' College, Cambridge*, ed. M. R. James (Cambridge, 1905), 16.

[45] *LP* VI. 1111(1).   [46] PRO, SP1/103, fo. 251 (*LP* X. 819).

[47] 'Petition of Edmund Dudley', 86.

as I would be saved'. He could not let the issue alone, repeating a few lines later that he would ask no pardon for treason 'for as I be saved I never offended His Grace in treason'.[48]

This attitude translated readily into action. As deputy lieutenant and then lieutenant of the Tower of London, Lovell was keeper of many of those who fell foul of tightening laws of treason and sedition, from 1487, when the council committed one Plomer to his charge, to 1524, when he produced a Greenwich schoolmaster and his accomplices for their trial.[49] In between came some of the greatest men of the kingdom. In 1499 he presented the young earl of Warwick, nephew of Edward IV and Richard III but a prisoner for fourteen years, for his trial and execution.[50] In 1521 he interrogated the duke of Buckingham about his designs on the throne and escorted him to and from his condemnation. On the return trip he offered Buckingham cushions and a carpet to sit on in the barge, which the duke theatrically refused.[51] His activity reached well beyond London and Westminster. In 1502 he and Bishop Fox lured Sir James Tyrrell, suspected of Yorkist plotting, out of Guînes Castle onto their ship and reportedly threatened to throw him overboard if he did not order his son to surrender the castle and accompany his father to the Tower.[52] In 1506 he went to Dover to collect the Yorkist claimant Edmund de la Pole, shipped over from Calais by Henry Wyatt with an armed escort sixty strong.[53] In 1509 he arranged for the safe return of the marquess of Dorset, imprisoned at Calais under suspicion of plotting in 1507, but now slated for release.[54] Sir Thomas's supreme trustworthiness in the eyes of his masters was summed up by the identity of one of his two household falconers at the end of his life: a certain Lambert Simnel.[55]

Others played their part in the same task. Poynings and Guildford started early, trying a rebel yeoman at Canterbury in December 1485.[56] Risley was a juror when Humphrey Stafford was indicted in 1486.[57] Bray, Guildford, and Lovell sat alongside peers and judges at treason trials in 1493–5, as Warbeck's sympathizers were hunted down.[58] Lovell sat on the commission to try Tyrrell in 1502; Poynings on that to try Sir John Wyndham in 1504; Brandon, Englefield, Hussey, Lovell, and Marney on that to try Dudley in 1509; Lovell and Marney on that to indict Buckingham in 1521, when Wyatt was a juror.[59] From his elevation to the peerage to his death Windsor took part in every treason trial of a peer except one, making

---

[48] PRO, SP1/121, fo. 2r (*LP* XII, ii. 2).

[49] *LP* I, i. 1732 (41); HL, MS El 2652, fo. 10v; PRO, KB9/492/2/9.

[50] L. W. V. Harcourt, *His Grace the Steward and the Trial of Peers* (London, 1907), 465–6.

[51] *LP* III, i. 1284 (5); E. Hall, *Hall's Chronicle* (London, 1809 edn), 623.

[52] *LPRH*, i. 181.

[53] *The Chronicle of Calais*, ed. J. G. Nichols, CS o.s. 35 (London, 1846), 6; PRO, E404/85/2/99.

[54] *Report on Manuscripts in Various Collections*, 8 vols, HMC 55 (London, 1901–13), ii. 304.

[55] Belvoir Castle, MS a/c no. 4, partially calendared in *HMC Rutland*, iv. 260–5.

[56] PRO, KB9/369/35.   [57] PRO, KB9/371/17.

[58] PRO, KB9/401/30; *Six Town Chronicles of England*, ed. R. Flenley (Oxford, 1911), 164–6.

[59] *CPR, 1494–1509*, 506; 4 Henry VIII c. 14; *Third Report of the Deputy Keeper of the Public Records* (London, 1842), App. ii. 226; *LP* III, i. 1284.

him one of the most assiduous noblemen of his generation in that grim business. He made up for missing one peer by trying Sir Thomas More.[60] Hussey sat at the trial of Lord Dacre in 1534, an acquittal, which redeems these treason hearings a little from the sense that once prosecution had begun, condemnation was inevitable.[61]

Within weeks of Henry VIII's accession Marney took on a particularly sensitive role as captain of the guard, responsible for the king's day-to-day security.[62] He supervised the guard from then until his death, protecting the king in the potentially risky diplomatic interviews of 1520 and 1522, and whenever else it was needed.[63] In 1518, when Henry was worried about the intentions of some of his nobles, Marney was, reported the king's secretary Richard Pace, both wise and faithful in limiting the size of the retinues great men were allowed to bring to court.[64] In 1521, accompanied by a hundred guardsmen, he arrested the duke of Buckingham on his barge and marched him up Thames Street to the Tower. While others questioned the duke, he investigated the possible involvement of Lord Willoughby de Broke in any plot and negotiated the submission of Lord Bergavenny to the king.[65]

The new men's intertwining commitments to crown, king, and royal house were easy to proclaim in visual terms. The imperially crowned royal arms stood for an English monarchy endowed with supreme temporal power.[66] The Beaufort portcullis and red rose spoke of Henry's descent from Edward III through his Beaufort mother and his upholding of the Lancastrian claim taken on from Henry VI. The double rose, combining the red of Lancaster and the white of York, carried the providential message that the offspring of Henry and Elizabeth were raised up to end England's troubles.[67] All were used by the new men to advertise their commitment to Henry's rule and to pass on the messages these symbols stood for to his other subjects. Lovell surrounded his portrait medallion with Tudor roses and put them in the windows at East Harling; he put the crowned royal arms in his new stained glass at Enfield parish church and the gatehouse at Lincoln's Inn, and at East Harling showed Henry VIII's arms impaling Katherine of Aragon's.[68] Poynings put roses and crowned royal arms on the plaster ceilings of his house at Westenhanger.[69] Wyatt had the imperial crown and the double rose drawn onto

[60]   H. Miller, *Henry VIII and the English Nobility* (Oxford, 1986), 45; *LP* VIII. 974.
[61]   *LP* VII. 962 (x).
[62]   *LP* I, i. 54 (9); A. Hewerdine, *The Yeomen of the Guard and the Early Tudors: The Formation of a Royal Bodyguard* (London, 2012), 42.
[63]   *LP* I, i. 118, ii. 2055 (37, 100), II, i. 1780, ii. 4251, III, i. 704, ii. 2288.
[64]   *LP* II, ii. 4057, 4061, 4085.
[65]   Hall, *Chronicle*, 622; *LP* III, i. 1290, 1320.
[66]   D. Hoak, 'The Iconography of the Crown Imperial', in D. Hoak (ed.), *Tudor Political Culture* (Cambridge, 1995), 54–103.
[67]   S. Anglo, *Images of Tudor Kingship* (London, 1992), 35, 74–97.
[68]   Starkey (ed.), *Henry VIII: A European Court in England*, 33; F. Blomefield, *An Essay towards a Topographical History of the County of Norfolk*, 11 vols (London, 1805–10), i. 333; *HMC Rutland*, iv. 265; *Historical Monuments in London*, ii. 47.
[69]   G. Clinch, 'Notes on the Remains of Westenhanger House, Kent', *AC* 31 (1915), 80–1.

the initial letter of the royal charter of free warren he obtained from the king in 1518.[70] Portcullises and red roses were less ubiquitous, but featured on cups owned by Dudley and Marney and the window glass of Cutt's house, Horham Hall. The ostrich feather of the Prince of Wales may have been a special token for those who served the heir to the throne or his duchy of Cornwall—it appeared issuing from an imperial crown in Marney's glass at Layer Marney—but it was also used by Cutt in his glass, this time with a crowned portcullis.[71]

APTITUDES

The inns of court provided the lawyers among the new men not just with an education in the law, but also with social and administrative skills, life-long connections, and institutional loyalties. At Lincoln's Inn, in addition to giving readings in Autumn 1475 and Lent 1482, Lovell organized revels as butler, kept order as marshal, made up accounts as pensioner, audited them as treasurer, and led the Inn as a governor. He shared rooms with Edmund Bedingfield and worked on the Inn's affairs with Hobart, both future colleagues on Henry VII's council. At the Inn, too, he would have met Yorkist courtiers like Daubeney, who would rise to be Henry's lord chamberlain, and John Fortescue, Henry's chief butler, for whose daughter's marriage settlement he served as a feoffee.[72] He recognized the obligations this start in life gave him. In 1508 he gave £3 6s 8d towards a new building, in 1516–17 £2 for work on the library, and between 1517 and 1521 at least £75 towards the construction of the new gatehouse which still survives on Chancery Lane.[73] Windsor, similarly, shared membership of the Middle Temple with his step-father, was a bencher by 1500 and carried weight as a senior member in the 1520s, just as Empson, called on for advice about a troublesome building project by his brethren in 1508, had once done.[74] Legal training opened the way not just to practice in the courts, but to wide-ranging careers in business and administration, because so many of society's dealings were framed in legal terms: as Eric Ives has put it, '"Lawyer" was obviously synonymous with "man of business".'[75] Other skills were

[70] PRO, E326/12541.

[71] PRO, E154/2/17; C. H. Cooper, *Memoir of Margaret, Countess of Richmond and Derby* (Cambridge, 1874), 134; A. Emery, *Greater Medieval Houses of England and Wales 1300–1550*, 3 vols (Cambridge, 1996–2006), ii. 116; P. Morant, *The History and Antiquities of the County of Essex*, 2 vols (East Ardsley, 1978 edn), i. 408n.

[72] *The Records of the Honourable Society of Lincoln's Inn: The Black Books*, ed. W. P. Baildon, R. Roxburgh, 5 vols (London, 1897–1968), i. 48, 50, 52, 55–8, 60, 68, 72–3, 83; *The Records of the Honourable Society of Lincoln's Inn: Admissions from AD 1420 to AD 1799* (London, 1896), 14–21; Ives, *Common Lawyers*, 36–59; *SCC*, xxxi, xxxv, 3–28; J. C. Wedgwood, *History of Parliament: Biographies of the Members of the Commons House, 1439–1509* (London, 1936), 349; *CIPM*, i. 977, 1175. For further links with Hobart and Fortescue, see *Paston Letters and Papers*, i. 183; NRO, Bishop's Register 12, fo. 23v; *CIPM*, ii. 392.

[73] *Lincoln's Inn Black Books*, i. 148, 184; *Historical Monuments in London*, ii. 45, 47.

[74] *Minutes of Parliament of the Middle Temple*, ed. C. T. Martin, 4 vols (London, 1904), i. 4, 5, 8, 25, 42, 69.

[75] Ives, *Common Lawyers*, 8–15.

gained in other settings. Financial competence was generally acquired in less formal ways than legal, usually by service as clerk to a more senior accounting official, as Heron served Lovell or Cope served Bray.[76]

Their material surroundings suggest that filing and accounting came naturally to the new men. In his house at Elsings in Enfield Lovell had a counting house with an 'old square large board covered with green say' and two 'long old chests with coffers in them', but he also kept a 'counting board covered with green cloth' in his great parlour and 'a little counting board of wainscot' in his London lodgings at Holywell Priory.[77] Dudley's London house at his fall was found to contain a counting house inside the little parlour, 'a coffer with bills and boxes with evidence' in the gallery next to the great chamber, 'divers evidence and other writings' in a closet within the great chamber, two 'gardeviances wherein be divers obligations concerning the king and other evidence and writings concerning to other persons' and 'a coffer with bills and writings' in the little wardrobe, 'a coffer wherein bills and other writings be' in the low gallery by the gardens, and—one senses the exhaustion of the cataloguers—five 'old coffers with evidence as they say' in the great gallery that lay beyond. Lawyer that he was, he also had 'a boke of the statutes written'.[78]

Removal from these surroundings could be disorientating. A letter describing the failure of one of Henry's ministers, probably Empson, to find some vital documents, records his excuse that in his 'other study from whence his books be now late transposed, he could have soon found them, but his books be removed to his new lodging and he kn[oweth not?] where they now lie'. 'He hath oft times promised to cause them to be searched', continued the frustrated petitioner, 'but he forgetteth'.[79] To lessen such difficulties, effective information management reached down to the level of individual documents. Wyatt's property deeds and manorial court rolls were carefully endorsed with identifying notes such as 'The indenture between John Lawrens and me for the lands in Chalk', or 'The court roll of Dame Elynsbery holden in my feoffees' names in anno xxiiº', many in his own hand.[80] Lovell's private estate and household administration consumed writing materials relentlessly: in 1522–3 alone two reams of paper for accounts, letters, and memoranda, three books of paper to record payments, a roll of parchment, three large skins of vellum, one and three-quarter pounds of sealing wax, and 6d worth of pin-dust, metal filings for blotting.[81]

Though they had little education in rhetoric by the standards of the generations that followed, the new men were suave letter-writers. Lovell promised one correspondent 'And that I can reasonably do to your pleasure, I shall be glad to my power . . .

[76] J. R. Hooker, 'Some Cautionary Notes on Henry VII's Household and Chamber "System"', *Speculum* 33 (1958), 70–2; PRO, E36/285.
[77] PRO, PROB2/199, mm. 1–2, 9.   [78] PRO, E154/2/17.
[79] KUL, Marquess of Anglesey papers, General Correspondence box 1 no. 2.
[80] PRO, E210/10765; SC2/153/18.
[81] Belvoir Castle, MS a/c no. 4 (*HMC Rutland*, iv. 263).

By your lover, Thomas Lovelle'.[82] Hussey characteristically opened with greetings 'In my most hearty wise' or 'In my right hearty manner' or declared himself 'right glad to hear of your good welfare'.[83] Faced with a long-running dispute among the Cinque Ports, Poynings offered that 'forasmuch as the said matter there depended before so many discreet persons . . . if they all could not make an end thereof . . . then he would be glad to take further pains in the premises'.[84] Having secured a lease of lands from York corporation for his nephew, a prebendary of the Minster, Bray told the mayor, aldermen, and citizens 'I heartily thank you and, for your kindness and good minds, ye shall be assured to have me your friend to do for you at your reasonable desire, with the help of Jesu, who preserve you.'[85] After years of legal practice, men like Lovell were probably quick with the right spoken words, too: when chosen speaker of the commons in 1485 he graciously 'thanked all the masters of the place'.[86]

At their best they were considerate about the demands their work placed on others, Wyatt warning Wolsey of a document he had drafted that 'it will be tedious to your grace to hear it read, it is so long'.[87] But they could be brisk, even brutal, when urgency was required or efficiency impaired. 'I marvel ye should be in any doubt for the matter ye wrote to me for', Lovell told a ditherer, 'for I showed you the king's mind in certain'.[88] As chancellor of the duchy of Lancaster, Marney rapped a peer of the realm over the knuckles for conduct the like of which 'none' had 'been seen nor used in the duchy'.[89] Dudley allegedly told a Londoner haggling over the price of a pardon, 'agree with the king or else you must go to the Tower'.[90] Belknap reportedly spoke his mind to the French commander trying to cut corners at the return of Tournai:

> Well, said Sir Edward Belknap, you must understand that we have a commission from the king our master to deliver you the city at a day appointed: wherefore we must show the king of England both your commission that you had authority to receive it from the French king, and also that you by your indenture sealed with your seal of arms shall confess that you receive the city as a gift, and not rendered as a right to the king your master, or else be you sure that the city shall not be delivered.[91]

The same brusqueness inspired their auditing. In 1506–7, Empson disallowed as unjustified an expense payment on one set of duchy of Lancaster accounts which had been allowed in every year since 1422.[92]

---

[82] *Records of the Borough of Nottingham*, iii. 402.

[83] PRO, SP1/70, fo. 202, SP1/72, fo. 41r, SP1/83, fo. 101 (*LP* V. 1238, 1556, VII. 516).

[84] *A Calendar of the White and Black Books of the Cinque Ports*, ed. F. Hull, Kent Records 19 (London, 1967), 171.

[85] *York Civic Records*, ed. A. Raine, 8 vols, YASRS 98, 103, 106, 108, 110, 112, 115, 119 (Wakefield, 1939–53), ii. 170.

[86] *The Red Paper Book of Colchester*, ed. W. G. Benham (Colchester, 1902), 62.

[87] PRO, SP1/17, fo. 38 (*LP* II, ii. 4400).

[88] *Materials*, i. 549.   [89] PRO, SP1/30, fo. 127 (*LP* IV, i. 103).

[90] M. R. Horowitz, '"Agree with the King": Henry VII, Edmund Dudley and the Strange Case of Thomas Sunnyff', *HR* 79 (2005), 330.

[91] Hall, *Chronicle*, 596–7.

[92] R. Somerville, *A History of the Duchy of Lancaster, I, 1265–1603* (London, 1953), 264.

With efficiency and persuasiveness went a shrewdness in judgment that appealed to Henry VII, who let them address him in straightforward terms. Wyatt wrote to him from the northern borders in 1496 of one local gentleman's efforts in the king's service 'I am sure he would promise largely, but I would he did half so mickle'.[93] In another letter, still extant in the seventeenth century but now lost, he reportedly told the king, 'Sir, by whose advice soever you take this course, give me leave to tell you, that it is not for your worship'.[94] Such habits left them free to offer Henry VIII equally direct advice, like Poynings's comment on an English spy in France, 'I think it expedient both in war and in peace that Your Grace have such one in the French king's court'.[95] Lastly, they combined martial ability with these administrative and political skills. They all fought when they had to, to win Henry the throne, keep him on it, and make a mark for him and his son on the European stage. His colleagues were credible soldiers, but Poynings was an independent commander of stature and a fighting man to inspire others. In Ireland, in 1494–5, Sir James Ormond, battle-hardened nephew to the earl of Ormond, called him 'as good a man as I know', and the Irish parliament praised his 'great wisdom and manhood'; sixteen years later, at the siege of Straelen, he 'ever was in the forward with his archers'.[96]

It is hard to say how self-consciously meritocratic they were. They did not scorn the dignity of ancestry when they happened to possess it. Poynings used the crowned key badge of his noble forebears at every turn, on his seals, on his war banner, carved over the entrance, and plastered on the ceiling of his house; and Thomas Spinelli must have got from somewhere the idea he passed on to Margaret of Austria in 1511, that she should call Poynings cousin because he was kin to the earl of Northumberland, one of the most notable men of the kingdom.[97] In his will Poynings insisted that his granddaughters by his daughter's marriage to Lord Clinton should 'marry with none but such as be of noble blood as they are'.[98] Dudley, who married into the parliamentary peerage whence his forebears had sprung, hanged his house with flowery heraldic tapestries matching his arms with those of his wife Lady Lisle, and had pots, cups, and cloths marked with the arms of Dudley.[99] Marney and Windsor displayed their long ancestry among the gentry of Essex and Middlesex in their armorial bearings.[100] Belknap had the arms of distinguished families to whom he was distantly related carved into the wood of his house at Weston under Wetherley.[101] Lovell, more

[93] A. Conway, *Henry VII's Relations with Scotland and Ireland, 1485–1498* (Cambridge, 1932), 238.

[94] BL, Addl. MS 62135, fo. 468r.   [95] PRO, SP1/8, fo. 139 (*LP* I, ii. 3025).

[96] Conway, *Scotland and Ireland*, 151; Hall, *Chronicle*, 523.

[97] BL, Addl. Ch. 1519, 9074; 'Banners, Standards and Badges, temp. Hen VIII', *Collectanea Topographica et Genealogica* 3 (1836), 60; Hasted, *Kent*, viii. 65; Clinch, 'Westenhanger House', 80–1; ADN, B30131.

[98] PRO, PROB11/20/21.   [99] PRO, E154/2/17.

[100] J. Ashdown-Hill, 'A Pyramidal Seal Matrix of Sir John Marney (1402–c1471)', *Essex Archaeology and History* 38 (2007), 120–5; *History from Marble, Compiled in the Reign of Charles II by Thomas Dingley, Gent.*, ii, ed. J. G. Nichols, CS, o.s. 97 (London, 1868), 146–7.

[101] C. Carpenter, *Locality and Polity: A Study of Warwickshire Landed Society, 1401–1499* (Cambridge, 1992), 200.

Figure 1. Biting dog from the tomb of Sir John Mordaunt, Turvey, Bedfordshire. Photograph by the author.

modestly, featured the cinquefoil of his great-grandmother's Muswell family in his own arms and badges.[102]

But just as common among the new men was the heraldic inventiveness, often based on verbal puns, which betrayed recent origins. Bray's arms featured a bray or brake, a tool used for breaking hemp; Mordaunt's badge, depicted on his tomb at Turvey (see Figure 1), was a dog biting, or mordant; Cutt's windows were painted with broom branches that had been cut; Heron's seal showed an elegant but predatory heron.[103] Such innovation could be bolstered by borrowing from patrons and a little imaginative genealogy. Bray included the eagle's foot of the Stanleys, the family of Lady Margaret Beaufort's last husband, in his own arms. Then, by 1497, he went to the heralds to grant him the right to quarter the arms of the old Bray family of Northamptonshire with his own, just as Wyatt got them in 1508 to confirm his arms as a variation of those of a better-established family of Wyatts, 'he being descended', as the grant put it with studied vagueness, of their 'house, blood and name'.[104] Bray, intriguingly, liked buying manors that had been owned by families called Bray, sometimes in the distant past.[105]

---

[102] *Historical Monuments in London*, ii. 45, 47; D. Pam, *A Parish near London* (Enfield, 1990), 30.

[103] M. M. Condon, 'Bray, Sir Reynold [Reginald]', *ODNB*; Emery, *Greater Medieval Houses*, ii. 116; Cornwall RO, DDME 624.

[104] M. M. Condon, 'From Caitiff and Villain to *Pater Patriae*: Reynold Bray and the Profits of Office', in M. A. Hicks (ed.), *Profit, Piety and the Professions in later Medieval England* (Gloucester, 1990), 139, 141; Bodl. MS Ashmole 858, fo. 28v.

[105] Condon, 'Profits of Office', 141.

They certainly invoked office and service to the king as a mark of status to a degree new among English elites. One way was to advance steadily up the chivalrous hierarchy. Guildford, Poynings, and Risley were knighted at Henry's landing in 1485, Bray at his coronation, Lovell at Stoke two years later. At Blackheath in 1497 Bray, Guildford, and Lovell were promoted to the senior rank of banneret and Brandon and Hussey were dubbed knights. Cutt, Empson, Englefield, Hobart, Marney, Mordaunt, and Southwell owed their knighthoods to the less bloody circumstances of Prince Henry's creation first as duke of York, then as Prince of Wales; Windsor and Wyatt to the festivities for his coronation. But the 1513 campaign in France saw Hussey, Poynings, Windsor, and Wyatt made bannerets and Belknap knighted.[106] Military service was matched with service in council, and it is striking that Dudley, Wyatt, and Sutton all used the title of king's councillor as part of their personal style as though it were a rank in the peerage or an office of state, while it came readily to others' minds that men such as Bray and Lovell were 'counsellors to the king's grace', as Cicely, duchess of York specified in naming them executors of her will in 1495, or that Hussey was 'one of the king's counsellors' or 'one of the king's most honourable council'.[107] Southwell's sister even recorded on her own funeral monument that her brother had been councillor to Henry VII and Henry VIII.[108]

Much of the new men's approach to the world was shaped by their Englishness. They were imbued with English law and English chivalry, and Dudley argued readily from English history: Edward the Confessor, Harold, Henry III, Richard II, Edward IV, Richard III, and the rebellion of 1497. Yet they were intrigued by the wider world. Dudley thought about law comparatively: the English king had greater need of discreet mercy in applying his laws than other kings, 'considering the great number of penal laws and statutes made in his realm for the hard and strait punishment of his subjects'. He compared the English polity with that of 'the Turks and the Saracens', acknowledging that they, too, have 'much delight to uphold the tree of common wealth' and reflecting on the earthly virtues they achieved despite their deficiencies in religion. In addition to a host of Biblical parallels—Lucifer, Adam, Pharaoh, Sampson, Saul, David, Solomon, Nebuchadnezzar—he cited Charlemagne and Nero and pointed out that the Jacquerie had done the French peasantry little good, for they ended up 'in more subjection and thraldom then ever they were before, the which yet continueth'.[109] His interest in the political lessons of wider history is suggested by his readership of John Lydgate's English version of Boccaccio's *Fall of Princes*.[110] Guildford's last

[106] Shaw, *The Knights of England*, i. 142, 144, 146, 148, ii. 22, 24, 28–9, 34, 36, 39.

[107] M. M. Condon, 'Ruling Elites in the reign of Henry VII', in C. D. Ross (ed.), *Patronage, Pedigree and Power in Later Medieval England* (Gloucester, 1979), 123; Bodl. MS Ashmole 858, fo. 28v; Brasenose College, Oxford, Muniments Cropredy 87 (NRA report); A. H. Johnson, *The History of the Worshipful Company of the Drapers of London*, 5 vols (Oxford, 1914–22), i. 369; *Wills from Doctors' Commons*, ed. J. G. Nichols and J. Bruce, CS, o.s. 83 (London, 1863), 8; WSHC, Register Blythe, fo. 13v; PRO, SP1/28, fo. 177, SP1/32, fo. 150v (*LP* III, ii. 3276, IV, i. 799).

[108] Bodl. MS Ashmole 784, fo. 29r.

[109] Dudley, *Tree*, 27–30, 37, 41, 51–2, 70–1, 80, 85–6, 91–2.

[110] D. Wakelin, *Humanism, Reading, and English Literature 1430–1530* (Oxford, 2007), 37.

pilgrimage took in not only shrine after shrine, but also Livy's tomb, the Venetian doge's ceremonial casting of a ring into the sea, the Murano glassworks, and the Venetian arsenal, where his party minutely examined the latest sea-going artillery. He finally reached Jerusalem riding on a camel, hired from the locals at 'outrageous cost'.[111] The new men's curiosity extended further yet, to the limits of their world. In the last months of his life, Lovell made special efforts to meet Sebastian Cabot, Bristolian explorer and chief pilot of the Casa de Contratación of Seville.[112]

THE CASE FOR THE PROSECUTION

Historians have generally approved of the new men: they smack of seriousness, hard work, meritocracy, professionalism, efficiency, and modernity. Wilhelm Busch, the Freiburg professor who inaugurated modern study of Henry's reign, explained how the 'hereditary nobility had to make way before the talent of the statesman'.[113] As Warbeck's charges might suggest, contemporaries were not so sure. Medwall let his characters question Lucrece's choice of Gaius Flaminius even after she had made it, opening up the debate on Gaius's true nobility rather than closing it down.[114] Meanwhile, another play, probably performed in or around Henry's court, *The World and the Child*, may have intended to give a less sympathetic picture of the new men than Medwall had done. Here the vices Covetous and Folly nearly ruin the knightly hero, Manhood. They are unscrupulous lawyers of base social origin: Folly boasts that he 'can bind a sieve and tink a pan'. They 'plead for the king' but will also take on cases for others, 'be it right or be it wrong'. They have experience of the royal court—'with the courtiers I am be-taught'—as well as the courts of law. They are aggressive, even inappropriately martial: Folly claims to be 'a curious buckler player' and duels with Manhood. They are veterans of the stews, and their attitude to the character Conscience who calls Manhood to his moral duty is that they 'would not give a straw for his teaching'. Yet they are welcomed in monasteries and 'greatly beloved with many a lord'. Their plan is to lead Manhood into evil living and thus strip him of his money. They are foiled at the last only by the timely appearance of Conscience's brother Perseverance, who persuades Manhood to repent. Low origins, versatile skills, good contacts, flexible consciences, and ruthless self-promotion through the exploitation of others' weakness: it was a plausible alternative characterization of the rising official class.[115]

---

[111] *The Pylgrymage of Sir Richard Guylforde to the Holy Land, A.D. 1506*, ed. H. Ellis, CS o.s. 51 (London, 1851), 6–9.

[112] *LP* IV, i. 366.

[113] W. Busch, *England under The Tudors*. Vol. I: *King Henry VII (1485–1509)* (London, 1895), 295.

[114] Lexton, '*Fulgens and Lucrece*', 175–82.

[115] *Here Begynneth A Propre Newe Interlude of the Worlde and the Chylde, otherwise called Mundus & Infans* (London, 1522), B4v–D4r; I. Lancashire, 'The Auspices of *The World and the Child*', *Renaissance and Reformation* 12 (1976), 96–105.

Thomas More, celebrating the accession of Henry VIII in polished Latin verse, wrote in less knockabout style, but his message was the same. Under Henry's father the nobility, 'whose title has too long been without meaning', were 'at the mercy of the dregs of the population', while merchants were 'deterred by numerous taxes', and all feared 'laws put to unjust ends' and were 'on many counts in debt to the king'. Then 'sycophants', 'informers', and 'thieves' with 'sly clutching hands' prospered, and indeed 'each rank in the state was changing character completely', as 'honours and public offices' were 'sold to evil men'. For More, young Henry's accession had put all this right at a blow, but the picture at least raised questions about the wisdom he attributed to Henry VII elsewhere in the poem.[116] His aim was to glorify the Tudors, Warbeck's had been to damn them. But the similarity of their portrayals should give us pause for thought.

Most pointed were the charges levelled at Empson in a poem written around the time of his fall. Two of his enemies seem to have been responsible, William Cornish of the chapel royal, who was in dispute with him in 1504, and the earl of Kent, who had lost land by sale to Empson and by forfeiture to the king at Empson's instigation.[117] This might explain the poem's personal venom against Empson, 'Thou pigman, thou gargoyle', his wife, 'that foul sow's image', and their son, 'prince Empson'. But it is the content of the charges against him that commands attention. Empson, 'a bond churl born' whose father made 'sieves round'—the same trade of sieve-making picked out in *The World and the Child*, which presumably reflects some now irretrievable joke at Empson's expense—was but a 'counterfeit gentleman', who had 'rent old arms down, and set up for them thine'. He rose by 'cunning' rather than valour, for his 'pen was feared' much more than his sword. He curried favour with 'dissembled courtesy' and 'false flattering'. Yet he built up his wealth and landholdings, 'won great good and ground', by 'extortion', ruining good men in the process, for he could 'safeguard' or put 'in jeopardy' whomever he chose. He flaunted his rise through conspicuous consumption, eating at a table 'fatly garnished' with 'briby presents' in rooms decorated with 'rich tapets' and taking in the high way to make himself a park, while his son 'jetteth with his men, like a lord of kind'. He lorded it over urban society 'as king of Northampton' and was sought out by suitors, such that

> About thy door, men should more people see
> Than any duke's gate, that lay in this city.

At his beck and call was a network of 'false naughty knaves' who worked to bring 'true men' 'in trouble', ranging

> . . . over this land wide
> To bring the prey, to your ravenous hand.

---

[116] *Complete Works of St Thomas More.* Vol. 3 part ii: *Latin Poems*, ed. C. H. Miller et al. (New Haven CT and London, 1984), 100–13.

[117] M. R. Horowitz, 'Richard Empson, Minister of Henry VII', *BIHR* 55 (1982), 48–9; S. Anglo, 'William Cornish in a Play, Pageants, Prison and Politics', *Review of English Studies*, n.s. 10 (1959), 353–7; G. W. Bernard, 'The Fortunes of the Greys, Earls of Kent, in the Early Sixteenth Century', *HJ* 25 (1982), 673, 676–7.

Being 'risen suddenly', he should not have counted that Fortune would continue to smile on him, because it was her habit to cast down those who reacted to her promotion with 'pride and covetise', as he had done. The proper outcome was that he should be raised higher still, 'First to be drawn, and then suffer hanging'.[118] This put rotten meat on the bones of More's elegant vagueness and *The World and the Child*'s comic caricatures. Perhaps Perkin Warbeck was right after all?

SERVICE, POWER, WEALTH, AND SURVIVAL

To test the importance of Henry VII's new men, this book will investigate their careers in the round. The next part, comprising Chapters 3 to 6, examines the different spheres in which they served the king. They were active at the centre of government, at court, in parliament, and in the king's council, where they both offered advice and dealt out justice. They were also vigorous officers in local administration, implementing justice as justices of the peace, as sheriffs and as arbitrators and tackling social problems such as enclosure and vagabondage. They took part in the king's increasingly elaborate and burdensome fiscal projects, helping him increase regular sources of income such as those from the crown lands, wardship, and the customs, make irregular direct taxation more effective, and introduce charges for appointments to office and painful fines and expensive pardons for offences old and new. As the money rolled in, they helped to audit income and expenditure and manned proliferating but flexible new financial institutions. They took some part in the government of areas distant from Westminster, in Wales, in Ireland, in Cornwall, and in the far North, but they were more prominent in the diplomacy and warfare that kept Henry's monarchy safe in Europe.

In serving the king the new men became powerful, and they in turn needed social and political power of various sorts to serve the king more effectively. The following part, Chapters 7 to 11, analyses the different means by which they exercised influence in society at the local and national levels. They enjoyed rich and productive relationships with the corporations of many towns, as recorders, stewards, patrons, and protectors, and even at London some won friends among the merchant elite though others generated outrage. Manorial stewardships and other local offices amplified their influence. Their activities depended on the construction of followings of servants, deputies in office, and licensed retainers. They exercised considerable patronage in the church, appointing parish clergy, encouraging the universities, and patronizing or exploiting the monasteries. They used their familiarity with the law and their access to able lawyers to force home their rights. They helped and relied on one another and on other trusted individuals in central politics, they built networks among the county gentry, and they both promoted and were sustained by their kin.

With growing power and in reward for service came growing wealth. Part four, Chapters 12 to 15, examines the accumulation and use of the new men's riches.

---

[118] *The Great Chronicle of London*, ed. A. H. Thomas and I. D. Thornley (London, 1938), 344–7.

Their offices and the fees people paid them for their assistance in dealing with the king gave them large cash incomes, but it was hard to convert cash into land: Henry was not generous with land grants, so marriages, wardships, and land purchases had to be pursued with skill. Once bought, land had to be managed to maximize income and different types of resources—pastures, woods, mills, urban properties, manorial rights—exploited to best effect. Money could not just be hoarded, but had to be spent in appropriate ways—ways that built social status and influence without breaching contemporary notions of what was appropriate. Buildings, clothes, horses, plate, food, entertainment, even tombs and funerals had to echo the new men's power without betraying the fatal 'pride and covetise' of which Empson was accused.

Henry's reign could not last forever. The last part, Chapters 16 to 18, sees how the new men faced the challenges of a new king and of their need to pass on their gains to a new generation. While Empson and Dudley were destroyed at Henry's death, others pressed on, working closely with Wolsey and helping their sons and nephews build careers in royal service. For those who lived past 1529, into the years of Henry's divorce and the break with Rome, events took a darker turn. Commitment to Princess Mary, to clerical colleagues and religious orders who felt bound to oppose the king, to the elaborate piety of the late king's court, caused them grief even when it did not, as it did in Hussey's case, take them to the block. Yet the families they had founded and endowed often survived in the English political elite for generations, sometimes to the present day.

In analysing the new men's careers we shall have to bear a number of questions in mind. How important were they in governing Henry's England, in comparison with the king himself, a man bent on personal monarchy but largely ignorant of the realm before he took the throne, and in comparison with others who served him, with great lords, churchmen, and courtiers? What did they contribute, by personal activity or the forging of institutions, to the perpetuation of the strengths and priorities of Henry's regime beyond 1509? How distinctive were the means by which they exercised power, either in their own behaviour or in the political bonds and local followings they built, when compared with more traditional magnates? Was their conduct in some ways counter-productive for a king who sought stability in the wake of civil war? As we shall see, in imposing justice and extracting revenue, they pressed uncomfortably hard on the peerage, the church, and London's trading elite, while in entrenching themselves in local society they disrupted the established systems of social and political power among the gentry and nobility. Some, perhaps all, abused their power for their own benefit: Dudley and Wyatt ruthless on the land market, Hussey repeatedly troubled for corruption. Could Henry afford servants like these, or was he perhaps protected by the readiness of his other new men to rein in those who went too far? A number of the new men failed in different ways: why did Guildford, Hobart, Empson, and Dudley not enjoy the long-running success of Lovell, Poynings, or Wyatt? And, standing back from their lifetimes, we should ask whether every generation produces individuals who rise to power by their talent, and whether earlier English kings had not had servants like these. How new were the new men really?

SERVICE

3

Council, court, and parliament

Determined to keep his throne, determined to govern well, Henry was an intensely personal monarch. In the end, the new men's power rested on their relationships with him. But they worked out their role in his government through institutions, first and foremost those most closely associated with the king, most firmly established in the traditional workings of the English polity, and best able to contain at the centre of political affairs the king's relationship with his subjects: the king's council, the royal court, and parliament.

COUNCIL

The most obvious place in which the new men made their mark was Henry's council. The council became the central institution of government in Henry's reign, in a way it had not been for previous English kings, though it remained a fluid body, meeting in smaller or larger groups at different times of year and in different places. Part of its importance lay in the way it brought together the great peers trusted by the king with the leading bishops, lesser clerics, household noblemen and knights, lawyers, and financial officers, coordinating the efforts and the advice of groups who in other ways served the king in separate spheres. In some ways, it might even be seen as a corporate substitute for the dominating individual will of the ideal medieval king, necessary perhaps at a time when government was becoming ever more complex and ambitious, and yet the occupant of the throne knew at first hand more about Brittany than Britain.[1] Matters of the greatest weight were discussed there—war, peace, and the defence of Henry's throne—but also matters of fine financial, judicial, and legislative detail.

Surviving records of the attendance and business at council meetings are patchy, and this makes it hard to discuss its activities in as much depth as their importance warrants. But it is clear that from its earliest recorded sessions in 1486–91 Bray, Guildford, Lovell, and Risley were among the most regular

---

[1] M. M. Condon, 'Ruling Elites in the reign of Henry VII', in C. D. Ross (ed.), *Patronage, Pedigree and Power in Later Medieval England* (Gloucester, 1979), 128–34; M. M. Condon, 'An Anachronism with Intent? Henry VII's Council Ordinance of 1491/2', in R. A. Griffiths and J. Sherborne (eds), *Kings and Nobles in the Later Middle Ages* (Gloucester, 1986), 228–53; J. L. Watts, '"A New Ffundacion of is Crowne": Monarchy in the age of Henry VII', in B. Thompson (ed.), *The Reign of Henry VII* (Stamford, 1995), 48–50.

attenders, and Brandon came from time to time.[2] In a rota of 1494, Bray, Guildford, and Lovell were marked to be continually present in the council alongside a handful of bishops and clerical lawyers and a rotating mix of courtier peers and judges, and minutes of 1493–5 show that this mix was often achieved, whether at the royal palaces along the Thames or on progress into Kent and the Midlands.[3] At various times in the 1490s others joined them: Empson, Hobart, Mordaunt, Poynings, and Wyatt.[4] In the last years of the reign, Bray, Mordaunt, and Guildford were removed by death, but the others remained active, and younger men came in, too: Dudley, Ernley, Lucas, and Southwell.[5] When contemporaries tried to name the most important councillors, whether to praise, influence, or condemn them, Bray and Lovell often featured, alongside officers of state such as Cardinal Morton, Bishop Fox, or, later, the earl of Surrey, and leading household peers such as Daubeney.[6] This fitted the facts that they were often with the king when they were not in council, and that other councillors away from court kept in touch with the king by writing to them.[7]

Over time, specialized groups within the council developed to deal with particular areas of business. The most notorious was the council learned in the law, a small body which generally met in the duchy of Lancaster council chamber at Westminster or in St Bride's parish in London. Bray, then Empson, led it, and its members included Mordaunt, Dudley, Lucas, and Hobart. It concentrated on the pursuit of the king's rights over his subjects and on turning them to profit.[8] Other conciliar tribunals, as we shall see, were designed to deal either with judicial matters or with those of audit. While the council might contract, it might also expand. At least four times Henry called together great councils of lords, prelates, judges, and town representatives to discuss major issues of war, peace, and dynastic security, though what role the new men played in promoting the king's agenda in such gatherings is unclear.[9]

OFFICES AT COURT

Henry's court played a complementary role to his council as an instrument of government. It was both a place to meet and negotiate with the leading men of his realm and a means to display his kingliness to his subjects in a way that would win their obedience. It could meet either need in different ways by basing itself at the

---

[2] *SCC*, 1–22.   [3] PRO, REQ1/1, fos. 1r, 40r–110r.

[4] *SCC*, 23, 28–32, 50–8; PRO, REQ1/1, fo. 91r.

[5] *SCC*, 33–46; *CSPS*, i. 564–71, 573–4; *CPR, 1494–1509*, 308, 419, 465, 471, 544.

[6] *CSPS*, i. 204; *CSPM*, 299, 335, 550; *CSPV*, i. 743; *Correspondencia de Gutierre Gomez de Fuensalida*, ed. Duque de Berwick y de Alba (Madrid, 1907), 419, 448; *The Great Chronicle of London*, ed. A. H. Thomas, I. D. Thornley (London, 1938), 278.

[7] *CCR 1500–9*, nos. 68, 142; PRO, E404/81/3.

[8] R. Somerville, 'Henry VII's "Council Learned in the Law"', *EHR* 54 (1939), 427–42.

[9] P. Holmes, 'The Great Council in the reign of Henry VII', *EHR* 101 (1986), 840–62.

great royal palaces around London or by moving around the country on progress, visiting towns, religious houses, and seats of aristocratic power. It was protean as well as mobile. It had an institutional core, the royal household, a body of clear but complex structure designed to provide for the practical needs of the king and his entourage. But it also had an important and fluctuating penumbra of lords, gentlemen, and hangers-on; and even some of the office-holders—esquires and knights for the king's body, for example—were not expected to be permanently in attendance on the king, but to use their household office to convey the king's authority into the localities.[10]

At the head of the two sides of the household were the lord steward and lord chamberlain, one responsible for the more practical side of its life and the other for the more ceremonial. But much of the work of running the household traditionally devolved onto senior officers of knightly rank, the treasurer and comptroller, and these were offices held by a succession of the new men. Lovell was certainly treasurer by May 1503, perhaps ten years earlier, and kept the post until 1519, when he was succeeded by Poynings.[11] Guildford was comptroller by 1494 and was followed by Hussey, who gave way at the accession of Henry VIII to Poynings, who, in turn, remained comptroller until he moved to the more senior post of treasurer.[12] These household officers welcomed outsiders to court on the king's behalf, the mayor and aldermen of London at Twelfth Night 1494, for example.[13] They took a lead in organizing court events: in 1519 Lovell, together with Windsor, Wyatt, and Cutt, planned the mourning for the Emperor Maximilian in St Paul's Cathedral 'and other honourable ceremonies as to the obsequies of so great a prince it appertaineth'.[14] That they were often at court by virtue of their offices—Hussey, for example, recalled in 1529 that he had been at Richmond as comptroller when Henry VII died, while Poynings stayed with the court on the plague-ridden progress of 1518—reinforced their position as prominent councillors.[15] These were men who could speak to the king, as contemporaries knew: one monk of Christ Church Canterbury reported to his prior that he had delivered a warrant to Guildford, 'and as soon as he may have the king at any leisure, he will speak to have it signed'.[16]

The treasurer and comptroller of the household together oversaw expenditure of some £14,000–£20,000 a year, peaking at the great festivals at Easter and Christmas

---

[10] S. J. Gunn, 'The Courtiers of Henry VII', *EHR* 108 (1993), 23–49; S. J. Gunn, 'The Court of Henry VII' in S. J. Gunn and A. Janse (eds), *The Court as a Stage: England and the Low Countries in the Later Middle Ages* (Woodbridge, 2006), 132–44.

[11] Shropshire Archives, 946/A427; *LP* II, ii. 3897, III, i. 223; C. S. L. Davies, 'The Crofts: Creation and Defence of a Family Enterprise under the Yorkists and Henry VII', *HR* 68 (995), 258n.

[12] Sean Cunningham, 'Guildford, Sir Richard', *ODNB*; *Memorials*, 106; *LP* I, i. 438(3 m. 8); PRO, E36/214, fo. 148r; E101/418/16, fo. 35v, 419/2.

[13] *Great Chronicle*, 251.   [14] BL, Addl. MS 45131, fos. 34v–35v.

[15] 11 Henry VII c. 62; 1 Henry VIII c. 16; BL, Cotton MS Vespasian C XIV, fo. 229r (*LP* II, ii. 4124); *LP* II, ii. 4075, 4266, IV, iii. 5774(5v).

[16] *Christ Church Letters*, ed. J. B. Sheppard, CS n.s. 19 (London, 1877), 70; dated by death of John Nethersole, *Reports of Sir John Spelman*, ii. 364n.

and for special events such as the arrival of Katherine of Aragon in 1501.[17] In practice the detailed cash-flow was more the responsibility of the cofferer, whose accounts survive in larger number and more detail and were more thoroughly audited.[18] This was the post that Cope held from 1494 to 1508, and one in which Henry told him he was expected to operate 'as if he were treasurer of our said household indeed', a responsibility recognized in the act of parliament of 1510 earmarking moneys for the household.[19] Characteristically, the system was more fluid than it might appear. The treasurer and comptroller signed off not only large drafts to the cofferer, but also smaller sums for events such as chapters of the order of the garter.[20] And while technically fulfilling an inferior role, tasked with items of irregular expenditure, such as payments to the heralds for their participation in court ceremonial, the treasurer of the chamber, first Lovell, then Heron, then Wyatt came, as we shall see, to occupy a central position in crown finance.[21]

The regular absence from court of lord stewards and lord chamberlains who were active military and diplomatic figures and great local magnates—Giles, Lord Daubeney; Robert, Lord Willoughby de Broke; Charles, Lord Herbert; George Talbot, earl of Shrewsbury—also made work for the new men who acted as their deputies. Lovell, for example, kept order in the court by presiding over the court of the verge as deputy to the lord steward, while Guildford deputized for the chamberlain at the great court gathering of All Hallows 1488.[22] By the 1490s, the captaincy of the king's guard had been linked to the office of vice-chamberlain, and Marney stood in for the lord chamberlain on some grand occasions, such as the peerage creation ceremony of February 1514 and the reception of the papal sword that May.[23] He was also involved in the care of visiting ambassadors.[24] His presence at court was sufficiently important that he always featured on lists of those who should be provided with lodgings there.[25]

Other household officers played distinct parts in providing for the king's needs and maintaining royal magnificence. As master of the horse from Easter 1498, a safe appointment in succession to the troubled Sir Edward Burgh, Brandon was in charge of the royal stables.[26] He led a staff more than eighty strong in caring for the horses and vehicles needed to transport the king and his entourage over

[17] PRO, E101/412/9, 413/9, 415/6, 416/15.

[18] PRO, E101/414/2, 415/6, 415/9, 415/12, 416/1, 416/14.

[19] D. M. Loades, *The Tudor Court* (Bangor, 1992 edn), 60, 74–6; J. R. Hooker, 'Some Cautionary Notes on Henry VII's Household and Chamber "System"', *Speculum* 33 (1958), 70–4; 1 Henry VIII c. 16.

[20] *LP* I, i. 404; *The Register of the Most Noble Order of the Garter*, ed. J. Anstis, 2 vols (London, 1724), i. 236.

[21] *The Herald's Memoir 1486–1490: Court Ceremony, Royal Progress and Rebellion*, ed. E. Cavell (Donington, 2009), 107, 180.

[22] PRO, KB9/427/79; *LP* I, i. 1266 (10), ii. 2055 (60); *Herald's Memoir*, 162.

[23] A. Hewerdine, *The Yeomen of the Guard and the Early Tudors: The Formation of a Royal Bodyguard* (London, 2012), 12; BL, Egerton MS 985, fos. 60v–61v.

[24] *LP* II, ii. 3446, 3471.   [25] *LP* III, i. 491, 528; *HMC Rutland*, i. 21.

[26] PRO, E404/81/2, writ of 13 May 1493; E404/81/3, writ of 18 December 1493; E404/83/1, writ of 21 June 1499?; E404/83/3, writ of 18 November 1500.

distances short and long. He spent, to judge from earlier and later accounts, £400 or more a year in addition to the supplies of horse harness sent him from the great wardrobe, some workaday, some luxurious, covered in crimson velvet edged with cloth of gold and studded with gilt copper bosses even in Henry VII's time.[27] It was his senior subordinates who did most of the administrative work, the successive avenors and clerks of the stable William Hatcliffe and William Pawne. They had served long apprenticeships in royal administration and, in Pawne's case, in the service of Henry's first master of the horse, Sir John Cheyney.[28] For a hunter and jouster like Brandon, the chance to preside over the finest stables in the kingdom and thereby to serve the king in an area close to his heart must have been enjoyable. A parallel role was played by Guildford as master of the armoury in supplying materials for the many tournaments with which Henry entertained himself and his court and kept his leading subjects tuned up for war.[29]

Wyatt's very different skills were well suited to his court office. He was appointed clerk of the king's jewels by September 1486, confirmed seventeen months later, and succeeded by 1492 to the more senior post of master of the jewels, keeping it till 1521 or 1524.[30] He was responsible for the care of the king's plate and jewellery, an important aspect of the magnificent monarchy Henry wished to display to foreigners and his own subjects and an important stock of reserve wealth should the king need to spend suddenly. Inventories suggest that he did a good job of conservation: it is likely that 735 of the 887 items in the jewel house listing of 1521 had belonged to Henry and many of them survived beyond Wyatt's time in the post, including two gold toothpicks monogrammed HE for King Henry and Queen Elizabeth.[31] Even Henry VIII, when he wanted to withdraw precious stones from Wyatt's stock for his own purposes, had to sign a receipt at top and bottom.[32] Wyatt was also responsible for repairs, such as those carried out to some of Henry VII's most impressive adornments so they could be taken on the French expedition of 1492 as the king campaigned in state.[33]

Wyatt took responsibility for acquisitions, too. In 1495 he travelled to Holt Castle to help inventory the forfeited goods of Sir William Stanley, including his 'great

---

[27] *LP* I, i. 20; S. J. Gunn, *Charles Brandon, Duke of Suffolk, c.1484–1545* (Oxford, 1988), 12; M. Hayward, *Dress at the Court of King Henry VIII* (Leeds, 2007), 275–76; *The Great Wardrobe Accounts of Henry VII and Henry VIII*, ed. M. Hayward, London Record Society 47 (Woodbridge, 2012), 40–1, 54–8, 60–1, 228–9, 238–9, 278, 280.

[28] *LP* I, i. 449(14); PRO, E404/86/2/100; *Materials*, ii. 20; S. T. Bindoff, *History of Parliament: The House of Commons 1509–1558*, 3 vols (London, 1982), ii. 308–9; A. R. Myers, *The Household of Edward IV* (Manchester, 1959), 65; *A Collection of Ordinances and Regulations for the Government of the Royal Household* (London, 1790), 144, 200–7.

[29] W. R. Streitberger, *Court Revels, 1485–1559* (Toronto, 1994), 22–6; S. J. Gunn, 'Chivalry and Politics at the Early Tudor Court', in S. Anglo (ed.), *Chivalry in the Renaissance* (Woodbridge, 1990), 122–4; Gunn, 'Courtiers', 34, 37, 39.

[30] *CPR, 1485–94*, 136, 433; *CCR 1485–1500*, 250; *LP* I, i. 20, III, ii. 2016(17); P. Glanville, 'Cardinal Wolsey and the Goldsmiths', in S. J. Gunn and P. G. Lindley (eds), *Cardinal Wolsey: Church, State and Art* (Cambridge, 1991), 142.

[31] Hayward, *Dress*, 77.   [32] Bodl. MS Rawlinson A290, fo. 4 (*LP* I, ii. 3571).

[33] Conway, *Scotland and Ireland*, 39n.

broad chain of gold', his 'little pax with St George gilt', and his £9,000 or so in cash.[34] Later in the reign, bequests of plate to the king, or the use of plate to pay off debts to the crown, were marked in the chamber accounts as Wyatt's area of responsibility.[35] He commissioned new work from goldsmiths when the king required it for his own use or for distribution as New Year's gifts.[36] He moved royal plate around to the palaces where it was needed or even overseas on campaign, and handed out appropriate supplies to members of the royal family leaving the court, again taking careful inventories.[37] He delivered chalices, patens, crucifixes, images, candlesticks, and bells to the clerk of the closet for the king's private devotions.[38] He led a stable and experienced staff, several of his half-dozen yeomen and grooms of the jewel house serving ten years or more, taking on increasing responsibility and winning various rewards from the king.[39] His expertise also made him a source of advice to those who wanted to know what kind of jewellery would please his royal masters.[40]

Yet more wide-ranging were the activities of the great wardrobe, of which Windsor became master 'in the meantime' in 1505 in succession to his step-father Sir Robert Lytton and permanently from 1506 to the end of his life.[41] From its base in Carter Lane, near St Paul's, and with ready access to London's luxury craftsmen and the Italian merchants who imported sumptuous fabrics, the great wardrobe provided the monarch and anyone else he cared to reward with clothing, accessories, and soft furnishings, a vital element of magnificent royal display.[42] For most of Windsor's time, annual expenditure ran at between £3,000 and £5,000, though it went beyond £8,000 in the heady days of 1511–12 and regularly rose beyond £6,000 in his last years. By the 1530s the wardrobe's capacity to overspend its budget and run up debts to impatient Londoners seems to have vexed Thomas Cromwell more than it did Windsor.[43] The staff was small, though once again experienced: Laurence Gower, the clerk who kept the accounts, had been at the wardrobe more than twenty years when Windsor took over and survived throughout his tenure.[44] Much of the final look of what was produced was determined by the king's tailor. But the keeper was in charge, held responsible by act of parliament for wardrobe expenditure.[45] Windsor's signature, not only on indentures about the delivery of annual accounts, but also on some warrants, shows his active engagement.[46] When things needed doing fast, he received notes like that from Wolsey in

[34] PRO, E154/2/5.
[35] BL, Addl. MS 21480, fos. 177r, 183r; PRO, SC1/58/52.
[36] *LP* I, ii. 3336, II, ii, pp. 1446, 1460, 1478–80, IV, ii. 3739.
[37] BL, Addl. MS 59899, fo. 15v; *LP* I, ii. 3360(1), II, i. 139, 284, ii, App. 6.
[38] *LP* IV, ii. 3085.
[39] *LP* I, i. 20, 749(10), II, ii, p. 1478, III, i. 102(18), 1114, ii. 2750, III, ii, p. 1535, V. 980(6), 1270(3), 1370(15), 1589.
[40] *LP* III, i. 1090.   [41] PRO, E404/85/113/1; *CPR, 1494–1509*, 470.
[42] For what follows, see Hayward, *Dress, passim*; *Great Wardrobe Accounts*, xi–li.
[43] *LP* VIII. 978, IX. 725(ii), X. 254, XII, i. 576, ii. 1122, 1151.
[44] *Great Wardrobe Accounts*, 3n; PRO, E101/423/6, m. 2d.
[45] 1 Henry VIII c. 17; 4 Henry VIII c. 17.
[46] PRO, E101/417/3/51, 52, 79; E101/420/1/33, 67; E101/420/14, 421/3, 421/16, 602/5; E315/455, 456.

March 1515, beginning 'Master Windsor, the king's pleasure is', instructing him to equip a herald going to Scotland with a tabard of the royal arms.[47] When the sums involved were large, he was personally involved in negotiations, as in the series of agreements drawn up in the 1520s between Florentine and Lucchese merchants and royal officers for the delivery of silks and cloth of gold to the king.[48] And he lived above the shop, since the great wardrobe was his London home: it was there, for example, that his wife died in January 1531.[49]

Royal tastes might vary and had to be accommodated. Late in his reign, Henry VII often wore black, though purple and russet also featured, and he did not have much liking for embroidery. Already in winter 1508–9 his son was showing a penchant for yellow cloth of gold and crimson velvet and, as king, he wore a much wider range of colours in more complex styles. Clothing also had to be fitted to the season or event, for weddings, lyings-in, christenings, feasts, or funerals. For the wider court, livery clothing was provided, often in the Tudor colours of green and white and well sprinkled with roses and portcullises. For departing members of the royal house or satellite households, whole stocks of clothing had to be provided: for Princess Mary on her way to France in 1514; for her niece and namesake in the Welsh Marches in 1525; and for Henry Fitzroy, duke of Richmond, sent north at the same time.[50] For those in the king's special favour, the best in dress had to be procured: Charles Brandon and William Compton in 1511–12, Henry Norris and Nicholas Carew in 1522.[51] For those who wanted to retain the king's favour, Windsor helped arrange appropriate gifts, like a bed costing £118 2s 1½d from Wolsey.[52] For those in the king's disfavour, there were tapestries, like Buckingham's, to be confiscated, and there was a regular supply of clothes to prisoners of state: some, like Lord William Courtenay, found release and restoration; some, like Edmund de la Pole, earl of Suffolk, release through execution; others, like the earl's brother William de la Pole, incarceration for twenty-five years or more.[53]

The great wardrobe's activities touched on many aspects of life at court and beyond. In wartime it provided banners for commanders—St George and the red dragon with flames for the earl of Surrey in 1512, St George and the duchy of Guyenne for the marquess of Dorset in the same year, St George and the royal arms for the duke of Norfolk in 1542—and small green and white pennons with imperially crowned red roses, to mark the carriages of the king's treasurer of war.[54] In peacetime it provided surplices for the choir of the chapel royal and gowns for the

[47] PRO, E101/418/5/2.

[48] PRO, E211/131, 202; E41/207 (with Windsor's signature); *LP* III, ii. 2835, IV, ii. 4699, 5350; *Great Wardrobe Accounts*, xxxviii–l.

[49] CA, MS I 15, fo. 145r; *LP* XV. 1029(68).

[50] *LP* I, ii. 3360(2), II, ii, p. 1470, App. 6, IV, i. 1577; Hayward, *Dress*, 311; *Great Wardrobe Accounts*, 244.

[51] BL, Addl. Ch. 7925; BL, Egerton MS 3025, fos. 21r, 25r, *Great Wardrobe Accounts*, 204, 252–3.

[52] *LP* VII. 923(xii).

[53] *LP* III, ii. App. 25; *Great Wardrobe Accounts*, 95–6, 196, 213–14, 261; PML, Rulers of England box 2/11.

[54] BL, Egerton MS 3025, fos. 26v, 40v; *LP* XVII. 725, 741.

poor men at the royal Maundy.[55] At parliament time it provided the red worsted or say hangings for the parliament chamber and gilt nails to pin them up.[56] When diplomacy was in hand it provided materials for court entertainments before visiting ambassadors or gifts for the king to give them.[57] To keep the royal palaces attractive and warm, it arranged regular repairs to tapestries and other hangings.[58] For Henry VII's most private needs it provided his close stool, covered with black velvet and equipped with six pewter basins.[59] For ease of transport in his last months it provided white and green cloth for covering his barge and his great boat.[60] And when there were deaths in the royal house or obsequies to be performed in honour of departed foreign princes, it supplied mourning cloth to the court and the many other fabrics required for a state funeral, in the case of Henry himself to the value of £6,000 and more.[61]

PARTICIPATION AT COURT

Participation in great ceremonial occasions was also an important part of life at court. In the early years, as the dynasty was established, Arthur christened and Queen Elizabeth crowned, Bray, Guildford, Lovell, Poynings, and Risley were much involved.[62] Later, for the funerals of Prince Edmund and the queen, and Princess Margaret's espousal, they were joined by newer arrivals such as Belknap, Heron, Hussey, Marney, Mordaunt, Southwell, and Wyatt.[63] At Henry's own funeral on 9–10 May 1509, as his coffin was brought first from Richmond to St Paul's, then from St Paul's to Westminster, the new men played their parts again. Lovell and Cutt were among the executors authorizing payments by Heron for the costs, while Windsor and Brandon were responsible for expenditure on cloth and horses and Wyatt for payments to messengers. In the funeral procession, Brandon as master of the horse led a courser trapped in black velvet embroidered with the royal arms, while also having responsibility for fifty men with staves to control the crowd. At the point of interment the leading household officers, including Lovell as treasurer and Hussey as comptroller, cast their rods of office into the grave. Belknap, Cope, Cutt, Hobart, Hussey, Lovell, Marney, Risley, Southwell, Windsor, and Wyatt all drew allowances of black cloth for themselves and their servants to join in mourning the king.[64] Six weeks later, the cloth being issued was red and

---

[55] *LP* V. 862–3; *Great Wardrobe Accounts*, 113–14, 234, 248–9, 284.
[56] *LP* V. 470, VII, 53; *Great Wardrobe Accounts*, 245, 284.
[57] *LP* II, ii, pp. 1443, 1541, IV, iii, App. 150.
[58] *Great Wardrobe Accounts*, 143, 145, 155–8, 231–2, 280.
[59] PRO, E101/416/3, fo. 21v.
[60] PRO, E101/417, warrant of 4 November 1508.
[61] *LP* I, i. 19, II, ii, pp. 1450, 1471, III, ii, pp. 1536, Addenda, i. 130.
[62] *Herald's Memoir*, 103, 105, 133, 148–9, 161–2, 165, 182; *LPRH*, i. 403.
[63] PRO, LC2/1, fos. 4v–5r, 59r–60r, 67v, 72r; *Joannis Lelandi Collectanea*, ed. T. Hearne, 6 vols (Oxford, 1774), iv. 260.
[64] *LP* I, i. 19, 20 (1, 4, 5).

scarlet for the coronation, most reprising their roles.[65] Then the sad duties revived, as Poynings, Windsor, Hussey, and Southwell saw young Prince Henry to his grave in 1511.[66]

Service at court remained personal service to the king. Early in the reign, Lovell and Brandon were esquires for the king's body and may well have waited on him in his most intimate moments. In 1489 Brandon was rewarded for his service with black satin cloth.[67] Those who held the same office later on, such as Hussey, may also have attended closely on the king, though Henry increasingly withdrew into a privy chamber staffed by more humble servants.[68] The king's chief relaxations were hunting and hawking, and in their different ways the new men provided for these diversions. In July 1493 Wyatt supplied the king with a white horse, and a year later Lovell was paid £3 for broad-headed arrows for hunting deer.[69] From 1494 to 1507, Brandon repeatedly supplied horses, hounds, hawks, and falcons, and once was rewarded for finding two hares.[70] In 1503 a servant of Poynings brought hawks to the king, and in 1505 Wyatt rewarded a man who had kept the king's deer in his pastures.[71] They also catered for a range of other diversions. Lovell laid bets with the king and provided clothing for a high-wire walker who entertained him, while Brandon rewarded minstrels and French visitors.[72] The king watched jousts with pleasure, and Brandon was an expert participant. At the tournament to celebrate Prince Henry's creation as duke of York in 1494, his horse trapper covered in his crowned lion's head badge, Brandon broke lances and swords, recovered from a near-unhorsing, and won the answerers' prize of a gold ring with a ruby.[73] Bernard André thought that his jousting skill gained his election to the garter.[74] His nephew, Charles, followed him into the lists and starred in the tournaments of the last years of the reign alongside Hussey's son William and Guildford's son Edward.[75]

Service at court was also service to the wider royal family. Hussey made his house at Dagenhams in Romford, Essex, available to the wife and children of Lord William Courtenay after Courtenay's arrest on suspicion of Yorkist plotting in 1502. He was doubtless prompted to do so by the queen, for Lady Katherine

---

[65] *LP* I, i. 82, 94(33).   [66] *LP* I, i. 707.

[67] *CPR, 1485–94*, 23; *Materials*, ii. 495; *Collection of Ordinances*, 109–16, 118.

[68] *CPR, 1485–94*, 455; D. R. Starkey, 'Intimacy and Innovation: The Rise of the Privy Chamber, 1485–1547', in D. R. Starkey (ed.), *The English Court from the Wars of the Roses to the Civil War* (London, 1987), 72–6.

[69] BL, Addl. MS 7099, fos. 11r, 18r.

[70] BL, Addl. MS 7099, fo. 14r; Addl MS 59899, fos. 20r, 41v, 48r; PRO, E101/414/6, fos. 13r, 24r, 70r, 414/16, fos. 33r, 44r, 61v, 63r, 64r, 415/3, fo. 49v, E36/214, fo. 107v.

[71] BL, Addl. MS 59899, fos. 32r, 96r.

[72] PRO, E101/415/3, 414/16, fo. 63v; *Great Wardrobe Accounts*, 257; BL, Addl. MS 59899, fo. 25r.

[73] *LPRH*, i. 397–400.   [74] *Memorials*, 122.

[75] *Lelandi Collectanea*, iv. 262–3; PRO, E36/214, fos. 10v, 16v, 20r, 24r; F. H. Cripps-Day, *The History of the Tournament in England and France* (London, 1918), xlvii; *Remains of the Early Popular Poetry of England*, ed. W. C. Hazlitt, 4 vols (London, 1864–6), ii. 109–30.

Courtenay was the queen's younger sister, and the queen paid for her children's upkeep.[76] He also accompanied Princess Margaret to Scotland for her wedding in 1503 and Princess Mary to France for hers in 1514, together with Windsor and Wyatt.[77] Such contacts could be informal and fleeting: at one point, Henry told Guildford to spend some time with the princes while he talked to Bray.[78] Marney's role in Prince Henry's household was something more substantial, tantalizingly hard to reconstruct, but clearly important; perhaps the stewardship. His patent of creation as a peer in 1523 spoke of how he had served Henry with probity, loyalty, and hard work since the king's tender years.[79] In 1501 he was with young Henry in St George's Fields to welcome Katherine of Aragon; in 1502 he had a pallet bed where he could sleep in the prince's lodgings; and in 1505 he was at the prince's side when he temporarily repudiated his betrothal to his brother's widow.[80] He was close to the prince's other servants. His son Thomas was one of Henry's carvers, cupbearers, and gentlemen waiters, and his daughter Grace one of his gentlewomen.[81] He was supervisor of the will of Ralph Pudsey, gentleman waiter and keeper of the prince's jewels, and executor to William Compton, Henry's closest body servant; and for Sir John Raynsford, another of the prince's household men, he felt, in the words of Raynsford's son, a 'hearty, old and assured love'.[82] He was in the inner circle of those to whom the prince gave New Year's gifts in 1508–9, and at Henry VII's funeral he marched with Compton and the prince's other men.[83]

The new men's wives often served the queen as they served the king. Lady Bray was close to Elizabeth of York from Arthur's christening and the coronation through to the queen's final years and funeral.[84] Lady Lovell, too, moved in her circle, sending her an ivory chest carved with the crucifixion as a gift in 1502.[85] By 1502–3, a Mistress Belknap, presumably Edward's wife or daughter, likewise served the queen.[86] The most remarkable record was that of Lady Jane Guildford. She served Elizabeth from her coronation to her death, having begun in the household of the king's mother, and went on to serve her daughters Margaret and Mary, ending by escorting Mary to the French court.[87] Lady Poynings seems not to have

---

[76] *Privy Purse Expenses of Elizabeth of York: Wardrobe Accounts of Edward the Fourth*, ed. N. H. Nicolas (London, 1830), 32, 62–3, 76–7.

[77] *Lelandi Collectanea*, iv. 292, 299; *LP* I, ii. 3348(3), II, i. 1374.

[78] Hooker, 'Some Cautionary Notes', 75.

[79] *Foedera, Conventiones, Literae et cujuscunque generis Acta Publica*, ed. T. Rymer, 20 vols (London, 1704–35), xiii. 787 (*LP* III, ii. 2936).

[80] *LPRH*, i. 410; PRO, E101/415/7, fo. 10; *CSPS*, i. 435.

[81] PRO, LC2/1, fo. 73r–73v.

[82] PRO, PROB 11/15/35; *LP* IV, ii. 4442(1); T. Penn, *Winter King: The Dawn of Tudor England* (London, 2011), 308; PRO, STAC2/20/26.

[83] *The Antient Kalendars and Inventories of the Treasury of His Majesty's Exchequer*, ed. F. Palgrave, 3 vols (London, 1836), iii. 397–8; *LP* I, i. 20.

[84] *Herald's Memoir*, 103, 105, 145, 159, 164; *Privy Purse Expenses of Elizabeth of York*, 10, 18, 21, 23, 28, 52–3, 54, 57, 67; PRO, LC2/1, fo. 78r.

[85] *Privy Purse Expenses of Elizabeth of York*, 15.

[86] *Privy Purse Expenses of Elizabeth of York*, 13, 38, 52, 99; PRO, LC2/1, fo. 78r.

[87] *Herald's Memoir*, 150, 164; *Privy Purse Expenses of Elizabeth of York*, 52, 99; B. J. Harris, *English Aristocratic Women, 1450–1550* (New York, 2002), 217–19; W. C. Richardson, *Mary Tudor, the White Queen* (London, 1970), 108–11.

been a great presence at court, but did join her husband in his posting to Tournai, riding into the city on 28 November 1513 at the head of a train of thirty gentle-women whose husbands were serving in the garrison.[88]

The greatest event staged by Henry's court, the wedding of his heir Arthur to Katherine of Aragon in 1501, shows the central part taken by the new men and their families, as organizers and participants, in the court's projection of Henry's magnificence. The best guides to the event's planning are two early schemes, one of them printed because so many people needed to know what was planned. They had to be modified as it became clear that Katherine would not arrive either at Southampton or by boat up the Thames, but by road from her landfall at Plymouth; however, they can be complemented by later, less complete plans, by chronicles, and heraldic accounts.[89]

Under the early plans, Risley was to help Lord Willoughby de Broke organize Katherine's arrival at Southampton while Lovell was to prepare lodgings in the Tower for Katherine's ladies.[90] Guildford, working with Sir Charles Somerset, cap-tain of the guard, was to organize the construction of barriers to manage the crowds around St Paul's and conduits running with wine, staging inside the cathedral so the couple could be visible without any 'impediment to the sight of the people', and a flower-strewn gallery along which they could walk to the high altar.[91] For the celebrations after the wedding, Guildford was in charge of cosmetic repairs to Westminster Hall and Westminster Bridge and the provision of tournament equip-ment, viewing stands, and a large tent.[92] Cope, as cofferer, was to see to the pay-ment for the feast after the wedding, while Bray handled negotiations with the London authorities about the costs of the pageants.[93] Wyatt must have been in charge of the stupendous display of plate at the wedding banquet, which he took the mayor of London, a goldsmith, to view together with other expert aldermen; their estimate of its value was £32,000.[94]

The new men and their relatives were also significant participants. In the early plans, Brandon and Hussey were to join Marney in the party with Prince Henry to welcome Katherine as she arrived by river at the Tower of London. All were to be marshalled by Lovell and Bishop Fox, and Brandon and Lovell were to ensure that only 'such honest persons as shall be thought convenient by the discretion of the said Sir Thomas Lovell' be admitted to the landing wharf.[95] These arrangements

[88] Robert Macquéreau, *Traicté et recueil de la maison de Bourgogne*, ed. J. A. C. Buchon, Choix de chroniques et mémoires sur l'histoire de la France 16 (Paris, 1838), 58.
[89] *The Receyt of the Ladie Kateryne*, ed. G. Kipling, EETS 296 (Oxford, 1990), xi–xii.
[90] *LPRH*, ii. 104; *Miscellaneous State Papers. From 1501–1726*, ed. P. Yorke, Earl of Hardwicke, 2 vols (London, 1778), i. 7.
[91] *Miscellaneous State Papers*, i. 12–15; *LPRH*, i. 413; *The Traduction and Mariage of the Princesse* (London, 1500), fo. 5r–5v.
[92] *Miscellaneous State Papers*, i. 17–18; *LPRH*, i. 405, 416; *Traduction*, fo. 7v; S. Anglo, 'The Court Festivals of Henry VII: A Study Based on the Account Books of John Heron, Treasurer of the Chamber', *Bulletin of the John Rylands Library* 43 (1960–1), 37.
[93] *Miscellaneous State Papers*, i. 16; *Great Chronicle*, 310.
[94] *Great Chronicle*, 312–13.
[95] *Miscellaneous State Papers*, i. 6–7; *Traduction*, fo. 3r.

were superseded, but when the welcoming party awaited her in St George's Fields it included not only Marney, Hussey, and Brandon, but also Poynings and Risley, with Risley—who had always been responsible for making sure Prince Henry was in the right place on the wedding day—now playing Lovell's role alongside Fox.[96] Jane Guildford was among the ladies appointed to meet Katherine of Aragon when she arrived, singled out to dance 'right pleasant and honourably' with Arthur to show off his skills on the day he first met his bride. Thomasina Risley and Isabel Poynings were also among the welcoming ladies.[97] In the procession on the wedding day, Brandon wore a gold chain reckoned to cost £1,400 and remarkable not for its length but for 'the greatness of the links'; and when he marshalled the tournaments, Guildford, too, sported a 'great and massy' chain.[98] On the morning after the wedding, Brandon's nephew Charles waited on the prince and he began his court jousting career at the celebration tournament.[99]

The great lords of the court of course played more conspicuous roles than the new men in the pageantry of the affair—Surrey, Oxford, Buckingham, Bergavenny, Willoughby de Broke, and Daubeney—as did the realm's leading clerics, but the new men's contribution was vital both behind the scenes and on the stage. Henry needed them not only for their courtliness, but for their flexibility and eye for detail. Early in the planning process, Guildford volunteered to take on any tasks which had been assigned to Willoughby de Broke, but which illness might prevent him from carrying out. Under both earlier and later versions of the plans, Robert Southwell was commissioned with Sir William Vampage to 'oversee and perfectly peruse' the book of plans and 'not only to advertise every man that hath any charge committed to him to be ready, and to do their offices, but also to call upon them for the execution of the same'.[100] In the new men's court service, dignity and efficiency were combined.

PARLIAMENT

Henry made vigorous use of parliament as a means to consult his subjects, bolster his finances, and legislate for the common good.[101] In his parliaments and those of his son, royal councillors were expected to take a leading role, and the new men did so. Though records are thin, we know that many of them sat as knights of the shire, the socially and politically weightier part of the commons' membership. Bray sat regularly for Hampshire, Lovell and Risley for Middlesex, Empson for Northamptonshire, Marney for Essex, Guildford for Kent, and Mordaunt for Bedfordshire; the

---

[96] *LPRH*, i. 410; *Miscellaneous State Papers*, i. 12.
[97] *Miscellaneous State Papers*, i. 2–3; *Receyt*, 8.
[98] *Great Chronicle*, 311; *Receyt*, 65.
[99] Gunn, *Charles Brandon*, 5; *Receyt*, 109.
[100] *Miscellaneous State Papers*, i. 19; *LPRH*, i. 406.
[101] P. R. Cavill, *The English Parliaments of Henry VII, 1485–1504* (Oxford, 2009).

first six were all there in 1491–2, for example.[102] Over time, others joined or replaced them: Englefield for Berkshire, Poynings for Kent, Hussey for Lincolnshire.[103] Younger or less powerful individuals took borough seats, like Cope at Ludgershall in 1491–2, or worked their way up: Dudley from Lewes in 1491–2 to knight of the shire for Sussex, Windsor from an unknown constituency in 1510 to the county seat for Buckinghamshire in 1529.[104] Others no doubt represented the many constituencies for which no evidence survives between the well-documented parliaments of 1491 and 1529.

Within the commons they took a lead in getting the government's business done. Most conspicuously, they often acted as speaker. Lovell in 1485 presided over the debates in which there was much 'commoning for the common weal of all the land', for example over the coinage, but in which some matters, such as the attainder of those who had fought for Richard III at Bosworth, were 'sore... questioned with'.[105] He also led the commons in asking Henry to marry Elizabeth of York, so that they might commence 'the propagation of offspring from the stock of kings'.[106] Mordaunt followed him as speaker in 1487, Empson in 1491–2, Englefield in 1497, Dudley in 1504, in a session with business almost as controversial as that of 1485, including an attempt to raise feudal aids diverted into a peacetime subsidy and a sharp act against retaining. Sheffield took up the baton in the new reign, as speaker in 1512.[107]

In the absence of commons' journals or parliamentary diaries, it is hard to document the role taken by the new men in processing parliamentary business from beyond the speaker's chair, but it seems to have been a large one. In 1495 it was Bray, Empson, and Guildford who led a delegation to the lords to announce that the commons had chosen their speaker; in 1497 it was Lovell; and in 1512 it was Poynings.[108] Lovell led the commons delegation to the lords to collect the customs bill on 23 February 1510 and brought the bill on enclosure and the decay of villages from the lower to the upper house on 27 February 1515.[109] In 1512 Sheffield led a delegation to the lords to discuss benefit of clergy and in 1515 he helped draft the act of resumption.[110] In 1523, when the commons found Wolsey's tax demands exorbitant, it was Hussey who broke the deadlock by suggesting that the richer landowners be more heavily burdened, a proposal which succeeded because his fellow members were unwilling to contradict it, but which earned him 'much evil

[102] R. Virgoe, 'Sir John Risley (1443–1512), Courtier and Councillor', *NA* 38 (1981–3), 144; J. C. Wedgwood, *History of Parliament: Biographies of the Members of the Commons House, 1439–1509* (London, 1936), 104–5, 300, 403–4, 575–6, 607–8; Bindoff, *Commons*, ii. 548–9; 'List of Members of the Fourth Parliament of Henry VII', ed. W. Jay, *BIHR* 3 (1925–6), 169–70.

[103] Bindoff, *Commons*, ii. 103–4, 423–4, iii. 146–7.

[104] Wedgwood, *Commons*, 219, 285–6; Bindoff, *Commons*, iii. 633–6.

[105] *The Red Paper Book of Colchester*, ed. W. G. Benham (Colchester, 1902), 63–4.

[106] *PROME*, vi. 278.

[107] J. S. Roskell, *The Commons and their Speakers in English Parliaments, 1376–1523* (Manchester, 1965), 298–316.

[108] *PROME*, vi. 458, 510; *LJ*, i. 11.   [109] *LJ*, i. 8, 29.

[110] Bindoff, *Commons*, iii. 305.

will'.[111] Engagement in parliament gave an opportunity to advance matters of personal interest: private acts for Windsor and Wyatt, provisos to bills that might affect Lovell's grants from the king.[112] But service to the common weal came first even when they regretted it. Hussey reported wistfully to his friend Lord Darcy on 6 July 1523 that 'We be yet so busied with common causes in the parliament that there is no leisure to solicit our own particular matters', and again ten days later that 'our common businesses have been and be so great that we cannot attend our own'.[113]

The new men featured in the lords, too. It was testimony to their dependability that Hussey and Windsor were among those promoted when Henry VIII wanted reliable lay peers in the house for the coming confrontation with the church, the queen, and the pope in the parliament of 1529.[114] The solicitor-general and attorney-general, who attended in the lords under writs of assistance, also played a central role in preparing and processing parliamentary business. Hobart, Lucas, and Empson, for example, negotiated a deal between the king and the nuns of Syon ready for statutory ratification in 1504.[115] Ernley and John Port, Lucas's successor as king's solicitor, took charge of forty-nine bills between them in the parliaments of 1510, 1512, and 1515.[116]

In parliament, as in court and council, the ubiquity of the new men gave Henry's regime its characteristic air of purposeful, if not always popular, activity. Their versatility was striking: the same men presented political advice and argument in council and parliament, organized household hospitality and display, kept the king company, participated in court ceremonial, and brokered the relationship between the king and his subjects in a multiplicity of institutional contexts. They were equally important in more specialized areas of government, judicial and financial.

---

[111] Hall, *Chronicle*, 657.
[112] *PROME*, vi. 286, 345; 11 Henry VII c. 48 s. 6, c. 63 s. 8; 14 & 15 Henry VIII c. 20 s. 7, c. 21 s. 6, c. 21 s. 21, cc. 31–2.
[113] PRO, SP1/28, fos. 105, 118 (*LP* III, ii. 3164, 3183).
[114] H. Miller, *Henry VIII and the English Nobility* (Oxford, 1986), 22–4.
[115] Cavill, *English Parliaments*, 117, 162.
[116] Christopher Whittick, 'Ernley, Sir John', *ODNB*.

4

The pursuit of justice

The pursuit of justice was a fundamental aim of Henry's government. As Dudley put it, the 'root of justice' was essential to the health of 'the tree of commonwealth' and must be secured by royal power: justice 'must needs come of our sovereign lord himself, for the whole authority thereof is given to him by God, to minister by himself or by his deputies to his subjects'.[1] The new men were essential agents of the king's judicial policy both at the centre and in the localities and of its perpetuation into the reign of his successor.

THE COUNCIL COURTS

Under Henry, the judicial activity of the king's council was of increasing importance in the resolution of disputes and the maintenance of order. It alone operated with the speed and flexibility to bypass the rigidities of the common-law courts and the power to impose settlements on the king's greatest subjects. Various conciliar tribunals were established by statute to deal with corrupt juries, miscreant courtiers, perjury, and illegal retaining, but none of them showed much vigour, since the tendency was always for business to be drawn into the wide scope of the council's general jurisdiction. Whether sitting in the Star Chamber at Westminster or on progress with the king, Henry's councillors heard cases of all sorts, concentrating on abuses of power, acts of disorder or perversion of justice, but inevitably also responding to the clever framing of suits to attract their attention.[2]

In the most significant cases, Henry VII and Wolsey after him used the council courts as a conspicuous means to do justice on great men or local magistrates. The new men were often present when they did so. Lovell was there with Henry in May 1488 when Lord Grey of Codnor and Sir Henry Willoughby were ordered to keep the peace and in November 1504 when the earl of Northumberland and archbishop of York were called to account for their disorder. He was there with Wolsey in October 1519 when Sir William Bulmer was punished for wearing the duke of Buckingham's livery, rather than the king's, at court, and in January 1520, when the justices of the peace of Norfolk and Suffolk were reprimanded for neglect of

---

[1] Edmund Dudley, *The Tree of Commonwealth*, ed. D. M. Brodie (Cambridge, 1948), 34.
[2] S. J. Gunn, *Early Tudor Government 1485–1558* (Basingstoke, 1995), 81–9, 107–8; *SCC*, xlix–lxxii, cxxii–cxxvi.

their duty in enquiring into murders, robberies, and other misdemeanours.[3] They were involved when the council settled disputes between mighty corporations. Marney was sitting, for example, when Wolsey made an award in the contention between Norwich city council and the cathedral priory that had lasted nearly a hundred years.[4] They also heard local cases in different regions as the council attendant moved with the king. In 1494–5, for example, Lovell sat on the council's judicial business not just at Sheen, but at Canterbury, Woodstock, and Langley.[5]

In Henry's reign much remained flexible, and councillors often investigated problems informally at the king's command. Thus, in 1502, when Margaret Kebell fled from her husband and arrived at Greenwich claiming to have been abducted and married against her will, the king detailed Lovell and Mordaunt to examine her husband's uncle about his role in the affair.[6] Yet expanding business encouraged formalization in the council's judicial structures. A president was appointed to lead its judicial sessions; here, the rise of the new men was shown in the appointment of Dudley as president in 1506 in succession to two bishops.[7] The council learned began to operate independently, mainly to pursue the king's rights, but also to hear suits between parties, sometimes remitted by the main body of the council.[8] As the success of the council courts led them under Wolsey to become choked with cases, so committees had to be set up to streamline their work, and again the new men— Belknap, Hussey, Wyatt, and above all Windsor—played a part.[9] The courts also used local commissions to question witnesses and conduct other investigations, and Hussey, for example, served on these.[10] In the 1530s the structure of the royal council mutated more drastically under the pressure of the politics of the royal divorce, and an executive privy council distinguished itself from judicial courts of star chamber and requests. For older councillors this might mean exclusion from the new privy council, but a continuing role in judicial affairs: Hussey, Windsor, and Wyatt continued to sign star chamber orders in the early 1530s, at a time when they were clearly no longer at the centre of policy-making.[11]

[3] *SCC*, 17, 42; HL, MS El 2653, fos. 1r, 16v; J. A. Guy, *The Cardinal's Court: The Impact of Thomas Wolsey in Star Chamber* (Hassocks, 1977), 32.

[4] Guy, *Cardinal's Court*, 68–9; *LP* III, ii, App. 12.

[5] S. J. Gunn, 'The Court of Henry VII' in S. J. Gunn and A. Janse (eds), *The Court as a Stage: England and the Low Countries in the Later Middle Ages* (Woodbridge, 2006), 137–8; PRO, REQ1/1, fos. 1r, 40r, 81r–110r.

[6] E. W. Ives, '"Against Taking Away of Women": The Inception and Operation of the Abduction Act of 1487', in E. W. Ives, et al. (eds), *Wealth and Power in Tudor England: Essays presented to S. T. Bindoff* (London, 1978), 40.

[7] *SCC*, xxxvii–xl; M. M. Condon, 'An Anachronism with Intent? Henry VII's Council Ordinance of 1491/2', in R. A. Griffiths and J. Sherborne (eds), *Kings and Nobles in the Later Middle Ages* (Gloucester, 1986), 240.

[8] R. Somerville, 'Henry VII's "Council Learned in the Law"', *EHR* 54 (1939), 430–4, 440–1.

[9] Guy, *Cardinal's Court*, 37–42; *LP* III, i. 571, IV, ii. 2837, iii, App. 67, Addenda, i. 64 (2); HL, MS El. 2655, fos. 12r, 16r, 18r.

[10] *Select Cases before the King's Council in the Star Chamber*, ii, ed. I. S. Leadam, SS 25 (London, 1911), 129–30; *REED Lincolnshire*, ed. J. Stokes, 2 vols (Toronto, 2009), i. 20.

[11] J. A. Guy, 'The Privy Council: Revolution or Evolution?', in C. Coleman and D. Starkey (eds), *Revolution Reassessed: Revisions in the History of Tudor Government and Administration* (Oxford, 1986), 68–85; PRO, STAC2/17/399, 19/205; *York Civic Records*, ed. A. Raine, 8 vols (Wakefield, 1939–53), iii. 164.

As in royal finances, in judicial matters the duchy of Lancaster formed a microcosm of the workings of the early Tudor regime. The duchy council heard disputes between tenants and others subject to its jurisdiction on the duchy's lands scattered across England and Wales, but was also engaged in the administration of justice in Lancashire by its oversight of the justices who sat at Lancaster. In February 1511, for example, it ordered the imprisonment of riotous Lancashire gentry in Lancaster Castle to await the king's pleasure and make fine for their offences.[12] Marney, busy at court, did not always preside over the council's judicial business, but was there for important sittings, whether they concerned the inheritance of Lord Fitzwalter or peat-cutting in the common marsh at Methwold in Norfolk.[13] When a new generation took the helm of the duchy in the person of Sir Thomas More, chancellor from 1525, the new men were there alongside him, Hussey and Windsor still active as members of the duchy council.[14]

THE COMMISSIONS OF THE PEACE
AND THE SHRIEVALTY

The everyday work of local justice rested on the justices of the peace, commissioners recruited mainly from local gentlemen and lawyers. Henry's regime increased the powers and duties of the JPs, increased the numbers of commissioners appointed in each county, and increased central supervision of their activities, making them a cornerstone of the king's provision of justice.[15] The new men played several parts in this process. They were named to commissions regularly in the counties where their lands or significant offices lay. From the start of the reign Lovell and Hobart were commissioned in Norfolk, Poynings and Guildford in Kent, Bray in Surrey, Risley in Middlesex, Mordaunt in Bedfordshire, and Empson in Northamptonshire. In the 1490s Lovell joined the Middlesex bench, Marney that for Essex, Hussey those for the different parts of Lincolnshire, Dudley that for Sussex, Belknap that for Warwickshire, Lucas that for Suffolk, and Southwell that for Norfolk. After 1500, Wyatt was named for Essex, Middlesex, and Surrey; Windsor for Hampshire, Middlesex, and Buckinghamshire; Cutt for Essex; and Cope for Oxfordshire. Such appointments of men trusted by the king to administer their home counties were to be expected, but at times of political crisis, such as the mid-1490s, Henry added his leading councillors, the new men prominent among them, to a wide range of commissions to oversee the local elites. This brought Bray, Guildford, and Lovell into commission in large numbers of counties, sometimes just for a year or two, but sometimes for much longer: Lovell remained a JP for eight counties to his death. Towards the end of Henry's reign, as

[12] R. Somerville, *A History of the Duchy of Lancaster, I, 1265–1603* (London, 1953), 280; PRO, DL5/5 fo. 16r.

[13] PRO, DL 5/5, fos. 37–57, 86–211.

[14] J. A. Guy, *The Public Career of Sir Thomas More* (New Haven CT and London, 1980), 28.

[15] Gunn, *Early Tudor Government*, 100–2.

justice took a more fiscal turn, Dudley, Hussey, and Southwell were each added to several further commissions. And after 1509 the surviving new men kept their places, often among the quorum of more honoured, though not necessarily more active, commissioners in each county, and in some cases—Wyatt in Kent, Marney in Middlesex and Cornwall—extended their reach further.[16]

These appointments were more than nominal. While most cases in quarter sessions were heard by legally trained local gentlemen, the new men sat from time to time.[17] Some changed their habits as their careers developed. Dudley was active in Sussex from the mid-1490s; but from 1504, as his work at London increased, he was more often seen at Southwark and Westminster.[18] Wyatt made occasional appearances on the Surrey bench between 1505 and 1521, doing his best to keep the peace as feuds among the older county families disrupted local politics, but made his presence felt in Kent only after retiring from his court offices.[19] Hussey cut his teeth in Lincolnshire on a spectacular case, accompanying Viscount Welles and others in April 1497 to take indictments against the king's master of the horse, Sir Edward Burgh. Burgh had broken into Robert Sheffield's house at West Butterwick and taken him away to Gainsborough, then, with two thousand followers, ambushed the king's justices on their way to Lincoln to investigate the deed. It was the start of a fall from grace for Burgh, which would end in imprisonment, financial ruin, and madness.[20] Hussey's appearances were occasional thereafter, but settled down in the 1510s and 1520s, when his duties at the centre of government were less pressing, into a comfortable routine of local authority at Boston, Folkingham, Sleaford, and Spilsby.[21] One of his local critics recalled in 1536 how he would gather men 'for his own pomp to ride to a sessions or assize'.[22]

Those whose work fitted the rhythms of the legal year, or whose estates lay closer to the usual haunts of the court, did duty more regularly. Hobart was the most assiduous JP of his generation in Norfolk and Suffolk.[23] Risley sat frequently in Middlesex, and Windsor did so again and again from 1505 to the mid-1520s and

---

[16] J. R. Lander, *English Justices of the Peace, 1461–1509* (Gloucester, 1989), 73, 112–20, 139–40; *CPR, 1485–94*, 481–508; *CPR, 1494–1509*, 629–69; *LP* I, ii, pp. 1533–44, II, i. 202, 207, 427, 430, 504, 674, 1220, 4435, 4437, III, i. 1081(24), 1186(13), 1379(19, 26), ii. 2074(14), 2415(6), 2993, IV, i. 464(2), ii. 2002(11), 5083(2), V. 1694; BL, Addl. MS 36773, *passim*.

[17] Lander, *Justices of the Peace*, 62–74; M. L. Zell, 'Early Tudor JPs at Work', *AC* 93 (1977), 125–43; for Empson, Guildford, Englefield, Belknap, and Cutt, see PRO, KB9/369/14, 369/35, 371/9, 398/44, 399/6, 403/14, 404/10, 405/16, 411/2, 411/7, 411/41, 415/18, 418/2, 419/20, 420/62, 421/11, 422/24, 430/10, 431/2, 437/83, 439/40, 440/42, 456/9; for Marney and Southwell, see PRO, KB9/389/17, 406/29, 415/42, 417/88, 436/7, 445/100, 446/43, 446/120; E137/11/4, mm. 11r, 13r.

[18] PRO, KB9/403/1, 406/70, 413/17, 416/53, 417/114, 417/116, 419/22, 425/55, 427/41, 435/54, 437/7, 437/29, 437/101, 443/58, 446/31, 447/30, 446/126, 448/113, 451/47.

[19] PRO, KB9/437/7, 437/29, 447/30, 479/5, 490/10, 518/44, 523/79, 526/40; S. Brigden, *Thomas Wyatt: The Heart's Forest* (London, 2012), 74–6.

[20] PRO, KB9/412/2; E404/81/3; S. J. Gunn, 'The Rise of the Burgh Family, c.1431–1550', in P. Lindley (ed.), *Gainsborough Old Hall*, Society for Lincolnshire History and Archaeology Occasional Papers 8 (Lincoln, 1991), 9–10.

[21] PRO, KB9/429/23, 435/45, 457/3, 508/24, 973/114; E137/20/4/1/3, 20/4/3.

[22] PRO, SP1/110, fo. 139r (*LP* XI. 969).

[23] Lander, *Justices of the Peace*, 36–7, 71.

as late as 1541, not just at Westminster, but at Uxbridge and St John Street in Clerkenwell.[24] He was also busy in Buckinghamshire. In 1508 he certificated with two other justices an alleged riot by the Stonor family at Eton; in 1511 he took indictments at Chalfont St Giles about a murder by a gentleman at Denham; and he sat fairly regularly at Aylesbury and Chipping Wycombe until about 1530, when age got the better of him, and his son William began to take over.[25] Another side of his activities is evident from the household accounts of his neighbour and fellow justice Sir Edward Don. These show both Windsor and his son at work with Don and other local officers to investigate offences, arrest suspects, and bind them over to appear at sessions. The relationship was not always smooth, William Windsor supposedly accusing Don in open sessions of supporting his park keeper in a bold career of robbery and corruption, but then JPs were there to keep an eye on each other as well as on everyone else.[26]

Most telling are the attendance records of Henry's busiest councillors, who prioritized cases that demanded careful handling or a show of conciliar authority. Among other significant matters, Bray oversaw the indictment of an esquire of the king's household for an attack on the keeper of the Fleet prison going about his business inside the Palace of Westminster in 1492.[27] Poynings attended the Kent sessions when he could, but made a special effort for cases important to the good order of the county: riots by the younger members of the Guildford family and their opponents the followers of Lord Bergavenny in May 1503, Bergavenny's own indictment for retaining in January 1507, investigations at the start of Henry VIII's reign into the injustices of the recent past.[28] Lovell sat occasionally in a number of counties, but concentrated on notable disorder, especially when it could be dealt with close to the route of the king's summer progresses and when he could add his legal expertise to the social weight of noble colleagues.[29] In August 1489 he joined the earl of Arundel at Lewes to tackle an epidemic of riotous poaching in Sussex and in July 1493, when the court was at Coventry, he accompanied Lords Daubeney and Willoughby de Broke to deal with an ambush and murder in Northamptonshire.[30] In July 1502, when the king was between Windsor and

[24] PRO, KB9/385/39, 385/40, 394/7, 394/9, 394/19–20, 397/73, 398/5, 398/8, 398/24, 398/36, 402/65, 402/72, 405/34, 408/16, 408/37, 410/57, 413/74, 417/17, 420/12, 423/121, 429/9, 439/35, 439/43, 440/2, 442/16, 442/21, 444/46–8, 445/89, 445/90, 445/109, 445/120, 446/31, 446/126, 447/11, 448/66, 448/112–14, 451/5, 451/29, 451/47, 452/67, 455/85, 455/87, 458/118, 459/87, 460/24, 461/20, 476/32, 476/35, 476/53, 497/58, 550/204, 974/32.

[25] PRO, KB9/448/109, 457/65, 487/15, 509/60, 509/124, 514/68.

[26] *The Household Book (1510–1551) of Sir Edward Don: An Anglo-Welsh Knight and his Circle*, ed. R. A. Griffiths, Buckinghamshire RS 33 (Aylesbury, 2004), 129–30, 160, 164–5, 185, 191, 287, 381; *LP* XIII, i. 532.

[27] M. M. Condon, 'Ruling Elites in the reign of Henry VII', in C. D. Ross (ed.), *Patronage, Pedigree and Power in Later Medieval England* (Gloucester, 1979), 125; PRO, KB9/388/42, 394/9, 394/19, 395/16, 398/25, 398/44, 404/36, 417/19–20, 417/28, 417/50, 420/12, 420/14, 423/121.

[28] PRO, KB9/369/14, 369/35, 399/6, 415/18, 417/61, 418/52, 419/55, 427/2, 429/1, 430/49, 433/31, 433/43, 436/1, 437/28, 437/83, 437/96, 439/40, 442/12, 443/2, 443/17, 444/3, 445/28, 447/19, 452/18, 452/395, 470/23, 475/48, 477/50.

[29] PRO, KB9/378/9, 395/32, 410/57, 410/68, 461/22, 464/102.

[30] PRO, KB9/379/48, 382/38–49, 383/106–7, 400/54; L. L. Ford, 'Conciliar Politics and Administration in the Reign of Henry VII', Univ. of St Andrews Ph.D. Thesis (2001), 230.

Woodstock, he rode over to Caversfield in Buckinghamshire with the marquess of Dorset, the earls of Essex and Surrey, and Sir John Mordaunt to try an Oxfordshire gentleman for armed burglary and arson.[31] In December 1514 he travelled to York to oversee, together with the earl of Northumberland, the indictments of the feuding gentry responsible for rioting at the August sessions in the city and for a series of local murders.[32]

The new men's focus on important cases was heightened by their frequent appointment to the smaller commissions appointed to try the prisoners accumulated in particular prisons or accused of heinous crimes such as treason.[33] Lovell featured on many of these, and Poynings, Marney, Hussey, Southwell, and Windsor also played their part.[34] A variation came in Henry's last years when orders began to be sent out by the council learned to selected JPs instructing them to investigate reported offences, with the aim not only of enforcing good order, but also of levying fines on offenders. Hussey, for example, was told to 'see it found' when word came of a riot between Lord Willoughby's servants and those of Sir William Ayscough in 1504, to probe the 'wilful escape' of a prisoner permitted by two priests in Lincoln, and to look into accusations of riot against William Hansard and his men in 1506.[35]

The post of sheriff, responsible for the coordination of legal process at county level, was also important. As Dudley put it, it was 'a singular furtherance to good and indifferent justice to be had... to appoint good sheriffs'.[36] Service as sheriff, requiring regular presence throughout a year, was harder to combine with central government office than the more flexible role of the JP. It also demanded a certain weight among the county gentry which it was not always easy for an upstart to command. Many of the new men filled the role, but often before their period of peak activity at the centre. Thus Marney was sheriff of Essex and Hertfordshire in 1486–7 and 1492–3, Guildford of Kent in 1493–4, and Hussey of Lincolnshire in the same year, Southwell of Norfolk and Suffolk in 1494–5, Belknap of Warwickshire and Leicestershire in 1501–2, and Ernley of Wiltshire in 1504–5.[37] Cutt served both before and after his busiest years: he was sheriff of Yorkshire in 1504–5, then waited until 1516–17 to be sheriff of Cambridgeshire and Huntingdonshire and until 1519 to fill a vacancy in Essex and Hertfordshire.[38] Others appeared on the

---

[31] PRO, KB9/442/110.   [32] PRO, KB9/373/3, 475/2, 478/8, 466/3.

[33] J. H. Baker, *The Oxford History of the Laws of England.* Volume vi: *1483–1558* (Oxford, 2003), 255–65.

[34] *CPR 1485–94*, 50, 73, 132, 163, 180, 239, 283, 348, 356, 397, 442, 477; *CPR 1494–1509*, 29–33, 53, 86–7, 118, 149, 179, 195, 210, 231, 248, 287, 289, 291, 293–4, 326, 328, 360, 361, 408, 474, 487, 546, 560, 580; *LP* I, i. 289(43), 731(27–8), 1732(2), ii. 2484(27), 2684(41), 3408(37), II, ii. 4444, III, i. 1036(24), 1081(14, 26), IV, iii. 6490(20), V. 278(16), 457(2), XIII, i. 1519(12), XV. 282(6), XVI. 580(18), XVIII, i. 226(8).

[35] Lander, *Justices of the Peace*, 112–20, 139–40; *CPR 1485–94*, 481–508; *CPR 1494–1509*, 629–69.

[36] Dudley, *Tree*, 35.

[37] *List of Sheriffs for England and Wales*, PRO Lists and Indexes 9 (London, 1898), 14, 45, 68, 79, 146, 153.

[38] *List of Sheriffs*, 14, 45, 163.

roll from which the king pricked the names of the sheriffs for each county, but were not selected to serve.[39] A less intensive role in the administration of justice was that of *custos rotulorum*, the justice of the peace charged with custody of the records of proceedings at quarter sessions. Hobart was probably *custos* in Suffolk, by 1515 Hussey was *custos* in Holland, and others may well have held the post.[40] Its importance increased in Henry's closing years as the search for old offences and debts to the crown was pursued. In 1507–9, Wyatt, as *custos* in Surrey, not only certified the surrender of suspects to Guildford Castle prison, but was also expected to ferret out bonds taken by the JPs fifteen years earlier in the hope that some might be forfeit.[41]

IMPRISONMENT

Sheriffs were also responsible for the custody of prisoners in county gaols. Escapes from prison and the failure to arrest recalcitrant suspects were the target of investigation and enforcement by Henry's regime, often by royal commissions on which the new men featured.[42] Those held liable for escapes could be fined, sometimes large sums. Lovell and Bray made arrangements in 1494 for the abbot and convent of Westminster to pay £666 13s 4d for a series of escapes.[43] Empson allegedly turned this policy to the king's profit by setting up arrests and escapes so that London magistrates could be fined for not preventing them.[44] But his colleagues were hit, too: Southwell lost £200 for prisoners escaped during his term of office as sheriff; Hussey and Sheffield £133 13s 4d for an escape at Lincoln; Humphrey Wellesbourne, Lovell's deputy, more than £100 for escapes from Wallingford Castle, plus a spell in the Fleet prison when he did not appear to explain himself.[45]

A more distinctive role in keeping the king's prisoners was occupied by Sir Thomas Brandon, as marshal of the king's bench prison in Southwark. His father had held this office from 1457 to his death in 1491 and it offered the potential for profit from supplying board and lodging or more elaborate comforts to prisoners.[46] Within days of his father's death the prisoners complained that they could buy food, drink, and firewood only at prison rates, where a pint of ale cost a steep half a penny.[47] Prisoners might also be subjected to discomfort, presumably to

---

[39] *LP* I, ii. 3499(12), III, ii. 2020

[40] Baker, *Laws of England*, 266; D. N. J. MacCulloch, *Suffolk and the Tudors: Politics and Religion in an English County 1500–1600* (Oxford, 1986), 36; *LP* II, i. 1374.

[41] *CPR 1494–1509*, 517, 558; M. R. Horowitz, '"Contrary to the Liberties of this City": Henry VII, English Towns and the Economics of Law and Order', *HR* 85 (2012), 39.

[42] *CPR 1494–1509*, 66, 294–5, 357, 361, 379.

[43] WAM 28204–7, 33088.

[44] J. P. Cooper, 'Henry VII's Last Years Reconsidered', *HJ* 2 (1959), 109.

[45] BL, Addl. MS 21480, fos. 94r, 165r, 166r; PRO, DL5/2, fos. 30v, 48r–48v, 50v, 52v, 57r; E404/85/100; KB9/415/5, 7.

[46] *CPR 1452–61*, 395; *PROME*, vi. 291–2; R. B. Pugh, *Imprisonment in Medieval England* (Cambridge, 1968), 120, 166–8, 175, 179.

[47] PRO, KB9/390/14; *CFR*, 136.

extort better payment: one complained that he had been put 'in a place called "paradise" all this holy time of Christmas that he was in point of death' and requested transfer to Newgate gaol instead.[48] There were other windfalls, like the £9 stolen from a merchant which came into Brandon's possession while the thief was in his care.[49] On the other hand, the marshal might be fined for escapes, as Brandon several times was, or sued for compensation by those whose debts were left unsatisfied when prisoners were released.[50]

Sir Thomas led a staff of an undermarshal and at least four keepers, and the undermarshal may have had considerable freedom of action to judge from Brandon's will, which talked of his true service but also of his accounts.[51] The standards of care they maintained may not have been good, to judge from the forty-four prisoners who died from disease in the prison between July 1498 and January 1502.[52] But those who did not die in prison, leave for execution, or escape, but survived to be redeemed by their friends and families or by the charity of the king or other donors, could leave with gracious letters encouraging those they met to support them with alms in any pilgrimage they had vowed to undertake, or to provide them with work.[53] Most of the prisoners were not of great political moment, but some were, whether in the most aggressive phase of Henry's government or in the reaction against it. In 1507–8 it was Brandon to whom Thomas Kneseworth, former mayor of London, and both his sheriffs, were committed while under investigation by Dudley.[54] In 1509 Brandon's prison was among those used to detain the informers arrested alongside Empson and Dudley; and in the months of investigation that followed he signed with other councillors several warrants sealing the fate of prisoners in his charge.[55]

ARBITRATION

The arbitration of disputes by great lords or panels of clerics, lawyers, and gentlemen was a characteristic response to late medieval disputes too complex to be readily resolved at the common law. The result was often a compromise solution which gave both parties an incentive not to renew the quarrel because, for example, one received the disputed land but had to pay the other compensation.[56] As powerful men with some legal training, the new men were much in demand as

---

[48] PRO, C1/145/33.   [49] PRO, PROB11/16/29.

[50] PRO, E404/82/1, warrant of 19 May 1496; KB27/926, m. 30v; BL, Lansdowne MS 127, fo. 49v.

[51] WSHC, G25/1/221; PRO, PROB11/16/29.

[52] PRO, KB9/417–24.

[53] WSHC, G25/1/221; PRO, E101/414/16, fo. 24r.

[54] *The Customs of London, otherwise called Arnold's Chronicle*, ed. F. Douce (London, 1811), xliii; M. R. Horowitz, '"Agree with the King": Henry VII, Edmund Dudley and the Strange Case of Thomas Sunnyff', *HR* 79 (2005), 352–4.

[55] *Great Chronicle*, 343; *LP* I, i. 190(36), 289(35).

[56] E. Powell, 'Arbitration and the Law in England in the Late Midde Ages', *TRHS* 5th ser. 33 (1983), 49–67.

arbitrators and this provided another means for them to pursue the strategy of pacification. Often, the royal council delegated the settlement of suits to councillors singly or in small groups, as it did under Henry VII to Bray, Guildford, Hobart, and Windsor and in 1518 to Lovell.[57] Often, councillors worked together in teams large or small: Bray and Lovell in a minor dispute of 1487; Bray, Lovell, three judges, Cardinal Morton, the earl of Derby, Lords Dynham, and Daubeney in a land dispute between Devon knights in 1499.[58]

Local office-holders were particularly suitable arbiters. Poynings, warden of the Cinque Ports and constable of Dover Castle, acted for Sandwich and Fordwich and settled matters between Dover corporation and Dover Priory.[59] Lovell's wide range of stewardships led him to arbitrate disputes involving St Alban's Abbey, Lenton Priory, and the boroughs of Nottingham and Walsall.[60] A wider prominence in local society might equally invite a role as arbitrator: as the monks of Norwich Cathedral Priory reminded Lovell in one case, they welcomed his involvement because they were 'longest acquainted with' him and he was 'of our country'.[61] Hussey arbitrated disputes among the Lincolnshire gentry; Wyatt among those of Kent; Lovell among those of Nottinghamshire and Norfolk; Windsor among those of Surrey, Berkshire, and Yorkshire; Hobart and Lucas among those of Norfolk and Suffolk.[62]

Hussey's arbitrations involving the Bussy family likewise engaged him with his neighbours, but in characteristically murky fashion. In 1500 he made an award with his fellow Holland JP Reynold Gayton in a dispute between Miles Bussy and the prior of Haverholme, but at about the same time, it was later alleged, he was representing Miles's uncles Edward and Edmund, his partners in land dealings, in an arbitration over the Bussy inheritance, colluding to divert part of it to them. When Miles died in 1525, his elder son John disputed the terms of his will, which left considerable estates to the executors, including his uncles, and the supervisors, of whom Hussey was one, to provide for his daughter and younger son. In 1531 Hussey arbitrated in the dispute between John and the executors. John had been encouraged by his father-in-law, Thomas, Lord Burgh, to put the matter in Hussey's hands, 'for I put no doubt he will be good to you'. But how impartial he could have

[57] PRO, REQ1/1, fos. 32v, 46v, 59v; Library of Birmingham, MS 3279/357335; *Registrum Caroli Bothe, Episcopi Herefordensis*, ed. A. T. Bannister, CYS 28 (London, 1921), 45.

[58] *CCR 1485–1500*, 198, 1096.

[59] KHLC, Sa/Fat 22, mm. 9–10; CCA, U4/8/11, U4/8/87; *A Calendar of the White and Black Books of the Cinque Ports*, ed. F. Hull, Kent Records 19 (London, 1967), 176; BL, Egerton MS 2107, fo. 96v.

[60] KUL, Marquess of Anglesey Papers, General Correspondence, box 1, no. 2; F. W. Willmore, *A History of Walsall and its Neighbourhood* (Walsall, 1887), 180; *Records of the Borough of Nottingham*, ed. W. H. Stevenson, 9 vols (Nottingham, 1882–1936), iii. 345–8, 402.

[61] *The Paston Letters 1422–1509*, ed. J. Gairdner, 3 vols (London, 1872–5), iii. 330–3, 392.

[62] Nottinghamshire Archives, DD/SR12/93/1; *LP* VII. 813; PRO, C146/10599; Berkshire RO, D/ESK/M28; *Plumpton Letters and Papers*, ed. J. Kirby, CS 5th ser., 8 (London, 1996), 190, 289–90; *CAD*, iii. C3436; *LP*, Addenda, ii. 1515; NUL, Mi 2/72/40; C. E. Moreton, *The Townsends and their World: Gentry, Law and Land in Norfolk c.1450–1551* (Oxford, 1992), 93–9, 102; Blomefield, *Norfolk*, iii. 178, vii. 55; NRO, Hare 136; W. A. Copinger, *The Manors of Suffolk*, 7 vols (London and Manchester, 1905–11), vi. 73; HL, MS El 1796.

been, given his role as supervisor of the will, seems open to question. The award did result in new settlements of the estates, but disputes rumbled on, and by 1547 they produced a full-blown denunciation of Hussey's 'crafty counsel and maintenance' in the case, his diversion of £1,000 received under the will to his own purposes, his offers to ignore the will if John would marry his son and heir to his daughter, and his failure to build the £10 tomb Miles had requested.[63]

Kinship imposed a special obligation to help make peace. In 1531 Hussey and his friend Lord Darcy made an award between his nephew George, son of his late brother Sir William, and Sir William's widow and her new husband, by which George was to hold three of Sir William's manors, but pay them £100 a year.[64] Shared service to the king also drew groups of councillors together to arbitrate disputes involving their colleagues. Lovell joined with Guildford and two judges to settle a dispute involving Thomas Garth, a long-serving captain in Ireland and the North, and with Guildford and Poynings to settle one involving their conciliar colleague Christopher Urswick as dean of Windsor.[65] Arbitrating disputes for relatives and friends was a way to strengthen ties of mutual assistance and admiration. Guildford assured his 'cousin' Sir William Scott, whose dispute with the prior of Horton he had been discussing with Scott's brother-in-law Poynings, that if Scott let him 'be a mean between you' to see the dispute 'indifferently heard' then 'ye may be sure I will not see your hurt nor dishonour, but will do for you as I would ye should do for me'.[66] As the new men used what influence they had to settle disputes, so they not only served the king's aim in maintaining order, but also developed their own power further.

SOCIAL POLICY

The work of judicial commissions extended beyond crime and civil litigation into what we might think of as social or environmental policy. One well-established area for this was drainage. In 1489 parliament extended for twenty-five years the powers established under Henry VI to issue commissions of sewers to men in every county who might make orders to promote good drainage and prevent the 'many great hurts and inconveniences... had by increase of water'.[67] Several of the new men were named to such commissions in their areas of influence: Marney and Wyatt in Essex and Middlesex; Poynings and Guildford in Kent, Surrey, and Sussex; Lovell in Lincolnshire, Sussex, and the counties around London.[68]

---

[63] Northamptonshire RO, Bru Dv 13, 21a–c, Dxx 1a, Hiv 41; LA, Mon3/29/40; *CCR 1500–9*, 664; PRO, C1/186/15, 385/33, 472/44–5, 942/74–6; C142/81/216; PROB11/22/4; E41/311.
[64] Hull History Centre, U DDEV/50/10, 25/4 (NRA report).
[65] ERO, D/DFa F12; *CCR 1500–9*, 275; J. C. Wedgwood, *History of Parliament: Biographies of the Members of the Commons House, 1439–1509* (London, 1936), 363–4; Windsor, The Aerary, MS IV.B.3, fos. 226v–130r.
[66] KHLC, U1115/C1.   [67] 4 Henry VII c. 1.
[68] *CPR 1494–1509*, 90, 181, 285, 328, 358–9, 592–3; *LP* I, i. 132(33, 51), 969(45), II, i. 2138, ii. 4573.

The most active among them was Hussey. By the late fifteenth century flooding was a major problem in the Lincolnshire fens and Hussey was named to fifteen commissions of sewers for the area between 1486 and 1531, eight of them between 1503 and 1511.[69] Lady Margaret Beaufort's estates in the hinterland of Boston were regularly damaged, and she paid him £40 in 1499 for works in the town to prevent flooding of the River Witham. Soon her discussions with royal councillors, including Bray, Guildford, and Lovell, led to a more far-reaching scheme, the construction of a sluice to scour the harbour at Boston, for which Hussey contracted with a Flemish engineer in 1500. The sluice was finished in 1502, but Hussey's involvement continued and in 1511 he was advanced £200 from the king's chamber for further expenditure.[70] Meanwhile related projects drew him in. In 1492 he was investigating illegal fishing and swan-hunting on local rivers, in 1507 he was involved in drainage of the land north of Boston, and in 1510 he was overseeing repair of sea banks in Holland.[71] As steward of the duchy of Lancaster manors south of Boston he agreed to speak to the king's council about a new turret and drain for Fleet, without which, he had been warned at the last manor court at Moulton, 'the town will be lost'.[72] As steward of what had been Lady Margaret's manors of Maxey and Deeping, he was commissioned to investigate the ownership of nearby fenland.[73] In 1520 he sat on a commission of sewers further north, at Spilsby.[74]

Between the 1480s and 1520s the king's council repeatedly tackled other social problems, such as enclosure, vagrancy, high food prices, excessive expenditure on clothing, food, and drink by various social groups, and an apparent decline in England's military capabilities. Henry VII's preferred remedies were statutory, but by 1504 his council was naming commissioners, Poynings and Guildford among them, 'for the reformation of idle people and vagabonds not set upon occupation to the great decay and ruin of cities towns boroughs and villages' and to deal with the 'great enormity of apparel, as well by great lords, as gentlemen and other persons, and the excess of meats and drinks and costly fare'.[75] Wolsey took commissions much further. The enclosure commissions of 1517 were a justly famous attempt to measure the depopulating effects of the conversion of arable land to pasture. Lovell and Heron served on the Middlesex commission, Ernley on that for Surrey and Sussex, but the most demonstrably active of the new men was Windsor, named, with one churchman and a Coventry merchant, to cover seven Midlands counties. Between August and October he sat at nine of the eleven hearings for

[69] *CPR 1485–94*, 10; *CPR 1494–1509*, 90, 358, 408, 457, 547; *LP* I, i. 257(48), 804(13), 969(52), ii. 3582(14), II, i. 695, ii. 4131, III, i. 1379(16), IV, i. 213(2), V. 278(17).

[70] M. K. Jones, 'Lady Margaret Beaufort, the Royal Council and an early Fenland Drainage Scheme', *Lincolnshire History and Archaeology LP* 21 (1986), 11–18; *LP* II, ii, p. 1452.

[71] *CPR 1485–94*, 416; PRO, DL3/23/R6; LP II, ii, p. 1449.

[72] PRO, DL34/1/43.

[73] M. K. Jones and M. G. Underwood, *The King's Mother: Lady Margaret Beaufort, Countess of Richmond and Derby* (Cambridge, 1992), 127–8, 276.

[74] PRO, KB9/974/49.

[75] 3 Henry VII c. 13; 4 Henry VII c. 16, 19; 11 Henry VII c. 2, 13; 19 Henry VII c. 12; *SCC*, 40–1.

which the attendance is known, at Bedford, Culham, Eton, Henley, Leicester, Lutterworth, Northampton, Remenham, and Turvey, missing just the two held at Allesley in Warwickshire, while a summons naming him survives for a twelfth session, at Abingdon. The evidence gathered was used to prosecute depopulating landlords.[76]

The new men were also active in nocturnal searches for vagrants in and around London. In summer 1519, Lovell, Marney, and others helped Wolsey plan them. Windsor was one of four commissioners charged with the sensitive areas around Westminster Palace and the abbey sanctuary. Lovell, as constable of the Tower, took care of the poor parishes nearby, as well as Shoreditch and Hoxton, around his London home at Holywell. Wyatt and Cutt took Holborn, Kentish Town, and Paddington, while Heron covered Hackney and Newington. The searches were a serious attempt to stem the tide of masterless men flooding the metropolis and the various moral and social abuses associated with them. In July, for example, Wyatt certified the arrest of three vagabonds and four all-night gamblers, and Heron took two suspect persons, while in the second wave of searches that November, Windsor took two suspect women and one man. Teams of councillors were deputed to examine those arrested, Hussey and Belknap serving for Southwark, Cutt for the eastern suburbs, Cutt and Wyatt for the northern.[77] In November 1524 and February 1525 the exercise was repeated, with Windsor and Wyatt taking responsibility for the same zones and Hussey added to Wyatt's group, while by 1528–9 Hussey was covering the area around St Martin's in the Fields.[78] This direct involvement in London, like that in the enclosure commissions, paralleled the activity of many of the courts over which the new men presided more or less actively as borough stewards. At Grantham, for example, harbouring vagabonds and suspect persons and enclosure of the commons had both been on the agenda during Hussey's time as steward.[79]

When it came to military inefficiencies, Wolsey's approach killed two birds with one stone by combining a survey of the nation's military capacity—the numbers of able men, the distribution of weapons, and the relationships of service and tenure that facilitated recruitment—with an assessment of personal wealth that could be turned to fiscal purposes. Lovell, Marney, Poynings, and Hussey were involved at an early stage, when the council resolved to overhaul the muster commissions in 1516.[80] In 1522 Hussey surveyed the weapons held by Londoners and Windsor personally brought the returns of the military survey for Buckinghamshire into

[76] J. J. Scarisbrick, 'Cardinal Wolsey and the Common Weal', in Ives et al. (eds), *Wealth and Power in Tudor England*, 45–67; P. A. Slack, *Poverty and Policy in Tudor and Stuart England* (London, 1988), 115–16; *The Domesday of Inclosures, 1517–1518*, ed. I. S. Leadam, 2 vols (London, 1897), i. 74, 84–6, 158, 318, 327, 339; Bodl. MS Ashmole 1148 part xi, pp. 5–6.

[77] *LP* III, i. 365.

[78] *LP* IV, i. 1082, Addenda, i. 430, 609, 655.

[79] PRO, SC2/185/39, mm. 1, 3, SC2/185/40, m. 3, SC2/185/41, m. 1.

[80] *LP* Addenda i. 160.

Star Chamber.[81] Attempts to regulate food prices, meanwhile, were in evidence as early as 1518, when Lovell and Marney sat in the council meeting that tried to enforce maximum prices for poultry on the merchants of London and investigate the high price of other meats.[82] In winter 1527–8 grain was short and more far-reaching action was taken, as county commissioners checked the stocks in barns to prevent profiteering. Englefield was named a commissioner in Berkshire and doubtless others elsewhere.[83] These initiatives could not arrest social and economic change, but their breadth and precision testify to the ambitions of the government the new men were helping to build.

JUSTICE AND THE CHURCH

Henry's reign saw a series of confrontations between the king's lawyers and judges and senior churchmen over the boundaries between the church's privileges and jurisdiction and the king's power as administered by them through the common law.[84] The new men might meet these tensions in any of the forums in which they did justice. The king's council, for example, heard cases in Henry's last years between the dean and chapter of Hereford Cathedral and Shrewsbury Abbey and the townsfolk of each place.[85] Under Marney, the duchy of Lancaster twice settled a dispute between the inhabitants of Ogmore and the prior of Ewenny about the priory's failure to provide the spiritual services required by the local population.[86] The post of steward to either university, responsible for the exercise of common-law jurisdiction over the members in order to preserve their privileges before the regular courts of town and county, placed several of the new men at another point where the king's agenda of enforcing order and justice met the liberties of ecclesiastical corporations.

Bray was steward at Oxford from 1493, representing the university's interests to the king, dealing with cases from the commissary's court, and giving generously to the rebuilding of the university church of St Mary the Virgin, while being greeted with wine, comfits, and gloves when he came to visit.[87] He was also steward at Cambridge, which outdid Oxford's hospitality with seals, pikes, tenches, rabbits, larks, and other delicacies, and there he was followed by Mordaunt, then Empson,

---

[81] J. J. Goring, 'The General Proscription of 1522', *EHR* 86 (1971), 681–705; LMA, Rep. 5, fo. 305v; *LP* III, ii. 3687.

[82] *LP* Addenda i. 206.

[83] P. Gwyn, *The King's Cardinal: The Rise and Fall of Thomas Wolsey* (London, 1990), 456–9; *LP* IV, ii. 3587(1).

[84] Baker, *Laws of England*, 237–44, 536–51.

[85] Hereford Cathedral Library and Archives, Hereford Cathedral Muniments 2971 (NRA report); H. Owen and J. B. Blakeway, *A History of Shrewsbury*, 2 vols (London, 1825), i. 279.

[86] PRO, DL5/5, fos. 40v–42v, 190r.

[87] R. L. Storey, 'University and Government 1430–1500', in J. I. Catto and T. A. R. Evans (eds), *History of the University of Oxford, Volume ii, Late Medieval Oxford* (Oxford, 1992), 743–6; *Epistolae Academicae Oxon*, ii, ed. F. Anstey, OHS 36 (Oxford, 1898), 616–17, 621–2, 673–4; *Medieval Archives of the University of Oxford*, ii, ed. H. E. Salter, OHS 73 (Oxford, 1921), 352; *Registrum Cancellarii 1498–1506*, ed. W. T. Mitchell, OHS n.s. 27 (Oxford, 1980), 143.

whom the university asked in 1506 for help in a praemunire suit.[88] Lovell succeeded first Bray at Oxford and then Empson at Cambridge. Oxford lauded him for his justice and prudence not only in the administration of public affairs but also in the defence of their commonwealth, though also complained he was too busy to respond rapidly to their requests; Cambridge made communication easier, at least in 1511–12, by having his chaplain, Thomas Thompson, vicar of Enfield, as vice-chancellor.[89] Meanwhile, Cutt and Hobart were lobbied by Cambridge, and Dudley was appointed in 1505 one of the lay external assessors to oversee the work of the Oxford steward's court.[90]

Other issues, such as churches' right to offer sanctuary to criminals and clerics' right to escape trial in the secular courts, provoked sharper debate. State security made sanctuary a question for Lovell, who cheerfully pulled a treason suspect out of the sanctuary of St Martin-le-Grand in London in 1518.[91] For others benefit of clergy was more important. Dudley fined many prelates for escapes from the special—and allegedly lax—prisons where they kept clerical convicts, and in February 1508 the London Dominicans had to deal with him over the arrest of a Breton friar accused of magical practices.[92] Hussey saw the abbot of Peterborough fined £100 in 1506 for an escape, a charge for which the monks prayed God forgive him, for it was unjust.[93] Meanwhile Hobart and Ernley, as attorneys-general, prosecuted churchmen under the statute of praemunire in a more wide-ranging and controversial assault on the business of the church courts. Others pounced on their victims when they could. Dr Thomas Hare, chancellor of Norwich diocese, claimed that Empson and Lucas tried to make him pay £333 6s 8d to the king for a praemunire offence first prosecuted by Hobart; he would not submit, but years of court appearances cost him over £100.[94]

This was not the only area, as we shall see, in which the king's desire to enforce the law and the new men's vigour in implementing it began to smack less of justice and more of extortion. But on balance, by their activity at the centre and in many corners of England the new men had contributed strongly to Henry's provision of justice, imposition of order, and cultivation of the common weal.

[88] R. Halstead, *Succinct Genealogies of the Noble and Ancient Houses of Alno or de Alneto etc* (London, 1685), 513; C. H. Cooper, *Annals of Cambridge*, 5 vols (Cambridge, 1842–1908), i. 277; C. H. Cooper and T. Cooper, *Athenae Cantabrigienses*, 3 vols (Cambridge, 1858–1913), i. 6–7, 9, 14; *Grace Book B*, ed. M. Bateson, 2 vols, Cambridge Antiquarian Society Luard Memorial Series, 2–3 (Cambridge, 1903–5), i. 119, 137–8, 153, 195.

[89] *Epistolae Academicae 1508–1596*, ed. W. T. Mitchell, OHS n.s. 26 (Oxford, 1980), 12–13, 25–6, 168–70; Cooper and Cooper, *Athenae Cantabrigienses*, i. 30, 32; *Grace Book B*, i. 251, ii. 11, 34, 46, 118.

[90] Storey, 'University and Government', 745; *Grace Book B*, i. 120, 136–8, ii. 11.

[91] *Reports of Cases by John Caryll*, ii. 694.

[92] BL, MS Lansdowne 127; *Memorials*, 109.

[93] *Peterborough Local Administration: The Last Days of Peterborough Monastery*, ed. W. T. Mellows, Northamptonshire RS 12 (1947), p. xi.

[94] P. R. Cavill, '"The Enemy of God and his Church": James Hobart, Praemunire and the Clergy of Norwich Diocese', *Journal of Legal History* 32 (2011), 127–43.

5

The king's revenues

From the start of his reign Henry and his councillors sought ways to strengthen royal finances. They continued the Yorkist kings' expansion and exploitation of the crown lands, drove up customs income, made parliamentary taxation more effective, and systematized profits from the king's feudal rights over landholders and judicial rights over all his subjects. At length, they built a more sustainably powerful fiscal system than any previous English regime. But in the process they gained the king a reputation for avarice and themselves too many enemies for comfort. Their operations were curtailed at the king's death, but often revived as Wolsey and Cromwell built on Henry's work. In these matters king and councillors worked together in ways now hard to unpick. Henry's negotiations with debtors, auditing of accounts, and checking of paperwork showed his full responsibility for policy, a responsibility his subjects recognized in charging him with avarice after his death. But he acted through, and no doubt exchanged ideas with, his ministers.[1]

THE CROWN LANDS

The new men were central to Henry's expansion of his income from the crown lands. At the most formal level, they served among the feoffees who held land to the king's use. In large settlements, such as those for the performance of the king's will, Poynings, Hobart, Empson, and Mordaunt joined or replaced Bray, Lovell, Guildford, and Risley as the reign went on.[2] In countless small transactions in which individual subjects' lands were secured for the king, either as he expanded the crown estate by purchase or confiscation or as he took guarantees for the payment of debts, Bray and Lovell, Hobart and Empson were prominent from the 1490s and Mordaunt, Dudley, Lucas, and Wyatt later in the reign. In the 1510s, Marney, Heron, and Englefield were doing the same for Henry VIII, still alongside

[1] S. Anglo, 'Ill of the Dead. The Posthumous Reputation of Henry VII', *Renaissance Studies* 1 (1987), 29–33.
[2] *CPR 1494–1509*, 353–4; M. M. Condon, 'The Last Will of Henry VII: Document and Text', in T. Tatton-Brown and R. Mortimer (eds), *Westminster Abbey: The Lady Chapel of Henry VII* (Woodbridge, 2003), 124–7.

Lovell; and Wyatt persisted into the late 1520s.[3] When Henry VIII made a will in 1513 before invading France, he turned to Lovell, Southwell, Englefield, Cutt, and Heron as feoffees.[4]

To draw income effectively from his enlarged estate the king needed a network of dependable officials: stewards to oversee manorial administration, feodaries to chase up the windfall profits that came from his seigneurial rights, receivers to collect his revenues. As we shall see, the new men often held stewardships, which were the most important of these offices at the political and military level. But many of them—Bray, Lovell, Southwell, Marney, Belknap—also operated as receivers or feodaries.[5] These were not sinecures. Southwell personally chased up the payment of rent from crown land in Norfolk with the widow of the executed Lord Fitzwalter.[6] Attention to detail was the key to profit, and from the start of the reign, but with growing intensity in its last years, the new men were also named to commissions to check the boundaries of the king's lands, value his estates and establish his rights.[7]

As the crown estate expanded, so the need grew for an institution to coordinate its administration and to audit the accounts it generated. By 1505, a court of general surveyors had emerged, led by Southwell and a bishop, first Roger Layburne of Carlisle, then Robert Sherbourne of St David's. The court negotiated leases, chased debts, ordered repairs, sales of wood, and the holding of manorial courts, investigated the king's rights, and settled disputes. It coordinated its work with that of Dudley, Empson, Hussey, and Wyatt, and it was complemented by another court of audit responsible for the prince's lands in Cheshire, Wales, and the duchy of Cornwall, where Southwell and Sherbourne were joined, among others, by Sheffield, Sutton, and Hussey. Southwell and his colleagues were interventionist in their concern to drive up the king's revenues. In the duchy of Cornwall they overrode decisions by Prince Arthur's councillors to let people off fines, and in the lordship of Bromfield and Yale they increased the receiver's fee to reward his diligence in chasing arrears.[8] Sometimes they resorted to extreme measures. In July 1508, Southwell and Lovell made two royal servants, more than £2,000 in arrears with the rent for lands in the Calais Pale, agree that they would pay by Christmas 1510 or face forfeiture of lands and goods and imprisonment at the king's pleasure.[9] The court's powers were too extensive to be palatable in the reaction against Henry's reign and it was abolished in 1509, but by 1512 Southwell

[3] *CPR 1494–1509*, 54, 260, 501, 583; *CCR 1485–1500*, 612, 1109, 1110; *CCR 1500–9*, 765, 976; *CAD*, iii. D819, D1094, iv. A7551, v. A13088; *CIPM*, ii. 861, iii. 366; *Report on the Manuscripts of the late Reginald Rawdon Hastings, Esq.*, 4 vols, HMC 78 (London, 1928–47), i. 298; BL, Addl. MS 21480, fos. 32r, 35r, 94r–94v; Harl. Ch. 44 I 59; PRO, C1/303/21; C54/379, m. 9d, 385, m. 2d, 386, m. 4d, 388, mm. 23d, 27d; KB27/983, m. 61r; LA, 2ANC3/A/46; ESRO, Firle Place MSS, 43/13, 22.

[4] *LP* I, ii. 2330(4).

[5] B. P. Wolffe, *The Crown Lands, 1461–1536* (London, 1970), 140; *CIPM*, iii. 926; *CPR 1494–1509*, 9; BL, Addl. MS 59899, fos. 33r, 37v, 38v; Addl. MS 1480, fos. 194r–194v, 196r–198r; *LP* I, i. 438(4 m. 5), 709(41), IV, i. 1298.

[6] PRO, C1/632/50.   [7] *SCC*, 3; *CCR 1500–9*, 106; PRO, DL5/4, fo. 55v.

[8] DCRO, DC Roll 211, mm. 7, 10, 11; PRO, SC6/Henry VII/1873, m. 3.

[9] PRO, E40/14648.

was again empowered as general surveyor, this time with Bartholomew Westby, an exchequer auditor. The new court never had quite the freedom of action or vigour of its predecessor, but under Southwell, then Belknap, it played a modest but effective role in the management of the crown estate.[10]

Throughout Henry's reign, the duchy of Lancaster, led successively by Bray, Mordaunt, and Empson, set the pace for effective exploitation of the crown estate, as it had done since the 1470s. Commissions of investigation were dispatched, feodaries invigorated, and ineffective officers removed. Rents were driven upwards, rentals renewed, and arrears chased down. Woodlands, fisheries, bondmen, and wards were turned to profit, fines for livery and respite of homage exacted with care. By the end of the reign, the duchy was generating about a quarter of the crown's landed income. In addition to the chancellors, a number of the new men took part in its administration. Cutt was receiver-general and toured the northern estates in 1497 forcing up income. Hussey, Lovell, and Hobart were named to commissions to improve revenue in Yorkshire, Northumberland, and East Anglia. Wyatt, Hussey, Lovell, Hobart, and Risley were stewards and Cope a feodary and receiver.[11]

Marney, appointed chancellor of the duchy in 1509, was from a more courtly mould than his predecessors. His most obvious impact came in the appointment of his friends and relations to offices: his colleague from Prince Henry's household Sir John Raynsford as chief steward in the north parts; his neighbour and feoffee Edward Sulyard as receiver in Essex and nearby counties; his son-in-law Thomas Bonham as receiver-general, keeper of Soham warren, and steward of the Savoy; his son John steward in half a dozen counties and constable of Pleshey Castle; for good measure he took for himself the chief stewardship of the south parts, with a reversion for his son.[12] Yet courtliness was not indolence. Marney regularly signed warrants for appointments to office, grants of leases, and presentations to benefices, sometimes counter-signing bills signed by the king, sometimes signing alone. In 1511 he directed the clerk of the duchy council to make out a grant of a park keepership, instructing him that 'this bill shall be your warrant...which I have assigned with my hand'.[13] The duchy council continued to seek out wardships and wastes of woodland, dismiss unsuitable officers, and commission local investigations, and after an initial lull the rate of business accelerated from 1511–12 and the drive to increase income revived. Marney did not attend every council session, but managed 79 per cent of those when attendance was recorded between 1515 and 1521, working with other councillors as appropriate: Lovell for a wardship, Windsor for the earl of Derby's lands.[14] He paid due attention to safe-keeping of

[10] Wolffe, *Crown Lands*, 71–86, 142–97; J. A. Guy, 'A Conciliar Court of Audit at work in the last months of the reign of Henry VII', *BIHR* 49 (1976), 289–95; *CCR 1500–9*, 774.

[11] R. Somerville, *A History of the Duchy of Lancaster, I, 1265–1603* (London, 1953), 242–77, 401–2, 522, 529, 574, 584, 595, 606, 618, 625; *The Honour and Forest of Pickering*, ed. R. B. Turton, 4 vols, North Riding Records, n.s. 1–4 (London, 1894–7), i. 135.

[12] Somerville, *Duchy of Lancaster*, 393, 402, 423, 430, 587, 601, 606, 608; T. Penn, *Winter King: The Dawn of Tudor England* (London, 2011), 308.

[13] PRO, DL12/11, 12.   [14] PRO, DL5/5, fos. 40r–211v, 236r; DL28/6/8–20.

the duchy's older records.[15] And he was insistent that control of its resources should remain at the centre and not devolve onto local noble office-holders. When it came to his attention that Lord Darcy and his deputies had been leasing out duchy land at Dunstanburgh in Northumberland on their own initiative, he wrote briskly to forbid it.[16]

The forest administration, in which Bray, Dudley, Brandon, and Lovell served successively as chief justices of the king's forests south of the Trent, combined judicial with financial and political business in idiosyncratic ways. The king's hunting rights over his forests legitimated both the prosecution of those who poached there and the gift of venison to those he favoured. Thus we find Bray pushing jurors hard in 1494 to extend the bounds of Whaddon Chase in Buckinghamshire, and Lovell granting a stag and a hind each to two officers of Windsor Forest in 1519.[17] Forest rights were as open to fiscal exploitation as any others, and Southwell was commissioned in 1505 to detect offences in the forests of the Midlands.[18] The woodlands in the forests were also a significant financial resource. Dudley and Lovell presided over profitable sales: more than £120 from sales of wood in 1505–6, £80 for one grant of permission to fell timber on 400 acres of Waltham Abbey's estates falling within the forests.[19] The king's rights and those of his subjects, meanwhile, had to be held in tension. In 1514 Lovell confirmed that a Northamptonshire widow might take wood for house repairs and pasture for her pigs out of a wood in Whittlewood Forest, but in 1521 he deprived the earl of Arundel of the keepership of two Hampshire forests for maladministration.[20] Even outside the forest jurisdiction, the new men kept an eye out for the king's woods. Empson operated as receiver-general for sales of woods across the entire crown estate and in 1521 Windsor tried to block the sale of woodland near Windsor on the grounds that the king needed building timber in the area and that the wood was also inhabited by top-quality goshawks, a fine breed for falconry.[21]

THE CUSTOMS

The customs on trade also rose dramatically under Henry, partly the result of a reviving European economy hungry for English cloth and an English economy more able to afford imports from the continent, partly the result of more efficient collection. As we shall see, Dudley took a controversial role in pressing Londoners for higher customs, and in 1505 the Southampton customs officers were in touch

---

[15] BL, Harl. Ch. 53D8.   [16] PRO, SP1/30, fo. 127 (*LP* IV, i. 103).

[17] *The Victoria History of the County of Buckingham*, ed. W. Page, 5 vols (London, 1905–28), ii. 139–40; *HMC Seventh Report* (London, 1879), App., 600.

[18] *CPR 1494–1509*, 437.

[19] NUL, Mi6/173/57, 93; BL, Addl Ch. 8404 (*LP* I, i. 1673); MS Lansdowne 127, fo. 42r; PRO, C1/467/37; *Descriptive Catalogue of the Charters and Muniments in the Possession of the Rt Hon Lord Fitzhardinge at Berkeley Castle*, ed. I. H. Jeayes (Bristol, 1892), 203.

[20] PRO, LR1/310, fos. 38v–39r; *LP* III, ii. 1437, 2145 (26).

[21] Wolffe, *Crown Lands*, 47; *LP* III, i. 1300.

with him about malmsey wine, cypress-wood chests, cotton, and other Mediterranean goods unloaded there.[22] As part of his campaign, the first ever book of rates was introduced, setting fixed values for commodities to combat under-valuation by merchants; several key products, such as woad, salt, and pewter, immediately yielded higher duties.[23] Lovell, too, was in the forefront of the campaign against customs evasion, working with Bray, Guildford, Dudley, Wyatt, and the king himself to follow up information about smuggling, interview suspect officials, and negotiate fines on offenders, engaging with the great ports such as Southampton and the great merchant companies such as the Staplers of Calais.[24] When Bray died and it emerged he had infringed the regulations on wool exports, Lovell, Dudley, and Wyatt negotiated with his executors a fine of £5,600. Henry pardoned £266 13s 4d and took lands worth over £290 a year to secure payment of the rest.[25] As Southwell's role in royal finances increased, he, too, chased up customs frauds and arrears.[26] Where customs revenue met state security, Wyatt was involved in the confiscation of wine traded by London merchants suspected of associating with Perkin Warbeck in the Netherlands.[27]

Henry engaged actively with foreign merchants at London to promote and manipulate trade, secure commodities he needed, and, where possible, turn a profit. His agents in these dealings included Bray, Lovell, Mordaunt, and above all Dudley, who did business on the king's behalf with members of Italian and German merchant houses, such as the Altoviti and Corsi of Florence, the Adorno, Centurione, Lomellini, Ponte, and Vivaldi of Genoa, the Bonvisi of Lucca, the della Fava of Bologna, various Venetians, and the Hochstetters of Augsburg.[28] Henry VIII dealt with merchants, too, and Wyatt and Lovell were engaged at various times with Giovanni Cavalcanti, supplier of luxury textiles and large-volume armaments, Lorenzo Bonvisi, and other Italians. Wyatt found one of them, Pier Francesco de' Bardi, particularly slippery: he wanted written notes of whatever had been agreed between him and Wolsey, 'for', he told the cardinal, 'I will give no credence to his saying'.[29] One of England's most distinctive exports was tin, and Cutt and Wyatt were commissioned in 1509 and again in 1518 to license merchants to buy and export it.[30] At the opposite end of the scale, Hussey held local offices in the customs administration. He was weigher of wools at Boston from

[22] BL, Addl. MS 21480, fos. 191v–192r.

[23] H. S. Cobb, '"Books of Rates" and the London Customs, 1507–1558', *Guildhall Miscellany* 4 (1971–3), 3–6.

[24] BL, Addl. MS 21480, fos. 67v, 130v, 159v, 168v, 176r, 177r, 188v, 190r.

[25] BL, Addl. MS 59899, fo. 182r

[26] BL, Addl. MS 21480, fos. 174v, 191r–192r.   [27] PRO, C1/251/1.

[28] Penn, *Winter King*, 198–204, 250–3; *CCR 1500–9*, 208, 403, 591; BL, Addl. MS 59899, fo. 139r; BL, MS Lansdowne 127, *passim*.

[29] C. M. Sicca, 'Consumption and Trade of Art between Italy and England in the First Half of the Sixteenth Century: the London House of the Bardi and Cavalcanti Company', *Renaissance Studies* 16 (2002), 166–70; *Great Wardrobe Accounts*, xxxviii–l; *LP* I, ii, App. 21, Addenda, i. 399, III, ii. 2835, IV, ii. 4231; *CAD*, iii. D1052; PRO, SP1/17, fo. 38 (*LP* II, ii. 4400); E40/14731; C54/392, mm. 1d–2d, 3d–4d, 395, mm. 24d–25d.

[30] *LP* I, i. 94(58), II, ii. 4347.

1494, tapping for the king the considerable if declining profits of raw wool exports from the rich wolds of Lincolnshire, and became customer at Hull in 1505.[31]

Several import duties on wine and a levy in kind, called prisage, were collected by the chief butler of England, an office held by Southwell from 1503 to 1514 and by Hussey from 1521 to 1537. The butler operated through a network of deputies based in sixteen major ports, mostly merchants like John Robinson of Boston, Hugh Elyot of Bristol, or Nicholas Coward of Southampton, often customs officers like Nicholas Turpyn at Newcastle or John Palmer at Great Yarmouth, but occasionally clerics such as Thomas Dalby, archdeacon of Richmond, at Hull, or even a peer, Thomas Lord De la Warr, at Chichester.[32] The butler's income stream was not large, around £600 a year, but he was charged with paying annuities and presenting rewards in wine to significant royal officers and favoured religious houses. Many of these issued receipts showing they had cheerfully received wine direct from the nearest port, but there were problems on the money side of the account.[33] Individual collectors built up significant arrears even under the brisk Southwell, who managed to deliver £750 of arrears to Henry VII in 1508, and by the end of his tenure he himself owed £335 10s 8d.[34] Hussey left more of the work to his deputies, Hugh Clerk in the 1520s and Richard Lyster, chief baron of the exchequer, in the 1530s, though he signed occasional receipts. Under him individual collectors ran up bigger debts—particularly the courtier Sir Hugh Vaughan for the port of London—and his own arrears rose from £289 10s 9d in 1526 to £786 13s 7d in 1533.[35]

The post could be stressful for the butler and his staff. Clerk wrote to William Symondes at Exeter one August in the mid-1520s, complaining that the king's servants had been pressing Hussey for payment of their annuities and Hussey had asked him what money he had from each collector. When he saw that Clerk 'had received but £20 of you for the whole half year, he marvelled greatly that there was no greater sum grown in your ports and caused the customers' books to be viewed'. They suggested that £80 or so was due. 'And then he was marvellously discontent with you', particularly because it 'put him in displeasure of those that were assigned, as my lord cardinal and others'. Hussey was infuriated at having to 'furnish the payments' to Wolsey and the rest 'of his own purse', the reverse of the usual situation where crown office-holders used public money as a private credit reserve. He told Clerk to sue Symondes on his bond for good behaviour in office, but Clerk refrained, thinking Symondes would send the money soon. He did not, so Clerk wrote 'as your friend' advising him 'to send up the residue of your whole sum with as short speed as ye may possible...as ye intend to avoid my master's displeasure and the indemnity of your bond'.[36] Such stresses had their

[31] *CPR 1485–1494*, 455; *LP* I, ii. 1819; BL, MS Lansdowne 127, fo. 12v.
[32] *LP* I, i. 158(37), 438(1 m. 9, 1 m. 14, 2 m. 32, 3 m. 14), 874(2), 1804(54); PRO, E101/86/35, m. 3r.
[33] *CAD*, i. A959, iii. A5811 PRO, E40/14743; E42/410; E329/79.
[34] PRO, E101/85/12, 15, 16; *LP* I, i. 874(2), ii. 3313(8).
[35] PRO, E101/84/37, 85/38, 86/34, 86/35, 87/9, 687/40.
[36] PRO, E101/85/38/7.

compensations. Powerful men might be obliged by meeting their requests: wine from Newcastle in 1524 for Lord Dacre, stationed at Morpeth in command against the Scots, at the request of the earl of Surrey.[37] Better still was the chance to help oneself. Hussey wrote in his own hand to the deputy at Boston, the port nearest his home, asking him to send him two hogsheads of wine, one red, one white, of the first that arrived. 'And let it be good', he added, 'as my trust is in you.'[38]

TAXATION

Much of Henry VII's strengthening of crown finances focused on recurrent sources of income such as the crown lands and customs. But he was also concerned to secure direct taxation from parliament at appropriate times, especially for war, and to make the assessment and collection of that taxation locally as effective as possible, breaking away from the established system of tenths and fifteenths, with its fossilized local quotas, towards a direct and realistic assessment of the wealth of individuals. Here, the new men's local influence came into play as many of them took an important part in the work of tax commissions. The aid granted by the 1504 parliament shows their reach. They were particularly prominent in East Anglia, where Lovell, Hobart, and Southwell served in Norfolk; Brandon, Hobart, and Lucas in Suffolk; and Marney and Cutt in Essex. They were predictably to the fore in the counties around the capital: Lovell, Risley, and Windsor in Middlesex, Guildford and Poynings in Kent, Sheffield in London, Brandon in Southwark. But their work spread outwards into the Midlands and beyond. Mordaunt served in Bedfordshire, Empson and Windsor in Buckinghamshire, Englefield in Herefordshire, Empson in Northamptonshire, Dudley in Sussex and on the Isle of Wight, Belknap in Warwickshire, Sheffield in Lindsey, and Hussey in all three parts of Lincolnshire.[39]

Those who enjoyed long careers assessed taxes again and again. In 1492 and 1497, it was the parliamentary knights of the shire and the commissioners of the peace who organized taxation in each county, bringing many new men into play.[40] By 1512–15 they featured in many county subsidy commissions: Belknap in Warwickshire, Cope in Oxfordshire, Englefield in Berkshire, Ernley in Sussex, Hussey in Lincolnshire, Lovell in Buckinghamshire, Lucas in Suffolk, Poynings in Kent, Sheffield in Lindsey, Wyatt in Surrey, Southwell and Hobart in Norfolk, Lovell and Heron in Middlesex, and Marney, Southwell, and Cutt in Essex. As senior officers of the royal household, Lovell, Marney, and Poynings assessed its members.[41] Lovell, Wyatt, and Hussey went on to levy the yet more demanding subsidies of the 1520s.[42] In 1496 Henry VII anticipated the income from

[37] *LP* IV, i. 28.   [38] PRO, E101/85/38/9.   [39] 19 Henry VII c. 32.
[40] 7 Henry VII c. 11; 12 Henry VII c. 13; *CPR 1494–1509*, 629–69.
[41] 4 Henry VIII c. 19, 5 Henry VIII c. 17, 6 Henry VIII c. 26.
[42] *LP* III, ii. 3282, 3504, IV, i. 214, 547; PRO, E179/136/313, m. 1.

parliamentary taxation by demanding loans from his subjects with the approval of a great council. Bray in London, Marney in Essex, Risley in Middlesex, and no doubt others, served among the commissioners haggling with individuals over how much they might lend.[43] Both Henry and his son also took direct taxation without parliamentary consent. In 1491 Henry levied a benevolence. Lovell and Risley headed the commission to assess it in Middlesex, Bray that in Surrey, while Empson and Mordaunt served in Bedfordshire, Buckinghamshire, and Lindsey.[44] Years later, the takings were still being accounted for, a process involving Wyatt and Cope as collectors and Lovell and Dudley as auditors.[45]

Sometimes the growing importance of an individual in enforcing taxation can be precisely charted. Windsor was the fourth most senior commissioner for the aid of 1504 in Buckinghamshire, and seventh out of eight in Middlesex, but he was set on an upward path. By the 1512 subsidy, he was the fourth most senior commissioner in Middlesex and leader at the borough of Windsor. By 1514 he also led the Buckinghamshire commission. In the 1520s he continued on all three commissions, bringing in the Buckinghamshire accounts to Westminster, and in 1522–3 he headed the forced loan commissions for Buckinghamshire and Middlesex, examining the more recalcitrant contributors on oath.[46] His local influence was precisely deployed by the way in which the commissioners divided their responsibilities. In Middlesex he presided over Isleworth and Spelthorne hundreds, nearest to his home at Stanwell, while in Buckinghamshire he took the three southernmost hundreds, in the Chilterns around his manor at Bradenham.[47]

Henry VIII would find another form of taxation in debasement of the coinage, but his father preferred to make it a solid expression of royal power and a reliable medium of exchange for a recovering economy. Wyatt aggregated posts in the royal mint in parallel with those in the jewel house: clerk and usher from 1488, comptroller and assayer from 1495. His main role seems to have been to keep an eye on the expert coiners, some of the same goldsmiths who provided the king with jewels and plate, to make sure the king was not being defrauded. He generally did so through his deputy Thomas Aunsham, an 'ancient honest man' who 'gave daily attendance' at the mint, though he signed some accounts and took responsibility in other ways. Whatever the balance of duties, Wyatt's period at the mint included the introduction of new designs with a profile portrait of the king in 1504, surges

[43] H. Kleineke, '"Morton's Fork"—Henry VII's "Forced Loan" of 1496', *The Ricardian* 13 (2003), 325–6; PML, Rulers of England, box 1 no. 41.

[44] *CPR 1485–94*, 354–5.

[45] BL, Addl. MS 21480, fos. 80v, 155r; *CPR 1494–1509*, 458; B. P. Wolffe, *The Royal Demesne in English History: the Crown Estate in the Governance of the Realm from the Conquest to 1509* (London, 1971), 208.

[46] 19 Henry VII c. 32, 4 Henry VIII c. 19, 5 Henry VIII c. 17, 6 Henry VIII c. 26; *LP* III, ii. 2485, 3282, IV, i. 214, 547, VII. 1496.

[47] *LP* IV, i. 969 (4); *Subsidy Roll for the County of Buckingham Anno 1524*, ed. A. C. Chibnall and A. V. Woodman, Buckinghamshire RS 8 (Bedford, 1950), 11.

in coin production in 1505–9, and, following revaluation in 1526, an attempt to reduce the proportion of clipped coins in circulation, so he was engaged with the coinage at a vibrant time.[48]

WARDSHIP

Wardship, the control of the lands and marriages of the under-aged heirs of royal tenants-in-chief, was the most lucrative right available to the king as feudal overlord, and Henry VII set out to exploit it systematically. With the advice of his lawyers, he restricted the opportunities for evasion of such feudal incidents by the enfeoffment of land to uses. By the issue of investigative commissions, he sought out heirs who should be his wards and others who had taken up their ancestors' lands without suing livery in due form. By selling custody of many of the wards thus uncovered and renting out the lands of others, he turned his rights into cash. Bray coordinated much of this work, but after his death, in December 1503, Hussey was appointed chief officer for overseeing, managing, and selling the wardships of lands in the king's hands, what would later come to be called master of the wards. If Henry had suspicions of Hussey's probity, he did his best to insure against them. Hussey was bound in £666 13s 4d, three sureties in £200 each and a fourth in £66 13s 4d that he would demean himself truly in the office, not displaying partiality or accepting any gifts save food and drink. Soon the directly administered wards' lands were bringing in £5,000, then £6,000 a year, while sales of wardships, thirty or so of them a year, raised more than £5,000 annually in cash and bonds for future payment.[49] Some of the sales Hussey negotiated were extremely lucrative. Three wardships in 1504–5 were sold for £900, £1,010, and £1,600 respectively.[50] He did not work alone. Lovell, Dudley, and Wyatt negotiated with major buyers; Southwell, Hobart, Lucas, Dudley, Empson, and the council learned undertook investigations or took bonds for payment; Hobart prosecuted those who had agreed bargains for wards but then tried to back out of them.[51] But Hussey's role was central. Cases about wards were marked 'Hussey' in the margin of the chamber accounts, the council learned ordered that wards be handed over to him, and £100 a year was assigned for care of the wards in his custody.[52]

[48] C. E. Challis, *The Tudor Coinage* (Manchester, 1978), 29–30, 37–9, 46–63, 67, 79, 311; C. E. Challis, 'Lord Hastings to the Great Silver Recoinage, 1464–1699', in C. E. Challis (ed.), *A New History of the Royal Mint* (Cambridge, 1992), 179–83, 197, 207–10, 213–15; *CPR 1494–1509*, 16; *LP* I, i. 185, 876, ii. 2316, 2781(ii), IV, iii. 6271, 6600(18); PRO, E101/298/35 (*LP* IV, i. 2338(7)); SP1/46, fos. 186–9 (*LP* IV, ii. 3867(2)).

[49] H. E. Bell, *An Introduction to the History and Records of the Court of Wards and Liveries* (Cambridge, 1953), 1–7; W. C. Richardson, *Tudor Chamber Administration, 1485–1547* (Baton Rouge LA, 1952), 166–75; SROB, Ac449/E3/15.53/2.8; *CPR 1494–1509*, 324; BL, Addl. MS 59899, fos. 117v–22v, 158v–79r; Addl. MS 21480, fos. 46v–49r, 104v–27r.

[50] BL, Addl. MS 59899, fos. 120v, 121v, 163v.

[51] BLARS, L24/427, 432; PRO, C1/325/14, 142/84; DL5/2, fo. 58v; DL5/4, fos. 32v, 58v, 153v; *CCR 1500–9*, 774; BL, Lansdowne MS 127, fo. 29v.

[52] BL, Addl. MS 59899, fo. 212r; Addl. MS 21480, fos. 189r–190v; PRO, DL5/2, fo. 67r; DL5/4, fo. 30v; PML, Rulers of England box 1, no. 43v.

After 1509 Hussey kept his post, but the machinery at his disposal seems to have atrophied and other councillors were involved in what sales there were.[53] In June 1513, Lovell replaced him and reinvigorated operations. He settled terms with grantees on the basis of an exact valuation of the lands involved, upset Lord Dacre by his independent-mindedness, and made even the duke of Buckingham understand that he should negotiate with him before suing to the king.[54] From August 1513 feodaries were appointed to pursue the crown's rights to wardships in every county and collect the resulting revenues. The team was regularly refreshed and periodically backed up by special commissions. Lovell chose experienced local administrators for the role, men like the JPs John Hales, Thomas Hall, Gregory Morgan, Robert Warcop, John Wellys, William Wymondeswold, and William Young, the naval administrator and customer of Southampton John Dawtrey, or the duchy of Lancaster feodary and Middlesex coroner Richard Hawkes. A dozen or more had served as county escheators or commissioners tracking the crown's rights. Four, William Young, John Monson, John a Lee, and Humphrey Hercy, were also Lovell's retainers.[55] His reach extended even to Ireland, for in 1519 the council told the earl of Kildare to deliver to Lovell the heir of the baron of Slane, a client house in the Pale peerage.[56] In 1520 Lovell, citing his age and the press of business, handed over to Belknap and he, Englefield and their colleagues developed Hussey's and Lovell's work to lay the basis for the court of wards and liveries.[57]

The key procedure to establish the king's rights to wardship and livery was the inquisition post mortem, in which local jurors, informed by documents furnished by the heirs or other parties, reported to escheators or commissioners what land was held by deceased tenants-in-chief. As Henry pressed to increase his income from such sources, the new men played an active, an accelerating, and perhaps a distorting role. Sometimes, they were specially commissioned to investigate particular estates; sometimes they took special care because they had a personal interest in the lands in question by royal grant or marriage. Individually and collectively, they kept up pressure on escheators to hold inquisitions and deliver findings beneficial to the crown.[58] But most telling are the instances in which they or their servants steered the reports of inquisitions through the central institutions to make sure the king received his due. In 1501–3, Hobart was prominent, he or his servants involved in

[53] Bell, *Wards and Liveries*, 8–10, 187–9; *CAD*, v. A12575, A12855; *LP* I, i. 1524(16), II, ii, pp. 1483–6.

[54] Richardson, *Tudor Chamber Administration*, 284–8; *LP* I, ii. 2055(80, 104), 2913, II, i. 950, 1391, ii. 3793, 3807, 4199, 4225, 4263, 4539, 4622, 4634, III, i. 1036(20), 1070, 1081(13); Staffordshire Record Office, D(W)1790/A/13/61 (NRA report); NUL, Mi6/177/94; PRO, E41/5, 42, 91.

[55] *LP* I, i. 1393(vii), 1414, ii. 2222(12), pp. 1534, 1542, 1544, 1546, II, i. 523, 1435, 1455, ii. 4412, III, i. 206(16), 529(28), 1081(28); Bindoff, *Commons*, ii. 275–6, 285–7, 321–2; *List of Escheators for England and Wales*, List and Index Society 72 (London, 1971), 64, 73, 82, 117, 125, 142, 158, 167, 176; PRO, C42/18/19, 21, 22/22–4, 24/35, 25/145–6; *HMC Rutland*, iv. 562–5.

[56] HL, MS El 2652, fo. 11r; G. Power, *A European Frontier Elite: The Nobility of the English Pale in Ireland, 1496–1566* (Hanover, 2012), 58–61.

[57] *LP* III, i. 1121; Bell, *Wards and Liveries*, 8–12, 187–9.

[58] M. A. Hicks (ed.), *The Fifteenth-Century Inquisitions Post Mortem: A Companion* (Woodbridge, 2012); *CPR 1494–1509*, 5, 209; PRO, C142/23/118, 119, C142/18/64–6; D. Luckett, 'Henry VII and the South-Western Escheators', in Thompson (ed.), *The Reign of Henry VII*, 54–64.

the delivery of twenty-four reports into chancery, often involving wardships, while Empson and Lucas were involved with half a dozen each.[59] From 1504 Hussey as master of the wards took an increasing role, usually in wardship cases. Between then and 1507 he or his servants were responsible for a hundred, while Empson, Lucas, and Hobart continued to be involved occasionally and Belknap and Dudley joined in.[60] Gradually the machinery became more elaborate, as Thomas Pole, Richard Clerk, and George Harebrowne took charge under Hussey's direction.[61] All this activity certainly delivered more information to the centre about the king's rights, though at times what came in was confused or self-contradictory.[62]

Hussey's orders were to see relevant inquisitions speedily found to the king's 'most profit and advantage as far as truth and justice shall require'.[63] No doubt he tried too hard. One hearing at Melton Mowbray in Leicestershire in May 1505, it was ruled in the 1530s, found lands to be the king's which should by right have descended to an heir. Hussey had presided with three other commissioners, and Dudley had processed the report.[64] It was possible to contest verdicts by suing a traverse even in Henry's reign, but not everyone had the stomach for a fight. Elizabeth, duchess of Norfolk, aged about sixty and thirty years a widow, explained in her will in 1506 that she had bought the wardship of Gilbert Pinchbeck from the earl of Oxford and paid off other claimants to her 'great charge'. An inquisition, 'to my pretence untrue', held in Lincolnshire and delivered by Hussey, found that the wardship should belong to the king. Henry gave her the choice whether to try to traverse the findings or to acquiesce, offering not to press her for past rents if she complied. She duly—though 'for none right I understood his highness had to him'—handed the ward and his lands over to Hussey. She left the king £100 to be good lord to her executors, but with the biting condition that 'if his grace be not so content, but look or by his royal power will take or have any more', he was not to have the £100 of her gift, but take what he could 'on his charge of conscience'.[65] It was telling that councillors' pursuit of inquisition returns ceased at Henry's death and did not revive even when Lovell took the reins at the wardship office.[66]

OTHER PREROGATIVE REVENUES

Henry set his councillors to chase many other revenues beside wardship, relentlessly expanding the range of means to profit from his powers. His three characteristic devices were the issue of investigative commissions, the taking of bonds to

[59] PRO, C24/15–16, 23. [60] PRO, C24/17–21, 23. [61] PRO, C24/20–3.

[62] Luckett, 'Escheators', 61–4. [63] *CCR 1500–9*, 913.

[64] J. Nichols, *The History and Antiquities of the County of Leicester*, 4 vols in 8 (Wakefield, 1971 edn), IV, ii. 965–68: *CIPM*, ii. 905; PRO, C24/18/84.

[65] G. R. Elton, 'Henry VII: A Restatement', in G. R. Elton, *Studies in Tudor and Stuart Politics and Government*, 4 vols (Cambridge, 1974–92), i. 73–6, 98–9; PRO, PROB11/15/25; C142/19/159; *CIPM*, iii. 187.

[66] PRO, C24/24–5, 28–30.

ensure that debts were paid, and the creation of specialized offices to exploit differ-
ent areas of revenue. In addition to raising revenue, such bonded debts were used
by the king as a means of political control. As Dudley put it, 'the pleasure and
mind of the king's grace...was much set to have many persons in his danger at his
pleasure'.[67] This put the new men in a particularly powerful but also a particularly
exposed position, as the financial obligations they set up between the king and his
subjects became the tools of the king's painful management of individual loyalty.

The investigation of the king's rights and his subjects' offences began early, as Bray
and Lovell checked on the king's mines and Bray, Empson, Guildford, and Mordaunt
on concealed lands and lands given to the church without licences for mortmain.[68]
Such commissions multiplied and their scope expanded as the reign went on.
Southwell, Hobart, and Lucas were appointed in 1500 to scour Norfolk, Sussex, and
Essex for concealed lands and wardships, treasure trove, the goods of convicts, mort-
main offences, and money lent in usury, and in 1504–6 Hussey, Southwell, and
Windsor were set to seek out an ever wider range of infringements.[69] By the end of
the reign, Hussey, Empson, Lucas, and Dudley were designing the terms under
which such commissions operated, and when the search revived in less virulent form
in the 1520s, Hussey's expertise was again called into play.[70]

Bonds were by no means invented by Henry's government—indeed, they were
a standard management technique in the duchy of Lancaster—but they were
adopted in his reign to a unique degree as the means to codify his subjects' obliga-
tions to him. New debts were set out in bonds and old debts recorded in bonds
were sought out and prosecuted. Bonds for good performance in office were
counted forfeit if officers' conduct did not meet the king's expectations, and special
debts were created to secure the political loyalty of those who would be financially
ruined if the debts were called in. In some instances, people were imprisoned with-
out charge until they agreed to enter bonds to the king's use. How much money
was raised is hard to calculate, but in the last five years of the reign bonds were
taken from more than 600 people each year, capable of yielding £100,000 or more
a year if fully realized, a sum peaking in 1508 at £163,443.[71]

By the end of the reign, the policy was controversial and it has remained so.
Preachers made 'open exclamations and clerkly monitions' at Paul's Cross, London's
major public preaching venue, against the depredations of the king's ministers, but
'the more they were preached against, the more they vexed the king's true subjects'. At
Henry's death, the outrage was focused on Empson, Dudley, and their minions, but a
wider debate was already in progress. Thomas More's accession poem for Henry VIII

[67] 'The Petition of Edmund Dudley', ed. C. J. Harrison, *EHR* 87 (1972), 86.

[68] Richardson, *Tudor Chamber Administration*, 64–97, 101–6, 119–23.

[69] *CPR 1494–1509*, 204, 404, 407, 420, 421, 459, 489, 592.

[70] M. R. Horowitz, 'Policy and Prosecution in the reign of Henry VII', *HR* 82 (2009), 436; *LP* III,
ii. 1451(15).

[71] Horowitz, 'Policy and Prosecution', 412–58; M. R. Horowitz, '"Agree with the King": Henry VII,
Edmund Dudley and the Strange Case of Thomas Sunnyff', *HR* 79 (2005), 329–35, 352–55;
M. R. Horowitz, 'Henry Tudor's Treasure', *HR* 82 (2009), 560–79; S. Cunningham, 'Loyalty and the
Usurper: Recognizances, the Council and Allegiance under Henry VII', *HR*, 82 (2009), 459–81.

framed the case for the prosecution. Laws 'put to unjust ends' had made it 'a criminal offence to own honestly acquired property', informers prospered, and 'the entire population used to be in debt to the king'. From that day to this, the defence has countered that the law was being applied strictly in the interests of strong government and public peace and that because it cost people money, they were bound to complain.[72]

All the new men were involved in the taking and processing of bonds to some degree. Bray, Lovell, Mordaunt, Hobart, and Lucas were prominent throughout the reign and Empson and Dudley central after 1504, backed up by Wyatt and Ernley.[73] Dudley worked especially closely with the king while others specialized, Hussey with wardships, for example, Lovell with prisoners under his care at the Tower.[74] Meanwhile, the king's concern that the sureties bound to support individual debtors in meeting their obligations should be of sufficient substance to act as credible guarantors, and that networks of suretyship should bind whole social groups to obey him, gave councillors and their local contacts a role in vetting proposed sureties and replacing those who died.[75]

One use for bonds was the sale of office. While there was no formal system of sale of government office in England like that developing in France, Henry accepted offers of cash from those petitioning for appointments. The new men forwarded these bids to the king and made the resultant financial arrangements. Lovell, for example, submitted Cutt's offer of £20 for the customs searchership of tin and lead in the port of London, while Bray and Guildford put in bids of hundreds of pounds from aspiring judges.[76] From 1504, Dudley became heavily involved, taking £20 for a castle constableship, a park keepership, an escheatorship or an estate receivership, £266 13s 4d for the mastership of the royal mint, the chancellorship of Prince Henry, or the chief justiceship of the common pleas, £1,000 for the mastership of the rolls in chancery.[77] The system was one of the many ways that the king set the new men to regulate one another. Dudley took £100 from Ernley for appointment as king's attorney, the same from Lovell for the stewardship of Wakefield and £200 from Windsor for the great wardrobe.[78] Bonds were also taken for good service. Belknap was bound in £666 13s 4d as surveyor of the prerogative, and Edward Cheeseman, cofferer of the household, in £8,000, together with Lovell, Empson, Dudley, and Wyatt, for due execution of the budget the five of them had worked out.[79]

---

[72] *Great Chronicle*, 335; *PVAH*, 129; *Complete Works of More ... Latin Poems*, 101–13; Cooper, 'Henry VII's Last Years Reconsidered', 103–29; G. R. Elton, 'Henry VII: Rapacity and Remorse', in G. R. Elton, *Studies*, i. 45–65, and 'Henry VII: A Restatement', in G. R. Elton, *Studies*, i. 45–99.

[73] Cunningham, 'Loyalty and the Usurper', 470; M. R. Horowitz, 'Richard Empson, Minister of Henry VII', *BIHR* 55 (1982), 41–2; *CCR 1500–9, passim*.

[74] Horowitz, 'Policy and Prosecution', 442–6; *CCR 1500–9, passim*; BL, Addl. MS 59899, fos. 118r–122v, 158v–165v, 169v–179r; Addl. MS 21480, fos. 171r, 187r.

[75] Cunningham, 'Loyalty and the Usurper', 466–8, 474–6.

[76] BL, Addl. MS 21480, fos. 173v, 185v, 187v.

[77] BL, MS Lansdowne 127, fos. 4v, 5r, 13v, 14r, 23r, 33r, 45v, 51v.

[78] BL, MS Lansdowne 127, fos. 23r, 45v, 49r.

[79] W. C. Richardson, 'The Surveyor of the King's Prerogative', *EHR* 56 (1941), 65; *CCR 1500–9*, 840, 852.

The most questionable aspect of the system was the sale of justice. Exactly what it meant for the king to take payments to show favour to litigants before his courts is not quite clear, but some of the payments recorded both in Bray's time and in Dudley's surely took Henry close to breach of his coronation oath. Bray put in a bid of £200 from Lady Scrope of Upsall 'so that the king's grace will commit her matter to the judges and to suffer her to have indifferent justice'.[80] Dudley took £1,000 for John Seyton 'to have the course of the king's common laws in assize against one Metcalff' and £66 13s 4d from James Beamount for the king's 'lawful favour' in a land dispute.[81] Perhaps most brazenly of all, Lovell, Dudley, and Wyatt indented with the earl of Derby that selected councillors would hear his suit against Thomas Middleton and if he won he would give the king lands worth £50 a year.[82]

Henry's fiscal exploitation of his subjects became an increasingly specialized affair. At first, Bray coordinated matters under the king: a memorandum of about 1489 shows him dealing with mortmain, prison escapes, wardships, and forfeited recognizances as well as the customs, the crown lands, and the royal household.[83] Later, he found that business expanded beyond his capacity. From around 1500, the council learned prosecuted a wide variety of offences that might end in fines—breaches of economic regulations, riots, abuses of office, entries into land without livery, failure to take up knighthood, and so on—and systematically called in debts.[84] Mordaunt seems to have been the first individual councillor besides Bray given a special role in managing the king's rights. His family recalled that in summer 1499 he was 'called into the king's house, and went thither wholly at Michaelmas'. Soon he was granted a royal annuity and became more prominent in processing forfeitures, mortmain licences, and similar business.[85] In 1504 Mordaunt succeeded Bray as chancellor of the duchy, and Dudley replaced him in his more general role. Dudley sold offices, wardships, and licences to marry the widows of tenants-in-chief; grants of livery of lands; renewals of liberties to town corporations; pardons for treason, sedition, murder, riot, retaining, hunting in the king's forests, and other offences. In less than four years he collected over £200,000 in cash and bonds for future payment, his accounts signed by the king on every page. As his activities accelerated, he was equipped with privy seal writs to summon individuals to appear before him, just as Hussey, Southwell, and Wyatt were for their various areas of responsibility.[86] In summer 1508, the structure changed again with the appointment of Edward Belknap as surveyor of the king's prerogative. Responsible for a number of the areas previously covered by Dudley, mulcting felons, outlaws, and king's widows, Belknap had both

---

[80] BL, Addl. MS 21480, fo. 179r.

[81] BL, Lansdowne MS 127, fos. 23v, 33v.   [82] *SCC*, xxxiv.

[83] Richardson, *Tudor Chamber Administration*, 73–4, 76–7, 123–4.

[84] R. Somerville, 'Henry VII's "Council Learned in the Law"', *EHR* 54 (1939), 434–42; Horowitz, 'Empson', 46–8.

[85] R. Halstead, *Succinct Genealogies of the Noble and Ancient Houses of Alno or de Alneto etc* (London, 1685), 65; BL, Addl. MS 21480, fos. 164v–192r; *CPR 1494–1509*, 226.

[86] Somerville, *Duchy of Lancaster*, 392; *CPR 1494–1509*, 506; BL, Lansdowne MS 127; M. R. Horowitz, '"Contrary to the Liberties of this City": Henry VII, English Towns and the Economics of Law and Order', *HR* 85 (2012), 38, 41–2; Horowitz, 'Sunnyff', 365–6.

new powers and new agents to execute them. He could confiscate and farm out the lands of offenders. He appointed a network of county deputies, naming those who had served recently as escheators or JPs, other gentlemen of administrative stamp or royal household servants. He was to be paid by results, taking one-ninth of the profits he made for the king and allowing his deputies one-tenth of the remainder. In less than a year of operation he seems to have raised more than £1,200 in cash and more than that in bonds for future payment.[87]

Yet for all the development of individual and institutional roles, fluidity in action at the king's command continued to characterize the system. The chamber accounts record individual councillors dealing with a wide range of matters. Southwell, for example, brought to the king's attention or investigated for him details of the aulnage tax on cloth, land descents and liveries, pensions to courtiers, and the revenues of vacant bishoprics.[88] Councillors tackled matters alone and in groups as seemed most appropriate. In one case of 1505, a knight was summoned before the council learned to explain why he had not met his debt to the king; the matter was passed to Hussey who discussed it with Heron; and Heron supplied written certification that it had been paid. In another case of 1506 someone appeared before the council learned but was sent away because his matter was being considered by Dudley and Wyatt.[89] In less happy instances victims were batted backwards and forwards between Empson, Dudley, and their respective underlings in a nightmare of exploitative prosecution.[90] And even as Henry neared death, he kept his grip on the system. One set of fines, Belknap's accounts recorded, were assessed by the king at Hanworth on 11 February 1509.[91]

These policies touched all the king's subjects, but they were particularly sensitive when applied to the peerage. Throughout the reign the new men negotiated settlements over land, wardships, marriages, and other matters of personal and political importance with the greatest lords in the kingdom or their representatives. Bray and Lovell, for example, charged the executors of the fourth earl of Northumberland £4,000 in 1489 for a marriage between the earl's daughter and the king's ward, the young duke of Buckingham. Ten years later, George Lord Tailbois was charged £533 6s 8d by Bray, Lovell, Hobart, Empson, and Lucas for an agreement that, should he be declared a lunatic, his lands would be entrusted to his friends. In 1505, Lovell, Dudley, and Wyatt secured the king's approval for a marriage between Buckingham's younger brother, Henry, Lord Stafford, and Cecily, widow of the marquess of Dorset; the price was £2,000, with a £1,000 discount for good behaviour. In the same year Lovell, Hobart, Empson, Dudley, and Wyatt confirmed the council's verdict that Edward, Lord Hastings, should inherit many of the lands of William, Viscount Beaumont, provided he paid £1,000.[92]

---

[87] Richardson, 'Surveyor', 63–75; *CPR 1494–1509*, 358, 421, 590, 637, 645; *LP* I, i. 438(2 m. 32, 4 m. 5), 1803(2 m. 4); *List of Escheators*, 47; PRO, E101/517/15.

[88] BL, Addl. MS 21480, fos. 174v, 178r, 189r, 190v, 191r; Addl. MS 59899, fos. 213r–213v; PRO, DL5/4, fo. 32v.

[89] PRO, DL5/4, fos. 68v, 93r.   [90] Horowitz, 'Sunnyff', 328–36.

[91] PRO, E101/517/15, fo. 8v.

[92] *Materials*, ii. 554–5; *CPR 1494–1509*, 176; *CCR 1500–9*, 471, 480.

Such dealings gave Henry a tighter grip on the nobility than most kings before or since, but the fear and resentment they generated were readily focused on his agents. It was surely Henry who drove on Lord Bergavenny's prosecution for retaining, his fine of £500 a year, his bonds in £5,000 and £3,333 6s 8d to keep his allegiance to the king and stay out of Kent, Surrey, Sussex, or Hampshire, the counties where most of his lands lay. But it was Dudley who had charge of the documents that recorded them all.[93] And the new men were persistent. In 1523, Wyatt sat with Wolsey, as 'commissioners... to common and conclude with such persons as been indebted to our sovereign lord', to negotiate terms on which Thomas, marquess of Dorset could meet the remaining £5,607 4s 4d of the debts his mother and her late husband Henry Stafford had contracted since 1505.[94]

If there were political difficulties about fining the peerage, there were political and moral difficulties about squeezing the church. Henry levied increasing taxation on the clergy, through benevolences and forced loans as well as grants in convocation, and Poynings tried to secure unprecedentedly heavy clerical taxation from the parliament he called in Ireland. The king charged heavy fines for the mortmain licences required to transfer land from lay ownership into that of ecclesiastical institutions, he asked large sums from newly appointed prelates for the restitution of their temporalities—the equivalent of livery fines for laymen—and he came perilously close to the heinous sin of simony in requiring hefty payments from churchmen for his favour in appointing them to bishoprics and other benefices. His approach worried the clergy, who complained about infringements of their liberties in the convocation of 1504 and the parliament of 1510. It worried the king himself, who asked in 1504 for additional power for his confessor to deal with cases of simony.[95]

Bray and Lovell handled such matters in the 1490s, but from 1504 they were built into Dudley's wide-ranging system of exactions.[96] He levied fines for mortmain, the restitution of temporalities and the appropriation of one religious institution's revenues to another, for offences under the statute of praemunire and escapes from episcopal and abbatial prisons; he took payments for arrears of clerical taxation, for the king's favour towards clerics in lawsuits, and for pardons for clergymen accused of treason or other offences. He raised large sums from the king's exercise of ecclesiastical patronage: £666 13s 4d from James Harrington 'for the king's most gracious favour in the deanery of York'. He raised even larger sums from the king's right to confirm privileges: £5,000 from all the Cistercian abbeys to elect their abbots freely, not have to sue for restoration of their temporalities, and other liberties 'according to their old usage in that behalf'. All in all, Dudley collected some

    [93] J. R. Lander, 'Bonds, Coercion and Fear: Henry VII and the Peerage' in J. R. Lander, *Crown and Nobility, 1450–1509* (London, 1976), 267–300; T. B. Pugh, 'Henry VII and the English Nobility', in G. W. Bernard (ed.), *The Tudor Nobility* (Manchester, 1992), 49–110; BL, Lansdowne MS 127, fo. 52r–52v.

    [94] PRO, E210/10514; C54/396, m. 25d.

    [95] *Records of Convocation*, ed. G. Bray, 20 vols (Woodbridge, 2005–6), xvi. 43–4, 310–12; S. J. Gunn, 'Edmund Dudley and the Church', *Journal of Ecclesiastical History* 51 (2000), 513–16.

    [96] Halstead, *Succinct Genealogies*, 211.

£38,112 10s 5¼d from English churchmen in four years, a little over a third of it in cash and the rest in bonds. Each year he was thus single-handedly extracting from the English church nearly twice as much as the pope. Here as elsewhere, he and his colleagues were straining the law to serve the king in his quest for financial and political strength. In this case they also sought their master's spiritual benefit. In 1508 Dudley settled with the master and fellows of Fotheringhay College after an inquisition, later condemned as falsely procured by Empson, threatened their tenure of their lands. They were to pay £200 and say daily and quarterly masses for the king. These exactions were certainly resented—in their accounts the monks of Battle Abbey described the £166 13s 4d they paid to elect their abbot freely as taken by the king's 'great power and unjust oppression'—and in the wake of Henry's death, some of them would be disowned.[97] The king's executors ordered the restoration of £8,406 13s 4d in fines taken in cash and bonds from four bishops, eleven abbots, and two priors.[98] But in their mobilization of royal rapacity and royal piety the new men had laid the foundations for future Tudor policy towards the church.

AUDIT AND CONTROL

The reigns of Edward IV and Richard III had seen a shift away from the traditional dominance of the exchequer in royal financial management towards coordination of royal income and expenditure by the treasurer of the chamber. At first, Henry reversed this trend, restoring exchequer supremacy. But by 1487 he was beginning to concentrate new streams of income in the chamber and soon it was more powerful than ever. Even parliamentary taxation and customs revenue, the collection of which was organized by the exchequer, were marshalled and spent through the chamber. The treasurer of the chamber, first Lovell, then Heron, who had begun the reign as Lovell's clerk, became in effect the king's chief financial administrator. The chamber dealt in cash rather than the assignments on crown debtors that were the characteristic means of payment in the medieval exchequer, but as it became more important, it became less mobile and developed its own staff and office routines. By 1501–5 two expert clerks, John Daunce and Robert Fowler, were receiving and paying out perhaps three-quarters of the crown's annual revenue from fixed offices at Westminster under Heron's supervision and sending large drafts of coin over to the Tower for deposit in the king's privy coffers. Meanwhile, Heron operated from a third office in Westminster Abbey, making up from their accounts the overall chamber books he discussed with the king. Heron continued as treasurer until 1521, formally denoted in 1510 general receiver of the king's revenues, and in January 1523 Wyatt took over, managing the king's money through difficult times until his retirement in 1528.[99]

[97] HL, MS BA272.   [98] PRO, SP1/1, fos. 102–3 (*LP* I, i. 308).

[99] Wolffe, *Crown Lands*, 51–88; Richardson, *Tudor Chamber Administration*, 109–32, 160–6, 216–48; J. R. Hooker, 'Some Cautionary Notes on Henry VII's Household and Chamber "System"', *Speculum* 33 (1958), 70–2; D. Grummitt, 'Henry VII, Chamber Finance and the "New Monarchy": Some New Evidence', *HR* 72 (1999), 229–43; JRL, Latin MS 241, fo. 33v; *LP* III, ii. 2750, 2835.

As treasurer of the chamber Wyatt was engaged, under the direction of Wolsey and the king, with every area of the crown's financial activity, as his signature on myriad documents attests. He oversaw collection of the forced loan of 1522–3, the lay and clerical subsidies of 1523–6, the anticipations of payments from richer taxpayers introduced to facilitate accelerated expenditure, and the abortive amicable grant of 1525, drawing in money collected by the exchequer as Heron had done.[100] He dispensed money for armies, navies, ambassadors, court festivities, the king's household, and those of his daughter Princess Mary and his illegitimate son Henry Fitzroy, duke of Richmond.[101] Diplomatic payments could require particular ingenuity, for example when he arranged payment to English ambassadors in Spain out of the revenues of the bishoprics given to Wolsey by the Emperor Charles V and then reimbursed the cardinal in England.[102] He took new bonds for debts to the king and monitored old bonds for payment or cancellation.[103] His activity left physical traces. For the spending boom of the war years his staff bought 22¾ yards of green cloth to count money on, four new coffers, and forty-one dozen canvas money bags.[104] It also left an auditing problem so complex that he received his final release only six years after leaving office.[105]

The exchequer was not eliminated by the rise of the chamber; indeed, its powers were partly reasserted in 1509, but its roles were clearly confined. It was nevertheless important that its activities be coordinated with those of the chamber and other newer agencies, and in this the new men played an important part by holding office in both. Bray was briefly lord treasurer, Heron deputy chamberlain of the exchequer, while Cutt was first receiver-general of the duchy of Lancaster, then undertreasurer of the exchequer. Lovell was chancellor of the exchequer from 1485, found posts there for his servants and clients, and corresponded cheerfully with his colleagues. At his funeral, he was mourned by the second baron, William Wotton, the foreign apposer, Thomas Pymme, the clerk of the pleas, William Young, and the comptroller of the pipe, Robert Waleys. His retainer John Daunce was simultaneously an exchequer teller and Heron's clerk and solemnly paid taxation received by himself acting in one capacity over to himself acting in the other.[106]

[100] *LP* IV, i. 214, 522, 638, 881, 1713, 2888(1), 2911(1, ii), ii. 2911(1), 3380(10), 3471, 3542, 3650, 4772, 5124, iii, Appendices 36, 37; *Records of the Borough of Leicester*, ed. M. Bateson et al., 7 vols (London, 1899–1974), iii. 23; ESRO, Rye 81/2; SROI, T4373/265; PRO, E179/141/109/9–12.

[101] *LP* IV, i. 214, 281, 1132, 1210, 1337, 1512, 1577(11), 1684, 1839, 2139, 2359, ii. 2852, 2876, 3023, 3104, 3375, 3597, iii. 6070, 6138, V, pp. 310, 312.

[102] *LP* IV, ii. 2682, iii. 5856, 5863.

[103] *CAD*, iii. D1052; *LP* III, ii. 2694(8), iii. 6798, V. 538, 1715; PRO, C1/585/42–3, 45.

[104] *LP* IV, i. 214.   [105] *LP* VII. 254, VIII. 633(2).

[106] J. D. Alsop, 'The Exchequer in late medieval Government, c1485–1530', in J. G. Rowe (ed.), *Aspects of Late Medieval Government and Society: Essays presented to J. R. Lander* (Toronto, 1986), 179–212; J. D. Alsop, 'The Structure of early Tudor Finance, c.1509–1558', in C. Coleman and D. Starkey (eds), *Revolution Reassessed: Revisions in the History of Tudor Government and Administration* (Oxford, 1986),143–7; *CPR 1485–94*, 18; *Materials*, i. 508, 549–50; PRO, SC1/52/76; J. C. Sainty, *Officers of the Exchequer*, List and Index Society Special Series 18 (London, 1983), 75, 83, 96, 102, 175, 199; M. M. Condon, 'From Caitiff and Villain to *Pater Patriae*: Reynold Bray and the Profits of Office', in M. A. Hicks (ed.), *Profit, Piety and the Professions in later Medieval England* (Gloucester, 1990), 139–40; Somerville, *Duchy of Lancaster*, 401–2, 595; PRO, C142/41/62; *HMC Rutland*, iv. 261; *LP* IV, i. 366; Grummitt, 'Chamber Finance', 233–4.

Audit was one of the main functions of the medieval exchequer, yet from the early 1490s Henry increasingly reserved the auditing of important accounts to himself or groups of his councillors. Until his death, Bray was much involved, but many other councillors, notably Lovell, took part, and by the end of the reign Southwell was working well beyond the general surveyors' remit for crown lands. He was present, for example, on 21 May 1507, when Sir Hugh Conway handed in his accounts as treasurer of Calais for 1505–6.[107] In the reaction of 1509, Southwell's role was squared with the reassertion of the exchequer's control as he was appointed its principal auditor on 30 June 1510. His powers were further expanded in 1511 and 1512 as Henry VII's system was slowly, though never wholly, reconstructed, concerns remaining about the legal status of the general surveyors as a 'by-court', insufficiently integrated with the common law system to give accountants legal discharge, and about the propriety of a single auditor, rather than the conventional pair, hearing and discharging accounts.[108] From then on, Southwell's activity was evident throughout the financial system, even when it involved chasing colleagues hard. It was on his orders that the duchy of Cornwall officers pursued Windsor for fees over-paid to his executed brother-in-law Dudley, though in the end it had to be admitted that as Dudley's wealth had been forfeited to the king there was no realistic prospect of repayment.[109] In the war of 1512–13 he audited accounts of all types, for the navy, for tents, for horses, for the defence of the Isle of Wight, for the army that fought at Flodden.[110]

Sometimes audit had a physical side, checking the stocks of the king's goods as well as the accounts of his money. Cutt and Wyatt surveyed the ordnance in the Tower of London in 1516, Windsor the king's armoury and stables in 1519 and the jewel house in 1524.[111] Sometimes it had specific targets, like the London goldsmiths investigated by Marney for their misconduct at the Tower mint or the executors of Lady Margaret Beaufort, checked by Southwell for their compliance with her intentions in setting up St John's College, Cambridge.[112] Audit was also a matter of the king's conscience. Henry VII, for all his obsessive pursuit of debt and control, did not wish to wrong his subjects. In 1504 he ordered it proclaimed that anyone who felt aggrieved in matters such as forced loans or purveyance should complain to a panel of seven councillors including Lovell and Mordaunt. Again, at the beginning of Lent 1509, reviewing his conduct with his confessor, he promised a general pardon to his subjects, one issued on 16 April. Meanwhile, he put the finishing touches to his will, signed on 31 March. This set up a committee of sixteen, Lovell, Ernley, Empson, and Dudley among them, to whom anyone might show 'any wrong to have been done to him by us, our commandment, occasion

---

[107] Wolffe, *Crown Lands*, 70–5; Richardson, *Tudor Chamber Administration*, 75–6, 176–92; BL, Addl. MS 21480, fo. 183r; *LP*, I, i. 582; JRL, Latin MS 241, fo. 33v.

[108] Sainty, *Exchequer*, 119; Wolffe, *Crown Lands*, 76–9; M. McGlynn, '"Of good name and fame in the countrey": Standards of Conduct for Henry VII's Chamber Officials', *HR* 82 (2009), 547–59.

[109] DCRO, DC Roll 215, m. 30r; Roll 218, m. 16v.

[110] *LP* I, i. 1531, ii. 2054, 2349, 2479, 2538, 2540, 2651.

[111] *LP* II, i. 1908, III, i. 576, IV, i. 695, V. 939.

[112] *LP* I, i. 1083(24); M. K. Jones and M. G. Underwood, *The King's Mother: Lady Margaret Beaufort, Countess of Richmond and Derby* (Cambridge, 1992), 245–6.

or mean, or that we held any goods or lands which of right ought to appertain unto him'. They were to deal with cases 'speedily, tenderly and effectually...duly and indifferently'.[113]

After his arrest, Dudley was in no position to serve on the committee, but composed a long list identifying which debts to the king among 'all such matters as I was privy unto' he thought reasonable, which excessive, and which mere tools of political management. He sent it to Lovell and Fox, knowing the trust Henry had placed in them 'especially for the help and relief of his soul'.[114] Though more than a dozen councillors were involved, including Marney, Wyatt, Cutt, and Englefield, it was indeed Lovell and Fox who took the lead in reviewing outstanding debts to Henry and the actions of those who had administered them. Southwell performed the technical work of audit under their guidance and Lucas, Hobart, and Ernley the legal assessment and, where necessary, prosecution. At least fifty-one bonds were cancelled on the grounds that they were made without any lawful cause, such that to pursue them would be to the 'evident peril' of the late king's soul.[115] Aggrieved parties wrote to Southwell at Belknap's suggestion, one insisting 'I had great wrong in that matter. I trust to be restored'.[116] One wrote to Dudley, who assured him that he thought in conscience he should be reimbursed; 'if I were of power', concluded Dudley, 'I would restore you myself.'[117] Some indentures kept by Dudley had to be looked out and returned to the parties involved by Marney, who had charge of his confiscated goods.[118]

Many other bonds, however, were judged reasonable and pursued by negotiation or prosecution, to be cancelled only on payment.[119] Within ten weeks of Henry's death, Lovell, Marney, Hussey, Wyatt, and others were taking bonds for debts to the new king, as they continued to do for payments large and small, from subjects great and obscure, for purposes many and varied, long into the new reign.[120] When money became short in the wake of the young king's first war, it was Lovell, Marney, Heron, and Englefield who negotiated with debtors to call in repayments, before handing over to a more urgent commission led by Wolsey.[121] When Sir John Savage and his son indented with Wolsey, Lovell, and Heron in November 1520 for the payment of £2,333 6s 8d for a pardon for the murder of a

---

[113] *CPR 1494–1509*, 380; Elton, 'Rapacity and Remorse', 61–5; S. J. Gunn, 'The Accession of Henry VIII', *HR* 64 (1991), 281; Condon, 'Last Will', 118–19.

[114] 'Petition of Edmund Dudley', 86–7.

[115] Lander, 'Bonds, Coercion and Fear', 298n; *LP* I, i. 218(54, 58), 448(4), 1493, Addenda, i. 105.

[116] PRO, SC1/44/87, 63/316.   [117] *LP* Addenda, i. 92.   [118] *LP* I, i. 391.

[119] Horowitz, 'Policy and Prosecution', 450–2; PRO, CP40/1010, m. 552r.

[120] *CAD*, iii. D1094, iv. A6220, v. A13033, A13207–8; *LP* II, ii. 2932, 3026, 3403, 3532, 4494, 4546, III, i. 1012(12), ii. 2074(7), IV, ii. 2927(20); PRO, C54/377, m. 3d, 379, m. 3d, 382, mm. 14d–15d, 383, mm. 1d, 5d, 10d, 12d, 384, m. 27d, 385, m. 2d, 386, mm. 2d, 3d, 388, m. 4d; CP40/1005B, m. 372v, 1022, mm. 429v, 621v, 1026, m. 533v, 1028, m. 716r, 1029, m. 531v, 1030, mm. 327v, 421r–421v, 1034, mm. 326v, 580v, 1037, mm. 127v, 637v, 1038, m. 439r, 1043, mm. 536v, 540v.

[121] PRO, E210/10103; S. J. Gunn, 'The Act of Resumption of 1515', in D. T. Williams (ed.), *Early Tudor England: Proceedings of the Fourth Harlaxton Symposium* (Woodbridge, 1989), 93–4.

neighbouring JP and abuses of local office, their estates being recovered by feoffees including Lovell, Marney, and Heron to ensure due payment, Henry VII's blend of forceful justice, fiscal pressure, and tight political management had come back with a vengeance.[122]

Even to the tidying of Henry's fiscal and moral legacy and its partial perpetuation, the new men brought both their political and moral judgment and their legal and accountancy skills. They were engaged in every area of his revenue raising, recurrent and occasional, traditional and innovative, acceptable and extortionate, and they gave him vital assistance in monitoring and disbursing his gains, both in their individual interactions with him and in their development of wider relationships and institutions.

[122] PRO, C54/388, m. 27d; E. W. Ives, 'Crime, Sanctuary and Royal Authority under Henry VIII: The Exemplary Sufferings of the Savage Family', in M. S. Arnold et al. (eds), *On the Laws and Customs of England: Essays in honor of Samuel E. Thorne* (Chapel Hill NC, 1981), 296–320.

6

Borderlands, war, and diplomacy

The circumstances of Henry's reign did not only demand that he rule lowland England effectively; he had equally urgently to control the peripheries of his realm and deal with his powerful neighbours. Significant areas under his rule were geographically, culturally, administratively, and strategically distinct from the core of the Anglo-Saxon kingdom. Large parts of Wales, Ireland, Cornwall, and the northernmost counties of England presented upland or boggy areas of sparse settlement and pastoral or transhumant farming. In Wales, Cornwall, and Ireland many of the population spoke a language other than English. Distinctive legal and administrative systems had survived complete English conquest in Wales and partial English conquest in Ireland, while the bishops of Durham and lords of the Welsh marches retained the jurisdictional liberties granted by earlier kings to bolster them against the Scots and the Welsh. Much of the armed disruption of the Wars of the Roses had its origin in these areas, as marcher lords drew their retinues into warfare in the heart of the kingdom. Richard, duke of York, used Ireland as a base and Henry himself appealed to Welsh support, the national redeemer foretold by the bards, as he marched from Pembrokeshire to Bosworth.

Those who challenged Henry saw the possibilities these borderlands offered. Lambert Simnel was crowned in Dublin and Perkin Warbeck tried Ireland, the northern borders, and Cornwall in turn as bases for his campaigns. The pretenders and their promoters also tried to exploit Henry's relations with his European neighbours to their advantage. The old rivalry with France, two centuries of confrontation with the Scots, and close but fraught commercial and dynastic relations with the Low Countries and Iberia made a difficult inheritance for a king of England concerned to keep his throne, uphold his honour, and defend his subjects. Skilful diplomacy and vigorous warfare in the right combination would be required to keep Henry and his England afloat.

BEYOND THE HEARTLAND

Much of the new men's work was done around the king, and even when they were apart from him they were often in the southern, eastern, and midland counties where they bought lands and held office. In contrast, Henry's power at the fringes of his realm depended heavily on the great lords whose military followings equipped them to impose order and mobilize local society for defence against the Gaelic lords of Ireland or the Scots: the Fitzgerald earls of Kildare, the Butler earls of

Ormond, the Percy earls of Northumberland, the Lords Dacre of the North.[1] In these areas, towns were fewer and judicial proceedings less regular than in most of England and, at least in Ireland and the far North of England, crown landholdings were smaller, all of which deprived the new men of handholds. Wales presented the rather different problems of the patchwork of jurisdictions created by the piece-meal Norman conquest of the Marches and the duality of legal and administrative structures that was the legacy of Edward I's subjugation of the remaining Welsh principalities. These issues the Yorkist kings had begun to address by the creation of regional royal councils headed by bishops or trusted southern peers, a policy Henry revived.[2]

It was in Wales and Cheshire, also part of the traditional endowment of the Prince of Wales, that the new men were most active. Englefield was a prominent member of Arthur's council and the Marcher council that succeeded it. He sat as a justice in the border counties and marcher lordships, arbitrated local disputes, and progressed from deputy justice to assize justice in Chester and North and South Wales.[3] Mordaunt was Arthur's attorney from 1490 to 1495 and a pensioned councillor thereafter, busy in the affairs of the duchy of Cornwall as well as the Welsh borders. He took the lead in pressing the prince's rights in a series of *quo warranto* investigations in Cheshire in 1499 and in negotiating in 1503–4 the terms of the charters by which the king, in return for large fines, abrogated the civil disabilities imposed on the Welsh of North Wales in the wake of the Edwardian conquest and Glyndŵr rebellion.[4] Bray was joint steward of Monmouth and, between 1495 and 1500, chamberlain of Chester.[5] Wyatt joined in briefly, on a commission tasked in 1495 with taking into the king's hands the forfeited estates of Sir William Stanley in Wales, the Marches and the border counties.[6] Efficient control, even at the cost of disaffection, tempered by efforts to cultivate loyalty, characterized Arthur's Wales like his father's England, and in that the new men played their usual part.

[1] S. G. Ellis, *Tudor Frontiers and Noble Power: The Making of the British State* (Oxford, 1995), 46–170.

[2] S. J. Gunn, *Early Tudor Government 1485–1558* (Basingstoke, 1995), 62–70.

[3] S. T. Bindoff, *History of Parliament: The House of Commons 1509–1558*, 3 vols (London, 1982), ii. 103; S. Gunn, 'Prince Arthur's Preparation for Kingship', in in S. Gunn and L. Monckton (eds), *Arthur Tudor, Prince of Wales: Life, Death and Commemoration* (Woodbridge, 2009), 13–14; W. R. B. Robinson, 'The Administration of the Lordship of Monmouth under Henry VII', *The Monmouthshire Antiquary* 18 (2002), 33; *CPR 1494–1509*, 229; J. B. Smith, 'Crown and Community in the Principality of North Wales in the Reign of Henry Tudor', *Welsh History Review* 3 (1966), 162–3, 168; T. Thornton, *Cheshire and the Tudor State, 1480–1560* (Woodbridge, 2000), 92, 144, 147; *Thirty-First Annual Report of the Deputy Keeper of the Public Records* (London, 1870), 195.

[4] Gunn, 'Prince Arthur's Preparation', 13–15; PRO, SC6/Henry VII/362, m. 7r, 1081, mm. 4–5, 1087, m. 1r; DCRO, DC Roll 211, mm. 7, 10, Roll 214, m. 6; E. W. Ives, *The Common Lawyers of Pre-Reformation England. Thomas Kebell: A Case Study* (Cambridge, 1983), 227; R. Stewart-Brown, 'The Cheshire Writs of Quo Warranto in 1499', *EHR* 49 (1934), 679–80; Smith, 'Crown and Community', 157–9, 168–9.

[5] R. Somerville, *A History of the Duchy of Lancaster, I, 1265–1603* (London, 1953), 648; Thornton, *Cheshire*, 150.

[6] *CPR 1494–1509*, 29.

Cornwall was in some ways similar to Cheshire, distant from London, but tied by tradition to the crown through the holding of the duchy by the king's eldest son. Tin mining made its economy distinctive and the French conquest of Brittany made it vulnerable to seaborne attack. Henry mostly governed it through trusted local men, but Arthur's councillors caused some disruption with their efforts to maximize revenue, contributing to the rising of 1497.[7] In 1509 Marney, with his small Cornish landed inheritance and his large claims to the new king's favour, became steward of the duchy and lord warden of the stannary courts that regulated the tin industry and much else in the mining communities, even exercising a legislative function as tinners' parliaments.[8] He operated through his deputy-warden Thomas Denys, a Devon lawyer with a successful future as Wolsey's, then Cromwell's, chief agent in south-western affairs, but this does not seem to have ensured an easy ride. In 1512, parliament and the royal council intervened when Denys imprisoned Richard Strode, a Plympton MP who had been agitating about the damage done by tinworks.[9] Two years later, the court of king's bench became involved when more than a hundred named opponents defied Marney's authority in a series of local stannary courts from Helston in West Cornwall to Chagford in mid-Devon. They included Strode again, John Cole, a Slade tinner, who ended up in Lydford prison under stannary law, and even Marney's disgruntled predecessor in the stewardship, Robert, Lord Willoughby de Broke.[10] The duchy's administration was consolidated three times between 1514 and 1521 with the appointment of successive groups of commissioners led by Marney and the bishop of Exeter, but the exercise of its local power probably became easier when Marney was succeeded by the great local magnate, Henry Courtenay, earl of Devon.[11]

Wyatt's Yorkshire roots made him a more natural agent for the king in the North than most of his fellows. In 1487–8 he dealt on Henry's behalf with the embattled supporters of James III of Scots both at court and on embassy to Scotland, and in 1489–90 he took them munitions and victuals by ship from Chester. From June 1491 he served for about ten years as captain of Carlisle, an office which separated control of the city and castle from the wardenship of the west march, which the king nominally held in person with the natural occupant, Thomas Lord Dacre, as his deputy. Wyatt's duties ranged from the transfer of defence funds from London to Durham and the direction of defensive building works, through the maintenance of English networks of espionage and subversion in Scotland, including attempts to kidnap Perkin Warbeck, to an embassy connected with the truce of 1497. He extended his remit to the surveillance and frank assessment for the king's benefit of the local gentry and peers who were conducting the defence of the

---

[7] A. L. Rowse, *Tudor Cornwall* (London, 1941), 77–140; J. P. D. Cooper, *Propaganda and the Tudor State: Political Culture in the Westcountry* (Oxford, 2003), 172–209.

[8] *LP* I, i. 54(26); G. R. Lewis, *The Stannaries: A Study of the English Tin Miner* (Boston MA and New York, 1908), 116–28.

[9] Bindoff, *Commons*, ii. 34–6, iii. 399–401; 4 Henry VIII c. 8; *LP* I, ii. 1474.

[10] PRO, KB9/465/104–9; KB27/1013, mm. 27r–28v; C1/359/33; D. A. Luckett, 'The Rise and Fall of a Noble Dynasty: Henry VII and the Lords Willoughby de Broke', *HR* 69 (1996), 261–5.

[11] A. L. Rouse, *Tudor Cornwall* (London, 1941), 82–3; *LP* II, ii. 3324(24), 4286, III, ii. 1391.

border.[12] Few of his colleagues ventured north of the Tees, but they were available when needed. In 1488 Cutt surveyed the defences of Berwick, Carlisle, Newcastle, Norham, and Wark.[13] In the 1490s, Hobart took the judicial priorities of the king's inner councillors to the far North as one of the bishop of Durham's assize justices.[14] In 1521 Windsor was sent to assist the bishop of Carlisle on the borders.[15] At other times, the new men worked at one remove, as when Bray and the council learned sent the serjeant-at-law Humphrey Coningsby to York in 1501 to check on the 'execution of justice' at the assizes and assist Bishop Sever in his pursuit of prerogative revenues.[16]

Poynings was the new man whose name became famously associated with Ireland through Poynings' Law, passed by the Irish parliament over which he presided, which empowered the king's council in England to vet all legislation for the Irish parliament and regulated relations between the English and Irish parliaments for nearly 300 years. Henry sent him to Ireland in October 1494 to deal with a series of urgent and interconnected problems. In recent decades, English government there had become more effective and better able to defend the Pale around Dublin and its settler communities against pressure from the Gaelic lords, but constant campaigning was necessary to maintain the English position. Such campaigns were best led by the great Anglo-Irish nobles, above all the Fitzgerald earls of Kildare. But Gerald Fitzgerald, the current earl, had proved himself unreliable by his support for Lambert Simnel and now the threat loomed that Perkin Warbeck would invade England from Ireland, as Simnel had done. Kildare was removed from the deputyship in 1492 and various stopgap measures failed before Henry resolved to send Poynings as lord deputy, at the head of an English army 653 strong and backed by a team of English administrators.[17]

Poynings dealt with his military duties to good effect. In his first few months he compelled many Gaelic lords to enter sureties to keep the peace and wasted the lands of those who would not. When Kildare's brother James Fitzgerald went into rebellion and occupied Carlow Castle, Poynings took it after 'long and painful lying at the siege of the same'. And when Warbeck came to Ireland and joined with the earl of Desmond, Kildare's disaffected cousin, Poynings managed, albeit narrowly, to break their siege of Waterford and drive them off. Political success was more mixed. He erred on the side of caution in arresting Kildare for treason and sending him to England, but this cost him the help of

---

[12] A. Conway, *Henry VII's Relations with Scotland and Ireland, 1485–1498* (Cambridge, 1932), 16–19, 28–9, 34, 36, 114–15, 140–5, 236–9; Ellis, *Tudor Frontiers*, 148–9; H. R. T. Summerson, *Medieval Carlisle: The City and the Borders from the Late Eleventh to the mid-Sixteenth Century*, 2 vols, Cumberland and Westmorland Antiquarian and Archaeological Society extra ser. 25 (Kendal, 1993), ii. 466–73.
[13] *HKW*, iv. 627.   [14] Durham University Library, CCB190309, m. 4r.
[15] *LP* III, ii. 1483.   [16] WAM 12247.
[17] Conway, *Scotland and Ireland*, 42–77; S. G. Ellis, 'Henry VII and Ireland, 1491–1496', in J. F. Lydon (ed.), *England and Ireland in the Later Middle Ages* (Blackrock, 1981), 237–43; I. Arthurson, *The Perkin Warbeck Conspiracy 1491–1499* (Stroud, 1994), 42–51.

the earl's following and indeed prompted James Fitzgerald's revolt. He learnt to cultivate the Gaelic lords by gifts of fine woollen cloth for themselves, velvet for their wives, and pay for their troops, but could never build up intricate cross-border alliance networks like the Fitzgeralds or the Butlers. Crown finances in Ireland were strengthened, but not to the point where an army the size of his could be sustained without large English subsidies. The initial effect of Poynings' Law was merely to restore to the king the initiative in the Irish parliament his predecessors had lost. Poynings's mission ended in December 1495 with the restoration to the deputyship of a chastened Kildare.[18] Yet he had done what was needed to resolve the crisis and his experience lent him a role in Irish policy thereafter. Though he was not in the council in 1506 when it was proposed that Henry himself might lead an expedition to Ireland, he was there to sign a warrant in 1508 approving legislation for the Irish parliament under the terms of the law that came to bear his name and his deputyship would remain a point of reference in Irish affairs.[19]

Others played smaller parts in Henry's rule of Ireland. Wyatt's skills, financial, political, and military, were transferable to the lordship, where he served in 1493 and 1495–6.[20] When Henry called the Anglo-Irish lords to his court, for example to reconcile Kildare to his rival Ormond and set terms for his conduct as deputy, councillors such as Bray and Lovell were involved.[21] Years later, Hussey was one of the peers who stood surety for Kildare's son when he in turn was called to the English court to be exhorted to good behaviour.[22] The new men were often there when king and council called to account others charged with rule of the king's more distant dominions. Bray, Guildford, and Brandon sat when Lord Dacre was fined for riots in 1488 and Lovell, Guildford, Poynings, Dudley, and Wyatt when his keeping of Redesdale was under investigation in 1504.[23] These or others were doubtless present when the council reined in two courtiers gone wild in their government of Jersey, Matthew Baker and Sir Hugh Vaughan, and laid down detailed orders for the island's government.[24]

In the end, their talent and trustworthiness carried them wherever the king needed them. Windsor, active Middlesex JP and supplier of the king's clothing, was as metropolitan a royal servant as could be. Yet even he took on a temporary but varied task in 1521–2 with his appointment as a royal commissioner to govern the estates of the Stanley earls of Derby, the great lords of the North-West, during the minority of the third earl. Together with John Hales,

[18] Conway, *Scotland and Ireland*, 78–87, 151, 171–83, 216; Arthurson, *Perkin Warbeck Conspiracy*, 103–6, 113–15; Ellis, 'Henry VII and Ireland', 243–50.

[19] *SCC*, 46; M. M. Condon, 'An Anachronism with Intent? Henry VII's Council Ordinance of 1491/2', in R. A. Griffiths and J. Sherborne (eds), *Kings and Nobles in the Later Middle Ages* (Gloucester, 1986), 238–9, 252; *LP* III, i. 1182, Addenda, i. 297.

[20] Conway, *Scotland and Ireland*, 55–9, 65–86.

[21] Conway, *Scotland and Ireland*, 93–4.

[22] PRO, C54/398, m. 35d.   [23] *SCC*, 20–1, 38–9.

[24] A. J. Eagleston, *The Channel Islands under Tudor Government, 1485–1642* (Cambridge, 1949), 7–11, 18–32.

attorney-general of the duchy of Lancaster, he took inquisitions into the late earl's lands at London and made appointments to offices in Berkshire, but he also went much further afield. He granted out offices and leases in Cheshire, Lancashire, Yorkshire, and Wales, and at one point travelled through Shrewsbury, presumably heading into North Wales. Admittedly, it looks as though he intervened in the Isle of Man, of which the earls were lords, from Hawarden, rather than voyaging to the island.[25] But his engagement is further testimony to the length of the new men's reach.

DIPLOMACY

Henry operated in a Europe in which diplomatic exchanges were intensifying with the rise of resident ambassadors and the spread of a diplomatic style bred in Italy and characterized by classicizing terminology and realist, we might say Machiavellian, political analysis. By the end of his reign, he began to station permanent representatives at foreign courts, and his son took the trend further. For the most part, however, he continued the traditional practice of sending missions to other rulers when he had specific business to transact with them. For these embassies he made wide use of clerics, particularly civil lawyers, but he often teamed them with courtiers or lay councillors, including the new men.[26]

Several were active in the crisis provoked by the death of Francis II, duke of Brittany in 1488, which led Henry to send troops to stave off a French takeover of the duchy in alliance with Maximilian of Habsburg and Ferdinand and Isabella of Spain. Wyatt went out to Brittany in spring 1489 to help Henry's commanders negotiate a truce, and Lovell and Guildford were commissioned for Anglo-Breton negotiations in the following year. In winter 1488–9 Risley went to forge an anti-French alliance with Maximilian, who was struggling against opposition to his rule in the Low Countries encouraged by the French, and in summer 1492 he visited Maximilian again to coordinate military action against France. Meanwhile, Lovell had settled a treaty with Maximilian's envoys at Woking. In autumn 1489 and again in autumn 1492, conversely, Risley was at the French court, first feeling for terms on which the French might conciliate Henry's claims to a say in Brittany's future and the return of

[25] *LP* I, ii. 3324(24), III, ii. 2820, IV, i. 980; *CAD*, iii. D1238; *Abstracts of Inquisitiones post mortem relating to the City of London, Tudor Period*, ed. G. S. Fry et al., 3 vols (London, 1896–1908), i. 34; PRO, E210/5562; Bindoff, *Commons*, ii. 275–6; Owen and Blakeway, *Shrewsbury*, i. 294; 'Bridge House Collection, Document No. 36: "1417–1570. An Abstract of the Earls of Derby, Govrs & Officers of this Island, for Sevll Years 1417–1570"', *Journal of the Manx Museum* 2/32 (1932), 71.

[26] G. Mattingly, *Renaissance Diplomacy* (London, 1955); J. Blanchard, *Commynes l'européen. L'invention du politique* (Geneva, 1996), 71–133, 285–333; J. M. Currin, 'England's International Relations 1485–1509: Continuities amidst Change', in S. Doran and G. Richardson (eds), *Tudor England and its Neighbours* (Basingstoke, 2005), 14–43; C. Giry-Deloison, 'Le personnel diplomatique au début du XVIe siècle. L'exemple des relations franco-anglaises de l'avènement de Henry VII au Camp du Drap d'Or', *Journal des Savants* (July–Sept. 1987), 205–53; S. J. Gunn, 'The Courtiers of Henry VII', *EHR* 108 (1993), 40–1.

his predecessors' French lands, then accompanying Daubeney to consolidate the peace Henry agreed after his brief invasion of France.[27]

Others joined in later in the reign. Brandon and Dr Nicholas West were sent to Maximilian with the order of the garter in November 1502, as Henry tried to neutralize Habsburg support for the exiled earl of Suffolk. Pinning Maximilian down was never easy. They reached Cologne in January 1503, but managed to see him only in February, at Antwerp. There was trouble over innumerable details: the precedence of the Spanish and English ambassadors; the place, time, and the form of words for Maximilian to swear to his agreement with Henry; the need for Maximilian to take the garter oath when he had been elected years ago though never properly installed; and the timing and wording of the proclamation Maximilian was to make expelling Suffolk from his present home in Aachen. But they held to their task, hawking with Maximilian, negotiating with his councillors, and dining with his courtiers, telling him of Suffolk's 'many offences' and Henry's sympathy for his crusade plans, drawing pointed parallels between his bugbear the duke of Guelders and Henry's rebel Suffolk. The results were less than conclusive, but the mission must have been thought successful enough, for in July 1508 Brandon was despatched to Maximilian again.[28] Hussey was ready to join the diplomatic corps at the start of the next reign, but his mission to Rome in 1509 was cancelled, just as Poynings's trip to the Lateran Council in 1515 was. Hussey had to make do with a trip to Bruges in 1520 to discuss trade disputes with the Hanseatic League.[29]

Henry's diplomats often concentrated on one court in particular. Poynings's special relationship was with the Burgundians. It rested on his repeatedly fighting alongside them and on unforgettable occasions like the party thrown by the German captain Wilwolt von Schaumburg in the siege-camp at Sluis in 1492, allegedly attended by all the prettiest women in Bruges.[30] The first attempt to make diplomatic capital out of this brotherhood in arms did not go well. In summer 1493 Poynings was sent with Dr William Warham, expert Oxford lawyer and future archbishop of Canterbury, to the court of Philip the Fair at Bruges and Mechelen to discourage support for Perkin Warbeck. They were armed with information discovered by Henry's spies about Warbeck's true origins in Tournai and

[27] J. M. Currin, '"The King's Army into the Partes of Bretaigne": Henry VII and the Breton Wars, 1489–1491', *War in History* 7 (2000), 394–5; J. M. Currin, 'Henry VII and the Treaty of Redon (1489): Plantagenet Ambitions and Early Tudor Foreign Policy', *History* 81 (1996), 353–4; J. M. Currin, 'Persuasions to Peace: The Luxembourg–Marigny–Gaguin Embassy and the State of Anglo-French Relations, 1489–90', *EHR* 113 (1998), 894–5; J. M. Currin, '"To Traffic with War"?: Henry VII and the French Campaign of 1492', in D. Grummitt (ed.), *The English Experience in France c.1450–1558: War, Diplomacy and Cultural Exchange* (Aldershot, 2002), 107, 115; Giry-Deloison, 'Le personnel diplomatique', 248; *Foedera, Conventiones, Literae et cujuscunque generis Acta Publica*, ed. T. Rymer, 20 vols (London, 1704–35), xii. 397–410, 451–2, xiii. 502–10; R. Virgoe, 'Sir John Risley (1443–1512), Courtier and Councillor', *NA* 38 (1981–3), 144.
[28] *Foedera*, xiii. 35–37; BL, Addl. MS 59899, fo. 3r; *CSPV*, i. 830, 833; *Memorials*, 125, 189–219.
[29] *LP* II, ii, p. 1467, III, i. 868, 925, VII. 1566.
[30] *Die Geschichten und Taten Wilwolts von Schaumburg*, ed. A. von Keller, Bibliothek des litterarischen Vereins in Stuttgart 50 (Stuttgart, 1859), 125–6.

Poynings was equipped with expenses at three times Warham's level so he could make a splash among his noble friends. Unfortunately, Warham's denunciation of the dowager duchess of Burgundy, Margaret of York, for her attachment to Warbeck struck too offensive a tone, and those of Philip's courtiers sympathetic to Warbeck gained ground. The ambassadors returned with equivocal replies at best, Henry took coercive measures against the Netherlands, and Margaret and the Habsburgs intensified their promotion of Warbeck, thereby prolonging the Yorkist threat.[31]

It took twenty years and another hard-fought military campaign in 1511 before Poynings ventured back. Four times between January 1513 and May 1516, for a total of some thirteen months, he was English ambassador at the court of Philip's son and Maximilian's grandson, the Archduke Charles, and his regent, Margaret of Austria. His tasks were multiple. First, he had to cultivate maximum support for Henry's campaigns in northern France and defence of his isolated conquest there, Tournai, in a Netherlands bent on official neutrality.[32] Then he had to negotiate a firm friendship with Charles, not long after his betrothed, Henry's sister Mary, had been taken away to marry Louis XII of France, without promising military support against the duke of Guelders; secure as far as possible the highly favourable trading terms negotiated with Philip in 1506 but never fully implemented; and pursue Richard de la Pole, brother of the earl of Suffolk, still plotting against Henry.[33] He could not achieve everything, but managed a great deal. As his colleague Cuthbert Tunstall said of his summer 1515 embassy, by his 'wisdom' and 'great diligence' he had done more 'to bring the king's mind in his affairs [to] pass' than 'a far greater personage than he is . . . could have done'.[34] His chivalrous networks stood him in good stead, making him, as it was said in 1516, as 'welcome to this court as is possible'—especially to anglophiles like Jan van Glymes, lord of Bergen, whose town of Bergen op Zoom hosted much English trade—and enabling him to provide Henry with expert advice on the state of opinion amongst 'the lords and other of these countries' and on the geography and military capabilities of the Netherlands.[35] He recruited leading noblemen such as Henry of Nassau, Floris van Egmond, lord of Ijsselstein, Jan van Glymes, lord of Walhain, Antoine de Ligne, count of Fauquembergues, and David, bastard of Aymeries, many of them brothers-in-arms from 1511, to serve Henry in the 1513 campaign and the defence of Tournai.[36] His fraternity with the Burgundians was never better evident than at

[31] *Foedera*, xii. 544; PRO, E404/81/2; Arthurson, *Perkin Warbeck Conspiracy*, 67–73; S. Thiry, 'De constructie van een vorstelijk imago: Perkin Warbeck in de Nederlanden en het Heilige Roomse Rijk', *Tijdschrift voor Geschiedenis* 124 (2011), 165–71.

[32] *LP* I, i. 1566, 1630, 1660, 1679, 1713, 1722–4, 1750, 1764, ii. 1824, 1848, II, i. 701.

[33] *LP* II, i. 423, 498, 538–40, 609, 649, 724, 742, 831, 858, 1574, 1668, 1679, 1684, 1706, 1727, 1755, 1764, 1823.

[34] BL, Cotton MS Galba BIII, fo. 297v (*LP* II, i. 904).

[35] *LP* I, i. 1566, 1774, ii. 1745, 1749, 1961, 2014, 2657, 3474; II, i. 11, 32, 70, 85, 568, 1541, 1679, 1824, 2444, 2363, ii. 3069, 3091; BL, Cotton MS Galba BIV, fo. 42r (*LP* II, i. 1666); PRO, SP1/9, fo. 108 (*LP* I, ii. 3247).

[36] *LP* I, i. 1792, ii. 1918, 1934, 1950, 2371, 2473, 2943, 2995, 3046, 3474; E. Hall, *Hall's Chronicle* (London, 1809 edn), 540.

Brussels on St George's day 1516, when the sixteen-year-old Charles swore to observe the new Anglo-Burgundian treaty and then dined with Poynings, both dressed in their garter robes.[37]

Welcoming those visiting the English court was another task for courtiers. Brandon, 'a distinguished knight' as one Venetian called him, was a past master.[38] In December 1507 he met the new French ambassador and took him to the king at the Tower; on Ash Wednesday 1508 he fetched the Spanish ambassador from his room at Richmond to meet the council; in July he greeted Maximilian's ambassador and took the Scottish ambassador to the king; and that winter he was in the welcoming party at Dartford for a large embassy from Flanders.[39] With hindsight, all those missions pale before that he undertook in October 1506, taking 'a goodly company with him of his own servants all verily well horsed unto the seaside' to greet Baldassare Castiglione, the ultimate expert on renaissance courtliness, as he came to receive the garter at Windsor on behalf of his master the duke of Urbino.[40] Risley, Windsor, and Hussey, too, sometimes escorted foreign ambassadors from the coast to the court, or met them on Blackheath as they neared London.[41] Poynings, naturally, was sent to welcome Burgundians, who often came armed with letters of introduction to him and messages for him to pass on to the king.[42]

When dealing with large embassies, those with linguistic skills and courtly polish were detailed to entertain their counterparts. At the peace negotiations with the French in 1492, Risley interpreted between the earl of Shrewsbury and the leader of the French delegation, while Brandon and Poynings took a French nobleman each. Meanwhile Bray, Lovell, and Guildford were with the king, Hussey in the welcoming party.[43] In 1518 Poynings escorted one of the leaders of the French embassy sent to negotiate the return of Tournai.[44] Diplomacy also needed a supporting cast. Four French courtiers resided at the English court as hostages for the payments due for the restitution of Tournai. When their behaviour became rather suspicious at a time of tension in 1521, they were sent to Lovell's house at Enfield, to be honourably entertained but secretly monitored. When war broke out and Frenchmen in England were arrested, they were each entrusted to a different councillor for safe-keeping: Lovell and Windsor took one each.[45]

Henry required his councillors to conduct negotiations with the envoys foreign rulers sent to him. Lovell helped forge a truce with the Scots in 1486, discussed with

[37] *Inventaire-sommaire des archives départementales antérieures à 1790: Nord*, ed. C. Dehaisnes et al., 10 vols (Lille, 1863–1906), vii. 256–7; *LP* II, i. 1818, 1822.

[38] *CSPV*, i. 830.

[39] *Memorials*, 102, 122–3; *Correspondencia de Gutierre Gomez de Fuensalida*, ed. Duque de Berwick y de Alba (Madrid, 1907), 419; 'The "Spouselles" of the Princess Mary', ed. J. Gairdner, *The Camden Miscellany* ix, CS n.s. 53 (1853), 6.

[40] *The Register of the Most Noble Order of the Garter*, ed. J. Anstis, 2 vols (London, 1724), 257.

[41] *The Herald's Memoir 1486–1490: Court Ceremony, Royal Progress and Rebellion*, ed. E. Cavell (Donington, 2009), 184; *LP* II, i. 395, IV, i. 614, 1633.

[42] *LPRH*, i. 369–70; *LP* II, i. 1539, (ii). 3872, 1469, App. 21, III, i. 419.

[43] *LPRH*, ii. 291–2.

[44] *LP* II, ii. 4409.

[45] *LP* III, ii. 1516; Hall, *Chronicle*, 635.

Ferdinand's envoy in 1508 and had to explain to Margaret of Austria's representative in 1514 why Henry VIII had repudiated his sister's marriage to her nephew Charles.[46] Those close about the king signed draft treaties or witnessed his confirmation of them, as Lovell and Guildford did for Henry VII and Lovell, Marney, Poynings, and Windsor for Henry VIII.[47] Diplomacy also required administrative support. As Henry found the exchequer's procedures too cumbersome for the fast-paced negotiations of the Breton crisis and early Italian wars, he placed Lovell as treasurer of the chamber in charge of payments to his own ambassadors and gifts to those visiting his court.[48] Household officers like Marney and Guildford organized entertainment, transport, and gifts from the king for foreign ambassadors.[49] Lovell was sufficiently trusted by the French ambassador Antoine de Pierrepont, seigneur d'Arisolles, that he made him one of the executors of his will when he died in London in 1511.[50]

On the rare occasions when sovereigns met, the whole court became an engine of diplomacy. In 1500, Henry met Philip the Fair at Calais, and Lovell, Guildford, Brandon, Poynings, and Marney were among the first eight knights named to accompany him, with Hussey and Risley further down the list.[51] In 1506 Philip, shipwrecked on the English coast on his way to Spain, was welcomed to Windsor, Richmond, and London. Many of the new men must have been among the councillors, household officers, knights of the garter, and 'knights of great haviour' prominent in the five weeks of entertainments and negotiations. Brandon had been sent to meet Philip when he landed and, when it was all over, he escorted him to Falmouth to begin his onward journey.[52] In 1520 and 1522 Henry VIII met Charles V, and Marney took a leading role both times, while Poynings fixed meeting sites, Belknap built banqueting houses, Wyatt garnished cupboards with plate, and Windsor and Hussey organized lodgings.[53] At the Field of Cloth of Gold in 1520 all the new men's diplomatic and administrative skills were in demand. Belknap helped construct the spectacular temporary palace at Guînes, Henry's home for the duration of the meeting, and the lists where the feats of arms were held. When the kings first met, he briefed the English contingent while Poynings checked over the French. Hussey assisted in marshalling the jousters and Poynings judged their efforts. Marney led the guard with their gilded halberds and made sure the king was comfortable while he watched the feats of arms. Wyatt procured enough plate to furnish the king's lodgings and entertain the French court to a banquet. Cutt, Heron, Lovell, and Windsor added to the crowd, Lovell's distinction marked by a retinue the size of a baron's rather than a knight's.[54]

[46] *Foedera*, xii. 285–93; *Fuensalida*, 448, 419; *LP* I, ii. 3268.
[47] *Foedera*, xii. 379, 711, 752–3, 761–2, 782–3; *Materials*, ii. 474; *LP*, I, i. 153, II, ii. 3437(6), 4469, 4475, 4504, III, i. 739(2), ii. 2333(24).
[48] J. M. Currin, '"Pro Expensis Ambassatorum": Diplomacy and Financial Administration in the Reign of Henry VII', *EHR* 108 (1993), 597–609.
[49] *LP* II, ii. 3446, 3471; Currin, 'Pro Expensis Ambassatorum', 605.
[50] BL, Addl. MS 45131, fos. 159v–60r; Giry-Deloison, 'Le personnel diplomatique', 252.
[51] *LPRH*, ii. 88.
[52] *Memorials*, 288, 293, 297, 300; *CSPV*, i. 865, 870.
[53] *LP* III, i. 804, 906, ii. 2288; *Rutland Papers*, ed. W. Jerdan, CS o.s. 21 (London, 1842), 50–2, 56, 73, 81.
[54] J. G. Russell, *The Field of Cloth of Gold: Men and Manners in 1520* (London, 1969), 31–46, 59, 110, 116–18; *LP* III, i. 702(3), 703, 704.

WAR

As the king's servants, the new men were expected to serve him in war. They did so most urgently when he faced rebellion, aware no doubt of what might happen if he were defeated. William Catesby, their closest model among the councillors of Richard III, had not been killed at Bosworth, but executed afterwards.[55] Poynings and Risley were prominent on Henry's armed progress into the North in 1486, when he had to confront several outbreaks of unrest.[56] Belknap, Hussey, Lovell, Marney, Mordaunt, and doubtless others fought at Stoke in 1487.[57] Two years later, when Henry marched against the rebels who had killed the earl of Northumberland in a tax protest in North Yorkshire, we can watch his army come together thanks to the account of one of his heralds. Lovell, Risley, and Brandon, with other household men, were already with the king at Hertford when he set out, and Brandon took charge of the royal standard. Guildford caught up with them in the south Midlands and Hussey in Yorkshire.[58] In the defence of Kent against the western rebels and at Blackheath in 1497, Belknap, Brandon, Bray, Cope, Guildford, Hobart, Lovell, Marney, Poynings, and Wyatt all took the field.[59]

When Henry fought his neighbours they likewise answered the call. Poynings was among those who went to assist Maximilian against the Flemings at Diksmuide in 1489.[60] In France, in 1492, Brandon, Bray, Guildford, Lovell, Risley, Southwell, and Wyatt served.[61] The abortive Scottish campaign of 1497 was to have featured Hussey, Lovell, and Wyatt.[62] Service continued into the next reign. In 1513, Poynings, Marney, and Windsor crossed to France on the same day as the king and Hussey and Wyatt also served in person.[63] Poynings, in particular, played a full part in the campaign. In the spring and early summer, he had used his contacts in the Netherlands and his expertise in continental warfare to raise thousands of horsemen, gunners, and German foot to bolster Henry's army and to secure the cooperation of the captain of the border fortress of Gravelines.[64] In France he was reckoned to be one of Henry's chief military advisers and was active in gathering intelligence.[65] Hussey's career went on longer than most, and in 1521 he was under consideration to serve as a captain in a force to be sent to assist Charles V.[66]

---

[55] R. Horrox, 'Catesby, William', *ODNB*.   [56] *Herald's Memoir*, 72.

[57] *AHPV*, 23*; *Herald's Memoir*, 120.   [58] *Herald's Memoir*, 166–70.

[59] *AHPV*, 94*, 95*; Shaw, *Knights of England*, ii. 28–9; HL, MS STT Personal box 1(4); BL, MS Stowe 440, fos. 82r–83v.

[60] *Herald's Memoir*, 172.

[61] *AHPV*, 52*; PRO, E36/285, fos. 28r–29r, 30v–31r, 45r–45v, 47v; E30/612; CA, MS M16bis, fos. 30v–31r, 41r, 48v, 57*v.

[62] I. Arthurson, 'The King's Voyage into Scotland: the War the Never Was', in D. Williams (ed.), *England in the Fifteenth Century* (Woodbridge, 1987), 19, 22.

[63] *The Chronicle of Calais*, ed. J. G. Nichols, CS o.s. 35 (London, 1846), 11, 13; *LP* I, ii. 2053.

[64] *LP* I, i. 1745, 1792, ii. 1918, 1934, 1961, 2414, 3614 (232).

[65] *PVAH*, 209; *LP* I, ii. 2105, 2151.   [66] *LP* III, ii. 1462 (2).

Poynings repeatedly exercised independent command, and under him English troops acquitted themselves more consistently well than under any other commander of his generation. In 1492 he took twelve ships and 2,500 men to cooperate with Albert of Saxony in the siege of Sluis, stronghold of Philip of Cleves, leader of Flemish opposition to Henry's Habsburg allies. His men's repeated, costly attacks on the lesser castle at Sluis, their bloody repulse of sallies by the garrison even as water rose around their siege guns at high tide, and their destruction of the bridge of boats joining the lesser castle to the greater played a significant part in persuading Philip of the benefits of surrender. Their conduct convinced Wilwolt von Schaumburg, commander of some of Albert's Germans, that what he had read in chronicles of the warlike qualities of the English was true, while the chronicler Molinet thought the English displayed more 'valour and prowess' than any of their allies. Poynings would have been delighted with their verdicts, having proposed single combat between a gentleman of his band and any member of the garrison once he heard that 'certain opprobrious words to the dishonour of the English nation' had been circulated by his opponents, but equally having intervened when murderous brawls broke out between his men and their German colleagues.[67] Victory at Sluis was valuable to Henry. It helped justify making peace with France in November without having captured Boulogne on the basis that one of the two sieges begun by his armies had been successful, 'to the king's great honour, assurance of his town of Calais' and benefit of 'all intercourse and feat of merchandise of England into the countries of Flanders, Zeeland, Brabant, and Holland'.[68]

In 1511 Poynings was back in the Netherlands, taking English troops to assist in the Habsburgs' campaign against the duke of Guelders. At Broekhuizen his men stormed the castle with minimal losses, and at Straelen they dug their siege trenches so near the gates that the garrison surrendered before the assault. The siege of the larger town of Venlo failed—it was incompletely surrounded, so that the final battery and attack were carried out under unfavourable conditions—but this seems to have been mostly the fault of Poynings's colleague Floris van Egmond, lord of Ijsselstein. Certainly, Margaret of Austria told her father Maximilian that the English had done better than any other troops on the campaign, indeed 'marvellously well'. They had offered to lead the storming of the walls and lost two ensign-bearers in the attack. Yet Sir Edward was not wasteful of his soldiers' lives, losing less than one hundred out of 1,500 to war and disease on the four-month campaign, and advising Henry to call them home before the bad weather cost them more.[69]

[67] J. Molinet, *Chroniques*, ed. G. Doutrepont and O. Jodogne, 3 vols (Brussels, 1935–7), ii. 309–18; *Geschichten und Taten*, 123, 127; Hall, *Chronicle*, 452; PRO, E36/208, pp. 65–85; E36/285, fos. 30v–31r, 37r–38v.

[68] *Foedera*, xii. 492.

[69] Hall, *Chronicle*, 522–5; *Correspondance de l'empereur Maximilian Ier et de Marguerite d'Autriche*, ed. A. J. G. Le Glay, 2 vols, Société de l'histoire de France (Paris, 1839), i. 426–7, 440–2; *Inventaris van de Nassause domeinraad. Tweede deel*, ed. S. W. A. Drossaers, 5 vols (The Hague, 1955), iv, nos 37–40; Robert Macquéreau, *Traicté et recueil de la maison de Bourgogne*, ed. J. A. C. Buchon, Choix de chroniques et mémoires sur l'histoire de la France 16 (Paris, 1838), 21–2; ADN, B18854/30300.

Poynings faced a final test of his military and political skills as governor of the newly conquered city of Tournai in 1513. In quick succession he declined 'very graciously' Francis, duke of Valois's request to surrender the city, broke up several conspiracies to betray it, and foiled a surprise attack on Christmas Eve 1513, while his 5,000 men raided profitably into French territory. Meanwhile, he convinced the citizens that he was 'a virtuous man' who wished them well, handling adeptly sensitive issues such as the confiscation of the banners of the city guilds, and keeping a benevolent eye on the election of town officials whom he judged to be 'by all likelihood of good condition'. He was said to have shown the leading townsfolk a furious letter from Henry about their disloyalty, prompting them to pledge their obedience so that he could write to reassure the king. Yet he was careful to keep a spy among the Tournaisien exiles at the French court and was not afraid to tell Henry that only the provost Jean Le Sellier was wholeheartedly committed to the English regime. He did exemplary justice on seven of his soldiers who had massacred a family and pillaged and burnt down their house in August 1514 and before departing his post in 1515 he helped calm the near-mutiny caused by the expenditure cuts announced by his successor, Lord Mountjoy. No wonder some thought he should be sent back when the French seemed to threaten Tournai in 1516; no wonder those he left behind there tried to use him as their contact at the English court; no wonder he was chosen to meet the disbanded garrison at Dover in 1519 and send them home in an orderly fashion.[70]

Held much longer than Tournai, Calais was England's most important fortress and centre of advanced weaponry, and Poynings and Lovell were much engaged with its upkeep.[71] Poynings reviewed the fortifications, artillery, and other armaments there in 1488 and 1517, led nearly 2,000 men to reinforce the garrison in 1492, and took command for a time in 1493.[72] Lovell oversaw its re-fortification to face siege-guns in 1512 with new works including 'Lovel's Bulwark' and in 1513 sent over extra armaments.[73] In 1514 he took some 400 men to strengthen the garrison and stayed more than two months, picking up intelligence, negotiating prisoner exchanges, and winding down the war with France with his usual skill.[74] He also visited regularly between 1497 and 1512, collecting first the substantial pensions payable from the king of France under the treaty of Étaples and then the war subvention due from Henry VIII's ally Maximilian, and making payments to the garrison from the stockpiled French coin.[75] Others took their turn at Calais, too, Belknap overseeing ordnance expenditure there in 1514.[76]

[70] Macquéreau, *Traicté et recueil*, 57, 59–60; C. G. Cruickshank, *The English Occupation of Tournai 1513–1519* (Oxford, 1971), 15, 46, 61–3, 67, 76, 116, 179, 223; A. de Lusy, *Le journal d'un bourgeois de Mons 1505–1536*, ed. A. Louant, Commission royale d'histoire (Brussels, 1969), 25, 34, 44–5; PRO, SP1/7, fo. 94 (*LP* I, ii. 2657); *LP* II, i. 1496, III, i. 82.
[71] D. Grummitt, *The Calais Garrison: War and Military Service in England, 1436–1558* (Woodbridge, 2008).
[72] *Materials*, ii. 344–5; *LP* I, ii. 3279, 3371; PRO, E36/285, fo. 79v–80r; *Foedera*, xii. 544.
[73] *HKW*, iii. 342; *LP* I, ii 3137 (16).
[74] Hall, *Chronicle*, 569; *Chronicle of Calais*, 15; PRO, SP1/8, fos. 126, 159 (*LP* I, ii. 2974, 3087).
[75] PRO, E404/82/3/unnumbered warrant of 3 December 1497, E404/85/1/85; *HMC Ninth Report* (London, 1883), App. 1, 146; CCA, FA2, fo. 413v, FA9, fos. 42v, 137v; *LP* I, i, 1280; BL, Addl. Ch. 74077.
[76] *LP* II, ii. App. 2.

Naval service also beckoned to the new men. In spring 1487 Brandon commanded the flotilla of six ships based in East Anglia designed, unavailingly, to intercept Lambert Simnel's invasion force.[77] Guildford served at sea on the *Regent* off the Breton coast in 1490 and his ship the *Mary Guildford* sailed in Brandon's flotilla.[78] Others provided ships for naval service, as Lovell and probably Guildford did in 1492.[79] Others again surveyed the king's ships and their equipment. In July 1514, Wyatt and Windsor led a team including a naval captain, an auditor, and a gunner ('for their more sure instruction and knowledge of the king's ordnance') to Erith and Woolwich to view thirteen ships and a storehouse. They travelled up and down the Thames by boat for six days, counted guns, shot, pikes, and ropes, watched the guns shot off, and refreshed themselves, as their expense account shows, with ale, beer, bread, butter, cheese, eggs, beef, chicken, duck, mutton, pigeon, pork, rabbit, oysters, shrimps, plaice, salmon, salt fish, sole, dates, prunes, and raisins.[80]

Military service was paid, sometimes handsomely: £6 13s 4d a day as governor of Tournai, 6s 8d for a banneret, 2s, or, later, 4s for a knight or other captain, 1s 6d for a spear or fully armoured cavalryman.[81] It offered protections from legal process for captains and those serving under them; Poynings even got an act of parliament passed to protect him against litigation while he was at Tournai.[82] But it must also have been expensive to fulfil—Southwell had to be loaned £20 'by the king's high commandment' to enable him to play his part in the 1492 campaign— and it is not clear that much profit could be made.[83] Prisoners and other spoils were not commonplace in early Tudor campaigns, though in 1513 Hussey apparently took a share of 4s 8d in a horse captured by one of his men.[84] Warfare could have costs of other sorts. Marney was to have led part of the middle ward in 1513, combining his own troops with those of his friend Sir John Raynsford, his feoffee John Vere, and his duchy of Lancaster subordinate Godfrey Foljambe, but he was kicked by a horse on 21 July, the day the army marched out of Calais, and so badly hurt with a broken leg that he needed surgical attention until 3 November.[85] The demands of war could also distract from other duties. One litigant claimed in 1513 that Marney could not 'be at leisure' to testify to a bargain he had witnessed 'because of his continual attendance on the king's grace in his wars'.[86]

Mustering troops before they were dispatched to the front was a role for ageing but experienced captains or dependable administrators. Commissions of array to

---

[77] *Materials*, ii. 104, 128; *Naval Accounts and Inventories in the reign of Henry VII 1485–8, 1494–7*, ed. M. Oppenheim, Navy Records Society 8 (London, 1896), 31, 35, 42; M. Bennett, *Lambert Simnel and the Battle of Stoke* (Gloucester, 1987), 59–60.

[78] Currin, 'Breton Wars', 404; *Naval Accounts*, 42; *Materials*, ii. 104, 297, 324.

[79] PRO, E36/285, fo. 65v; E36/208, p. 70.

[80] PRO, SP1/230, fos. 194r–197v (*LP* I, ii. 3137).

[81] Cruickshank, *Tournai*, 69; *LP* III, ii. 3288; PRO, SP1/6, fo. 45 (*LP* I, ii. 2414); E36/285, fos 30v, 47v.

[82] *LP* I, ii. 1948 (55), 2617 (16), 2684 (74, 92); 5 Henry VIII c. 18.

[83] PRO, E36/285, fo. 47v.   [84] *LP* II, ii, p. 1513.

[85] *Chronicle of Calais*, 13; *LP* I, ii. 2053 (3, 5, 6), 2391, 3501.

[86] PRO, C1/360/62.

levy troops often featured the new men: Lovell in Norfolk and Marney in Essex in 1490, Hussey in Kesteven and Poynings in Kent in 1496.[87] In 1512, Lovell, Poynings, Marney, Hussey, and Wyatt were all involved in musters at the ports and in arranging payments for forces on land and sea.[88] In 1513, Lovell, who had stayed behind with Southwell and Englefield to advise the queen while the king was in France, levied Midlanders and mustered Surrey's southern retinues before they set off for the Flodden campaign.[89] Their financial skills often gave the new men a role in campaign finance. Bray was treasurer of war in Henry's early campaigns, from Brittany in 1489 through France in 1492 to Ireland in 1494, though he did not always travel with the armies.[90] Wyatt bought food for the army in 1492, was sent in to overhaul the income and expenditure of the Irish government in 1495 so that Poynings's army was properly paid, and advanced money to German mercenary captains in 1513.[91] Belknap was paymaster for a planned raid on Brittany in spring 1513.[92] Windsor served as treasurer of the middle ward in France in 1513 and treasurer of war on the 1523 campaign there, dispensing £52,000 with the aid of two clerks and a messenger, and was slated to do the same for the cancelled expedition of 1525.[93] Financial expertise was also needed at home. As preparations got underway for the large campaigns of 1513, Lovell and Poynings were appointed to authorize payments for weaponry and munitions.[94] In wartime, the crown sequestrated the property of enemy aliens, and Lovell and Hussey served on commissions to find Frenchmen's and Scotsmen's goods and settle disputes over their confiscation.[95]

The new men seem to have put their ingenuity to work as much in warfare as elsewhere. Guildford served as master of the armoury and master of the ordnance from 1485, presiding over premises in the Tower and on Tower Wharf and a team of a dozen gunners. Soon he was procuring armour and weaponry for the king's soldiers and ships. By 1487, he had extended his activities to fortification and ship-building, overseeing the construction of a coastal tower near Camber and of the king's great new ship, 'a right substantial and a royal vessel', armed with hundreds of guns, the *Regent*.[96] Lovell was much engaged with firearms in the wars of 1511–14, organizing the procurement of powder, shot, arquebuses, copper guns, falcons, serpentines, demi-culverins, and a set of twelve guns 'called the xii sisters'.[97] He kept an eye on quality, specifying of 4,000 sets of infantry armour he ordered in 1512 that each was to be 'as good and large in all things, stuff and workmanship

[87] *CPR 1485–94*, 348–9; *CPR 1494–1509*, 67.
[88] *LP* I, i. 1170(7), 1176(2), 1221(6), 1414, II, ii, p. 1457.
[89] *LP* I, ii. 2163, 243, 2330(3), 2269; 3408(37); Hall, *Chronicle*, 555; PRO, E101/417/3/95.
[90] Currin, 'Breton Wars', 387n; PRO, E36/208, fo. 2r; Conway, *Scotland and Ireland*, 64, 170.
[91] PRO, E36/285, fo. 82r; Conway, *Scotland and Ireland*, 65–77; *LP* II, ii. 2073.
[92] *LP* I, ii. 2575, 2598.
[93] *LP* II, ii, p. 1461, IV, i. 214, 1261; PRO, SP1/28, fo. 207v (*LP* III, ii. 3288).
[94] *LP* I, ii. 3612(58), p. 1457.
[95] *LP* I, ii. 2222(16); LMA, Rep. 5, fos. 305v–305*r.
[96] *CPR 1485–94*, 18, 77–8, 467; *Materials*, ii. 38, 136–7, 296, 322, 431–2; D. M. Loades, *The Tudor Navy: An Administrative, Political and Military History* (Aldershot, 1992), 39–41.
[97] *LP*, I, i. 1427, 1589, ii. 1903, 2604, 3377, pp. 1509, 1515, App. 14.

as the one pair of harness' provided 'for an example'.[98] After Flodden, he had the poignant task of selling off the armour stripped from the fallen Scots.[99] In his last years, he was experimenting with the manufacture of 'engines and caltrops net fashion for the war to pitch in a strait for horsemen', the sixteenth-century equivalent of tank traps.[100] In 1492 he had made use of another new technology, distributing the first printed statutes of war to the captains of the army.[101] He also involved himself with ships, negotiating the purchase for the king from a Lübeck shipmaster of his ship the *Salvator* in 1514. The deposit was £333 6s 8d, but the balance of £2,000 would be paid only when the ship reached Erith from Veere.[102]

Poynings, too, though his command of English archers in continental wars involved the technology of Agincourt or Crécy—barrels of bowstrings and a stake for each man to plant in the battlefield—soon learnt new ways.[103] From 1492, when two companies of German mercenaries were hired to serve under his command, he was familiar with the world of the *Landsknechte*, with their pikes and handguns.[104] In 1513 the king expected him to equip even some of his English recruits with the new-fangled 'morris-pikes'.[105] At Sluis, he also saw the latest in siege gunnery, commanding many German or Dutch gunners and learning from Wilwolt von Schaumburg how to set up guns under the protection of gabions.[106] Poynings put what he learnt there into practice in Ireland, where his heavy guns helped break Perkin Warbeck's siege of Waterford; at Broekhuizen, where his artillery, six English curtalls, broke down the bulwarks around the castle; and at Venlo, where it was set up to fire into the town from an artificial mound and beat down the towers of the walls.[107] Such familiarity with modern siege warfare was also useful at Calais and at Tournai, where he helped pick the sites for the new English citadels.[108]

RECRUITMENT

The new men also played their part in war and showed their loyal commitment by raising men vigorously to serve the king. Hussey, pleading his devotion to Henry VII, claimed that in wartime 'I never left friend of mine at home that was able to serve you and would be with me as far as my power would extend', assembling never fewer than 160 men for campaigns in England and eighty overseas. The

---

[98] BL, Lord Frederick Campbell Ch. V 1 (*LP* I, ii, App. 21).

[99] *LP* I, ii 2325.

[100] *HKW*, iii. 342; *HMC Rutland*, iv. 264.

[101] C. Richmond, *The Paston Family in the Fifteenth century: The First Phase* (Cambridge, 1990), 202.

[102] PRO, E326/12265.   [103] *LP* I, i. 1004.

[104] PRO, E36/208, pp. 72–3.   [105] *LP* I, ii. 1820.

[106] PRO, E36/208, pp. 72–81;*Geschichten und Taten*, 122.

[107] Conway, *Scotland and Ireland*, 85–6; Hall, *Chronicle*, 523–4; *Correspondance de Maximilian et de Marguerite*, i. 442; *LP* I, i. 1529, ii. 2609.

[108] *HKW*, iii. 344, 376.

numbers were exaggerated as regards his early years, but in 1512 he sent a hundred men to Guyenne and in 1513 he led more than 300 to France.[109] To raise a company was also a vivid demonstration of importance to one's neighbours. Retinues wore their captain's badge: Hussey's white hind, Lovell's falcon's wing, Belknap's lizard. They marched under their captain's banner: Windsor's with the unicorn and five stags' heads, Wyatt's with the demi-lion rampant and nine horse barnacles or blacksmith's bits, Poynings's with the unicorn with the golden horn and ten gold-crowned silver keys.[110] Bray's executors duly found among his goods 'a standard with the banner of his arms' and two 'streamers with his beast and brakes'.[111]

We know little of the forces the new men led on Henry's first campaigns, but from the French campaign of 1492 onwards they fielded surprisingly large contingents. In that year Poynings led 192 men, Bray 156, Lovell 143, and Risley 134, more than many barons and some earls; even Hussey brought forty-four, and Wyatt twenty-three.[112] Indentures and muster lists show the composition of the companies in more detail. In 1492 Risley planned to bring four men-at-arms including himself, eight demilances or more lightly-armed horsemen, twenty-five mounted archers, forty-five archers on foot, and eighteen billmen; Bray twelve men-at-arms, twenty-four demilances, seventy-seven mounted archers, and 231 archers and billmen on foot.[113] Lovell's company when mustered comprised three men-at-arms with their custrells and pages, sixteen demilances, three mounted archers, a hundred archers, and thirty-three billmen, and Guildford's two men-at-arms with custrells and pages, twenty-four archers, thirty-three billmen, and at least fifty-five labourers with the guns.[114] Numbers rose again by the Scottish campaign of 1497: Lovell had 493, Hussey seventy-nine, and Wyatt thirty-one.[115]

The composition of these companies showed the sources of the new men's power. Household servants and estate officers provided the core of the armed force at any gentleman's disposal. With Lovell in France in 1492 were William Kyrkeby and Robynet Walter, whom he rewarded as old servants in his will thirty-two years later.[116] Two of those who remembered riding with Guildford to the battle of Blackheath, as they testified twenty-five years later, were his servant James Tyrrell and his keeper of Halden Park, William Deryng.[117] Two servants of Windsor were noted in the Buckinghamshire musters of 1522, one a good

---

[109] PRO, SC1/51/179; SP1/2, fo. 113r, SP1/6, fos. 45, 107, 134, 196 (*LP* I, i. 1176, ii. 2414).

[110] *Banners, Standards and Badges from a Tudor Manuscript in the College of Arms*, ed. [T.] Lord Howard de Walden (London, 1904), 107, 120, 170, 174, 181, 210; 'Banners, Standards and Badges', 68.

[111] PRO, E154/2/10, fo. 7.

[112] NUL, Mi Dc 7, fo. 43r–43v; PRO, E36/285, fos. 30v, 45r–45v; CA, MS M16bis, fo. 41r.

[113] E101/72/3/15, 20.

[114] CA, MS M16bis, fos. 30v–31v, 57v*–58r*.

[115] Arthurson, 'King's Voyage', 19, 22; BL, MS Stowe 440, fos. 82r–83v.

[116] CA, MS M16bis, fo. 57v*; PRO, PROB11/23/27.

[117] *Inquisitiones post mortem London*, i. 39–40.

billman, the other a good archer.[118] Wider manpower was drawn from the tenantry of their estates and those of their kin. Sometimes such service was explicitly required. Hussey's yeoman tenant Henry Laxston of Great Casterton was 'retained to' him and Wyatt stipulated in 1525 that while Walter Wacton held a tenement in Ashill 'he shall not be retained with any person or be in their leading of time of war other than with the said Sir Henry and his heirs'.[119] Hussey's men always came from Lincolnshire, the centre of his landed estate.[120] Windsor's companies grew steadily larger as his lands expanded. In 1513 he raised eighty-one footmen plus a captain and petty captain for the middle ward of the king's army. They came from every part of his landed estate, four from his grandmother's manor of Baylham in Suffolk, twelve from his wife's lands in Derbyshire, eighteen from his paternal inheritance in Middlesex, eight and the petty captain from Buckinghamshire, where he had purchased lands. Fifteen set out from the home of his son-in-law Peter Vavasour, who apparently served as captain of the whole company, at Spaldington in Yorkshire.[121]

Poynings's campaigns illustrated the way in which relations of kinship, friendship, and clientage shaped whole armies, just as much for a knight like him as for such great lords as the dukes of Norfolk and Suffolk.[122] Sir Matthew Browne, his half-brother, led companies under his command in 1492 and in 1511.[123] William Hattecliffe, who oversaw the finances of both the 1492 and 1495 expeditions, was married to his aunt, while the treasurer of war in 1495 was a fellow veteran of the Kent rising of 1483, John Pympe.[124] Henry Aucher, captain in 1492, was involved like Poynings in the affairs of the town of Rye.[125] Henry Raynsford and probably John Hattecliffe served as captains both at Sluis and in Ireland, while Sir Roger Cotton commanded the fleet that carried Poynings to Sluis and that sent to his aid in Ireland in 1495.[126] In 1511 his son-in-law, Thomas, Lord Clinton, followed him to Guelders together with his nephew, John Scott, and his neighbours Sir Francis Cheyney, James Darrell, John Fogg, and John Norton. Cheney, Darrell, and Fogg were the sons of men who had risen with him in 1483, and Scott was

---

[118] *The Certificate of Musters for Buckinghamshire in 1522*, ed. A. C. Chibnall, Buckinghamshire RS 17 (London, 1973), 106, 227.

[119] *The County Community under Henry VIII*, ed. J. Cornwall, Rutland Record Series 1 (Oakham, 1980), 40; PRO, E210/5651.

[120] PRO, E36/285, fo. 45r–45v; BL, MS Stowe 440, fo. 81r.

[121] PRO, SP1/2, fo. 113r (*LP* I, i. 1176); SP1/28, fo. 205v (*LP* III, ii. 3288); PRO, E101/56/25/21; *LP* I, i. 438 (1, m. 17), 519 (39), XI. 580 (2, 5); SP1/231, fos. 224–5 (*LP* Addenda, i. 113).

[122] S. Gunn, D. Grummitt, and H. Cools, *War, State and Society in England and the Netherlands, 1477–1559* (Oxford, 2007), 140–2; S. J. Gunn, 'The Duke of Suffolk's March on Paris in 1523', *EHR* 101 (1986), 598–9.

[123] PRO, E36/285, fo. 37v; *LP* I, i. 1463 (xii); J. C. Wedgwood, *History of Parliament: Biographies of the Members of the Commons House, 1439–1509* (London, 1936), 122–3.

[124] *British Library Harleian MS 433*, ed. R. Horrox and P. W. Hammond, 4 vols (Gloucester, 1979–83), ii. 48; Conway, *Scotland and Ireland*, 65–6, 70.

[125] ESRO, Rye 60/3, fos. 55v, 56v, 61r, 68v, 74v, 93r, 100v; 'List of the Gentry of Kent in the Time of Henry VII', ed. J. Greenstreet, *AC* 11 (1877), 395.

[126] PRO, E36/208, pp. 10, 66–71; Conway, *Scotland and Ireland*, 77, 166–7, 193.

married to John Pympe's niece.[127] Another captain, Richard Whetehill, was Pympe's nephew, the son of Poynings's old Calais colleague Adrian Whetehill and probably the brother of his much favoured servant Rose Whetehill.[128] Darrell, Fogg, Norton, and Scott were knighted by the future Charles V at the end of the campaign and ten years later Poynings would name Norton supervisor of his will.[129] It was brotherhood in arms like this that was commemorated by a lost stained glass window at Ashford College depicting Poynings, Fogg, Darrell, and Sir William Scott in armour.[130] At Tournai, finally, his captains included his son-in-law Lord Clinton, his ward Henry Pympe, son and heir to John, and his lieutenant of Dover Castle, John Copledike.[131]

Poynings was a powerful recruiter. For his last campaign in the field in 1513, the king asked him to raise 500 men. His response suggested that he could easily draw that number from Kent—in the end he led 511—though it would be difficult to find the fifty demilances the king had asked for, because few local men were apt to serve on horseback. Instead, drawing on the military experience of his entourage and his strong continental contacts, he offered six fully armoured men at arms on armoured horses, if he could be permitted to hire cavalrymen from the Netherlands to make up the band of fifty.[132] What his expeditions meant for Kent could be seen when Archbishop Warham's officials visited his diocese in 1511. The rectors of Hawkinge and Lower Halstow were away on campaign with Poynings, but so was Richard Ricard of Kennington, whose reported crimes included threatening to kill the vicar, planning to flee overseas with one neighbour's wife, fathering an illegitimate child with another's, committing or projecting acts of incontinence with seven more women, slandering his fellow-villagers, and spending his money at alehouses rather than maintaining his wife and children.[133] Poynings gave his neighbours both glory and catharsis.

Stewardships played a large role alongside landlordship and kinship in the new men's ability to recruit. Lovell's recruitment was dependent from the first on a combination of his own limited estates, the more extensive holdings of his brother-in-law Lord Roos, and the offices he held under the crown. In 1492 he brought forty-four men from Enfield, where he was making his home, but more came from the Roos centres in Lincolnshire, Norfolk, Nottinghamshire, and Yorkshire: twenty-two from Belvoir and nine from Wragby, fourteen from Holt and eight from Hackford, six from Warsop, and four from Thornton in Craven. They met up at

---

[127] A. E. Conway, 'The Maidstone Sector of Buckingham's Rebellion, Oct. 18, 1483', *AC* 37 (1925), 106, 109, 114; R. Griffin, 'An Inscription in Little Chart Church', *AC* 36 (1923), 139–41; Wedgwood, *Commons*, 183, 342; J. R. Scott, *Memorials of the Family of Scott of Scot's-Hall* (London, 1876), 159; for Morton, see KHLC, DRb/Ar1/13, fo. 21v.

[128] W. G. Davis, 'Whetehill, of Calais', *New England Historical and Genealogical Register* 102 (1948), 249–51, 103 (1949), 5–12; *Materials*, ii. 344–5; PRO, PROB11/20/21.

[129] *Chronicle of Calais*, 8; Hall, *Chronicle*, 523; PRO, PROB11/20/21.

[130] *Lost Glass from Kent Churches*, ed. C. R. Councer, Kent Records 22 (Maidstone, 1950), 4.

[131] *LP* I, i. 1313, I, ii. 3057, II, ii, pp. 1513–14; *CIPM*, i. 1224; PRO, PROB11/20/21.

[132] PRO, SP1/3, fo. 167 (*LP* I, ii. 1820); *LP* I, ii. 2053.

[133] *Kentish Visitations of Archbishop Warham and his Deputies, 1511–1512*, ed. K. L. Wood-Legh, Kent Records 24 (Maidstone, 1984), 126, 203–5, 260.

Canterbury with men probably recruited through stewardships, including thirty-seven from Clipstone, Nottinghamshire, centre of Sherwood Forest.[134] In 1497, the weight was again on the Roos lands and crown offices, especially in Yorkshire and Nottinghamshire.[135] Lovell raised smaller contingents in 1512–14 as the Roos lands passed out of his control, but as late as 1523 his offices were still in play, as he ordered his lieutenant in Sherwood Forest to raise ten men to serve against the Scots.[136]

Hussey used town stewardships to raise soldiers, fifteen from Grantham to serve on the king's ships in 1514, fifteen from Stamford, twenty-five from Boston.[137] Poynings's recruiting, similarly, drew heavily on the Cinque Ports. In 1511, Dover, New Romney, and Sandwich equipped archers to serve with him in Guelders. Sandwich mended its bridge for him to march over on his departure and Dover refreshed him with wine on his return.[138] Again in 1513 Sandwich provided ten men with armour, bows, bills, or halberds 'to pass over the sea' with Poynings 'in the king's wars', Dover sent seven, similarly armed, and New Romney perhaps two.[139] In 1511 Poynings also deployed men from the archbishop's estates, of which he was steward.[140] Wyatt's recruitment balanced land and office. In 1492 his retinue included John a Trysse, probably a subordinate from the jewel house.[141] In 1512 his thirteen soldiers reflected his scattered landed estate, but in 1513 he turned decisively to his offices, taking to France a petty captain and four men from Doncaster, Mirfield, and Hooton Pagnell and fifty-six others from Lancaster 'and other places thereabouts'.[142] Only in 1536, after a lifetime's concentrated land-buying, did the government reckon on his raising significant numbers from Kent.[143]

Marney's substantial retinues—150 men in 1512, 818 in 1513, 200 Cornish miners in 1522—were strongly coloured by his office-holding. In 1513 some of his captains and petty captains were drawn from his family—John Marney his son, Edmund Bedingfield his son-in-law—but more were his subordinates in the duchy of Lancaster: Ralph Carr the receiver of Dunstanburgh, Roger Cholmeley the deputy steward of Pickering, Henry Morgan the future receiver of Kidwelly, Richard Throckmorton the steward of Kenilworth, Richard Venables the bailiff of West Derby Hundred. The duchy of Cornwall stood behind his 182 soldiers from Devon and Cornwall, the duchy of Lancaster behind the 148 from Pickering, Easingwold, Pontefract, and other Yorkshire manors and from Northumberland. The two duchies gave him fifty-two men from the Midlands, from Wiltshire and Berkshire to Bolingbroke, Kenilworth, and Tutbury. Lancashire and Cheshire provided

[134] PRO, E36/285, fos. 28r–29v.   [135] BL, MS Stowe 440, fo. 81v.
[136] PRO, SP1/2, fo. 113r (*LP* I, i. 1176); E101/56/10/70; *LP* I, i. 1661 (3); *Chronicle of Calais*, 15; *HMC Rutland*, iv. 264.
[137] PRO, E101/56/10/72 (*LP* I, ii. 3614 (72, 75, 101)).
[138] BL, Egerton MS 2092, fos. 57v, 58r, 62v, 65r; KHLC, NR/Fac 3, fo. 121r; Sa/FAt 19, m. 5.
[139] KHLC, Sa/FAt 20, mm. 7–9; NR/FAc 3, fo. 123r; BL, Egerton MS 2092 fos. 90r, 92r–92v.
[140] Hall, *Chronicle*, 524.   [141] CA, MS M16bis, fo. 41r; *LP* I, i. 20.
[142] PRO, E36/2, m. 4v (*LP* I, i. 1453); PRO, E101/56/25/40.
[143] *LP* XI. 580 (1, 2).

sixty-eight men and Kidwelly forty-two. Somerset's forty-two may have been tenants of Bath Priory, whom Marney served as steward. Seven Norfolk recruits returned with Bedingfield to Oxburgh, but eighteen to the duchy of Lancaster centres of Snettisham and Thetford. Only the single soldier from Suffolk and the sixty-four from Essex look likely to have been Marney's own tenants, though even seven of the Essex men went home to the duchy of Lancaster manor of Walden.[144] It is striking that his son, who did not succeed him in his offices, was asked to levy only 101 men in 1523.[145]

To equip the men they raised, Henry's councillors established considerable private arsenals. At his fall, Dudley had 157 bows, sixty bills, thirty-five sheaves of arrows, twenty spears, four crossbows, at least forty-one complete German-style and English-style armours for footmen and ten incomplete, plus thirty brigandines, twenty-nine sallets, and twenty-nine white coats with green fringes so his men could turn out in the Tudor livery colours.[146] At his death, Lovell, who kept an armourer on his household staff, had full body, head, and arm defences, 'coats of plates with sallets and splints belonging to them', for ninety-nine infantrymen, plus forty bows and sheaves of arrows. Some of this equipment had been bought only recently, 105 sallets and ninety pairs of splints coming from a London ironmonger in 1522–3.[147] In his will Lovell directed that such of his household servants as were 'able to serve the king's grace in his wars' should each have 'a whole harness to serve his grace therewith'.[148] Bray was not far behind, with a mixed bag of arms and armour including nine halberds, fifty-three bows, twenty sheaves of arrows, sixty-four 'yeomen sallets', eighteen brigandines, five corslets, and six hagbushes or handguns.[149] Aged though he was, Bray was ready to go with his men, sleeping on his 'bedstead for the wars'.[150] Marney must have had quite an arsenal, too, for in his will he desired each archer among his servants to have a bow and a sheaf of arrows and just two years later his son left a set of almain rivets, German body-armour, to every servant, with a bow for the archers, and a bill for the billmen.[151]

Although Southwell generally recruited on a smaller scale than his colleagues, gathering thirteen men at Norwich for the 1492 campaign and raising twenty-five for the fleet in 1513, he geared up for war in 1512–13 by spending £13 14s 3d on forty bills, a hundred bows, and more than forty sheaves of arrows, and gave his carpenter 2s 1d to make 'a standing for arrows'. As the prospect of fighting grew closer in August and September 1513, he added, for a further £3 10s 5d, a brigandine, perhaps from a high-class Italian armour workshop as he bought it from the Florentine merchant Giovanni Cavalcanti, a mail collar and hauberk, some leg armour, and a handgun with powder horn, powder, and match. In the

---

[144] PRO, SP1/2, fo. 113r (*LP* I, i. 1176); *LP* III, ii. 2374, 2560; E101/56/25/7–10; Somerville, *Duchy of Lancaster*, 505, 534, 539, 561, 643; *The Military Survey of Gloucestershire, 1522*, ed. R. W. Hoyle, Gloucestershire Record Series 6 (Stroud, 1993), 22, 37.
[145] PRO, SP1/28, fo. 200v (*LP* III, ii. 3288).
[146] PRO, E154/2/17.   [147] *HMC Rutland*, iv. 261, 264; PRO, PROB2/199, m. 4.
[148] PRO, PROB11/23/27.   [149] PRO, E154/2/10, fo. 6.   [150] PRO, E154/2/10, fo. 3.
[151] 'Ancient Wills', ed. H. W. King, *TEAS* 4 (1869), 150, 157–8.

event he stayed with the queen while the king was in France and Flodden was fought, but he topped up his stores with 2s 2d worth of powder and match in February 1514.[152]

Poynings needed larger supplies, and, as ambassador in Brussels in 1513, found it easier to obtain them, buying up 200 sets of armour, 300 pikes, a hundred each of bills, bows, and sheaves of arrows, a tent, a pavilion, a hale or wooden-framed tent, and two wagons to carry them all on the summer's campaign.[153] Matters were not so simple in the Midlands that year, where Windsor's local bailiff grumbled that the 'cost that I was at to see that your soldiers well harnessed in Staffordshire and Derbyshire' was 'xx times what it please your mastership to reward me to my costs'.[154] Hussey may have been best equipped of all. Faced with rebellion in 1536, and fearing what his neighbours might do, he hid 300 sets of armour in a hay barn.[155]

The new men, then, wielded the sword as much as the pen in defence of Henry and of his England and in the promotion of the powers of his crown. They were important agents of royal judicial and social policy at the centre and in the counties, important agents of royal fiscal policy through a constellation of institutions and expedients, important managers of politics in parliament, in the council, at court, and on embassy, important impresarios of magnificence. Many of these functions they continued to perform after the king's death, preserving the strengths of Henry's monarchy into the reign of his son. At every turn they displayed vigour and adaptability, but their achievements were not unshadowed. When the imposition of Henry's will hurt his subjects, it was easy for those subjects to blame the king's executives, especially when those executives seemed so eager to impose the king's power and when they prospered from their service to the king. And the fact that to serve the king well, as the recruitment of troops shows with particular clarity, the new men had to increase their own power, could only increase suspicion of their motives and resentment at their rise.

[152] PRO, E36/285, fo. 47v; E101/417/3/95; *LP* I, i, 1661 (3); SP1/230, fos. 110v, 111r, 113r, 113v, 115r, 115v, 116r, 120v (*LP* I, ii. 2765).
[153] PRO, SP1/3, fo. 167 (*LP* I, ii. 1820).
[154] PRO, SP1/231, fos. 224–5 (*LP* Addenda, i. 113).
[155] PRO, SP1/109, fo. 73r (*LP* XI. 852).

POWER

7

Towns and stewardships

In serving Henry VII, his new men became powerful, and their increasing power equipped them better to serve the king. That power was in part a question of office-holding and other formal functions, but much more a matter of informal relationships. In a society governed as much through favour, clientage, lordship, kinship, and friendship as through institutions and procedures, the new men had to make contacts if their power were to work and to last. In that process, their engagement with towns would be vital. Urban self-government was vigorous. Most towns had elaborate structures of councils, wards, and guilds through which urban elites, sometimes in dialogue with wider sections of the population, did justice and regulated the economic and moral affairs of their community. Towns were centres of trade, wealth, and culture as well as of local rule. In the Wars of the Roses they had manoeuvred uneasily between rival noblemen and rival dynasties, trying to maintain their safety from attack, their economic health—a challenge at times of trading depression—and their powers of self-government. Henry VII's regime promised a greater stability and even enhanced autonomy from other local powers, but demanded that certain standards of order and compliance with royal policy be met and enforced obedience, as elsewhere, by aggressive fiscal policies. With their role in the king's council and court, their engagement in judicial and fiscal policy, and their developing local influence, the new men were often important intermediaries between king and urban elites in the relationships that developed on this basis.[1] In those towns where lords retained some measure of manorial jurisdiction, meanwhile, the new men might be lent influence by appointment as steward, as they were in many other communities. Estate stewardships were a particularly suitable way for the new men to develop their power in local society, for they combined judicial and administrative functions with military.

TOWNS AND PATRONS

Many towns actively sought out the new men's protection. Some appointed them to the office of recorder to provide legal advice, expert judgments in borough

[1] R. Horrox, 'Urban Patronage and Patrons in the Fifteenth Century', in R. A. Griffiths (ed.), *Patronage, the Crown and the Provinces in Later Medieval England* (Gloucester, 1986), 145–66; J. Lee, 'Urban Policy and Urban Political Culture: Henry VII and his Towns', *HR* 82 (2009), 493–510; M. R. Horowitz, '"Contrary to the Liberties of this City": Henry VII, English Towns and the Economics of Law and Order', *HR* 85 (2012), 32–56.

courts and skilled representation with central government.[2] Northampton chose Empson as recorder in 1490 and Coventry did the same not long afterwards, apparently on the king's advice.[3] Norwich approached Hobart for help as early as 1487, chose him for its recorder by 1496, and regularly sent him gifts. He represented the city at great councils, attended sessions assiduously, gave £26 13s 4d towards the rebuilding of the council chamber in the Guildhall when the roof fell in, and was on hand to offer counsel on such tricky matters as a contested treason accusation in 1512.[4] At Great Yarmouth, he provided 'good and discreet advice' when the townsfolk made a new set of ordinances in 1491 and he was useful to Colchester, too, where the townsfolk turned after his death to Marney, father-in-law of their recorder Thomas Bonham.[5]

Even without recorderships, the new men offered assistance and won reward. The bailiffs and burgesses of Huntingdon found Hussey 'a special good master and friend' to the town, who bore 'good mind and favour unto the furtherance of all manner rightful causes concerning the weal and profit of the same town', so they granted him a £1 6s 8d annuity in February 1509.[6] Chichester was right next to Ernley's home at Sidlesham and duly retained his advice with a 13s 4d fee.[7] Cambridge wooed Lucas and Cutt with fees, wine, and fish.[8] Sir Andrew Windsor, chosen steward of Windsor, secured a proviso to protect the borough's financial interests in an act of parliament of 1510.[9] When Bray won Bedford a permanent reduction in the fee-farm paid to the king, the townsmen gave him the patronage of one of the town's hospitals in perpetuity, a grant his nephew would exploit to expropriate its endowment.[10]

Poynings was an influential neighbour at Canterbury. It was one of the kingdom's ten greatest cities, the archbishop was prominent in its affairs, and it called on many Kentish gentlemen and courtiers for counsel or aid.[11] Yet Poynings won a place among its friends soon after Bosworth, and intensified his engagement after

[2] J. Lee, 'Urban Recorders and the Crown in Late Medieval England', in L. Clark (ed.), *Authority and Subversion*, The Fifteenth Century 3 (Woodbridge, 2003), 163–79.

[3] *The Coventry Leet Book*, ed. M. D. Harris, 4 vols, EETS 134–5, 138, 146 (London, 1907–13), ii. 537, 547; M. R. Horowitz, 'Richard Empson, Minister of Henry VII', *BIHR* 55 (1982), 40; PRO, KB9/396/49, 418/47.

[4] F. Blomefield, *An Essay towards a Topographical History of the County of Norfolk*, 11 vols (London, 1805–10), iii. 173, 178, 191–2, 218; *Records of the City of Norwich*, ed. W. Hudson, J. C. Tingey, 2 vols (Norwich, 1906–10), i. 307–10, 316–17, iv. 228; NRO, NCAR 1502–3, m. 10, 1503–4, mm. 8–9.

[5] H. Manship, *The History of Great Yarmouth*, ed. C. J. Palmer (Great Yarmouth, 1854), 357; ERO, D/Y2/3, pp. 6, 8, 9, 12; *The Red Paper Book of Colchester*, ed. W. G. Benham (Colchester, 1902), 25, 27.

[6] PRO, E327/598.

[7] Christopher Whittick, 'Ernley, Sir John', *ODNB*; West Sussex RO, Chichester City Records AE/1, fo. 3v.

[8] C. H. Cooper, *Annals of Cambridge*, 5 vols (Cambridge, 1842–1908), i. 256; Cambridgeshire Archives, PB/X/71A, m. 11.

[9] Bodl. MS Ashmole 1126, fo. 41 (*LP* I, i. 1528); S. T. Bindoff, *History of Parliament: The House of Commons 1509–1558*, 3 vols (London, 1982), i. 33.

[10] John Leland, *The Itinerary of John Leland in or about the Years 1535–1543*, ed. L. T. Smith, 5 vols (London, 1906–10), i. 101.

[11] *HMC Ninth Report* (London, 1883), App., 134–52.

his return from Ireland. He and his servants were regular visitors and recipients of gifts.[12] He sat with Guildford and other commissioners to investigate disorders prompted by the labour legislation of 1495, to regulate mayoral elections, and to look into the dispute between the city and Christ Church Priory over the moving of the fish market.[13] He escorted a relative of the pope through the city in 1498–9, gave advice on receiving the Flemish ambassadors in 1508, and liaised with the mayor about the regulation of the local grain trade.[14] But the jolliest occasion seems to have been in summer 1502, when he and Chief Justice Fyneux presided over the civic archery and wrestling competitions while dining on lamb, pigeons, capons, currants, dates, and prunes.[15]

Canterbury and Dover saw many of the king's councillors on their way to and from the continent and made gifts to them in passing. Brandon got wine at Canterbury in 1506–7, and Windsor the same at Dover when the Emperor Charles V landed in 1520.[16] Lovell was treated to a range of gifts at Dover—wine, lampreys, capons, chickens—and reciprocated with a donation of £6 13s 4d towards repair work on the harbour in 1510.[17] He was regularly given wine at Canterbury, too, usually at the Swan Inn, and sometimes with fish or strawberries.[18] York saw those around the king less often, but still called on the advice of Bray, Lovell, Mordaunt, and Cutt.[19] The corporation was particularly insistent in its requests for Bray's help in its dispute with St Mary's Abbey in 1500–2, and happy to do him favour 'for to have him good master unto this city'.[20]

In dealing with the greatest towns, the new men struck a balance between conciliating the urban leaders, enforcing the king's rights and promoting their own interests. At York and Lincoln, Lovell agreed, of his 'charitable and loving mind', to take only a fraction of the fee-farms he could have claimed in the name of Lord Roos.[21] Hussey was not so obliging. He sent his brother Robert to the Lincoln common council in 1511 to protest against their choice of Christopher Burton of Branston, the neighbouring village of which he was lord, as sheriff of the city. The council would not back down over Burton, but agreed that if Hussey paid £20 no householder of Branston should have to perform any civic office without his consent.[22]

---

[12] CCA, FA7, fos. 26v, 41r, 230r, FA2, fo. 307r, FA9, fos. 8r, 137v, FA10, fos. 41v, 42r, 395r.

[13] CCA, FA7, fos. 265r, 282r–283v, FA9, fos. 98r, 158v, FA2, fos. 333v–334r, 361r–362r, 379r, 393r.

[14] CCA, FA2, fos. 295r, FA9, fo. 158r, FA10, fo. 393v.

[15] CCA, FA2, fos. 364v–365r.

[16] CCA, FA9, fo. 8r; BL, MS Egerton 2092, fo. 220r.

[17] BL, MS Egerton 2092, fos. 64r, 71r, 97v, 2107, fos. 54v, 62r, 97v, 2108, fos. 2r, 4v.

[18] CCA, FA2, fos. 295r, 361r, 394r, 413v, FA7, fo. 137r, FA9, fos. 42v, 137v.

[19] *York Civic Records*, ed. A. Raine, 8 vols (Wakefield, 1939–53), ii. 53, 85, 137, 143, 157, 165, 193; J. Hughes, 'Sever [Senhouse], William', *ODNB*.

[20] *York Civic Records*, ed. A. Raine, 8 vols, YASRS 98, 103, 106, 108, 110, 112, 115, 119 (Wakefield, 1939–53), ii. 154, 166, 169–70, 178–9.

[21] *LP* Addenda, i. 628; *CCR 1500–9*, 952; *York Civic Records*, iii. 34–5, 42–4, 81–2, 94; *The Manuscripts of Lincoln, Bury St Edmunds, and Great Grimsby Corporations*, HMC 37 (London, 1895), 31; LA, L1/1/1/1, fo. 186r; PRO, C1/860/8.

[22] G. A. J. Hodgett, *Tudor Lincolnshire* (Lincoln, 1975), 123; *HMC Lincoln*, 24.

In smaller towns, stewardships drew the new men deep into urban life. As royal steward at Walsall, Lovell ratified a new set of borough ordinances, arbitrated a dispute between the town and a neighbouring landlord, was included with his late wife among the beneficiaries of a chantry established in Bloxwich chapel by three leading townsmen, and secured a licence for a guild to keep seven chaplains in the parish church.[23] At Wallingford, he was granted the advowson to the Hospital of St John the Baptist by the townsfolk in 1504 and nominated Dr Stephen Bereworth, already dean of the castle chapel and formerly Prince Arthur's doctor. By 1507, he and Bereworth had done such good work in securing a new charter for the town at the cost of only £40—admittedly with the help of Lovell's local associates, Henry Reynolds and William Young—that the town council ordered that each should be prayed for in the town's four churches every Sunday for the rest of his life and an annual mass said for his soul thereafter.[24]

At Grantham, Hussey was steward and his friend Edmund Bussy receiver by July 1504, when they presided over the town courts.[25] Hussey and his son led the feoffees entrusted in 1508 with a property bequeathed to help the town pay its taxes, one of the town's mercers left him £5 in 1506 'to be good master to my wife and to my children in their rights as my special trust lies in him', and in 1534 the town sergeant brought him an ox as a gift from the aldermen.[26] In 1505, a Grantham man, Ralph Harbottle, stood surety for Hussey to the king, and in the 1530s it was a Grantham alderman, James Carter, who collected his rents in the town.[27] When a Grantham merchant, who had been in the company of the exiled Richard de la Pole, contacted the English embassy in Brussels in the hope of a pardon, Hussey was the councillor who knew him.[28] Similar pictures could no doubt be drawn for the many other towns where the new men held stewardships: Hussey at Stamford, where he presided over the swearing-in of the alderman, Belknap at Warwick, Bray at Kingston-upon-Thames, Bray, then Empson, then Belknap at Banbury, Dudley at Alford, Devizes, and Marlborough, Empson at Higham Ferrers, Mordaunt at Marlow and Newport Pagnell, Windsor at Amersham and Buckingham, and so on.[29]

Another route to influence in towns was through religious confraternities. The grandest drew together noblemen and gentry with high-ranking local clergy and

---

[23] *HMC Third Report* (London, 1872), App., 290; Willmore, *Walsall*, 180; *LP* II, i. 201, III, i. 1033.

[24] Berkshire RO, W/AC/1/1/1, fos. 1r–1v, 3v, 4r–4v, W/FAb 4; HL, MS El. 1518, fo. 40v; A. B. Emden, *A Biographical Register of the University of Oxford to AD 1500*, 3 vols (Oxford, 1957–9), i. 125.

[25] PRO, SC2/185/39, m. 6r.

[26] LA, FL Deeds 1431; *Lincoln Wills*, ed. C. W. Foster, 3 vols, Lincoln RS 5, 10, 24 (Lincoln, 1914–30), i. 27; PRO, E36/95, fo. 52v.

[27] *CCR 1500–9*, 444; PRO, E36/95, fo. 17r; *LP* XII, i. 199, XIII, i. 646 (10).

[28] *LP* II, ii. 3048, 3060, III, ii. 2356 (25).

[29] *William Browne's Town: Stamford Hall Book 1465–1492*, ed. A. Rogers (Stamford, 2005), 149; Bindoff, *Commons*, i. 138; PRO, KB9/434/15; SC6/Henry VIII/1345, m. 3v; Kingston Museum and Heritage Service, Kingston-upon-Thames Borough records, KF1/1/7; LA, Bishop's Register 22, fo. 86r, 24, fo. 327r; Bodl. MS dd Bertie c24/1; *CPR 1494–1509*, 412, 554, 589; R. Somerville, *A History of the Duchy of Lancaster, I, 1265–1603* (London, 1953), 587; Library of Birmingham, MS 3279/347140; *The Certificate of Musters for Buckinghamshire in 1522*, ed. A. C. Chibnall, Buckinghamshire RS 17 (London, 1973), 29, 230.

leading townsfolk, who might use them as agencies of local government and social control, while less pretentious village and small-town guilds were led by yeomen and burgesses.[30] Either way, guilds offered the new men contact with the leaders of local society, an opportunity Hussey clearly took. In 1507 he served as alderman of the Corpus Christi guild at Boston, a body which incorporated not only many Boston merchants and Lincolnshire gentry, but also the local peers Viscount Welles and Lord Willoughby d'Eresby, the king's mother, and the heads of many of the local religious houses that Hussey served as steward.[31] In 1517 he was alderman of the town's other leading confraternity, the St Mary's Guild, giving him further links to the life of the town: the guild kept thirteen poor beadsmen, ran a grammar school, and provided Noah's Ark for the annual mystery plays.[32] In contrast, though he was involved as a principal parishioner with the perpetual chantry in the parish church at Sleaford, he took no part in the town's Trinity Guild. There the dominant figure was Robert Carr, the townsman whose pointed evidence of his wavering in 1536 would help bring Hussey to the block.[33]

Others played their parts elsewhere. Belknap was a member of the high-status guild of the Holy Cross at Stratford and of the guild at Knowle in Warwickshire, where Empson and Poynings were also brethren.[34] Southwell, Englefield, and Cutt were members of the popular London Fraternity of St Nicholas.[35] There were guilds in the Norfolk parish churches of Beachamwell, East Harling, and Terrington where Lovell was lord, but it is not clear whether he was involved.[36] Perhaps other members of his family were, as Hussey's brother Robert was at Boston and Brandon's brother Robert was as alderman of the guild of St Katherine at Newton in Cambridgeshire.[37] Certainly some of Lovell's retainers in St Albans and Hitchin were members of the Holy and Undivided Trinity and Blessed Virgin Mary Guild of Luton, a privilege they shared with senior St Albans monks, bishops, courtiers, councillors such as Sheffield and Sutton and even members of the royal family.[38]

Three further ways in which the new men brokered the relationship between towns and the wider polity were through parliamentary representation, the governance of

[30] V. Bainbridge, *Gilds in the Medieval Countryside: Social and Religious Change in Cambridgeshire c.1350–1558* (Woodbridge, 1996), 135–43; D. J. F. Crouch, *Piety, Fraternity and Power: Religious Guilds in Late Medieval Yorkshire 1389–1547* (Woodbridge, 2000), 63, 89–90, 182–4, 200–1, 203–6, 2210–14; K. Farnhill, *Guilds and the Parish Community in Late Medieval East Anglia c.1470–1550* (Woodbridge, 2001), 51–8, 92–8.

[31] BL, Addl. MS 4795, fos. 50r–61r.

[32] P. Thompson, *The History and Antiquities of Boston* (Sleaford, 1997), 139; BL, Egerton MS 2886, fos. 5v, 7r, 8v, 15v–19v, 25v, 26v.

[33] *Chapter Acts of the Cathedral Church of St Mary of Lincoln, AD 1520–1536*, ed. R. E. G. Cole, Lincoln RS 12 (Lincoln, 1915), 29; BL, Addl. MS 28533, fos. 9r–16v.

[34] *The Register of the Gild of the Holy Cross, the Blessed Mary and St John the Baptist, of Stratford-upon-Avon*, ed. J. H. Bloom (London, 1907), 212; *The Register of the Guild of Knowle in the County of Warwick*, ed. W. B. Blickley (Walsall, 1894), 91, 150, 172, 186, 214.

[35] *The Bede Roll of the Fraternity of St Nicholas*, ed. N. W. James and V. A. James, 2 vols, London RS 39 (London, 2004), 481, 549, 554–5.

[36] Farnhill, *Guilds*, 176, 182–3, 204–5.

[37] BL, Addl. MS 4795, fos. 56v, 64r; PRO, PROB11/21/28.

[38] *The Register of the Fraternity or Guild of the Holy and Undivided Trinity and Blessed Virgin Mary in the Parish Church of Luton, in the county of Bedford, from AD MCCCCLXXV to MVCXLVI*, ed. H. Gough (London, 1906), 19, 38–9, 45, 48, 52, 72, 79, 95, 113, 118, 147.

the duchy of Lancaster, and arrangements for royal visits. Electoral influence is hard to track, but at Stamford and Grantham Hussey surely played a part in his brother's and his eldest son's choice as burgesses in 1512 and 1529 and Windsor must have assisted his son's election at Chipping Wycombe in 1529.[39] Poynings's role in elections in the Cinque Ports presumably helped his nephew Sir John Scott sit for New Romney in 1512.[40] The duchy of Lancaster exercised some electoral sway, but its influence on the duchy towns was much wider. Under Marney's chancellorship the duchy council heard disputes between the residents of Newcastle-under-Lyme and Uttoxeter, and those of Godmanchester and the abbot of Ramsey. It dealt with a reluctant mayor of Higham Ferrers and a recalcitrant bailiff of Leicester, and it intervened in election disputes in Monmouth.[41] As for visits, Nottingham sent to Lovell in 1503 to ask his 'mind how we should meet the king', and Dover in 1498 and Canterbury in 1520 asked Poynings the same question.[42]

The interests of crown, new men, and urban oligarchs met most clearly in the concern to maintain order by restricting the political involvement of the lesser townsfolk and punishing those who questioned the wisdom of the councillors' rule. At Nottingham in 1512, Lovell reacted to popular agitation for a widening of the franchise by reminding the recorder of 'the inconveniences that hath ensued upon the calling of the commons together in the city of London, and in other cities and boroughs', backing up the line taken by the recorder, Thomas Babington, that such participation was 'contrary to all good and politic order and rule'.[43] At Walsall, the only new borough ordinance he approved as steward concerned the punishment of anyone who 'misordaineth himself in words or deeds' against the town's rulers.[44] At Wallingford, it was enacted soon after Lovell helped the town get its new charter that 'any man that misbehaveth himself against master mayor or to any of the aldermen' be fined 6s 8d, while disobedience to any other officer would cost 3s 4d.[45] He was quite prepared to see these principles put into practice. At Dover in 1506, he advised the mayor and jurats to take order that 'one Richard Yong, Scottishman born, for divers offence and slandering with his tongue, that he shall have his ear nailed to a cart wheel and so be banned the town for ever'.[46] At London in 1517, he joined Cutt and others in trying the Evil May Day rioters.[47] Thus the new men played their part in the consolidation of oligarchy which marked English urban government in Henry's reign and beyond.[48] Like the king they

[39] Bindoff, *Commons*, i. 134, ii. 427, iii. 638.
[40] Bindoff, *Commons*, i. 253–4, iii. 282–3.
[41] Bindoff, *Commons*, i. 121, 130, 153–4, 187–8; PRO, DL5/5, fos 40r, 45v, 93r, 103r, 126r–127r.
[42] *Records of the Borough of Nottingham*, ed. W. H. Stevenson, 9 vols (Nottingham, 1882–1936), iii. 317; BL, Egerton MS 2107, fo. 59r; CCA, FA10, fo. 394r.
[43] *Records of the Borough of Nottingham*, iii. 341–2.
[44] Walsall Local History Centre, MS 277/238, m. 4d.
[45] Berkshire RO, W/AC/1/1/1, fo. 1v.
[46] BL, Egerton MS 2094, fo. 1r.   [47] PRO, KB9/478/8.
[48] S. H. Rigby and E. Ewan, 'Government, Power and Authority 1300–1540', in D. M. Palliser (ed.), *The Cambridge Urban History of Britain*. Vol. i: *600–1540* (Cambridge, 2000), 309–12; Lee, 'Urban Policy', 499–509.

expected certain standards to be upheld and towns were keen not to be embarrassed in front of them. Southampton fined an Italian trader 'that made two women drunk when Master Bray was in town'.[49]

POYNINGS AND THE CINQUE PORTS

A unique role was played by Poynings among the Cinque Ports of Kent and Sussex. The ports were not especially large, Dover and Rye on the edge of the top forty English towns by size, Faversham, Folkestone, Hastings, Hythe, Lydd, and Sandwich outside the top hundred, Fordwich, New Romney, and Winchelsea tiny. Yet they were important to the crown as the gateway to Calais, a source of information about movements in the Channel, and the home of ships for transport, warfare, or privateering. Over time, this utility had been parlayed by the ports into a series of political and legal privileges, and the warden was the key intermediary between crown and ports.[50] Poynings was an ideal candidate, as he knew the ports well. His father-in-law Sir John Scott was lieutenant of Dover Castle and deputy warden in the 1460s and remained involved with the ports to his death in 1485.[51] Poynings himself became a freeman of New Romney on 29 January 1482 and visited Lydd in 1483, while his wife and brother-in-law were entertained at Rye in 1481.[52] On his return from exile, he became a regular visitor, correspondent, and recipient of gifts of wine at Rye, Dover, and New Romney.[53] He did not have sufficient social status to serve as warden in the wake of such luminaries as the earls of Warwick and Arundel, so in April 1493 Henry appointed his younger son Prince Henry as warden and Poynings as his lieutenant.[54] From 1505, Poynings was the king's rather than the prince's deputy, and from 1509 warden in his own right, 'the right honourable and our singular good lord the lord Ponynges protector and defender of the v ports', as the mayor and jurats of Fordwich called him.[55] George, Lord Bergavenny, seems to have stood in while Poynings was away on embassy and at Tournai in 1513–16, but otherwise he kept the post till he died.[56]

Poynings's duties ranged from the routine to the highly sensitive. Within the ports he substituted both for the sheriff and for the lord admiral, passing on orders

[49] Southampton Archives Office, SC5/3/1, fo. 7r.

[50] A. Dyer, 'Appendix: Ranking Lists of English Medieval Towns', in Palliser (ed.), *Cambridge Urban History*, 762–3; P. Clark and J. Hoskins, *Population Estimates of English Small Towns 1550–1851*, 2nd edn (Leicester, 1993), 77–81, 151–3; K. M. E. Murray, *The Constitutional History of the Cinque Ports* (Manchester, 1935).

[51] J. C. Wedgwood, *History of Parliament: Biographies of the Members of the Commons House, 1439–1509* (London, 1936), 750–2; ESRO, Rye 60/3, fos. 17v, 22v, 23r, 38r, 39r; KHLC, NR/FAc 3, fos. 74r, 93r, 94v, 95r, 97v; *Records of Lydd*, ed. A. Finn (Ashford, 1911), 201–63, 302, 304, 310, 314.

[52] KHLC, NR/FAc 3, fo. 93v; *Records of Lydd*, 311; ESRO, Rye 60/3, fo. 14v.

[53] ESRO, Rye 60/3, fos. 61, 68v, 74v; BL, MS Egerton 2107, fos. 5v, 15v, 20r; KHLC, NR/FAc 3, fo. 99r–99v.

[54] *CPR 1485–94*, 423; KHLC, Sa/ZB1/23; CCA, U4/12/20.

[55] *CPR 1494–1509*, 427; CCA, U4/12/21.

[56] BL, MS Egerton 2092, fos. 70v, 71r, 106r; CCA, U4/8/6; KHLC, NR/FAc 3, fos. 121v, 126r–126v; NR/CPl 36; *White and Black Books*, 155, 157.

for the appearance of portsmen in royal courts, arrest warrants, and royal procla-mations.[57] When necessary, he imprisoned local troublemakers on his own initia-tive, while his court at Dover provided a forum for appeals from the courts of individual towns.[58] He also convened admiralty courts to deal with issues of wreck and piracy.[59] He mustered troops from the ports, levied taxation on them, and organized the ship service due when the king needed to cross the sea.[60] He imple-mented royal policy on such matters as the supply of food to Calais and the ban-ning of plays at dangerous times.[61]

He was on the front line at moments of international tension, sending on urgent instructions about Perkin Warbeck, the fugitive earl of Suffolk, dangerous Scottish ships, and Frenchmen who might burn the king's bark.[62] He warned the ports to receive foreign ambassadors well, a courtesy for which the bishop of Paris, perhaps after a rough crossing, was grateful in 1518.[63] Sometimes he had to think particularly fast. In May 1517, some Dieppe sailors were detained at Winchelsea, presumably until a dispute was resolved. When another Dieppe ship appeared in the harbour, they warned it not to enter. The second vessel headed back to Dieppe, and a crisis was in the making: as Poynings calculated, 'sinister bruits' of the arrest of French mer-chants in England might cause the arrest of English merchants in France. He took the situation in hand, writing to the governor of Dieppe and telling the mayor of Winchelsea to let some other Dieppe ships sail. Then he apologized to the king for being 'so bold' as to take all these steps without consulting him.[64]

The ports needed the warden as much as the king did. Their privileges were con-stantly in question, as outsiders challenged their legal immunities and the king pressed them for taxation. Collectively, they lobbied Poynings about court sum-monses under the privy seal, seizures of goods by the Merchant Adventurers, exemp-tion from parliamentary subsidies, the terms of their ship service, their rights over the Yarmouth herring fair, and, indeed, 'divers matters and causes touching and concern-ing the universal weal and profit of the whole corporation'.[65] In 1507–9, Poynings led their opposition to Empson's attempts to assert the duchy of Lancaster's rights over Pevensey.[66] He also served as an honest broker to settle disputes among them.[67]

[57] Murray, *Cinque Ports*, 70–138; PRO, C1/291/76; C1/392/62; DL5/4, fo. 120r; *LP* I, i. 1313; ESRO, Rye 45/17.
[58] *LP* Addenda, i. 46; KHLC, NR/CPl 1/1–4.
[59] *LP* II, i. 1379, ii. 3526, 3541, 3632, 3636, 3642, 3650, III, i. 315, 330, 355, 593, 618, 638, 656, 1372.
[60] *LP* I, i. 1360, ii. 1948(70), 2862(7).
[61] KHLC, NR/CPw2; W. A. S. Robertson, 'The Passion Play and Interludes at New Romney', *AC* 13 (1879), 218.
[62] KHLC, NR/Fac3, fos. 109r, 111r, 112v; ESRO, Rye 60/4, fo. 52v; *HMC Fifth Report* (London, 1876), 553; BL, MS Egerton 2092, fo. 236r.
[63] *LP* II, ii 4401; BL Egerton MS 2092, fo. 145v.
[64] PRO, SP1/15, fo. 121 (*LP* II, ii. 3244).
[65] *A Calendar of the White and Black Books of the Cinque Ports*, ed. F. Hull, Kent Records 19 (London, 1967), 119–20, 121, 137, 153, 161, 173–4, 178, 180–2.
[66] *Reports of Cases by John Caryll*, ed. J. H. Baker, 2 vols, SS 115–16 (London, 1999–2000), ii. 549–51.
[67] *White and Black Books*, 123, 162–3, 165–6, 168; ESRO, Rye 60/4, fo. 2v.

For individual ports, too, it became a reflex reaction to any problem to seek out Poynings for advice. Rye tackled him as soon as he was appointed about a dispute with Hastings, sending the mayor to Westenhanger and Dover to deal with him face to face.[68] Fordwich, too, sent its mayor to Westenhanger from time to time, usually about the town's lawsuits.[69] Security concerns prompted Rye to ask him about a hermit taken with writings in 1499, a friar taken with letters in 1502, and a felon who took sanctuary in the town friary in 1506.[70] Sandwich, worried about a prisoner they had taken, tracked Poynings down in Canterbury in 1516–17.[71] Romney regularly sent jurats and messengers to Westenhanger, Dover, London, or the Pympes' house at Nettlestead, to discuss the town's liberties or the preparation of armed men to serve the king.[72] Sandwich made contact up to ten times a year, sending Poynings 'certain articles of certain words spoken by one mariner of Newcastle' and lobbying him hard to protect their share of the ports' tax rebate.[73] Dover sent messengers, sometimes the mayor himself, 'to have his counsel in certain matter concerning our liberties', or 'for answer of the complaint of men of Calais in the parliament for the passage here', or 'for communication of the return for the writ of the king's service'.[74] Even individual townsmen, like Thomas Cokkes, who wanted to be customs collector at Dover and Sandwich, badgered Poynings for intercession with the powers that be.[75] He also visited the ports in person, to help Romney with their salt marsh and Dover with their harbour repairs and their disputed mayoral election.[76]

The ports could be demanding. In 1496 they resolved to send men to Poynings 'immediately after his coming home out of Ireland', twice they sent to him at Tournai, in 1516 they allowed him only four days to recover from his embassy in Flanders before tackling him and in 1518–19 Fordwich's mayor set out to catch him 'when he came from beyond the sea'.[77] But they were generous. On his appointment in 1493 they bought him collectively a tun of wine worth £4 10s 7d, in 1496–7 they gave him another, and when he became warden in 1509 they welcomed him with £66 13s 4d in cash.[78] In 1500–1, when he was helping them negotiate with the king over their charter, they dined him at London on beef, mutton, lamb, pork, goose, capon, and conger eel, washed down with white wine and

[68] ESRO, Rye 60/3, fos. 110v–112r.
[69] CCA, U4/8/4a, 11–12, U4/11/1, U4/12/21.
[70] ESRO, Rye 60/4, fos. 82r, 120r.
[71] ESRO, Rye 60/4, fo. 182v; KHLC, Sa/Fat 22, m. 6.
[72] KHLC, NR/Fac3, fos. 106v, 108r, 110r–110v, 114r, 117r, 118r, 120r, 127v, 128r, 129v, 132v, 133r.
[73] KHLC, Sa/FAt 12, m. 5, 14, mm. 1–2, 17A, m. 7, 19, m. 4, 20, mm. 7–8, 22, mm. 6, 23, 24 mm. 5–6, 9, 25, mm. 3, 5.
[74] BL, Egerton MS 2107, fos. 62r, 72v, 84r, 97v, 105r, 109v, 2092, fos. 63r, 65r, 97v, 142r, 146v, 169r, 170r, 171r, 174r, 196r–196v, 202r, 216r, 218r, 220r, 221v, 223r, 266r, 267r, 269v.
[75] PRO, C1/529/62.
[76] KHLC, NR/Fac3, fo. 128r–128v; BL, Egerton MS 2108, fo. 25r; Murray, *Cinque Ports*, 92–93.
[77] *White and Black Books*, 119–20, 161, 163, 189; CCA, U4/8/11.
[78] *White and Black Books*, 115, 145; BL, Egerton MS 2107, fo. 54r; KHLC, NR/Fac 3, fo. 108r.

claret.[79] When he visited any port he was treated to dinner or a drink.[80] Romney and Dover entertained him in London at parliament time in 1497, 1504, and 1512, and Dover gave him a hogshead of wine, over 50 gallons, when lobbying for tax exemption in 1516–17.[81] When asking advice, each port sent him signature gifts. From Fordwich, sited inland but on a river, it was trout, up to four a year, or occasionally capons.[82] New Romney, between the marshes and the sea, chose between wildfowl and fish.[83] Sandwich, bigger and richer, ranged from oranges, raisins, and quarter- or half-porpoises to a whole pipe of wine, but its real speciality was whelks, sometimes hundreds or even a thousand of them at a time.[84] Rye, larger still and with a prosperous fishing fleet, showered him with fish.[85] Dover rivalled Rye with a tempting and cosmopolitan array: halibut, bass, mullet, conger, trout, porpoise, cranes, capons, wine, sugar, oranges, and pomegranates.[86] In return Poynings sent venison to Dover and Rye, to be ceremoniously dined on by the mayor, jurats, and leading townsmen, and cash contributions to Dover's wall and harbour repairs.[87]

Poynings's intense relationship with the ports drew in his family, friends, and servants. John Copledike, long-serving deputy at Dover Castle, often took his place in holding admiralty courts, preparing ships or men for royal service or attending borough elections, but his senior servant Edward Thwaites also stood in at times.[88] John Norton, a former mayor of Faversham who would be supervisor of Poynings's will, levied money and men from the ports.[89] Sir William Scott, his brother-in-law, was active especially when Poynings was busy in Ireland or the Netherlands.[90] Sir Anthony Browne, his step-father's brother, accompanied him to Dover once and George Browne his servant went there twice on his behalf.[91] Lord Clinton, his son-in-law, checked on the watch kept over the anchorage in the Downs and led royal commissioners to Dover.[92] Individual servants were continually rewarded for carrying letters.

[79] *White and Black Books*, 126–8.

[80] BL, Egerton MS 2107, fos. 47r, 54r, 83v, 84r, 91v, 96v, 104r, 2092, fos. 58v, 172v; 'Expenses of the Corporation of Faversham, temp. Hen. VIII', ed. F. F. Giraud, *AC* 10 (1876), 234–5; KHLC, NR/Fac3, fos 106v, 111r; Sa/FAt 11, m. 5, 12, m. 5, 22 m. 11; ESRO, Rye 60/4, fos. 5v, 53v, 67r–67v, 69r, 70r–70v, 86r.

[81] KHLC, NR/Fac3, fos. 110v, 121v; BL, Egerton MS 2107, fo. 92r, 2092, fo. 169v.

[82] CCA, U4/8/4a, 10–12, U4/11/1, U4/12/21.

[83] KHLC, NR/Fac3, fos. 106v, 108r, 110v, 117r, 120r, 124r, 126v, 127v, 129v, 131r, 133v.

[84] KHLC, Sa/FAt 12, m. 4–5, 14, m. 2, 22 m. 6, 24, mm. 5–6.

[85] G. Mayhew, *Tudor Rye* (Falmer, 1987), 18–19; ESRO, Rye 60/3, fo. 111r, Rye 60/4, fos. 7r–11r, 30v–33r, 41r–43v, 51r–52r, 56r, 65r, 68r, 82r, 83r–83v, 85r, 103v, 104r, 116r, 118v, 119r, 120v, 121r, 122r, 133v, 135r, 141r, 151r, 152v, 154r, 156r, 167r, 168r, 169v, 171r, 181r–181v, 182v, 183r, 185v, 198r, 201v, 213r–213v, 217r, 229v.

[86] BL, MS Egerton 2107, fos. 50v, 58r, 62r, 97v, 114v, 2092, fos. 55v, 57r, 63r, 63v, 64v, 145v, 146v, 169r, 170r–170v, 172r, 173v, 196v, 198r, 216v, 217v, 221v, 261v, 262v, 264v, 265v, 266v, 267v.

[87] BL, MS Egerton 2107, fos. 25r, 37v, 41r, 102v; ESRO, Rye 60/4, fos. 11r, 82r, 122v, 211v, 230r.

[88] KHLC, NR/CPw 3; NR/FAc 3, fos. 91r, 117r, 121r, 123r, 128r, 132v; Sa/Fat 22 m. 9, 25 m. 4; *LP* I, i. 1313, ii. 2862(7); Sa/Fat 20, m. 7, 22 mm. 6, 9, 11, 25 m. 4; BL, MS Egerton 2092, fos. 107r, 144r, 146v, 171r, 173r, 197v, 221v; ESRO, Rye 60/4, fo. 183v.

[89] KHLC, Fa/Z33, fos. 5v, 13r, 19v, 282r; Sa/Fat 20, m. 7; *LP* I, ii. 2862(7).

[90] KHLC, NR/Fac 3, fos. 107r, 109r, 111r, 116r, 120v, 122r, 126r; ESRO, Rye 60/3, fos. 55v, 61r, 100v, 109v, 60/4, fos. 5v, 7r, 16r, 20v, 30r, 33r, 40v; BL, MS Egerton 2107, fo. 50v.

[91] BL, MS Egerton 2107, fo. 84r, 2092, fos. 171r, 173v.

[92] KHLC, NR/Fac 3, fo. 123r; Sa/Fat 20, m. 7; BL, Egerton MS 2092, fos. 39v, 56v, 68r, 89r, 170v.

Poynings could not aspire to an exclusive mastery of the ports. Sometimes he visited them with Archbishop Warham, Chief Justice Fyneux, Lord Bergavenny, or Sir Richard Guildford, great men of the county, whom the ports naturally court-ed.[93] At Rye, next door to his drained estate at East Guldeford and the River Rother where he was involved with the king's ships, Guildford was particularly important. His sailors visited the mayor in 1487 'for to have mariners'; the mayor called on him in 1491 'to be our good friend unto us for the matter of Tenterden'; the town paid for a local man held prisoner at Dieppe to go to London in spring 1492 to tell him 'such tidings as he heard in France' and despatched fish to his house at Halden when the king came to visit.[94] No wonder Guildford's son Sir Edward was a natural successor to Poynings as warden in 1521.[95] But even in their choice of other patrons, the ports took Poynings's advice. In 1512, Dover sent halibuts to Poynings and Lovell together at London and when Rye gave Lovell fish in 1497, it was explicitly 'by Mr Ponynges desire'.[96]

LONDON

London was by far the largest, richest, and most significant of England's cities, controlling much of the country's external trade as well as serving, with its suburb at Westminster, as the political and administrative capital of the kingdom. No single royal councillor could take London into tutelage. Yet three of the new men played central roles in the relations between the king, the civic government of mayor, aldermen, and common council, the livery companies that represented the economic and political interests of the freemen, the Merchant Adventurers who dominated the cloth export trade, and leading individual Londoners. Bray came first, organizing loans to the king from the first days of the reign and regularly joining council delegations to discuss matters, usually financial, with the mayor and his brethren or the Merchant Adventurers.[97] He was close to the Shaw family of goldsmiths. Edmund, mayor in 1482–3, named Bray, his 'right especial and tender loving friend', an executor in 1488, and Edmund's nephew John, mayor in

---

[93] 'Corporation of Faversham', 234–5; KHLC, Fa/Z33, fos. 16v, 18r, 21v; NR/Fac 3, fos. 99r–102v, 107r–109r, 111r–111v, 120v, 127v; Sa/Fat 9, m. 8, 12, m. 5, 17A, m. 6, 20, mm. 7–8, 19, m. 5, 21, m. 3, 22, mm. 6, 8–9; ESRO, Rye 60/4, fos. 7v, 10r, 30v, 42v; BL, Egerton MS 2107, fos. 5v, 14r, 19r–20r, 36v, 37r, 47r, 50v, 54v, 59r, 61v, 69r, 91v, 96v, 104v, 109v, 2108, fo. 25r, 2092, fos. 57r, 71v, 87v, 106v, 169r, 198r.

[94] ESRO, Rye 60/3, fos. 55v, 61r, 80r, 82v, 88r–88v, 89v, 92r, 93r, 99v, 100v–101v, 108r, 109v–110v, 113r, 60/4, fos. 5r, 7r–7v, 10r-v, 16v, 18r, 28v, 40v, 43v, 51r, 53v, 54r, 156r, and *passim*.

[95] Bindoff, *Commons*, ii. 262–3.

[96] BL, MS Egerton 2092, fo. 63r; ESRO, Rye 60/3, fo. 42r–42v, 60v, 80r, 82v, 88r–88v, 89v.

[97] M. M. Condon, 'From Caitiff and Villain to *Pater Patriae*: Reynold Bray and the Profits of Office', in M. A. Hicks (ed.), *Profit, Piety and the Professions in later Medieval England* (Gloucester, 1990), 140–1; *The Great Chronicle of London*, ed. A. H. Thomas, I. D. Thornley (London, 1938), 240, 263, 274–5, 310; A. F. Sutton, *The Mercery of London: Trade, Goods and People, 1130–1578* (Aldershot, 2005), 325–6.

1501–2, served Bray as feoffee and executor.[98] He was also courted by the tailors' company, a rising force in both overseas trade and civic politics.[99]

Dudley's relations with the Londoners were, predictably, more controversial. He began well, serving as undersheriff, hearing cases in the city courts, from 1496 to 1502, 'with favour of the citizens', a favour confirmed by the grant of an annual robe and £1 fee after he demitted office.[100] The favour soon evaporated as he served as speaker of the commons in the parliament of 1504, which rejected legislation proposed by London and passed two acts prejudicial to the city's privileges.[101] Thereafter he took over as the king's leading negotiator with London, extracting £3,333 6s 8d for confirmation of the city charter and considerable sums from individual townsmen.[102] On the streets it was said that his attempt to dictate the choice of sheriff in October 1506 was 'an utter derogation unto the liberties of the city' and that 'whosoever had the sword borne before him, Dudley was mayor, and what his pleasure was, was done'.[103] In the court of aldermen the language was more diplomatic, but equally fearful. On 14 December 1507 it was resolved to increase Dudley's annual fee to £3 6s 8d and to 'feel Mr Dudley's mind whether it will stand with the king's pleasure' for them to petition for a general pardon.[104]

Meanwhile, Dudley leant hard on the Merchant Adventurers in the effort to force up customs rates. His style in matters of trade was interventionist, confiscating shipments of pepper, organizing the king's deals in the lucrative alum trade, holding foreign merchants under arrest in his house, and taking huge obligations for the payment of customs.[105] Such confiscations may account for the seventy-nine broad white cloths, twenty-six ells of canvas, twenty-one bags of pepper, and forty-six bags of alum found in the great gallery of his London house.[106] Lawsuits and chronicles tell shocking tales of his harassment of individuals such as the haberdasher Thomas Sunnyff, imprisoned for months to force him to pay £500 for a pardon for an offence he did not commit, or the ex-mayor Thomas Knesworth, locked up until he paid the same sum for a pardon for trading offences.[107] Dudley admitted in his petition that he had dealt harshly with several Londoners, and his accounts are full of fines from individual citizens, livery companies,

---

[98] P. Tucker, 'Shaw, Sir Edmund', *ODNB*; Condon, 'Profits of Office', 151; C. M. Barron, *London in the Later Middle Ages: Government and People 1200–1500* (Oxford, 2004), 346, 348.

[99] *The Merchant Taylors' Company of London: Court Minutes 1486–1493*, ed. M. Davies (Stamford, 2000), 157; M. Davies and A. Saunders, *The History of the Merchant Taylors' Company* (Leeds, 2004), 64–6, 84–7.

[100] *Great Chronicle*, 348; LMA, Rep. 1, fo. 118r.

[101] H. Miller, 'London and Parliament in the Reign of Henry VIII', *BIHR* 35 (1962), 132–4.

[102] Horowitz, 'English Towns', 44–50.

[103] *Great Chronicle*, 333, 348.

[104] LMA, Rep. 2, fo. 36r–36v.

[105] Sutton, *Mercery of London*, 343; PRO, C1/473/26, 546/24–6, 1022/57; Penn, *Winter King*, 204, 251–2.

[106] PRO, E154/2/17.

[107] M. R. Horowitz, '"Agree with the King": Henry VII, Edmund Dudley and the Strange Case of Thomas Sunnyff', *HR* 79 (2005), 325–66.

the Merchant Adventurers, London churchwardens, London religious houses, and foreign merchants trading at London.[108] Meanwhile, he worked his associates, notably the grocer and brothel-keeper John Camby, into positions of power— weigher of wools in the London customs, keeper of the Poultry Counter prison— whether the London elite liked it or not.[109]

Lovell's metropolitan relationships were altogether smoother. He spoke to the city for the king throughout the reign, but came into his own after Bray's death. By 1504–5 the mayor was spending £6 13s 4d on 'a pleasure given to Mr Lovell' and further gifts of fish and wine followed, while deputations lobbied him about the city's liberties in 1508 and 1511.[110] In 1510, it was to him and Bishop Fox that the Merchant Adventurers turned, armed with spiced wine and wafers, in the hope that customs rates might be reduced. The advice they got sounds like Lovell. It was pragmatic, sympathetic, but firm: customs were to be paid at the established rate, 'all the council was thus minded', and so 'to labour to the contrary it was but folly'.[111] In other matters Lovell was generous. Twice he offered loans of £100 or even £200 towards the establishment of a civic store of wheat.[112] More lavish still was the gift of plate he made in May 1523: a full silver dining set, two chargers, twelve plates, twelve dishes, and twelve saucers, to the value of £184, marked with his arms, to pass from mayor to mayor in perpetuity.[113] He was also an open-handed patron of the grocers' company, of which he was a brother, buying and rebuilding the Weighhouse in Cornhill at a cost of £300 and endowing the company with properties worth £15 10s a year.[114]

Lovell's affection was reciprocated. The aldermen sent the mayor and recorder to his house at Holywell to thank him in person for the plate and returned the mortmain fine he paid on the land he gave the grocers, since 'he of long continuance hath been a special benefactor to this city'.[115] When he asked for his servants and friends to be made freemen, granted city offices or leases, or remitted fines, the favours were readily accorded.[116] Lovell's associates among the London elite were often wardens or masters of the grocers' company: Ralph Aleyn, city auditor and future alderman, who brought in the money for his mortmain fine and attended his funeral; John Billesdon, who handled his donation to the company and its

---

[108] 'The Petition of Edmund Dudley', ed. C. J. Harrison, *EHR* 87 (1972), 87, 89–91, 96–9; HL, MS HA 1518, *passim*.

[109] Horowitz, 'Sunnyff', 346–7, 357.

[110] *Great Chronicle*, 263, 274; LMA, Rep. 2, fos. 48v, 72r, 112r; Miller, 'London and Parliament', 137.

[111] Sutton, *Mercery of London*, 344–5; *Acts of Court of the Mercers' Company 1453–1527*, ed. L. Lyell and F. D. Watney (Cambridge, 1936), 349–50, 353–4.

[112] LMA, Rep. 5, fos. 26r, 263v, 266r.

[113] LMA, Rep. 4, fos. 150v–151r, Rep. 6, fos. 74r, 162v.

[114] J. Stow, *A Survey of London*, ed. C. L. Kingsford, 2nd edn, 2 vols (Oxford, 1971), i. 192; *Calendar of Wills proved and enrolled in the Court of Husting, London, A.D. 1258–A.D. 1688*, ed. R. R. Sharpe, 2 vols (London, 1889–90), ii. 635–6; LMA, Rep. 4, fos. 161r, 164v; *HMC Rutland*, iv. 264.

[115] LMA, Rep. 4, fos. 164v, 172v, Rep. 6, fo. 54r.

[116] LMA, Rep. 3, fos. 125v, 127v, 178r, 218r–218v, Rep. 4, fos. 43r–43v 102r, 149r, 151r, Rep. 5, fos. 73v, 100r, 107r, 109v.

provisions for his soul; Mayor John Wyngar, who sent him the gifts in 1504–5; Mayor John Ward, who bequeathed him a standing cup.[117] His servants' petitions for membership of the company were warmly received.[118] But his connections ran wider still. His deputy at the Tower, Simon Digby, showed such a 'good loving mind' towards the city that they granted him the freedom, and his executor Richard Broke was under-sheriff for eight years and recorder for a further ten.[119] Mayors Brown, Shaw, and Rede, a mercer and two goldsmiths, named him executor or supervisor of their wills, and three of the mayors of the early 1520s attended his funeral.[120]

Others had London connections. Brandon served as a feoffee to the draper Robert Brograve and Poynings's stints at Calais and in the Netherlands gave him contacts with the Staplers and Merchant Adventurers.[121] Cutt regulated weights and measures and promoted John Heron, the London mercer who replaced John Myllys, removed in 1509 for the 'manifold misdemeanours' associated with the Dudley regime, as surveyor of the London customs.[122] Windsor's weight was felt in the parish of St Andrew by the Wardrobe, where his arms were in the church's windows and he vigorously defended the tenants of the properties adjacent to the great wardrobe against demands they should serve in the London watch, telling Cromwell that Henry VII had commanded him to see their privileges preserved.[123] Wyatt's work at the jewel house and mint linked him to the goldsmiths, including his successor Robert Amadas and the former mayor Sir Bartholomew Rede.[124] Southwell's role as chief butler gave him some leverage for complaints that he had been deprived of lands near London Bridge.[125] Marney's sudden rise made it 'behoveful for the wealth of this city' that he be granted the same privilege of direct water supplies to his house as Dudley had enjoyed, and Windsor, too, could pull strings, securing a forty-year corporation lease of a garden in 1516 despite a resolution against long leases.[126]

The new men's relationships with London interacted with their other roles in the urban nexus and the wider polity. Windsor asked the London authorities in 1517, presumably as steward of the borough of Windsor, to release cloths

[117] J. A. Kingdon, *List of Wardens of the Grocers' Company from 1345 to 1907* (London, 1907), 13–16; *London and Middlesex Chantry Certificate 1548*, ed. C. J. Kitching, London RS 16 (London, 1980), xvi, 89; LMA, Rep. 4, fo. 172v; Wedgwood, *Commons*, 921; A. P. Beaven, *The Aldermen of the City of London temp. Henry III–1908*, 2 vols (London, 1908), ii. 30.

[118] *Acts of Court*, 571, 671.

[119] LMA, Rep. 1, fos. 37v, 77v, Rep. 6, fo. 54r; Bindoff, *Commons*, i. 504–6.

[120] Wedgwood, *Commons*, 758–9; Sutton, *Mercery of London*, 526n; T. F. Reddaway and L. E. M. Walker, *The Early History of the Goldsmiths' Company, 1327–1509* (London, 1975), 201; *LP* IV, i. 366; Stow, *Survey*, ii. 181.

[121] LMA, A/CSC/663–8; *Acts of Court*, 577.

[122] Sutton, *Mercery of London*, 345; LMA, Rep. 3, fo. 113v; H. S. Cobb, '"Books of Rates" and the London Customs, 1507–1558', *Guildhall Miscellany* 4 (1971–3), 6–7.

[123] *History from Marble, Compiled in the Reign of Charles II by Thomas Dingley, Gent.*, ii, ed. J. G. Nichols, CS, o.s. 97 (London, 1868), 146–7; *LP*, XIII, i. 25.

[124] *LP* IV, i. 643; *CPR 1494–1509*, 475; *CIPM*, iii. 94.

[125] LMA, Rep. 1, fos. 35r, 71r, 89v, 175r, Rep. 2, fos. 3v, 10r.

[126] LMA, Rep. 2, fo. 73v, Rep. 3, fo. 100r.

confiscated from a resident of Eton, and in 1518 Poynings settled terms with them for the delivery of fish by wholesalers from the Cinque Ports.[127] At parliament, London interests promoting legislation curried favour with the speaker or the king's attorney, Mordaunt receiving 'new fashioned' plate worth £1 7s 4d from the pewterers in 1487 and Hobart £1 from the carpenters ten years later, while Marney was among the councillors presented with wine by the corporation before parliament in 1512.[128] At every level of the urban hierarchy and in almost every part of England, the new men's relationships with towns increased the king's grasp on society and amplified their personal power.

MANORIAL STEWARDSHIPS

Almost every corner of England was subject to a more or less active manorial jurisdiction in the hands of a nobleman, knight, gentleman, bishop, religious house, or other institution, or sometimes of the king. The courts were the lords' courts, but their business had to be conducted in dialogue with juries of tenants and through the activity of manorial stewards. Stewards supervised the operation of low-level justice over minor assaults and public nuisances, misplaced dunghills, wandering pigs, and those who broke hedges for firewood. This was a sensitive task at a time when the leading men of many small towns and villages were keen to regulate the unruly young and mobile poor, as population levels began to recover from their fifteenth-century trough, the cloth industry spread and markets around London expanded. Stewards and their courts also managed the allocation of land to tenants holding by copyhold tenures. These were derived from the servile tenures of the high Middle Ages, though most, but by no means all, had lost the taint of serfdom as peasants' negotiating position became stronger in the wake of the Black Death; but the exact terms on which they were held, including the entry fines paid at the changeover from one tenant to another, were open to manipulation. Finally, the stewards of crown and ecclesiastical estates normally led the men of those manors to war in their own retinues, thus amplifying the numbers of men they could raise to serve the king from their own resources. When one kind of ideal steward was a skilful lawyer with an eye to the lord's financial interests and another was a loyal courtier-knight with a military bent, the new men's blend of skills fitted them perfectly for the role.[129]

All the new men collected stewardships, but Lovell's and Bray's assemblages ranged widest. Bray held stewardships from the crown, from religious houses and

[127] LMA, Rep. 3, fos. 158r, 189v.
[128] C. Welch, *History of the Worshipful Company of Pewterers*, 2 vols (London, 1902), i. 64–5; M. Davies, 'Lobbying Parliament: the London Companies in the Fifteenth Century', *Parliamentary History* 23 (2004), 144; Miller, 'London and Parliament', 137–8.
[129] M. K. McIntosh, *Controlling Misbehaviour in England, 1370–1600* (Cambridge, 1998); P. R. Schofield, *Peasant and Community in Medieval England, 1200–1500* (Basingstoke, 2003), 11–76; D. Luckett, 'Crown Office and Licensed Retinues in the reign of Henry VII', in R. E. Archer and S. K. Walker (eds), *Rulers and Ruled in Later Medieval England: Essays presented to Gerald Harriss* (London, 1995), 223–38.

from lay lords in the area of his own landed interests and far beyond.[130] Lovell had longer to build up his portfolio and it was correspondingly even more impressive. He began with royal grants in his native East Anglia, reaching across to Essex and Hertfordshire, on the duchy of Lancaster estates, the queen's jointure, and the lands of the duke of Buckingham and earl of Warwick while under royal control.[131] Further afield he accumulated stewardships from the honour of Wallingford in Berkshire and the neighbouring counties, through Walsall in Staffordshire, Bolsover and Horsley in Derbyshire, Sherwood Forest and Mansfield in Nottinghamshire to Wakefield and Halifax in Yorkshire.[132] Where the king led, others followed, and Lovell was steward to the dowager duchess of York at Bromsgrove and King's Norton in Worcestershire, the earl of Ormond at Fulbourn in Cambridgeshire, the bishops of Lincoln and of Coventry and Lichfield for their towns of Newark, Dorchester, Thame, and Lichfield, the abbeys of Peterborough and St Albans, the priories of Lenton, Wallingford, and Sheen, and St George's College, Windsor, where he succeeded Bray as chief steward.[133] The importance of these posts can be judged in several ways. Some had been held by the most powerful politicians of the previous generation, Edward IV's chamberlain, William Lord Hastings, for example.[134] Some of the towns involved were substantial, St Albans and Hitchin the largest in Hertfordshire, Newark, Mansfield, and Worksop three of the five largest in Nottinghamshire.[135] And other records, as we shall see, show that stewardships made Lovell a powerful presence in many communities.

In contrast to Lovell's steady accumulation, Marney leapt forward after 1509, before which he held only the stewardship of the Essex estates of Higham Ferrers College.[136] In June 1509, he secured the reversion after the earl of Oxford, who was to die in 1513, of the chief stewardship of the duchy of Lancaster in the South Parts and of a collection of East Anglian stewardships and other posts centred on Rayleigh, Thaxted, Clare, and Castle Rising. In 1514 he added the duchy of Lancaster stewardship in Essex and Hertfordshire and a further group of Essex

---

[130] M. M. Condon, 'Bray, Sir Reynold [Reginald]', *ODNB*; *CPR 1485–94*, 54, 114; Somerville, *Duchy of Lancaster*, 593; *LP* VII. 1634; *Calendar of the Manuscripts of the Dean and Chapter of Wells*, 2 vols, HMC 12 (London, 1907–14), ii. 163; HL, MS HAM Box 10(5), m. 7.

[131] *CPR 1485–94*, 38; Somerville, *Duchy of Lancaster*, 595; *Muster Roll for the Hundred of North Greenhoe (circa 1523)*, ed. H. L. Bradfer-Lawrence, Norfolk RS 1 (Norwich, 1930), 48, 52; M. K. McIntosh, *Autonomy and Community: The Royal Manor of Havering, 1200–1500* (Cambridge, 1986), 271; *LP* I, i. 132 (35).

[132] *CPR 1485–94*, 265, 273; *Certificate of Musters for Buckinghamshire*, 84, 286; *LP* III, ii. 1451 (20), IV, i. 390 (27); HL, MS El 1518, fo. 49r.

[133] *The Court Rolls of the Manor of Bromsgrove and King's Norton 1494–1504*, ed. A. F. C. Baber, Worcestershire Historical Society n.s. 3 (Kineton, 1963), 9; PRO, SC2/210/35, mm. 3–4; SC6/Henry VII/1341; E315/272, fo. 62r; E315/464, fos. 58v, 60v, 65v; E210/1478; *Peterborough Local Administration: The Last Days of Peterborough Monastery*, ed. W. T. Mellows, Northamptonshire RS 12 (1947), xlvii; *The Manuscripts of Lord Middleton, preserved at Wollaton Hall*, HMC 69 (London, 1911), 124, 515; *Certificate of Musters for Buckinghamshire*, 181, 195, 266, 271, 291; Windsor, The Aerary, MSS XV.48.60, XV.49.6, XV.49.13.

[134] HL, MS HAP oversize box 5 (11, 15, 18); *Registra Johannis Whethamstede, Willelmi Albon, et Willelmi Walingforde, Abbatum Monanasterii Sancti Albani*, ed. H. T. Riley, Rolls Series 28 (London, 1873), 199–200; *Peterborough Local Administration*, xlvi.

[135] Clark and Hoskins, *Population Estimates*, 69, 115.   [136] *CAD*, ii. C2650.

offices. Meanwhile, he took the stewardships of all the duchy of Cornwall's estates in Cornwall and Devon and of Mere in Wiltshire.[137] The one post he gained that really did not fit with his own landed influence, the stewardship of Galtres Forest near York, he soon arranged to be granted in reversion to the local courtier Sir Anthony Ughtred.[138] Seeing him bask in the new king's favour, the abbot and convent of Westminster gave him in 1510 the leadership of all their tenants in Essex and elsewhere for internal and defensive campaigns—though not overseas expeditions—and added in 1514 the offices of gatekeeper of the monastery, keeper of its prison, and steward of the manors of the prior's portion, held jointly with his fellow-councillor Thomas Neville.[139] Neville's brother Edward made Marney steward of his manor at Nayland, on the Suffolk-Essex border, as the queen did at Sudbury, a little deeper into Suffolk.[140] Further away, but still no doubt sensitive to the king's favour, the prior of Bath gave him the stewardship of his Gloucestershire manors of Cold Ashton and Olveston.[141]

Hussey's collection of stewardships was densely concentrated in Lincolnshire and patiently accumulated. It started in survivorship with his father at Lord De La Warr's manor of Swineshead, between Boston and Sleaford, and continued with three Lincolnshire manors in temporary royal custody within seven months of Bosworth.[142] In 1496, he and Bray became jointly stewards and receivers of Grantham and Stamford and bailiffs of Stamford; Stamford was the second or third largest town in the county and Grantham the fourth or fifth.[143] More royal grants followed in Henry's reign and beyond, on the forfeited estates of Lord Fitzwalter and William de la Pole, on the duchy of Lancaster manors of Long Bennington, Long Sutton and Spalding, on the Lincolnshire and Rutland lands granted to Anne Boleyn.[144] Meanwhile, Lady Margaret Beaufort gave him parallel advancement, as steward of her manors of Deeping and Maxey and perhaps also of Bourne and Boston, posts he kept when her lands passed to Henry VIII and then to his bastard son the duke of Richmond.[145]

Other landlords followed suit. Viscount Beaumont made him steward of Folkingham, Ruskington, Blankney, and other manors, Lord Latimer steward at Helpringham, Lord Darcy steward of Knaith, Lord Hastings and the duke of Norfolk steward of their Lincolnshire manors, the earl of Derby steward of Epworth in the Isle of Axholme.[146] Ecclesiastical lords joined in with a will, some

[137] *LP* I, i. 54 (26); DCRO, DC Roll 215, m. 15r.
[138] Somerville, *Duchy of Lancaster*, 393, 606; *LP* I, i. 94 (96), ii. 3324 (6).
[139] WAM, Lease Book II, fos. 13r, 67r.
[140] *The Military Survey of 1522 for Babergh Hundred*, ed. J. F. Pound, Suffolk RS 28 (Woodbridge, 1986), 19, 30.
[141] *The Military Survey of Gloucestershire, 1522*, ed. R. W. Hoyle, Gloucestershire Record Series 6 (Stroud, 1993), 22, 37.
[142] PRO, LR14/916; *Materials*, i. 411; *CPR 1485–1494*, 85.
[143] *CPR 1494–1509*, 39; Dyer, 'Ranking Lists', 761–3; Clark and Hoskins, *Population Estimates*, 95–101.
[144] *CPR 1494–1509*, 44, 383; Somerville, *Duchy of Lancaster*, 574; *LP* VII, 352.
[145] M. K. Jones and M. G. Underwood, *The King's Mother: Lady Margaret Beaufort, Countess of Richmond and Derby* (Cambridge, 1992), 276; *LP* I, i. 132 (56); 22 Henry VIII c. 17 s. 23.
[146] *LP* I, i. 158 (14, 17), IV, ii. 2527; Alnwick Castle, Syon MS X.II.6 box 1n; PML, Rulers of England box 1 no. 44v; PRO, SC6/Henry VIII/6305, fo. 239v; E326/12389.

from the last years of Henry VII's reign, a flood by the 1520s. The bishop of Lincoln made him steward of Sleaford, the bishop of Carlisle steward of Horncastle, both towns among the top dozen in a large county.[147] He was the dean and chapter of Lincoln's steward at Navenby, Fotheringhay College's at Spittlegate, Kirkstead Abbey's at Harmston, Tattershall College's and Crowland Abbey's in Kesteven, Vaudey Abbey's at Hanbeck, and Peterborough Abbey's at Gosberton, as well as high bailiff of the abbey's liberty.[148] He was steward of all the Lincolnshire lands of Magdalen College, Oxford, and of St Mary's Abbey, York, and of some of those of Thornton Abbey.[149] He was chief steward of St Gilbert's Priory, Sempringham, St Katherine's Priory by Lincoln, Bardney Abbey, Barlings Abbey, Bourne Abbey, Haverholme Priory, Ramsey Abbey, Revesby Abbey, Spalding Priory, and Swineshead Abbey.[150] The list is imposing, but the concentration of these grants suggests the strongly focused nature of Hussey's power. All lay within a radius of forty miles or so from Sleaford, with Stamford, Peterborough, and Ramsey at one extreme and Knaith, just south of Gainsborough, at the other. The exception that proved the rule was the surveyorship of the Welsh marcher lordship of Ruthin, a post he held briefly before 1511 as part of his rather exploitative relationship with his feeble brother-in-law the earl of Kent.[151]

Southwell's stewardships, like Hussey's, were narrowly concentrated geographically. Bishop Alcock of Ely, Bury St Edmunds Abbey, and the dowager duchess of Norfolk all gave him stewardships in Norfolk and Suffolk—mostly Norfolk—and Henry VII and Henry VIII did the same, with occasional additions stretching into the Midlands and West.[152] Poynings, similarly, held only the chief stewardship of the estates of the archbishop of Canterbury.[153] Windsor's concentration of office-holding, built slowly from his earliest days at court, was similarly intense. In London and Middlesex he was steward by the 1530s for Holy Trinity Aldgate, for Syon's manor of Isleworth, for the House of Captives of Hounslow, and the London Priory of the Order of St Clare. In Buckinghamshire he held stewardships on the estates of the Knights of St John, Ankerwyke Priory, Burnham Abbey, and St George's College, Windsor. Ranging more widely about the same centres of gravity, he served as steward of the duke of Buckingham's estates in Buckinghamshire, Bedfordshire, Hampshire, and Northamptonshire and Westminster Abbey's in Buckinghamshire, Middlesex, Oxfordshire, and

---

[147] PRO, SC6/Henry VIII/1981; *VE*, iv. 5, v. 274; Clark and Hoskins, *Population Estimates*, 95–101.

[148] *VE*, iv. 11, 36, 43, 87, 99, 283, 288; *Peterborough Local Administration*, 16–17; Jones and Underwood, *King's Mother*, 132.

[149] *VE*, ii. 281, iv. 74, v. 5.

[150] *VE*, iv. 34, 45, 82, 96, 98, 102–3, 118, 130, 273.

[151] *LP* I, i. 784 (34).

[152] 'Ely Episcopal Registers', ed. J. H. Crosby, *Ely Diocesan Remembrancer* 288 (1909), 76; NRO, Rye MS 74, part 2; PRO, SC6/Henry VII/1693; *CPR 1494–1509*, 355, 526; *LP* I, i. 158(71), 632(66); DCRO, DC Roll 215, m. 19r.

[153] CCA, Dean and Chapter Register T, fos. 68v–69v.

Surrey, and as bailiff of Lord Dacre of Gilsland's Suffolk estates.[154] Windsor did hold royal stewardships, for the queen at Langley Marish and Wraysbury in Buckinghamshire and for the king at Thurrock in Essex, but they were less central in his career than those of a Lovell or a Marney.[155]

Wyatt's stewardships and other local offices reflected the dispersed nature and ultimate frailty of his local power. His first grants came in Norfolk in autumn 1485, for his services in England and beyond the seas: the keepership of the duchy of Lancaster's rabbit warren at Methwold, the bailiffship of the manor there, and the keepership of Norwich Castle.[156] Then he moved his sights to his native Yorkshire, where he collected between 1487 and 1509 the stewardships of Conisbrough, Hooton Pagnell, Bradford, Tickhill, Hatfield, and Thorne. The mismatch between these grants and his developing landed estate in Kent forced him to associate himself with other, more locally powerful, men in each position, Sir John Savile, Sir Thomas Fitzwilliam, and John Melton at Conisbrough, and Sir Thomas Boleyn at Norwich, while at Bradford he and Richard Tempest sued out alternating grants until in 1524 Tempest was appointed jointly with Wyatt's son Thomas.[157] In practice, it became clear in 1536, Sir Brian Hastings, another local knight, had been used to calling out the king's tenants in Conisbrough and Tickhill for war with Wyatt's blessing.[158] Stewardships could amplify the influence brought by landed power—Hussey's in Lincolnshire, Marney's in Essex, Lovell's through the Roos estates—but they could not substitute for it.

PARKS AND CASTLES

With stewardships often went other local offices such as the constableships of castles and the keepership of parks. At first sight Brandon's local offices were unimpressive. Like others he secured stewardships in the area of his—or in his case his wife's—landed power, but they were few, covering a scatter of manors from Cornwall to Wiltshire, and were granted late in life.[159] Even this grant, with its specification that he was to be master of the hunt in all the south-western chases and parks held by the king's late grandmother, betrayed that his interest lay more in deer than court rolls. In 1504, he had been made parker of Freemantle Park, Hampshire, with an expense account for carrying water for the deer to the park in

[154] M. C. Rosenfield, 'Holy Trinity, Aldgate, on the eve of the Dissolution', *Guildhall Miscellany* 3 (1969–71), 172; *VE*, i. 398, 402, 406, 418, 426, iv. 221, 222; WAM, Lease Book II, fo. 11v; *LP* III, ii. 3695; Windsor, The Aerary, XV.49.10–21; *A Subsidy collected in the Diocese of Lincoln in 1526*, ed. H. Salter, OHS 63 (Oxford, 1913), 247; S. G. Ellis, *Tudor Frontiers and Noble Power: The Making of the British State* (Oxford, 1995), 102.
[155] PRO, KB9/467/1; *LP* I, i. 158 (57); *Certificate of Musters for Buckinghamshire*, 222.
[156] *Materials*, i. 81, 564, 581, ii. 30; *CPR 1485–94*, 74, 136; *Rotuli Parliamentorum*, ed. J. Strachey et al., 6 vols (London, 1767–77), vi. 371, 377.
[157] *Materials*, ii. 112; *CPR 1485–94*, 314; *LP* I, i. 54 (61), 1003 (11), 1083 (26), II, i. 699, 1309, III, ii. 2074 (16), 2214; Somerville, *Duchy of Lancaster*, 522, 529, 522.
[158] *LP* XI. 519 (4), 1026; Somerville, *Duchy of Lancaster*, 529–30.
[159] *LP* I, i. 218 (52).

summer.[160] In May 1509, he had become chief justice and warden of all royal forests and parks south of the Trent, a post that gave him supreme responsibility for the premises on which his successive royal masters pursued their favourite pastime, just as his mastership of the horse gave him charge of the horses vital for that pursuit.[161] For one whose centre of political gravity lay unequivocally at court, such offices were as valuable as any stewardship.

The pleasures of the chase were such that many others sought a few park keeperships. Bray was keeper of Guildford and Henley parks in Surrey.[162] Hussey, who asked to borrow his friend Lord Darcy's hunting dog in summer 1523 'for my fantasy now is set on hunting', was keeper of Viscount Beaumont's park at Folkingham and master of the game in the earl of Derby's parks in Axholme; for the king, he was master forester of the Huntingdonshire forest of Weybridge and Sapley and surveyor of the game of Ridlington Park in Rutland, with three bucks in summer, three does in winter, and free run for his greyhounds and bloodhounds; in Leighfield Forest, Rutland, he was variously comptroller, master, or lieutenant for the king and Lord Hastings.[163] Wyatt was keeper of Hatfield Park in Hertfordshire for the bishops of Ely, Baddow Park in Essex for the queen, and Conisbrough Park in Yorkshire for the king.[164] In addition to his keepership of Sherwood Forest, Lovell was master forester of Enfield Chase and keeper of the parks there from 1501, convenient for his great house at Elsings.[165] Marney was master forester of Dartmoor, ranger of the chase, and forester at Rising, and, most usefully for his own hunting and dining at Layer Marney, keeper of half a dozen royal parks in Essex and the bishop of London's park at Clacton.[166] Such offices allowed one not only to take recreation, but also to allow others to do the same, and were thus a significant source of patronage.[167]

Castle constableships were also distributed to the new men. Lovell was constable of Nottingham Castle for the king, Wallingford Castle for the Prince of Wales and Newark Castle for the bishop of Lincoln, while Englefield was constable of Banbury, Bray of Oakham, Hobart of Wisbech and Marney of Pleshey, Clare, and Castle Rising.[168] Wyatt's charges at Conisbrough and Tickhill included the constableship of the castles, but the suspicion that these were sinecures is strengthened by his need to secure exemption from the terms of a statute of 1504 voiding appointments to such posts 'not requiring actual exercise in any of the same offices by them to whom such grant or office is made or granted or by their deputy or

[160] *CPR 1494–1509*, 412.   [161] *LP* I, i. 94 (12).   [162] *CPR 1485–94*, 139.

[163] PRO, SP1/28, fo. 118v (*LP* III, ii. 3183); E326/12389; E36/5524; *LP* I, i. 158 (14, 88); *CPR 1494–1509*, 428, 433.

[164] 'Ely Episcopal Registers', 284 (1909), 12; PRO, SC6/Henry VIII/783; *CPR 1485–94*, 314.

[165] *CPR 1485–98*, 265, 295; Somerville, *Duchy of Lancaster*, 612; BL, Harley Roll Y28.

[166] Somerville, *Duchy of Lancaster*, 606; *LP* I, i. 94 (96), IV, i. 1264.

[167] M. A. Havinden, 'The Resident Gentry of Somerset, 1502', *Somerset Archaeology and Natural History* 139 (1996), 4.

[168] *CPR 1485–94*, 64, 265, 273; LA, BP Accounts 8, mm. 9r, 21r; 'Ely Episcopal Registers', 280 (1908), 133; *LP* I, i. 94 (96).

deputies'.[169] Certainly, the commissioners who surveyed both castles after his death were unimpressed with their condition. Three storeys of the keep at Conisbrough were 'well reparelled', but otherwise each needed several hundred pounds' worth of masonry repairs and large quantities of woodwork and ironwork, the wells were jammed with earth or gravel, and, perhaps most suspiciously, significant amounts of lead roofing and guttering were either missing entirely or stored up inside the castle, maybe ready for sale.[170] His keepership of Norwich Castle and the prison it housed may have been more demanding, as he was paid £40 towards repairs there in 1488.[171]

Lovell, similarly, seems to have let even the new buildings put up by Edward IV at Nottingham Castle start to crumble.[172] Poynings's constableship of Dover Castle, in contrast, was a real job. It functioned as the administrative centre of the Cinque Ports and still had a role in coastal defence and as a staging post for royal visits to the continent. In 1494 he was spending money at the king's command on repairs to the church and the keep, between June 1511 and June 1515 he received £366 13s 4d for further repair work, and in 1513 five barrels of gunpowder were supplied to him for the castle's defences.[173] Nor did he neglect the castle's spiritual needs, for it emerged in 1511 that he had enticed away the rector of St Peter's church to celebrate mass regularly in the castle church.[174] More inviting as homes and places to host the king were the royal palaces. Courtiers and royal body servants were more often appointed keepers of these than were more senior councillors, but Risley was keeper of Eltham Palace.[175]

Constableships and park keeperships played a less obvious role in the construction of the new men's power than stewardships or relations with towns. Their output could not be measured in retinues raised, burgesses elected to parliament, clients advanced, advice taken, gifts received. But they served as one more way in which the importance of the new men in local society was embedded and normalized, one more way in which they were equipped to act as the great men they were not born to be.

---

[169] *CPR 1485–94*, 314; Somerville, *Duchy of Lancaster*, 529; 19 Henry VII c. 10 s. 7.
[170] '"View of the Castles of Tickhill and Conisbro" made by Special Commissioners 29 Henry VIII', ed. W. Brown, *Yorkshire Archaeological Journal* 9 (1885–6), 221–2.
[171] *Materials*, ii. 393.   [172] *HKW*, iii. 284.
[173] *HKW*, iii. 242; SP1/5, fo. 14 (*LP* I, ii. 2834).
[174] *Kentish Visitations of Archbishop Warham and his Deputies, 1511–1512*, ed. K. L. Wood-Legh, Kent Records 24 (Maidstone, 1984), 130.
[175] S. J. Gunn, 'The Courtiers of Henry VII', *EHR* 108 (1993), 23–49; S. J. Gunn, 'The Court of Henry VII' in S. J. Gunn and A. Janse (eds), *The Court as a Stage: England and the Low Countries in the Later Middle Ages* (Woodbridge, 2006), 45–6; *HKW*, iv. 78–9.

8

Followers

The new men could not be everywhere at once, and much of their power was exercised through deputies. More generally, they did much of what they did through their servants, like many people in their age, when domestic servants and apprentices were commonplace even in quite humble households. Beyond their deputies and servants lay a circle of retainers who had sworn to serve them in return for a fee, a grant of livery clothing, or merely the promise of good lordship. Servants, deputies, and retainers alike had to be chosen and managed with care if their masters' affairs were not to run into difficulties and if they were to serve the king to maximum effect.[1] The operations of the followings of great lords, composed of affinities of gentry and yeomanry radiating outwards from great households, have been studied intensively for the fourteenth and fifteenth centuries and to some extent for the sixteenth.[2] So have the household secretariats and clientage networks of sixteenth-century royal ministers such as Thomas Cromwell and William Cecil.[3] The followings of the new men represented, as we might expect, a transitional phase between the lordly and the bureaucratic affinity and like them they blended private service, the service of the patron's wealth and comfort, with public service, the execution of governmental functions in the name of the king.

SERVANTS

At the top of their private administrations most of the new men had one particularly trusted factotum, usually the receiver-general of their estates. At the end of his life, Lovell's right-hand man was John Carleton. He was in his service by 1500 and receiver by 1511.[4] He was a very active manager of Lovell's estates. In 1522–3, for example, he spent twenty-four days touring through Norfolk to check on the

[1] R. E. Horrox, *Richard III: A Study of Service* (Cambridge, 1989), 1.

[2] M. A. Hicks, *Bastard Feudalism* (London, 1995); S. Adams, 'Baronial Contexts?: Continuity and Change in the Noble Affinity, 1400–1600', in J. L. Watts (ed.), *The End of the Middle Ages? England in the Fifteenth and Sixteenth Centuries* (Stroud, 1998), 155–97.

[3] G. R. Elton, *The Tudor Revolution in Government: Administrative Changes in the reign of Henry VIII* (Cambridge, 1953), 304–12; M. L. Robertson, 'The Art of the Possible: Thomas Cromwell's Management of West Country Government', *HJ* 32 (1989), 793–816; A. J. Slavin, *Politics and Profit: A Study of Sir Ralph Sadler, 1507–1547* (Cambridge, 1966), 14–45; R. C. Barnett, *Place, Profit, and Power: a Study of the Servants of William Cecil, Elizabethan Statesman* (Chapel Hill NC, 1969); A. G. R. Smith, *Servant of the Cecils: the Life of Sir Michael Hickes, 1543–1612* (London, 1977).

[4] WSRO, Chichester City Archives, AY136.

effects of another landlord's drainage works on the harbour at Cley next the Sea, investigate a dispute between two tenants and administer the transfer of two estates to Lovell from Sir William Paston, in addition to the normal audit trips to Belvoir, East Harling, and London.[5] He also dealt with various officials on Lovell's behalf, collecting his fees for offices or conduct money for his retinue.[6] It was to him that Lovell confided his instructions for charitable provisions to benefit his soul, and for bequests to his friends and relations. He enjoyed the use of a well-furnished chamber at Elsings, and Lovell left him the remaining fifty-four years of a lease on a house in London.[7] His servant Robert Ferley travelled even more on Lovell's business than he did himself, taking in Cambridgeshire, Huntingdonshire, Norfolk, Suffolk, Sussex, and Kent on his rent-collecting trips in 1523.[8] Though his work is harder to document, it look as though Carleton's predecessor John Thomson had been equally active.[9]

Richard Ward, Hussey's receiver, a clergyman, was just as busy, taking money to London, searching through documents at Sleaford, holdings courts at Gonerby, checking wine and coal deliveries at Boston, travelling around Lincolnshire talking to anyone who had business with his master, dispatching other servants to the places he could not reach himself, and writing from Sleaford to his 'right worshipful master' at London to keep him abreast of developments.[10] Marney's receiver Thomas Ashby and Southwell's Henry Palmer, based at Woodrising in Norfolk or his own home at Moulton while Southwell was at Hackney, served as feoffees on their masters' estates, trustees in whom the formal tenure of the land was vested, as well as collecting rent.[11] Their masters' confidence gave them power. It was either Palmer or his colleague Robert Holdich who brought Godfrey Vyncent to Southwell with the request to help him secure some lands in Dereham in the teeth of local opposition, which Southwell, persuaded that Vyncent had a good title, duly did.[12]

Early in his career Poynings was dependent on William May, the receiver who toured his estates calling in the rents while Sir Edward pressed on with his military and diplomatic career. In 1488 alone, May registered receipts at Crawley, London, Bourton-on-Dunsmore, Coventry, Milton Keynes, and many unspecified places on twenty-eight different days of the year.[13] In Poynings's last years, however, his right-hand-man was Edward Thwaites, feoffee on his lands, sole executor of his

[5] *HMC Rutland*, iv. 263; Belvoir Castle, MS a/c no. 4; BL, Addl. MS 12463, fos. 4v, 67v, 82v–83r, 117v (*LP* IV, i. 367).

[6] Belvoir Castle, MS a/c no. 4; *LP* I, ii, p. 1518.

[7] PRO, PROB2/199, m. 2; PROB11/23/27.

[8] Belvoir Castle, MS a/c no. 4.

[9] *Feet of Fines for Cambridgeshire Henry VIII to Elizabeth*, ed. W. M. Palmer (Norwich, 1909), 22; Hampshire RO, 21M65/A1/16, fo. 19r; *CCR 1500–9*, 338; WSRO, Chichester City Archives, AY133–8; Bodl. MS Kent ch. 231; PRO, E210/10993.

[10] PRO, E36/95, fos. 33r–33v, 63r, 64r, 99v; *LP* IV, i. 799.

[11] PRO, C142/40/7–9; SC6/Henry VII/160, 162, 163; PRO C1/455/44, 469/47; C142/29/15; *LP* I, i. 438(4 m. 10); F. Blomefield, *An Essay towards a Topographical History of the County of Norfolk*, 11 vols (London, 1805–10), xi. 110.

[12] PRO, C1/593/20–2.   [13] Alnwick Castle, Syon MS X.II.I, box 16b.

will, charged with managing his sons' estates until they came of age, rewarded with an annuity of £13 6s 8d, which he soon set out to earn by defending the boys' interests.[14] Thwaites apparently came to Poynings through his connections at Calais, as the son of Thomas Thwaites esquire, spear of the Calais garrison, who died at Westenhanger in 1523, and nephew of John Thwaites, whom Poynings presented to the rectory of Horsmonden in 1509.[15] He called his daughter Rose, perhaps a tribute to Poynings's close friend Rose Whetehill.[16]

Wyatt's voluminous collections of deeds enable us to track several generations of his team of men of business and the variety of work they did. Either side of 1509 Edward Baynes, John Bedell, George Emerson, and John Germyn handled many of his land dealings.[17] Servatius Frank, probably a Netherlander, was working with them by 1511 and soon became Wyatt's most valued servant, a regular feoffee from 1514, receiver-general of his lands in Kent by 1520, left a £6 13s 4d annuity in his will.[18] Between 1515 and 1535 it was most often he who was on the spot to negotiate the terms of Wyatt's land deals, whether in Kent, Essex, or Norfolk, hand over money to the sellers, receive possession of lands, or enforce disputed ownership.[19] Frank lived first at Chalk, then at Shorne, leasing land from Wyatt.[20] He died not long after his master, naming Wyatt's prosperous tenant Robert Brownyng his executor—he left him his damask coat—and Wyatt's step-son Roger Wilde, the parson of Milton, his supervisor.[21]

For twenty years from about 1513, Frank's closest colleague was Robert Draper.[22] Draper stood surety for Wyatt's debts, took seisin of land and then transferred it to Wyatt and his feoffees, and acted as Wyatt's proctor in ecclesiastical presentations in the diocese of Norwich.[23] Edmund Cusshyn, presumably a relative of other Cusshyns earlier associated with Wyatt, joined the team in the later 1520s.[24] George Multon entered Wyatt's service only in the last years of his life but still qualified for a grateful annuity of £2 13 4d in his will, while Edward Westbye,

[14] PRO, CP40/1022, m. 130v; PROB11/20/21; C1/450/4; J. R. Scott, *Memorials of the Family of Scott of Scot's-Hall* (London, 1876), lxiv.

[15] *LP* I, i. 833 (66–7), ii. 2684 (40), II, i. 1058, 1908, III, ii. 2145 (2); KHLC, PRC32/13, fo. 186r–186v; DRb/Ar1/13, fo. 35r.

[16] KHLC, PRC32/13, fo. 186r–186v.

[17] *CAD*, i. C421, iii. D1058, vi. C7345; *Feet of Fines for Essex*, ed. R. E. G. Kirk et al., 6 vols (Colchester, 1899–1993), iv. 108, 125; PRO, C54/382, m. 6d; CP25/1/186/42/28, CP25/1/281/169/136, CP25/1/232/79/130; SC2/153/18, m. 4; E210/10053; E326/8218, 8760, 8673; BL, Addl. Ch. 5674; Brasenose College, Oxford, Muniments Shelswell 3, 7, 10 (NRA report); *CCR 1500–9*, 720, 737, 953, 984; BLARS, L19, L132, L136, L509.

[18] PRO, CP25/2/19/104/4; E210/9917, 10030; SC6/Henry VIII/1684; PROB11/26/7; *CAD*, iii. D476, D1308.

[19] PRO, E210/4865, 6402, 6806, 9896, 9916, 10011, 10160; E326/7112, 8218, 8736, 8750, 11336, 11340; KB27/1094, m. 31r–31v; STAC 2/19/198.

[20] PRO, E210/10160; SC2/181/87, fo. 7r.

[21] KHLC, DRb/Pwr 9, fos. 254v–255r.

[22] PRO, CP25/2/3/11/32, 28/188/40, 37/245/4; E101/56/25, m. 40; E326/7786, 10416; *CAD*, iii. D1165.

[23] PRO, E36/215, fo. 343r; E326/8760, 8763; *LP* IV, ii. 3087(24); NRO, Bishop's Register 14, fos. 187r, 198r.

[24] PRO, E326/6961, 7112, 8736, 8740, 10072; KB27/1094, m. 31r–31v; CUL, Addl. MS 2994, fo. 209v.

active with Multon in Sir Henry's final land settlements, got £1 a year.[25] Wyatt's staff in Yorkshire was partly separate from that in Kent, but there was some overlap. John Savile, grandson of Sir John Savile of Thornhill, was associated with his interests in Yorkshire and Nottinghamshire in the 1520s, enfeoffed Wyatt and several of his associates on his lands in 1525, married a Wyatt cousin from Essex, and got a small annuity under his will.[26] But he was also active on Wyatt's lands in Kent in 1528 and 1535, just as Frank ventured up to Yorkshire in September 1535 to take possession of lands in Erringden leased by the king to Thomas Wyatt.[27]

These central financial and estate officers interacted with networks of local officers. Estate stewards were often lawyers who toured round holding manorial courts. Ideally they combined professional skill with local knowledge. On his Norfolk manors, Lovell used Thomas Abbs of Buxton, a local gentleman worth £40 a year in lands.[28] Henry Lacey, Lovell's steward in Lincolnshire and Northamptonshire towards the end of his life, was a Kesteven subsidy commissioner, alderman of Stamford and Hussey's deputy as steward there.[29] Wyatt named Simon Fitz of Barton-le-Clay, soon to be JP and escheator, steward of the Bedfordshire manors he had acquired from the earl of Kent in 1512.[30] More isolated estates, in contrast, might need locally powerful stewards to keep an eye on them and fees to match. Where Wyatt paid Fitz only £1 6s 8d a year, Poynings paid £6 13s 4d to Sir Thomas Green as steward of Milton Keynes, and Lovell £5 a year to Sir Marmaduke Constable as steward of his Yorkshire estates.[31] Stewards' legal expertise made them useful to their fellow-officers as well as their masters. Lovell's farmer and collector of rents at Harston in Cambridgeshire, John Bennet, had his will witnessed by John Hynd, Lovell's steward for the county and by then a serjeant-at-law.[32] Auditors tended to be less grand than stewards, but might still be men of substance. Hussey's Humphrey Walcot, paid a fee of £3 6s 8d a year, called himself esquire, mixed with the local gentry and merchant wool-exporters, had his own family chapel in Walcot parish church and left money to four other parish churches and a selection of gold rings and silver spoons to his relations.[33]

More local in their interests were the bailiffs who collected rents and enforced manorial jurisdiction. They were generally yeomen rather than gentry, men like

[25] PRO, E326/7782, 10551; PROB11/26/7.
[26] *LP* Addenda, i. 317; Nottinghamshire Archives, DD/SR209/150; PRO, CP25/2/33/220/40; PRO, PROB11/26/7; S. Brigden, *Thomas Wyatt; The Heart's Forest* (London, 2012), 80.
[27] *Yorkshire Star Chamber Proceedings*, ed. W. Brown et al., 4 vols, YASRS 41, 45, 51, 70 (1909–27), ii. 147–8, iii. 71–4; PRO, E210/9917; E326/6961, 8736.
[28] *Muster Roll for the Hundred of North Greenhoe (circa 1523)*, ed. H. L. Bradfer-Lawrence, Norfolk RS 1 (Norwich, 1930), 64; 'A Muster Roll and Clergy List in the Hundred of Holt, circa 1523', ed. B. Cozens-Hardy, *NA* 22 (1923–5), 57; 'Norfolk Subsidy Roll, 15 Hen VIII', *Norfolk Antiquarian Miscellany* 2 (1883), 403; Blomefield, *Norfolk*, vi. 446.
[29] LA, FL deeds 224; Northamptonshire RO, D1086, m. 11; S. T. Bindoff, *History of Parliament: The House of Commons 1509–1558*, 3 vols (London, 1982), ii. 488.
[30] BLARS, L17; *LP* I, i. 438 (3 m. 4), ii. 1533; *List of Escheators for England and Wales*, List and Index Society 72 (London, 1971), 7.
[31] Alnwick Castle, Syon MS XII.I, box 16b; *HMC Rutland*, iv. 260.
[32] Cambridgeshire Archives, VC10, fo. 10r–10v; BL, Addl. MS 12463, fo. 49v.
[33] PRO, E36/95, fo. 100r; LA, LCC wills 1538–40, fos. 118r–120r.

Thomas and Henry Inman, Hussey's bailiffs of Castle Bytham and half a dozen other manors, or William Swan, his bailiff of Burton Hussey. They practised mixed farming across a range of land tenancies, including demesnes leased from Hussey, and could afford to bury themselves in church rather than in the churchyard, leave tens of pounds in cash, and train their younger sons for the priesthood.[34] The post of bailiff often went with a substantial lease on the manor. Hamo Sutton senior and junior, Hussey's bailiffs of Branston, leased the watermill there and various holdings in the manor and its fen. William Wallhed, his bailiff of Kneesall, leased the herbage of the park for £25 a year. Henry Sleford, bailiff at Stretton, held a more modest landholding in the village.[35] Lovell's bailiffs were similar. Simon Pynder, bailiff at Higham Bensted in Walthamstow, was again a substantial tenant, John Dedyk, bailiff at Terrington by Tilney and Tydd St Giles, farmed the demesnes at Beachamwell and Wereham, while William and Thomas Netlam, bailiffs at Ryhall and Uffington, were yeomen each taxed on £80 in goods and busy buying up land.[36]

Bailiffs of central manors might also have a role in the household. Charles Nowell, Lovell's bailiff of Enfield, was a household servant pensioned in his will; he died not long after his master, requesting burial in St Andrew's Enfield.[37] Household sizes are notoriously hard to calculate, but the signs are that the new men maintained establishments smaller than the greatest noblemen of their generation—the duke of Buckingham and earl of Oxford had well over a hundred servants each—but easily comparable to those of less ambitious earls, lesser peers, and bishops.[38] Lovell, who spent around 16 per cent of his household expenditure on wages, as high a proportion as these great peers, had the most servants. Eighty-nine were waged and dressed in light tawny orange livery coats of Reading broadcloth in 1522–3 and many of them paid taxes on their wages at Enfield in the subsidy collected soon afterwards.[39] Others were not far behind. Belknap reckoned his executors would need fifty mourning gowns for his servants.[40] The household Marney's son inherited at Layer Marney numbered at least thirty-two, five of them foreigners, three conveniently surnamed 'Frenchman' and two 'Ducheman'.[41] Hussey paid wages to 22 servants in 1534–5 and bought his blue liveries for 23 in 1533–4.[42]

---

[34] PRO, E36/95, fos. 90–8; SC6/Henry VIII/6237; LA, LCC wills 1538–40, fos. 173v–174r; LCC wills 1566&c, fos. 66–8.

[35] PRO, E315/393, fos. 21r, 24v, 26r, 27r, 49r, 50r, 83v.

[36] ERO, D/DFc185, pp. 29, 33; BL, Addl. MS 12463, fos. 2v, 54v, 56r, 81v, 84v (*LP* IV, i. 367); *HMC Rutland*, iv. 562; *The County Community under Henry VIII*, ed. J. Cornwall, Rutland Record Series 1 (Oakham, 1980), 42, 97; *Muniments of Hon Mrs Trollope Bellew at Casewick* (NRA report, 1958), 4–6.

[37] BL, Addl. MS 12463, fo. 95v; PRO, PROB11/21/28, 23/27.

[38] C. M. Woolgar, *The Great Household in Late Medieval England* (New Haven CT and London, 1999), 10–17; S. J. Gunn, 'Henry Bourchier, Earl of Essex (1472–1540)', in G. W. Bernard (ed.), *The Tudor Nobility* (Manchester, 1992), 148.

[39] Belvoir Castle, MS a/c no. 4 (*HMC Rutland*, iv. 262); Woolgar, *Great Household*, 20; PRO, E179/141/111.

[40] HL, MS STT Personal box 1(7).   [41] PRO, E179/108/154, m. 15r.

[42] PRO, E36/95, fos. 26r, 51v, 52r.

Bequests in wills show the value placed on loyal servants. It was conventional to leave up to two years' wages to every household servant or to keep the household running for a few months after the testator's death while they found a new position. Those with direct heirs, like Windsor, might instruct them to keep in service all those who wished to stay.[43] Those without, like Lovell, might ask that the household be fed, paid, and liveried for a whole year.[44] Annuities of between £1 and £6 13s 4d a year, leases of land or grants of estate offices might be given to a handful of exceptional individuals, as Brandon, Lovell, Poynings, Windsor, and Wyatt did.[45] Beyond that, Brandon directed his executors to reward each servant as his service had been, but Lovell was more specific.[46] He listed 92 servants, from chaplains and senior household officers to labourers, to receive between £1 and £20 each, and followed it with a selection of 17 of them longest in his service who were to have divided among them £200 worth of plate, plus bedding and household goods.[47] One very special case was Poynings' servant Rose Whetehill, left an annuity of £26 13s 4d a year, the bedding and hangings for two of his best beds, two great parcel-gilt silver pots, a flagon, a drinking-pot, and 12 covered silver bowls. These were said to be in recompense for money and plate she had given him, but we cannot but speculate that there was more to their relationship than that.[48]

Valued servants were cared for long before their masters died. Southwell spent £1 3s 4d getting his servant Thomas cured of the 'great pox'.[49] Hussey gave his horse-keeper Richard an extra 8d 'for keeping of my lady horses when he was sick' and paid 8s for the burial of his servant George Pilffote.[50] He wanted his servants to enjoy themselves, particularly when it reflected well on him, sponsoring their attendance at a shooting match at Lincoln in 1535.[51] On the other hand, when he thought Edward Missenden had taken some of his money, he took him into the privy with a candle, produced a dagger and said 'Thou hast my money; give it me again and tell truth or I shall slay thee.'[52] The threat of violence was real enough, for he had been convicted of assault in London in 1496.[53] Servants could be rewarded with other benefits: Lovell gave John Thomson an advowson and put the exchequer's jurisdiction at the disposal of his men.[54] Masters might secure their servants' land acquisitions by acting as their feoffees, as Poynings did for Thwaites or Lovell for Thomson.[55] Proximity to powerful men also paid off more indirectly.

---

[43] PRO, PROB11/23/27.   [44] PRO, PROB11/29/23.

[45] PRO, PROB11/16/29, 20/21, 23/27, 26/7, 29/23.   [46] PRO, PROB11/16/29.

[47] PRO, PROB11/23/27.   [48] PRO, PROB11/20/21.

[49] PRO, SP1/230, fo. 111v (*LP* I, ii. 2765).   [50] PRO, E36/95, fos. 26r, 28v.

[51] PRO, E36/95, fo. 61v.   [52] PRO, SC1/51/179.

[53] J. H. Baker, *The Men of Court 1440 to 1550: A Prosopography of the Inns of Court and Chancery and the Courts of Law*, 2 vols, SS supplementary ser. 18 (London, 2012), i. 915.

[54] LA, Bishop's Register 23, fo. 54v; PRO, E13/178, rot. 35r, E13/180, rot. 17d, E13/181, rot. 23d, E13/190, rot. 17d.

[55] PRO, CP25/1/30/101/15, CP25/1/117A/350/411; CP25/2/19/110/21.

When Battle Abbey was negotiating the election of a new abbot in 1508–9, they paid Dudley's servant Richard Page 10s, presumably to get access to his master.[56] When Shrewsbury corporation was in dispute with Shrewsbury Abbey in May 1507, they paid another of Dudley's servants 1s 8d, while the London drapers' company admitted one to membership, presumably to placate his master.[57] It was the same everywhere. St George's College, Windsor, paid Bray's clerk in 1500–1 for writing a letter to the bishop of Lincoln on their behalf.[58] The London vintners, pleased to conclude some business with Sir Andrew Windsor in February 1517, slipped his clerk 12d for his assistance.[59] The dedication of servants to generous masters was expected to show in adversity, and in some cases it did. One of Poynings's followed him into exile, returning to be rewarded after Bosworth with the keepership of a royal wood.[60] Two of Dudley's got involved in his plans to escape from the Tower after his attainder and found themselves in trouble for it, while another recalled much later how he was 'pensive and sorry for the trouble of his said master'.[61]

DEPUTIES

Widespread office-holding both central and local made it essential that the new men exercised many of their roles by deputy. Where they were stewards, manor courts were held and instructions issued in their names, but they rarely signed the copies of court roll that proved tenants held land or other court orders, and deputies must always have done much of the work.[62] In the honour of Wallingford, for example, it was Lovell's deputies Humphrey Wellesbourne, mayor of Wycombe, Richard Hampden of Great Kimble, and William Young of Little Wittenham who presided over manorial courts, surveyed woods, and renewed rentals.[63] William Belson of Brill claimed he had ridden more than 800 miles a year holding courts as Lovell's last deputy in the stewardship of Wallingford; Lovell's executors did not dispute this, but refused his claim to a share of Lovell's fee because the understewardship itself was so profitable.[64]

[56] HL, MS BA 272.

[57] H. Owen and J. B. Blakeway, *A History of Shrewsbury*, 2 vols (London, 1825), i. 279; A. H. Johnson, *The History of the Worshipful Company of the Drapers of London*, 5 vols (Oxford, 1914–22), i. 159.

[58] Windsor, The Aerary, MS XV.48.2.   [59] BL, MS Egerton 1143, fo. 55r.

[60] *Materials*, i. 272.   [61] *LP* I, i. 559; PRO, C1/917/27.

[62] PRO, SC6/Henry VII/1802; DL30/94/1283, m. 4r; DL5/2, fos. 133v–134v; BL, Addl. Ch. 32911; Harl. Ch. 58F26; *LP* VII. 606; *The Manuscripts of St George's Chapel, Windsor Castle*, ed. J. N. Dalton (Windsor, 1937), 163.

[63] PRO, KB9/433/4; SC6/Henry VII/1087, mm. 2r–4r, 1091, mm. 1r–3r; *LP* I, i. 438(2 m. 14); E. J. Payne, 'The Montforts, the Wellesbournes and the Hughenden effigies', *Records of Buckinghamshire* 7 (1896), 394.

[64] PRO, C1/383/4–5.

As with those appointed to posts on the new men's own estates, local knowledge was a prime qualification for effective deputy stewards and receivers. At Bromsgrove and King's Norton the courts were held for Lovell first by John Symons, one of the richer tenants, and then, from 1502, by William Grevill, a rising lawyer who had become recorder of Bristol in 1498 and had just joined the Worcestershire commission of the peace.[65] In the East Anglian courts of the duchy of Lancaster, Lovell's and Hobart's deputy was an even safer pair of hands, William Elys, one of the most hard-working JPs of his generation.[66] Yet the great man did stand behind the deputy, a distant but meaningful presence. At Peterborough in 1517, Lovell's deputy tried to defuse a confrontation with the townsfolk in open court with the words:

> Neighbours and friends, I let you wit that my singular good master Sir Thomas Lovell is high steward of this lordship and all other my lord's of Peterborough and I am but his deputy and of your demeanour I will certify him and when I know his pleasure I will demean me thereafter.[67]

The most dependable deputies might accumulate responsibilities almost as widely as their masters. The way Simon Digby, a veteran of Bosworth, stood in for Lovell at London and in the Midlands was neatly brought out when he was pardoned in 1509 as of London, Coleshill in Warwickshire, his family home, and Clipstone in Nottinghamshire, administrative centre of Sherwood Forest.[68] As deputy lieutenant of the Tower he arranged the burial of Sir William Stanley after his execution in 1495, was paid by the imprisoned dean of St Paul's for his servants' board, and was granted a £5 pension by the dean after his release.[69] In Sherwood Forest he was keeper of Thornwood Forest and bailiff of Mansfield, arbitrated disputes amongst the Mansfield tenantry, and served under Lovell on the 1511 muster commission for Nottinghamshire.[70] By 1509–10 he was also Lovell's deputy in the constableship and stewardship of Newark.[71] He died in 1520 leaving lands worth more than £80 a year.[72] His relatives were also drawn into Lovell's service, his brother, executor and fellow muster commissioner Roland acting as his under-constable at Nottingham Castle, his brother or perhaps nephew Libeus serving in Lovell's household, while the Nottingham chamberlains presented his wife Alice with two

[65] *The Court Rolls of the Manor of Bromsgrove and King's Norton 1494–1504*, ed. A. F. C. Baber, Worcestershire Historical Society n.s. 3 (Kineton, 1963), 9, 15, 25, 78; *CPR 1494–1509*, 155, 665.
[66] R. Somerville, *A History of the Duchy of Lancaster, I, 1265–1603* (London, 1953), 595, 600; J. R. Lander, *English Justices of the Peace, 1461–1509* (Gloucester, 1989), 71.
[67] *Select Cases before the King's Council in the Star Chamber, ii*, ed. I. S. Leadam, SS 25 (London, 1911), 141.
[68] *TBPV*, 221; *LP* I, i. 438 (4 m. 24).
[69] BL, Addl. MS 7099, fo. 24r; *The Estate and Household Accounts of William Worsley, Dean of St Paul's Cathedral 1479–1497*, ed. H. Kleineke and S. R. Hovland, London RS 40 (London, 2004), 14, 16.
[70] PRO, E13/187, rot. 1r; *LP* I, i. 833 (50), III, i. 854 (16), ii. 3376 (12); Nottinghamshire Archives, DD/P/17/2, fo. 22v.
[71] LA, BP Accounts 8, m. 9r; *LP* IV, i. 366; PRO, SC6/Henry VII/1981, fo. 2.
[72] Library of Birmingham, Wingfield Digby A696.

gallons of red wine in 1503–4.[73] Thus Lovell tapped into the influence of the ramified Digby clan, who between them served as sheriffs in various Midlands counties eleven times between 1485 and 1524.[74]

It was a token of the new men's versatility that while gentlemen soldiers like Simon Digby were appropriate deputies for some roles, lawyers, accounts clerks, or clergymen were needed for others. Richard Lyster, on his way to the top as king's solicitor, king's attorney, chief baron of the exchequer, and eventually chief justice of king's bench, apparently did much of the work of Lovell's chief justiceship of the forests, then deputized for Hussey as chief butler.[75] Lovell gratefully left him a gilt cup and £5 in his will and led the feoffees on his lands.[76] William Wotton deputized for Lovell as duchy of Lancaster steward at Fulmodeston in Norfolk and went on to rise to second baron of the exchequer, serve as a feoffee on his estates and attend his funeral.[77] But a captain and diplomat like Poynings needed men of a different stamp, like Thomas Partrich. He went to Calais to pick up the money allocated to Poynings for retaining foreign soldiers in 1513, toured Holland that spring hiring ships to transport the English army, and was back in Flanders in 1514 preparing for another campaign.[78]

Sometimes lawyers, clerics, and local gentlemen served in combination. Lovell's commissioners to hear the pleas of Sherwood Forest in 1505 were two laymen and two clergymen.[79] One was John Port, a lawyer with lands in Cheshire and Derbyshire who would succeed Lucas as king's solicitor in 1509 and seems to have been more widely involved in Lovell's administration of the forest.[80] Another was Robert Nevell, a Nottinghamshire esquire, lawyer, JP, and local commissioner.[81] A third was Simon Stalworth, a colourful and well-connected cleric with a papal licence for pluralism, sub-dean of Lincoln, and clerk of the hanaper in chancery, whom Lovell had presented to a rectory in 1492. He collected books on the Turks, wrote breathless reports to the Stonors on the events of 1483 and was indicted for rape and burglary at Westminster in 1484.[82] The fourth was John Cutler, treasurer

---

[73] PRO, C1/192/24; PROB11/19/29; J. Nichols, *The History and Antiquities of the County of Leicester*, 4 vols in 8 (Wakefield, 1971 edn), II, i. 261–2; *LP* I, i. 833 (50); *Records of the Borough of Nottingham*, ed. W. H. Stevenson, 3 vols (Nottingham, 1885), iii. 315; Warwickshire RO, H2/64.

[74] *List of Sheriffs for England and Wales*, PRO Lists and Indexes 9 (London, 1898), 104, 113, 146.

[75] BL, Addl. Ch. 8404; PRO, LR1/310, fo. 39r; *LP* III, ii. 1437; *The Reports of Sir John Spelman*, ed. J. H. Baker, 2 vols, SS 93–4 (London, 1976–7), ii. 383, 360, 391–2.

[76] PRO, PROB11/23/27; CP25/2/7/33/28.

[77] Somerville, *Duchy of Lancaster*, 595; PRO, C142/41/62; *LP* IV, i. 366; Baker, *Men of Court*, ii. 1704–5.

[78] *LP* I, ii. 1918, 1745, 2009, 2850.

[79] YAS, MD218/331; Bodl. MS Ashmole 1145, fos. 68r–70r.

[80] *The Notebook of Sir John Port*, ed. J. H. Baker, SS 102 (London, 1986), xi–xiv, xxvi–xxvii.

[81] *CPR 1494–1509*, 145–6, 422, 488, 654; *LP* I, i. 438 (1 m. 22), 804 (29), 833 (50), 1948 (94); Baker, *Men of Court*, ii. 1151.

[82] A. B. Emden, *A Biographical Register of the University of Oxford to AD 1500*, 3 vols (Oxford, 1957–9), iii. 1753; *CEPR*, xv. 244, xix. 1049, 1515; W. C. Richardson, *Tudor Chamber Administration, 1485–1547* (Baton Rouge LA, 1952), 486; *Kingsford's Stonor Letters and Papers 1290–1483*, ed. C. Carpenter (Cambridge, 1996), 159–61; PRO, KB9/369/33; LA, Bishop's Register 22, fo. 215r.

of Lincoln Cathedral.[83] It is a measure of Henry VII's use of interwoven commissions of trusted men to implement all manner of royal policies that Cutler, Stalworth, and Nevell were named together on commissions of sewers and commissions to search out concealed royal rights in 1504–5 and Port and Nevell on commissions to try the prisoners in Nottingham gaol from 1507.[84] It is a measure of the intricate interconnections of the new men that Port was involved with Sutton's foundation of Brasenose College and Stalworth named Hussey his executor in 1511 and left him the house he had built in the close at Lincoln.[85]

The boundaries between service to the new men in their private affairs and deputising for them in service to the king were predictably blurred. Roger Delle managed Southwell's household expenses, but also collected the income from prisage and butlerage at London and delivered money from his master to those gathering horses for the army in 1513.[86] Southwell's more junior servants John Walpole and John Grace similarly kept books recording butlerage payments.[87] Richard Radclyff was clerk of the great wardrobe under Windsor and received funds from the exchequer for departmental expenditure, but also collected the conduct money due to Windsor's troops in 1513.[88] Edward Thwaites served as clerk of the council at Tournai under Poynings and visited Brussels to collect his master's pension from the Habsburgs.[89] Lovell's receivers John Thomson and John Carleton doubled up as the crown's receivers on estates where he was steward.[90] Edward Cheeseman had been an executor to Windsor's father in 1485 and by 1507–8 was acting as Windsor's deputy at the great wardrobe.[91] Kin, too, might provide natural deputies. At Walsall Lovell's deputy steward was William Hussey, husband of his niece Ursula.[92]

Wyatt's many posts drew his servants and kin into a web of service and when he became treasurer of the chamber all hands were called on deck. His son Thomas twice took £2,000 in cash to York to pay the king's army in the North.[93] His servant Robert Draper, who doubled up as yeoman of the king's jewels, carried money to Calais in September 1523, and twice took money to York.[94] John Trees, another of Wyatt's jewel house staff, took money to Ireland.[95] Richard Trees deputized for Wyatt at the chamber, as he had done for Heron, but also served under Wyatt at

[83] *LP* I, i. 1803(m. 4).   [84] *CPR 1494–1509*, 358–9, 420–1, 457, 507, 560, 608.
[85] *Notebook of Sir John Port*, xv–xvi; PRO, PROB11/17/21.
[86] *LP* I, ii. 2765, II, ii. 2054(2); PRO, E101/85/12.   [87] PRO, E101/84/16.
[88] BL, Egerton MS 3025, fo. 42v; PRO, E101/417/8, 419/8; *LP* I, ii. 2480.
[89] *LP* I, ii. 2767, II, i. 2223, II, ii, 3588, pp. 1512, 1514.
[90] PRO, SC6/Henry VIII/5730, m. 1r; *LP* I, i. 833(55).
[91] BL, Addl. MS 28623, fo. 8r; J. R. Hooker, 'Some Cautionary Notes on Henry VII's Household and Chamber "System"', Speculum 33 (1958), 73; J. C. Wedgwood, *History of Parliament: Biographies of the Members of the Commons House, 1439–1509* (London, 1936), 954.
[92] Staffordshire RO, D260/M/T/1/1a/8; D260/M/T/7/3.
[93] *LP* IV, i. 214.
[94] *LP* I, ii. 3343, III, i. 1114, ii, p. 1535, IV, i. 214, 2322, V. 980(6), 1370(15).
[95] *LP* III, ii. 2750.

the jewel house.[96] A similar osmosis drew Wyatt's official deputies into his private affairs. Richard Lee, his right-hand man at the jewel house, acted as a feoffee on his estates.[97] Thomas Kendall, his deputy constable at Tickhill Castle, and Thomas Strey, a Doncaster lawyer, who served as deputy steward there and was named supervisor of his will by Nicholas Boswell, bailiff at Conisbrough, were often among Wyatt's feoffees in Yorkshire and adjoining counties.[98] Service, friendship, and kinship joined hands as Kendall stood in for Wyatt's brother Richard at his installation as a canon of Southwell Minster.[99] The gratitude shown by the new men to those who worked for them was fully earned.

LOVELL'S RETAINERS

Henry needed loyal noblemen and gentlemen to retain followers who would serve under them in war and bolster their power in local communities. Yet he was wary of the way such retaining might provoke instability and took vigorous action to regulate it. He used Edward IV's statute against retaining of 1468 to prosecute those he did not trust and secured a stricter statute in 1504. The new men both implemented these policies—for example against Lord Bergavenny—and fell foul of them. Poynings had to seek a pardon for retaining offences in 1494 and in 1505 a Pevensey gentleman intimidated his neighbours by claiming, falsely, to be Guildford's retainer.[100] Meanwhile Henry issued licences to retain to those he trusted, who were to submit lists of their followers to his secretary. Such a list, dated 6 May 1508, survives for the retinue of Sir Thomas Lovell, providing a remarkable window on his ability to recruit and on the wider articulation of his local power.

The list names 1,365 men drawn from thirteen counties, ranging from 355 in Yorkshire, 197 in Nottinghamshire, and 149 in Staffordshire to seven in Northamptonshire and three in Sussex.[101] His household servants are not listed, presumably because under the statute no licence was needed to retain them. Hardly any of the retainers were drawn from his own manors, handfuls from East Harling or Ryhall. About one in six came from the Roos estates, but even these were heavily outnumbered by those recruited through stewardships he held under the crown, about one-third of the total, and a further one-fifth raised through monastic and episcopal stewardships, some of them admittedly those of Roos family foundations

[96] *LP* I, i. 19, 20, III, ii. 3471, IV, i. 366; D. Grummitt, 'Henry VII, Chamber Finance and the "New Monarchy": Some New Evidence', *HR* 72 (1999), 235–6; PRO, E179/141/109/9.

[97] PRO, E326/7885; *CAD*, iii. D476, D1308, vi. C7345.

[98] BI, Prob. Reg. 9, fo. 263r; Prob. Reg. 10, fos. 15r–16r, 104v–105r; Somerville, *Duchy*, i. 529; *CCR 1500–9*, 954; *Feet of Fines of the Tudor Period*, ed. F. Collins, 4 vols, YASRS 2, 5, 7, 8 (Wakefield, 1887–90), i. 24, 25, 29, 63; YAS, DD5/41, mm. 1v, 3v; PRO, CP25/2/25/159/38, 40.

[99] *Visitations and Memorials of Southwell Minster*, ed. A. F. Leach, CS n.s. 48 (London, 1891), 151.

[100] *CPR 1494–1509*, 6; PRO, KB9/439/5.

[101] Belvoir Castle, Addl. MS 97, calendared in *HMC Rutland*, iv. 559–66.

such as Rievaulx, Warter, and Bolton in Glendale.[102] The final fifth consisted of the personal followings of individual gentlemen and yeomen, some using their own offices on the crown estate to recruit, as Robert Hasilrigge seems to have done at Castle Donington in Leicestershire.[103]

The companies raised from the Roos lands resembled those one might expect in any aristocratic retinue. At the top were gentlemen-bailiffs such as James Carr of Thornton-in-Craven, Ralph Elwick of Seaton Ross, Thomas Heven of Wragby, or William Pye of Warsop and Eakring, generally able to equip themselves as demi-lances and have themselves buried in the chancels of their parish churches, taxed on around £40 in goods or £25 in lands in the subsidies of the 1520s and steady in their loyalty: Heven, Pye, and perhaps Elwick had served Lovell in 1492.[104] Beneath them served humbler estate officers like John Thompson, yeoman, bailiff of Freiston, equipped as a billman, taxed at £2 10s, and able to leave just over £30 in cash bequests, or substantial tenants like John Screven of Melton Ross or Ralph Calcraft of Bottesford, taxed on £20 to £30 in goods.[105] From Helmsley came comfortable yeomen and tanners.[106] Prosperous in a more unusual way was John Symondes of Cley next the Sea, owner of five ships and lands in eight townships, able to commission a pair of candlesticks for the church and a brass to mark his burial.[107] In the ranks stood husbandmen from Holt, Bottesford, or Thornton-in-Craven taxed on £1 or £2 or a little more in goods; parishioners from Chilham, Freiston, or Boston where the Roos arms shone down from the stained glass to remind them of their duty.[108]

Lovell's retaining through stewardships gave his retinue a more impressive grasp on local society in town and countryside alike. At Walsall his retainers included four past and three future mayors, seven churchwardens of the parish church, and the town's five richest inhabitants in the subsidy of 1525.[109] These and others, describing themselves variously as yeomen, loriners, spurriers, or chapmen, had significant property in the town and its fields and business interests that spread into the surrounding counties. They were tightly bound together as feoffees and witnesses in one

---

[102] W. Dugdale, *Monasticon Anglicanum*, ed. J. Caley et al., 6 vols in 8 (London, 1817–30), v. 277, vi (i), 297; E. Bateson et al. (eds), *A History of Northumberland*, 15 vols (Newcastle, 1893–1940), vii. 202–17.

[103] Somerville, *Duchy of Lancaster*, 574, 773; Leicestershire RO, 1D50/XII/8; HL, MS HAM Box 8 (3, 4); G. F. Farnham and A. H. Thompson, 'The Castle and Manor of Castle Donington', *Transactions of the Leicestershire Archaeological Society* 14 (1925), 65–6.

[104] *Early Tudor Craven: Subsidies and Assessments 1510–1547*, ed. R. W. Hoyle, YASRS 145 (Leeds, 1987), 4, 50, 61; BI, Prob. Reg. 9, fos. 64v, 349v; Prob. Reg. 10, fo. 77r–77v; PRO, E179/203/183, m. 15d; LA, LCC wills 1535–7, f. 42r–42v; CA, MS M16bis, fo. 57v*.

[105] P. Thompson, *The History and Antiquities of Boston* (Sleaford, 1997), 500; LAO, LCC Wills 1520–31, fos. 71r–73r; PRO, E179/133/108, m. 6r, 136/311, m. 1r.

[106] BI, Prob. Reg. 9, fos. 145r–145v, 232v; Prob. Reg. 11, fos. 15r, 29v, 163v, 334v.

[107] PRO, PROB11/16/20; Blomefield, *Norfolk*, ix. 379.

[108] G. F. Farnham, *Leicestershire Medieval Village Notes*, 6 vols (Leicester, 1929–33), vi. 204; *Early Tudor Craven*, 4, 50, 61; PRO, E179/150/236; C. R. Councer, 'The Medieval Painted Glass of Chilham', *AC* 58 (1945), 9, 11; Thompson, *Boston*, 192, 507, 518.

[109] F. W. Willmore, *A History of Walsall and its Neighbourhood* (Walsall, 1887), 171, 202, 262; 'Church-wardens' Accounts All Saints' Church Walsall 1462–1531', ed. G. P. Mander, *Collections for a History of Staffordshire*, 3rd ser. for 1928 (1930), 178, 182, 230–40; PRO, E179/177/97, m. 4.

another's transactions.[110] At Lichfield, similarly, fourteen of his forty-four retainers served in town office in the five years between 1494 and 1507 for which court rolls survive: four members of the Twelve, the bench of jurors at the borough court, eight tithingmen, and two borough constables.[111] At Wakefield nine of Lovell's sixty retainers had £10 or more in lands or goods in 1524, and another four had £3 or more in lands.[112] Again, this local elite stuck together as feoffees, executors, and witnesses to wills.[113] From the sprawling, booming clothmaking parish of Halifax, Lovell drew 142 men. Sixty-nine of them can be tentatively identified in the 123 lay wills surviving for Halifax between 1494 and 1532 and these and their subsidy assessments show the place many of them occupied amongst the circle of yeoman clothier families who dominated local life. They were tied up with one another as feoffees, executors, and witnesses; their younger brothers were the clergy serving the local chapels; some of them, like Brian Otes who supervised four wills between 1494 and 1509, were leaders even among the leaders.[114] Many of Lovell's men served as graves, constables, and jurors in the manor courts that presided over the affairs of Halifax, Wakefield, and the surrounding townships.[115]

It was the same further south. At Hitchin Lovell recruited seven of the nine richest men in the 1524 subsidy from an elite again tightly interwoven in property settlements.[116] At Thame, seven of Lovell's nineteen named retainers served as churchwardens, two bore lesser parochial office, and another was a tithingman. They included innholders, butchers, fishmongers, brewers, chandlers, and tailors, and some were of substantial means. In the course of a busy career John Goodwin managed to be churchwarden, guildwarden, constable, chandler, whitebread baker, fishmonger, and innkeeper while amassing the £60 worth of goods on which he was taxed in 1524, while Geoffrey Dormer, the biggest farmer in the fields around the town, was richer still.[117] At Henley ten of the twenty-four named retainers

---

[110] 'Church-wardens' Accounts', 236–9, 246–7; Staffordshire RO, D260/M/T/1/1a/2, 3, 6, 8–19, 26–9; D260/M/T/1/11a; D260/M/T/7/3, 4; D593/A/2/20/1, 10, 17, 26, 31, 43, 44, 47; D593/A/2/22/19; D593/B/1/26/6/31/9; D593/B/1/26/6/39/13; *Calendar of the Deeds and Documents belonging to the Corporation of Walsall*, ed. R. Sims (Walsall, 1882), 22–9; KUL, SP10, unnumbered deed of 24/4/1495; PRO, C1/593/23–5; LJRO, Wills PR1, p. 90; NUL, MiD3878–80.

[111] Staffordshire RO, D(W)1734/2/1/597, mm. 15–25; *The Victoria History of the County of Stafford*, ed. W. Page et al., 14 vols (London, 1908–), xiv. 74.

[112] 'A Subsidy Roll for the Wapentake of Agbrigg and Morley of the 15th Henry VIII', ed. J. J. Cartwright, *Yorkshire Archaeological Journal* 2 (1873), 52–3.

[113] BI, Prob. Reg. 8, fos. 56r–56v, 99r; Prob. Reg. 9, fos. 49v, 60v, 95r, 206r; Prob. Reg. 11, fos. 82r, 88v, 646r.

[114] R. B. Smith, *Land and Politics in the England of Henry VIII: The West Riding of Yorkshire, 1530–1546* (Oxford, 1970), 8, 24–5, 147–8; *Testamenta Eboracensia*, ed. J. Raine and J. W. Clay, 6 vols, Surtees Society 4, 30, 45, 53, 79, 106 (London, 1836–1902), iv. 251; *Halifax Wills*, ed. J. W. Clay and E. W. Crossley (Halifax, 1904), 27–84, 184–6; 'Subsidy Roll for the Wapentake of Agbrigg and Morley', 57–60.

[115] YAS, MD225/1/224–34.

[116] PRO, E179/120/110; Hertfordshire Archives, Miscellaneous vol. X/67125; PRO, PROB11/17/20, 14/22, 25/31.

[117] F. G. Lee, *The History, Description and Antiquities of the Prebendal Church of the Blessed Virgin Mary of Thame* (London, 1883), *passim*; Bodl. MS dd Bertie c16/20, 22–4; PRO, E179/161/198; *The Victoria History of the County of Oxford*, ed. W. Page et al., 17 vols (London, 1907–), vii. 190.

were part of the thirty-strong circle of burgesses, most from its richer, office-holding section, some of them taxed on £40 or £80 in goods. John Wyllys, warden of the town in 1508 as he had been for seven of the past twelve years, did not serve in person, but did provide the service of two, presumably younger, men.[118] Only at Newark did the borough elite, for reasons which are not apparent, seem to hold themselves back from Lovell's service.[119]

In three areas Lovell's retinue suggests that his influence spread more widely still. In Nottinghamshire, his recruitment rested on Roos estates, urban and monastic stewardships, and the constableship of Nottingham Castle and associated keepership of Sherwood Forest. In military terms, the foresters of Sherwood, expert archers, may have been particularly significant, and five of them served in both 1492 and 1508, a higher rate of retention than in any other contingent.[120] But the retinue was also politically weighty. Three Nottinghamshire JPs, Henry Boson, Thomas Meryng, and James Savage, two of them very active at quarter sessions, signed up to serve in person at the head of their tenants. So did Humphrey Hercy and Simon Digby, who would soon join the bench. These five furnished two sheriffs and two escheators between 1491 and 1519.[121] They and other esquires who led sub-contingents, such as Thomas Leek and Roland Digby, served on commissions to assess and collect taxes or find concealed lands.[122] Hugh Annesley, Thomas Leek, Humphrey Hercy, and William Wareyn, clerk of the peace, served under Lovell in the administration of the forest, as did Humphrey Hercy in the stewardship of Mansfield.[123] These were established members of the gentry, listed among the county's leading families, their landed incomes running from £20 to £100 and beyond, able to bequeath hundreds of pounds in cash, equipped to animate Lovell's local rule.[124]

In Hertfordshire, Lovell had some land, and there was one Roos manor, but the keys to his power were the stewardships of Hitchin and Standon and of the Abbey of St Albans. The liberty of St Albans had its own commission of the peace, on which William Skipwith, John Stepneth, bailiff of the liberty, and Richard Goodere and John Purse, each of whom raised men for Lovell, regularly sat.[125] With the

---

[118] R. Peberdy, 'The Economy, Society and Government of a Small Town in late medieval England: a study of Henley-on-Thames from c1300 to c1540', University of Leicester Ph.D. Thesis (1994), 198–249; *Henley Borough Records: Assembly Books i–iv, 1395–1543*, ed. P. M. Briers, ORS 41 (Oxford, 1960); PRO, E179/161/195.

[119] C. Brown, *A History of Newark-on-Trent*, 2 vols (Newark, 1904–7), i, *passim*; BL, Egerton Roll 8447.

[120] CA, MS M16bis, fos. 57v*–58r*.

[121] *CPR 1494–1509*, 653–54; *LP* I, ii, p. 1542; PRO, KB9/413/34, 417/41, 425/6, 428/22, 436/45, 437/17, 438/15, 438/85, 440/22, 441/18, 442/13, 442/106, 443/46, 446/18, 449/2, 464/60, 470/41, 477/6, 28, 496/52; *List of Sheriffs*, 104; *List of Escheators*, 113.

[122] 12 Henry VII c. 13; *CPR 1494–1509*, 420; *Abstracts of the Inquisitiones post mortem relating to Nottinghamshire*, i, ed. W. Phillimore, Thoroton Society Record Series 3 (Nottingham, 1905), 34; PRO, E36/285, m. 56r.

[123] Nottinghamshire Archives, DD/2P/27/9; NUL, Mi6/175/13; *LP* Addenda, i. 252.

[124] HL, MS 19959; PRO, E179/159/124, m. 5; *Testamenta Eboracensia*, v. 25n; *Inquisitiones post Mortem Nottinghamshire*, i. 74–77, 108–15; Newark Parish Church, Magnus Charity Deeds I/65 (NRA report).

[125] *LP* I, i. 438(3 m. 6), ii. 2684(41); PRO, KB9/386/26, 396/21, 408/54, 437/94, 442/79, 444/9, 446/109, 428/23, 480/69, 485/23, 25.

exception of Skipwith, an esquire with lands in four counties and a newly granted coat of arms who was equally busy on the main county bench, these men could not match their Nottinghamshire equivalents for wealth or standing, but in the little world of the liberty they carried genuine weight.[126] Several of them were members of the abbey's confraternity for leading townsfolk.[127] Some of these retainers and abbey tenants had interests that spread beyond the county, like Thomas Roos, the surgeon of St Albans and London.[128] Some had a deeper relationship with Lovell, like Ralph Buckberd, who used him as a feoffee in 1514.[129]

In Oxfordshire, there were no Roos estates, and Lovell held only one manor, but his retinue was larger than in any county except Yorkshire. He combined the stewardship of towns such as Thame and Henley with that of the duchy of Cornwall honour of Wallingford and those of other south Oxfordshire estates such as those of St George's College, Windsor. As in Nottinghamshire, this drew into his service the administrative gentry who served as his deputies and colleagues in local offices, men like John Daunce, Henry Reynolds, Hugh Shirley, and William Young, who led contingents of their own and whom he in turn promoted at Lincoln's Inn, at the exchequer, and in the wards office.[130] Like their counterparts further north, they took on much of the everyday work of local government. Young was escheator of Oxfordshire and Berkshire continuously from 1505 to 1510 and again in 1513–14, three other members of the retinue served as escheators in these counties between 1492 and 1515, and a fourth as sheriff.[131] William Young, Edmund Bury, Henry Reynolds, and Hugh Shirley were regularly named to the investigative commissions of Henry VII's last years.[132] Bury was an active Oxfordshire JP and became recorder of Oxford while Daunce and Young joined the bench there or in Berkshire after 1509.[133]

In the richer southern countryside, Lovell's office-holding also tied him to scores of lesser gentlemen and yeomen who served alone or with one or two followers,

---

[126] PRO, KB9/426/72, 427/13, 430/47, 431/24, 106, 433/61, 446/73, 124, 136, 448/123; E179/120/114; HL, MS 19959; Hertfordshire Archives, 2AR, fos. 139r–139v, 237r–237v; *A Catalogue of Manuscripts in the College of Arms: Collections*, i, ed. L. Campbell and F. Steer (London, 1988), 347.
[127] BL, MS Cotton Nero DVII, fos. 78r–79v; J. G. Clark, 'Monastic Confraternity in Medieval England: the Evidence from the St Albans Abbey *Liber Benefactorum*', in E. Jamroziak and J. Burton (eds), *Religious and Laity in Western Europe 1000–1400: Interaction, Negotiation and Power* (Turnhout, 2006), 329–30.
[128] PRO, PROB11/23/11.
[129] PRO, SC2/178/5, mm. 1–3; *Herts Genealogist and Antiquary*, ed. W. Brigg, 3 vols (St Albans, 1896–8), i. 77.
[130] PRO, SC6/Hen VII/1091, mm. 2r–4r; SC6/Hen VIII/5978; Bodl. MS dd Bertie c24/1; Windsor, The Aerary, MS XV.49.11; *LP* I, i, 190 (28), 438 (3 m. 7); *CPR 1494–1509*, 312, 619; *The Records of the Honourable Society of Lincoln's Inn: The Black Books*, ed. W. P. Baildon and R. Roxburgh, 5 vols (London, 1897–1968), i. 167; J. C. Sainty, *Officers of the Exchequer*, List and Index Society Special Series 18 (London, 1983), 96; *LP*, I, ii. 2222(12).
[131] *List of Escheators*, 125; *List of Sheriffs*, 108; D. A. Luckett, 'Henry VII and the South-Western Escheators', in B. Thompson (ed.), *The Reign of Henry VII* (Stamford, 1995), 60–1.
[132] *CPR 1494–1509*, 421, 437, 458, 491, 507, 582, 593, 608.
[133] PRO, KB9/440/44, 442/38, 466/73; *CPR 1494–1509*, 655; *LP* I, ii, pp. 1533–4, 1542; *Selections from the Records of the City of Oxford*, ed. W. H. Turner (Oxford, 1880), 5.

but who were substantial men in their villages. There were bailiffs and demesne farmers from each set of estates: Thomas Skydmore from Watlington and Edmund Mason from Beckley, William Bigger from Hook Norton and Thomas Calcote from Aston-Tirrold, Thomas Boldrey from Great Haseley and Edmund Gadbury from Pyrton.[134] There were a number who were the richest or second richest tax-payers in their villages in 1524, some very prosperous like Thomas Boldrey with his £133 6s 8d in goods or Humphrey Elmes of Bolney with his £40 in lands, others more modest but still thriving like Richard Grymsby and John Petty of Tetsworth, William Tanner of Bix Gibben, Richard Dawbery of Bensington, or Edmund Whitehill of Buckland, each taxed on between £16 and £40 in goods.[135]

The local influence exercised by such men was evident in many ways. Some served the crown in minor but responsible posts, eleven as subsidy collectors in 1523–4.[136] Others held manorial offices: Richard Blackhall of Nettlebed was woodward at Pyrton.[137] Some were named umpires or arbitrators in disputes.[138] Some made their mark through philanthropy: Richard Beauforest, the richest man in Dorchester in 1524, bought the abbey church for the townsfolk, while Christopher Swan, draper, grazier, clothmaker, and yeoman of Abingdon, left his house to St Nicholas's church.[139] Some made their impression in a more aggressive way, as enclosers and large-scale sheep farmers, following the example of such gentlemen of the retinue as Henry Reynolds, Edmund Bury, and William Cottesmore.[140] Leading yeomen and gentry alike were bound into circles of feoffees, witnesses, and executors which gave the retinue internal cohesion.[141]

Such penetration into local society was vital not only to the military security of Henry's regime, but also to its judicial ambition and fiscal aggression. The Oxfordshire retainers, like those elsewhere, were equipped to fight, as the weaponry mentioned in their wills and in muster books shows.[142] But they also sat on juries. Eight inquisition post mortem juries gathered by William Young at Dorchester, Oxford, Crowmarsh, and Henley in 1505–7 featured nineteen or

[134] PRO, SC6/Hen VII/1091; KB9/440/14; C54/388, m. 7; DCRO, DC Roll 211, m. 11; Windsor, The Aerary, MSS XV.48.58, XV.49.10, XV.49.15.
[135] PRO, E179/161/195, 198; E315/464, fo. 73r.
[136] PRO, E179/161/198.
[137] Bodl. MS Top. Oxon. c207, fos. 44r, 46r, 47r.
[138] *Registrum Cancellarii*, 118, 183, 186, 188; *Records of the City of Oxford*, 11.
[139] *The Victoria History of the County of Oxford*, ed. W. Page et al., 17 vols (London, 1907–), vii. 47, 59; A. E. Preston, *The Church and Parish of St Nicholas Abingdon*, OHS 99 (Oxford, 1935), 80–1.
[140] *The Domesday of Inclosures, 1517–1518*, ed. I. S. Leadam, 2 vols (London, 1897), i. 145; *VCH Oxfordshire*, v. 103, 243, vi. 164, vii. 13, 47, 190, viii. 28, 268–69; *Some Oxfordshire Wills proved in the Prerogative Court of Canterbury, 1393–1510*, ed. J. R. H. Weaver and A. Beardwood, ORS 39 (Oxford, 1958), 88; OHC, MS Wills Oxon. 178, ff. 96r–97v, 135v–136v; PRO, C1/142/39, 317/23.
[141] Bodl. MSS dd Barrett a2 (i18), (i20), (k2), (k6), (m12), (o1); MS Oxon. ch. 274; Brasenose College, Oxford, Muniments Faringdon 34, Wheatley 12 (NRA report); Merton College, Oxford, MCR 887, 3342; OHC, DD Par Great Haseley c4/2; MS Wills Oxon. 178, fo. 45v; *Oxfordshire Wills*, 88, 91–3.
[142] *Oxfordshire Wills*, 81; *Henley Borough Records*, 118, 167; PRO, E315/464, fo. 72v; PROB11/16/35; BI, Prob. Reg. 9, fo. 232v; Prob. Reg. 11, fos. 312v, 334v; *Halifax Wills*, 72–3; LJRO, will of John Slanye, 9 May 1541; Northamptonshire RO, Archdeaconry Court, First Series Wills, vol. B, Will of Henry Bellers, 4 October 1521.

twenty of Lovell's retainers, seven of whom also sat at quarter sessions in 1504–6.[143] Altogether some fifty-four of the retinue sat at quarter sessions, inquisitions post mortem, coroner's inquests, or before commissioners of sewers in Oxfordshire in the years 1499–1525, and at least four more on Berkshire juries in the same period. The assiduous John Richardson appeared at least thirteen times between 1502 and 1508. Some panels were as packed as any in Henry VII's dreams: at one hearing into concealed lands at Henley, Edmund Bury, Henry Reynolds, and two other commissioners questioned a jury of twelve, only three of whom were not Lovell's men.[144] With less intensity, the same pattern can be found elsewhere, in Hertfordshire, Lincolnshire, Nottinghamshire, Staffordshire, and Yorkshire.[145]

What long-term loyalties were fostered is hard to say. Manorial court and quarter sessions presentments suggest that those retained by Lovell were not transformed overnight into law-abiding Tudor subjects, though in several cases members of the retinue were prepared to return indictments against other members.[146] That some deeper loyalty to the king's purposes may have been planted is hinted at by events in Thame in 1537. Thomas Striblehill, one of Lovell's retainers in 1508, challenged the vicar when he held a solemn feast on the banned festival of St Thomas Becket. 'I think thou art of the Northern sect', he told him, 'thou wouldst rule the King's Highness and not to be ruled.' John Benet, his fellow from 1508, backed him; Sir John Daunce, organizer of Lovell's Thame contingent and his successor as steward, was one of the two justices to whom they reported the confrontation.[147]

EMPSON AND DUDLEY

So far as is known, no comparable list survives for any other licensed retinue, but a very different source enables us to sketch the outlines of two others. The charges against Empson and Dudley in 1509 named those to whom they had written that spring to prepare men and send them to London in the event of Henry's death, allegedly with the aim of traitorously governing the new king and his council. In Empson's case, in particular, they went into great detail about the process of retaining,

[143] PRO, C142/19/40; C142/20/35, 122, 150; C142/22/38; C142/23/266; E150/783/11, 13; KB9/436/72; KB9/439/32; KB9/440/14, 44, 46; KB9/442/38.

[144] PRO, C142/16/28; C142/20/42; C142/24/16; C142/28/36; C142/29/41, 64, 121; C142/30/92; KB9/422/23; KB9/426/12; KB9/427/1; KB9/434/26; KB9/435/38; KB9/446/51; KB9/447/22, 24; KB9/453/69; KB9/459/51; KB9/461/17; KB9/464/95; KB9/466/24; KB9/467/4; KB9/468/2; KB9/473/32; KB9/475/46; KB9/479/27–8; KB9/480/42; KB9/482/27; KB9/489/44; KB9/491/10; KB9/495/59; KB9/497/51, 90.

[145] PRO, C142/16/90, 18/66, 25/114, 119, 30/103; DL3/23/R6; KB9/429/11, 457/47, 461/31–2, 462/25, 467/24, 473/55, 475/35, 476/9, 488/41–2; *Calendar of Nottinghamshire Coroners' Inquests 1485–1558*, ed. R. F. Hunnisett, Thoroton Society Record Series 25 (Nottingham, 1966), 12, 19, 20, 24.

[146] PRO, KB9/439/17, 32; KB9/440/14, 43; LA, Misc. Dep. 511/1; FL Deeds 224.

[147] *LP* XII, ii., 357; *Chapter Acts of the Cathedral Church of St Mary of Lincoln, AD 1520–1536*, ed. R. E. G. Cole, Lincoln RS 12 (Lincoln, 1915), 48.

coordinated by his son Thomas from the family seat at Easton Neston. He wrote to four south Northamptonshire gentlemen and three Towcester yeomen and asked them to be ready at one hour's summons. At least one of the gentlemen then retained some of his neighbours to serve Empson, giving them each a penny. When the time came to ride to London, Thomas set off with a gentleman from Kislingbury and seven yeomen and a chaplain from Byfield, Caldecote, Easton Neston, Heathencote, Pury End, Stony Stratford, and Wood Burcote, all within fifteen miles of Towcester and most much closer. John Thorne of Abthorpe, three miles west of Towcester, one of the four gentlemen to whom Thomas had written, left home with three Abthorpe yeomen and a weaver, while another, Robert Saunders of Stoneton, just over the Warwickshire border, brought one servant with him.[148] A number of these men already had links with Empson. Henry Barker and Benedict Davey of Towcester and John Thorne of Abthorpe served as his attorneys or feoffees.[149] Davey, who led an advance party ahead of Thomas Empson and was denounced in 1509 as Sir Richard's 'knave' and 'ready handmaid' in his exactions, had used Sir Richard as his surety when appointed bailiff of Kenilworth Castle in 1492.[150]

Dudley's retinue was, as we might expect, grander, featuring several justices of the peace and sheriffs and even a peer. It was described in less detail, but clearly blended his landed interests in Sussex with his kinship connections in the West Midlands, the interest he had acquired in Wiltshire by buying the wardship of Lord Stourton's heir for the marriage of his daughter, and the unpopular team of servants and associates who helped him enforce the king's prerogatives.[151] The retinues Henry had licensed his trusted servants to retain were intended to be available for use against disorder as well as for external war, 'on any urgent occasion' as an Italian observer put it.[152] At one point between 1504 and 1507 the king instructed Thomas, Lord Darcy, to 'take the musters and put in readiness' some of the men he had prepared when Henry wrote to him 'for the retaining of such persons as...you might conveniently make in those parts to serve us in our wars', in order to assist Archbishop Savage of York against riots in Knaresborough Forest.[153] It was ironic that it was the summoning of such retinues to preserve good order at the accession of his son that became the means to destroy two of Henry's most dedicated servants. But even in their ruin the painstaking construction of power involved in the new men's retinues was made manifest.

[148] *Third Report of the Deputy Keeper*, App. ii. 227–8.
[149] Northamptonshire RO, MTD/D/13/2; *CCR 1500–9*, 708.
[150] *The Great Chronicle of London*, ed. A. H. Thomas and I. D. Thornley (London, 1938), 345; Northants RO, MTD/D/13/2; Somerville, *Duchy of Lancaster*, 562.
[151] *Third Report of the Deputy Keeper of the Public Records* (London, 1842), App. ii. 226; Bindoff, *Commons*, ii. 18, 486–7, 543–4; Wedgwood, *Commons*, 600, 752; *CP*, iv. 480–1, xi. 303, xii. 305–6; *CCR 1500–9*, 885; *CPR 1494–1509*, 589, 627; *LP* I, i. 11 (10), 158 (74), 438 (3, m. 9); *Great Chronicle*, 337, 339, 365; PRO, E36/214, fos. 78v, 93r, 147r.
[152] *A Relation, or rather a True Account, of the Island of England*, ed. C. A. Sneyd, CS o.s. 37 (London, 1847), 39.
[153] PRO, SC1/58/53.

The followings of the new men, then, looked like the noble affinities of their day in that the staffs of households and estate administrations formed their core, in that relations between landlords and tenants and estate officers underpinned their military recruitment, and in that they looked most able to steer the government of a county when, like Lovell's following in Nottinghamshire, they numbered some active justices of the peace from established gentry families. They also displayed the horizontal connections of mutual support between servants, officers, and retainers which were encouraged by vertical ties of service to the lord and helped in turn to strengthen those vertical ties.[154] They were less ambitious than the greatest lordly affinities, for the new men did not have the personal weight to draw the leading knightly families of an area into their service, as the earls of Oxford or Derby did. In any case under the Yorkists and Henry VII more of the county gentry, perhaps disillusioned by the noble factionalism of the Wars of the Roses, were entering into direct relations with the king through the court and the crown lands. But they were recognizable affinities none the less.[155]

In other ways they were distinctive. They echoed the followings of Edward IV's designated regional magnates in the interpenetration of royal service and loyalty to a patron and in the extension of the landed base from which they retained tenants well beyond their own lands through stewardships and other arrangements.[156] They differed from them, however, in the way in which the new men's responsibilities in royal administration drew lesser officials into their followings and in which their engagement with the inns of court drew in fellow lawyers, characteristically so at a time when lawyers dominated many areas of administration, public and private, and the university-educated laymen who would cluster around a Cromwell or a Cecil were not yet numerous.[157] Their blurring of private and government service foreshadowed that in Cromwell's household, but they were also characteristic of Henry's reign. Lovell's and Dudley's affinities in particular looked deftly shaped not just to raise troops and to spread their masters' influence, but also to impose royal fiscal and judicial policy.

[154] Hicks, *Bastard Feudalism*, 43–109, 137–200; C. Carpenter, *Locality and Polity: A Study of Warwickshire Landed Society, 1401–1499* (Cambridge, 1992), 615–44.
[155] S. J. Gunn, *Early Tudor Government 1485–1558* (Basingstoke, 1995), 28–48; C. Carpenter, *The Wars of the Roses: Politics and the Constitution in England, c.1437–1509* (Cambridge, 1997), 262–5; J. Ross, *John de Vere, Thirteenth Earl of Oxford (1442–1513): 'The Foremost Man of the Kingdom'* (Woodbridge, 2011), 181–202; S. Cunningham, *Henry VII* (London, 2007), 180–6.
[156] Horrox, *Richard III*, 27–88; M. A. Hicks, 'Lord Hastings' Indentured Retainers?', in M. A. Hicks, *Richard III and His Rivals: Magnates and their Motives in the Wars of the Roses* (London, 1991), 229–46.
[157] E. W. Ives, *The Common Lawyers of Pre-Reformation England. Thomas Kebell: A Case Study* (Cambridge, 1983), 9–16; G. R. Elton, *Reform and Renewal: Thomas Cromwell and the Common Weal* (Cambridge, 1973), 18–31, 38–65; Barnett, *Place, Profit, and Power*, 12–13.

9

Church and churchmen

The new men engaged with the church in a wide variety of ways. As fiscal officers and lawyers they taxed its revenues for the king and pinned back its jurisdiction. Their personal piety we shall consider later. But the church and its clergy also formed part of the structures of public life in which they exercised power and patronage. Dudley wanted the church to live up to the standards it professed, avoiding worldliness, vainglory, profiteering, simony, pluralism, and nepotism, rebuking sin, and practising charity.[1] He wanted the king to 'support and maintain his church and the true faith thereof in all rights as far as in him lieth'.[2] He wanted the laity to take their religion seriously, not allowing their 'delectation in worldly prosperity' to cause their thoughts to wander at matins or mass.[3] Yet he apparently saw no contrast between these ideals—which he shared with reform-minded churchmen like John Colet, dean of St Paul's, and his friend John Yonge, future warden of New College, Oxford—and the extraction of huge sums of money from churchmen on the king's behalf.[4] Clearly the new men's relationship with the church was complex.

DUDLEY AND LOVELL AS CLERICAL PATRONS

At the individual level, the new men's most direct impact came through the appointment of clergy in parishes where they held advowsons or rights of presentation. These often came with purchased or inherited manors, but there were other ways to obtain them. The king granted his rights to present to livings to favoured individuals. Lovell got one at St Stephen's, Westminster, in 1489, one at St George's, Windsor, in 1490, and one at Ampthill under Henry VIII.[5] Peers and gentlemen might surrender their rights to present for one occasion to a patron they wished to oblige, a Lovell in the 1490s, a Wyatt in the 1520s.[6] Wardships, too, for Empson, Hussey, Southwell,

---

[1] E. Dudley, *The Tree of Commonwealth*, ed. D. M. Brodie (Cambridge, 1948), 24–26, 32, 43, 57, 65–6, 73–5, 77, 103.

[2] Dudley, *Tree*, 24.   [3] Dudley, *Tree*, 78

[4] S. J. Gunn, 'Edmund Dudley and the Church', *Journal of Ecclesiastical History* 51 (2000), 511–12, 517–18, 520–1; A. B. Emden, *A Biographical Register of the University of Cambridge to AD 1500* (Cambridge, 1963), iii. 2135–7.

[5] *CPR 1485–94*, 266, 332; LA, Bishop's Register 27, fo. 258v.

[6] NRO, Bishop's Register 12, fo. 183r; Bishop's Register 14, fo. 198r; LA, Bishop's Register 23, fo. 99r–99v; LJRO, B/A/1/14i, fo. 62v; BI, Bishop's Register 27, fo. 88v; Devon RO, Chanter 14, fo. 32r; Cheshire RO, DCH/C/442.

Windsor, and Wyatt, provided the opportunity to present clergy to livings.[7] So did executorships or tenure as feoffees on the estates of those recently deceased.[8] However obtained, advowsons were valuable and worth litigating over. Lovell recovered that at Thornton-in-Craven in common pleas and fought a long king's bench suit over that at Buckland in Hertfordshire.[9] Poynings failed to establish his claim to present to Milton Keynes in an enquiry set up by the bishop of Lincoln and faced protracted common pleas litigation over the advowson at Hockwold cum Wilton.[10] Wyatt lost that at Weston in Nottinghamshire in common pleas, but Windsor won a suit before the archbishop of Canterbury's court over that at Midley, Kent.[11]

Dudley had decided views on clerical promotion. Bishops should take the lead in advancing clergy 'such as be virtuous and cunning and not given to fleshliness' and should 'search in the universities' to find them. They should encourage other patrons in their dioceses to do the same. Everyone, led by the king, should work to reverse not only the growth of pluralism but also the trend by which, allegedly, increasing numbers of parish livings had been appropriated to support monastic houses.[12] Yet Dudley did not live up to these prescriptions himself, presenting a pluralist civil lawyer in subdeacon's orders to one rectory in 1500 and the head of a house of Austin canons to two others in 1502 and 1506, the second time using an advowson granted to him by the prior and canons themselves, an arrangement sufficiently corrupt to require a special papal dispensation.[13] But how typical was he?

Lovell was the mightiest clerical patron among the new men, by dint of his longevity and of his control of the Roos estates. In all he made over fifty presentations between 1487 and 1524, mostly as sole patron, but occasionally acting in concert with others. In some respects, he matched Dudley's prescriptions well. He promoted an unusually high proportion of graduates or clergy studying at university, accounting for nearly half his presentations, apparently with a special liking for New College, Oxford, men.[14] Some at least, to judge from their wills or the

[7] WSHC, Bishop's Register Audley, fos. 30r, 36r; LA, Bishop's Register 27, fos. 6v, 47r–47v; Worcestershire Archives, BA2648/8(i), Ref:b716:093, 226; NRO, Bishop's Register 12, fo. 180r; Bishop's Register 13B, fo. 78r.

[8] Hampshire RO, 21M65/A1/19, fo. 5v; LJRO, B/A/1/14(i), fo. 8r; 'Ely Episcopal Registers', *Ely Diocesan Remembrancer* 312 (1911), 88.

[9] *The Register of Thomas Rotherham, Archbishop of York 1480–1500*, ed. E. E. Barker, CYS 69 (1976), 125; PRO, CP40/925, m. 265r; *The Victoria History of the County of Hertford*, ed. W. Page, 5 vols (London, 1902–23), iv. 48.

[10] LA, Bishop's Register 23, fos. 323v–324r; PRO, CP40/937, m. 413r–413v, 962, m. 547r, 965, m. 346r.

[11] BI, Bishop's Register 27, fo. 11v; LPL, Canterbury Register Warham II, fos. 386r–387v.

[12] Dudley, *Tree*, 26, 63.

[13] LA, Bishop's Register 23, fos. 319v–320r; Emden, *Oxford to 1500*, i. 115–16; Hampshire RO, 21M65/A1/17, fo. 1v; WSHC, Bishop's Register Audley fo. 27v; *CEPR*, xviii. 207–9, 289.

[14] Emden, *Oxford to 1500*, i. 84, 354, ii. 892, iii. 1932; A. B. Emden, *A Biographical Register of the University of Cambridge to AD 1500* (Cambridge, 1963), 132, 139, 582–3, 649; S. L. Ollard, *Fasti Wyndesorienses* (Windsor, 1950), 137; BI, Bishop's Register 25, fo. 63v; LMA, MS 9531/8, fo. 4r; Hampshire RO, 21M65/A1/19, fo. 5v; LA, Bishop's Register 23, fos. 295v, 306v, 373v, 377r; Bishop's Register 27, fo. 192r; LPL, Canterbury Register Warham II, fo. 332v; NRO, Bishop's Register 12, fos. 125r, 191v; Bishop's Register 13B, fo. 64v; *Register of Thomas Rotherham*, 166.

shape of their careers, were taking their university training back into pastoral work in the areas where they had grown up, while others settled down as rectors of large city parishes even after hectic careers as pluralist royal chaplains.[15] The choice of preacher for Lovell's funeral, Dr William Goodrich, was symbolic of his commitments: an Oxford theologian with eighteen years' study of logic, philosophy and theology, three times university preacher, and rector for over twenty years of a London church patronized by the newly powerful merchant taylors.[16] Many of Lovell's non-graduate appointees are mere names in a register, but some seem to have made committed parish clergy.[17] Richard Pemberton stayed in post thirty-one years at Cholderton in Wiltshire, requested burial there, and left sixty sheep to the church when he died and grain to his poor parishioners.[18] Others settled down for as long as thirty-six years, came from local families, or were at least found to be resident when bishops investigated.[19] One did have financial disputes with his flock, but agreed to satisfy them when the bishop's court stepped in.[20]

Further investigation suggests, however, that much of Lovell's patronage met needs other than those of the parishioners involved. Like Dudley, he sometimes appointed regular clergy to parochial livings, despite the wide resentment evident against the practice in episcopal visitations.[21] Like Dudley, he also promoted pluralist graduates who used their benefices to fund their work as royal or episcopal administrators, men like Dr Thomas Perte, the archbishop of Canterbury's commissary-general, Dr William Thornburgh, who played the same role in the diocese of Ely, or Simon Stalworth, sub-dean of Lincoln Cathedral and clerk of the hanaper of chancery; his most valuable living, at Bottesford in Lincolnshire, went first to Stalworth, then to Perte, whom he

[15] Hampshire RO, 21M65/A1/19, fo. 5v; Wills B1524/7, B1534/2, 1534/3; Emden, *Oxford to 1500*, i. 84; Ollard, *Fasti Wyndesorienses*, 67; A. B. Emden, *A Biographical Register of the University of Cambridge to AD 1500* (Cambridge, 1963), 82; PRO, PROB11/15/34; LA, Bishop's Register 27, fo. 110v; J. Venn and J. A. Venn, *Alumni Cantabrigienses*, 10 vols (Cambridge, 1922–54), iv. 98; J. I. Catto, 'Theology after Wycliffism', in J. I. Catto and T. A. R. Evans (eds), *History of the University of Oxford*. ii: *Late Medieval Oxford* (Oxford, 1992), 263–80.

[16] W. Robinson, *The History and Antiquities of Enfield, in the County of Middlesex*, 2 vols (London, 1823), i. 137; Emden, *Oxford to 1500*, ii. 790; M. Davies and A. Saunders, *The History of the Merchant Taylors' Company* (Leeds, 2004), 25.

[17] BI, Bishop's Register 26, fo. 48v; LMA, MS 9531/9, fo. 41v; LJRO, B/A/1/13, fo. 155r; LA, Bishop's Register 22, fos. 149r, 154r; LPL, Canterbury Register Warham II, fos. 348v, 360r, NRO, Bishop's Register 12, fo. 191v; Bishop's Register 13B, fo. 64r; *Register of Thomas Rotherham*, 125.

[18] WSHC, Bishop's Register Blythe, fo. 13v; Bishop's Register Campeggio, fo. 4v; PRO, PROB11/22/1.

[19] BI, Bishop's Register 26, fo. 46v; Bishop's Register 29, fo. 42r; LA, Bishop's Register 22, fo. 160v; Bishop's Register 23, fo. 97r; Bishop's Register 27, fos. 22r, 23r; LCC wills 1535–7, 94; NRO, Bishop's Register 13B, fo. 91r; Bishop's Register 14B, fo. 14v; Bishop's Register 15, fo. 6v; *VE*, v. 182; *Visitations in the Diocese of Lincoln 1517–1531*, ed. A. H. Thompson, 3 vols, Lincoln RS 33, 35, 37 (Lincoln, 1940–7), i. 79.

[20] LA, Bishop's Register 23, fo. 382r; *Visitations in the Diocese of Lincoln*, i. 1; *An Episcopal Court Book for the Diocese of Lincoln 1514–1520*, ed. M. Bowker, Lincoln RS 61 (Lincoln, 1967), 101.

[21] P. Marshall, *The Catholic Priesthood and the English Reformation* (Oxford, 1994), 184.

named as supervisor of his will.[22] Dudley berated those who promoted 'young scholars of x or xii years of age right near of your blood', and here Lovell offended in the case of Edward Chamberlain. Apparently a relative, and armed with a dispensation to hold benefices as a scholar of minor age, he received a vicarage and two rectories inside seven years from Lovell; he did at least use them to attain an MA.[23] The use of benefices to support those in education was accepted practice. Bridget Hogan, wife of the king's master cook, had her eye on Wyatt's living at Ashill in Norfolk, half a mile from her home, to support one of her sons at school when it became vacant in 1531.[24] But Dudley, in his more idealistic moments, would have expected better.

Dudley did not tackle the issue of household chaplains, but the parliament of 1529 did, limiting the numbers that might be maintained by patrons of different ranks.[25] Here, Lovell was conspicuous in his use of livings in distant parts of the country to fund the religious life of his household at Enfield and East Harling. His will left £6 13s 4d to each of four beneficed chaplains and two unbeneficed.[26] They were a close-knit group. William Dengayne, rector of Adderley in Shropshire, made his will at Enfield in 1509, requesting burial in St Andrew's, Enfield, and naming Nicholas Kirkby and Gerard Michaels his executors and Richard Jekell a witness.[27] Dengayne owed Adderley to Lovell's patronage, as Jekell owed the rectory of Holt in Norfolk, and Kirkby those of Woolley, Buckland, and Eakring in Huntingdonshire, Hertfordshire, and Nottinghamshire.[28] Michaels was still one of Lovell's chaplains and oldest servants when his master made his will.[29] Of the other chaplains named there, George Wyndham was given the rectory at Kirby Misperton in Yorkshire in 1514, Cuthbert Owrys that at Gunby in Lincolnshire in 1521, and Henry Smythe that at Braunston in Northamptonshire in 1524.[30] Other sources make mention of yet more men who passed through Lovell's service as chaplains and others to whom he gave multiple benefices or who were found absent at visitation probably did the same.[31] The parish churches at Enfield and East Harling, near his homes, were the final elements of Lovell's system. In 1501 he gave the

[22] LA, Bishop's Register 22, fo. 215r; Bishop's Register 23, fo. 267r; Bishop's Register 25, fo. 46r; *The Register of Thomas Langton, Bishop of Salisbury, 1485–93*, ed. D. P. Wright, CYS 74 (Oxford, 1985), 41; Emden, *Cambridge*, 451, 584; Emden, *Oxford to 1500*, iii. 1753; *CEPR*, xv. 244, xix. 1049, 1515; W. C. Richardson, *Tudor Chamber Administration, 1485–1547* (Baton Rouge LA, 1952), 486; *VE*, iv. 156; PRO, PROB11/23/27.
[23] Dudley, *Tree*, 65–6; Hampshire RO, 21M65/A1/16, fo. 19r; LMA, MS 9531/8, fo. 100r; LA, Bishop's Register 23, fo. 209v; Bishop's Register 27, fo. 110v; PRO, PROB11/23/27.
[24] *LP* VI. 245.   [25] 21 Henry VIII c. 13.
[26] PRO, PROB11/23/27.   [27] PRO, PROB11/16/32.
[28] BI, Bishop's Register 27, fo. 8v; LMA, MS 9531/9, fo. 42r; LA, Bishop's Register 23, fo. 377r; LJRO, B/A/1/13, fo. 224r; NRO, Bishop's Register 13B, fo. 63r.
[29] PRO, PROB11/23/27.
[30] BI, Bishop's Register 26, fo. 46v; LA, Bishop's Register 27, fos. 22r, 110v.
[31] PRO, C1/156/44; *Episcopal Court Book for Lincoln*, 125; LMA, MS 9531/9, fo. 17v; LA, Bishop's Register 23, fos. 68r, 127r; *Visitations in the Diocese of Lincoln*, i. 65.

vicar of Enfield, Dr John Hobyll, the rectory at Ducklington in Oxfordshire.[32] In 1523, Hobyll's successor at Enfield, Dr Thomas Thompson, named Lovell as his 'sometime good master and benefactor' when he left land to St John's College, Cambridge, to pray for both their souls and fund preaching fellows.[33] Lovell had made him rector of Oswaldkirk in Yorkshire in 1504, while he was still completing his doctorate in theology.[34] Meanwhile, his appointee at East Harling, William Borrows, must have been another household chaplain, witnessing a will at Enfield in 1508.[35]

VARIATIONS ON A THEME

Many of the themes of Lovell's patronage were repeated in that of his colleagues. Poynings had the next largest fund of livings at his disposal, making thirty-four presentations. Only a third of them went to graduates, a blend of Oxford and Cambridge theologians and lawyers, some hailing from the counties where he promoted them.[36] The most intellectually adventurous was Richard Sparchford, a young humanist cleric and future correspondent of Erasmus, presented to the rectory of Hockwold cum Wilton in Norfolk in March 1514 presumably as a favour to Poynings's diplomatic colleague Cuthbert Tunstall, whose chaplain Sparchford was.[37] The most pastorally unsuitable was the Yorkshire-born Cambridge junior proctor and university preacher John Robynson, canonically deprived of the rectory at Fawkham in Kent by Bishop John Fisher.[38] In general it was his richer livings like Bourton on Dunsmore or Horsmonden, worth around £20 or more, that attracted graduate clergy.[39] The poorer livings went to the less qualified.[40] Yet some of them seem from their wills and engagement in local ecclesiastical affairs to have made well-settled parish priests, whatever their lack of learning.[41] One, William Edwardson, requesting burial in the

[32] Emden, *Oxford to 1500*, ii. 939; LA, Bishop's Register 23, fos. 284v, 295v.
[33] M. Underwood, 'The Impact of St John's College as Landowner in the West Fields of Cambridge in the early Sixteenth Century', in P. Zutshi (ed.), *Medieval Cambridge: Essays on the Pre-Reformation University* (Woodbridge, 1993), 181–2.
[34] BI, Bishop's Register 25, fo. 63v.
[35] NRO, Bishop's Register 13B, fo. 27r; PRO, PROB11/16/12.
[36] KHLC, DRb/Ar1/13, fos. 35r, 38v; LMA, MS 9531/9, fo. 25r; LJRO, B/A/1/12, fo. 34r; B/A/1/13, fo. 206r; NRO, Bishop's Register 12, fo. 196r–196v; Bishop's Register 13B, fo. 68v; Emden, *Oxford to 1500*, i. 464, ii. 1229, iii. 1454, 2050; Emden, *Cambridge*, 481, 594, 600, 605; *CEPR*, xviii. 773.
[37] NRO, Bishop's Register 14, fo. 114r; P. G. Bietenholz and T. B. Deutscher (eds), *Contemporaries of Erasmus*, 3 vols (Toronto, 1987), iii. 269.
[38] Emden, *Cambridge*, 483; KHLC, DRb/Ar1/13, fo. 29v; PRO, PROB11/18/16.
[39] *VE*, i. 112, iii. 62.
[40] *VE*, i. 41, 49, 66, 70, 108, 111, 117, 118; KHLC, DRb/Ar1/12, fos. 8v, 15v; DRb/Ar1/13, fos. 6v, 29r, 40v, 42v, 58r, 84v; *The Register of John Morton, Archbishop of Canterbury 1486–1500*, ed. C. Harper-Bill, 3 vols, CYS 75, 78, 89 (Leeds and Woodbridge, 1987–2000), i. 140–1, 143, 160; LPL, Canterbury Register Morton II, fo. 170v; Canterbury Register Warham II, fos. 347v, 366v, 387v; WSRO, EPI/1/5, fo. 7v; *Registrum Thome Bourgchier, Cantuariensis Archiepiscopi, A.D. 1454–1486*, CYS 54 (Oxford, 1957), 343.
[41] KHLC, DRb/Ar1/13, fos. 22r, 56v; DRb/PWr7, fos 78v–79r, 270r–270v.

church he had served for fourteen years at Eastwell, even left money to be bestowed 'in almsdeeds by the good advisement and oversight of my master Mr Ponnynges', whom he made supervisor of his executors.[42]

Poynings's engagement fitted with the sense that lordship over a village carried obligations towards the spiritual welfare of the residents. At Milton, Wyatt agreed with Bishop Fisher that his chantry chaplains should make provision for the rector to have rooms in the chantry house and say mass in the chantry chapel, since that was 'much commodious and beneficial' to the inhabitants of the town, the parish church being distant.[43] At East Guldeford the Guildfords built a completely new brick church for those farming the marsh they had drained and presented the first incumbent in 1505.[44] Marney rebuilt Layer Marney church in brick, with dia-pered decoration and a battlemented tower, in parallel with his domestic building works.[45] Windsor may have been responsible for the significant rebuilding work in yellow brick at Midley.[46] Yet such enterprises risked the sort of self-advertisement against which Dudley warned, seeing vainglory as 'the pestiferous core' of the 'wholesome fruit of...good works' and detecting it in the habit of marking pious gifts with 'escutcheons, badges or scriptures, or both...to declare openly the doers thereof'.[47] Hobart completely rebuilt the church at Loddon at his own cost in three years, an event commemorated by a painting of him and his wife showing the church and the nearby St Olave's bridge, built in stone at his wife's expense, and requesting prayers for their souls.[48] Lovell marked the church tower at Monken Hadley and the new stone clerestory at Enfield with his badges and showed the nuns of Holywell Priory praying for him in the Enfield windows.[49]

Southwell and Windsor, like Poynings, seem to have made a distinction between their poorer and richer parish livings. To his richer livings, Southwell appointed those either studying for university degrees in arts or canon law or already equipped with them.[50] Windsor found well-qualified clerical administrators and scholars for Midley, enticing at £30 a year, and Marsh Baldon, conveniently close to Oxford.[51] Southwell generally gave parishes worth £8 or less to non-graduates.[52]

[42] LPL, Canterbury Register Warham II, fos. 322r, 366v; KHLC, PRC17/13, fo. 307v.

[43] PRO, C1/1144/37.

[44] T. Tatton-Brown, 'Church Building on Romney Marsh in the Later Middle Ages', *AC* 107 (1989), 262; WSRO, EpI/1/4, fo. 43r.

[45] RCHM *Essex*, iii. 155–56; D. Andrews et al., 'Plaster or Stone? Some Observations on Layer Marney Church and Tower', *Essex Archaeology and History* 17 (1986), 172–6.

[46] Tatton-Brown, 'Church Building', 262.

[47] Dudley, *Tree*, 73–5, 77.

[48] *The Reports of Sir John Spelman*, ed. J. H. Baker, 2 vols, SS 93–4 (London, 1976–7), ii. 391n.

[49] E. Ford, *A History of Enfield* (Enfield, 1873), 270–1, 275–6.

[50] NRO, Bishop's Register 13B, fos. 41r, 80r; Bishop's Register 16, fo. 22v; LMA, MS 9531/9, fo. 40r; LPL, Canterbury Register Warham I, fo. 247r; *VE*, i. 336, iii. 296, 375; J. Le Neve, *Fasti ecclesiae anglicanae 1300–1541: Hereford*, ed. J. M. Horn (London, 1962), 37.

[51] LPL, Canterbury Register Warham II, fos. 386r, 395v, 401r; LA, Bishop's Register 25, fo. 44v; Bishop's Register 27, fos. 189v, 191r; *VE*, i. 50, ii. 171; Emden, *Oxford to 1500*, i. 452; A. B. Emden, *A Biographical Register of the University of Oxford 1500–40* (Oxford, 1974), 200–1, 331; Emden, *Cambridge*, 45.

[52] NRO, Bishop's Register 12, fo. 180r; Bishop's Register 13A, fo. 13v; Bishop's Register 13B, fo. 93r; LMA, MS 9531/8, fo. 18v; *VE*, i. 449, iii. 319, 333, 360.

Windsor did the same with Bradenham in Buckinghamshire and Baylham in Suffolk.[53] Marney seems to have had few if any livings fit to tempt graduates.[54] Wyatt gave, if his kin are excluded, three-quarters of his livings, even some of the richer ones, to non-graduates.[55] Hussey's situation was the same.[56] Only his richest parishes could attract the well-qualified, and they were pluralists moving rapidly through a series of promotions; at least one was probably a useful contact, William Witter, the bishop's commissary for Bedfordshire and Huntingdonshire.[57] Brandon, too, gave patronage to local graduates or ecclesiastical administrators whether in the West Country or in Suffolk.[58]

For the parishioners, again, the best parish priests may have been less qualified but less pre-occupied than these high-fliers. Edmund Wotton, an Oxford MA who was Windsor's choice for the modest but not impoverished rectory of Greatworth, Northamptonshire, in 1537, stayed on through the changes of Edward's reign to face deprivation in 1554.[59] John Kirkby was a Cambridge BA who, once Wyatt had named him rector of Gonalston, Nottinghamshire, in 1527, stayed there 59 years, whether as an idle time-server or a dedicated village pastor it is hard to guess.[60] Richard Redberd, rector of Bradenham, who died in 1522, left bequests to his parishioners, requested burial in the church, and was commemorated by a brass noting that he had been incumbent by the patronage of Sir Andrew Windsor as lord of the manor.[61] At Brambeltye in East Grinstead, where there was no benefice, Windsor even seems to have allocated part of his rent to maintain a priest in a chapel of ease.[62]

Others' household chaplains are harder to trace than Lovell's, but were certainly given promotion. The 1519 Lincoln visitation found that Richard Gibbe, rector of

---

[53] LA, Bishop's Register 23, fos. 343r, 348v; Bishop's Register 27, fos. 200v, 210v; NRO, Bishop's Register 13B, fo. 52v; Bishop's Register 14B, fos. 2v, 14v; *VE*, iii. 404, iv. 252

[54] Devon RO, Chanter 12 (ii), fo. 103r; Chanter 13, fo. 34r.

[55] BI, Bishop's Register 27, fos. 11v, 31r, 69v; KHLC, DRb/Ar1/13, fos. 54r, 141v; LA, Bishop's Register 27, fos. 114r, 123v; LPL, Canterbury Register Warham II, fos. 352r, 381r, 392v; NRO, Bishop's Register 12, fo. 156r; Bishop's Register 13B, fos. 65r, 78r; Bishop's Register 14, fo. 95r; Bishop's Register 14B, fos. 10r, 14r; Bishop's Register 16, fo. 40v.

[56] *The Registers of Oliver King, Bishop of Bath and Wells, 1496–1503, and Hadrian de Castello, Bishop of Bath and Wells, 1503–1518*, ed. H. C. Maxwell Lyte, Somerset RS 54 (London, 1939), 28, 93; Worcestershire Archives, BA2648/8(i), Ref:b716:093, 103; WSHC, Bishop's Register Audley, fo. 59r; LA, Bishop's Register 23, fos. 101r, 197v; Bishop's Register 25, fo. 16v; Bishop's Register 27, fos. 47r–47v, 55v, 62r, 133v.

[57] LA, Bishop's Register 23, fos. 212r, 222v, 247r, 396v, 402r–402v; Bishop's Register 25, fos. 2r, 33r; *VE*, iv. 329; Emden, *Cambridge*, 500–1; Emden, *Oxford 1500–40*, 633.

[58] Emden, *Oxford to 1500*, ii. 814; LPL, Canterbury Register Warham I, fo. 203r; Devon RO, Chanter 13, fos. 5r, 11v, 26v; PRO, PROB11/21/37; NRO, Bishop's Register 14, fo. 87r; Emden, *Cambridge*, 88; *VE*, iii. 480. For presentations made collectively with the other Dynham co-heirs in right of his marriage to Lady Fitzwarin, see Devon RO, Chanter 12 (ii), third foliation, fos. 8v, 9r, 10v, 11v; Chanter 13, fos. 5r, 11v; *Registers Oliver King*, 113.

[59] LA, Bishop's Register 27, fo. 137v; Emden, *Oxford 1500–40*, 639; *VE*, iv. 336.

[60] BI, Bishop's Register 27, fo. 88v; Venn and Venn, *Alumni Cantabrigienses*, ii. 24; C. Marsh, *Popular Religion in Sixteenth-Century England* (Basingstoke, 1998), 87–90.

[61] *The Courts of the Archdeaconry of Buckingham 1483–1523*, ed. E. M. Elvey, Buckinghamshire RS 19 (Aylesbury, 1975), 379; K. Glass, *Bradenham Manor, Past and Present* (n.p., 1985), 13.

[62] *Sussex Chantry Records*, ed. J. E. Ray, Sussex RS 36 (Cambridge, 1930), 184.

Stickney, was absent acting as Hussey's chaplain.[63] In 1494 Guildford and Lovell presented Guildford's household chaplain Thomas Lark, a man with a bright future as royal chaplain and building surveyor, brother of Cardinal Wolsey's mistress and master of Trinity Hall, Cambridge, to the valuable rectory at Folsham, and in 1504 Brandon and his brother added the rectory at Thorndon to take his income past £50.[64] Robert Shuldham and John Baker were graduate lawyers promoted by Wyatt, one from Cambridge, one from Oxford, and were probably his chaplains; Shuldham was involved in land dealings with him and their benefices at Barnes and Milton were near his homes in London and Kent.[65] William Hudson looks like another Wyatt chaplain, as rector of Barnes and of Tickhill, where Wyatt was the crown's steward, and Wyatt's proctor in the execution of his brother's will.[66]

SERVANTS AND RELATIVES

More open to criticism than the employment of chaplains was the diversion of livings that should have sustained scholars and pastors to support 'stewards of households and clerks of kitchens', those expert in 'casting of accounts' who 'with good policy can survey your lands' or 'can surely and wisely be your receiver of your rents and revenues'.[67] Dudley denounced this amongst the bishops, but it was equally common among powerful laymen. Richard Ward, armed with a papal dispensation for pluralism, held the rectories of Pickworth in Northamptonshire and Moorby in Lincolnshire, but absented himself from both benefices to act as steward of Hussey's household and receiver-general of his lands.[68] Hobart's household steward was Thomas Leman, whom he presented to the rectory of Southacre in Norfolk.[69] Robert Sympson, a Cambridge MA, was rector of Layer Marney in 1488, added in 1505, once papally dispensed, the rectory of Great Stanway, where Marney's son-in-law Thomas Bonham was patron, and topped the collection off with the family's prebend in St Endellion church in Cornwall in 1524.[70] He repaid Marney with constant activity in the running of his estates and close cultivation of his tenantry, several of whom named him executor or supervisor of their

[63] *Visitations in the Diocese of Lincoln*, i. 76; LA, Bishop's Register 25, fo. 13v.

[64] *Abstracts of Inquisitiones Post Mortem relating to the City of London, Tudor Period*, ed. G. S. Fry et al., 3 vols (London, 1896–1908), i. 39; NRO, Bishop's Register 12, fo. 182r; Bishop's Register 13B, fo. 36r; *CEPR*, xix. 680; *VE*, iii. 359, 480; Venn and Venn, *Alumni Cantabrigienses*, iii. 48; A. F. Pollard, *Wolsey* (London, 1953 edn), 306–7; S. Thurley, 'The Domestic Building Works of Cardinal Wolsey', in S. Gunn and P. G. Lindley (eds), *Cardinal Wolsey: Church, State and Art* (Cambridge, 1991), 80.

[65] Emden, *Cambridge*, 527; Emden, *Oxford to 1500*, i. 94; LPL, Canterbury Register Warham II, fo. 331v; KHLC, DRb/Ar1/13, fo. 90r; *CPR 1500–9*, 737.

[66] LPL, Canterbury Register Warham II, fo. 352r; BI, Bishop's Register 27, fo. 159r–159v.

[67] Dudley, *Tree*, 64–5.

[68] *Visitations in the Diocese of Lincoln*, i. 56, 66; *Episcopal Court Book for Lincoln*, 26; *VE*, iv. 344; PRO, E36/95, fo. 15r.

[69] *LP* I, i. 438 (3 m. 16); F. Blomefield, *An Essay towards a Topographical History of the County of Norfolk*, 11 vols (London, 1805–10), vi. 85.

[70] Emden, *Cambridge*, 574; LMA, MS 9531/7, fo. 217r; *CEPR*, xviii. 509; Morant, *Essex*, ii. 191; Devon RO, Chanter 14, fo. 18v.

wills.[71] Most unusual was the career of Robert Hedcorn, Cistercian monk from Boxley and close associate of Sir Henry Wyatt. He was dispensed to hold a rectory in 1509 and Wyatt duly appointed him to Allington in 1514, where he stayed for sixteen years.[72] While there he witnessed Wyatt's property dealings and doubled up as hermit at Allington Castle; he was expected to say the daily prayers ordained for the hermit, but not to abandon his rectory to live in the hermitage, though to keep up appearances he was to visit it once a month.[73] Other clerics may have been of practical help in other ways. John Bonevassell, presented to a rectory by Poynings, and Lovell's chaplain Gerard Michaels, perhaps a Netherlander, were apparently involved in the production and care of luxury manuscript books.[74] Guillaume Poullain, a Norman whom Poynings made rector first of North Cray and then of Milton Keynes, may well have been useful on his continental travels.[75]

Lovell's promotion of his relatives was put in the shade by Wyatt's use of ecclesiastical patronage to advance the careers of his prolific clerical family. In this, Dudley, the critic of clerical nepotism, had set him a powerful example. His cousin Richard Dudley saw a remarkable upturn in his career once Edmund moved close to the centres of power, bringing him inside four years three rectories, six prebends, and the precentorship of Salisbury Cathedral.[76] There were grants from the king, the bishop of London, and the marquess of Dorset, all doubtless eager to reward Edmund or keep him sweet.[77] But more suspicious still were rewards to Richard from those with whom his cousin was in negotiation for fines or pardons on the king's behalf, the abbot and convent of Ramsey, James Stanley, warden of Manchester College, and Bishop Edmund Audley of Salisbury, whom Edmund had just charged £666 13s 4d for a general pardon 'for a very light cause'.[78]

Wyatt had two brothers in orders. John Wyatt, a Cambridge graduate armed with a papal dispensation for non-residence, managed to collect two rectories, a vicarage, a chantry in York, and the mastership of a college in Norfolk between 1487 and 1516, with the help among others of Bishop Alcock and Sir Thomas Lovell. Lovell presumably would have approved of his decision to be buried at Cley next the Sea, the Roos living he had held since 1493, leaving bequests to the guilds,

---

[71] PRO, SC6/Henry VII/162; C142/40/8; D. Keene and V. Harding, *Historical Gazeteer of London before the Great Fire, I, Cheapside* (Cambridge, 1987), no. 11/6; ERO, D/ACR1, fos. 141r–142r; D/ACR2, fos. 25v–26v, 119v–120r, 240r–241r.

[72] KHLC, DRb/Ar1/13, fos. 54r–54v, 141v; PRO, E326/7877.

[73] PRO, E326/7112, 7876, 8736, 8740, 10072.

[74] LPL, Canterbury Register Warham II, fo. 325v; PRO, PROB11/7/15; *HMC Rutland,* iv. 264.

[75] KHLC, DRb/Ar 1/13, fo. 29r; LA, Bishop's Bishop's Register 23, fos. 316r–316v, 347r; *LP* I, i. 1602(4); F. Markham, *A History of Milton Keynes and District,* 2 vols (Luton, 1973–5), i. 144.

[76] Emden, *Oxford to 1500,* i. 598–9.

[77] *CPR 1494–1509,* 534, 539, 586; J. Le Neve, *Fasti ecclesiae anglicanae 1300–1541: St Paul's London,* ed. J. M. Horn (London, 1963), 33; LA, Bishop's Register 23, fo. 204v.

[78] LA, Bishop's Register 23, fo. 372v; *The Victoria History of the County of Lancaster,* ed. W. Farrer and J. Brownbill, 8 vols (London, 1906–14), iii. 7; WSHC, Bishop's Register Audley, fos. 32r, 72v; BL, MS Lansdowne 127, fos. 16v, 23v, 28v, 31r, 60r; 'The Petition of Edmund Dudley', ed. C. J. Harrison, *EHR* 87 (1972), 88.

lights, and parishioners there.[79] Richard Wyatt did even better. His studies in Cambridge, supported by a Norfolk rectory to which his brother presented him together with Sir Thomas Lovell and Sir Henry Heydon in 1494, were crowned with a doctorate in theology and the mastership of Christ's College in 1506–8; but like Richard Dudley he suddenly collected a raft of rectories, canonries, and prebends from the crown, bishops, and other patrons in the last years of Henry VII, finishing his career as precentor of York Minster.[80] Richard, it seems, was also closer to Sir Henry than was John. Both named him an executor, but Richard left him some land and £100 towards the marriage of his daughter Margaret.[81] Both acted as feoffees in his land transactions, but Richard was bound for his debts to the king.[82] Such favours could be returned. It was Sir Henry who met the payment for dilapidations due to Richard's successor in one of his livings.[83] One of the witnesses to Richard's will and recipient of one of his best gowns was a fellow-priest, John Hughson, whom Sir Henry presented to two Nottinghamshire rectories.[84]

Wyatt's steps-sons John and Roger Wilde also pursued clerical careers, but were more directly dependent on his patronage. John, about five years the senior, studied at Oxford, Roger at both Oxford and Cambridge.[85] John's first livings were presentations by monastic houses in which his stepfather may or may not have had a hand, but in the 1520s Sir Henry presented him to Milton, in the heart of his Kent estates, and then to Charleton in Devon.[86] Roger's first rectories, Wotton in Northamptonshire and Ashill in Norfolk, came from Sir Henry in 1524; in 1525 he succeeded John Wyatt at Cley next the Sea; and then in 1531 he followed his brother at Milton.[87] Each step-son was thus equipped with a set of benefices bringing in a comfortable £40 a year or more.[88] Like the Wyatts, they acted in land transactions for Sir Henry.[89] Wyatt and Dudley were not alone. Richard Empson junior enjoyed a successful ecclesiastical career in parallel with that of Richard Dudley.[90] John Ernley presented William Ernley to a Wiltshire living on the death

[79] Emden, *Cambridge*, 661; *CEPR*, xx. 540; NRO, Bishop's Register 12, fo. 165v; Blomefield, *Norfolk*, ii. 195; PRO, PROB11/21/34.

[80] Emden, *Cambridge*, 661–2, 687; *CEPR*, xvii(i). 532; NRO, Bishop's Register 12, fo. 183r; BI, Bishop's Register 25, fos. 31v, 157r; *Calendar of Institutions by the Chapter of Canterbury Sede Vacante*, ed. C. E. Woodruff and I. A. Churchill, Kent Archaeological Society Records Branch 8 (Canterbury, 1924), 57; *The Victoria History of the County of Lancaster*, ed. W. Farrer and J. Brownbill, 8 vols (London, 1906–14), iv. 62.

[81] PRO, PROB11/21/34; BI, Bishop's Register 27, fos. 159r–159v.

[82] PRO, CP25/2/3/11/32; CP25/2/19/105/34; CP25/2/19/109/10; E36/215, fo. 298v; *CAD*, iii. D1308, vi. C7435; BL, Addl. Ch. 5674; Addl. MS 21480, fo. 80v.

[83] PRO, E326/6960.

[84] BI, Bishop's Register 27, fos. 31r, 69v, 159r–159v.

[85] Emden, *Oxford 1500–40*, 644.

[86] *The Victoria History of the County of Oxford*, ed. W. Page et al., 17 vols (London, 1907–), vi. 307; R. Newcourt, *Repertorium ecclesiasticum parochiale Londinense*, 2 vols (London, 1708–10), ii. 186; KHLC, DRb/Ar1/13, fos 112r–112v; Devon RO, Chanter 14, fo. 32r.

[87] LA, Bishop's Register 27, fo. 110v.

[88] *VE*, i. 108, ii. 371, iii. 339, 363, iv. 328.

[89] PRO, PRO, E210/9867; E326/5772, 7786, 8760, 11264; CP25/2/20/119/24.

[90] LA, Bishop's Register 23, fos. 202r, 214r.

of another William Ernley in 1522.[91] Windsor joined his step-father Sir Robert Litton in three presentations of Litton's brother Christopher in 1502–4, giving him £75 to top up his canonry of St Stephen's Westminster.[92] Three small Brays— Edward, John, and Reynold—began their clerical careers at the ages of seven or eight in the years around 1500, presumably with the backing of Sir Reynold, who certainly helped John Bray, newly appointed prebendary of Fridaythorpe in York Minster, in his negotiations with York city council over land leases in 1501.[93]

THE UNIVERSITIES

Turning to his positive injunctions, Dudley was concerned that the universities be well maintained. 'Look well upon your two universities' he urged the church, 'how famous they have been and in what condition they be now.'[94] He especially wanted theologians to be encouraged, rather than the civil and canon lawyers who had grown to outnumber them two to one at Oxford over the previous fifty years.[95] He may well have been inspired in these views by his cousin Richard, to whom he left twenty marks in his will as one of his executors. Richard was a fellow of Oriel College, Oxford, from 1497 to 1506, and later proved a generous benefactor to the college. Oriel was one of the colleges in which theology remained the dominant higher faculty throughout the fifteenth century and Richard was a theologian with a doctorate from Turin.[96] But a sense that clergy should be theologians also went with a sense that common lawyers and other educated laymen should run the country, for when clerics held temporal office 'thereby most commonly is destroyed the church and the office'.[97]

In various ways Dudley's colleagues seem to have followed these injunctions, often with the same penchant for theology. Risley was a significant patron of Jesus College, Cambridge, building the nave of the chapel, roofing the cloister and bequeathing £160 to finish and glaze these buildings and funds to maintain a lecturer in divinity at the college, to teach only on the Old and New Testaments in line with the biblical emphases of the founder, Bishop Alcock, for fifteen years his colleague on the king's

---

[91] WSHC, Bishop's Register Audley, fo. 90v.

[92] LA, Bishop's Register 23, fo. 183r; LMA, MS9531/8, fo. 73v; NRO, Bishop's Register 13B, fo. 31r; PRO, PROB11/14/40; *VE*, i. 433, iii. 428, iv. 323.

[93] *CEPR*, xvi. 539, xvii(i). 688–9; *HMC First Report* (London, 1874), App., 96; J. Le Neve, *Fasti ecclesiae anglicanae 1300–1541: Bath and Wells*, ed. B. Jones (London, 1964), 56; *Salisbury*, ed. J. M. Horn (London, 1962), 101; *York Civic Records*, ii. 170, 178–79.

[94] Dudley, *Tree*, 62.

[95] T. A. R. Evans, 'The Numbers, Origins and Careers of Students', in Catto and Evans (eds), *Late Medieval Oxford*, 497n; S. L. Greenslade, 'The Faculty of Theology', in J. K. McConica (ed.), *History of the University of Oxford. Volume iii: The Collegiate University* (Oxford, 1986), 304–5.

[96] Emden, *Oxford to 1500*, i. 598–9; G. C. Richards and C. L. Shadwell, *The Provosts and Fellows of Oriel College, Oxford* (Oxford, 1922), 42; H. S. Grazebrook, *The Barons of Dudley*, Collections for a History of Staffordshire 9/2 (London, 1888), 81–2; A. B. Cobban, 'Colleges and Halls 1430–1500', in Catto and Evans (eds), *Late Medieval Oxford*, 603.

[97] Dudley, *Tree*, 25.

council.[98] Bray was a benefactor of Jesus, as he was of Pembroke.[99] Hussey chased up his mother's executors to make sure that his parents' benefactions to Jesus College library and a university readership in divinity had been fulfilled and procured a mortmain licence to endow Pembroke with lands worth £20 a year.[100] Lucas left money for an exhibition to support a student at Cambridge.[101] Lovell left £20 each to Oxford and Cambridge, and £10 to Gonville Hall, to which he had earlier given £30 for building works. Gonville had strong links with East Anglia and concentrated on arts and theology; Robert Carlton, patronized both by Lovell and by religious houses where he had some influence, had been a fellow there.[102]

Lovell also encouraged learning at second hand through the benefactions of his chaplains. Thomas Thompson, former master of Christ's, left bequests there and to Michaelhouse and St John's.[103] George Wyndham left £400 to endow a school 'to the honour of God and profit of the common weal of England'.[104] Wyatt showed flickers of theological interest to match Lovell's, presenting Robert Cutler, a Cambridge university preacher and president of Michaelhouse, to Finningley in Nottinghamshire in 1512 and delegating one presentation at Ashill in Norfolk in 1534 to a team of patrons led by the Cambridge theologians John Crayford, master of Clare College, and John Chesewright.[105] Those around the king's mother were linked with her extensive projects in Cambridge: Hussey, Southwell, and Cutt were in attendance when she visited Christ's College in autumn 1506 for its dedication and the election of her scholars.[106] Meanwhile, at Oxford, Sutton was centrally involved in the foundation of Brasenose, again charged with the study of arts and theology, and Hussey gave the college more than £30 between 1517 and 1527, though he may have been discharging a debt.[107] Mordaunt, though not an executor of Morton, nominated one of the scholars maintained in Oxford under his will.[108]

[98] A. Gray and F. Brittain, *A History of Jesus College Cambridge* (London, 1979), 27, 29; D. N. J. MacCulloch, *Thomas Cranmer: A Life* (New Haven CT and London, 1996), 22–3, 32; *SCC*, 1–3, 8–23, 28.

[99] M. M. Condon, 'From Caitiff and Villain to Pater Patriae: Reynold Bray and the Profits of Office', in M. A. Hicks (ed.), *Profit, Piety and the Professions in later Medieval England* (Gloucester, 1990), 158–9.

[100] PRO, E111/107; PROB11/14/22; *LP* I, i. 1732(26).

[101] J. H. Baker, *The Men of Court 1440 to 1550: A Prosopography of the Inns of Court and Chancery and the Courts of Law*, 2 vols, SS supplementary ser. 18 (London, 2012), ii. 1036.

[102] PRO, PROB11/23/27; C. N. L. Brooke, *A History of Gonville and Caius College* (Woodbridge, 1985), 15–17, 31–3; *The Annals of Gonville and Caius College by John Caius MD*, ed. J. Venn, Cambridge Antiquarian Society 80 ser. 40 (Cambridge, 1904), 9; LA, Bishop's Register 23, fo. 146v; Emden, *Cambridge*, 124; G. Poulson, *The History and Antiquities of the Seignory of Holderness*, 2 vols (London, 1840–1), ii. 94; H. Chauncy, *The Historical Antiquities of Hertfordshire*, 2 vols (Dorking, 1975 edn) i. 451.

[103] Emden, *Cambridge*, 582–3.

[104] PRO, PROB11/29/23.

[105] NRO, Bishop's Register 17, fo. 27r–27v; Emden, *Oxford 1500–40*, 115–16, 148–9; Emden, *Cambridge*, 173; BI, Bishop's Register 26, fo. 26r.

[106] M. K. Jones and M. G. Underwood, *The King's Mother: Lady Margaret Beaufort, Countess of Richmond and Derby* (Cambridge, 1992), 223.

[107] J. G. Clark, 'Sutton, Sir Richard', *ODNB*; J. K. McConica, 'The Rise of the Undergraduate College' in McConica (ed.), *The Collegiate University*, 7–17; I. S. Leadam, 'The Early Years of the College', in *Brasenose College Quartercenenary Monographs. Volume ii Part i*, OHS 53 (Oxford, 1909), 135; PRO, CP40/1007, m. 428v.

[108] *Canterbury College Oxford*, iii, ed. W. A. Pantin, OHS n.s. 8 (Oxford, 1950), 232.

THE RELIGIOUS ORDERS

Dudley had less to say about the regular orders than about universities, bishops, or parish life. But they were important to the new men in various ways. Poynings, unsurprisingly, took the most lordly attitude to houses of religion, leaving £2 each to the Trinitarian house at Mottenden and the Abbey of St Radegund's 'where I am founder' to pray for his soul and those of his forebears.[109] When St Radegund's elected an abbot without consulting him in 1514 he secured papal letters for redress of the 'considerable prejudice and injury' done to him.[110] Others acquired rights of presentation or confirmation as they built up their estates: Lovell over the nuns of Gokewell and Hussey over Thurgarton Priory.[111] With larger houses, still a powerful social and political presence in local society, rising men perhaps had a more equal relationship. Poynings received letters of confraternity from the monks of Christ Church, Canterbury, in 1490; Prior Thomas Goldstone put his arms, together with those of the Guildfords, Scotts, and other leading Kentish families on the priory's new gatehouse; and Poynings named Goldstone's successor, Thomas Goldwell, one of the overseers of his will. In return, Poynings stood surety for the prior's payments to the king for escapes from his prison.[112] In his complex dealings over land and drainage Guildford worked closely with the abbots of Battle and Robertsbridge, but when his career collapsed it was they who took responsibility for sorting out his debts.[113] Marney's links were with St Osyth's, whose abbot, John Vyntener, he made one of his executors.[114] Hobart, much involved with the city of Norwich, was a benefactor of Norwich Cathedral Priory.[115] Windsor was a dinner guest at the great London priory of Holy Trinity, Aldgate in December 1513, when fresh salmon and shrimps were added to the usual fare.[116]

The new men exercised their religious patronage in favour of monastic clerics. Lovell appointed the heads of several houses to rectories in his gift; each lay in a different sphere of his influence. Rievaulx, like Belvoir which granted him confraternity in 1499, stood under the patronage of the Lords Roos whose lands he controlled. St Mary Graces was next to the Tower of London, where he was lieutenant.[117] Dudley's presentations of Robert Bremner, prior of Tortington, similarly cultivated mutually beneficial relations. Dudley's first wife was buried at the priory, his father had been a benefactor there and he held lands nearby; the prior gave him

[109] PRO, PROB11/20/21; *The Victoria History of the County of Kent*, ed. W. Page, 3 vols (London, 1908–32), ii. 172–5, 205–8.

[110] *CEPR*, xx. 242.

[111] PRO, CP25/2/25/156/6; C54/383, m. 5d; E315/393, fo. 20r.

[112] *HMC Ninth Report*, App., i. 118; E. Hasted, *The History and Topographical Survey of the County of Kent*, 12 vols (Wakefield, 1972 edn), xi. 506n; PRO, PROB11/20/21; BL, Addl. MS 21480, fo. 104r.

[113] S. Cunningham, 'Guildford, Sir Richard', *ODNB*; *CPR 1494–1509*, 110–11; PRO, C1/138/60; SC6/Henry VII/1874, m. 8v; HL, MS BA263; BL, Addl. MS 59899, fo. 158v.

[114] 'Ancient Wills', ed. H. W. King, *TEAS* 4 (1869), 154.

[115] W. Dugdale, *Monasticon Anglicanum*, ed. J. Caley et al., 6 vols in 8 (London, 1817–30), iv. 6.

[116] PRO, E36/108, fo. 70v.

[117] LA, Bishop's Register 23, fo. 169r; BI, Bishop's Register 25, fo. 66v; LPL, Canterbury Register Morton II, fo. 359v; *CEPR*, xx. 542; J. Nichols, *The History and Antiquities of the County of Leicester*, 4 vols in 8 (Wakefield, 1971 edn), II-I, app. 21–2.

use of the garden of his London house, and he appointed Richard Bremner, presumably a relation, as bailiff of two of his Sussex manors.[118] Calculations of the same sort presumably underlay Guildford's appointment of the abbot of Robertsbridge to a rectory in 1501 and Poynings's and Wyatt's presentations of an Austin canon and two monks.[119]

Hussey exercised a wider influence among quite a network of religious houses, allegedly conspiring as one of the 'nigh friends and lovers' of the abbot of Swineshead to divert property to his house and writing to Cromwell on behalf of the abbot of Holme Cultram and of the abbot of Vaudey, who, the abbot of Fountains had assured him, was being treated unjustly by the abbot of Woburn.[120] In 1534–5 alone, the abbots of Kirkstead, Revesby, Swineshead, and Vaudey and the priors of Catley, Haverholme, Spalding, and St Katherine's sent him gifts, payments, or letters.[121] He also used local houses such as Catley and Sempringham to board, and presumably educate, the young ladies of his household.[122] Bray was seen as a friend by the English knights of St John, whose prior, Thomas Docwra, asked him in 1503 to look after the order's interests while he stayed on Rhodes to fight off an Ottoman attack.[123]

Relations could be more predatory. At Luffield Priory in Buckinghamshire, Empson first took a fee and leased individual estates on beneficial terms, then, in 1496, supervised the house's surrender into the king's hands for the endowment of his new foundation at Westminster, and finally, in 1504, secured a forty-year lease of all the temporalities and spiritualities from Westminster Abbey.[124] After Empson's fall, it became possible to suggest openly, as the abbot of St James's Abbey beside Northampton did, that the fees religious houses paid him were a form of protection money. First Empson's 'adherents and servants' suggested the abbey should pay him £2 a year 'in avoiding of his displeasure'. Then, three or four years later, he sent a servant to ask for a joint grant to himself and his son. The abbot hesitated for a year, then, because Empson was 'a man of great might and power in that country', he conceded. Nonetheless he did the house not a 'pennyworth of good', promising to forward the abbot's suit to the king for the lands of Cold Norton Priory, but then securing the farm of the lands for himself.[125] Abingdon Abbey had an even more spectacular story, Empson having allegedly framed their abbot for treason, kept him sixteen weeks awaiting a hearing and then had a friend suggest that the grant of a fee might sweeten a request to go home.[126]

---

[118] *LP* I, i. 559; *Transcripts of Sussex Wills*, ed. W. H. Godfrey, 4 vols, Sussex RS 41–3, 45 (Lewes, 1935–41), iv. 252; J. Stow, *A Survey of London*, ed. C. L. Kingsford, 2nd edn, 2 vols (Oxford, 1971), i. 224; PRO, SC6/Henry VIII/6217.

[119] KHLC, DRb/Ar1/13, fos. 19r, 54r; LPL, Canterbury Register Morton II, fo. 169v; NRO, Bishop's Register 14, fo. 95r.

[120] PRO, C1/318/40; *LP* V. 1556, VII. 516.

[121] PRO, E36/95, fos. 31v–32r, 52v–53v.

[122] PRO, E36/95, fos. 28v, 56r, 97v.

[123] G. O'Malley, *The Knights Hospitaller of the English Langue 1460–1565* (Oxford, 2005), 155.

[124] *Luffield Priory Charters*, Part ii, ed. G. R. Elvey, Buckinghamshire RS 18 (n.p., 1975), xxxiv–xxxvi, 441–2.

[125] PRO, C1/360/66.   [126] PRO, C1/462/43.

With cash went religious patronage. In 1505 St James's appointed Richard Empson junior, aged about twelve, to the mastership of the Hospital of the Holy Trinity in Kingsthorpe, Northamptonshire.[127] Other Midlands houses, such as Chacombe Priory and Notley Abbey, granted advowsons to Sir Richard so he could make his own appointments.[128] Caldwell Priory did the same for Bray and Mordaunt; Croxden Abbey and Thurgarton Priory for Hussey; St Mary's Hospital outside Bishopsgate for Lovell; Holy Trinity Aldgate for Poynings; Blyth Priory in Nottinghamshire, St Benet's Abbey in Norfolk, and the dean and chapter of St Paul's Cathedral for Wyatt.[129] In such a climate it is easy to suspect that even grants of purely spiritual benefits, like the letters of confraternity Durham Priory gave Empson and Dudley on 10 February 1509, were an attempted exchange of heavenly for worldly protection.[130]

The church's wealth and power, its role in education and government as well as pastoral care, made it the site for some of the new men's most elevated undertakings, but also some of their most sordid. In that they were not untypical of their age. Sir Thomas More, while arguing for the highest standards in the selection of clergy, used his patronage to promote a similar mixture to the new men of pluralist graduates—crown servants and ecclesiastical administrators—and active parish clergy, though he did not approve of household chaplains and did not use his presentations to meet the obligations of kinship.[131] Other patrons integrated their relations with the church more naturally into their wider systems of clientage, building local reputation and family power.[132] When combined with aspirations to make the clergy better, powerful laymen's acceptance of royal power over the church and preparedness to exploit the church's wealth would help drive the English Reformation, and the new men exemplified such attitudes.

---

[127] LA, Bishop's Register 23, fo. 202r; *CEPR,* xix. 449.

[128] LA, Bishop's Register 23, fo. 278r, Bishop's Register 27, fo. 207v.

[129] R. Halstead, *Succinct Genealogies of the Noble and Ancient Houses of Alno or de Alneto etc* (London, 1685), 506; LA, Bishop's Register 25, f. 16v; Bishop's Register 27, fo. 62r; Hampshire RO, 21M65/A1/16, fo. 19r; LMA, MS 9531/9, fo. 25–25e; BI, Bishop's Register 27, fo. 11v; NRO, Bishop's Register 16, fo. 40v; LPL, Canterbury Register Warham II, fo. 392v.

[130] *Historiae Dunelmensis Scriptores Tres,* ed. J. Raine, Surtees Soc. 9 (London, 1839), ccccx–ccccxi.

[131] S. B. House, 'Sir Thomas More as Church Patron', *Journal of Ecclesiastical History* 40 (1989), 208–18.

[132] S. J. Gunn, *Charles Brandon, Duke of Suffolk, c.1484–1545* (Oxford, 1988), 20, 25, 87, 98–100, 104–5, 116, 120, 160–4, 199–200, 208–9.

10

Law and power

The new men were familiar with the law and what it could do for them as well as for the king's power. Law framed social, political, and financial relationships and many transactions needed a lawyer.[1] They knew the costs of litigation and the risk of failure too well to be frantic litigants, as some of their contemporaries were: the duke of Buckingham fought 128 lawsuits in common pleas and king's bench alone, many against his own servants, and seems to have won only six of them.[2] But they pursued their interests through suits in a range of courts and did their best to get maximum benefit from the effort involved. At times they were tempted to use their expertise or power to take unfair advantage, but when they did so the law stood ready—at least in theory—to put matters right.

LAWYERS

They did not stint to hire the best lawyers they could get. Great men and corporations retained lawyers with a fee of £1 or £2 a year to provide counsel when needed, but when they had special business to do or suits to fight they added others to the team.[3] Lovell and his executors matched this pattern. For general purposes he retained his Enfield neighbour Robert Wroth, a future attorney-general of the duchy of Lancaster, paying him extra in 1522–3 for drafting indentures and managing individual cases, and leaving him a covered cup and £5 in his will.[4] Meanwhile, Sir Richard Broke, justice of common pleas and soon chief baron of the exchequer, lent advice over conveyancing.[5] And when his tenants at Cley next the Sea were sued in star chamber by their neighbours at Blakeney for destroying a drainage bank made without leave on Lovell's land, he hired on their behalf John Spelman, a Norfolk lawyer who had just become a serjeant-at-law and would end as a king's bench justice.[6] For the suits that followed his death, his executors

---

[1] E. W. Ives, *The Common Lawyers of Pre-Reformation England. Thomas Kebell: A Case Study* (Cambridge, 1983), 97–100.

[2] B. J. Harris, *Edward Stafford, Third Duke of Buckingham, 1478–1521* (Stanford CA, 1986), 96–100.

[3] Ives, *Common Lawyers*, 131–43.

[4] *HMC Rutland*, iv. 260; Belvoir Castle, MS a/c 4; S. T. Bindoff, *History of Parliament: The House of Commons 1509–1558*, 3 vols (London, 1982), iii. 666–7; PRO, PROB11/23/27.

[5] *HMC Rutland*, iv. 263; Bindoff, *Commons*, i. 503–4.

[6] Belvoir Castle, MS a/c no. 4; *The Reports of Sir John Spelman*, ed. J. H. Baker, 2 vols, SS 93–4 (London, 1976–7), i. pp. ix–xvii.

retained not only John Spelman and Richard Lyster, Lovell's deputy in his forest justiceship, but also John Rowe, serjeant-at-law, the assize clerk and versatile advocate Thomas Fitzhugh and Henry White, common serjeant and soon to be under-sheriff of London, plus the rising stars John Baldwin, William Coningsby and William Whorwood, respectively future chief justice of common pleas, justice of king's bench, and attorney-general.[7] Different courts demanded different expertise, so for exchequer business they turned to John Smith, the treasurer's remembrancer, and Humphrey Bowland, clerk to the treasurer's remembrancer and future king's remembrancer.[8] The church courts, which dealt with matters of probate, called for canon lawyers rather than common lawyers, but here, too, they found expert counsel. When dealing with the joint probate commission set up by Wolsey and Warham they were advised by Thomas Cockes, Oxford Bachelor of Canon Law, as their proctor, and chose as their counsel Dr William Bretton, Cambridge Doctor of Civil Law and Dr Rowland Lee, future bishop of Coventry and Lichfield.[9]

Others spotted rising talent, too. Wyatt, who, one opponent claimed, had 'all the learned men ... of Essex ... of fee and retained of counsel', used Thomas Audley, the future lord chancellor, to draft property agreements in the 1520s.[10] Hussey retained the local lawyer Richard Clerk, recorder of Lincoln, for his counsel with £3 6s 8d a year, but, when he needed special advice, paid 6s 8d to Edward Montagu, future chief justice of king's bench.[11] Windsor was represented in chancery by Humphrey Brown and Edmund Mervyn, future justices of common pleas and king's bench; Hussey by John Baldwin, future chief justice of common pleas; Wyatt by Roger Cholmley, future chief justice of king's bench, and Walter Hendley, future attorney-general of the court of augmentations, whom he made one of his executors and paid an annuity for his good counsel.[12] In other courts the new men chose attorneys with years of experience: John Franklyn, John Heron, John Jenour, and Thomas Strey had each been in common pleas more than twenty years when they represented Wyatt, Oliver Southworth more than twenty years in king's bench.[13] Often their attorneys knew the court in question from the inside as

[7] *LP* IV, i. 366; J. H. Baker, *The Men of Court 1440 to 1550: A Prosopography of the Inns of Court and Chancery and the Courts of Law*, 2 vols, SS supplementary ser. 18 (London, 2012), i. 259–60, 515, 678–9, ii. 1382–3, 1661–2; Bindoff, *Commons*, i. 372–3, iii. 605, 608–11.

[8] J. C. Sainty, *Officers of the Exchequer*, List and Index Society Special Series 18 (London, 1983), 54; Baker, *Men of Court*, i. 344.

[9] *LP* IV, i. 366; P. Gwyn, *The King's Cardinal: The Rise and Fall of Thomas Wolsey* (London, 1990), 277–9; A. B. Emden, *A Biographical Register of the University of Oxford 1500–40* (Oxford, 1974), 125; G. D. Squibb, *Doctors' Commons: A History of the College of Advocates and Doctors of Law* (Oxford, 1977), 136, 138.

[10] PRO, C1/590/53–5; STAC 2/19/198.

[11] PRO, SC6/Henry VIII/1937; E36/95, fo. 31v; Baker, *Men of Court*, i. 480; J. H. Baker, 'Montagu, Sir Edward', *ODNB*.

[12] PRO, C1/456/34, 525/71, 597/13, 588/44, 922/65; PROB11/26/7; Baker, *Men of Court*, i. 259–60, 379–80, 472–3, 850, ii. 1085.

[13] PRO, CP40/998, m. 436r, 1003, mm. 128v, 533r, 1049, m. 135v, 1051, m. 124r, 1066, m. 323r; KB27/1073, m. 78r–78v, 1075, m. 33v, 1094, m. 31r; Baker, *Men of Court*, i. 708–9, 856, ii. 945–6, 1435–6, 1475.

officers: several filazers, a clerk of outlawries, a clerk of the king's remembrancer in the exchequer, a clerk to the chief clerk of the king's bench.[14] Sometimes other factors came into play. Windsor consistently chose men from his own inn, the Middle Temple: Brown, Mervyn, John Felgate, and Henry Digby.[15] Lovell, similarly, had preferred his Lincoln's Inn colleagues for much of his career—Guy Crafford, George Emerson, Leonard Knight—though by the end of his life he ranged far and wide.[16] Hussey and Poynings often used their neighbours: Thomas Archer of Hougham and Anthony Irby of Gosberton in Lincolnshire, Robert Maycote and John Holme of Faversham, and William Fisher of Maidstone in Kent.[17]

Lawyers were also active in land transactions as working feoffees and might be especially important if titles needed defending.[18] Wyatt often used Reynold Pegge, a minor but busy south Midlands lawyer, as a feoffee and surety in 1502–8, and later deployed John Hales and his cousin Christopher, his highly successful Kent neighbours, as well as lesser lawyers such as Robert Chidley and Thomas Strey.[19] Marney used John Fitzjames, baron of the exchequer and former attorney-general of the duchy of Lancaster, John Hales, his successor at the duchy, and Edmund Knightley of the Middle Temple.[20] Lovell was similarly well supported, with Robert Blagge, a career exchequer lawyer, named a feoffee to his will alongside his usual legal counsel.[21]

Legal activity had costs beyond lawyers' fees. It was conventional to entertain legal advisers to dinner, and Lovell's executors took theirs to a tavern called the King's Head at a cost of 18s 11d.[22] Documents cost money. Lovell had to pay 3s 4d to a notary to take down testimony to his title to property he had bought in London and 12d for a handwritten copy of an act of parliament, while his executors had to pay 13s 4d for a copy of the will of the father of one of his wards and some other business.[23] Spelman's standard fee of 6s 8d was a little over a third of the cost of the star chamber suit Lovell undertook for his tenants at Cley next the Sea, for there was 5s for a copy of the complaint and 1s 8d for a clerk searching for it,

[14] PRO, E159/288, recorda m. 7v; KB27/980, m. 35r–35v, 984, m. 71v, 1000, m. 79r, 1073, m. 78r–78v, 1075, m. 37r–37v, 1089, m. 63v; Baker, *Men of Court*, i. 303, 521, 674, ii. 889–90, 945–6, 1034–5, 1092, 1435–6.
[15] PRO, CP40/1048B, m. 123r, 1059, 122r; Baker, *Men of Court*, i. 379–80, 592–3, 661, ii. 1085.
[16] PRO, CP40/925, m. 265r, 997, m. 437v, 998, m. 516v; Belvoir Castle, MS a/c 4; Baker, *Men of Court*, i. 537, 637–8, ii. 974–5.
[17] PRO, KB 27/963, m. 21v, 965, m. 72v, 969, mm. 39v, 94r, 352r; CP40/1014, m. 432r; LA, Mon3/29/40; Baker, *Men of Court*, i. 221, 674, 889–90, 929–30, ii. 1077–8.
[18] Ives, *Common Lawyers*, 94–7.
[19] *CCR 1500–9*, 954; Bindoff, *Commons*, ii. 274–6; *Essex Fines*, iv. 108; *CCR 1500–9*, 720, 737, 984, 986; PRO, C1/175/55; CP25/1/170/197/106, 186/42/28, 294/81/162; C54/386, m. 16d; E210/9917; E326/8750; BLARS, L132, L136; BL, Addl. MS 59899, fo. 138r; Baker, *Men of Court*, i. 468, ii. 1215, 1475.
[20] PRO, CP25/2/51/363/18; C142/40/8; R. Somerville, *A History of the Duchy of Lancaster, I, 1265–1603* (London, 1953), i. 407; Bindoff, *Commons*, ii. 275–6, 476–8.
[21] PRO, C142/41/62; Sainty, *Exchequer*, 45; Baker, *Men of Court*, i. 318.
[22] Ives, *Common Lawyers*, 305; *LP* IV, i. 366.
[23] *HMC Rutland*, iv. 264; Belvoir Castle, MS a/c 4; *LP* IV, i. 366; PRO, C1/546/52.

3s 4d for writing up an answer and submitting it to Wolsey, and 2s given to the tenants.[24] Lovell used the exchequer to chase up debts, exploiting his privilege as chancellor, and the writs there came fairly cheap through Robert Castleton, whom he had appointed as clerk of the pleas. But three terms suing two men for debt through his attorney Guy Crafford cost 36s 10d and another suit cost 33s 6d.[25] Most expensive of all was common pleas, but then the business it dealt with was correspondingly weighty: the costs at Westminster to ratify the purchase of two manors added up to £10 10s 5d, more than half Lovell's litigation bill for 1522–3.[26]

LITIGATION

The skills, contacts, and determination of the new men made them formidable legal adversaries. The language of legal pleadings was of course full of the sort of accusations levelled at Windsor in one chancery suit, decrying his 'great power, might and maintenance', his 'great bearing and sinister means'.[27] But when the Pastons and their servants confessed in private letters, as early as 1488, that they were 'half dismayed' at the prospect that Wyatt would have them condemned in a £40 debt, it was clear that the new men were a force to be reckoned with.[28] The complexity of the legal system invited imaginative use by those who knew it well, and they were sometimes accused of exploiting such flexibility. Southwell, it was claimed, pursued a suit for his father in king's bench in 1499 while the same matter was under consideration in chancery. At first, he would not appear when called into chancery although he was present in Westminster Hall, where both courts sat; when he did appear he was bound over not to pursue the matter further, but did so regardless.[29] In 1507 Hussey was fined £10 for pushing his claim to a horse through the London mayor's court and the exchequer while his opponent defended himself in chancery.[30] In 1518 Poynings tried suing a case about land in Romney Marsh in common pleas in defiance of the marsh's privileges, but found it remitted to the court of the marsh at Dymchurch.[31] In 1524 one of Windsor's suits was likewise remitted from common pleas to the London court of hustings.[32]

They used different types of suit in different courts for different purposes. They went to chancery for complex disputes, ill suited to the set forms of action of king's bench and common pleas, often about property purchases where something had gone wrong, or where perhaps they had deliberately bought a questionable title in the hope of making it good through litigation. Wyatt fought suits of this type in each decade from the

[24] Ives, *Common Lawyers*, 295–305.
[25] Belvoir Castle, MS a/c 4; Sainty, *Exchequer*, 96; Bindoff, *Commons*, ii. 616–17.
[26] Belvoir Castle, MS a/c 4.   [27] PRO, C1/513/15.
[28] *Paston Letters and Papers of the Fifteenth Century*, ed. N. Davis, 2 vols (Oxford, 1971–6), i. 656.
[29] PRO, C1/216/85–6.   [30] PRO, C1/342/1.
[31] PRO, CP40/1022, m. 130v.   [32] CP40/1044, m. 328r.

1490s to the 1530s, alleging mishaps and deceptions of every sort in his purchases of land, while defending himself against similar suits from rival claimants.[33] Windsor was equally active, sometimes in intractable disputes like that over displaced boundary markers in the salt marshes of Kent, where the best evidence he could find came from tours of the disputed lands given to his farmer eleven years previously by septuagenarian locals.[34] Complex debt cases also came to chancery, sued both by the new men and against them. Wyatt sued a man who owed money to a debtor of his for his failure to obey the debtor's deathbed instructions to clear the debt by paying Wyatt.[35] The suppliers of eighty embroidered raven's head badges to the previous husband of Marney's second wife sued Marney for the unpaid bill.[36]

Most king's bench suits were trespasses, often related to disputes over the ownership or use of land. The new men accused their rivals, or their rivals' tenants and servants, of breaking into their closes and causing damage, often by consuming pasture with their animals.[37] Sometimes they used the statutes against forcible entry or older procedures, such as the assize of novel disseisin.[38] They also joined in the expansion of procedure by bill in king's bench to take a wide range of actions against opponents while they were in the court's custody, sometimes charged with a fictitious offence against land in Middlesex.[39] The complexities that underlay apparently straightforward trespass suits sometimes became clearer in the course of pleading. In 1529–30 Wyatt proceeded against a gentleman and a yeoman for breaking his closes at Rainham and Gillingham in Kent. It emerged that the land had been held by a William Arnold, who had died in 1513. In his will he had bequeathed it to Edward Whyte, who had leased it to Wyatt's opponents. But Wyatt claimed that Arnold had been only seventeen years old at the time of his death and therefore incapable of making a valid will of his lands, which should have descended to his first cousin, a Sussex gentleman who had granted them to Wyatt. A jury at the Maidstone assizes believed Wyatt's version of events and he won at least one of the two cases involved.[40]

Common pleas cases, in contrast, were mostly a matter of debts, the origins of which are often now unclear.[41] Even when the debt derived from a bond made to guarantee an obligation or ensure the payment of sums of money, the underlying transaction remains obscure.[42] Occasionally, the issue comes more clearly into

---

[33] PRO, C1/112/55, 143/36–7, 175/55, 555/38–40, 590/53–5, 597/13–14, 922/65.

[34] PRO, C1/217/19, 268/24–5, 456/34, 559/32–5, 588/44, 588/57–62, 690/44, 783/20.

[35] PRO, C1/918/40.   [36] PRO, C1/191/8.

[37] Baker, *The Oxford History of the Laws of England.* vi: 1483–1558 (Oxford, 2003), 720–4; PRO, KB27/933, m. 91r, 961, m. 20v, 962, m. 27v, 963, m. 21v, 964, m. 85r, 984, m. 71v, 990, m. 68r, 999, m. 75r, 1000, m. 79r, 1046, m. 26r, 1047, m. 63r-v.

[38] Baker, *Oxford History*, 719–20; PRO, KB27/965, m. 72v, 969, m. 39v, 987, m. 69r–69v, 1001, m. 29v, 1040, m. 73r.

[39] Baker, *Oxford History*, 151–6; PRO, KB27/1001, m. 103v, 1003, m. 26v, 1005, mm. 25r, 109v, 1075, mm. 33v, 73r, 1089, m. 63v, 1094, m. 31r–31v.

[40] PRO, KB27/1073, m. 78r–78v, 1075, mm. 29r, 37r–37v.

[41] PRO, CP40/918, m. 274v, 980, m. 35r–35v, 989, mm. 580v, 582v, 607r, 1041, m. 339r; *CPR 1494–1509*, 331, 494, 548.

[42] PRO, CP40/1003, m. 128v, 1025, m. 526v, 1023, m. 332r–332v, 1024, m. 438r, 1033, m. 340r, 1039, m. 433r.

focus: a sale of timber gone wrong, or payments related to marriage settlements left incomplete, or 600 sheep not delivered in time.[43] Some were debts incurred in the execution of crown office, like those due to Marney as sheriff or on behalf of the duchy of Lancaster, those prosecuted successfully by Wyatt as treasurer of the chamber and Windsor as keeper of the wardrobe or, presumably, those sued on jointly by Lovell, Empson, and Dudley in 1506–8.[44] Common pleas was also used for trespasses of the sort more usually pursued in king's bench, involving the cutting of timber or underwood, the distraint of livestock to enforce the payment of rent, or the destruction of hedges round enclosed land.[45] Finally, it had a role in ratifying land settlements by the action of common recovery.[46]

Other central jurisdictions were used more rarely. Southwell brought at least one suit into Henry VII's council and Wyatt used star chamber against those who had attacked his manorial pound at Ashill.[47] Lovell used the privilege of the office of chancellor of the exchequer to pursue trespass and debt suits through the exchequer of pleas and Windsor also sued there for debts due to him as keeper of the wardrobe.[48] Local courts were no doubt often brought into play, but their records either do not survive or are hard to search. Criminal prosecutions were brought against offenders like the three Greenwich yeomen who allegedly stole a cow and two heifers belonging to Lovell in 1490 or the twenty Enfield residents who, it was claimed, riotously broke into his land at Edmonton in 1518 and set their horses, oxen and cows to eat his grass in what may well have been an enclosure dispute. The indictment in the latter case was brought into king's bench from the Middlesex quarter sessions by Thomas Roberts, the county coroner, on Lovell's instruction as a Middlesex JP.[49]

Many suits petered out without result: debt suits worked as reminders to pay and trespass suits as invitations to negotiate. Some ran on inconclusively for a decade or more, like Brandon's defence against a trespass suit by the Lestranges over land in Hampshire.[50] But when they forced suits home, the new men won damages and costs sufficient to compensate for the effort they put into litigation. Lovell won £12 10s against the abbot of Fountains in a dispute over rights of presentation to a benefice and £2 6s 8d costs and damages against an executor who failed to pay him a £25 debt.[51] Poynings won 10s damages in a suit for a £10 debt in 1519 and 6s 8d damages in one for a £20 debt in the same year.[52] Wyatt was particularly

[43] PRO, CP40/1014, m. 432r, CP40/1014, m. 532v, 1039, m. 538r.
[44] PRO, CP40/903, m. 100r–100v, 990, m. 27r, 1027, mm. 509r, 535v, 1028, m. 130v, 1060, m. 436r.
[45] PRO, CP40/918, m. 213v, 995, m. 533r, 997, m. 437v, 998, mm. 516v, 522r, 1002, m. 140r, 1011, m. 436, 1027, m. 437v, 1029, mm. 537v, 587v, 1032B, m. 307v, 1034, m. 321r, 1038, m. 520r, 1059, m. 122r.
[46] PRO, CP40/1004, m. 124r, 1035, m. 535r, 1046, m. 124r, 1048B, m. 123r, 1049, m. 135v, 1051, m. 124r, 1056, m. 428r, 1062, m. 438r–438v, 1066, m. 123v, 1083, m. 324r.
[47] PRO, REQ1/1, fo. 85v; STAC 2/34/50.
[48] PRO, E13/186, rot. 1, 187, rot. 18d, 198, rot. 14; Baker, *Oxford History*, 170n.
[49] PRO, KB9/389/18. 476/53, 101.
[50] PRO, KB27/933, m. 30r, 934, m. 27r, 936, m. 20r, 950, m. 39v, 959, m. 24v, 970, m. 37v.
[51] PRO, CP40/925, m. 270r, 998, m. 131r.
[52] PRO, CP40/1024, m. 438r, 1025, m. 526v.

prolific, so the Pastons' worries were probably justified. He was awarded £3 costs and 6s 8d damages in a trespass suit of 1494—when admittedly he started by claiming damages of £40—£1 costs in a suit for £5 damages in 1513, 6s 8d damages on a £15 debt and 10s damages on a £40 debt in 1519, 5s costs in winning a suit for a £5 debt in 1530 and in the same year 27s costs and damages in king's bench from a suit a Kent jury thought worth only 10s 4d.[53] Perhaps it was his precision that served him well. He claimed in one suit that a local butcher had taken not only ten cows and eleven bullocks from his land at Hitcham in Suffolk, but also one marsh gate, two stakes and two buckets.[54]

Arbitration was a standard way to solve difficult disputes and it was one the new men were happy to pursue when it promised an acceptable outcome. The king's council delegated a difference between Lovell and Christopher Urswick in 1504 to arbitration by the Londoners Sir Bartholomew Rede and Sir Henry Colet.[55] Lovell submitted to arbitration again in 1504, this time in a difference with Sir William Say over the stewardship of St Alban's Abbey, though he can hardly have been unhappy with the terms settled by William, Lord Mountjoy and Anthony Fetiplace: Say was to relinquish the stewardship to him and pay him £20 cash and £3 6s 8d a year, while Lovell in return was merely to be 'favourable and loving unto the said Sir William in such causes and matters reasonable as he shall have hereafter to do'.[56] In 1495 the council, Lovell among them, ordered Wyatt and Southwell to break off their lawsuits over a property in Bishop's Lynn pending their judgment, and in 1528 Wyatt and Thomas Boleyn, Viscount Rochford, promised Wolsey 'on their faith and honour' that they would abide by the arbitration of three judges in a land dispute in Kent.[57] Poynings was persuaded to put his dispute with the Woodhouse family over the Norfolk manor of Flitcham Poynings to arbitration by the two chief justices in 1503 after a dozen years of litigation.[58] Even Hussey submitted to arbitration by judges, in his case over the Hertfordshire manor of Oxhey Richard, disputed between him and Sir John Talbot, but perhaps predictably things went wrong: the process commenced in 1515, was still running in 1524 and ended with a chancery suit in which Hussey claimed he had failed to pay over the money he was to give Talbot in return for title to the manor for perfectly understandable reasons and now Talbot was reneging on the whole settlement.[59]

In the legal system as in other respects, the new men's intimacy with the institutions of government helped them. Lovell's executors knew they needed ten copies of his will disposing of his lands, costing a shilling each, to deliver to the juries in the ten different counties where his inquisitions post mortem would be held. They knew they needed a clerk working for their master's old colleague Sir John Daunce

[53] PRO, KB27/933, m. 91r, 1075, mm. 37r–37v, 73r; CP40/1002, m. 140r, 1025, mm. 336v, 338r, 435r.
[54] PRO, KB27/962, m. 27v.   [55] PRO, DL5/2, fo. 60v.   [56] PRO, E210/1478.
[57] PRO, REQ1/1, fo. 104r; SP1/46, fo. 222r (*LP* IV, ii. 3926).
[58] NRO, FLT 838; PRO, CP40/918, m. 426r–426v.
[59] BL, Addl. Ch. 72951–6; PRO, C1/525/71.

to list the money the king owed Lovell, at a cost of 6s 8d, and two clerks of Sir Henry Wyatt, charging 8s 8d, to search the king's book for discharge for those debts. They knew that it would cost only 10s for the lawyer Humfrey Rowland to write out the king's pardon on parchment, but that it would cost £333 6s 8d to get the pardon from the king. More disreputably, they knew that 6s 8d to the sheriff of Middlesex would stop him serving a writ on them at the suit of the dowager Lady Roos, just as Lovell had known that 6s 8d to the sheriff of Norfolk would make sure the writs in his exchequer debt suits and his common pleas conveyancing would be served to good effect.[60] That familiarity equipped them to bend the rules in more drastic ways, but how far did they go?

ABUSES OF POWER

Contemporaries would not have been surprised by Dudley's warning that royal councillors might use their power under the king 'for their proper advantage and sometimes for avenging of their own quarrels, grudges or malice'.[61] When he and Empson fell, many accusations of the maintenance of unjust causes for their own profit, of procuring assaults on their enemies, of perverting justice to defend their accomplices were thrown at them.[62] Most must of course be taken with a pinch of salt. They were easy to kick when they were down, and many charges related more to the money they had extracted for the king than to any private profit for themselves. But there were already complaints before 1509. Two gentlemen claimed they could get no justice at the Northampton assizes against Empson's steward John Seyton, who was 'greatly masterfast and friended in the said court' through Empson's 'supportation and assurance', so much so that no lawyer would represent them.[63] By 1509, Sir Robert Plumpton had been complaining bitterly for eight years about Empson's manipulation of the legal system to strip away his lands.[64] Dudley, as we shall see, was still more adept at using the legal system to take advantage of others in the land market. And it was claimed that they made profits for themselves while extracting money for the king. Londoners said there were proven cases where the king had £200 and Dudley and his 'affinity by means of bribing and polling' had £300.[65]

Empson and Dudley may have been unusually good at using their power to their own benefit, but they were not alone. The terms of Belknap's appointment as surveyor of the king's prerogative, by which he was to have one-ninth of all the money he raised for the king, might be thought an open invitation to maximize

---

[60] Belvoir Castle, MS a/c 4; *LP* IV, i. 366.
[61] E. Dudley, *The Tree of Commonwealth*, ed. D. M. Brodie (Cambridge, 1948), 37.
[62] PRO, C1/325/1–5; PRO, KB9/452/126, 133, 135–6, 138–9, 143, 146, 348–9, 387, 456, 458–61.
[63] PRO, C1/339/82.
[64] PRO, KB9/452/87; *Plumpton Letters and Papers*, 10–12.
[65] *The Great Chronicle of London*, ed. A. H. Thomas and I. D. Thornley (London, 1938), 348.

oppression to make himself rich.[66] But of the other new men it was Hussey who was most often in trouble. One cluster of accusations concerned his spell as sheriff of Lincolnshire in 1493–4. Dudley stressed the importance for good justice of appointing 'good sheriffs and such as will not be affectionate or bribers'.[67] Hussey had a questionable record, for, as he put it to the king, 'misusing your laws'. He accepted £5 cash and two geldings for releasing a prisoner at the Lincoln assizes and £6 13s 4d tied up in a kerchief for not saying any more about an accusation that the abbot of Louth Park was seeking to make gold or silver by alchemical means. When a chain of accusations about a robbery implicated one of his own former servants, Hussey let him go, purportedly for lack of evidence. At Stamford he had a Coventry mercer arrested on information from a thief and confiscated his spices, though he claimed he released him after three or four days and took nothing from him. He was pardoned for all his actions as sheriff of Lincolnshire on 16 January 1496, but his trouble was not at an end.[68] His role in the customs system was also problematic. He was said to have deceived Henry VII to his own profit as weigher of wools at Boston, but he insisted that the wool 'was given from the beam as largely to your profit since I was weigher as it was any time before' and that he 'had never in wages nor reward otherwise than they that occupied it before this many years'.[69] He investigated evasion of the wool customs in Yorkshire and Lincolnshire, but then evaded them himself, selling wool in France for a good price and buying silks and furs so he could look good for Prince Arthur's wedding: 'I would fain', as he admitted, 'have been fresh against that time'.[70]

Allegations continued to the end of Henry's reign and well beyond. He paid a £133 16s 4d fine for 'extortion or bribery', and bought a pardon for murder.[71] He was accused of cancelling a debt of £200 by the simple expedient of cutting up the deed that bound him to pay it.[72] His 'great might and maintenance' allegedly prevented a litigant from gaining redress from the JPs at Sleaford for the armed expulsion of his family from his home, since 'no man there will find nor dare find it contrary to his mind', unlike the king's uncle Lord Welles, who was 'very well and nobly disposed to the ministration of justice'. In star chamber cases he was accused of procuring charges against his local rivals and partiality in investigative commissions. One complainant claimed that at the Sleaford sessions Hussey had asked for the names of inquest jurors who would 'do truly and find the truth' about a murder 'according to their oaths and conscience', but then had these men replaced by his 'tenants and servants' who 'would find nothing contrary to his pleasure', especially when presented with evidence from his friends. Fellow JPs said that he maintained murderers and other felons and practised extortion.[73]

---

[66] W. C. Richardson, 'The Surveyor of the King's Prerogative', *EHR* 56 (1941), 64.
[67] Dudley, *Tree*, 35.
[68] PRO, SC1/51/179; *CPR 1494–1509*, 40.   [69] PRO, SC1/51/179.
[70] BL, Addl. MS 21480, fos. 67r–67v, 78v, 175r, 178r; PRO, SC1/51/179.
[71] PRO, SC1/51/179; BL, Addl. MS 21480, fos. 66v, 76r.
[72] PRO, KB27/969, m. 94r.
[73] PRO, STAC1/1/12, 25; STAC2/29/40; E. Trollope, *Sleaford and the Wapentakes of Flaxwell and Aswardhurn in the County of Lincoln* (London, 1872), 196–201; WAM 566, 33022, 33023.

In most of these cases, of course, Hussey, or those he supported, could put forward another side to the story. He was helping the coroner's inquest find the truth about the murder; those taking the house had legal judgments in their favour; if accused felons were not guilty, then standing surety for them and giving them food and drink did not make him an accessory to their crimes. But Hussey was criticized in far more insistent and detailed ways than others who survived 1509. Windsor was a pale imitation: it was suggested that a Middlesex jury found an improbable verdict in a land suit after nine hours' discussion because three or four of the jurors, 'somewhat for dread and somewhat for affection' towards him, or perhaps even 'corrupt by promise', favoured his 'feigned interest and title'.[74] Wyatt was accused of 'supportation, great bearing and sinister importunity and means' in a complex case he may just have been trying to sort out, involving a London brewer who stabbed his wife and unborn child and the brother-in-law who took some of his goods hoping to save them from confiscation.[75]

When the new men's self-help did overstep the mark, kings and colleagues made efforts to restrain them. Accusations against Hussey were collected by Mordaunt and Richard Sampson, clerk of the council, and Bray and Lovell assessed his customs evasion fine.[76] He produced a long justification of his actions to Henry VII when the king pressed him, but also threw himself on the king's mercy—'I submit me to the pleasure of your most noble grace and beseech you of your most gracious favour and am content to be ordered after your pleasure'—and offered to list the offences he did admit in even more detail 'upon pain of jeopardy of your displeasure, which I will not offend'.[77] Wolsey put him out of the council for a time, 'to his great miscomfort and heaviness', and removed him from certain local commissions, 'to the diminishment of his worship, saving only the perfect love and favour that divers of his country did bear unto him'.[78]

Others faced similar treatment. Empson was bound over in 1504 to stop his quarrel with William Cornish, composer and gentleman of the chapel royal, who seems to have been beaten up and imprisoned for criticizing him.[79] When Sir William Meryng took his quarrel with Sir Edward Stanhope, in which Empson had supported Stanhope even when he attacked Meryng on the streets of London, to parliament in 1504, the king and other councillors promoted a settlement.[80] When Windsor fell out in 1517 with Thomas Pygot, king's serjeant-at-law, over the wardship of George Bulstrode, whom Windsor claimed as his tenant by knight service, his fellow councillors, led by Wolsey, stepped in. Their servants had fought, and one man been killed, leaving the cardinal fuming that they must be taught

---

[74] PRO, C1/513/15.   [75] PRO, SP1/42, fos. 126–45 (*LP* IV, ii. 3212).
[76] BL, Addl. MS 21480, fos. 67r–67v, 178r.   [77] PRO, SC1/51/179.
[78] WAM, 33022.
[79] M. R. Horowitz, 'Richard Empson, Minister of Henry VII', *BIHR* 55 (1982), 48–9; T. Penn, *Winter King: The Dawn of Tudor England* (London, 2011), 163–5.
[80] A. Cameron, 'A Nottinghamshire Quarrel in the Reign of Henry VII', *BIHR* 45 (1972), 27–37.

'the new law of star chamber'. In the end, however, it was the more traditional route of arbitration that settled the affair, as two judges in 1519 gave the wardship to Pygot but ordered him to pay Windsor £200.[81]

The law courts were more often involved when it was a matter of the new men's deputies or servants misbehaving. Chancery heard of the excesses of Roland Digby, Lovell's under-constable at Nottingham Castle, who imprisoned the sheriff's bailiffs in irons in 1499 because they had arrested one of his servants, and of Stephen Draper, his understeward at Thetford, who, by his 'crafty handling' and 'politic counsel', supposedly set up and then judged a lawsuit to win a friend £4 6s 8d damages.[82] The council learned in the law pursued Lovell's lieutenant at Wallingford Castle, Humphrey Wellesbourne, over escapes from the prison there, though blame had originally fallen on Wellesbourne's own deputy, William Plattys, keeper of the castle prison.[83] Belknap's deputy Philip Warton was charged in 1509 with offences including the extortion of 9s 8d from a Southwark man on a false claim of outlawry.[84] Empson's associate Benedict Davey, entrusted by Dudley with the sale of the timber from some crown woodland, was said to have made £230 but handed over only £68 10s of it.[85] In some cases the subordinates' actions were hard to separate from their masters', and agents of Empson and Dudley like John Camby, Richard Page, and Henry Toft were swept away with them in 1509.[86] Distinctions were also hard to make where relatives were involved. A commission led by Hobart looked into all manner of abuses by Southwell's brother Francis as farmer of the duchy of Lancaster manor of Gimingham in Norfolk, including the claim that his servants had killed two of the king's deer 'and carried them to Sir Robert Southwell'.[87]

In some cases—Empson and Dudley would have argued in theirs—the servants were serving not just their masters but the king. Wyatt and his men were called into star chamber in around 1520 by the Yorkshire clergyman Dr Thomas Drax as part of a long-running tangle of suits. Drax's brother Robert had married Wyatt's sister Joan and died leaving a son, also called Thomas. Dr Thomas painted a dire picture of Wyatt's henchman Thomas Kendall taking a dozen or more followers, in one case including the young Thomas Wyatt, to rustle his cattle from his lands and impound them at Tickhill Castle at Sir Henry's command, even while the dispute between him and Sir Henry was under arbitration, then refusing to release the cattle under a writ of replevin. Wyatt countered that young Thomas Drax was his ward, the lands in question were his, and the case was already being heard in the court of requests. Kendall proudly reported that he had 'the keeping of the castle of Tickhill under his master, Sir Henry Wyatt' and that he refused the replevin

[81] *LP* II, ii, App. 38; Buckinghamshire RO, D/P320.

[82] PRO, C1/192/24, 530/26.

[83] PRO, DL5/2, fos. 38v, 48r–48v, 50v, 52v, 57r; E404/85/100; KB9/415/5, 415/7; BL, Addl. MS 21480, fo. 166r.

[84] PRO, KB9/452/424–6, 428–9.   [85] PRO, KB9/452/125.

[86] Penn, *Winter King*, 266–9, 276, 346–8.   [87] PRO, DL3/9/R8, R8a.

because it was not issued by an officer of the duchy of Lancaster and 'he would obey no replevin made by none stranger contrary to the liberties of the said duchy'.[88]

Sometimes servants just got out of hand. Star chamber took detailed evidence about the bloody end of Marney's servant Michael Brasebrigge, who took sanctuary at Colchester after killing a servant of the earl of Shrewsbury, reportedly fought one acquaintance who came to visit him with a dagger and the stones he kept up his sleeve, and was killed in the abbey cloister in a murky scuffle involving, according to various accounts, a tailor called Black Tom, a relative of another man he had killed and the son of Marney's great friend Sir John Raynsford, whom he apostrophized while dying as 'thou coward gentleman'.[89] Seven of Southwell's men were accused of maiming his Norfolk neighbour John Lestrange of Little Massingham, gentleman, when a dispute over rival claims to grazing land at Great Bircham generated a confrontation in 1510 in which Southwell's servant John Whitney was wounded by Lestrange's servants; the council, Poynings among them, had to order Southwell and Lestrange and their servants to keep the peace.[90] Lovell seems to have tried to keep his deputies in line with stringent financial penalties like those used by the king. After his death his executors sued Richard Tempest of Bradford for £2,000, most likely on a bond given by Tempest for good conduct as deputy to Lovell at Halifax.[91] Equally predictably, Hussey's servants were not well thought of. His cook was charged with assault in London in 1508, another servant was a prisoner in Newgate in 1522, and in 1532 suspicion pointed to his men when hundreds of pounds were stolen from the prior of Spalding.[92] Authority could not always be exercised without hard-nosed subordinates and strong-armed servants. When they got out of hand the new men faced the same problem as great lords, that to disown them might discourage their other followers from zealous pursuit of their master's interests.

In the circumstances, the collective check on their men's misbehaviour provided by the judicial institutions they themselves helped to operate was the best means available to keep good order while preserving their own social power. In this area as in others, the new men's relationship with legality and justice was not unambiguous. While claiming to act according to law and in pursuit of good order and the common weal, they used their legal expertise and their access to the best lawyers to defend and promote their private interests and extend their power. They would no doubt have argued that their conduct was preferable to the violent self-help they decried in others, but it did not always seem that way to their victims.

---

[88] *Yorkshire Star Chamber Proceedings*, i. 107–15, 174–6, iii. 15–17; PRO, CP40/1021B, m. 236r; KB27/1079, mm. 29v, 36v, 1081, m. 61v; C1/690/36.

[89] PRO, STAC2/18/283, 20/26, 100.

[90] PRO, KB27/1000, m. 37v, 1001, m. 34r, 1002, mm. 40v, 72v, 1003, m. 87r, 1004, m. 62v, 1005, m. 29v; STAC10/4/2/356.

[91] PRO, CP40/1056, m. 530v.   [92] PRO, KB9/453/424; *LP* III, ii. 2648(29), V. 1576.

11

Families and friends

The new men's dealings with towns and manors, deputies, retainers, churchmen, and lawyers blended formal office-holding with informal transactions of clientage, influence, and favour. Equally important in exercising power were relationships of friendship and kinship yet further detached from official structures. Families and friends were the means to get things done, especially to get things done at a distance for men busily engaged in central government: as it was crisply explained in a lawsuit, Southwell helped his favoured candidate gain title to lands in Norfolk 'by the assistance of his friends and kinsfolks'.[1] And both kinship and friendship tied them not only to those who were, like servants or retainers, their dependants, but also to those who were their equals or superiors among the gentry, higher clergy, and peerage, and around them at court and in council.

FAMILIES

Kinship provided the new men with helpers, friends, and followers. Brothers, sons, uncles, and nephews in the male line were the most obvious allies on whom to call, though recent events demonstrated that brothers, uncles, and nephews such as Edward IV, George duke of Clarence, Richard III, and Edward V could not be guaranteed to get along. Uncles and cousins on the mother's side might also be important. Marriages built on alliances of property and power aimed to bind in-laws together. Meanwhile, high death rates and ready re-marriage created all sorts of relationships between step-parents, step-children, and step-siblings which might prove particularly close or particularly bitter. Much might be expected of kin, and they might in turn expect much from the new men. Poynings's father-in-law Sir John Scott, dying two months after Bosworth, named Sir Edward supervisor of his will, 'heartily putting trust in' him 'to be the great comfort cheer and aider to my said wife, my son William and to all my servants'.[2]

Family members played an important role in looking after the local interests of those absorbed in the business of court and council. Many served as sheriffs, keeping county administration ticking over in a way that suited their powerful kinsmen. Windsor's son William and son-in-law Roger Corbet held the shrievalty in Bedfordshire and Buckinghamshire, his brother-in-law Sir George Puttenham, and brother Sir Anthony in Hampshire. Hussey's son Sir William served in

[1] PRO, C1/593/21.   [2] PRO, PROB11/7/15.

Lincolnshire, Poynings's brother-in-law Sir William Scott in Kent, Marney's son-in-law Thomas Bonham in Essex.[3] Some were also active JPs. After 1509 Marney rarely sat in Essex, but Thomas Bonham did so frequently and from 1517 Sir John Marney sometimes joined him.[4]

Until his death in 1521, Lovell's brother Sir Robert, married to a minor local heiress, played the roles in Norfolk society for which Sir Thomas did not have time, keeping up contact with their first cousin Sir Gregory Lovell, head of the senior line of the family seated at Barton Bendish, supervising local wills, acting as a feoffee for local gentry, and overseeing the rebuilding of the church tower at Swaffham.[5] He served on county commissions for inquests, musters, concealed lands, and the seizure of Scotsmen's goods, held some crown land stewardships, and as sheriff, in 1489, took Norfolk and Suffolk's tax revenues to the Exchequer with an armed escort of a dozen men.[6] He was also a vigorous Norfolk JP, conspicuously so at Lynn, near the bulk of his brother's lands.[7] The value of his presence is evident from an indictment taken before him at the quarter sessions at Norwich on 31 May 1491. A yeoman, a chaplain, and a housewife were indicted for forcibly depriving Sir Thomas and others of a small property in Hingham, and the indictment was delivered into the king's bench by Robert in person.[8] In return for his support, Sir Thomas generously financed the marriages of his brother's daughters into neighbouring gentry families.[9]

Brandon's brother Sir Robert similarly looked out for his interests in Norfolk and Suffolk as a JP, muster and tax commissioner, sheriff in 1491–2 and 1507–9, and knight of the shire for Norfolk in the 1491–2 parliament.[10] He was trusted as a feoffee by local landowners and counted as one of 'the worshipful of this shire' by John, Lord Fitzwalter, but was certainly not averse to throwing his weight around in local affairs.[11] In a string of lawsuits, indictments, and appearances before the council learned he was accused of unjust imprisonment, failure to deliver writs, letting

[3] *List of Sheriffs for England and Wales*, PRO Lists and Indexes 9 (London, 1898), 3, 45, 55, 69, 80, 88.

[4] PRO, KB9/459/39, 461/76, 463/14, 464/81, 467/9, 472/80, 473/14, 476/19, 477/49, 479/20, 479/109, 481/13, 481/28, 482/25, 482/46, 485/27, 487/13; E137/11/4, mm. 6r–18v.

[5] PRO, C142/84/54, 89/54; C1/536/30–2; F. Blomefield, *An Essay towards a Topographical History of the County of Norfolk*, 11 vols (London, 1805–10), i. 484, ii. 349, vi. 208, ix. 497; *Register of John Morton*, iii. 53.

[6] *CPR 1485–94*, 357, 393; *CPR 1494–1509*, 265, 408, 424; *LP* I, i. 132 (26), 833 (58), 2222 (16); Blomefield, *Norfolk*, ii. 329; 'Income Tax Assessments of Norwich, 1472 and 1489', ed. M. Jurkowski, in *Poverty and Wealth: Sheep, Taxation and Charity in Late Medieval Norfolk*, ed. M. Bailey, M. Jurkowski, and C. Rawcliffe, Norfolk RS 71 (Norwich, 2007), 108.

[7] PRO, KB9/389/72, 396/18, 402/11, 403/9, 417/16, 429/29, 429/33, 441/30, 449/15, 459/119, 463/18, 464/7, 469/48, 470/94; DL5/4, fo. 125v.

[8] PRO, KB9/389/72.

[9] PRO, PROB11/23/27.

[10] J. C. Wedgwood, *History of Parliament: Biographies of the Members of the Commons House, 1439–1509* (London, 1936), 102; KB9/376/17, 434/60; D. N. J. MacCulloch, *Suffolk and the Tudors: Politics and Religion in an English County 1500–1600* (Oxford, 1986), 352–3; *CPR 1485–94*, 278, 349; *Rotuli Parliamentorum*, ed. J. Strachey et al, 6 vols (London, 1767–77), vi. 536.

[11] Blomefield, *Norfolk*, viii. 94; PRO, CP25/1/170/195/13, 14, 20; *The Paston Letters 1422–1509*, ed. J. Gairdner, 3 vols (London, 1872–5), iii. 342–3.

prisoners escape, contempt of court, forcibly withholding his step-son's inheritance, cutting down 400 of his neighbour's trees, retaining—though he argued that all those to whom he had given livery were genuinely his servants, including one who was his 'swan-herd', caring for swans and chickens—and various riots featuring his servants and kin.[12] In the light of all this, the instructions he was supposed to have given one of his men, sent to kidnap an heiress he claimed as his ward, 'break no doors for her nor make no affrays, but deal under good manner', sound rather improbable.[13] This rough-and-ready influence nonetheless made him a useful partner to his brother in royal grants of land and office in Suffolk, while his third marriage, to the widow of John Carew of Haccombe, Devon, gave him links in the West Country to match his brother's.[14] In Brandon's will he was thanked with £10 and a luxurious russet gown, of tinsel satin furred with genets.[15]

The Brandons' cousin Humphrey Wingfield complemented Sir Robert as an up-and-coming lawyer and active Suffolk JP.[16] He worked astutely in land purchase negotiations, reporting to Sir Thomas on one rival buyer that 'as I feel by him he will not have your displeasure for the advantage of the said bargain; and so I see not but that ye may have your pleasure in the matter'. He also oversaw the building of an aisle at Wangford church, where the Brandons' parents were buried, paying £40 to the builder and arranging for the purchase of lead at London to roof it, since the builder thought 'if it should lie uncovered all this winter it should be much damageous to the church'.[17] Other members of the ramified Wingfield clan helped Sir Thomas in other ways, including Sir Robert who took on the main financial role among his executors and others who acted as feoffees and sureties.[18] Brandon's bonds to them were evident not only in his standing surety for their debts, but also in his request to be buried as near as possible to the tomb of his uncle Sir John Wingfield, father to Sir Robert and Humphrey.[19]

Brandon's sister Mary and her husband John Redyng helped him out in rather different ways. They connected him to successive generations of the royal family, Mary serving Elizabeth of York, Prince Henry, and Princess Mary as a gentlewoman and John acting as treasurer of Prince Henry's household between 1499 and 1503. More concretely, they boarded various members of his household, perhaps when he was away at war or on embassy, his wife Lady Berkeley and sixteen servants for

[12] PRO, C1/146/53; KB9/401/25, 432/3; KB27/941, Rex m. 7; KB27/952, m. 28v; E404/81/3, writ of 19 November 1494, E404/85/100, writ of 27 May 1505; DL5/4, fos. 34v, 51v, 68v, 84v, 90v, 91v; BL, Addl. MS 59899, fos. 179v, 183v; *CIPM*, ii. 468; *Records of the City of Norwich*, ed. W. Hudson, J. C. Tingey, 2 vols (Norwich, 1906–10), i. 307.
[13] PRO, STAC2/7, fo. 85
[14] NRO, Bishop's Register 13B, fo. 36r; PRO, C1/286/85; PROB11/21/28; KB27/981, m. 60v; C1/118/52, 284/3, 286/76, 329/64–5.
[15] PRO, PROB11/116/29.
[16] Bindoff, *Commons*, iii. 640–1; PRO, E137/42/3/1, 11; KB9/442/119; MacCulloch, *Suffolk*, 356, 372–4; S. J. Gunn, *Charles Brandon, Duke of Suffolk, c.1484–1545* (Oxford, 1988), 45–50.
[17] WAM 16091; PRO, PROB11/9/7; CP40/950, m. 307r–307v.
[18] BL, Addl. MS 45131, fo. 154r; *CPR 1494–1509*, 503; *Abstracts of Feet of Fines relating to Wiltshire 1377–1509*, ed. J. L. Kirby, Wiltshire RS 41 (Devizes, 1986), 174–5; BL, Addl. MS 59899, fo. 153v; PRO, E101/414/16, fo. 210v.
[19] PRO, E101/426/16, fo. 210v; PROB11/16/29; BL, Addl. MS 59899, fo. 153v.

nearly eight months and Lord Saye and his man for three years. They even agreed to adapt their house for the purpose, building 'a closet over the chapel...for the said Lady Berkeley to sit or be at her divine service and mass'. Brandon died, they alleged, owing them over £100 towards the costs.[20]

Sir Robert Hussey was another supportive brother. He married an heiress and assembled a landed estate worth some £500 a year around Linwood and Blankney, either side of Lincoln.[21] He developed relationships with various religious houses and parish churches, lent out money to local men, and supervised their wills.[22] From 1507 he served on a variety of local commissions, in 1533 he was reckoned 'of great substance and power', being 'of kin and ally to the most part of all the honourable and worshipful men' in the county, and even in the immediate aftermath of his brother's downfall he was accounted 'a man of worship and a great ruler in the country, greatly friended and allied within the same', well able to sway a jury at Lincoln.[23] His brother relied on him heavily in the running of his estates and made him the primary executor of his will, offering in exchange financial support for Robert's son's expensive marriage to a royal ward.[24]

Step-kin might have bonds as lasting as those of blood. Windsor asked his step-father Sir Robert Litton to stand godfather to his eldest son George, was supervisor of Litton's will and served for three decades as a feoffee on the lands of Litton's son and grandson.[25] Poynings, similarly, was feoffee, surety and testamentary supervisor for his step-father's brother, Sir Anthony Browne.[26] Brothers-in-law, too, might stick together. Marney was executor to his brother-in-law Sir John Arundel, while Windsor and his brothers-in-law Sir Richard Fowler and Sir George Puttenham acted as feoffees to one another.[27]

---

[20] PRO, E404/83/1; LC2/1, fos. 73r, 74r; C1/671/18; BL, Addl. MS 59899, fo. 26r; *LP* I, ii. 3324(14).

[21] *Lincolnshire Church Notes*, ed. R. E. G. Cole, Lincoln RS 1 (Lincoln, 1911), 238; *LP* I, i. 438 (4 m. 15); LA, LCC Wills 1545–6, i, fos. 227r–237r; PRO, CP25/2/25/160/9, CP25/2/25/162/23, CP25/2/25/162/31, CP25/2/25/167/27; E315/393, fos. 14r, 16r; E36/95, fo. 47r.

[22] *The Manuscripts of the Duke of Leeds, the Bridgewater Trust, Reading Corporation, the Inner Temple*, HMC 11th report 7 (London, 1888), 66; *VE*, iv. 36, 38, 117, 123, 234; LA, Bishop's Register 27, fo. 65r–65v; BL, Egerton Charters 480, 482; *Illustrations of the Manners and Expenses of Antient Times in England*, ed. J. Nichols (London, 1791), 228; PRO, C1/534/74; E118/1/31, fo. 41v; *Lincoln Wills*, ed. C. W. Foster, 3 vols, Lincoln RS 5, 10, 24 (Lincoln, 1914–30), ii. 77, 133, iii. 54; *Lincoln Wills, 1532–1534*, ed. D. Hickman, Lincoln RS 89 (Lincoln, 2001), 187.

[23] *CPR 1494–1509*, 648; *LP* I, i. 804 (13), 969 (52), ii. 2222 (16), 3582 (14), p. 1540, III, i. 1081 (14, 26), ii. 3504, IV, ii. 5083 (2), V. 119 (69), 278 (17), 1694, VII. 1498 (13), VIII. 149 (44), XI. 202 (13); 4 Henry VIII c. 18; 5 Henry VIII c. 17; 6 Henry VIII c. 26; PRO, C1/855/16.

[24] PRO, E36/95, fos. 16r–17r, 20r, 82r; SP1/122, fo. 173 (*LP* XII, ii. 187 (3)); C54/400, m. 32d.

[25] PRO, CP25/1/294/80/67; *LP* VII. 761(18); *CAD*, vi. C7473; PRO, PROB11/14/35.

[26] *CPR 1494–1509*, 339; *CCR 1485–1500*, 1006; *Testamenta Vetusta*, ed. N. H. Nicolas, 2 vols (London, 1826), ii. 489.

[27] *Cornish Wills 1342–1540*, ed. N. Orme, Devon and Cornwall RS n.s. 50 (Exeter, 2007), 154; *CIPM*, iii. 519; OHC, M/112/D/1; Wi/I/i/2; PRO, C1/487/10; C54/387, m. 12d; CP25/1/191/31/63; *Bedfordshire Wills proved in the Prerogative Court of Canterbury 1383–1548*, ed. M. McGregor, Bedfordshire Historical RS 58 (Bedford, 1979), 132, 134; *Abstracts of Surrey Feet of Fines 1509–1558*, ed. C. A. F. Meekings, 2 vols, Surrey RS 45–6 (Frome, 1946), 10; *Herts Genealogist and Antiquary*, ed. W. Brigg, 3 vols (St Albans, 1896–8), i. 79; 'Fines of Mixed Counties', ed. G. Wrottesley, *Collections for a History of Staffordshire* 12/1 (London, 1891), 178–9.

Kinship bonds often crossed the generations. Poynings kept up contact with his mother's family, the Pastons.[28] Hussey's relative on his mother's side, Thomas Marmyon of Ringstone, stood surety for his debts and feoffee on his estates in 1505–15. Elizabeth Marmyon lived in his household in 1533–4 and he paid to board Dorothy Marmyon at Catley Priory. At the end of his life, he asked the king to meet his large debts to his aunt Marmyon and her daughter.[29] Further alliances might be built by the marriages of children. In 1499, Marney's daughter Katherine married Edward Knyvett of Stanway, a neighbouring esquire, as his second wife. He survived the marriage less than three years, but left her with dower lands in Essex and Suffolk, which she took into a second marriage with Thomas Bonham, a rising Inner Temple lawyer who settled down at Stanway to help govern Essex.[30] In 1510, her sister Grace married Edmund Bedingfield, third son but eventual heir of a Norfolk knightly family.[31] Bonham and Bedingfield were duly enfeoffed with lands to the use of Marney's will.[32]

The use of kinsfolk in property settlements spread the net of affinity wide and combined representation of the powerful parental generation with that of their juniors, so that any children endowed would not find all their protectors had died by the time they needed them. Marney, for example, in settling lands for his daughter Grace in 1510, used not only his son John, but also some of the younger members of the Tyrrell family, relatives through his sister's marriage to Sir Thomas Tyrrell of Heron.[33] Windsor used Andrew Sulyard, first cousin on his mother's side, in some of his feoffments, and Wyatt used John Skinner, his father-in-law.[34] Equally, the new men consolidated their bonds with their kin by marriage by acting as their feoffees or as sureties for their debts to the king. Marney did so for Sir William Capel, who had married the sister of Marney's first wife, and his son Sir Giles, though he was shrewd enough to extract bonds from them protecting him against the consequences should they default.[35] Poynings did so for his sister-in-law Margaret Bedingfield and went on to stand surety for his nephew's livery.[36]

[28] PRO, CP25/1/170/196/84, 197/113; *Paston Letters and Papers of the Fifteenth Century*, ed. N. Davis, 2 vols (Oxford, 1971–6), i. 196; Blomefield, *Norfolk*, v. 60.

[29] LA, H1/10; *CCR 1500–9*, 444, 586; PRO, E36/215, fo. 325r; E36/95, fos. 28v, 97v; SP1/121, fo. 2v (*LP* XII, ii. 2).

[30] *CIPM*, ii. 417–19, iii. 457, 537; R. Somerville, *A History of the Duchy of Lancaster, I, 1265–1603* (London, 1953), i. 402; PRO, CP25/2/51/358/2, 363/18.

[31] BL, Addl. Ch. 5515; *The Visitation of Norfolk in the Year 1563*, ed. G. H. Dashwood and E. Bulwer Lytton, 2 vols (Norwich, 1878–95), i. 158.

[32] 'Ancient Wills', ed. H. W. King, *TEAS* 4 (1869), 150; D. Grummitt, 'Radcliffe, Robert, first earl of Sussex', *ODNB*.

[33] BL, Addl. Ch. 5515; *The Visitations of Essex by Hawley, 1552; Hervey, 1558; Cooke, 1570; Raven, 1612; and Owen and Lilly, 1634*, ed. W. C. Metcalfe, 2 vols, HS 13–14 (London, 1878–9), i. 113–14.

[34] 'Fines of Mixed Counties', 178–9, 182–3; Blomefield, *Norfolk*, viii. 287; S. Brigden, *Thomas Wyatt; The Heart's Forest* (London, 2012), 65–6; PRO, CP25/1/232/79/116.

[35] W. Minet, 'The Capells at Rayne, 1486–1622', *TEAS* n.s. 9 (1906), 259, 262; BL, Addl. MS 21480, fo. 49r; PRO, C146/9666, 9782.

[36] J. R. Scott, *Memorials of the Family of Scott of Scot's-Hall* (London, 1876), 125; *CIPM*, ii. 4; BL, Addl. MS 21480, fos. 53v, 80v.

The employment of kin as servants produced dependable subordinates and offered them the chance of advancing themselves. William Sidney, for example, Brandon's nephew, was brought up for seven years in his uncle's household and 'continually waited upon him in the court', launching a career that would make him chamberlain to Prince Edward, his son lord deputy of Ireland, and his grand-sons the Elizabethan hero Sir Philip Sidney and the Jacobean earl of Leicester.[37] Southwell's nephew Robert Holdich served in his estate administration, witnessed his will, and went on to become receiver-general for the third duke of Norfolk.[38] Thomas Lovell of Enfield, apparently descended from Lovell's uncle William Lovell of Chesterton, was tightly bound into the leading circle of Sir Thomas Lovell's household servants, while Gregory Lovell of Harlington, a more distant relation, entered Sir Thomas's service by 1514, carried the banner of the Trinity at his funeral, and used him as a feoffee.[39]

Kin also linked the new men to powerful allies. Sir Robert Lovell was a leading retainer of the earl of Oxford and Brandon's Wingfield cousins also served him, Walter as a household officer, Anthony a gentleman of the household, Humphrey a legal councillor.[40] Lewis Wingfield served in the household of Bishop Fox, even-tually as comptroller.[41] Sir Robert Hussey served the Lords Roos, and Lovell before them, as bailiff and constable of Belvoir Castle, while he later drew close to the duke of Norfolk, in whose service his son, Hussey's nephew Thomas, did well.[42] In the 1530s, Andrew Windsor's brother Sir Anthony was active in managing the affairs of Arthur Plantagenet, Viscount Lisle, while he was absent in command at Calais. It was the culmination of a career on the Lisle estates dating back to Lady Lisle's marriage to his and Andrew's brother-in-law Edmund Dudley, though it cannot always have been comfortable, for the Lisles' London agent John Husee clearly did not like him.[43]

Kinship was particularly important for those whose landed wealth or office-hold-ing gave them little traction in local society. Southwell's eight sisters provided him with many brothers-in-law among the Norfolk gentry, several of them active in

[37] PRO, C24/29; Bindoff, *Commons*, iii. 318; P. W. Hasler, *The House of Commons 1558–1603*, 3 vols (London, 1981), iii. 382–7.

[38] PRO, C1/593/20–2; C142/29/15; PROB11/18/5; D. M. Head, *The Ebbs and Flows of Fortune: the Life of Thomas Howard, Third Duke of Norfolk* (Athens GA, 1995), 260–1.

[39] PRO, PROB11/20/22; PROB11/23/27; Blomefield, *Norfolk*, i. 45–6; *LP* III, ii. 2016(29), IV, i. 366; *The Victoria History of the County of Middlesex*, ed. W. Page et al., 13 vols (London, 1911–), iii. 262; PRO, E13/190, m. 17d; LMA, Acc/0530/M9, m. 9a.

[40] ERO, D/DWd1; BL, Addl. Ch. 41711; 'The Last Testament and Inventory of John de Veer, thirteenth earl of Oxford', ed. W. H. StJ. Hope, *Archaeologia* 66 (1915), 318; BL, Addl. Ch. 41711; PRO, C24/29; Longleat House, Misc. vol. 11, fos. 81v, 82v, 83r, 114r, 126r, 129r, 131r, 133r; CA, MS M16bis, fo. 55v; J. Ross, *John de Vere, Thirteenth Earl of Oxford (1442–1513):'The Foremost Man of the Kingdom'* (Woodbridge, 2011), 187–8, 192, 194–5, 233–4, 238–9.

[41] CA, MS M16bis, fo. 28r; *LP* I, ii. 1948 (17), 2055 (72, ii).

[42] Belvoir Castle, Addl. MS 97; *HMC Rutland*, iv. 171; *LP* VI. 633; Bindoff, *Commons*, ii. 425–6.

[43] *The Lisle Letters*, ed. M. St C. Byrne, 6 vols (Chicago, 1981), i. 155–6, 164, 277–85; *LP* VI. 814, 1339, 1436, VII. 24, 291, 350, 773, 856, 917, 929, 959, 979, 1471, 1491, 1521, VIII. 40, 663, 773, 1017, IX. 460, 571, 643, 850, 859, 860, X. 708, 780, 856, 994, XI. 46, 264, 370, 478, 1181, 1222, 1256, 1282, XII, i. 759, ii. 166, XIII, i. 382, ii. 485–6.

county government.[44] He made good use of them and they of him. John Berney, Ralph Berney, Anthony Hansard, Edmund Jenney, and William Wotton served him as feoffees, as did his more distant relatives by marriage Philip Calthorp, Robert Holdich, and John Sturgeis and his cousin Robert Southwell of Barham, Suffolk.[45] Anthony Hansard supported him in buying wardships.[46] He named 'my brother' William Wotton one of his executors and Wotton duly helped his widow buy the wardship of his nephew and heir.[47] When Wotton died a dozen years later, he requested burial before the altar where mass was sung daily for Southwell's soul.[48] Wotton and John Berney used Southwell as a feoffee; Berney named him supervisor of his will and Southwell did his best to see Berney's daughters, two of whom were brought up as attendants to his wife, well married.[49] Such men's local influence presumably worked in tandem with Southwell's own, Wotton receiving a fee from Thetford priory, for example, as did Southwell's brother Francis.[50]

Yet relations could also be a liability. Sir Robert Brandon had his demanding moments, Sir Thomas and three of the Wingfields having to stand surety for his release from prison in 1495 when he was condemned to pay damages in a trespass suit.[51] Hussey had bigger problems. His uncle or older cousin, Peter, archdeacon of Northampton, was caught on the fringes of Yorkist plotting in the mid-1490s, and Hussey's own name came up in some of the evidence against him.[52] Worse was to come with his brother, William. He married into land in Yorkshire, was active at court, and from 1526 spent much of his time at Calais, as comptroller.[53] But he fell foul of the council learned in 1501, 'detected of felony', and John had to strike a deal with Bray, Lovell, and others by which William's wife's inheritance was made over to the king to yield £100 a year.[54] Then, allegedly at the prompting of Dudley's associate John Baptist Grimaldi, William was held to have broken the terms of bonds given for his true allegiance to the king, apparently through involvement with the fugitive earl of Suffolk. From 1502 to the end of the reign John, their mother, their brothers-in-law the earl of Kent and Lord Willoughby d'Eresby, William's relative by marriage John Salven, and Lincolnshire and Nottinghamshire

---

[44] *Visitation of Norfolk 1563*, i. 124–5; *LP* I, i. 414(4), 833(58), ii, p. 1541; 12 Henry VII c. 13; 4 Henry VIII c. 19.
[45] PRO, C142/29/15, 32, 44; E150/617/1; *The Visitation of Suffolk, 1561*, ed. J. Corder, 2 vols, HS n.s. 2–3 (London, 1981–4), i. 176.
[46] PRO, E36/215, fo. 331v.
[47] PRO, PROB11/18/5; WARD9/147; E36/215, fo. 340r–340v; *LP* II, i. 96.
[48] PRO, PROB11/22/40.
[49] *CIPM*, iii. 239; *Feet of Fines for Essex*, ed. R. E. G. Kirk et al., 6 vols (Colchester, 1899–1993), iv. 114; PRO, C1/469/46–8.
[50] *The Register of Thetford Priory*, ed. D. Dymond, 2 vols, Norfolk RS 59–60 (Oxford, 1995–6), 220, 223, 234, 245, 248, 259, 260, 263, 273, 275, 285, 287.
[51] PRO, KB27/947, m. 23r.
[52] I. Arthurson, *The Perkin Warbeck Conspiracy 1491–1499* (Stroud, 1994), 77, 135–7; *LPRH*, ii. 318–23.
[53] Bindoff, *Commons*, ii. 427; *Yorkshire Deeds*, v., ed. C. T. Clay, YASRS 69 (Wakefield, 1926), 35–6; PRO, C67/93, m. 2; *LP* II, ii. 3446, pp. 1504, 1507, III, i. 704 (2–3), 906, IV, i. 1945 (27), ii. 2661, 2972, 2975, 3556, 3569, 3655, 4321, 4552, 4601–2, 4689, 4726, 5102 (5), iii. 5947, V. 220 (14).
[54] BL, Addl. MS 21480, fo. 178v; PRO, DL5/2, fo. 22v; *CPR 1494–1509*, 501–2.

neighbours from the Bussy, Byron, Copuldike, Dunham, Marmyon, Quadring, Tyrwhit, and Wymbish families were sucked into a series of large payments and bonds to the king while William spent some time in prison.[55] William was almost as troublesome at the end of his life, dying intestate to leave John and his son George to try to sort out his affairs.[56]

THE GENTRY

The new men's links in local society reached beyond their kin to integrate them into networks of county gentry, harnessing the local expertise and social sway of their neighbours, and in return serving as powerful trustees or executors that troublemakers were unlikely to challenge. Such links were particularly important as the leading gentry of many counties seem to have moved from the 1450s away from dependence on noble leadership in local affairs and towards greater cooperation among themselves and closer links with the crown.[57] Lovell's early legal practice involved him as a feoffee in various East Anglian settlements, and after 1485 his activity increased with his influence.[58] Leading local gentry such as Sir William Paston, Sir Thomas Wyndham, and Sir John Heydon served among his own feoffees, while Paston was executor to Lovell and Lovell supervisor to Sir Henry Heydon.[59] Southwell, too, collaborated with his East Anglian neighbours, acting as a feoffee or executor to Sir William Boleyn, Sir Robert Clere, Sir Robert Drury, and Sir Roger Lestrange and to lesser men such as Peter Blake, John Walpole, and the duchy of Lancaster officer Thomas de la Haye, while standing surety with Sir Robert Drury, Sir Henry Heydon, and Sir William Knyvet.[60] Marney did the same in Essex. His feoffees included his fellow JPs Sir Richard Fitzlewis, Sir Thomas Tey, Sir John Vere, and Edward Sulyard and lesser gentlemen from the county such as Anthony Darcy and Robert Foster, even yeoman tenants like Richard and William Badby.[61] He featured in enfeoffments or stood surety for Roger Darcy, John Doreward, Wiliam Tey, Humphrey Tyrrell, Sir Robert Tyrrell, and Sir Roger Wentworth.[62] Similar pictures might be drawn for Poynings in Kent and Sussex,

[55] PRO, E101/413/2/3, fos. 37v, 66r; KB27/986, m. 28v; KB27/1002, m. 35v; BL, Addl. MS 21480, fos. 42v, 44r, 49r–49v, 104v, 158v; *CCR 1500–9*, 939, 955(xix); Penn, *Winter King*, 78–80, 267–9.

[56] PRO, C1/827/47.

[57] C. Carpenter, *Locality and Polity: A Study of Warwickshire Landed Society, 1401–1499* (Cambridge, 1992), 599–614; S. J. Gunn, *Early Tudor Government 1485–1558* (Basingstoke, 1995), 45–8.

[58] BL, Addl. Ch. 27694; PRO, CP25/1/170/196/75; *CAD*, i. A726, v. A13127; *CIPM*, i. 444, ii. 946, iii. 435; *Essex Fines*, iv. 109, 124, 132; *CCR 1485–1500*, 460; *CCR 1500–9*, 395, 474, 868; *Feet of Fines, Divers Counties*, ed. E. F. Kirk (London, 1913–24), 43.

[59] PRO, C142/41/62; PROB11/23/27; *Visitation of Norfolk 1563*, ii. 221.

[60] *CAD*, iv. A7760; *CCR 1500–9*, 179; PRO, CP25/1/170/196/85; NRO, Hare 3618; *Visitation of Norfolk 1563*, i. 376; Somerville, *Duchy of Lancaster*, i. 598; 'Will of Sir Roger le Strange, Knt', ed. H. Le Strange, *NA* 9 (1880–4), 239; BL, Addl. MS 21480, fos. 77v, 83r, 95r.

[61] PRO, CP25/2/51/358/2; C142/40/8, 9; SC6/Henry VII/160; *LP* I, 969(23), ii, p. 1536, III, ii, p. 1367; ERO, D/ACR2, fos. 119v–120r, 240r–241r.

[62] *CCR 1485–1500*, 1015; *CIPM*, i. 1144, ii. 613, iii. 555, 935; BL, Addl. MS 21480, fos. 78v, 99r.

Empson in Northamptonshire and Buckinghamshire, and Dudley in Sussex and beyond.[63]

Those with scattered lands cultivated different circles in different places. Lovell had associates in Middlesex and Kent as well as East Anglia.[64] Wyatt mostly used as feoffees his neighbours Sir Francis Cheyney, Sir Henry Isley, Sir John Legh, Sir Thomas Neville, John Crowmer, John Culpepper, Robert Fisher, and John Scott, all active in the government of Kent and Surrey or the administration of the bishopric of Rochester.[65] But his continuing links with Yorkshire were evident in his use of Sir Richard Cholmley as a feoffee and in East Anglia he added in different feoffees again, leading local gentry such as Sir William Paston, Sir John Heydon, and Sir Roger Townsend.[66] He acted as a feoffee for Kent and Surrey neighbours great and small, close associates and more distant, but also for minor Yorkshire gentry.[67]

Some faced a shaky start. In Warwickshire Belknap was caught up in disruptive feuds among the county's leading families, but eventually built bonds with his neighbours.[68] For others longevity paid off. Windsor's widespread land-holding and long career made him a prolific feoffee for gentry families in Bedfordshire, Berkshire, Buckinghamshire, Derbyshire, Essex, Hampshire, Hertfordshire, Middlesex, Northamptonshire, Oxfordshire, Surrey, Sussex, and Warwickshire.[69] Windsor, like other lawyers, also did favours for brothers from his inn, the Middle Temple, men such as John Fitzjames and Guy Palmes and crown officials such as the auditor Thomas Tamworth. Palmes in turn helped him settle his wife's estates.[70]

---

[63] *Testamenta Vetusta*, ii. 448, 525; PRO, C1/106/41, 251/4–6; CP25/1/117A/348/314, 348/331, 350/444, 351/469, 352/512, 352/533; CP25/2/19/102/21, 111/23; PROB11/20/21; W. L. King, 'Pedigree of the Family of De Fynes', *AC* 28 (1909), 24; *CIPM*, i. 686, 824; *CPR 1485–94*, 326; *CPR 1494–1509*, 339; *CCR 1500–9*, 22; *The Reports of William Dalison 1552–1558*, ed. J. H. Baker, SS 124 (London, 2007), 116–17; Scott, *Memorials*, lxii–lxiii; *Feet of Fines for the County of Sussex*, iii, ed. L. F. Salzmann, Sussex RS 23 (London, 1916), 299, 300; *Early Northampton Wills*, ed. D. Edwards et al., Northamptonshire RS 42 (Northampton, 2005), 164, 184; *The Courts of the Archdeaconry of Buckingham, 1483–1523*, ed. E. M. Elvey, Buckinghamshire RS 19 (Aylesbury, 1975), 196; Wedgwood, *Commons*, 495; *HMC Middleton*, 126.

[64] *CCR 1500–9*, 258; *Feet of Fines, Divers Counties*, 13; *HMC Rutland*, iv. 565; PRO, C142/41/62; Bindoff, *Commons*, ii. 230–1.

[65] *CAD*, iii. D476, D1308, D1058; *CCR 1500–9*, 953; PRO, CP25/2/34/225/18, 37/245/4; E210/9917; E326/7102; *LP* I, i. 289(10), II, i. 1220, III, ii. 4437, App. 45*, VII 1498(13), VIII 149(40); Bindoff, *Commons*, ii. 136, 274–6, iii. 10–11.

[66] PRO, E210/6831, 10160; E326/10416, 8218; *Herts Genealogist and Antiquary*, i. 82.

[67] PRO, CP25/2/19/102/18, 19/107/4, 19/108/14, 19/109/11, 21/123/17, 42/286/36, 42/287/34, 43/297/32; Bodl. MS Yorks ch. 191.

[68] Carpenter, *Locality and Polity*, 563–83, 592.

[69] PRO, CP25/1/6/83/11, 22/120/106, 179/97/20; CP25/2/1/2/35, 31/212/15, 34/225/9, 42/286/46, 43/296/14, 51/359/7–9, 51/364/10; E326/5630, 5636; C1/502/35–7, 559/29, 586/29; WSRO, Addl. MS 4200; Shakespeare Birthplace Trust RO, DR3/275, 283, 286, 294; *CAD*, i. B870, ii. B3460, iii. D1078; *CCR 1485–1500*, 706; *CIPM*, i. 682, iii. 195, 279, 463, 1139; *Derbyshire Feet of Fines 1323–1546*, ed. H. J. H. Garratt and C. Rawcliffe, Derbyshire RS 2 (Chesterfield, 1985), no. 1216; *Essex Fines*, iv. 151; *Herts Genealogist and Antiquary*, i. 2, 6–7, 78; *A Calendar to the Feet of Fines for London and Middlesex*, ed. W. J. Hardy and W. Page, 2 vols (London, 1892–3), ii. 34; F. Markham, *A History of Milton Keynes and District*, 2 vols (Luton, 1973–5), i. 154–5; *Surrey Fines 1509–1558*, 8, 21; *Some Oxfordshire Wills proved in the Prerogative Court of Canterbury, 1393–1510*, ed. J. R. H. Weaver and A. Beardwood, ORS 39 (Oxford, 1958), 90.

[70] E. W. Ives, *The Common Lawyers of Pre-Reformation England. Thomas Kebell: A Case Study* (Cambridge, 1983), 103–9; PRO, CP25/1/145/165/80; CP25/2/2/8/8; *Wiltshire Fines*, 181; *LP* VI. 1195(20); *Feet of Fines, Divers Counties*, 61; 'Fines of Mixed Counties', 178–9; PRO, CP25/2/3/11/9; OHC, Wi/I/i/2.

Hussey, too, had time to build up the wide network among the gentry of Lincolnshire and the adjoining counties evident in the list of those whose servants brought gifts to his household in 1534–5. They included the Kesteven JPs Edmund Bussy, Thomas Hall, Anthony Irby, and Sir John Thimbleby, the Holland JP Blaise Holland, the Lindsey JP John Littlebury, the Nottinghamshire JP Sir John Markham, and perhaps the Leicestershire JP Sir John Villers.[71] Below the level of the bench, they included members of inter-married local gentry families such as the Disneys of Norton Disney and Carlton-le-Moorland, the Suttons of Washingbrough and the Walcots of Walcot.[72] Reciprocal service as feoffees and sureties suggests that he was especially close to the Bussys, but he had enduring connections with other families of similar rank.[73] He paid a £3 fee to his Kesteven neighbour John Fitzrichard of Sedgebrook, for example, and John's father Sir Simon named Hussey, his 'especial and singular good master and friend and well-beloved in Christ', supervisor of his will, bequeathing him a crossbow.[74] Beyond the county boundaries he had connections to such prominent Midlanders as Sir Richard Basset, Sir Nicholas Byron, Sir John Byron, Sir William Gascoigne, Sir George Hastings, Sir George Manners, Sir William Meryng, Sir Nicholas Vaux, and Sir Henry Willoughby and to the Yorkshire families of Tempest, Hopton, and Constable.[75] And when it came to influence in local administration, it was the lawyers who served him as feoffees and attorneys who were vital, men such as Thomas Archer, Anthony Irby, county coroner before he became a JP, and Thomas Gildon, duchy of Lancaster feodary for Lincolnshire.[76] Gildon and Irby in particular were useful men to know, with reputations for bending the law to suit their own interests and those of their friends.[77]

None of the new men was in the position to build up a following of dependent gentry in the same way that the greatest aristocrats could, but where land-holding and local office permitted, they could generate a small imitation of one. In north-west and central Norfolk, Lovell retained four gentlemen, but they were not at the level of his knightly associates. John Cusshyn was taxed on £80 and his interests were confined to his home village of Hingham and those around.[78] William Greve was taxed on £100 or more, but in goods; he called himself Lovell's servant when

---

[71] PRO, E36/95, fos. 31v–62v; *LP* V. 166(9, 10), 838(27), XI. 202(13), XII, i. 1104(10).

[72] *Lincolnshire Pedigrees*, ed. A. R. Maddison, 4 vols, HS 50–2, 55 (London, 1902–6), i. 303–4, iii. 939–40, 1032.

[73] LA, H1/10; BLARS, L24/429; BL, Addl. MS 21480, fo. 42r; PRO, E211/130; CP25/2/112/9; CP25/2/25/163/50; *CCR 1485–1500*, 807, 914–15; *CCR 1500–9*, 444, 913.

[74] PRO, E315/237, p. 100; LA, LCC wills 1520–31, fos. 126v–127r.

[75] *Testamenta Eboracensia*, ed. J Raine and J. W. Clay, 6 vols, Surtees Society 4, 30, 45, 53, 79, 106 (London, 1836–1902), v. 149; *Feet of Fines, Divers Counties*, 103–4; *CIPM*, ii. 750, 755, 759, 761; PRO, CP25/2/51/368/25; C54/378, m. 15d; *CCR 1500–9*, 131, 904, 913; BL, Addl. MS 21480, fos. 42r–42v, 64v, 97v; NUL, Mi6/173/63–4; PRO, CP25/2/51/364; *Feet of Fines, Divers Counties*, 56–7, 59–60; PRO, E36/95, fos. 97r, 99v.

[76] PRO, CP25/1/145/165/38; CP25/2/33/220/37; CP25/2/51/364; E211/130; *Feet of Fines, Divers Counties*, 56–7, 59–60; Oriel College, Oxford, Shadwell 1161.

[77] PRO, REQ2/4/82; STAC2/15/67–72, 20/292, 31/20.

[78] 'Norfolk Subsidy Roll, 15 Hen VIII', *Norfolk Antiquarian Miscellany* 2 (1883), 403; PRO, PROB11/24/14.

suing those who had broken into his house at West Winch in 1501.[79] Richard Gousell of Fordham was a younger son, endowed with one manor and making his way by leasing other lands and serving in offices such as the constableship of Clackclose hundred and the bailiffship of Ramsey Abbey.[80] Lewis Orwell was apparently the most substantial of them but also the most unstable, charged at various point with piracy off the coast of Normandy and accusing the abbot of West Dereham of being a bondman, and prone to sell off parts of his inheritance, two manors of it to Lovell.[81] Nonetheless, Lovell took Orwell's son James into his household and left him some land.[82]

Office-holding created bonds for the new men even outside the areas where their lands and natural influence lay. It was the chancellorship of the duchy of Lancaster that made Marney a suitable supervisor for the will of Godfrey Foljambe, head of the leading gentry family of north-east Derbyshire.[83] It was his local offices, together with his custody of the Roos estates, that drew Lovell into local politics in the Midlands and Yorkshire, where service alongside him brought even the greater gentry partially into his orbit.[84] His intrusion into Nottinghamshire reduced the dominance of the sometimes unruly local knights who had previously held the Sherwood Forest offices, but did not eliminate from power those prepared to cooperate in serving the king, such as the rich and well-connected Sir Henry Willoughby of Wollaton, whom Lovell nominated in 1509 for election to the garter.[85] Sir John Markham, similarly, served as his lieutenant in Sherwood Forest and attended his funeral, Sir Gervase Clifton named him supervisor of his will, and Richard Whalley served in his household.[86] In Oxfordshire, he retained William Cottesmore, son and heir to Sir John Cottesmore, while Sir John Longford, sheriff in 1508–9, recruited four yeomen for Lovell's retinue though he did not serve himself.[87] In Staffordshire, his stewardships at Walsall and Lichfield heralded a different political style from that of his predecessor, Sir Humphrey Stanley, a loyal household knight and active local governor, but one with a strong penchant for violent self-help. Just enough of the Stanleys' local power was preserved to assist Lovell and the king, as Sir Humphrey's son John collected the names of men willing to serve in Lovell's

[79] 'Norfolk Subsidy Roll', 401; *Muster Roll for the Hundred of North Greenhoe (circa 1523)*, ed. H. L. Bradfer-Lawrence, Norfolk RS 1 (Norwich, 1930), 66; PRO, E13/80, rot. 17d.

[80] Blomefield, *Norfolk*, vii. 367, 411; *LP* I, i. 438(2 m. 26).

[81] Blomefield, *Norfolk*, vii. 300, 504; *CPR 1494–1509*, 527; *LP* I, ii. 2856; PRO, C1/269/25, 404/38–41; REQ2/10/178; KB27/1000, m. 21.

[82] PRO, PROB11/23/27; *HMC Rutland*, iv. 563; *LP* IV, i. 366.

[83] S. M. Wright, *The Derbyshire Gentry in the Fifteenth Century*, Derbyshire RS 8 (Chesterfield, 1983), 61, 239.

[84] Library of Birmingham, Hampton 1910; PRO, CP25/2/51/359/2, 15; *Report on the Manuscripts of Lord de L'Isle and Dudley*, 6 vols, HMC 77 (London, 1925–66), i. 14; *The Victoria History of the County of Buckingham*, ed. W. Page, 5 vols (London, 1905–28), iv. 193; *CCR 1485–1500*, 468.

[85] A. Cameron, 'Sir Henry Willoughby of Wollaton', *Transactions of the Thoroton Society*, 74 (1970), 10–21; A. Cameron, 'Complaint and Reform in Henry VII's Reign: The Origins of the Statue of 3 Henry VII, c.2?', *BIHR* 51 (1978), 86; *The Register of the Most Noble Order of the Garter*, ed. J. Anstis, 2 vols (London, 1724), i. 271.

[86] *HMC Rutland*, iv. 264; *LP* IV, i. 366; *Testamenta Eboracensia*, iv. 276–7; Bindoff, *Commons*, iii. 594.

[87] *Oxfordshire Wills*, 100–1; *List of Sheriffs*, 109; Belvoir Castle, Addl. MS 97.

retinue.[88] Lovell's arrival at Halifax and Wakefield again disappointed the ambitions of the two competing local families, the Saviles and the Tempests, as the Saviles lost the stewardship and the Tempests were relegated to serving as deputies to Lovell, their 'especial good master', but such disappointment was surely the king's aim as he broke up established power structures to insert the men he trusted into local politics.[89]

BISHOPS AND NOBLEMEN

With two powerful groups, senior churchmen and noblemen, the new men often had more ambivalent relationships than with the gentry. As the traditional leaders in national politics such great men might well feel uneasy at the rise of these upstarts. As Francis Bacon later reflected, 'men of noble birth, are noted, to be envious towards new men, when they rise'.[90] The new men, close to the king, were in a position to put forward suits and petitions from great men and women with more confidence than they might do it themselves: Bray and Lovell especially, but also Guildford, Mordaunt, Lucas, Hobart, and others.[91] Worse still, peers and bishops were often prime targets for the policies of fiscal exploitation and coercive control the new men administered for the king. As we shall see, some reacted by placating the new men with grants of pensions and offices and patronage for their friends and relations. Others—Bishop Nykke and the duke of Buckingham stick out—were aggressive. Others again found their way to cooperation.

Several bishops named Bray executor or supervisor of their wills, among them Thomas Langton of Winchester and Edward Storey of Chichester. Archbishop Henry Deane was the most fulsome, naming that 'venerable man my dearest Reynold Bray, knight, most faithful counsellor of our most serene lord his majesty the king of England' first among his executors, while recognizing that Bray was so busy in the king's affairs that he might have time to do little more than offer advice.[92] Poynings had served with Deane in Ireland and on embassy with Deane's successor Warham. He stood surety for Deane's payments to the king as bishop of Salisbury in 1500 and acted as chamberlain at Warham's enthronement feast in 1505.[93]

---

[88] S. J. Gunn, 'Sir Thomas Lovell (c.1449–1524): A New Man in a New Monarchy', in J. L. Watts (ed.), *The End of the Middle Ages? England in the Fifteenth and Sixteenth Centuries* (Stroud, 1998), 117–18.

[89] R. B. Smith, *Land and Politics in the England of Henry VIII: The West Riding of Yorkshire, 1530–1546* (Oxford, 1970), 67, 147–50, 158; *Testamenta Eboracensia*, iv. 250–1; R.W. Hoyle, 'The fortunes of the Tempest family of Bracewell and Bowling in the sixteenth century', *Yorkshire Archaeological Journal* 74 (2002), 169–89.

[90] Francis Bacon, *Essays* (Oxford, 1937), 33.

[91] S. J. Gunn, 'The Courtiers of Henry VII', *EHR* 108 (1993), 30, 46; BL, Addl. MS 21480, fos. 155r, 157r, 164r–87v.

[92] *Sede Vacante Wills*, ed. C. E Woodruff, Kent Archaeological Society records branch 3 (Canterbury, 1914), 99, 111, 114.

[93] BL, Addl. MS 21480, fo. 59v; *Joannis Lelandi Collectanea*, ed. T. Hearne, 6 vols (Oxford, 1774), vi. 18, 25.

Younger clerics built more wide-ranging networks. Thomas Ruthal was secretary to Henry VII for ten years before his promotion to the bishopric of Durham in 1509. At his funeral in 1523, Hussey, Windsor, and Wyatt were three of the leading mourners.[94] Cuthbert Tunstall, appointed bishop of London in 1522, borrowed money to pay his fees from Lovell, whom he served as a feoffee and supervisor of his will; he was also executor to Marney.[95] Southwell bridged the generations. Christopher Urswick, one of Henry's leading clerical councillors and diplomats, who had been close to Bray and was Southwell's neighbour at Hackney, was one of his executors. Richard Sampson, a rising civil lawyer, diplomat, and future bishop, was supported by Southwell in his studies abroad and served as a feoffee on his lands and a witness to his will.[96] Sampson lamented on Southwell's death that he had lost one of his 'great friends' and Tunstall recalled in 1522 that Urswick 'greatly favoured' Sampson 'for Mr Southwell's sake'.[97]

Noblemen close to the king and active at court generally found accommodation with the new men without undue difficulty. The lord steward, Robert, Lord Willoughby de Broke, used Bray and Lovell as feoffees in his grand-daughter's marriage settlement, and the lord chamberlain, Charles Somerset, Lord Herbert, used Hussey and Southwell as feoffees, while Lovell in turn used him.[98] The queen's chamberlain, the earl of Ormond, named Lovell as a feoffee, the chivalric author John, Lord Berners, named Windsor, and the court jouster Henry Bourchier, earl of Essex, named Marney and stood surety for Hussey as master of the wards.[99] The executors of John, Lord Cheyney, master of the horse, included Bray and Empson, and those of John, Lord Dynham, lord treasurer, Bray and Litton.[100]

Shared local interests also drew peers and new men together. Marney and his neighbour Robert, Lord Fitzwalter served as each other's feoffees; Marney nominated Fitzwalter repeatedly for membership of the order of the garter and Fitzwalter solemnly presented Marney to the king at his creation as a baron in 1523; eventually Fitzwalter's son married Marney's grand-daughter.[101] Marriages often strengthened such ties. Hobart married his son to Fitzwalter's daughter.[102] Wyatt included George Brooke, son of his neighbour Lord Cobham, in feoffments in the 1520s, presumably as a consequence of his son Thomas's marriage to George's sister.[103] Hussey had

[94] BL, Addl. MS 45131, fo. 149r.

[95] *LP* IV, i. 1264; PRO, C142/41/62; PROB11/23/27; 'Ancient Wills', 162.

[96] PRO, PROB11/18/5; C142/29/15; *LP* I, ii. 2765; J. B. Trapp, 'Urswick, Christopher', *ODNB*; A. Chibi, 'Sampson, Richard', *ODNB*.

[97] BL, Cotton MS Caligula DVI, fo. 290r (*LP* II, i. 29); PRO, SP1/24, fo. 57 (*LP* III, ii. 2136).

[98] PRO, C54/379, m. 7d; CP25/2/19/111/19, 32, CP25/2/27/178/49; *LP* I, ii. 3049; *CCR 1485–1500*, 1201.

[99] Longleat House, NMR 1127; *CAD*, v. A13511; PRO, CP40/934, cartae irrotulatae, mm. 2r–3r; BL, Addl. MS 59899, fo. 117v.

[100] Wedgwood, *Commons*, 183; R. P. Chope, 'The Last of the Dynhams', *Transactions of the Devonshire Association*, 50 (1918), 492.

[101] PRO, C142/43/8; CP25/2/51/359/16; *Register of the Garter*, i. 279, 284, 288, 292, 358; *LP* III, ii, App. 41; Grummitt, 'Radcliffe, Robert, first earl of Sussex'.

[102] Bodl. MS Norfolk ch. 257, 338.

[103] PRO, CP25/2/20/114/6, 115/13; E326/6961, 8750, 12736; *CAD*, iii. D1058; Brigden, *Wyatt*, 54, 92–4.

similarly good relations with his neighbour and brother-in-law William, Lord Willoughby d'Eresby, and by the end of his career was integrated into the social networks of the wider Midlands aristocracy.[104] In 1531 the earl and countess of Rutland were involved in the christening of one of his sons, and he attended the wedding of Francis Lord Hastings, son of the earl of Huntingdon, to Katherine Pole, daughter of Lord Montague, at the earl of Shrewsbury's house at Chelsea.[105] Windsor similarly came to blend in with the baronage, serving as a feoffee to the lords Stourton and Hastings.[106]

With the greatest peers, most of the new men's relationships were necessarily more deferential. Many of them moved in the orbit of the earl of Oxford. Marney and Hobart served him as feoffees, Oxford referred to Marney as his cousin in his will, and Southwell offered up the earl's sword at his funeral.[107] Marney's servants took gifts of venison, pheasants, and herons to Oxford's household.[108] Lucas was happy to refer a dispute involving a tenant of Oxford's from the council learned to the earl for resolution.[109] In the next generation, Thomas Howard, third duke of Norfolk played a similar role. He consistently promoted Windsor's admission to the garter, and Windsor named him supervisor of his will.[110] Hussey was Norfolk's chief estate steward in Lincolnshire; lesser men used him as an intermediary with the duke and Norfolk tried to help him clear his name in 1536.[111] Even Buckingham found a *modus vivendi* with some of the new men. Windsor was steward on his estates in four counties and justice in his lordship of Brecon, surety for his debts, and feoffee on his lands. In 1519 he was joined by Belknap, Englefield, and even Lovell as feoffees in the marriage settlement for the duke's son and Lady Ursula Pole.[112]

Others, dowager noblewomen for example, were in more need of the new men's assistance. Southwell was councillor and chief steward of the estates of Elizabeth, duchess of Norfolk, thirty years a widow, and led her executors.[113] Bray was supervisor and chief executor to Jane, Viscountess Lisle, who reckoned him her 'most singular good friend in the world'.[114] Anne, Lady Scrope, twice widowed before she married John, Lord Scrope of Bolton, left Lovell a gold garter and Southwell a silver spoon.[115] Alice, Lady Morley, widowed a second time by the death of Sir Edward Howard, made Lovell an executor.[116]

[104] *CCR 1500–9*, 444; BL, Addl. MS 59899, fos. 117v, 157r; *The History of Methley*, ed. H. S. Darbysire and G. D. Lumb, Thoresby Soc. 35 (Leeds, 1937), 97–98; *Lincolnshire Pedigrees*, ii. 528.
[105] *HMC Rutland*, iv. 270; *Registra Stephani Gardiner et Johannis Poynet Episcoporum Wintoniensium*, ed. H. Chitty and H. E. Malden, CYS 37 (Oxford, 1930), 25.
[106] *The Antiquarian Repertory*, ed. F. Grose et al., 4 vols (London, 1809), iv. 672; HL, MS HAP oversize box 5(25); MS HAD 2132, 2137, 3497; *HMC R. R. Hastings*, i. 308–9; PRO, CP25/1/191/31/62.
[107] ERO, D/DWd 1; 'Last Testament', 317; BL, MS Harley 295, fo. 155v.
[108] Longleat House, Misc. vol. 11, fos. 9v, 33r, 40v, 46r.
[109] R. Somerville, 'Henry VII's "Council Learned in the Law"', *EHR* 54 (1939), 441.
[110] *Register of the Garter*, i. 368–422; PRO, PROB11/29/23.
[111] *StP* i. 369 (*LP* IV, iii. 6588); PRO, SC6 Henry VIII 6305, fo. 239v; SP1/111, fo. 9 (*LP* XI. 1007); *LP* XI. 1045.
[112] PRO, E36/215, fos. 303v, 327v (*LP* II, ii, p. 1482); C54/384, m. 11d; B. J. Harris, *Edward Stafford, Third Duke of Buckingham, 1478–1521* (Stanford CA, 1986), 228; HL, MS HAD/3413.
[113] NRO, Rye MS 74/2; PRO, PROB11/15/25; *CCR 1500–9*, 527.
[114] *Sede Vacante Wills*, 142.
[115] *Testamenta Eboracensia*, iv. 152–4.   [116] PRO, PROB11/19/15.

Peers and clerics in trouble were similarly grateful for help. James Stanley, a churchman with a turbulent role in regional politics, pointedly included Lovell and Bray among the beneficiaries of a chantry he established in 1498, while Brandon stood surety for the young earl of Derby's fine for livery of his lands in 1504.[117] Edward Courtenay, earl of Devon, dying in May 1509 while his son and heir was in prison for treasonable plotting, thought it wise to join Marney to Bishop Fox as supervisors of his will.[118] Windsor stood surety for huge payments to the king by John, Lord Audley, restored in 1512 after his father's attainder in 1497, and Wyatt was one of the many neighbours of Lord Bergavenny bound for his good behaviour in 1522 after he was arrested in connection with Buckingham's fall.[119] Such transactions bring out the ambiguities of the new men's dealings with many of those around them. Were they helping out, even if winning friends and influencing people in the process? Or were they gaining ever better handholds in the lives of those upon whom they might at any moment turn, to strip them of their power and wealth in the king's interest or their own?

FRIENDS

The new men's power coursed through Henry's England, but it had to be maintained above all at the centre of government, since it had its origins in their relationship with the king, with those around him at court and in council, and in the institutions of central administration. This made relations with others at the centre of power important to them, as they would be for those who aspired to play a role in the court-centred politics of Henry VIII and his children. The new men reinforced one another's power by the way they stuck together. They often, for example, named one another as executors or overseers in their wills. Bray used Empson, Cutt, and Cope; Brandon used Lovell and Poynings; Sheffield used Lovell; Cutt used Lovell and Wyatt.[120] God-parenthood was another badge of confidence. Sir Thomas Neville, a colleague of the new men in Henry VIII's council, asked Lady Anne Wyatt and Lady Margaret Heron to be godmothers to his daughter Margaret, born in 1520.[121] To secure their land settlements they named one another as feoffees. Lovell acted as a feoffee for Wyatt, Southwell, and Dudley, and used Cutt, Ernley, Heron, Poynings, Southwell, Windsor, and Wyatt as feoffees on his own estates.[122] Cutt used Wyatt, and Wyatt used Cutt, Poynings, Windsor, and

---

[117] WAM 13119; BL, Addl. MS 59899, fo. 175r.

[118] PRO, PROB11/16/15.

[119] PRO, C54/379, m. 17d; *CP*, i. 342; *LP* III, ii. 2712.

[120] *CPR 1494–1509*, 366; PRO, PROB11/16/29; H. W. King, 'Descent of the Manor of Horham, and of the Family of Cutts', *TEAS* 4 (1869), 33; *Testamenta Vetusta*, ii. 556–7.

[121] *The Manuscripts of the Marquess of Abergavenny, Lord Braye, G. F. Luttrell, Esq., &c*, HMC 10th report 6 (London, 1887), 1.

[122] *Essex Fines*, iv. 97; *CAD*, i. A650; *CCR 1500–9*, 755, 843; PRO, C142/41/30, 62; CP25/2/25/155/14, CP25/2/28/189/45, CP25/2/19/111/9, 32.

Southwell.[123] The East Anglians helped one another—Lucas, Cutt, Hobart, and Southwell—and in the South-East Guildford, Marney, Poynings, and Brandon did the same.[124] Cooperation secured the interests of the next generation, as Poynings and Brandon served as feoffees in the marriage settlement between Lovell's niece and Hussey's son and Southwell and Wyatt in that for Cutt's son.[125]

The new men befriended courtiers, too, men who might both value their support and assist in their ready access to Henry, and even more crucially to his son. Hugh Denis, Henry VII's most intimate servant as groom of the stool, named Heron among his executors and used Dudley and Wyatt as feoffees.[126] Richard Weston, another of Henry's privy chamber men, used Hussey as a surety and was counted together with Lovell and Guildford as a friend to Sir Robert Plumpton in his dispute with Empson.[127] Marney was nominated executor to Sir John Peche, a lively presence at court before and after 1509, and to Sir William Compton, Henry VIII's powerful groom of the stool.[128] Brandon was close to John Roydon, a serjeant-at-arms since 1485. He named Roydon one of his executors and Roydon avowed in his own will that he loved Brandon's 'blood' and 'name' before all others.[129] Powerful household knights of successive generations, from Sir John Huddlestone of Sudeley, survivor of Richard III's plantation of the south with Cumbrian loyalists, through Sir Richard Nanfan and Sir Thomas Cokesey, to Sir William Sandys and Sir Nicholas Vaux, both raised to the peerage by Henry VIII, used Brandon and Poynings, Lovell and Southwell as feoffees, sureties and executors, or were used by them in turn.[130]

Other connections tied the new men into other groups. Prominent for much of the reign was the powerful network around the king's mother. Bray, Cope, Cutt, Heron, and Hussey served her, as did rising clerics such as William Smith, Hugh Oldham, John Fisher, and Christopher Urswick and high-flying lawyers such as

---

[123] *CAD*, i. D1308, vi. C7345; PRO, CP25/2/28/188/40; CP25/2/33/220/14; E210/9917, 10030; C54/382, m. 6d; C54/386, m. 16d; *Abstracts of Surrey Feet of Fines 1509–1558*, ed. C. A. F. Meekings, 2 vols, Surrey RS 45–6 (Frome, 1946), i. 5; *Essex Fines*, iv. 125, 127; *CCR 1500–9*, 720; *Abstracts of Inquisitiones Post Mortem relating to the City of London, Tudor Period*, ed. G. S. Fry et al., 3 vols (London, 1896–1908), i. 33–34.

[124] PRO, CP25/1/117A/350/407; CP25/1/170/196/51, 197/91; CP25/2/224/123/70, 90, 92; C142/43/8; C1/266/30; CUL, Hengrave MS 116; BL, Harl. Ch. 78/I/22–3; Addl. Ch. 5515; SROB, Ac449/2/570; *CCR 1500–9*, 501, 521, 927; *Paston Letters*, i. 495, 594; *Household Books of John Howard*, i. 165, ii. 488–9.

[125] *CCR 1500–9*, 338; 22 Henry VIII c. 21.

[126] PRO, E211/291; CP25/1/294/81/133.

[127] *Plumpton Letters and Papers*, ed. J. Kirby, CS 5th ser. 8 (London, 1996), 170; *CCR 1500–9*, 675.

[128] W. A. S. Robertson, 'Peche of Lullingstone', *AC* 16 (1886), 235; *Testamenta Vetusta*, ii. 593–4.

[129] PRO, PROB11/16/29; *Materials*, i. 11–12; A. N. Palmer, 'Isycoed, County Denbigh', *Archaeologia Cambrensis*, 6th ser. 10 (1910), 242.

[130] Wedgwood, *Commons*, 477–8, 623; R. Horrox, *Richard III: A Study of Service* (Cambridge, 1989), 84; *CPR 1485–94*, 140; PRO, C1/135/18, 172/11, 260/8, 318/1–3; CP25/1/260/29/7; *CCR 1500–9*, 459, 745, 773, 789; C. C. Brookes, *History of Steeple Aston and Middle Aston* (Shipston-on-Stour, 1929), 73; *Abstracts of Feet of Fines relating to Wiltshire 1377–1509*, ed. J. L. Kirby, Wiltshire RS 41 (Devizes, 1986), 174–5, 180–1; BL, Addl. MS 59899, fo. 156v; *CIPM*, iii. 365.

Humphrey Coningsby and Robert Brudenell.[131] Bray remained close throughout his life to those with whom he had shared in her service, and Smith, Oldham, and Coningsby were among his executors.[132] Even those on the fringes of her circle felt the demands and rewards of exposure to her powerful personality. One June, probably in 1504, she wrote to Mordaunt from Collyweston as her 'full trusty counsellor' asking for his help in securing the establishment of a commission of sewers manned by her associates to deal with the flooding of the River Witham and the issue of a writ to help her tenants at Coningsby amortize lands for their guild. In 1504 she recommended him for the university stewardship at Cambridge.[133] Lovell and Marney were among the executors of her will and played some part in implementing its provisions, though Fisher was the dominant figure.[134] Other members of the royal kin had a similar if weaker pull. Cecily, duchess of York—'the queen's grandmother', as she called herself—named Bray and Lovell among her executors and had Lovell's friend Sir Henry Heydon among her household officers.[135]

By the end of the reign, new connections were emerging. Hussey, comptroller of the household in Henry's later years, forged a lasting friendship with the captain of the guard, Thomas, Lord Darcy. Both lost their offices in 1509 but they stuck together, corresponding in the 1520s with greetings to one another's families, news of domestic and international politics, and advice about the king and his court.[136] In July 1523, for example, Hussey assured Darcy that the king 'as far as I can perceive ... is very good lord unto you', while Sir Richard Wingfield, Marney's successor as chancellor of the duchy of Lancaster, 'as far as I can perceive is your very good friend in all things'.[137] Meanwhile, Yorkshiremen in disfavour with Darcy hoped that Hussey would 'make' his friend their 'good lord'.[138] In correspondence they called one another 'cousin', but in describing their relationship to the imperial ambassador in 1534 Hussey called Darcy his brother.[139] The two old courtiers supported one another in financial transactions for thirty years or more, and in the revolts of 1536 they met their doom together.[140] Hussey was, as he signed one letter to Darcy, 'yours assuredly during my life'.[141]

[131] M. K. Jones and M. G. Underwood, *The King's Mother: Lady Margaret Beaufort, Countess of Richmond and Derby* (Cambridge, 1992), 79–80, 105–7, 140, 144–5, 151–2, 193–4, 196, 223; Ives, *Common Lawyers*, 454, 457–8.

[132] M. M. Condon, 'From Caitiff and Villain to *Pater Patriae*: Reynold Bray and the Profits of Office', in M. A. Hicks (ed.), *Profit, Piety and the Professions in later Medieval England* (Gloucester, 1990), 148; *CPR 1494–1509*, 366.

[133] R. Halstead, *Succinct Genealogies of the Noble and Ancient Houses of Alno or de Alneto etc* (London, 1685), 512–13; *CPR 1494–1509*, 358–9.

[134] C. H. Cooper, *Memoir of Margaret, Countess of Richmond and Derby* (Cambridge, 1874), 119, 180–214.

[135] *Testamenta Vetusta*, ii. 422–3; PRO, SC2/185/38, m. 5v; R. Fleming, 'The Hautes and their "Circle": Culture and the English Gentry', in D. T. Williams (ed.), *England in the Fifteenth Century* (Woodbridge, 1987), 99.

[136] *LP* III, ii. 3164, 3276, IV, i. 880, XII, ii. 186(17, 25, 32, 33).

[137] PRO, SP1/28, fo. 118r–118v (*LP* III, ii. 3183).

[138] *LP* IV, iii. 6746; Bindoff, *Commons*, iii. 280–1.

[139] *LP* VII. 1206.

[140] BL, Addl. MS 21480, fo. 42r; BL, Addl. MS 59899, fo. 115r; *CCR 1500–9*, 913; *Surrey Fines*, i. 30.

[141] PRO, SP1/231, fo. 290 (*LP* Addenda, i. 163).

Empson and Dudley similarly grew closer to one another and more isolated from their colleagues in Henry's last years. The king's failing health made them take on more independent administrative responsibility, while those who had been their patrons and allies—Bray, Mordaunt, and Litton—died in 1503–5.[142] Dudley in particular had risen fast in a way that must have been jarring to older royal servants. As Francis Bacon noted, 'those that are advanced by degrees, are less envied, than those that are advanced suddenly'.[143] Of the other new men, only Wyatt, Cutt, Cope, and Ernley, Dudley's colleague at Gray's Inn, seem to have been much associated with them.[144] They had little traction among the peerage, with the exception of minor figures such as Edward Sutton, Lord Dudley, or Richard Beauchamp, Lord St Amand, or among the bishops, apart from Richard Fitzjames, bishop of London, Dudley's executor.[145] Kinship bound Windsor to his brother-in-law Dudley. They bought wardships together and allegedly arranged a divorce between Sir Edward Bray and the heiress Elizabeth Lovell so that she could be married to Windsor's younger brother Anthony. But from 1509 all Windsor could do was to work with Dudley's other executors to salvage something for his sons.[146]

Most powerful of all were the bonds that held together the tight circle at the centre of Henry VII's council. They crossed ties of older allegiances and the differences of perspective between new men, clerics, and peers, and they survived even beyond the king's death. Giles, Lord Daubeney, named his 'singular good lords and friends' Bishop Richard Fox, John, earl of Oxford, and Sir Thomas Lovell as overseers of his will in May 1508, 'for the singular trust and confidence that I have and long have had in them'. They also led the feoffees on his estates.[147] Eleven months later, Oxford named 'mine old friend' Lovell as the first of his executors, and when Lovell died fifteen years later, rooms in his house at Enfield were still known as 'my Lord of Oxford chamber' and 'my Lord of Oxford's closet'.[148] Lovell continued until his last years to name Fox as a feoffee and just months before his death, on 19 July 1523, they dined together on a buck sent to Lovell by the abbot of Waltham, two old men perhaps reminiscing about their long years at the top.[149]

---

[142] M. R. Horowitz, 'Richard Empson, Minister of Henry VII', *BIHR* 55 (1982), 39–44; *Plumpton Letters and Papers*, 10–12, 162–3; Wedgwood, *Commons*, 104–5, 565–6, 607–8; E. Dudley, *The Tree of Commonwealth*, ed. D. M. Brodie (Cambridge, 1948), 3.

[143] Bacon, *Essays*, 35.

[144] Somerville, *Duchy of Lancaster*, i. 263, 267; *Historiae Dunelmensis Scriptores Tres*, ed. J. Raine, Surtees Society 9 (London, 1839), ccccx–ccccxi; Durham University Library, Durham Priory Register 5, fo. 115r; Dudley, *Tree*, 3 n. 8; PRO, C1/473/78; DL5/4 fo. 93r; BL, Addl. MS 59899, fo. 174v; *CPR 1494–1509*, 591; *LP* I, i. 54(88), 709(26); *Readings and Moots at the Inns of Court*, ed. S. E. Thorne, J. H. Baker, 2 vols, SS 71, 105 (London, 1952, 1989), ii. pp. lxxxi–lxxxv, ci; Cheshire RO, DCH/B/44; *Final Concords of the County of Lancaster ... part III ... AD 1377–1509*, ed. W. Farrer, Record Society of Lancashire and Cheshire 50 (Manchester, 1905), 159–60, 163–4.

[145] *Third Report of the Deputy Keeper*, App. ii. 226; *CP*, iv. 480–1, xi. 303; *CCR 1500–9*, 885; *CPR 1494–1509*, 589; *Testamenta Vetusta*, ii. 491; PRO, C54/379, m. 12d.

[146] PRO, C1/473/78; C54/391, mm. 16d–17d; CP25/1/294/83/48; E326/5714; STAC2/28/110; BL, Addl. MS 21480, fos. 98v, 120v; Addl. MS 59899, fos. 156r, 174r; Cheshire RO, DCH/B/44; *Final Concords of the County of Lancaster*, 159–60, 163–4; OHC, Wi/I/i/2; *CCR 1500–9*, 13, 283, 617, 629, 663, 762, 972; *CAD*, i. A1492; *CIPM*, iii. 1039; *Lisle Letters*, i. 278; *LP* III, ii. 2266.

[147] PRO, PROB11/16/16; BLARS, L155; Devon RO, Chanter 13, fo. 35v.

[148] 'Last Testament', 313; PRO, PROB2/199, mm. 2–3.

[149] PRO, C142/41/30, 62; Belvoir Castle, MS a/c no. 4.

The new men's power spread through relationships of many sorts. Some, like kinship or the employment of servants, were common to many societies, others very specific to their time and place. Their local office-holding and their relationships with urban elites made them intermediaries between the king and communities urban and rural, a relationship sometimes formalized in their retaining of leading members of small town and village society to serve the king under their leadership. Their role in the enforcement of royal fiscal and judicial policy made them intermediaries between the king and individuals great and small, as did their ability to speak to the king on behalf of petitioners. Their role as church patrons spread their influence through clerical networks and into parishes, religious houses and university colleges. Their skilful use of the law put them at an advantage in many of their dealings.

In central politics they were not, individually, the greatest of the king's ministers, but they readily built alliances with those who were. In local politics they could never be great lords, but that did not stop them being important in county society, and that was valuable to the king. Some, like Lovell, exercised an extended local influence on the basis of permanent or temporary landed endowment and regional office; others, like Hussey, a more localized sway based on landholding, long residence, and engagement in county administration; others, like Poynings, a power more tied to specific office, in his case in the Cinque Ports. Such arrangements enabled Henry to re-structure local politics in less dramatic ways than Edward IV had done by his establishment of regional hegemonies for trusted noblemen, a system which had worked well in his lifetime but which proved dangerously inflexible at his death.[150] The new men were the king's men as much as Edward's lords had been, in some ways more so, as they had even less claim on local loyalties by ancestry or private landed power. But their multiplicity and versatility made Henry's regime supple and durable: if Londoners feared Dudley, they could honour Lovell; if Buckingham hated Lovell, he could work with Windsor; and Bray, or Empson, could come and go and the king, or his son, retain control.

When viewed in longer perspective, the means by which Henry's new men exercised power appear transitional between those of Edward's great lords and those of the great ministers of the later Tudor reigns. Where engagement at court and in the king's council was complemented by local office-holding and the construction of a retinue designed to serve the king in the career of William, Lord Hastings, the same was true for Lovell and others.[151] Yet in their combination of local leadership in the area where they were building their landholdings with informed dominance of the bureaucratic machinery of government, engagement with the London elite and cultivation of urban oligarchies, they also foreshadowed the *modus operandi* of William Cecil, Lord Burghley, and those who led the Elizabethan state.[152]

[150] C. Carpenter, *The Wars of the Roses: Politics and the Constitution in England, c.1437–1509* (Cambridge, 1997), 183–92; D. A. L. Morgan, 'The King's Affinity in the Polity of Yorkist England', *TRHS* 5th ser. 23 (1973), 18–25.
[151] T. Westervelt, 'The Changing Nature of Politics in the Localities in the Later Fifteenth Century: William Lord Hastings and his Indentured Retainers', *Midland History* 26 (2001) 96–106.
[152] A. Wall, 'Patterns of politics in England, 1558–1625', *HJ* 31 (1988), 955–6; S. Alford, *Burghley: William Cecil at the Court of Elizabeth I* (New Haven CT and London, 2008); G. D. Ramsay, *The City of London in International Politics at the accession of Elizabeth Tudor* (Manchester, 1975), 54–9; Hasler, *Commons*, i. 586–7.

WEALTH

12

The profits of power

The new men's service to Henry VII and their power over his subjects gave them opportunities to become wealthy. The Spanish ambassador Pedro de Ayala recognized that both the king and his ministers had 'a wonderful dexterity in getting other people's money'.[1] Money was not enough: like lawyers, merchants, soldiers, and anyone else with a cash income, the new men had to accumulate land to entrench themselves and their families in English society. The lines were far from clear between legitimate and illegitimate ways of converting influence into bags of cash or landed acres and success was only to be achieved by close oversight and judicious risk. The tangled relationship between Guildford's heavy debts, apparent financial irregularities in office, and political downfall served as a warning to his colleagues.[2]

Others were more careful. Wyatt and Windsor signed the accounts of their estates and bills for repairs and Lovell heard the accounts of his household officers in person.[3] Windsor went to Lydd in September 1507 to investigate a disputed rent due him from Bilsington Priory, which he was still pursuing in the courts twenty-one years later.[4] Like their master the king they chased up debts, Windsor taking large bonds from those who owed him money and pursuing the sureties or distraining the livestock of defaulting tenants.[5] Like their master they dealt in ready money. Marney took many of his rents in cash in person in the 1490s, and Wyatt, Hussey, and Windsor did the same, even as their careers got busier.[6] Lovell was grandest of all, collecting up £868 1s 1½d in cash, some of it specifically 'in gold', from his lands in 1522–3, though he did hand £153 1s 1½d of it straight back to his receiver to spend on household bills.[7]

MODERATE RICHES

It is hard to work out just how rich the new men were, but we can start with their tax assessments. Early Tudor regimes levied a range of taxes which tell us either

---

[1] *CSPS*, i. 207.　　[2] S. Cunningham, 'Guildford, Sir Richard', *ODNB*.
[3] PRO, SC6/Henry VIII/1684, m. 2v; SC6/Henry VIII/7146; Belvoir Castle, MS a/c no. 4.
[4] PRO, C1/588/58; *VE*, i. 51.
[5] *LP* XI. 867, 871; PRO, C54/419, m. 37d; KB9/500/19.
[6] PRO, SC6/Henry VII/160; SC6/Henry VIII/1684, m. 3r; E36/95, fos. 36v–37r, 66r–69v, 101r–102v; SC6/Henry VIII/7146; Hampshire RO, 25M75/M2, mm. 16–18 and unnumbered.
[7] Belvoir Castle, MS a/c no. 4.

how much they were expected to pay compared with their contemporaries or, even better, what their income in lands and fees or wealth in goods were reckoned to be. Such assessments, moreover, seem to have been quite accurate when judged against other sources such as private accounts or probate records, catching a half or two-thirds of the total income or wealth of those assessed.[8] These round figures are corroborated by assessments of their landed incomes made for other purposes, by the government or by their private administrations. Inquisitions post mortem listed all their estates at death and when their valuations can be compared with private estate documents do not seem to be wildly inaccurate.[9] Valors, giving a snapshot of the total income from estates in a given year, also give impressive totals. Other sets of accounts can shed further light. But the survival of such records is patchy at best, and there must always be a certain amount of guesswork in estimating the revenues the new men drew from their lands. At death, goods were listed for probate purposes, and while these listings seem to have been thorough, the values assigned to old or hastily viewed objects may not always have reflected their real worth or purchase price. The estimates of wealth included in the indictments of those tried for treason constitute a final, grim source.

The richest of the new men rated highly by any of these measures. For the subsidy of 1523, Lovell was reckoned to have goods worth £2,000, and an incomplete probate listing of his goods a year later totalled over £840. In the benevolence of 1491, he had been asked for £400 and in the forced loan of 1522 he paid £500.[10] These valuations marked him as richer than all but the wealthiest half-dozen peers.[11] Listings for a possible forced loan or benevolence in 1524–5 planned that Lovell's executors might be asked for £666 13s 4d, when the richest bishops and noblemen were put down for £1,000 and only Wolsey himself for more.[12] Bray was probably richer than Lovell. In 1491 he had paid £500, the largest contribution by anyone in the kingdom bar a few churchmen and the king's mother.[13] His probate inventory, likewise incomplete, totalled over £770, though more than half was accounted for by building materials for his new houses.[14]

Dudley, Windsor, Hussey, and Marney were in the rank behind them, but still very prosperous. In his indictment, Dudley's landed income was reckoned at £333 6s 8d and his goods at more than £5,000.[15] Rumour on the London streets put his

---

[8] R. Schofield, 'Taxation and the Political Limits of the Tudor State', in C. Cross et al. (eds), *Law and Government under the Tudors: Essays Presented to Sir Geoffrey Elton on his Retirement* (Cambridge, 1988), 233–55.

[9] M. Holford, "Notoriously Unreliable": The Valuations and Extents', in M. A. Hicks (ed.), *The Fifteenth-Century Inquisitions Post Mortem: A Companion* (Woodbridge, 2012), 117–44.

[10] PRO, E179/141/109/3; PROB2/199; E36/285, fo. 10v; *HMC Rutland*, iv. 263.

[11] J. Cornwall, *Wealth and Society in Early Sixteenth-Century England* (London, 1988), 143–4.

[12] *LP* III, ii. 2483(2).

[13] M. M. Condon, 'From Caitiff and Villain to *Pater Patriae*: Reynold Bray and the Profits of Office', in M. A. Hicks (ed.), *Profit, Piety and the Professions in later Medieval England* (Gloucester, 1990), 158.

[14] PRO, E154/2/10.

[15] *Third Report of the Deputy Keeper of the Public Records* (London, 1842), 227.

worth much higher, at £800 in lands, fees, and offices, £20,000 in coin and jewels, plate and rich household stuff.[16] The inventory of his goods at their confiscation did not value them, but certainly gives the impression of opulence.[17] The listings of 1524–5 recommended Windsor for a contribution of £200, among the richest knights, and put Marney's son higher, at £366 13s 4d, while the subsidy assessments of 1535–6 reckoned Windsor worth £600 a year, with Hussey some way behind at £266 13s 4d.[18]

In a third rank, but still amongst the richer gentry, came the rest. Fines for substantial landowners who had not yet taken up knighthood in 1501 rated Hobart and Belknap at an income of £200, Englefield at £133 6s 8d, Mordaunt and Empson at £100, and Southwell at £66 13s 4d, though Southwell's father, whose land he would shortly inherit, counted for £133 6s 8d.[19] Empson, who had paid £40 to the 1491 benevolence, the same as Cutt, was thought at his fall to be worth only £65 6s 8d a year in lands and £100 in goods, but this was surely an underestimate.[20] In the 1523 subsidy Sutton paid on £133 13s 4d in goods, Hobart's son on £180 in lands.[21]

Contemporaries were not shocked at the absolute size of these fortunes—a leading peer or bishop was worth several of the new men put together—but at the speed with which they were assembled. Dudley's wealth was, as a London chronicler put it, 'shortly gathered', and though none of the others moved quite as fast as he did, they were all profiting from their power at a disconcerting rate.[22] They knew how to spend, too. By the end of his life Lovell was spending around £900 a year on his household, a third or a quarter what the duke of Buckingham spent, but more than the average taxable income of a peer of the realm.[23] And like their master, what was striking was how much of their wealth was readily available in cash. They lent money regularly to those whose assets were less liquid, Lovell £100 or £200 a time to the duke of Buckingham and the earl of Northumberland and £500 to Queen Elizabeth of York.[24] Much of the new men's income in any given year came from land, but for those who started with little inherited wealth, land, except in rare cases of direct royal endowment, had to be bought or gained by marriage. Both cost money, money which had to be generated through office-holding or the more nebulous profits of power.

---

[16] *The Great Chronicle of London*, ed. A. H. Thomas and I. D. Thornley (London, 1938), 348.

[17] PRO, E154/2/17. [18] *LP* III, ii. 2483 (2); *LP* XI. 139. [19] HL, MS HM 19959.

[20] PRO, E36/285, fo. 11r; *Third Report of the Deputy Keeper*, 228.

[21] PRO, E179/141/109/3; 'Norfolk Subsidy Roll, 15 Hen VIII', *Norfolk Antiquarian Miscellany* 2 (1883), 399–410, 402.

[22] *Great Chronicle*, 348.

[23] Belvoir Castle, MS a/c no. 4; B. J. Harris, *Edward Stafford, Third Duke of Buckingham, 1478–1521* (Stanford CA, 1986), 101–2.

[24] *LP* III, i, 1070, 1285 (5); PRO, E36/226, fos 42r, 59r, 71v, 87r, 101v (*LP*, IV, ii, 3380 (5)); *Privy Purse Expenses of Elizabeth of York: Wardrobe Accounts of Edward the Fourth*, ed. N.H. Nicolas (London, 1830), 110.

THE PROFITS OF OFFICE

Offices in the crown's service paid attractive fees. At the peak of his career Lovell was in receipt of £100 as constable of the Tower of London, £100 as master of the wards, probably the same as chief justice of the forests, £66 13s 4d as treasurer of the household, and £26 13s 4d as chancellor of the exchequer, so nearly £400 in total.[25] At least briefly, Marney could match him, with £365 a year as lord privy seal and £66 13s 4d as chancellor of the duchy of Lancaster, plus £28 fixed expenses for attendance in London.[26] Windsor's official fee as keeper of the great wardrobe was £100, but that seems to have been topped up by an additional £300 annuity while he held the office.[27] Bray's fees for crown offices totalled over £130.[28] Hussey had £100 a year as master of the wards, then £100 as chief butler.[29] Southwell had £66 13s 4d a year as chief butler and Brandon £40 a year as master of the horse.[30] Wyatt patiently added fee to fee. He got £13 6s 8d as clerk of the jewels, then £50 as master of the jewel house; £8 4s 3d as clerk of the mint, then £26 13s 4d as comptroller.[31]

Annuities from the crown sometimes amplified these rewards, or substituted for them in newly created posts. Southwell with his wide-ranging auditing responsibilities was granted a £100 annuity in 1513, plus £200 a year backdated to the start of the reign.[32] Mordaunt had £100 as a retained royal councillor, Dudley £66 13s 4d.[33] Brandon was granted a £40 annuity in 1498, 'by way of reward', renewed in 1509, Wyatt one of £20 in 1504, likewise renewed.[34] Even scraps were welcome, like Hussey's £5 annuity from the manor of Bourne, Lincolnshire, granted in 1509.[35] The queen paid fees to the king's lawyers to look after her interests, Empson, Hobart and Mordaunt among them in 1502–3.[36]

Local offices, granted by the king or other lords or institutions, likewise paid fees. Again Lovell probably accumulated the highest income, starting with significant items like £50 at Wallingford or £26 13s 4d at Nottingham, through £16 as chief steward of St Albans, £15 2s 1d at Enfield or £13 6s 8d from St George's Windsor, down to single or shared stewardships worth £2 a year; the total must

[25] *LP* II, i. 2736, ii. App. 58 (10), XX, ii. 34; PRO, E36/215, fo. 196r.

[26] *LP* III, ii. 2830; PRO, DL28/6/14, fo. 5v

[27] *The Great Wardrobe Accounts of Henry VII and Henry VIII*, ed. M. Hayward, London Record Society 47 (Woodbridge, 2012), 163; *LP* II, i. 2736; *Trevelyan Papers Prior to AD 1558*, ed. J. P. Collier, CS o.s. 67 (London, 1857), 165.

[28] Condon, 'Profits of Office', 140.   [29] *LP* III, i. 1379(1).

[30] PRO, E101/85/15; E404/83/3, writ of 18 November 1500; *LP* III, ii. 2395.

[31] *CCR 1485–1500*, 250; *Materials*, i. 405; C. E. Challis, 'Lord Hastings to the Great Silver Recoinage, 1464–1699', in C. E. Challis (ed.), *A New History of the Royal Mint* (Cambridge, 1992), 183.

[32] *LP* I, ii. 1836 (4), 2315 (1).   [33] *CPR 1494–1509*, 226, 506.

[34] PRO, E404/83/3, writ of 18 November 1500; E405/479, fo. 2r; *CPR 1494–1509*, 367; *LP* I, i. 54(60), II, i. 2736.

[35] *LP* I, i. 132 (55).   [36] *Privy Purse Expenses of Elizabeth of York*, 101.

have been well over £150.[37] Marney's duchy of Cornwall offices paid a grand total of £75 11s 11d; when they were temporarily interrupted by the act of resumption of 1515, he secured a privy seal letter ordering their payment in full.[38] Southwell's estate stewardships provided at least £48 a year in fees and probably nearer £70.[39] Hussey's crown stewardships and those from lay lords were worth nearly £40, those from ecclesiastical lords over £50.[40] Poynings's Canterbury stewardship alone was worth £40 a year.[41] Windsor's estate stewardships were worth at least £31 a year.[42]

These fees were not pure profit. Some must have been spent on deputies or servants needed to do part of the work involved, while simply getting the fees paid cost fees to others in the royal administration, like the 3s 4d paid to the clerk of the receipt in the exchequer by Lovell's men in 1522–3 to 'search what sums of money were owing' to Lovell for various positions.[43] Some had to be surrendered in advance in the payments Henry VII required in return for appointment, systematized towards the end of the reign by Dudley. But what did come came in cash, helping to build the new men's impressive liquidity. Meanwhile, constant alertness to opportunity maximized profit. This was Wyatt's forte. One of the manors he bought from the earl of Kent, Ashill, carried the unusual obligation of acting as grand serjeant of the table linen at every royal coronation, an honour he duly claimed at the court of claims before the coronations of 1509 and 1533. No doubt the performance of the associated duties marked his stake in society, but there was a baser motive to insist on his claim. In 1513 he sued two officers of the royal household for detaining twelve table cloths, ten towels, and six napkins which should have come to him as his perquisites for the coronation four years earlier, winning £9 6s 8d in costs and damages.[44]

Two problems might bedevil the attempt to profit from office-holding. Busy royal councillors were heavily dependent on honest and efficient subordinates, but they could not always find them. Cope, for example, had trouble with his deputies as cofferer of the household. His chief clerk Richard Ward fled his service owing

[37] *LP* II, i. 2736, III, ii. 3695; PRO, E315/272, fo. 62r; SC6/Henry VII/1091, m. 6v; SC6/Henry VIII/783; E210/10993; BL, Harley Roll Y28; Windsor, The Aerary, MS XV.49.6; *HMC Middleton*, 124; *Certificate of Musters for Buckinghamshire in 1522*, ed. A. C. Chibnall, Buckinghamshire RS 17 (London, 1973), 181.
[38] DCRO, DC Roll 215, mm. 14–17; S. J. Gunn, 'The Act of Resumption of 1515', in D. T. Williams (ed.), *Early Tudor England: Proceedings of the Fourth Harlaxton Symposium* (Woodbridge, 1989), 102.
[39] *CPR 1494–1509*, 9; NRO, Rye MS 74, part 2; PRO, SC6/Henry VII/1693, 1802; 'Ely Episcopal Registers', ed. J. H. Crosby, in *Ely Diocesan Remembrancer* (Cambridge, 1908–11), 288 (1909), 76; *LP* I, i. 632 (66).
[40] *LP* I, i. 604 (31), IV, ii. 2527; Alnwick Castle, Syon MS X.II.6, box 1n; PRO, SC6/Henry VIII/6305, fo. 239v; *VE*, ii. 281, iv. 5, 34, 45, 74, 82, 96, 98, 102–3, 118, 130, 273, v. 5, 274; PRO, E36/95, fo. 24r.
[41] CCA, Dean and Chapter Register T, fos. 68v–69v.
[42] *VE*, i. 398, 402, 406, 418, 426, iv. 221, 222; M. C. Rosenfield, 'Holy Trinity, Aldgate, on the eve of the Dissolution', *Guildhall Miscellany* 3 (1969–71), 172; Windsor, The Aerary, MS XV.49. 10–21; *LP* III, ii. 3695.
[43] Belvoir Castle, MS a/c no. 4.
[44] *LP* II, i. 120; E. Hall, *Hall's Chronicle*, ed. H. Ellis (London, 1809), 798; PRO, CP40/1003, m. 533r.

him large sums of money and took sanctuary, leaving Cope heavily in debt to the king and uncertain how much was owed him by Ward and how much by his other deputy, Thomas Spencer. Eventually, careful auditing showed that Ward was £4,080 short and Spencer £1,460 9s 5d; but before that, Cope had drawn in Spencer's brother John, his tenant and relation by marriage, to guarantee his brother's debts, creating problems that generated litigation after his death. Cope's resourcefulness was evident in his persuasive line to Spencer, who alleged that he told him 'Cousin Spencer, this obligation that ye shall make for your brother shall be but only to put your brother in dread, to make him in the more fear and be the more ready to make his account, for I know well he is able to pay me all that he oweth me'. But as Cope's executors pointed out, the root of the problem was the 'singular trust and confidence' Cope had placed in his subordinates.[45]

The second problem was that the temptation to spend money first and account to the king for it later—in effect, to use government finances as a source of private credit—could unravel when the political climate changed. In 1509 Hussey already owed £266 13s 4d to the king, which Lovell and Englefield bound him to pay off in instalments by 1514, but he continued to build up debts to the crown thereafter.[46] These made him vulnerable when Wolsey decided to bolster the king's coffers by pursuing those who owed him money.[47] In 1515 royal auditors began to crawl over his accounts for the past nine years. Hussey tried to explain why this sum or that, for sales of woods, for wards' lands, for estates he had exchanged with the crown, for lands confiscated from others by Henry VII and put into his hands, was not really his responsibility; the auditors made notes to check further records. On one auditor's circuit alone, Hussey managed to negotiate down the crown's claims from over £2,000 to £195 18s 1¾d.[48] On 11 July 1515 Hussey acknowledged before Wolsey, Bishop Fox, and John Heron debts to the crown of £3,118 19s 8½d, a mixture of funds borrowed from the king, advances of money unaccounted for, arrears of accounts in office, and overdue payments for wardships. The terms of his repayment were favourable, explicitly because of the king's 'goodness and benign grace' towards him and in recognition of his 'acceptable service': he was to pay off £200 a year, and his first wife's lands were put in the hands of feoffees led by Wolsey to guarantee the payment.[49] By October 1520, £800 had duly been paid, and Hussey managed to persuade the king, of his 'further benign grace and goodness', to reduce the payments to £100 a year.[50] A decade or so later the debt was down to £918 19s 8½d, but things were still tight.[51] Hussey borrowed money from Cromwell in 1527 and corresponded anxiously with him in the mid-1530s about new, or newly discovered, debts of hundreds of pounds he owed (or claimed

[45] PRO, C1/360/13–14.   [46] PRO, SP1/12, fo. 155 (*LP* XII, ii. 187(1)).
[47] PRO, E36/215, fos. 295r, 302v, 328r, 332v, 337v; Gunn, 'Act of Resumption', 93–4.
[48] PRO, SC6/Henry VIII/1952.   [49] PRO, E211/130, 152.
[50] PRO, E210/10102.   [51] PRO, SP1/58, fo. 256 (*LP* IV, iii. 6792).

not to owe) the king.[52] In February 1534 one of his servants had to send him his grant of pardon from 1509 so he could wield it once again.[53] If power slipped away, its profits became harder to hold.

GIFTS AND PENSIONS

Harder still to quantify, but clearly important, were the benefits the new men derived from their power in the form of gifts and pensions. These came from petitioners who hoped they would use their proximity to the king to sway him in their favour, or otherwise deploy their influence on the payer's behalf. A very special case was the king of France, who paid annual pensions to Henry's councillors to encourage them to maintain the peace of 1492. Bray and Lovell got 525 and 350 *livres tournois* respectively, smaller than the sums paid to the leading bishops and noblemen, but by no means insubstantial, at around £62 and £42. When peace was renewed in 1514 Poynings was added to the list at 1050 *livres tournois*, some £125, and in 1518 Belknap joined, too, with 1000 *livres tournois*.[54] Keen not to be left behind, the Habsburgs pensioned those they thought well-disposed to amity between their house and the Tudors, and Poynings was the major beneficiary here, with an annual pension of 1000 *livres parisis*, nearly £150, from January 1516, granted in thanks for his help in forging friendship between the future Charles V and Henry VIII and to make him 'all the more inclined to put his hand to and employ himself in the maintenance, augmentation and firm continuation of the said amity and confederation'.[55] The French soon dropped their payments to Poynings, but the Habsburgs kept paying him and even topped up the pension with a further 500 ducats, some £166, in July 1520, after Charles and Henry had met, in a round of tipping that also included Marney.[56]

On the domestic scene, noblemen and bishops paid generous fees. Lovell had £10 each from the earl of Derby, Viscount Beaumont, and Lord Willoughby d'Eresby, £6 13s 4d from the earl of Northumberland, and £3 6s 8d from the earl of Huntingdon, most of them granted by 1491.[57] Bray had annuities from Northumberland, Ormond, Devon, Dynham, Hastings, Audley, and Archbishop Deane.[58] The fifth earl of Northumberland continued his father's payments to Lovell and Bray and added fees and stewardships for Ernley and Lucas.[59]

---

[52] *LP* IV, ii. 3250, VII. 1259, 1566, VIII. 169 (2); PRO, C54/404, m. 26d.

[53] PRO, E36/95, fo. 33r.

[54] C. Giry-Deloison, 'Money and Early Tudor Diplomacy. The English Pensioners of the French Kings', *Medieval History* 3 (1993), 140–6.

[55] BL, Addl. Ch. 1521 (*LP* II, i. 2223).

[56] *LP* II, i. 2676, ii. 3443; ADN, B2292/80614; B3336, fo. 74.

[57] *LP* IV, i. 976, 1857; PRO, SC6/Hen VIII/345, m. 51v; SP1/27, fo. 58r (*LP* III, ii. 2822); SROB, Ac 449/E3/15.53/2.8.

[58] M. M. Condon, 'Ruling Elites in the Reign of Henry VII', in C. D. Ross (ed.), *Patronage, Pedigree and Power in Later Medieval England* (Gloucester, 1979), 123; HL, MS HAM Box 10(5), m. 7; *HMC Eighth Report* (London, 1881), App. I, ii. 331a.

[59] CUL, Hengrave MS 88, vol. iii, 6.

Lesser peers with more regional interests paid smaller fees and targeted them towards the most relevant members of the new elite. As early as 1489–90, Richard Hastings, Lord Willoughby, with his Lincolnshire lands, paid John Hussey £3 6s 8d a year.[60] In 1499–1500 Edward, Lord Hastings, and Richard Neville, Lord Latimer, both with estates in the Midlands, were paying Empson £4 and £2 13s 4d for his counsel.[61] Wyatt's collection was more eclectic: £7 a year from Thomas Lord Dacre, once his colleague on the borders, and £2 a year from Bishop Veysey of Exeter.[62]

Religious houses, too, paid fees to those whose favour might protect their interests. Peterborough Abbey paid Lovell £3 a year and St George's College, Windsor £2 before either made him chief steward, while Holy Trinity Aldgate paid him £5.[63] St George's also paid Wyatt £1 6s 8d a year from 1505 and Windsor £2 a year from 1509–10.[64] Hobart was paid £2 a year by St Osyth's Priory and £2 13s 4d by Wymondham Priory as its chief steward.[65] In addition to his many stewardship fees, Hussey got £2 each from Louth Park Abbey and Croxton Priory.[66] Westminster Abbey, recognizing his sudden rise, granted Marney £6 13s 4d a year in 1510 and by the 1520s Peterborough Abbey paid Windsor a £1 fee.[67] Empson was a systematic collector of small fees: £2 each from Durham Priory, Kenilworth Abbey, St James's Abbey beside Northampton, £1 6s 8d from an unidentified house, £6 13s 4d from Abingdon Abbey.[68] Dudley, predictably, thought bigger, ranging upwards from £2 from the abbot of Quarr on the Isle of Wight through £3 from the abbot of Peterborough to £20 as chief steward of the estates of the bishop of Durham.[69]

Payments by those involved in specific litigation or petitioning could be just as lucrative. At the more legitimate end they were fees for professional assistance, like the £1 10s St George's College, Windsor paid Hobart for advice about one of their lawsuits in 1504–5.[70] At the less legitimate end they constituted extortion, of the sort alleged against Lucas in the reaction of 1509–10. He was said to have kept a Suffolk jury waiting on the council learned at London, accused of delivering a false verdict, until one member granted him a £1 annuity.[71] In between lay a world of

---

[60] HL, MS HAM Box 74(3); *CP*, vi. 385–87.

[61] HL, MS HAM Box 10(5), m. 7; Alnwick Castle, Syon MS X.II.6, box 1n.

[62] S. G. Ellis, *Tudor Frontiers and Noble Power: The Making of the British State* (Oxford, 1995), 103n; Devon RO, Chanter 1072.

[63] *Account Rolls of the Obedientiaries of Peterborough*, ed. J. Greatrex, Northamptonshire RS 33 (Northampton, 1984), 178, 192; Windsor, The Aerary, MSS XV.48.53, XV.59.1; PRO, E36/108, fo. 37v.

[64] Windsor, The Aerary, MSS XV.49.6–21.

[65] PRO, SC11/984; SC6/Henry VII/1746.

[66] *A Subsidy Collected in the Diocese of Lincoln in 1526*, ed. H. Salter, OHS 63 (Oxford, 1913), 49, 122.

[67] WAM, Lease Book II, fo. 67r; *Subsidy Collected in the Diocese of Lincoln*, 166.

[68] *Extracts from the Account Rolls of the Abbey of Durham*, ed. J. T. Fowler, 3 vols, Surtees Society 99, 100, 103 (Durham, 1898–1901), ii. 306; PRO, C1/360/66, 462/43, 783/57, 786/12.

[69] *The Charters of Quarr Abbey*, ed. S. F. Hockey, Isle of Wight Records Series 3 (Newport, 1991), no. 59; *Account Rolls of the Obedientiaries of Peterborough*, 178, 192; Durham University Library, Durham Priory Register 5, fo. 102.

[70] Windsor, The Aerary, MS XV.49.6.

[71] PRO, KB9/452/40.

bribes, gratuities, and protection money. William Worsley, dean of St Paul's, found himself in the Tower in 1495, accused of plotting with Warbeck; he came out with a royal pardon that cost him £200 a year to the king for the rest of his life and a £10 pension each to Lovell and Bray.[72] Litigation before the council was a good opportunity for gifts, like the £3 Shrewsbury corporation gave Empson in 1507.[73] So was parliament, particularly for those chosen as speaker of the commons. In 1485–6 the dean and canons of Windsor were lobbying hard to protect their interests under the new regime. Lovell had £3 6s 8d from them on the day after parliament returned from the Christmas recess, and a share in a further £6 13s 4d at the end of the session.[74]

In such matters Dudley came into his own. In London it was said that he and his kind 'provoked men by sundry ways and means to give unto them rich and great gifts of value and yet their causes full hardly sped'.[75] We do not know what lay behind the £1 6s 8d a year Sir Richard Carew paid Dudley or the £2 13s 4d from Lord Willoughby d'Eresby, a fee the peer cheerfully crossed out of his annual accounts for 1509.[76] Single payments are easier to trace. Shrewsbury corporation, litigating against Shrewsbury Abbey in May 1507, paid £6 13s 4d 'for a reward to Mr Dudley', nearly half the cost of that phase of the suit, which they seem to have lost despite their efforts.[77] Sir Robert Wotton paid him the same sum in 1508, perhaps in connection with the fine Dudley negotiated for Wotton's grant of the portership of Calais.[78] The London goldsmiths' company paid him £2 for his favour in their suit before the king's council against a goldsmith from Bridgwater.[79] Even the king's mother had to pay Dudley for his 'diligent labours with the king' when arranging the transfer of the assets of Creake Abbey to Christ's College, Cambridge in July 1507.[80] The new men's rise to wealth was testimony to their acuity in turning every opportunity to profit.

ROYAL FAVOUR

The most straightforward way to convert power into land was to seek a grant from the king, but Henry VII, determined to maintain a large crown estate to fund a strong monarchy and provide a landed base for direct intervention in local politics,

[72] *Estate and Household Accounts of William Worsley, Dean of St Paul's Cathedral 1479–1497*, ed. H. Kleineke and S. R. Hovland, London RS 40 (London, 2004), 15–16, 100, 107.

[73] H. Owen and J. B. Blakeway, *A History of Shrewsbury*, 2 vols (London, 1825), i. 279, 281.

[74] H. Kleineke, 'Lobbying and Access: The Canons of Windsor and the Matter of the Poor Knights in the Parliament of 1485', *Parliamentary History* 25 (2006), 156–8; Windsor, The Aerary, MS XV.48.50.

[75] *Great Chronicle*, 326.

[76] SHC, 281/2/1, fo. 5v; PRO, C1/132/30; SC6/Henry VIII/1976.

[77] Owen and Blakeway, *Shrewsbury*, i. 279; *LP* I, i. 132 (43).

[78] BL, Addl. MS 73523, fo. 4r; HL, MS HA 1518, fo. 57r.

[79] T. F. Reddaway and L. E. M. Walker, *The Early History of the Goldsmiths' Company, 1327–1509* (London, 1975), 197.

[80] M. K. Jones and M. G. Underwood, *The King's Mother: Lady Margaret Beaufort, Countess of Richmond and Derby* (Cambridge, 1992), 222.

granted very little land to his trusted servants. Most of the new men received some grants, but they were almost always dwarfed by their purchases. Bray was given a few manors, but sometimes had to buy out the titles of previous owners to make his possession sure.[81] Lovell got one substantial reward in 1486, the manor of Ducklington in Oxfordshire, worth over £50 a year with its satellite at Fringford. Eight years later Henry added a grant of Grimston in Norfolk, forfeited by John, earl of Lincoln as Ducklington had been by Francis, Viscount Lovell. Even here there were limits to the king's bounty. The second grant was merely for life and was treated for accounting purposes as a farm, Lovell paying the king £10 a year; and as the first was made in tail male, Lovell in the end failed to pass it on to his heirs.[82] In 1488 Lovell appeared to have been given another major prize, the forfeited Cornish estates of Sir Henry Bodrugan, worth £80 or more a year, but the intention was always that he would grant an annuity out of the revenues to Nicholas Crowmer, which would revert to the king on Crowmer's death, and then pass the estates on to Sir Richard Edgecombe, comptroller of the household and one of the king's key supporters in the county. Nothing was simple in Henry VII's England.[83] Brandon, too, got one forfeited manor, Duddington in Northamptonshire, granted by 1493 and worth £20 or more a year.[84] Between 1487 and 1492 Wyatt was given a house in London, a sixty-year term in some lands in Berkshire, a confiscated manor in Norfolk and some scraps of land in Suffolk; he made sure he got his due by personally bringing the inquisition describing the Norfolk lands into chancery.[85]

Poynings, born a gentleman and prominent in war, may have been less controversial to reward than mere pen-pushers. In 1488 Henry gave him seven manors in Buckinghamshire, Leicestershire, Northamptonshire, and Warwickshire, forfeited by the rebel Humphrey Stafford. They were worth a handsome £200 or so a year, and Poynings's rights were protected when Stafford's heir petitioned for restoration by act of parliament in 1515 and paid £900 to the king for it. Lady Poynings even managed to claim dower in them after his death.[86] Others had to wait until Henry VIII's reign for anything from the king. Southwell had less than a year to live when granted four manors and two hundreds in Norfolk for life.[87] Marney's reward was more generous but equally ill timed. In March 1522, fourteen months before his death, he gained three manors in Buckinghamshire and the lordship of the borough

[81] Condon, 'Profits of Office', 141–5.
[82] *CPR 1485–94*, 25, 474; *The Victoria History of the County of Oxford*, ed. W. Page et al., 17 vols (London, 1907–), vi. 127; BL, Addl. MS 21480, fo. 32v; *Reports of Cases from the Time of King Henry VIII*, ed. J. H. Baker, 2 vols, SS 120–1 (2003–4), i. 59–60.
[83] *CPR 1485–94*, 224; Cornwall RO, DDME 621–4, 1839, 1923; *CAD*, i. A545; BL, Addl. MS 59899, fo. 111r.
[84] *LP* II, i. 1190; PRO, E150/677/2; Northamptonshire RO, J(D)540/24.
[85] *LP* I, i. 833 (70); *CPR 1485–94*, 433; PRO, C142/23/118.
[86] *CPR 1485–94*, 250; *CIPM*, iii. 990; Alnwick Castle, Syon MS X.II.I, box 16b; PRO, C142/36/14, 39/85, 81/193, 81/194, 81/197; C54/381, m. 16d; CP40/1038, m. 425v; Worcestershire Archives, BA7335, Ref:705:7/20/7; *Certificate of Musters for Buckinghamshire*, 310, 317, 327; 5 Henry VIII c. 13.
[87] *LP* I, ii. 1836 (4).

of Buckingham, all forfeited by the duke of Buckingham and worth some £65 to £85 a year.[88] Buckingham's fall benefited Hussey, too, with a grant in April 1522 of the manor of Kneesall, Nottinghamshire, worth around £30 a year.[89] Wyatt, who had improved on the terms of his grants from Henry VII in 1511 and obtained some land in Northamptonshire forfeited by Empson, joined in the jamboree of 1522 with the grant of a manor in Yorkshire.[90]

Poynings was also fortunate in that Henry VII's favour made it easy to pursue his inherited claims to two major estates, those of his grandfather Robert, Lord Poynings, and his more distant ancestor Sir Guy de Brian, even against such powerful competitors as the earls of Northumberland and Ormond. By 1488–9 he had managed to secure more of the Poynings lands than his father ever held, 'by what title is unknown', as Northumberland's receiver sniffily put it. They were concentrated in Kent and Sussex, though with outliers in East Anglia. Meanwhile in December 1488 a settlement arbitrated by his colleagues on the king's council gave him the Kent portion of the Brian estates plus three manors in Somerset. Together, these estates brought in some £315 a year.[91] Yet even he failed sometimes. He pursued his claim to Poynings manor in Flitcham, Norfolk, through litigation against the Woodhouse family in 1491, a trespass suit against their farmer in 1501–8, and arbitration by the two chief justices in 1503, but seems never to have secured it.[92]

MARRIAGE

For those with less favourable pedigrees than Poynings's, marriage was the easiest route to the acquisition of land. It was one that could be much facilitated by royal favour and that could be turned to extra advantage by those skilful or unprincipled enough to divert or sell off an inheritance or delay its passage to the heirs of a wife's previous match. Lovell's marriage did not bring him any land to pass on to his heirs, but made possible his control of a major estate while he lived. In 1485–6, doubtless with royal encouragement, he married Isabel, the sister of Edmund, Lord Roos, who may have been the widow of the Yorkist household knight Sir Thomas Everingham.[93] Roos, though his father's attainder was reversed and his lands

[88] *LP* III, ii. 2145 (18); *Certificate of Musters for Buckinghamshire*, 29, 63, 136, 336; PRO, C142/40/7.

[89] *LP* III, ii. 2214 (19); PRO, SC6/Henry VIII/6237.

[90] *LP* I, i. 833 (70), III, ii. 2415 (19).

[91] R. Jeffs, 'The Poynings–Percy Dispute: an Example of the Interplay of Open Strife and Legal Action in the Fifteenth Century', *BIHR* 34 (1961), 162; J. M. W. Bean, *The Estates of the Percy Family 1416–1537* (Oxford, 1958), 114–25; *CCR 1485–1500*, 410; Alnwick Castle, Syon MS X.II.I, box 16b.

[92] PRO, CP40/918, m. 426r–426v; KB27/961, m. 20v, 964, m. 85r, 968, m. 26v, 971, m. 35v, 972, m. 31v, 989, m. 77v; NRO, FLT396, 396a, 838; F. Blomefield, *An Essay towards a Topographical History of the County of Norfolk*, 11 vols (London, 1805–10), viii. 412–13.

[93] *A Visitation of the North of England circa 1480–1500*, ed. C. H. Hunter-Blair, Surtees Soc. 144 (Durham, 1930), 163; E. L. Meek, 'The Career of Sir Thomas Everingham, "Knight of the North"', in the Service of Maximillian, Duke of Austria, 1477–81', *HR* 74 (2001), 238–48.

restored in 1485, was counted 'not of sufficient discretion to guide himself and his livelihood' and, just as important from Henry's point of view, not 'able to serve his Highness after his duty'. So, by summer 1486, perhaps even earlier, his lands, and the power to serve the king that accompanied their control, were entrusted to Lovell.[94] They gave him a significant stake in the North and East Ridings of Yorkshire, where over one-third of the estates lay, with manors of a similar value leading away across the Midlands through Nottinghamshire, Lincolnshire, Leicestershire, and Northamptonshire to Shropshire. Of the remainder, half lay in East Anglia—a tenth of the total in Lovell's home county of Norfolk—and half scattered around the South-East. From their revenues Lovell was to pay the king £466 13s 4d a year, and he duly did so.[95] But once he had shaken off most of the other claimants who occupied parts of the estate, he must have made £800 a year or more from the Roos lands, for their total clear income was valued in 1524 at £1,310 16s 3/4d, while a valuation of some of the manors in 1513 rated them about 21 per cent higher in clear yield than that.[96] Under terms guaranteed by act of parliament in 1492, Lovell was even allowed to keep the estates for his lifetime if Roos predeceased him, as he did, dying at Lovell's house, Elsings in Enfield, in 1508. From 1509 the rent previously paid to the crown went to Roos's eventual heirs, the Manners of Etal, but Lovell gave up no land until Sir George Manners agreed in February 1513 to marry his son to Lovell's niece. Lovell then passed about one-third of the Roos inheritance, almost the entire Yorkshire holdings, into the Manners' hands, some of it to serve as his niece's jointure.[97] The rest Lovell kept until he died.[98]

Hussey made three marriages, each profitable in a different way: one to an heiress, one to a dowager, one to a well-connected aristocrat. His first wife, Margaret, was daughter and heiress to Simon Blount, a Gloucestershire esquire who died young. Hussey's father obtained her wardship from Edward IV, they were married by 1490, and in 1492, she having been proved to be of age to inherit, they took control of her lands.[99] They consisted of some sixteen manors and other holdings concentrated around Bath, where Somerset met Wiltshire and Gloucestershire, worth at least £200 a year.[100] She died in June 1508, and a year later Hussey married again, to Anne, the widow of Richard Beauchamp, Lord St Amand, who had been dead less than a year, leaving lands in Wiltshire, Berkshire, Buckinghamshire, and Huntingdonshire. They rapidly set about securing her dower rights on her late

---

[94] *CP*, xi. 106–7; *PROME*, vi. 310–11; 7 Henry VII c. 20.

[95] PRO, E404/54/3, unnumbered warrant of 12 November 1503.

[96] PRO, C54/392, mm. 30d–31d; SC6/Hen VII/1242; C1/158/13; SHC, LM/1842/4.

[97] *LP* I, i. 289 (32); PRO, PROB11/17/24.

[98] *Certificate of Musters for Buckinghamshire*, 44; 'Muster Roll and Clergy List in the Hundred of Holt, circa 1523', ed. B. Cozens-Hardy, *NA* 22 (1923–5), 57; Northamptonshire RO, D1086, m. 9; LAO, FL Deeds 224; Misc. Dep. 511/1.

[99] *CPR 1494–1509*, 279; *A Catalogue of the Medieval Muniments at Berkeley Castle*, ed. B. Wells-Firby, 2 vols, Gloucestershire Record Series 17–18 (Bristol, 2004), ii. 843; *CCR 1485–1500*, 620; *CIPM*, i. 869.

[100] *Calendarium Inquisitionum Post Mortem sive Escaetarum*, ed. J. Caley and J. Bayley, 4 vols (London, 1806–28), iv. 382; PRO, C140/59/79; E211/152.

husband's lands and defeating his attempt to endow his illegitimate son, but less than two years later, on 2 March 1511, she too was dead.[101] Hussey soon found solace in his third marriage, to Anne, sister of Richard earl of Kent, who was already married to his sister. Anne had been betrothed in 1506–7 to the eldest son of Charles Somerset, Lord Herbert, but either she must have refused the match or her incompetent brother proved unable to provide for it. On 15 November 1512 it was agreed she would marry Hussey instead. He, Kent, and Herbert struck a three-cornered deal that gave Hussey three of Kent's manors as Anne's marriage portion and Somerset five others in compensation for the lost match.[102]

Southwell, too, married an heiress, Ursula, one of the two daughters of John Bohun, while her elder sister, Mary, married Sir David Owen, illegitimate uncle to Henry VII.[103] When Bohun died in 1492, followed some years later by his widow, most of their Sussex estates went to Owen, though two manors were divided, as was the single manor in Surrey, while those in Essex, Hertfordshire, Middlesex, and London came to the Southwells. Southwell and Ursula had no issue, but somehow, presumably by a mixture of payments and pressure, he induced Owen's son Henry to agree early in 1513 that he and his second wife Elizabeth, daughter of Sir Philip Calthorp, whom he had married by 1508, could keep Ursula's lands for his life, commit some to his executors for four years, and even pass the most important manor, Fillol's Hall in Kelvedon Easterford, on to his own heirs.[104] Bray, similarly, married a minor heiress in the 1470s, but seems to have needed to exercise some influence after 1485 to draw maximum benefit from her lands.[105]

Windsor married only once, but it was so profitable that John Leland, touring England around the time of his death, thought it worthy of note: 'The old Lord Windsor or his father had the daughter and heir of the Lord Mountjoy in marriage, by whom he had 500 marks of land by the year.'[106] His details were a little foggy—Elizabeth Windsor and her sister Anne were left co-heirs to their grandfather, Walter Blount, Lord Mountjoy, by the deaths of their father William and brother John—but the gist was right.[107] Chancery litigation was necessary to secure the estates and some passed to the Blounts' heirs male, but what remained was impressive.[108] In 1504 the inheritance was formally split down the middle, moieties of five manors in Sussex, three in Kent, four in Derbyshire, and one in

[101] *CP*, vii. 17, xi. 303; *Memorials*, 121; *The Victoria History of the County of Berkshire*, ed. P. Ditchfield et al., 4 vols (London, 1906–27), iii. 459; PRO, CP40/989, m. 352r; 'Early Berkshire Wills from the PCC, ante 1558', ed. G. F. T. Sherwood, *Quarterly Journal of the Berks Archaeological and Architectural Society* 3 (1893–5), 148–9.

[102] PRO, C54/380, m. 10d; BLARS, L15.

[103] J. C. Wedgwood, *History of Parliament: Biographies of the Members of the Commons House, 1439–1509* (London, 1936), 654–5.

[104] W. H. StJ. Hope, *Cowdray and Easebourne Priory* (London, 1919), 10; *Feet of Fines for the County of Sussex*, iii, ed. L. F. Salzmann, Sussex RS 23 (London, 1916), 303; *CAD*, i. A644, A650, iii. A5810, v. A12276; PRO, E41/188; C142/29/15.

[105] Condon, 'Profits of Office', 138–39.

[106] J. Leland, *The Itinerary of John Leland in or about the Years 1535–1543*, ed. L. T. Smith, 5 vols (London, 1906–10), iv. 132.

[107] Wedgwood, *Commons*, 86–7.

[108] PRO, C1/217/9, 268/24; Leland, *Itinerary*, iv. 132.

Staffordshire, and of over 4,000 acres of land, settled on Andrew and Elizabeth with remainders to their sons, and beyond them to Anne and her husband Sir David Owen, who had married her as his second wife.[109] Anne's half was settled in the same way, and it was she who died without issue, leaving the entire estate to the Windsors.[110] Gambling on the fecundity of relations by marriage similarly paid off at length for Dudley, whose second wife's title to the lands of her brother John Grey, Viscount Lisle eventually endowed Edmund's son John, created Viscount Lisle in 1542.[111]

Heiresses were so much in demand that even the most ambitious men might have to settle for widows instead. Here the king's right as feudal lord to direct the marriages of the widows of his tenants-in-chief, notionally so that he could ensure they married men suitable to perform the military service owing from their lands, became useful to those who could access the king's favour. Marney's first marriage, to Thomasine, daughter of Sir Thomas Arundel of Lanherne, brought him no land and was probably to the advantage of those who held his wardship, just as Poynings's marriage, made when his family was under a cloud, brought him little gain.[112] Marney's second match, in contrast, made by 1486, to Isabel, daughter of Nicholas Wyfold and widow of John Norreys, did bring land temporarily under his control, especially when reinforced by the grant in 1491 of the wardship of her son Edmund Norreys.[113] There were two manors in Hertfordshire, scraps in Kent and Buckinghamshire, and four houses on the corner of Cheapside and Honey Lane in London, which Marney managed to re-settle in 1503–5 on his children by Isabel.[114] Hobart married a widow as his third wife after two marriages that forged connections among the Norfolk gentry.[115] Englefield married as his second wife a widow who brought with her dower lands from two previous marriages in Oxfordshire.[116] Wyatt married the widow of another royal servant, Anne, sometimes known as Agnes, daughter of John Skinner of Reigate, Surrey, and widow of John Wilde of Camberwell, clerk of the green cloth in the king's household. Wilde died in 1502 and by June 1503 Anne was settling the descent of her grandmother's lands at Rudgwick, Sussex, and Coulsdon, Surrey, on her heirs by Wyatt in expectation of their marriage.[117] Her grandmother was still alive in 1511 and her mother in 1513, but Wyatt did eventually get hold both of Rudgwick and of her mother's

[109] *Sussex Fines*, iii. 300–1; Wedgwood, *Commons*, 654–5.
[110] *The Victoria History of the County of Sussex*, ed. W. Page et al., 9 vols in 11 (London, 1905–), ix. 273; *Sussex Manors, Advowsons etc recorded in the Feet of Fines, Henry VIII to William IV (1509–1833)*, ed. E. H. W. Dunkin, Sussex RS, 19–20 (1914–15), 130–1.
[111] D. M. Loades, *John Dudley, Duke of Northumberland 1504–1553* (Oxford, 1996), 8, 25–6, 48–9.
[112] *CAD*, iv. A6298.
[113] *CAD*, i. C1230; *CPR 1485–94*, 345.
[114] *The Victoria History of the County of Hertford*, ed. W. Page, 5 vols (London, 1902–23), iii. 48, 411; PRO, SC6/Henry VII/1062; D. Keene and V. Harding, *Historical Gazeteer of London before the Great Fire, I, Cheapside* (Cambridge, 1987), no. 11/6.
[115] E. W. Ives, 'Hobart, Sir James', *ODNB*.
[116] S. T. Bindoff, *History of Parliament: The House of Commons 1509–1558*, 3 vols (London, 1982), ii. 103.
[117] WSRO, MP23/R4; Addl. MS 35530; KHLC, U908/T454.

Surrey manors of Aglondes More and Henfold, which he re-settled in 1511–13 in conveyances involving her mother's family the Gaynsfords.[118] Wilde's own lands do not seem to have been large, but there were some meadows in Kew; Wyatt and his wife apparently sold off them off, in cooperation with Wilde's son Hugh, in 1522.[119]

Of all the new men, marriage was proportionately most important to Brandon, though the benefits it brought him were only short-term. Ever the dashing courtier, he specialized in charming aristocratic widows. First he married Anne, dowager marchioness of Berkeley, whose aged husband died in February 1492 after settling much of his inheritance on the king.[120] By August 1495, they had received a papal dispensation enabling them to marry and Thomas set about taking control by negotiation and litigation of her share of her husband's lands and goods. Her five manors in Gloucestershire, two in Essex, and one in Somerset were worth in total at least £300 a year and perhaps nearer £450, while one of the houses, Great Chesterford in Essex, had eight 'great chambers' newly built by the spendthrift marquess.[121] The goods over which the couple tussled with her late husband's servants were also worth having, fine textiles decorated with designs of foliage, chariots, and the white lions rampant of the Berkeleys' Mowbray forebears.[122] Unfortunately, she lived only two more years, dying in September 1497, leaving Sir Thomas to make a favourable settlement with her disinherited brother-in-law Maurice.[123]

Brandon next set his sights on Elizabeth, dowager Lady Fitzwarin, whose first husband had died as long ago as 1479, but who had since then been married for over twenty years to Sir John Sapcotes, giving her two sets of dower lands. Sapcotes died on 5 January 1501, and before the month was out his widow became in addition co-heir with her three sisters to the estates of her brother, John, Lord Dynham.[124] 'Sapcotes is deceased', noted the king's chamber accounts, 'and his wife is the king's widow, a great marriage'. Shortly afterwards Brandon and Lovell promised £100 in gold for a letter of recommendation from the king, presumably directed to Lady Fitzwarin, and between August and November 1502 they married.[125] Sapcotes had left her his lands in Huntingdonshire and Berkshire, worth £50 or more a year, his goods and his debts, though Brandon sought to avoid

[118] PRO, E326/10551; *The Victoria History of the County of Surrey*, ed. H. E. Malden, 4 vols (London, 1902–14), iii. 137; *Abstracts of Surrey Feet of Fines 1509–1558*, ed. C. A. F. Meekings, 2 vols, Surrey RS 45–6 (Frome, 1946), i. 4, 6.

[119] *Surrey Fines*, i. 15–16.

[120] *CP*, ii. 135.

[121] *CEPR*, xvi. 371; *CIPM*, i. 778, 832, 834, iii. 839, 865; PRO, SC6/Henry VII/1071–2; *CAD*, iii. D819; *Descriptive Catalogue of the Charters and Muniments in the Possession of the Rt Hon Lord Fitzhardinge at Berkeley Castle*, ed. I. H. Jeayes (Bristol, 1892), 198–9, 203.

[122] PRO, KB27/932, mm. 22v, 36v, 936, m. 24v; CP40/934, m. 47r; *CIPM*, i. 778.

[123] J. Smyth, *The Berkeley Manuscripts: The Lives of the Berkeleys, Lords of the Honour, Castle and Manor of Berkeley in the County of Gloucester from 1066 to 1618, with a Description of the Hundred of Berkeley and of its Inhabitants*, ed. J. Maclean, 3 vols (Gloucester, 1883–5), ii. 157–8.

[124] *CP*, iv. 380–81, v. 509–10; PRO, C1/135/13.

[125] BL, Addl. MS 21480, fos. 178r, 184r; Devon RO, Chanter 12 (ii), third foliation, fos. 6v, 8v; *Wiltshire Fines*, 174–5.

paying those.[126] More important were the Fitzwarin estates. Most of those she held in dower were in Devon, so much so that Sapcotes had left his native Huntingdonshire to settle there. They lay spread from north to south across the middle of the county from Marwood through Tawstock and Bampton to Combeinteignhead.[127] But there were also manors in Cornwall, Somerset, Wiltshire, and Berkshire.[128] The Dynham inheritance was more impressive still, two dozen manors concentrated in Devon and Cornwall but extending into Somerset, Hampshire, Oxfordshire, Buckinghamshire, and Warwickshire.[129] The lands were held in common by the heiresses and their descendants, the revenue split four ways and grants of tenements and presentations to benefices made in their joint names.[130] But with neither the Fitzwarin nor the Dynham lands was Brandon content to let matters rest. Gambling on surviving his bride, in 1507 he handed some of the Fitzwarin estates over to his step-son, John, Lord Fitzwarin, in return for a grant of others to last his own lifetime as well as his wife's.[131] In the same year, hoping to endow his nephew Charles, he secured a royal licence to settle on him a reversionary life interest in some of the Dynham lands in Devon, an arrangement which Charles and Lord Fitzwarin were still untangling in the 1520s.[132]

A further settlement in 1509 ensured that Lady Fitzwarin would be able to pass some of her inheritance on to her son by Sapcotes rather than to Lord Fitzwarin, but in other respects she may have had cause to regret her final venture into matrimony.[133] In his will, though Brandon left her plate worth £333 6s 8d and half of all the goods she had brought into their marriage, he did so on condition that she not interfere with the rest of his provisions. He left his house in Southwark and its contents together with some of his purchased lands to Lady Jane Guildford, Sir Richard's widow, ten or twenty years younger than his wife, who would request prayers for his soul immediately after those of her husbands in her own will twenty-eight years later. Perhaps he just felt sorry for the reduced circumstances in which Sir Richard's financial problems had left Lady Jane, but his reward to her servants 'for their kind labour about me in time of my sickness'

---

[126] CCA, Christ Church Register F, fo. 106v; *CIPM*, ii. 406, 442; PRO, C1/333/30.

[127] Wedgwood, *Commons*, 740–1; R. Polwhele, *The History of Devonshire*, 3 vols (London, 1793–1806), ii. 143–4, 378–9, iii. 410; PRO, KB9/432/29; Devon RO, Chanter 12(ii), second foliation, fos. 9r, 14v, 15r, Chanter 13, fos. 26v, 54r; PRO, C1/135/117.

[128] *The Victoria History of Wiltshire*, ed. R. B. Pugh et al., 18 vols (London, 1953–), xi. 170–1; *VCH Berkshire*, iv. 260; J. Collinson, *The History and Antiquities of the County of Somerset*, 3 vols (Bath, 1792), iii. 111; *Calendarium Inquisitionum Post Mortem*, iii. 397–8.

[129] *Abstracts of Feet of Fines relating to Wiltshire 1377–1509*, ed. J. L. Kirby, Wiltshire RS 41 (Devizes, 1986), 174–5; *Feet of Fines, Divers Counties*, ed. E. F. Kirk (London, 1913–24), 7.

[130] Devon RO, 346M/T423; Z17/3/19; Chanter 12(ii), third foliation, fos. 6v, 8v, 9r, 11v, Chanter 13, fos. 5r, 11v, 49r, 63r; Somerset Heritage Centre, DD/HI/517, roll 5, m. 9; *Certificate of Musters for Buckinghamshire*, 127; *The Registers of Oliver King, Bishop of Bath and Wells, 1496–1503, and Hadrian de Castello, Bishop of Bath and Wells, 1503–1518*, ed. H. C. Maxwell Lyte, Somerset RS 54 (London, 1939), 113.

[131] *Wiltshire Fines*, 180–1.

[132] *CPR 1494–1509*, 503; PRO, CP25/2/7/32/4; CP40/1037, m. 793, CP40/1043, m. 566; C54/391, m. 18; *LP* IV, i. 1136 (16).

[133] *Feet of Fines, Divers Counties*, 72–3.

makes the arrangement look more like cohabitation than charity.[134] Matters may have been further complicated by the fact that Lady Elizabeth's son Richard Sapcotes was married to Lady Jane's niece, Alice Vaux.[135] Either way Sir Thomas's widow had had quite enough of marrying courtiers. Within three months of his death she appeared before Bishop John Fisher in Beckenham parish church to take an oath of perpetual chastity and receive the mantle and ring of a vowed widow.[136]

WARDSHIPS

Another means to expand the lands under one's control was to secure the wardship of those who inherited while under-age. Henry's aggressive assertion of his feudal rights over the landed classes expanded the stock of wardships coming into his hands and enforced the priority of royal over private wardship. He could grant the care of a ward's lands to whomever he chose, and the choice was determined by a variable mixture of favour and payment. The new men were well placed to compete on both levels, and to overcome any subsequent hitches: in 1519 Poynings extracted Jane Tilney from the hands of Giles Claybroke on the grounds that she was a royal ward, not a city orphan, and the king's grant to him trumped the city's to Claybroke.[137] The trade in wards was not entirely heartless, and attempts were made to ensure that aristocratic orphans were given a fit start in life. One ward of the king in Lovell's care was provided at royal expense in 1499 with doublets, gowns, a jacket, hose, shirts, bonnets, shoes, slippers, pinsons or pumps, and a hat, some in velvet or camlet.[138] But, in general, wardship operated as a spoils system conditioned by genetic fortune and royal favour.

The trade in royal wardships moved fast. In 1503 Mordaunt obtained the king's signature for the wardship of John Leventhorpe and sold it on to his brother-in-law Wistan Browne for £100 before any of the inquisitions post mortem necessary to demonstrate the king's title to the wardship had been held, a process that took more than two years.[139] Most of the new men secured some wardships from the king—Bray, Empson, Guildford, Belknap, and so on—but their purposes varied.[140] Some aimed at control over family estates which might otherwise pass into less sympathetic hands. Marney, for example, knew about wardship at first hand, having been subject to it himself, entrusted by Edward IV in 1472 to his brother Richard duke of Gloucester, who passed him on within four months to Robert

---

[134] PRO, PROB11/16/29, PROB11/17/28, PROB11/27/21.
[135] *Feet of Fines, Divers Counties*, 72–3.
[136] KHLC, DRb/Ar1/13, fo. 37r–37v; J. A. F. Thomson, *The Early Tudor Church and Society, 1485–1529* (London, 1993), 336–7.
[137] LMA, Rep. 4, fo. 5v.
[138] PML, Rulers of England, box 1, no. 48c.
[139] R. Halstead, *Succinct Genealogies of the Noble and Ancient Houses of Alno or de Alneto etc* (London, 1685), 518–19, 525; *CIPM*, iii. 899.
[140] Condon, 'Profits of Office', 147; PRO, C1/174/58; *CPR 1485–94*, 167, 343, 425.

Tyrell and Thomas Green.[141] His sole acquisition was defensive, the marriage and lands of his step-son Edmund Norreys, though it did achieve a wider fame when Robert Constable used it as an illustration of one of the rules governing wardship in his influential reading on *Prerogativa regis* four years later.[142] Other grantees sought other outcomes. Some were looking for suitably endowed marriage partners for their children, grandchildren, or other dependants. Some sought strategic, if temporary, accretions to their landed power, some simple profit.

Many wardships, of course, mixed several motives. Four grants to Poynings illustrate the variety. In 1497 the king confirmed his purchase from Sir Thomas Cokesey of the custody of the lands and determination of the marriage of Humphrey Stafford, then about to come of age. The estates, scattered across the Midlands and worth perhaps £40 a year, complemented the forfeited lands of Humphrey's father, granted to Poynings in 1488.[143] It was also in 1497 that he was granted the wardship and marriage of Henry, son and heir of John Pympe of Nettlestead, Kent, who had served as his colleague in Ireland. This brought control of another section of the Stafford estates, granted to Pympe, and of lands in Kent worth between £25 and £50 a year, with a similar amount to fall in if Henry's mother died before he came of age.[144] Sir Edward's tenure of Pympe's Stafford estates might be doubly temporary—until Pympe came of age or Stafford's son secured their restoration—but could still be made to pay by vigilant exploitation. In 1512, as both possibilities loomed, Poynings was making ninety-nine-year leases on some of the lands, presumably for premium fines, and in 1514 he demanded that the local escheator be stopped from holding inquisitions into Pympe's lands to his disadvantage while he was at Tournai.[145] In 1503 Poynings and his comrade-in-arms John Norton of Faversham bought for £200 the wardship and marriage of the two daughters of John Norwood of Norwood in Milton, Kent. Their lands lay in Kent, Hampshire, and Wiltshire, and in due course Norton married one of them and established himself at Norwood.[146] In 1518, finally, Poynings paid £200—of which the king then pardoned him £66 13s 4d—for the wardship and marriage of Edward Fiennes, Lord Clinton. In terms of landed income alone the deal was a good one, for the lord was five years old and his estates worth more than £80 a year even when the portions of his mother and grandmother were deducted. The lands were in Kent and Warwickshire, near Sir Edward's own. But he was also Poynings's grandson through his daughter Jane, widow of Thomas, Lord Clinton, and Poynings would not have wanted him to slip out of the family's control.[147]

---

[141] *CAD*, iv. A6298; R. E. Horrox, *Richard III: A Study of Service* (Cambridge, 1989), 75.

[142] *CPR 1485–94*, 345; Robert Constable, *Prerogativa Regis, Tertia Lectura Roberti Constable de Lyncolnis Inne Anno 11 H 7*, ed. S. E. Thorne (New Haven CT, 1949), 35.

[143] *CPR 1494–1509*, 84; *Materials*, ii, 66–7; *CIPM*, i. 224–6, 230, 236.

[144] A. E. Conway, *Henry VII's Relations with Scotland and Ireland, 1485–1498* (Cambridge, 1932), 65–6; *CPR 1494–1509*, 105; *CIPM*, i. 1224, 1235; Scott, *Memorials*, xlv.

[145] Worcestershire Archives, BA3964, Ref:705:95/1(ii); BA7335, Ref:705:7/64(iv); PRO, SP1/8, fo. 144 (*LP* I, ii. 3057).

[146] *CPR 1494–1509*, 338; BL, Addl. MS 21480, fo. 101r; *CIPM*, i. 1169, ii. 713; *The Victoria History of Hampshire and the Isle of Wight*, ed. H. A. Doubleday and W. Page, 6 vols (London, 1900–14), iv. 247–8; E. Hasted, *The History and Topographical Survey of the County of Kent*, 12 vols (Wakefield, 1972 edn), vi. 179–80.

[147] *LP* II, ii. 4260; PRO, WARD9/147, unfol.; C54/409, m. 6d.

Brandon's motives seem to have been less complex. In 1491 Henry gave him the wardship of Richard Fiennes, Lord Saye, with the keeping of his estates in Oxfordshire, Hampshire, and Somerset. Saye, who had already passed through the hands of Richard III as duke of Gloucester and Sir Richard Harcourt, was about to come of age and Brandon quickly sold his marriage on to an Oxfordshire gentleman, who married him to his daughter.[148] Ten years later he was dead, and his son's wardship was in the king's hands. Henry VII seems to have kept hold of it, but in the early months of the next reign, perhaps after a good day's hunting—the grant was signed at the royal hunting lodge at Wanstead in Essex—Brandon secured his wardship, too. His will directed that Saye's marriage should be sold and the proceeds spent to the benefit of his soul while control of the lands, worth some £190 a year, should pass to his nephew Charles, and another nephew William Sidney should have a wardship attached to the estates.[149] Lovell, too, was a profiteer. In 1503–5 he paid £66 13s 4d in four instalments for the wardship of his godson Thomas Elrington, whose lands lay in Middlesex near his own. By the time Elrington came of age, it was alleged in a later lawsuit, Lovell had taken £2,289 11s 3d income from the lands and maximized profit by leaving more than £420 of repairs undone. Whatever the details, the matter must have rested on his conscience, for his executors offered his former ward compensation.[150]

Wyatt, predictably, traded hard in wardships both royal and private. In 1489 the king gave him the wardships of three daughters of Jasper Ruskyn esquire, co-heiresses with their elder sister to his lands in Leicestershire. One died, one married, and one was sold by Wyatt back to the care of her mother and promptly became a nun.[151] As guardian of John Spelman of Great Ellingham, Norfolk, Wyatt insisted on his right to present to Norfolk churches and it was presumably as guardian of the sisters of John Wyse that he sued those who had failed to pay him towards the cost of their marriages.[152] In 1512 he defended himself against the bishop of Lincoln's suit for taking away William Taillard, whom the bishop claimed as his ward under feudal tenure, by arguing the superiority of the earl of Kent's claim, which Wyatt had acquired in 1506 from a London goldsmith, who no doubt received it in payment of the earl's debts; though he seemed to concede the bishop's claim in court, he still held the wardship some years later.[153] And always Wyatt told people he was doing them a favour. When he bought the wardship of Anne, daughter and heir of Henry Chaloner of Camberwell, Surrey, from her mother in 1518, it was not just for money but 'also for the other great benefits and promotions that the said Sir Henry hath preferred her unto aforetimes'.[154]

[148] *CPR 1485–94*, 345, 439; *CP*, xi. 483; PRO, C1/93/19.
[149] BL, Addl. MS 21480, fos. 39r–39v, 162r, 182v; *LP* I, i. 218 (30); PRO, C54/389, m. 19; PROB11/16/29.
[150] BL, Addl. MS 59899, fo. 151v; PRO, C1/546/52; *LP* IV, i. 366.
[151] *CPR 1485–94*, 291; *CIPM*, i. 457, ii. 934.
[152] Blomefield, *Norfolk*, vii. 298; *The Visitation of Norfolk in the year 1563*, ed. G. H. Dashwood and E. Bulwer Lytton, 2 vols (Norwich, 1878–95), i. 258; PRO, CP40/1014, m. 532v.
[153] PRO, CP40/998, m. 436r; *Registrum Annalium Collegii Mertonensis 1483–1521*, ed. H. E. Salter, OHS 76 (Oxford, 1923), 501.
[154] PRO, C54/386, m. 18d.

Southwell's close involvement with the royal financial machinery left him well placed to bid for attractive wardships. Between 1501 and 1512 he was granted those of George Stratton, Margaret and Elizabeth Pykenham, Robert Crane, John Bardfeld, and Thomas Felton, paying £100 for Stratton, the Pykenhams, and one other heiress in a job lot. Their lands lay in Suffolk and Essex, as Southwell well knew in at least one instance, where he had served on the commission that identified them.[155] Crane's in particular were attractive enough—taxable at £100 a year by 1524—to make him a fine match for Southwell's half-sister Elizabeth.[156] Felton was married to a daughter of the Suffolk gentleman Thomas Seckford, presumably at a good price for Southwell.[157] John Bardfeld did not live to inherit his lands, but did receive a share of his uncle's plate and his gold chain, which Southwell seems to have kept hold of when young John died.[158] Between 1502 and 1512 Southwell was also involved in half a dozen other bids for wardships, though whether as an active participant or a financial guarantor for his friends is hard to say.[159] As so often with Southwell, his extended family loomed large in these dealings. One bid in 1511 was made with his brother-in-law Anthony Hansard and in 1513 he sold another brother-in-law, William Wotton, the wardship of Elizabeth Bardwell, which he had obtained from Sir Edward Howard and his wife, Alice, Lady Morley, so Wotton could marry her to his son.[160] After Southwell's death his kin returned the favour, Wotton joining with his widow to secure the wardship of his nephew and heir.[161]

Windsor likewise often obtained grants with associates, first his step-father Sir Robert Lytton, then his brother-in-law Edmund Dudley. With the former he gained the wardship of Germain Pole in 1494 and bid £100 in 1503 for the wardship of the heir of William Tendring, whose land-holdings he had just investigated for the king.[162] With the latter, for a payment of £400, he secured control of the lands and marriages of Elizabeth and Agnes, daughters of Henry Lovell esquire, of Harting, Sussex, who were rapidly married off to Empson's younger son John and Windsor's younger brother Anthony.[163] With a set of colleagues he gave £80 in 1505 for the two young daughters of William Tauke with their lands, worth perhaps £25 a year, in Hampshire and Sussex.[164] The next reign saw him still busy, but with unpredictable results. In 1515 he had to sue Elizabeth, widow of Sir Thomas Frowyk, over the abduction of Frowyk's daughter and heiress Frideswide, whose

---

[155] *CPR 1494–1509*, 235, 309, 538; *LP* I, i. 1524 (22); *CIPM*, ii. 231, 363, 396, 889; Wedgwood, *Commons*, 739; BL, Addl. MS 21480, fo. 70r.

[156] *Visitation of Norfolk 1563*, i. 124–25; *Suffolk in 1524*, ed. S. H. A. Hervey, Suffolk Green Books 10 (Woodbridge, 1910), 16.

[157] *The Visitation of Suffolk, 1561*, ed. J. Corder, 2 vols, HS n.s. 2–3 (London, 1981–4), i. 200.

[158] PRO, C1/334/43.

[159] BL, Addl. MS 21480, fos. 77v, 78r, 83r; PRO, E36/215, fo. 335r; *LP* I, i. 1221(56); Bindoff, *Commons*, iii. 640.

[160] PRO, E36/215, fo. 331v; Blomefield, *Norfolk*, x. 43, 263.

[161] *LP* II, i. 96.

[162] *CPR 1494–1509*, 10, 209; BL, Addl. MS 21480, fo. 89r.

[163] *CPR 1494–1509*, 396, 542, 612; BL, Addl. MS 59899, fo. 174r.

[164] BL, Addl. MS 21480, fo. 178r; *CPR 1494–1509*, 415; *CIPM*, ii. 804, iii. 824.

marriage he claimed.[165] In 1522–3 he bought the wardship of Henry Fortescue for great sums from Sir Francis Bryan, to whom the king had lately granted it on Bryan's marriage to Fortescue's widowed mother, but a dozen or so years later, and before Windsor could arrange a marriage for him, Henry slipped away. Allegedly, his mother took advantage of Windsor's soft-heartedness in letting him leave Stanwell to visit her, but William Stafford, whose daughter he eventually married, seems also to have had a hand in the affair.[166]

The opportunities and difficulties of the quest for wardships were exemplified by the saga of Hussey and the wardship of Lord Monteagle. Hussey, as former master of the wards, knew his way around the system. He discovered and secured for himself the wardship of Isaac Sybyllys, with his £44 a year of landed income, and between 1511 and 1516 bid, apparently as an agent for other grantees, for a number of other wardships in and around Lincolnshire.[167] In 1522–3 he moved to protect the interests of his daughter when her prospective father-in-law, Maurice Berkeley, died, by buying up the wardship of John Berkeley and his inheritance, lands worth some £100 clear of charges scattered across the Midland counties. Disputes with Maurice's widow were amicably settled, and in the early 1530s the Berkeley estates on the borders of Leicestershire and Rutland were being administered together with Hussey's own.[168] In 1526 he secured the wardship of Gerrard Foster of Brampton, Huntingdonshire, in 1530 that of Henry Ryther of Harewood, Yorkshire, in 1533 he found a husband for another of his daughters, Dorothy, by buying the wardship of Thomas Wimbush with his £30 a year of lands and in 1536 yet another ward, Roland Sherrard, was being brought up in his household.[169]

The Monteagle wardship was an altogether more complex business. Edward Stanley, Lord Monteagle, died on 6 April 1523. Towards the end of his life, the old lord had drawn close to Thomas, Lord Darcy, and made him and his friend Hussey executors of his will, together with his neighbour Sir Alexander Ratcliffe and his estate officers Laurence Starkey and Richard Banks, telling Darcy that he placed his trust in them to obtain his fourteen-year-old son's wardship and care for him.[170] They sought the grant in the teeth of competition from the duke of Norfolk and others, Darcy negotiating with Monteagle's servants and Hussey with Sir Richard Weston, master of the wards, with Wolsey and with the king; 'Cousin', Darcy told

[165] PRO, CP40/1011, m. 420v.
[166] *LP* III, ii. 2145 (8); PRO, C1/917/57–8; Bindoff, *Commons*, i. 526; P. W. Hasler, *The House of Commons 1558–1603*, 3 vols (London, 1981), ii. 148.
[167] *CCR 1500–9*, 774; *CIPM*, iii. 895; PRO, C54/387, m. 13d; E36/95, fo. 20v; E211/152; E36/215, fos. 334r, 337v, 349v, 350r (*LP* II, ii, pp. 1486, 1488); WARD9/147; *LP* I, i. 731 (30), 833 (31), II, ii. 3902.
[168] J. Nichols, *The History and Antiquities of the County of Leicester*, 4 vols in 8 (Wakefield, 1971 edn), ii-i. 413; *The Victoria History of the County of Rutland*, ed. W. Page, 2 vols (London, 1908–36), ii. 160; *LP* IV, i. 799, XII, ii. 567; PRO, E41/45/6; E210/10100; E36/95, fos. 6r, 26v; LA, Bishop's Register 27, fos. 26v, 47v, 54r.
[169] PRO, WARD9/148; E36/95, fos. 20v, 97r; SP1/122, fo. 165 (*LP* XII, ii. 187(3)); *LP* IV, iii. 6751(16), VI. 196(39), XII, ii. 2.
[170] *LP* III, ii. 2664, 2834, 2855, 2915, 2927; *Testamenta Vetusta*, ed. N. H. Nicolas, 2 vols (London, 1826), ii. 601–2; R. Somerville, *A History of the Duchy of Lancaster, I, 1265–1603* (London, 1953), 462–3.

Hussey, 'spare for no costs and reasonable to be above all others to speed'.[171] Hussey and his agents worked on through the summer and beyond, Hussey shuttling between Sleaford, London, and Darcy's home at Temple Hirst, until in February 1524 the young lord's marriage was granted to Darcy, Hussey, and Ratcliffe for £800—haggled up from their offer of £666 13s 4d—and his lands, worth some £500 or £600 a year, rented to them for £450 a year.[172]

In April they divided the spoils. Banks would preside at Hornby Castle and put the old lord's affairs in order, Darcy would control some manors and Ratcliffe others, and Hussey would keep young Monteagle and marry him to one of his daughters.[173] By the end of the year things were going wrong. Hussey had kept his ward at Sleaford for most of the year, taking him to visit Hornby and Lancaster in the summer, and then, from Michaelmas, put him into Wolsey's household, a great centre for young aristocrats to learn the ways of the court, kitted out in a jacket of cloth of gold and purple velvet, a cloth of gold doublet, and gowns of satin and damask.[174] But Monteagle's servants wished that Darcy, not Hussey, were bringing up their young master, and the young lord was conniving at their refusal to hand over rents to Hussey's representatives, so that if nothing were done to stop the rot, Hussey's receiver-general Richard Ward thought, Hussey might 'look for no profit, nor to have so much as will pay the king'.[175]

For the next five years, until Monteagle came of age, quarrels multiplied. Banks, Starkey, and other Monteagle servants fell out among themselves and Banks fell out with Hussey. Settlements were attempted by which Banks would control the lands but compensate Hussey for his costs, but they fell through. At the worst points Banks was spreading rumours in Lancashire that Hussey was in the Tower and accusing him and Darcy of worming their way into the late lord's confidence to get their hands on his money; Hussey was accusing Banks of wasting the late lord's goods, having him imprisoned at London, and sending Ward to Lancashire to make new leases of the Monteagle lands; and each party was generating competing accounts of how the Monteagle wealth had been spent and who was now owed compensation.[176] By one set of reckonings, Hussey had been paid £1,768 17s 8½d from Monteagle's lands between Easter 1523 and Michaelmas 1527, but £475 11s 8d was still owing to him.[177] It looks as though the real revenues of the lands were never sufficient to compensate Hussey and his friends for the effort they had put into obtaining them. Perhaps worst of all, Monteagle would not marry Hussey's daughter. In June 1528 a settlement was arbitrated with his father's executors that left him free to make his own marriage and control his father's lands, but promised

[171] PRO, SP1/27, fo. 167v (*LP* III, ii. 2944).

[172] *LP* III, ii. 2273, 2734, 2960, 2982, 3070, 3164, 3183, 3187, 3276, IV, i. 13, 48, 120, Addenda, i. 653(6); PRO, DL10/403; C54/398, mm. 13–14; SP1/45, fo. 309r (*LP* IV, ii. 3724).

[173] PRO, SP1/30, fo. 295 (*LP* IV, i. 221).

[174] PRO, E314/79/25; SP1/38, fos. 58–9 (*LP* IV, i. 2130(2)); P. Gwyn, *The King's Cardinal: The Rise and Fall of Thomas Wolsey* (London, 1990), 174–5.

[175] *LP* IV, i. 235; PRO, SP1/32, fos. 150r, 247r (*LP* IV, i. 799, 958(3)).

[176] *LP* IV, i. 634, 689, 880, 958, 1125, 1281, 2130(2), ii. 2526, 2935, 2989, 2990, 4350, 4570, 5105, iii. 5339; Addenda, i. 434; PRO, C1/456/16, 476/24.

[177] PRO, SP1/45, fo. 312v (*LP* IV, ii. 3724(2)).

that he would take over their debts to the king for his wardship and reimburse the expenses they had laid out on his behalf.[178] Meanwhile, Hussey, Darcy, and Ratcliffe—whether in compliance with Monteagle's wishes or not is unclear—managed to transfer the wardship to the duke of Suffolk, whose daughter Monteagle married. They lived unhappily ever after, a sorry end to a sorry tale.[179]

In the new men's scramble for land, royal favour, marriage, and wardship were powerful tools. Their positions around the king, within the administration and in local society put them in a strong position to use them, but they might break in the user's hand. Each was dependent on the vagaries of mortality, fertility, and personal choice. Each in its way was also dependent on the backing of a king who might die, change his mind or, as in Hussey's case, call in his debts. More dependable was hard cash purchase, but that presented challenges of its own.

[178] PRO, SP1/59, fos. 106–7 (*LP* IV, iii, App. 109).
[179] PRO, C54/398, mm. 13–14; DL10/403; Gunn, *Charles Brandon*, 93, 95, 130–1, 174–5.

13

The land market

Those who wanted to pass on a substantial estate could not in general rely on Henry VII's generosity, marrying into an inheritance, or exploiting a wardship. The new men had to buy, and did so with a will. What they achieved is not always easy to show. Some properties were only temporarily or controversially in their hands; property settlements and other financial dealings often involved fictitious conveyances; and contracts, setting out the terms of sales and purchases in detail, survive less often than other documents registering title in more formal terms. No complete deed collections survive for their families, and even where receivers' accounts exist, as they do for Dudley, Lovell, Wyatt, and Hussey near the end of their respective lives, these have their dangers, unaccountably missing out properties and using measures of value which are not always congruent with our ideas of profit and loss. Nonetheless, it is possible to sketch what they achieved on a land market which was much less fluid than it would become from the 1530s, when the dissolution of the monasteries opened the floodgates to buyers and sellers alike.

BUILDING GREAT ESTATES

Bray led the way as a purchaser. He bought estates at breakneck speed—nine manors in 1499, nine in 1502—and his land acquisitions were so confusing that even those who claimed to be his heirs could not agree what estates they were arguing over. Yet it is clear that he established a coherent belt of properties running through the south Midlands from Bedfordshire and Northamptonshire to Oxfordshire and Berkshire, with a large subsidiary group in Sussex and Surrey, and more scattered manors elsewhere, probably worth in total more than £1,000 a year.[1] Lovell's purchases added up to about half that amount, his accounts for 1522–3 giving a clear total of £454 15s 6d, though they missed out at least one significant manor. Nearly a quarter of his lands by value were in his home county of Norfolk, many in the west and north-west of the county around Beachamwell, Denver, Tydd St Giles, and Wereham, where they lay near the one-sixth of his acquisitions located in Cambridgeshire; with smaller holdings in Suffolk, Huntingdonshire, and eastern Rutland these made up half his estates. Another quarter was scattered across

---

[1] M. M. Condon, 'From Caitiff and Villain to *Pater Patriae*: Reynold Bray and the Profits of Office', in M. A. Hicks (ed.), *Profit, Piety and the Professions in later Medieval England* (Gloucester, 1990), 148–50, 155–6.

Hampshire, Wiltshire, Sussex, and Kent, a tenth in Yorkshire and Lincolnshire, and rather more than that in Middlesex and Hertfordshire, though the small cash income recorded from the latter underestimates their importance in providing for his household at Enfield.[2]

Lovell seems to have started by trying to reassemble the inheritance of John Tiptoft, earl of Worcester, which had been divided between his wife's mother, Philippa, Lady Roos, Lady Joan Ingoldsthorpe, and Edward Sutton, Lord Dudley. Some of Philippa's lands, including those in Enfield where he made his home, were in his hands by 1487–9, though on what terms is unclear: in the 1490s some of his receivers still claimed to be acting for all three co-heirs.[3] By the 1520s, her inheritance made up more than one-third of his estate.[4] In 1490 he added three manors from Dudley, who had just come into his inheritance and was also selling land to Bray.[5] Soon afterwards he began to make acquisitions from other sources. By 1499 he had made the major purchase of East Harling from Sir Edmund Bedingfield, which Bedingfield had valued at £1,000 when he bought the reversion to it in 1490.[6] Elsewhere, the 1490s brought Lovell the manors of Parkers and Masons in Brumstead and Walcott, Norfolk, and lands and rents in Cambridgeshire and Huntingdonshire.[7] We cannot reconstruct all his purchases in detail, but he clearly pressed on past 1509 with Willy's in Choseley (Norfolk) in 1513, Manby (Lincolnshire) in 1515–19, lands in Cheshunt (Hertfordshire) in 1518, and Wereham Hall and Ironhall (Norfolk) in 1519.[8] In the last months of his life he was buying Sporle in Norfolk from Sir William Paston.[9]

Lovell's patience in reconstituting divided estates or combining adjacent ones was a virtue. He apparently had to wait to 1519 to add Ashfields in Beachamwell to his father's manor of Well Hall there.[10] He held Felderland in Worth, Kent, by 1488, but did not buy Uptons in the same parish until 1504.[11] He bought the two halves of the manors of Castlethorpe and Broughton, Lincolnshire, slightly more

[2] BL, Addl. MS 12463 (*LP* IV, i. 367).
[3] *CP*, xii, pt ii. 846; *The Victoria History of the County of Middlesex*, ed. W. Page et al., 13 vols (London, 1911–), v. 233; *The Estate and Household Accounts of William Worsley, Dean of St Paul's Cathedral 1479–1497*, ed. H. Kleineke and S. R. Hovland, London RS 40 (London, 2004), 90; WSRO, Chichester City Archives AY133–8.
[4] BL, Addl. MS 12463 (*LP* IV, i. 367).
[5] *The Victoria History of the County of Rutland*, ed. W. Page, 2 vols (London, 1908–36), ii. 270; *The Victoria History of Wiltshire*, ed. R. B. Pugh et al., 18 vols (London, 1953–), xi. 32; *Feet of Fines for Cambridgeshire Henry VIII to Elizabeth*, ed. W. M. Palmer (Norwich, 1909), 22; W. R. B. Robinson, 'Family and Fortune: The Domestic Affairs of Edward Sutton (d. 1532), Lord Dudley', *Staffordshire Studies* 10 (1998), 42–3.
[6] *CIPM*, ii. 114; NRO, MC49/8; *Testamenta Vetusta*, ed. N. H. Nicolas, 2 vols (London, 1826), ii. 434, 436.
[7] *CCR 1485–1500*, 745; *Cambridgeshire Fines*, 22; *A Calendar of the Feet of Fines relating to the County of Huntingdon*, ed. G. J. Turner, Cambridge Antiquarian Society 37 (Cambridge, 1913), 115.
[8] F. Blomefield, *An Essay towards a Topographical History of the County of Norfolk*, 11 vols (London, 1805–10), x. 349; PRO, CP25/2/28/188/36, 189/45; C54/383, m. 5d; CP25/2/25/156/6; *Feet of Fines, Divers Counties*, ed. E. F. Kirk (London, 1913–24), 43–4.
[9] PRO, CP25/2/28/190/58; C142/41/62.   [10] Blomefield, *Norfolk*, vii. 288–9.
[11] PRO, KB9/379/6; Bodl. MS Kent ch. 231.

than two years apart in 1511–13.[12] It seems to have taken much longer to put back together the Tiptoft manors of Barford and Redlynch in Downton, Wiltshire, one of which had gone to Lady Roos and the other to Lady Ingoldsthorpe.[13] The drive to accumulate did not preclude sales, but they had to be profitable, tactically convenient, or both. In 1486, for example, he obtained two manors in Appleton-le-Street in the North Riding of Yorkshire from James Nesfield and, in 1491, eliminated the life interest held by the widow of the Ricardian John Nesfield. These acquisitions were far from his other lands and in 1497 the chance came to sell to Robert Constable, a successful local lawyer, for £533 6s 8d, perhaps as much as twenty-four times the annual value, so he took it, probably recycling the money into other purchases.[14]

Dudley was another big buyer. While inquisitions post mortem and his will suggested that he had assembled an estate spread across thirteen counties, his accounts for 1509 show lands in only nine. Though he had bought fast, he had been able to concentrate his purchases in the area where he had first inherited lands, roughly two-thirds of his income deriving from Sussex, Hampshire, and the Isle of Wight. The gross receipts from his estate were some £550 a year and allowances were low, so his net landed income may have been as much as £500, on a par with Lovell's if the Roos lands are discounted.[15] Hobart similarly bought Norfolk manors and smaller parcels of land steadily from the 1480s to the 1500s, though the end result was an estate around half the size of Dudley's.[16] Empson was a regular buyer around Towcester and then further afield, into Oxfordshire, Warwickshire, and Hampshire, reaching a total landed income of perhaps £300 a year, placing him among the richest gentry though not quite as grand as some of his colleagues.[17]

EXPANDING MODEST ESTATES

Hussey provides a clear contrast to those who created landed endowments almost from scratch, since he started with the very considerable estates built up by his father the judge. These accounted for perhaps half of what he himself held in

---

[12] PRO, CP25/2/25/155/10, 14.   [13] *VCH Wiltshire*, xi. 32, 53.

[14] *The Victoria History of the County of York: North Riding*, ed. W. Page, 2 vols (London, 1914–25), i. 467–8; *CIPM*, ii. 567; *Yorkshire Deeds*, vii, ed. C. T. Clay, YASRS 73 (Wakefield, 1932), 150–1; W. E. Hampton, 'John Nesfield', in J. Petre (ed.), *Richard III: Crown and People* (London, 1985), 176–83.

[15] E. Dudley, *The Tree of Commonwealth*, ed. D. M. Brodie (Cambridge, 1948), 10; PRO, SC6/Henry VIII/6217.

[16] Blomefield, *Norfolk*, v. 476, vii. 220, 243, 265, viii. 13, ix. 110–11; CA, Norfolk and Suffolk Deeds 326/41 (NRA report); PRO, C1/321/34.

[17] M. R. Horowitz, 'Richard Empson, Minister of Henry VII', *BIHR* 55 (1982), 39; M. M. Condon, 'Empson, Sir Richard', *ODNB*; J. Cornwall, *Wealth and Society in Early Sixteenth-Century England* (London, 1988), 145–7.

1535–6, though not all were available to him until his mother's death in 1504.[18] Yet he was certainly not content to rest on his father's laurels, and relentlessly built up his holdings in central and southern Lincolnshire and the adjoining areas. Between 1501 and 1509 he made acquisitions in Careby, Castle Bytham, Culverthorpe, Firsby, Haydor, Little Bytham, and Rippingale, all within 30 miles of Sleaford, as well as consolidating his estates by exchange, buying out rival claims to his father's valuable manors of Woodhead and Bridge Casterton in Rutland, and securing a small estate in Greenwich, convenient for service at court.[19]

Meanwhile, Hussey joined in the crowd of courtiers stripping his unfortunate brother-in-law, the earl of Kent, of his lands. Kent's troubles started within months of his succeeding his father in 1503.[20] Hussey's mother had promised £1,333 6s 8d in February 1498 to secure the young lord's marriage to Hussey's sister Elizabeth, and well over £1,000 of it had been paid by 1503. Having paid so much, one of Hussey's concerns in his dealings with Kent was the integrity of his sister's jointure lands, on which he made sure that he, his son William and his friends Thomas, Lord Darcy, Sir Miles Bussy, and Edmund Bussy were feoffees.[21] But the earl's financial incompetence was such that he kept turning to Hussey to pay off his debts, owed to Italian merchants, to Londoners, and to the king: in total, Hussey paid at least £1,868 to the earl or on his behalf in 1506 and 1507 alone. Although Hussey was acting, as one indenture put it, out of good counsel and aid and fraternal love towards the earl, he made sure his advances were secured on land. At one time or another he had title, in possession or reversion, to Brampton in Huntingdonshire, to Castle Ashby, Towcester, and Yardley Hastings in Northamptonshire, to Ampthill and Millbrook in Bedfordshire, and to half a dozen other manors, plus a twenty-year lease of the lordship of Ruthin and seven further estates. But Kent's grip on his affairs was so shaky that the same manor had often been mortgaged or sold to several claimants, leaving them to sort things out among themselves. To complicate matters further, the king took a hand in August 1507, forbidding Kent to make further alienations without his consent, appointing royal officers to run his household, and commanding him to attend at court daily, going on to secure title to many of his estates in November 1508.[22] After deals with Empson, Dudley, the king, some of the earl's relatives and the earl himself, who began a new spree of alienations once Henry VIII released his father's tight grip on his affairs, Hussey came out with a £50 rent on Towcester, payable for the life of his sister, Brampton, worth £90 or £100 a year, which he kept, and Castle Ashby, which he seems to

---

[18] PRO, E36/95, fos. 90–104; PROB11/14/22; *CCR 1500–9*, 338; *CIPM*, i. 1166, 1209; *VCH Rutland*, ii. 233.

[19] PRO, CP25/1/145/165/38, 64; CP40/958, m. 21v; E326/5667, 5675, 6033; KB27/984, m. 20r; *CCR 1500–9*, 264, 338, 968; BL, Addl. Ch. 6419.

[20] G. W. Bernard, 'The Fortunes of the Greys, Earls of Kent, in the Early Sixteenth Century', *HJ* 25 (1982), 671–85.

[21] *CAD*, iii. D1194; *CCR 1500–9*, 473; *CPR 1494–1509*, 512–13; PRO, C54/393, m. 4: E326/5594; SP1/34, fos. 158r, 160v (*LP* IV, i. 1309).

[22] *CCR 1500–9*, 554, 702, 724, 740, 757, 794, 797; PRO, E328/46; E40/14645; *CAD*, v. A13485; BLARS, L24/429.

have sold to Sir William Compton between 1512 and 1514.[23] In June 1522, two years before he died, Kent also gave Hussey control of Ampthill and Millbrook, but swift action in the court of chancery made sure the crown took hold of them as soon as the earl was gone, while defending Hussey's other titles against the earl's half-brother, furious at his disinheritance.[24]

Hussey's purchases slowed to a trickle under Henry VIII as his finances became more constrained. Suspicions about his financial probity in office entangled him in debts to the crown and he had to find cash to provide for his four younger sons and four daughters. His main strategy was now to liquidate his holdings in other counties while preserving or expanding his land in and around Lincolnshire. Near Sleaford he would sell on occasion, but only under special circumstances: a small manor in Rutland in 1495 to his associate Edmund Bussy, some lands in Dunsby, Lincolnshire, in 1507, to Sir Henry Willoughby; not only did Sir Henry already hold the main manor there, but he had done 'certain pleasures' to Hussey in addition to the £40 cash price.[25] From his wives' property, in contrast, he raised thousands of pounds. With the holdings of his first wife, Margaret Blount, in the South-West, he and his eldest son William played a long game. The first four manors and some smaller estates were sold in 1515, the next in 1518, one more manor and a few hundred unattached acres in the 1520s; then, in 1531, eight manors and nearly 2,500 acres went in one sale.[26] Hussey took all the cash, though by 1529 he was at least promising William lands in Huntingdonshire to compensate him for the loss of his mother's inheritance.[27] With the lands of his second wife, Lady St Amand, he moved much faster, selling one or two manors in dispute between her and her husband's bastard in the winter of 1509–10.[28] He was almost as spritely with the manors the earl of Kent gave him on the occasion of his third marriage. His new wife surrendered all her rights to them on 22 November 1512, within a week of the marriage agreement, and on 3 January 1513 Hussey contracted to sell Gooderstone in Norfolk to the London merchant Sir William Capel. In the following year, he disposed of one Buckinghamshire manor, he soon disposed of the other, and that was the last Lady Anne saw of her portion.[29] He was equally unsentimental about land acquired by his father. In 1512 he traded the judge's two manors in Havering, Essex, for two in Lincolnshire in a four-way deal involving the crown, the London grocers' company, and the heirs of the company's benefactor

---

[23] *CCR 1500–9*, 763, 765; PRO, SP1/33, fo. 58r (*LP* IV, i. 977); C54/380, m. 9d; KB27/1005, m. 110v; Northamptonshire RO, MTD/D/21/1d–1g, MTD/D/27/1, 3; LA, Bishop's Register 23, fos. 212r, 222v; Bernard, 'Fortunes of the Greys', 672–3.

[24] PRO, SP1/34, fos. 162v, 163v (*LP* IV, i. 1309); C1/567/16; C4/14; C54/393, m. 5; CP25/2/1/2/13; Bernard, 'Fortunes of the Greys', 679, 683–4.

[25] *CCR 1485–1500*, 914; NUL, Mi6/173/63; Cameron, 'Sir Henry Willoughby', 12.

[26] PRO, CP25/2/14/80/17–18, 26; CP25/2/35/236/17; CP25/2/46/318/40; CP25/2/51/368/5; CP25/2/53/382/2; C54/386, mm. 12d–13d; Oriel College, Oxford, SII.III.59.

[27] PRO, SP1/57, fos. 244–8 (*LP* IV, iii. 6525).

[28] *The Victoria History of the County of Berkshire*, ed. P. Ditchfield et al., 4 vols (London, 1906–27), iii. 459; PRO, CP25/2/2/7/3; CP25/2/25/155/2.

[29] PRO, C54/380, mm. 11d, 19d; CP25/2/3/11/32, CP25/2/28/188/26; *The Victoria History of the County of Buckingham*, ed. W. Page, 5 vols (London, 1905–28), iv. 471.

Sir John Crosby.[30] By the mid-1530s, his strategy had brought him an estate centred on Lincolnshire worth around £600 a year, once the profits of leases and sales of demesne produce were added to the survey value of £566 7s 2½d, a very comfortable income for a baron.[31]

Southwell, likewise, could build on his father's landed acquisitions, admittedly more modest than Chief Justice Hussey's. The estate he inherited consisted of five manors in Norfolk with various attached parcels of land, bringing in by the time of his own death a little over £50 a year, but half as much again of his father's land never came into his possession, as his step-mother outlived him.[32] By judicious purchases and the sale or exchange of small or outlying properties he raised that income to some £250 drawn from two sets of estates, the larger stretching across north Norfolk from Yarmouth to Lynn, whence some three-quarters of his income derived, and the smaller between Colchester and Chelmsford, which accounted for a further one-sixth, while he had £100 or more a year in addition from the lands of his first wife.[33] Belknap also started with an inheritance, a share in the lands of the Lords Boteler of Sudeley, but added to it steadily. He sold estates in southern Warwickshire to consolidate his holdings in the east of the county, until his clear landed income, to judge from a surviving rental, was nearly £450.[34]

Windsor, Marney, and Poynings came from old landed families but still bought land. Poynings did so primarily to endow his illegitimate sons. The major purchase was Westenhanger, where he took up residence by around 1493. The price is unknown, but in conveyances of the title it was treated as worth up to £666 13s 4d.[35] He certainly had access to such large sums. To settle a dispute over a manor in Ash in 1497, in a deal which Guildford apparently helped broker, he bought out both parties' claims for a total of £533 6s 8d.[36] Smaller purchases nearby, sometimes of as little as 20 acres of marsh, followed in the last decade of his life, in Newchurch, Saltwood, and Postling, in Burmarsh, Sellindge, and Lymne.[37] They probably took his total landed income to around £600 by the time of his death.[38] Marney was a less active purchaser, but there were reasons for that. His inheritance was scattered but significant: the Essex core worth perhaps £55 a year after he had sold two small manors in 1479, with outliers in Cornwall, Somerset, Oxfordshire,

[30] PRO, E41/171; *LP* I, i. 1316 (4).

[31] PRO, E315/393, fo. 96r; E36/95, fos. 24v, 36r, 48v, 96v; SC6/Henry VIII/1937.

[32] PRO, C54/394, m. 1d; C142/29/15; E150/617/1; 'Norfolk Subsidy Roll, 15 Hen VIII', *Norfolk Antiquarian Miscellany* 2 (1883), 402; Weasenham Hall Muniments, nos. 136, 146 (NRA report).

[33] *CIPM*, iii. 561; *The Victoria History of the County of Cambridge and the Isle of Ely*, ed. L. F. Salzman et al., 10 vols (London, 1938–2002), v. 191; PRO, SP1/2, fo. 5v (*LP* I, i. 559); PROB11/18/5; C1/669/34, 36; CP25/2/188/48; C54/394, m. 1d; C142/29/15; E150/617/1.

[34] C. Carpenter, *Locality and Polity: A Study of Warwickshire Landed Society, 1401–1499* (Cambridge, 1992), 132–3; HL, MS STT 37.

[35] J. Leland, *The Itinerary of John Leland in or about the Years 1535–1543*, ed. L. T. Smith, 5 vols (London, 1906–10), iv. 34, 44; J. Stow, *A Survey of London*, ed. C. L. Kingsford, 2nd edn, 2 vols (Oxford, 1971), i. 134; PRO, C1/76/3, 79/2; CP25/1/117A/345/120, 348/298; KHLC, NR/FAc 3, fo. 106v; ESRO, Rye 60/3, fo. 111r.

[36] *CPR 1494–1509*, 107–8.

[37] PRO, CP25/2/19/106/18, 109/14, 111/3.

[38] PRO, C54/390, m. 16; C142/36/14, 38/39, 39/85, 81/194, 81/197.

and Buckinghamshire totalling another £125 or so.[39] To it he added one manor in Oxfordshire by purchase, but much more by the marriages he arranged for his son and by grants from a grateful king.[40] Nonetheless, on a total income of perhaps £325 his descendants would have been hard pressed to maintain a lifestyle fitting the baronial rank he had won for them.

Windsor's inheritance was in part as old as Domesday Book, but scattered and unprofitable. Besides Stanwell in Middlesex, his father left him an assemblage of small manors in Hampshire and one in Berkshire, all valued in 1486, perhaps rather pessimistically, at about £25 a year.[41] His mother brought him one manor in Suffolk, at Baylham, and a share of one in Norfolk.[42] His marriage really made his landed fortune, but he was also an ardent buyer in half a dozen counties from the 1490s to his death. In Suffolk he bought around his mother's estate at Baylham; in Hampshire near his father's manor of Bentworth Hall; in Sussex near his wife's manors of Dixter and Gatecourt in Northiam.[43] In Kent, Surrey, Oxfordshire, and Derbyshire he picked up occasional manors or smaller units.[44] In Buckinghamshire and Middlesex he rounded off a lifetime's acquisitions in 1539 with manors, demesne lands, and a rectory from the dissolved Ankerwyke Priory and Chertsey Abbey.[45] Like others, he sold or exchanged land occasionally to help him concentrate his holdings.[46]

Windsor's ability to buy throughout his career suggests the advantage of retaining office, even comparatively minor office, over a long period. But what royal favour gave, it could also take away. In 1542 an exchange between Windsor and the crown deprived him of Stanwell and the associated complex of lands, plus £2,197 5s 8d to even out the valuations of the estates involved, in return for the estates of Bordesley Abbey in Worcestershire and other ex-monastic manors in Buckinghamshire, Gloucestershire, Middlesex, Surrey, and Sussex.[47] Dugdale was told by Andrew's great-great-grandson the dramatic story that Henry VIII,

---

[39] PRO, C142/40/9–11; *Feet of Fines for Essex*, ed. R. E. G. Kirk et al., 6 vols (Colchester, 1899–1993), iv. 67, 77; J. Polsue, *Lake's Parochial History of the County of Cornwall*, 4 vols (Wakefield, 1974), iii. 206–7.

[40] PRO, CP25/2/51/363/18.

[41] *CIPM*, i. 12, 28, 29; *CCR 1485–1509*, 27.

[42] W. A. Copinger, *The Manors of Suffolk*, 7 vols (London and Manchester, 1905–11), ii. 256; Blomefield, *Norfolk*, viii. 287.

[43] PRO, CP25/2/39/257/48, 39/259/36, 40/268/7, 43/296/20; C1/456/34; Copinger, *Manors of Suffolk*, v. 310; *VCH Hampshire*, ii. 476, iv. 69; *The Victoria History of the County of Sussex*, ed. W. Page et al., 9 vols in 11 (London, 1905–), ix. 173, 273.

[44] PRO, CP25/1/117A/345/107; *The Victoria History of the County of Surrey*, ed. H. E. Malden, 4 vols (London, 1902–14), iii. 291, 423; PRO, C1/588/44; BL, Addl. MS 6705, fo. 62v; *The Victoria History of the County of Oxford*, ed. W. Page et al., 17 vols (London, 1907–), v. 34; OHC, Wi/I/i/1.

[45] *CIPM*, i. 16; PRO, C1/559/32; CP25/2/3/11/9, 3/16/90; PROB11/29/23; *Certificate of Musters for Buckinghamshire in 1522*, ed. A. C. Chibnall, Buckinghamshire RS 17 (London, 1973), 96, 104, 138, 211, 218, 223, 228, 243, 264, 267, 271, 294, 297, 352; *VCH Buckinghamshire*, ii. 367–8, iii. 36, 297, 324; *LP* XIV, ii. 113 (10); *The Victoria History of the County of Middlesex*, ed. W. Page et al., 13 vols (London, 1911–), iii. 39, v. 282.

[46] NRO, Hare 873–5, 963; 1 Henry VIII c. 19 s. 9; PRO, CP25/2/19/103/29; SC6/Henry VIII/7146.

[47] *LP* XVII. 231, 276, 285 (18); PRO, E326/12909.

determined to make the dissolution of the monasteries irreversible, invited himself to dine at Stanwell and then pressed Windsor to give it to him in exchange for Bordesley. It was an offer that could not be refused, and the old lord left his house full of its Christmas provisions and with it the home of his forebears for nearly five centuries and the seat of his own peerage title.[48] Perhaps the family had the story right but the season wrong: the indentures for one part of the exchange were dated 14 March 1542, three and a half weeks before Easter.[49]

WYATT

By a quirk of family history, the new man whose landed acquisitions we can document in most detail is Wyatt. His grandson's rebellion in 1554 brought the confiscation of his papers, and with them the evidence of Sir Henry's painstaking assembly of the inheritance Sir Thomas the younger had just gambled and lost. Wyatt started buying land in 1489 or earlier, but accelerated between 1500 and 1509. In this phase he made purchases for as little as £4 and as much as £200, spending perhaps £2,000 in total, often paying cash in hand. He bought in Surrey, where most of his wife's lands lay.[50] He bought in Norfolk, around Methwold where he was the king's bailiff and warrener from 1485, and northwards to Ashill, Fincham, and Watlington.[51] He bought in Yorkshire, around Conisbrough where he farmed the royal park from 1500, and further north, to the east of Leeds.[52] He bought in Bedfordshire, Oxfordshire, Northamptonshire, Nottinghamshire, and Lincolnshire.[53] He bought all round London, at West Ham, Hackney, Stepney, Kensington, Westminster, and Walworth and in the extramural parishes of St Clement Danes and St Sepulchre-without-Newgate.[54] And he began, slowly but surely, his lifetime accumulation of estates in Kent, where he bought Allington Castle, which he would make his home, sometime between 1493 and 1509.[55]

After 1509, unlike some of his colleagues, he rolled ever onwards. By his death in 1536 he had spent a further £8,000 or so on land in a hundred or more separate transactions. Though he still had property in eleven or twelve counties when he died, he did sell off some of his earlier acquisitions, or bought estates and then

[48] William Dugdale, *The Baronage of England*, 2 vols (London, 1675), ii. 307–8.
[49] BL, Addl. MS 5705, fos. 48v–49r.
[50] *CCR 1500–9*, 985.
[51] *Materials*, i. 564, 581; *CCR 1485–1500*, 509, 720; *CCR 1500–9*, 265, 720, 737; NRO, Hare 1870–1, 1875–6; PRO, CP25/1/170/197/106.
[52] *CPR 1485–1509*, 219; *CCR 1500–9*, 954, 988; PRO, CP25/1/281/169/136, CP25/2/48/330/11.
[53] *CCR 1500–9*, 720, 988; *VCH Oxfordshire*, vi. 287, xii. 425; PRO, CP25/1/294/81/162; R. Thoroton, *The Antiquities of Nottinghamshire*, 3 vols (Wakefield, 1972), iii. 438; *LP*, Addenda, i. 1233 (7).
[54] PRO, CP25/1/152/100/46, CP25/1/232/79/116, 130; KB27/989, m. 69; C54/382, m. 6d, C54/379, m. 1d; SHC, LM/1659/21; *CAD*, iii. C3170.
[55] *CCR 1500–9*, 953, 984, 987; PRO, E326/7879, 7885, 7888, 11252; CP25/2/19/102/5; C54/377, m. 21d; C1/1355/55; W. M. Conway, 'Allington Castle', *AC* 28 (1909), 345; *LP* I, i. 438 (3, m. 10).

disposed of them, presumably at a profit.[56] Elsewhere, he made efforts to concentrate his holdings, adding to his wife's inheritance in East Sussex, consolidating his Norfolk lands around Ashill and Watlington and making acquisitions in Nottinghamshire.[57] In Essex and Bedfordshire he tried to arrange an exchange with the owner of the other halves of three estates so they would each end up with whole manors, though the affair ended in a lawsuit in 1527.[58] But it was in Kent, where two-thirds of his transactions after 1509 were made, that Wyatt really set to work.

Kent was, admittedly, a comparatively easy place in which to build up an estate. The peculiar local land tenure, gavelkind, tended to break up estates among co-heirs and this combined with the proximity of London investment capital to produce a lively land market.[59] Wyatt took advantage of his metropolitan contacts and bought not only from local men, but also from Londoners. Yet his assembly of a coherent endowment took determination and patience. The estate he put together was densely concentrated between Allington, Barming, and Maidstone in the south and Gravesend and St Mary Hoo on the coast to the north, running east to Meopham and Northfleet and west to Gillingham and Detling, an area 10 miles by 20. Nineteen of his transactions included land in Chalk, ten in Milton, nine in Boxley, eight in Shorne. Beyond this core, a penumbra of smaller holdings reached out to Eynsford, Yalding, Staplehurst, Canterbury, Sittingbourne, and Sheppey.[60] Though occasionally he paid over £100, once even £260, for an estate, most of his purchases were small, made from yeomen, husbandmen, or even labourers, of a couple of tenements, a few dozen acres, or less, bought for sums as small as £2 10s, £2, £1 10s, or even £1.[61] These plots often adjoined land he already held as he consolidated his hold on the area. One three-acre plot bought from a

---

[56] PRO, E326/10551; C142/82/64; C146/9164; KB27/1094, m. 31; C54/386, m. 16d; CP25/2/16/92/38, 25/159/38, 40, 48/330/20, 24, 48/339/22, 28, 33, 49/340/26,/49/342/35; E210/10495; *CAD*, vi. C7345, C7525; *Essex Fines*, iv. 120, 125, 147, 151; *Abstracts of Surrey Feet of Fines 1509–1558*, ed. C. A. F. Meekings, 2 vols, Surrey RS 45–6 (Frome, 1946), 4–6, 15–16; *VCH Surrey*, iii. 137; SHC, 212/7/1; *VCH Oxfordshire*, vi. 287, xii. 425; Brasenose College, Oxford, Muniments Shelswell 1–16 (NRA report); *Testamenta Eboracensia*, ed. J Raine and J. W. Clay, 6 vols, Surtees Society 4, 30, 45, 53, 79, 106 (London, 1836–1902), v. 105.

[57] PRO, C54/396, mm. 10d, 12d; CP25/2/33/220/33, 40, 188/40; E210/6831, 9906, 10011, 10038–41, 10453–5; E326/12780; C1/922/65; *CAD*, iii. D1165.

[58] PRO, C1/590/53–5.

[59] A. Brown, 'London and North-West Kent in the Later Middle Ages: The Development of a Land Market', *AC* 92 (1976), 145–55.

[60] PRO, SC6/Henry VIII/1684; E210/4791, 4832, 4835, 4843, 4864–5, 6402, 6806, 9437, 9837, 9857, 9861, 9867, 9896, 9916–17, 10056, 10030, 10034–5, 10110, 10501, 10160, 10164, 10765, 10779, 11058; E326/5639, 5772, 6061, 6961, 7102, 7112, 7213, 7782, 7785–6, 8218, 8727, 8736, 8739–40, 8747, 8749–50, 8752, 8760, 8763, 10072, 10416, 11264, 11336, 11340, 12736–7, 13624; CP25/2/19/103/20, 28, CP25/2/19/104/18, CP25/2/20/114/6, 22, 38–9, CP25/2/20/115/13, CP25/2/20/118/13, 17, 29, 30, 32, CP25/2/20/119/24, CP25/2/21/121/59, CP25/2/21/124/36, CP25/2/21/127/16, CP25/2/21/128/45, 57, 69, CP25/2/21/129/34, 57, CP25/2/21/131/4; CP40/1035, m. 124r; C54/386, m. 16d, C54/388, m. 23d, C54/396, m. 14d; C1/597/13; *CAD*, iii. D1308, D476, D1058; *Feet of Fines, Divers Counties*, 78.

[61] PRO, C1/597/13; E210/4832, 9387, 10765; E326/8740, 10072, 13624; CP25/2/21/127/16; *Feet of Fines, Divers Counties*, 78.

Gravesend yeoman in 1525 abutted Wyatt's land to the south, east, and west and the common marsh in Milton, which Wyatt was about to enclose, to the north.[62] An enclosed meadow of an acre and a half bought from a yeoman of Boxley the following year was sandwiched between the River Medway, two meadows already bought by Wyatt from the same seller, and one small meadow the yeoman still owned.[63]

With this sharpness of focus went a certain ruthlessness. Having benefited from gavelkind in the assembly of his estates, Wyatt then made sure that it would not incommode him in passing them on intact to his descendants, securing an act of parliament in 1523 that converted all his holdings to standard common-law tenures.[64] The prices he paid were often much less than twenty times the annual value and several of the purchases were made on mortgage, as Sir Henry, flush with the money he handled as keeper of the jewel house and treasurer of the chamber, extended credit to his poorer neighbours and then foreclosed.[65] One mortgage, drafted in Wyatt's characteristic style, pointed out that he was extending credit to Robert Darknoll, a royal household servant, 'of his own free will and for the special love favour and good mind that he beareth towards the said Robert'.[66] It can be no coincidence that nearly one third of all the purchases Wyatt made in Henry VIII's reign fell in 1523–8, while he was treasurer of the chamber and could, if careful, use almost the entire revenue of the English crown as a credit account. He was doing on a larger scale what one of those who sold to him had done in a smaller way: William Wodlake, under-bailiff of the Savoy, spent money he had collected in rents and fines for the duchy of Lancaster on buying land in Gravesend and Cobham, which he then sold on to Wyatt, leaving his executors to chase Wyatt for the outstanding part of the price when the duchy officers asked where the rent money had gone.[67] Wyatt also practised a kind of mortgage in reverse, selling land to his poorer neighbours which would be forfeited back to him if they did not pay an instalment of the price in full every year for twenty years: one such grant survived among his papers endorsed with a note that the land had duly returned to him for lack of payment.[68]

Wyatt showed the same pitiless accumulative streak in his dealings with the hapless earl of Kent. Like Hussey, but without his brotherly concerns, he latched onto the earl fast, buying the reversions of two manors in Bedfordshire and one in Northamptonshire in 1506, then returning them by the end of the year in exchange for the reversions of six other Bedfordshire manors and one in Norfolk, Ashill. Early in 1507 he bought immediate possession of these estates, while granting the earl annuities secured on the revenues of the Bedfordshire manors, £22 a year out of an income of £40. The reversions cost Wyatt £266 13s 4d, immediate possession further unspecified 'great sums of money'. Since it was not clear whether Kent had already sold one of the manors in question to Giles, Lord

---

[62] PRO, E210/6402.   [63] PRO, E326/8752.   [64] 14 & 15 Henry VIII c. 32.
[65] PRO, C1/784/62–3; E210/10161; E326/8727, 8752.
[66] KHLC, U1515/T50.   [67] PRO, DL1/22/W13.   [68] PRO, E326/7098.

Daubeney, Daubeney and Wyatt had to make a separate agreement over how to divide the lands, endorsed by Wyatt with characteristic meticulousness 'the indenture betwixt my Lord Chamberlain and me for Caynhow and Clophill'.[69] The king then intervened to block Kent's dispersal of his inheritance, but in November 1512 Wyatt paid £2,000 to regain the estates, including Wootton in Northamptonshire, in a deal supposedly mediated by the friends of both parties to avoid disputes between them. This time the countess was a party to the agreement, a fact perhaps recognized by Wyatt in the grant of an annuity of £6 to her 'for the love kindness and favour that I have found in the right noble lady Elisabeth countess of Kent, and for that she shall so continue good lady unto me hereafter'.[70]

The earl's half-brother, Sir Henry Grey, also had to be brought into line. In March 1513, Wyatt cut a deal with him, selling him titles to most of the Bedfordshire estates for £300, while Grey accepted £10 for confirming Wyatt's title to Ashill and the Bedfordshire manor of Dame Ellensbury in Ampthill and Houghton Conquest. The £300 was duly paid over the next five years, and Grey got the lands. In his usual way, Wyatt had it recorded what a favour he was doing Sir Henry, letting him have the manors for 'a far lesser sum of money' than would be expected, and 'with long days of payment to his great loss and damages', because Grey was 'next heir in blood' to the earl.[71] Sir Henry thought otherwise, later claiming that Wyatt had hustled him into an agreement when the manor house at Wrest was about to be demolished so Wyatt could sell the materials and when he could not wait to negotiate because he had been summoned to fight on the Scottish border.[72] Soon Wyatt went back to the earl to buy out the annuities payable from the lands he had secured. Kent was chronically short of cash, writing to Wyatt one January to ask if half the next £50 due in annuities might be paid early so he could stock up his household for Lent.[73] In 1518–19 Wyatt paid him £66 13s 4d to extinguish the £14 annuity due from Wootton, a bargain at less than five years' purchase. He capped the deal, at the earl's 'great suit and request and for the more larger recompense for the annuity', by throwing in £9 6s 8d for Kent's collar of the order of the garter, and with it perhaps the last vestige of the ruined peer's self-respect.[74] Meanwhile he looked for opportunities to take a profit he could plough back into his Kentish expansion, selling Dame Ellensbury to Sir William Gascoigne for £300 in 1518, as his son would sell Wootton, leaving only Ashill as the Wyatts' portion of the plunder of the Greys.[75]

[69] Bernard, 'Fortunes of the Greys', 673; *CCR 1500–9*, 720; BLARS, L24/15–16, L24/411, L132–3, L135–6, L151; PRO, E210/10053.

[70] PRO, E41/365; E210/4916; SP1/34, fo. 159r (*LP* IV, i. 1309); *LP* I, i. 1503.

[71] Bernard, 'Fortunes of the Greys', 678–80; BLARS, L18–22, L24/15, L25–6, L26/325, L509–10; PRO, LR14/6.

[72] BLARS, L24/16.   [73] *LP* Addenda, i. 369.

[74] PRO, E326/12187; C54/387, m. 17d.

[75] BLARS, L29; PRO, E326/10438; SC2/153/21; *The Victoria History of the County of Northampton*, ed. W. Adkins et al., 7 vols (London, 1902–), iv. 293; Blomefield, *Norfolk*, ii. 353.

PURCHASING PATTERNS

All this activity shows how much cash the new men had at their disposal. Some of the sums involved were staggering. Bray spent over £10,000 buying land between 1485 and 1503, usually paying cash quickly rather than spinning things out.[76] Heron paid £666 13s 4d for the manors of Great and Little Rycote, Oxfordshire, fortunately for him in instalments.[77] By the 1530s, large cash purchases were becoming more commonplace as the dissolution opened up the land market, but Windsor's ability to put £400 down in cash when buying monastic lands in 1539 was still impressive.[78] Empson bought small plots for cash like Wyatt, building up his lands in Towcester, Hulcote, and Easton Neston.[79] But he also had enough money to swoop on a big deal when the time came: £166 13s 4d for the manor of Hulcote in 1493, £466 13s 4d for the reversion of the manor of Towcester in 1506.[80] Mortgages were a powerful device for those who could take advantage of neighbours suffering the liquidity problems that plagued the late medieval economy. The terms on which Ernley contracted to buy the manor of Houghton, Sussex from Thomas Cheyne of Houghton, gentleman, in 1516, are unusually well documented. Ernley lent Cheyne £100; if Cheyne failed to repay it, Ernley was to have the manor at the attractive price of sixteen times the annual value, the £100 counting towards the price.[81] Lucas, too, seems to have bought lands on mortgage, while Dudley's acquisition of Penkridge in Staffordshire by mortgage from the troubled Robert, second Lord Willoughby de Broke, was probably halted only by the minister's fall.[82] Something similar may have been going on between Windsor and John Touchet, Lord Audley, in the 1530s.[83] Superior liquidity also apparently enabled them to forestall bargains between sellers and other buyers to obtain the lands themselves.[84]

Another common feature was the drive to consolidate land not only within certain counties, but also by accumulating small holdings to form larger, more compact estates, as we have seen Wyatt doing in Kent. Marney occasionally bought up messuages and lands to add to manors he had inherited.[85] Southwell, too, bought small estates throughout his career, collections of closes or tenements, or even single messuages with a few acres of land in villages where he was already a

---

[76] Condon, 'Profits of Office', 158.

[77] F. G. Lee, *The History, Description and Antiquities of the Prebendal Church of the Blessed Virgin Mary of Thame* (London, 1883), 335.

[78] PRO, E323/1/part2, m. 8 (*LP* XIV, ii. 236).

[79] Northamptonshire RO, MTD/D/13/2, 13/6, 15/1, 24/1, 28/1, MTD/E/29/5, 29/6, 29/10, 30/6, 31/3, MTD/F/32/6.

[80] Northamptonshire RO, MTD/E/20/2, MTD/D/27/5.

[81] PRO, C54/383, m. 11d.

[82] SROB, 449/2/125–6, 138–41(NRA report); *The Victoria History of the County of Stafford*, ed. W. Page et al., 14 vols (London, 1908–), v. 109; D. A. Luckett, 'The Rise and Fall of a Noble Dynasty: Henry VII and the Lords Willoughby de Broke', *HR* 69 (1996), 261–4.

[83] PRO, C54/404, m. 13d; C1/783/20.

[84] PRO, C1/325/1–5; SP1/2, fo. 5r (*LP* I, i. 559); C54/378, m. 1d.

[85] *CAD*, i. C1061, vi. C5064; PRO, CP25/2/51/358/2.

manorial lord, for sums as small as £8 13s 4d.[86] Lovell's supreme achievement in this vein was the estate he built up in Enfield. To the manor of Worcesters, acquired from the Tiptoft heiress Philippa, Lady Roos, he added separate tenements called Elsings—from which his great house took its name—Gilberts, Hamonds, Lepers, Leynams, Lowdes, Meryweathers, Okebornes, Snellings, Wilkynsons, Wodehams, and Wyberds, amounting in all to 280 acres of arable land, 150 of pasture, 97 of meadow, and 50 of wood.[87] He seems to have put together a smaller assemblage over an equally long period at Greenwich and Woolwich in Kent.[88]

Prices were judged carefully. A calculation survives in which Guildford worked out how much to pay for two estates worth £30 a year 'after xviii year purchase'.[89] But they were not always got right at the first attempt. When Hobart bought the manor of Chedgrave in Norfolk from William, Lord Willoughby d'Eresby, he initially agreed a price of £228, or just over fourteen times the estimated value of £16 a year. The final price was to be dependent on a fresh valuation, but this was not at first carried out. In 1506 it was urgently rearranged, because Hobart had found that the cost of clearing an estate overrun with furze and bushes was drastically cutting his profits.[90] Southwell bought the manor of Wood Norton in Norfolk for £500 in 1508, apparently at a rate of between ten and fifteen years' purchase. The title was a complex one, which required further claims to be negotiated away, but the sellers claimed Southwell tried to get it cheaper still, by paying them only £300 and then suing them on their bond to complete the conveyance.[91] Sometimes there must have been special reasons, now impenetrable, for a particular price to be paid: why else would Thomas, Lord Howard, have sold Lovell on 14 November 1507 for £120 a manor he had bought two days earlier for £160?[92] Wyatt bought two estates in Sussex from the same seller five months apart, one at twenty years' purchase and one at sixteen.[93] Ideally, of course, sales had to be at a better rate than purchases. Hussey made sure to set a price 'after the rate of xix years' purchase' when he sold Gooderstone in 1513.[94] He did better still with Bitton and Mangotsfield in Gloucestershire two years later, £1,000 for manors worth £41 4s a year, more than twenty-four years' purchase, but he had to agree that if the actual income fell below that stated, then twenty-two times the shortfall should be deducted from the final instalment of the price.[95] Sometimes, too, the demands of royal service had to be taken into account in terms of sale. Wyatt inserted into a contract of 1491 the proviso that he might make a payment due at Michaelmas 1492 belatedly without penalty, if he were then 'in the king's our sovereign lord's

[86] *CAD*, i. A832; PRO, C1/271/48; C142/29/15; E150/617/1.
[87] PRO, C142/41/79; E150/479/2; BL, Addl. MS 12463, fos. 95v–111r.
[88] PRO, KB9/389/18; CP25/2/19/111/9, 32.
[89] WAM 12242.   [90] NRO, Phi/85 (NRA report).
[91] PRO, C1/358/97; C54/394, m. 1d; Bodl. MS Rawlinson D1480, fo. 521.
[92] *CCR 1500–9*, 802, 867.   [93] PRO, C54/396, mm. 10d, 12d.
[94] PRO, C54/380, m. 19d.   [95] PRO, C54/383, mm. 24–5d.

service beyond the sea, as he is very like to be'.[96] Reversions were a good way to secure land in the long term at more reasonable short-term prices. Lovell, Wyatt, and Southwell each bought reversionary titles to manors held by widows.[97] Southwell, for example, paid £226 13s 4d for the reversion to the manor of Coggeshall Hall in Essex after the death of the widow of the previous owner. In the event she outlived him, but when the manor fell in, it would bring in over £29 a year.[98] Reversions could go wrong, however, as Wyatt discovered when he paid for one, but found the current holders of the land would not consent to the necessary conveyance.[99]

PURCHASING POWER

A number of the new men bought up questionable titles in the hope of establishing them through successful litigation or intimidation. The claim to have bought an estate, but to be unable to prove it because another claimant had the relevant deeds, though sometimes a convenient legal fiction, might suggest such a situation: Dudley, Lovell, Lucas, Southwell, Windsor, and Wyatt all fought such suits.[100] Bray bolstered purchased claims with vigorous litigation, and Southwell bought disputed titles to scraps of land from widows or executors and then sued those in possession.[101] Guildford was accused of buying titles he knew to be open to challenge because he had been involved in arbitrating disputes over them.[102] Wyatt bought one title from an heir in defiance—in ignorance, he claimed—of the will in which the seller's father bequeathed part of the land to one of his executors and one from a claimant whose title depended on proving the invalidity of a relative's will.[103] He bought two from heirs too poor to litigate in defence of their claims and allegedly encouraged claimants to another estate to reject an arbitrated settlement detrimental to a reversionary title he hoped to buy from them.[104] He sued sellers who refused to carry out their bargains and feoffees who refused to make estates over to him.[105] In one bargain he stipulated that the seller should compensate him at a rate of twelve years' purchase for any lands for which he was successfully sued within a year of the conveyance, and other contracts included similar, if

---

[96] PRO, C54/379, m. 1d.
[97] PRO, CP25/2/19/109/8; C142/45/56; C142/29/15; E150/617/1; C54/394, m. 1d; *VCH Hampshire*, iii. 225.
[98] PRO, E41/197; C54/394, m. 1d.
[99] PRO, C1/175/55.
[100] PRO, C1/100/28, 112/55, 130/8, 131/1, 131/52, 132/12, 166/29, 266/41, 273/33, 303/13, 303/55, 330/1, 371/88, 456/34, 588/44, 690/44, 922/65; J. H. Baker, *The Oxford History of the Laws of England*, vi: *1483–1558* (Oxford, 2003), 189.
[101] Condon, 'Profits of Office', 141–2; PRO, C1/225/6, 271/48.
[102] PRO, C1/315/53–6.
[103] PRO, C1/555/38–40; PRO, KB27/1073, m. 78, 1075, m. 37.
[104] *CCR 1485–1500*, 509; *VCH Oxfordshire*, vi. 287; *LP* Addenda, i. 317.
[105] PRO, C1/232/10, 376/40.

less detailed, provisions.[106] Dudley, it appears from a letter sent to him in the Tower, obtained estates without proper payment and then sold them on for 'a great sum of money' to owners—in this case the shrewd John Spencer—whose title remained open to challenge.[107] Disputed titles doubtless came cheap. Hussey paid only £186 13s 4d in 1507 for lands worth £16 a year, less than twelve years' purchase, but then had to fight a chancery action to secure them.[108]

There were other ways to make sure lands came in the right direction. Mordaunt was accused of ensuring that the childless Edward Stafford, earl of Wiltshire, left his lands to distant relatives, including Mordaunt's daughter-in-law, by turning up at his deathbed and reading him a new will he had drafted when the earl had already received extreme unction and was 'in extreme pains of death, so that the said earl neither heard nor understood what the said Mordaunt read'. The earl's chaplain and auditor testified that the will was drafted by the earl's council and that he was quite compos mentis when he sealed it, but the ensuing dispute lasted sixteen years.[109] Yet more underhand methods sometimes came to light. Sutton was accused of using his powers as steward of Syon to put someone in the stocks at Isleworth until he agreed to sell him his land.[110]

The ability to access the king's favour for those in need of it was a strong card for the new men. Bray bought out Lord Zouche's title to the manors that would become the core of his own landed base in Bedfordshire in 1495 thanks to the fact that Zouche had, as he acknowledged, 'by the especial labour, assistance and means of the said Sir Reynold attained the singular favour and the especial grace' of the king.[111] Other purchases, too, seemed to depend on Bray's ability to intercede with the king or work the mechanisms of royal administration in favour of those who sold to him, some of them men as great as Zouche—William, marquess of Berkeley, Henry, Lord Grey of Codnor—others much smaller fry.[112] For those who needed to buy back the king's favour, like Robert, Lord Fitzwalter, recovering from his father's attainder, the fact that the new men had the cash to make quick purchases was reason enough to sell to them, as he did to Windsor.[113] Those who needed the reversal of forfeitures piloted through parliament found a deal with the grantees of their lands just as useful. It was Wyatt, who had held the confiscated manor of Thorpe Parva since 1492, who introduced a bill in 1515 for its restoration to the White family. They were still paying him off fourteen years later.[114]

Dudley was in a class of his own. A sense of his techniques emerges from the questions put to Roger Lewkenor, a Sussex gentleman, in a lawsuit of 1512 about

[106] PRO, E326/13624; E210/9437.
[107] BL, Althorp Papers A8, A13/10; HL, MS HAD 1598.
[108] *CCR 1500–9*, 968; PRO, C1/323/1.
[109] R. Halstead, *Succinct Genealogies of the Noble and Ancient Houses of Alno or de Alneto etc* (London, 1685), 218–21, 225–7; Northamptonshire RO, SS3752.
[110] PRO, C1/391/13.
[111] Condon, 'Profits of Office', 144.
[112] Condon, 'Profits of Office', 140, 149–56.
[113] NRO, Hare 873, 963.
[114] 6 Henry VIII c. 22; *LJ*, i. 26; Bodl., MS Tanner 106, fos. 1, 4.

the sale of his manor of Sheffield. First Lewkenor was asked whether he had sold it to Dudley or to someone else. Later the questions became more interesting:

Who paid for his meat and drink while he was in prison and such fees as belonged to the officers of the prison; And for such apparel as he had new made for him when he was delivered out of prison; Item who got him his charter; And what his charter cost; And who paid for it; [And] who paid the fees and charges when he pleaded his charter; And who agreed with the heir of the man that was murdered?

Though Lewkenor denied it, the answer to all these questions was probably Edmund Dudley. Lewkenor was indicted for murder before the Sussex justices of the peace at Horsham on 13 July 1507. Dudley was not sitting, but his associate John Caryll was. On 30 January 1508 Lewkenor was pardoned, a pardon that cost £200 paid to the king in a deal negotiated by Dudley. By 1509, Dudley had all Lewkenor's land, land he guiltily made provision in his will for Lewkenor to buy back from his executors.[115]

Lewkenor was not the only person whose land Dudley bought in return for paying off debts to the king he had himself arranged. We may suspect something of the sort in the cases of Lords Willoughby de Broke and Dacre of the South, who both appeared in the account book of his dealings for the king around the time they sold him land.[116] The evidence is clearer in other instances. In winter 1506–7 he secured two manors in Cheshire, in a complex deal based on his payment of a debt of £266 13s 4d from the owner to the king, a debt he had himself imposed in July.[117] Other complaints rang variations on this theme. One John Maryng claimed that Dudley, 'being of great rule and authority and in high favour' with Henry VII, had arranged for him to mortgage his lands to a third party, then redeemed the lands himself when Maryng defaulted because he was imprisoned in the Tower. When Dudley was in the Tower in his turn, Maryng visited him. Dudley 'lamented and showed himself to be very penitent and sorry for the said injuries and wrongs', but Maryng lost—this is where his story wears rather thin—the petition Dudley wrote to the king on his behalf.[118] Dudley was not the only such predator. Cope, for instance, paid off the fine for a pardon for treason for a man in his custody in return for the grant of a manor.[119] But Dudley was the fastest operator and apparently the most shameless.

When the king's title crossed their own, the new men could come off worse. Southwell featured ominously in a list in the back of the king's chamber accounts of forty-two landowners who had not sued livery for lands descended to them; in the end he escaped fairly lightly, paying Dudley £80 10s 10d for livery of his

[115] PRO, C1/305/42–52; C1/473/48; KB9/446/130; SC6/Henry VII/6217; SP1/2, fo. 4v (*LP* I, i. 559); *CPR, 1494–1509*, 572; HL, MS El. 1518, fo. 55v; *LP* I, i. 709 (26).
[116] BL, MS Lansdowne 107, fos. 11v, 16v; *Final Concords of the County of Lancaster ... part III ... AD 1377–1509*, ed. W. Farrer, Record Society of Lancashire and Cheshire 50 (Manchester, 1905), 159–60.
[117] Cheshire RO, DCH/B/42–4; PRO, C1/377/16; *LP* I, i. 559; HL, MS El. 1518, fo. 26a.
[118] PRO, SP1/46, fos. 2–7 (*LP* IV, ii. 3727).   [119] Condon, 'Profits of Office', 153.

mother-in-law's lands, less than twice their yearly value.[120] Mordaunt found the king 'took displeasure' with his attempts to secure part of the landed inheritance of his father-in-law Sir Nicholas Latimer, who owed the king money. When Mordaunt did not hold back, the king bypassed him to have the lands put in the hands of royal feoffees, including Bray and Lovell. The deaths of Mordaunt and Latimer then put Mordaunt's son at the mercy of the king and his new agent Dudley, to whom Henry directed him despite his protests 'that they had as good leave the land for the hard dealing they knew of Dudley'. Dudley said they must pay £1,200 to the king, although, as an enquiry after 1509 would find, the king had no title; Dudley himself later admitted the deal was made on 'a slender ground'. Then came a final twist. Mordaunt's son agreed to pay the king £1,000 at £200 a year; Dudley said he would make up the balance of the £1,200 in cash in return for the title to one of the Latimer manors.[121] There was little taboo on financial cannibalism amongst Henry's predatory executives. But the greatest devourer was the king himself, not during his ministers' lifetimes, perhaps, but certainly once they were dead. When Bray died, his executors faced a demand from Henry for £3,333 3s 4d for a pardon, plus £800, later reduced to £533 3s 4d, for an additional pardon for customs offences, and the loss of a vital wardship he had paid for, but not yet been granted.[122] If Henry let his servants profit at the expense of his subjects while they served him, he was determined to take his share once their term of service was complete. Dudley faced a worse fate still at the hands of Henry VIII, but even he admitted that 'the executors of Mr Bray were hardly dealt with at divers times'.[123]

These qualifications notwithstanding, the new men were remarkably effective in buying land. They found it easier in some counties than others, notably those with active land markets because of proximity to the capital or the prevalence of small estates, but between them they made significant acquisitions across lowland England. Their successes were not unprecedented or unparalleled. Sir John Fastolf, the most financially successful English soldier of the fifteenth century, spent more than Wyatt, probably more than Lovell and Bray, building up his East Anglian estates over the thirty years following Agincourt and showed comparable attention to detail and concern to get a good price and a secure title.[124] Thomas Kebell, Roger Townshend, and other fifteenth-century lawyers used their inside knowledge of the land market, their access to liquid cash, their preparedness to buy reversions and offer mortgages, and their confidence in litigation to buy, lease, and consolidate compact sets of estates at bargain prices.[125] London merchants also put

[120] BL, Addl. MS 59899, fo. 192r; MS Lansdowne 127, fo. 53v.
[121] Halstead, *Succinct Genealogies*, 64–9; 'The Petition of Edmund Dudley', ed. C. J. Harrison, *EHR* 87 (1972), 90.
[122] Condon, 'Profits of Office', 156–9.
[123] 'Petition of Edmund Dudley', 88.
[124] A. Smith, '"The Greatest Man of that Age": The Acquisition of Sir John Fastolf's East Anglian Estates', in R. Archer and S. Walker (eds), *Rulers and Ruled in Late Medieval England: Essays presented to Gerald Harriss* (London, 1995), 137–53.
[125] E. W. Ives, *The Common Lawyers of Pre-Reformation England. Thomas Kebell: A Case Study* (Cambridge, 1983), 330–44, 374–9; C. E. Moreton, *The Townshends and their World: Gentry, Law and Land in Norfolk c.1450–1551* (Oxford, 1992), 116–33.

their profits successfully into land, though they tended to buy in more scattered fashion.[126] In the frenetic 1530s Thomas Cromwell spent thousands of pounds buying and leasing estates across England from Kent and Sussex to Cornwall, Shropshire, and Yorkshire.[127] Yet the new men's achievement still stands out. The absolute scale of their gains was larger than that of the lawyers or the merchants. Fastolf got fewer bargains than they did, perhaps because he generally bought from those he or his advisers knew and trusted.[128] Cromwell used his political power to buy as they did, but frequently re-sold his acquisitions, apparently regarding land, like his London merchant friends, as a short-term and flexible investment. Even his concentration of holdings around Lewes in Sussex was, it has been argued, more a move in the politics of court and parliament than a family power-base.[129] Not till the great families of the mid-sixteenth century, the Russells, Riches, Wriothesleys, Paulets, and Cecils, did the new men meet their match, and that was in the very different context of an open-handed monarchy and a land market energized by the dissolution. How successfully, though, would the new men exploit the estates they had won?

[126] S. L. Thrupp, *The Merchant Class of Medieval London, 1300–1500* (Chicago IL, 1948), 122–30, 282–7; M. Albertson, 'London Merchants and their Landed Property During the Reign of the Yorkists', Bryn Mawr Ph.D. thesis (1932), 45–77; A. F. Sutton, 'Colet, Sir Henry', *ODNB*; S. T. Bindoff, *History of Parliament: The House of Commons 1509–1558*, 3 vols (London, 1982), i. 569–70, ii. 248–50, 359–60, 611–13, iii. 203–4, 649–51.

[127] M. L. Robertson, 'Profit and Purpose in the Development of Thomas Cromwell's Landed Estates', *Journal of British Studies* 29 (1990), 317–46.

[128] Smith, 'Acquisition', 145–52.

[129] Robertson, 'Profit and Purpose', 324, 329–7.

14

Landlordship

Economic conditions in the years either side of 1500, as England emerged from the slump of the mid-fifteenth century, provided both challenges and opportunities for new men bent on drawing income from the lands they had acquired. The long depression in population that had followed the Black Death and encouraged landlords to let their lands out to farm was starting to lift, increasing demand for arable farming tenancies. Prices for wool were rising to feed growing cloth exports to continental Europe, and pastoral farming also offered opportunities to meat and cheese producers as standards of living and nutrition remained much higher than before the plague. But the speed and nature of change varied greatly from region to region, rents rose consistently only from the 1520s or later, and different landlords chose different strategies to meet the needs of the moment. In the fifteenth century, as landlords sought stability in a difficult market, servile tenures had mutated into more favourable copyhold tenures, rents had declined, and periods of tenure had generally got longer. In the sixteenth century, as opportunity beckoned and inflation threatened, lords tried to convert copyhold land to leasehold, make leases shorter, raise rents, and charge higher entry fines on both leasehold and copyhold land. But variations in manorial custom and local economic conditions confuse any attempt at generalization.[1]

RENTS AND TENURES

The first requirement for any ambitious landlord was accurate information. The renewal of rentals kept a clear check on what income was due from every holding on every estate. Marney had new rentals drawn up for Layer Marney in 1486 and for Layer Marney and Gibcracks in Great Totham in spring 1497, Empson for his lands in ten Northamptonshire villages in 1507, Belknap for Stondon Massey in

---

[1] J. M. W. Bean, 'Landlords', in E. Miller (ed.), *The Agrarian History of England and Wales*, iii: *1348* (Cambridge, 1991), 568–86; R. Britnell, *Britain and Ireland, 1050–1530: Economy and Society* (Oxford, 2004), 368–450, 499–524; J. Whittle, *The Development of Agrarian Capitalism: Land and Labour in Norfolk, 1440–1580* (Oxford, 2000), 28–84; M. Mate, *Trade and Economic Developments, 1450–1550: The Experience of Kent, Surrey and Sussex* (Woodbridge, 2006); M. Yates, *Town and Countryside in Western Berkshire c.1327–c.1600: Social and Economic Change* (Woodbridge, 2007); K. Wrightson, *Earthy Necessities: Economic Lives in Early Modern Britain, 1470–1750* (London, 2002 edn), 132–7.

1517.[2] As soon as Windsor had bought Marsh Baldon, he ordered all his tenants to produce their copies of court roll to show on what terms they held their lands, and there and at Bentworth Hall he regularly had his rentals renewed.[3] Southwell's rentals at Hainford were renewed in 1508–10, recording many farms of lands but also surviving bond rents and rents in kind, in barley, capons, and hens.[4]

However well informed landlords were, there were many constraints on maximizing the return on estates. In Kent, gavelkind tenure imposed particular restrictions, so Guildford, Wyatt, and Windsor converted their land to other tenures by royal grant or act of parliament.[5] Copyhold rents were often inflexible and standard concessions of land, not for terms of years but for two or three lives, like those Hussey was making at Bitton and Swainswick between 1490 and 1520, made it hard to predict when holdings would next come into the lord's hand.[6] Tenants in manorial courts might restrict landlords' freedom of manoeuvre by claiming ancient demesne tenure, as Hussey's tenants at Brampton did, or defining manorial custom conservatively, as Windsor's tenants did over heriots at Bentworth Hall and inheritance practices at Tardebigge.[7] The main opportunity on most manors was to increase copyhold entry fines. Where Windsor's father had taken a third or a fifth of the annual rent of a copyhold as a fine at Bentworth Hall, he took on average a half.[8] His fines ran at similar levels at Baylham, Beddingham, and Marsh Baldon.[9] Wyatt's and Poynings's fines were higher, usually fixed at a year's rent.[10] Lovell's fines at Higham Bensted in Walthamstow and Uffington were higher still, at more than a year's rent and often more than £1 a time.[11] At Uffington, in 1522, he did without a fine on one cottage and parcel of lands, but only on the grounds that the new rent was some 38 per cent higher than that previously charged.[12] By the 1530s, Hussey was taking fines more than four times the annual rent.[13]

The new men made money from their manorial demesnes, like most landlords at the time, by leasing them out rather than farming them directly, balancing the stability of longer leases to dependable tenants against the flexibility of shorter terms. Windsor generally let demesne farms for twenty-one years, but sometimes ventured eight-year leases with an increase in rent after the first four years.[14]

---

[2] PRO, SC11/40; SC12/7/40; SC6/Henry VII/160, m. 2; Bodl. MS dd Ewelme a7/A52; HL, MS STT 37, fos. 19r–26r.

[3] Bodl. MS Rolls Oxon 166, mm. 1, 4; Hampshire RO, 25M75/M2, mm. 11–14.

[4] NRO, FOS293 (MF/X/134/17).

[5] 11 Henry VII c. 49; 14 & 15 Henry VIII c. 32; 31 Henry VIII c. 3.

[6] *A Catalogue of the Medieval Muniments at Berkeley Castle*, ed. B. Wells-Firby, 2 vols, Gloucestershire Record Series 17–18 (Bristol, 2004), ii. 843, 851; Oriel College, Oxford, S.II.III.59.

[7] PRO, E315/393, fos. 86r–91r; B. M. S. Campbell, 'The Land', in R. Horrox and W. M. Ormrod (eds), *A Social History of England 1200–1500* (Cambridge, 2006), 194; Hampshire RO, 25M75/M2, m. 4; Worcestershire Archives, BA1146, Ref:705:170/11; PRO, C1/1138/46.

[8] Hampshire RO, 25M75/M1, M2.

[9] SROI, HB8/1/254; ESRO, GLY986; Bodl., MS Rolls Oxon 166.

[10] PRO, SC2/181/81, 87–8; SROI, HB26/371/57, fos. 1r–7v.

[11] ERO, D/DFc 185, pp. 24–39; LA, FL Deeds 224.

[12] LA, FL Deeds 224.   [13] PRO, E315/393, fos. 31v, 82r.

[14] Hampshire RO, 25M75/M2, mm. 16–19 and unnumbered; *Sussex Chantry Records*, ed. J. E. Ray, Sussex RS 36 (Cambridge, 1930), 183–4; *HMC Various Collections*, vii (1914), 358.

Wyatt's leases, of demesnes, parks, or whole manors were shorter: for seven, ten, or twelve years.[15] Lovell's preference was for ten, twenty, or twenty-one year leases, but he raised rents where he could, leasing the manor of Adderley in Shropshire, which had been let at £28 in 1467, to a local gentleman in 1503 for twenty-one years at £34 a year.[16] Hussey's leases in the 1520s and 1530s were rather longer, mostly for twenty years, sometimes for thirty and sometimes for life; but the life grants attracted large fines, up to eight times the annual rent, and they were still shorter than the three lives for which he used to lease manorial demesnes on his wife's south-western estates.[17]

The land available for leasing might be expanded and the restrictions of customary tenures bypassed when landlords bought up copyholds within their own manors and then combined them into farms. Marney was a past master. In at least eight separate deals between 1491 and 1519 he bought up six tenements in Layer Marney with hundreds of acres of land, some in parcels as small as 7 acres. Once leased out as part of consolidated farms each parcel was worth between three and seven times the rent payable to the manor; together they yielded just over £7, increasing the value of the estate by nearly 20 per cent.[18] Such manoeuvres were aided by the loyalty of his tenants. In May 1508, John Wade of Tollesbury, long-serving receiver of his Essex estates, specified in his will that three portions of his customary lands were to be sold by his executors, 'and if it please Master Sir Harry Marney to buy my foresaid lands, I will that he shall have them v mark within the price they be worth'.[19] Belknap, Empson, Hussey, and Windsor similarly consolidated and sub-let holdings within their manors, Hussey leasing them for forty-year terms.[20] Wyatt concentrated copyholds around Allington in his own hands and bought up the combined copyhold and freehold tenures of one of his deceased tenants at Ashill in 1524, in a deal with careful provisions for compensation if the lands turned out to be part of his demesne after all.[21]

The market in farms seems to have been lively, with little continuity in tenants from generation to generation, but the farmers attracted by demesnes or consolidated copyholds were substantial men. William att Wode, Poynings's demesne farmer of Ash, left lands in six places, bequests to four churches, and £10 each to marry his three daughters, while Thomas Walter, his demesne farmer at Fawkham, built up a 165 acre holding.[22] Marney's and Wyatt's farmers were men of similar stature. John Causton of Tollesbury, farmer of the Layer Marney demesnes at £44 a year, left cash bequests totalling over £113—including 6s 8d for repairs to Layer

---

[15] PRO, SC6/Henry VIII/1684; E210/5651; BLARS, L899.

[16] BL, Addl. MS 12463, fos. 27v, 44v, 72v (*LP* IV, i. 367); Shropshire Archives, 946/A426–7.

[17] PRO, E315/393, fos. 13r, 22v, 37r, 31v, 38r, 42r, 48r, 51r; LR2/254. fos. 266r, 270v; C1/1354/74–5; Somerset Heritage Centre, DD/WHb/453.

[18] PRO, C142/40/8, 43/8; CP25/2/11/52/13; SC11/40.

[19] ERO, D/ACR1, fos. 141r–142r; PRO, SC6/Henry VII/160.

[20] HL, MS STT 37, fos. 1r–1v; Bodl. MS dd Ewelme a7/A52; PRO, E315/393, fos. 17v, 22v, 39r, 65r; LR2/254, fo. 267; Hampshire RO, 25M75/M2, m. 10.

[21] PRO, SC6/Henry VIII/1684; E210/100041.

[22] Alnwick Castle, Syon MS X.II.I, box 16b; KHLC, DRb/PWr 5, fos. 408v–410r; U947/M1/1, M2/1, 2; Petworth House, 5731.

Marney church and £6 13s 4d to the poor—in addition to 120 sheep and 14 cows.[23] Robert Brownyng farmed sheep and barley on Wyatt's land in Chalk, but also leased an inn called the White Hart and lands in Gravesend and Milton. He left £40 to marry his daughters and a gown furred with black coney to his son; and he could sign his name.[24] Robert Stokmede was similarly literate, a Gravesend yeoman who owned a gilt silver goblet and a salt with a gilt cover, and left £140 to his nieces and nephews.[25] Lovell's farmer at Beachamwell and Wereham, John Dedyk, was taxed on an income of £50 in 1523 and William Bendish at Layham was equally rich.[26] Most of his farmers were smaller than that, but steady enough. William Pyle, farmer of Over Wallop, farmed another manor, too, and left hundreds of sheep.[27] John Disborow, farmer of Wolves in West Wickham, seems to have had only that farm, but was farming wheat, barley, and cattle there.[28] Thomas Rypyngale, farmer of part of the demesnes at Woolley, was equally diversified, with sheep, cattle, and barley; his probate inventory added up to £40.[29] Anthony Malory, farmer of Castle Manor in Bassingbourn, was a regular contributor to the parish church, giving malt, wheat, and money to church ales, plays, and bells.[30] Occasionally farms were let to members of the gentry, one of Lovell's to the widow of Sir Robert Peyton, another to George Henningham, taxed on £366 6s 8d in goods.[31] Other tenants were firmly upwardly mobile. Cope let out the whole manor of Wormleighton to John Spencer, the grazier who would found a great landed family partly with the help of his links by marriage to Cope and Empson.[32]

In leasing land, flexibility and attention to detail were the keys to profit. Hussey kept his freedom of manoeuvre by letting a manor in Ingoldsby to a local yeoman for twenty years in 1533, but on the understanding that 'if any of the young sons of the said Lord Huse be at any time hereafter disposed to dwell themselves in the said manor' then the tenant would have to vacate on two years' notice.[33] Marney encouraged the farmers at Layer Marney and other manors nearby to keep his household supplied, counting deliveries of wheat, oats, hay, wood, sheep, cattle, and pigs and even the costs of carriage of herrings from Maldon and payments to a Colchester beer-brewer against their rent.[34] Windsor had to keep an eye on his

[23] PRO, SC6/Henry VII/163; ERO, D/ACR1, fo. 199v–200r.

[24] PRO, SC6/Henry VIII/1684, m. 1v; SC2/181/81, m. 1; KHLC, DRb/Pwr 10, fos. 62v–63r.

[25] KHLC, DRb/Pwr 9, fos. 173r–174r; PRO, E210/4832.

[26] BL, Addl. MS 12463, fos. 40v, 54v, 56r, 81v, 84v (*LP* IV, i. 367); 'Norfolk Subsidy Roll, 15 Hen VIII', *Norfolk Antiquarian Miscellany* 2 (1883), 406; *Suffolk in 1524*, ed. S. H. A. Hervey, Suffolk Green Books 10 (Woodbridge, 1910), 153.

[27] BL, Addl. MS 12463, fo.27v; Hampshire RO, WR2, pp. 223–4.

[28] BL, Addl. MS 12463, fo. 21v; Cambridgeshire Archives, VC8, fo. 168r–168v.

[29] BL, Addl. MS 12463, fo.10v; Huntingdonshire Archives, Archdeaconry wills vol. 8, fos. 157v–158r.

[30] BL, Addl. MS 12463, fo. 13v; Cambridgeshire Archives, P11/5/1, fo. 10r; P11/5/2, fos. 38r, 46v, 54r, 55v, 70*r.

[31] BL, Addl. MS 12463, fos. 53v, 114v; PRO, E179/141/109.

[32] BL, Althorp Papers A14; M. E. Finch, *The Wealth of Five Northamptonshire Families, 1540–1640*, Northamptonshire RS 19 (Oxford, 1956), 38–9.

[33] PRO, E326/9079.   [34] PRO, SC6/Henry VII/163, 674; *CAD*, iii. C3158, C3339.

farmers, such as Christopher Swan at Marsh Baldon who took the bars of the farmhouse windows away with him.[35] But he also saw to their needs, going to Lambeth Palace to negotiate with Archbishop Warham's officials over the pannage rights available to his farmers in archiepiscopal parks.[36] What caused him problems was the enforced exchange with the crown at the end of his life, which gave him ex-monastic estates where his control of fishing rights, for example, was not well established and the relevant evidence could not be extracted from the king's auditors.[37] Wyatt tried to provide for every eventuality. One ten-year lease he made to a Sittingbourne yeoman specified that, while Wyatt would keep the house wind-tight and watertight, the tenant would bear the cost of repairs if it were damaged by his cattle or by fire through his negligence; that he could have shreddings from the trees for fuel, but was not allowed to pollard them for this purpose; that he would keep the dovecote not only repaired but stocked with doves; that he could not sell the lease on without Sir Henry's permission; and, perhaps most telling of all, that if Sir Henry's receivers had to wait for late rent payments, the tenant would pay their expenses.[38]

PASTURE FARMING AND LAND IMPROVEMENT

Most of the new men made the best of the market conditions of the years either side of 1500 by engaging directly in pastoral farming. The lands they acquired were often well suited to it. Southwell had hundreds of acres of pasture in Norfolk and Essex, a number of closes ideal for livestock farming and, like Lovell, Hussey, and Wyatt, some foldcourses on which animals could be pastured across his tenants' lands after the harvest.[39] Wyatt and Poynings bought extensive marshlands.[40] By 1487, Lovell's pasture lands in Enfield were already worth twice what the arable lands were and by his death his estate there comprised at least 150 acres of pasture and 102 of meadow.[41] Wyatt and Hussey likewise had estates where the pasture and meadow were more extensive than the arable.[42]

Sheep made the biggest impression on the contemporary imagination as the means to profit from pasture. Poynings left his wife 200 sheep, Lovell left his nephew 500 and Windsor spent £4 16s on ewes in 1496–7, but the best-documented sheep

---

[35] Bodl. MS Rolls Oxon 166, m. 6.   [36] ESRO, GLY986, m. 3.

[37] PRO, C1/1169/67–70.   [38] PRO, E315/215, fos. 36v–37r.

[39] PRO, C142/29/15, 32, 41/62; E150/617/1; CP25/2/28/188/26, 36, 40, 189/45, 190/58.

[40] PRO, CP25/2/19/106/18; CP25/2/20/115/13, 119/24; CP25/2/21/127/16, 129/34; CP25/2/28/188/40; CP25/2/38/220/33; *Feet of Fines, Divers Counties*, ed. E. F. Kirk (London, 1913–24), 78.

[41] *The Victoria History of the County of Middlesex*, ed. W. Page et al., 13 vols (London, 1911–), v. 226; PRO, E150/479/2.

[42] PRO, CP25/1/145/165/64; CP25/2/25/155/34; C142/82/64; CP25/2/34/225/18; CP25/2/37/245/4; CP25/2/48/331/2; CP25/2/49/339/33, 342/35; *Feet of Fines for Essex*, ed. R. E. G. Kirk et al., 6 vols (Colchester, 1899–1993), iv. 147.

farming operation is Hussey's.[43] He took long leases from monasteries of estates ideal for sheep-runs, hired up to five shepherds, and probably ran flocks of several thousand sheep. One year he sold 320 sheep, another over 600 sheepskins. One year his shearers, fed on bread, ale, cheese, eggs, fish, and veal and backed up by labourers to handle the sheep and wool, took thirty-one man-days to clip his flocks, another year fourteen, suggesting several thousand animals were involved.[44] With wool sales worth at least £52 12s in 1531–2 and £57 15s in 1533–4, he was farming sheep on less than half the scale of the greatest flock-masters of the age, but still making perhaps a tenth of his income from wool.[45] Others surely did the same. Bray traded in wool, shipping it in the great new royal warship the *Sovereign*.[46] Dudley had wool at the Leadenhall in London when he fell, perhaps from his own sheep, and in 1514 Wyatt had two licences to export wool grown in Norfolk and Kent.[47] Lovell owned a ship by 1492, and may well have used it to trade, while Wyatt bought and used a ship captured from Warbeck's forces in Ireland in 1495.[48] Sheep were not alone. Raising beef cattle was a promising venture at a time when meat consumption was high. Wyatt had bullocks at Hitcham in Suffolk in 1494 and Southwell sold oxen from his farm at Hackney for nearly £1 each.[49] The new men had dairy cattle, too, though these may have been for their own household needs. Lovell had cows and heifers at Greenwich in 1490.[50] Hussey kept his cattle at Folkingham Park, where they had to be fed on hay when it snowed, and sold fifty-three assorted bulls, cows and steers in 1533–4 alone.[51]

The enclosure of fields with hedges or fences was necessary for efficient pastoral farming. Often, where settlement had contracted naturally, it was achieved uncontroversially, but where it involved the displacement of arable farming tenants or breached their rights of common it caused trouble, all the more so as population levels revived.[52] The enclosure commissions of 1517–18 and 1549 found that Belknap had enclosed land, perhaps some 600 acres in all, forearming himself with a pardon from the dying Henry VII which covered not only past but also future breaches of the anti-enclosure statute, and pleading that his enclosures benefited the local community, which had had too much arable land but was now so prosperous that mass on holidays was sung 'by note' as never before.[53] Certainly, a

[43] PRO, PROB11/20/21; *LP* IV, i. 366; Hampshire RO, 25M75/M2, m. 18.

[44] PRO, E36/95, fos. 23r, 25r, 27r–27v, 97v, 99r; PRO, E315/393, fo. 99r–99v; P. J. Bowden, *The Wool Trade in Tudor and Stuart England* (London, 1962).

[45] PRO, E36/95, fos. 7r, 23r, 27r, 95v, 99r; C. E. Moreton, *The Townshends and their World: Gentry, Law and Land in Norfolk c.1450–1551* (Oxford, 1992), 176.

[46] M. M. Condon, 'From Caitiff and Villain to *Pater Patriae*: Reynold Bray and the Profits of Office', in M. A. Hicks (ed.), *Profit, Piety and the Professions in later Medieval England* (Gloucester, 1990), 147.

[47] *LP* I, i. 381 (47), ii. 2684 (52), 2861 (27).

[48] PRO, E36/285, fo. 65r; A. E. Conway, *Henry VII's Relations with Scotland and Ireland, 1485–1498* (Cambridge, 1932), 86.

[49] PRO, KB27/962, m. 27v, 1003, m. 26v.   [50] PRO, KB9/389/18.

[51] PRO, E36/95, fos. 12v, 22v, 30r, 46v.

[52] Britnell, *Britain and Ireland*, 371–3, 412–13, 419.

[53] *The Domesday of Inclosures, 1517–1518*, ed. I. S. Leadam, 2 vols (London, 1897), ii. 424–7, 478–80, 655–7; HL, MS STT Personal box 1(4); *CPR 1494–1509*, 599.

rental of his lands made after his death found many closes and pastures.[54] Cope enclosed in Northamptonshire and Warwickshire, raising the value of estates and then selling them on.[55] Windsor and Empson enclosed land and converted it to pasture and one of Marney's farms at Layer Marney was turned over from plough-ing to grazing in around 1505.[56] Lovell's newly erected hedges at Wragby were attacked by his neighbours in 1511 and Hussey's officers at Boston, Sleaford, and elsewhere claimed for the costs of hedging.[57] But we should hesitate always to blame landlords for such changes. At Bentworth Hall in Hampshire it was Windsor's larger tenants who were reported to the manor court for enclosing land with hedges to the detriment of others.[58]

At Milton by Gravesend the enclosure of the townsman's marsh, as it was called, was achieved by agreement between Wyatt and his tenants, but it looks very much like agreement on Wyatt's terms. On 20 September 1525 seven leading tenants put their names to an undertaking that Sir Henry might enclose the marsh with fences, gates, and ditches, and the tenants would present to him and his advisers their claims to pasture animals there. At the next manor court, on 23 May 1526, seventeen named tenants were allocated rights to pasture their animals, but eleven of them were allowed just one cow each. Even William Burston, gentleman, only qualified for one horse and three cows, and if the priests of the local chantry chapel had no horses then they had no rights to pasture. Even for these rights there would be an annual charge of 8d for each head of cattle and 12d for each horse. Last-minute negotiation seems to have secured a concession, written in darker ink, that those with no cow might substitute a horse, provided they paid at the higher rate. These rights were operable only from 1 May to Michaelmas. From Michaelmas to 1 March, Wyatt was to have all the profits of the pasture on the marsh, and from 1 March to 1 May, he was to keep control, though the tenants were to have the profits. He retained the right to prosecute outsiders interloping on the marsh and impound their beasts, but did agree not to increase the rent per animal without the tenants' consent. Subsequent courts dutifully checked whether these orders for the marsh were being well kept and occasionally endorsed the rights of a new tenant to keep a cow.[59]

There were other ways to improve the value of land. In many places stewards and receivers worked through manor courts to order tenants to keep their houses, lands, fences, and ditches in good repair.[60] Sutton 'substantially repaired' lands after he bought them in order to raise their value.[61] Cutt, Leland noticed, bought lands 'much overgrown with thorns and bushes', but then had them 'cleansed, and the value much enhanced'.[62] Near the coasts drainage was an option. Guildford

---

[54] HL, MS STT 37, fos. 1v, 9r–9v, 11v.

[55] *Domesday of Inclosures*, i. 287, ii. 403–4, 485–7.

[56] *Domesday of Inclosures*, i. 204–5, 218, 384; *VCH Middlesex*, iii. 44.

[57] PRO, CP40/997, m. 437v; E36/95, fos. 75v, 81r, 115v, 118v.

[58] Hampshire RO, 25M75/M1, m. 9; 25M75/M2, m. 8.

[59] PRO, SC2/181/81, 88 mm. 4–5.

[60] For Lovell's estates see NRO, MC1898; LA, Misc. Dep. 511/1; FL Deeds 224.

[61] PRO, C1/391/14.

[62] J. Leland, *The Itinerary of John Leland in or about the Years 1535–1543*, ed. L. T. Smith, 5 vols (London, 1906–10), ii. 30.

worked with Robertsbridge Abbey under royal licence between 1478 and his death to drain thousands of acres of salt marsh on the coast near Rye and create the parish of East Guldeford, letting out the resultant pasture in blocks of up to 300 acres.[63] Dudley seems to have drained lands and built sea walls on the coastal marshes of Sussex, and Windsor had claims to profitably improved salt-marshes in the same county, just as he was involved in drainage by Dutch engineers in Stepney marshes.[64] Undrained areas were also open to exploitation, Hussey leasing out fishing, fowling, and peat-cutting rights in the fens at Branston.[65]

Livestock did not stop at sheep and cattle. Hussey leased out rabbit warrens at Pickworth and Grantham, one for a rent that included forty rabbits a year.[66] Wyatt let his warrens in Shorne for seven years from Michaelmas 1514 at a rent rising from 6s 8d in the first year to 26s 8d thereafter.[67] He took an even closer interest in those at Allington, using his powers as a JP to question those who had taken more than thirty rabbits illegally from his warren and that of the abbot of Boxley on a succession of winter nights: 'the confession of the hunters of my warren', he wrote with satisfaction on the resulting investigation.[68] Windsor's manor court at Baylham forbade his tenants to hunt his rabbits, as did Lovell's at Higham Bensted.[69] Wyatt and Lovell each bought dovecotes and we have seen how carefully Wyatt rented his.[70]

TIMBER, MILLS, TOWNS, AND MANORS

The sale of timber could bring a regular income or a large injection of cash if one were needed. Wyatt sold timber steadily from many of his estates and bought up small parcels of woodland inside his manors from his own tenants.[71] Poynings, too, made substantial sales, though he was short of timber when he needed to rebuild a fire-damaged house in 1517.[72] Lovell made wood sales from several manors in 1522–3 and reserved the wood from others for his own use, while on the Roos estates he sold timber from manors such as Helmsley and turves and peat from Storthwaite Moor.[73] Marney made regular sales from Colquite woods,

[63] *The Victoria History of the County of Sussex*, ed. W. Page et al., 9 vols in 11 (London, 1905–), ix, 149, 151; *The Wiston Archives: A Catalogue*, ed. J. M. L. Booker (Chichester, 1975), no. 2169; *HMC De L'Isle and Dudley*, i. 154–56; *CPR 1494–1509*, 110; *CCR 1500–9*, 618.

[64] *LP* XVI. 220 (22); PRO, SC6/Henry VIII/6217; C1/1169/66, 1279/73–5; 27 Henry VIII c. 35.

[65] PRO, E315/393, fos. 25r–26r.

[66] PRO, E315/393, fo. 42r; C1/1139/32; *LP* XIII, i. 646 (10).

[67] PRO, SC6/Henry VIII/1684, m. 1v.   [68] KHLC, U301/E1.

[69] SROI, HB8/1/254, mm. 1, 7r; ERO, D/DFc 185, pp. 24–5, 27–8, 38.

[70] PRO, CP25/1/232/79/117; CP25/2/20/114/38; CP25/2/21/130/24; CP25/2/27/178/49; E326/12737; *Feet of Fines, Divers Counties*, 63.

[71] PRO, SC6/Henry VIII/1684; SC2/181/88/1.

[72] Alnwick Castle, Syon MS X.II.I, box 16b; *LP* II, ii. 3244.

[73] BL, Addl. MS 12463, fos. 19v, 45v, 59v, 63v (*LP* IV, i. 367); SHC, LM/1842/4.

sometimes for charcoal.[74] Windsor's wood sales were more intermittent, though his local officers did their best to protect timber supplies. He provided 180 oak trees from his Suffolk manors for Wolsey's college at Ipswich and had further stocks in his park at Brambletye.[75] Further reserves of timber are shown in the lawsuits waged against those who felled them without permission, Lovell, Poynings, and Wyatt suing over oaks, ashes, elms, and underwood.[76] The best evidence for woodland management comes from Hussey's estates. He was already active in 1515, selling 200 oaks from Bitton to his neighbour Sir Maurice Berkeley for £20.[77] By 1525–36, his sales brought in over £85 a year, more than his wool, peaking at £187 18s 2½d in 1534–5.[78] Yet he felled responsibly, replanting as he went, so that in 1537 his stocks of oaks, ashes, elms, hazels, aspens, and maples in sixteen different localities ranged in age from one to twenty years.[79] Best of all, he had 150 acres of woods at Branston which were divided into thirty parts, so that 5 acres were felled and sold each year.[80] Fruit trees were equally made to pay: he leased out orchards, as Lovell and Wyatt did in Kent.[81]

Mills were a means for landlords to benefit from wider economic revival and their numbers and revenues were rising in the early sixteenth century.[82] Watermills were widespread and Brandon, Dudley, Hussey, Lovell, Poynings, Southwell, and Wyatt each had one or more.[83] Hussey's rented for 6s 8d, 13s 4d, or even 26s 8d with an attached close of land.[84] Windmills were rarer. Hussey's brought in 13s 4d or 18s a year, though one which might have made 33s 4d yielded nothing in 1534–5 because it had fallen down some years before.[85] Wyatt and Windsor did better. The first let his windmill at Milton for twelve years at £3 6s 8d.[86] The second let his on Beddingham Down for just 6s 8d a year, but took an entry fine of £3 6s 8d and a fine of £2 two years later for his consent to a transfer of the tenancy.[87]

The developing wealth of the cloth industry might be tapped by investment in fulling mills. Windsor spent at least £6 on making one at Bentworth Hall in

---

[74] *CAD*, i. C1285, ii. C2750, vi. C4683; PRO, C146/9272.

[75] Hampshire RO, 25M75/M2, mm. 2–9, 16–19, and unnumbered; PRO, SP1/47, fo. 294r (*LP* IV, ii. 4229 (11)); *LP* Addenda, i. 71.

[76] PRO, CP40/998, m. 516v, 1002, m. 140r, 1011, m. 437v.

[77] *Descriptive Catalogue of the Charters and Muniments in the Possession of the Rt Hon Lord Fitzhardinge at Berkeley Castle*, ed. I. H. Jeayes (Bristol, 1892), 203; PRO, CP40/1014, m. 432r.

[78] PRO, E36/95, fos. 15v, 66r, 72r, 73v, 81r, 106v, 111r, 112v, 120r, 127r; SC6/Henry VIII/1937, 1951; E315/393, fo. 38v.

[79] PRO, E315/393, fos. 4r, 11v, 12v, 20r, 32v, 36v, 42v, 43r, 53r, 59r–60r, 78v, 83v, 84r, 95v.

[80] PRO, E315/393, fo. 27r.

[81] PRO, E315/393, fo. 85r; E315/215, fos. 36v–37r; E315/215, fos. 36v–37r.

[82] J. Langdon, *Mills in the Medieval Economy: England 1300–1540* (Oxford, 2004), 26–64.

[83] *Abstracts of Feet of Fines relating to Wiltshire 1377–1509*, ed. J. L. Kirby, Wiltshire RS 41 (Devizes, 1986), 174–5; *Feet of Fines, Divers Counties*, 7; PRO, SC6/Henry VIII/6217; C142/29/32; PRO, C54/383, m. 25d; Somerset Heritage Centre, DD/WHb/1049; BL, Addl. MS 12463, fo. 62v (*LP* IV, i. 367); Petworth House 5731, m. 7; PRO, CP25/1/117A/345/120; SC2/181/88, m. 5r.

[84] PRO, E315/393, fos. 24v, 52r, 57v.

[85] PRO, E36/95, fos. 84v, 106v; E315/393, fo. 46v; CP25/2/49/342/35.

[86] PRO, SC6/Henry VIII/1684, m. 2r.   [87] ESRO, GLY986, m. 6.

1495–7 and then let it to an Alton fuller for twenty years, at a rent rising from £2 a year for the first ten years to £2 6s 8d thereafter.[88] Wyatt and Hussey had fulling mills in Kent and Wiltshire, and in Huntingdonshire Hussey found one tenant who would pay £20 a year for three corn mills and a fulling mill.[89] Other industries beckoned. Wyatt and Windsor had stone quarries, though Wyatt kept his in his own hands, perhaps for his building operations at Allington.[90] Wyatt bought a blacksmith's forge at Sandling and Hussey leased out a 'kilnhouse' in the fen common at Blankney.[91] Trade might be harnessed by renting out ferries, like Hussey's Martin Ferry at Timberland, or tolls on fairs like that at Corby.[92]

Urban property needed good management just as much as rural did. Inns ranged from grand establishments to barely dignified alehouses. Lovell's Swan Inn and Greyhound Inn at Cheshunt were let together with a brewery to a widow for £20 a year.[93] Wyatt's Seven Stars and Saracen's Head in Milton rented for 10½d and 6d a year respectively.[94] In between came Hussey's Angel in Sleaford and his White Hart and Saracen's Head in Boston, Wyatt's Clement and Christopher (formerly The Vine) in the parish of St Clement Danes, London, and Poynings's ancestral home in Southwark, used as a commercial inn called The Crown Key before he let it to the king at £4 a year for use as an armoury.[95]

Wyatt's other London houses were let to tradesmen—a skinner, a joiner—at £2 a year each.[96] In smaller towns rents were lower, but Hussey managed 16s 8d each for shops and houses in Boston, with an extra 2s if docking for a ship was included, 10s or 12s 8d at Grantham, 6s 4d or 7s on the Market Place at Sleaford.[97] Constant repairs were necessary to maximize income. Nearly half the rent of Lovell's inns in Cheshunt went on repairs in 1522–3 and royal surveyors thought Hussey's Grantham properties would have done better had the houses not been 'fallen down and utterly decayed'.[98] Fire was always a threat. In 1534–5 Hussey had to spend over £20 rebuilding fire-damaged houses in Sleaford and reduce some rents.[99] But there were other opportunities. Suburban pastures, used for fattening meat, attracted high rents, at Boston up to 6s 8d or even 7s 2d an acre.[100] For those with an eye to profit from London's expansion, finally, the equivalent of enclosure for urban landlords was to allow the infilling of plots with small dwellings for the poor. The properties in London that Lovell gave to the grocers' company included rent

[88] Hampshire RO, 25M75/M2, mm. 18, unnumbered.
[89] PRO, CP25/2/21/128/45; CP40/989, m. 352r; E315/393, fo. 94v.
[90] Hampshire RO, 25M75/M2, mm. 16–18 and unnumbered; PRO, SC6/Henry VIII/1684, m. 1r; E326/11340.
[91] PRO, E326/7112, 8740; E315/393, fo. 16v.
[92] PRO, E315/393, fos. 19v, 46v.
[93] BL, Addl. MS 12463, fo. 93v (*LP* IV, i. 367).
[94] PRO, SC2/181/88, m. 4r.
[95] *LP* V, 806; PRO, C54/382, m. 6d; PRO, E315/393, fo. 8v, 68v; M. Carlin, *Medieval Southwark* (London, 1996), 51n, 65; *LP* II, ii. 1477.
[96] *CAD*, ii. C2092; PRO, KB27/1061, m. 24r–24v.
[97] PRO, E315/393, fos. 9v, 33v–34r, 71r–71v.
[98] BL, Addl. MS 12463, fo. 93v; PRO, E315/393, fo. 35r.
[99] PRO, E36/95, fos. 56v, 79r, 80r, 117v–118v.
[100] PRO, E315/393, fos. 72r–73v.

from an 'alley…where poor people dwelleth'.[101] And ambitious men always encroached on common resources: in St Clement Danes Wyatt built a fence 41 yards long that carved off part of the king's highway.[102]

The profits of manorial jurisdiction and feudal incidents did not play a very large part in any late medieval English landlord's revenues. Some courts brought in nothing because none were held, as on Wyatt's Kent estates in 1520–1 or some of Lovell's in 1522–3.[103] Most others, indeed Wyatt's in other years, brought in modest sums from the heriots payable by those inheriting land; fines paid by brewers, bakers, and perpetrators of minor assaults, or those who had failed to keep their animals under control, their ditches scoured, or their houses repaired; or more unusual levies like the tallage on pigs payable at Lovell's manor of Adderley.[104] Sometimes they heard local pleas of debt, as Marney's court at Colquite or Poynings's at Wrentham Poynings did.[105] Occasionally they offered the chance to exercise charity, as when Wyatt graciously declined to impose fines on the half-dozen poor women and men breaking hedges for firewood at Milton in 1528.[106] Over time their powers tended to decay, as royal courts drew business away, parishes overtook manors as units of local administration, and the crown's lawyers attacked courts with pretensions to wide jurisdictions, such as Windsor's at Stanwell and South Mimms.[107]

Generally, stewards were left to run courts, though Windsor himself appeared to back up the steward of Baylham in 1496 when there was a dispute about the tithes due from Baylham mill.[108] Bailiffs did the hard work of enforcing lordly rights, distraining livestock to enforce the payment of dues, but running the risk of resistance. Windsor's bailiff at Baylham, John Scoot, suffered the violent recovery of a cow in 1508, his bailiff at Stanwell, John Wodward, assault by a husbandman, two labourers, and a miller in their efforts to recover a horse in 1525.[109] At times, estate officers' zeal in their master's cause became an embarrassment as they obstructed the rights of royal officials to levy fines or execute other business. At Holt in Norfolk, the duchy of Lancaster's bailiff found that Lovell's bailiffs 'will suffer none officer to come within that fee without great business', an attitude which encouraged other lords' bailiffs to be equally awkward; he hoped the chancellor of the duchy might have a word with Sir Thomas, so that things might be quietly sorted out, thinking 'the default is not in him but in his servants'.[110] Wyatt, the duchy officers thought, needed speaking to in similar vein. His bailiffs certainly enforced his rights with vigour, impounding a bull and a cow belonging to a yeoman of

---

[101] LMA, Rep. 6, fo. 61r.   [102] PRO, KB9/491/9.

[103] PRO, SC6/Henry VIII/1684, m. 2r; BL, Addl. MS 12463, fos. 10v, 27v, 84v (*LP* IV, i. 367).

[104] PRO, SC2/181/42; Shropshire Archives, 327/1; ERO, D/DFc185, pp. 24–39; LAO, Misc. Dep. 511/1; FL deeds 224.

[105] PRO, SC2/158/37, mm. 18–22; SROI, HB26/371/57, fos. 1r–5v.

[106] PRO, SC2/181/87, fo. 5v.

[107] H. Garrett-Goodyear, 'The Tudor Revival of Quo Warranto and Local Contributions to State Building', in M. S. Arnold et al. (eds), *On the Laws and Customs of England: Essays in Honor of Samuel E. Thorne* (Chapel Hill NC, 1981), 281, 285.

[108] SROI, HB8/1/254, m. 10r.

[109] SROI, HB8/1/254, m. 3d; PRO, KB9/500/19.   [110] PRO, DL1/1/D3a, D3cv.

Stoke Hammond when he failed to pay his rent and stepping up manor court fines when tenants persisted in disobedience.[111]

The manumission of serfs, on the hundreds of manors where servile tenure had survived the erosion of the fifteenth century, was another profitable business. It was most easily organized by initiating a fictitious lawsuit in which the lord denied the tenant succession to an acre of land on the grounds that he was of illegitimate descent. The services of a bishop were then procured to certify that the tenant in question was indeed a bastard, so could not have inherited servile status. This manoeuvre was at its most popular between 1490 and 1520 and Lovell seems to have done it for at least two men and perhaps many more.[112] Windsor had serfs at Beddingham and Marsh Baldon, where he took the more troublesome route of repeated attempts to fine them for moving out of the manor.[113]

Private wardship could be lucrative, so much so that Lovell specifically reserved his claims to wards when letting out manors. At Braunston he just missed his chance to claim the wardship of the fourteen-year-old son of his leading free tenant Thomas Willoby, as he himself died about the same time as the tenant.[114] Poynings claimed at least two wards in Kent, but one case, in which he joined with the other lords involved to sell the wardship and marriage to his neighbour John Norton, went better than the other, in which the boy was taken into his possession, but opportunistically removed at his death.[115] The new men's legal knowledge and influence encouraged them to push their rights to the uttermost. Hobart allegedly claimed that the manor of Narborough in Southacre was held of him by knight service and thus that its heiress, Katherine Bockyng, was his ward. He used the claim to unnerve her stepfather George Willoughby into paying him £6 13s 4d to 'be in peace' and keep control of the manor, money Willoughby was all the more ready to pay because Hobart was 'in great authority and room'.[116] Windsor apparently fought a series of collusive court actions in 1519 to establish his wardship over the heir of the Bulstrode family and reinforce it with a grant from their other overlords. By 1529–30, it put him in charge of their estates, holding courts, leasing out lands, and levying rents, 'as guardian in chivalry'.[117] On occasion, their claims brought the new men into conflict with those capable of standing up to them. It was Windsor's riotous dispute with Thomas Pygot, king's serjeant-at-law, about 'a seizure of a ward' that famously aroused the ire of Cardinal Wolsey.[118]

When it is possible to judge, it looks as though all these techniques paid off in enabling the new men to extract increasing amounts of income from their lands.

[111] PRO, DL1/1/DCBv; CP40/1027, m. 437v; SC2/153/20, m. 2.

[112] D. N. J. MacCulloch, 'Bondmen under the Tudors', in C. Cross et al. (eds), *Law and Government under the Tudors: Essays Presented to Sir Geoffrey Elton on his Retirement* (Cambridge, 1988), 91–109; BL, Addl. Ch. 14200; PRO, CP40/1020B, m. 324v.

[113] ESRO, GLY986, m. 1; Bodl. MS Rolls Oxon 166, mm. 3, 7–9.

[114] Shropshire Archives, 946/A427; Northamptonshire RO, D1086, m. 9; Bean, 'Landlords', 571–3.

[115] PRO, C54/379, m. 3d; KB27/1050, m. 32r.   [116] PRO, C1/376/22.

[117] PRO, CP40/1025, m. 331v, 1026, m. 522r; LMA, Acc/0928/1/14–16.

[118] PRO, SP1/16, fo. 16v (*LP* II, ii, App. 38).

For fourteen of Poynings's manors, or sets of manors, the difference can be calcu-
lated between what was paid or owed him in 1488–9 and what a valor of 1520–1
suggested was the clear income when he died, corroborated by accounts from
1523–4. Twelve of the fourteen had increased in yield, six of them by between
45 per cent and 70 per cent, and two had nearly doubled.[119] A similar comparison
between what was paid or owed on fourteen Roos manors spread from Yorkshire
to Kent in 1485–6 and the valor taken at Lovell's death suggests that all had
increased in yield under his administration. The smallest increase was 7 per cent,
the largest 248 per cent, the mean 55 per cent.[120] Lovell's accounts in 1522–3
showed minimal arrears and healthy expenditure on repairs; arrears on Hussey's
lands in the 1530s fluctuated but were generally declining; Windsor clawed back
arrears by binding the debtors in large sums for quick repayment.[121] Wyatt
ploughed back the profits of his lands into the expansion and improvement of his
estate. In 1520–1 his receiver-general paid out not only £15 12s 5½d for repairs to
tenements and scouring ditches, but also £40 10s, a fifth of the rental income of
the Kentish estates, to those from whom his master was buying land. No wonder
many of the plots of land in his accounts were described as 'lately purchased'.[122]

LEASES

Not content with their own lands, the new men looked to turn a profit by taking
lands on lease from other landlords and making them pay. Lovell was an expert. He
rented crown manors from 1485, first at Wratting in Suffolk, then at Walthamstow
Frannceys and Higham Bensted in Essex, then at Tolworth in Surrey.[123] From
about 1502 to 1516 he leased the demesne lands at Castle Rising in Norfolk for
£50 a year, and for 3s he rented a scrap of land in London just before he died.[124]
Further farms were taken from religious institutions and lay lords. In Cheshunt,
near Enfield, he farmed St Giles in the Bushes from Cheshunt Priory.[125] In north-
west Norfolk he acquired the farms of Choseley, held from the hospital of Burton
Lazars, and used to pasture his sheep, and of Southmere in Docking, held from the
dowager Lady Fitzwalter.[126] At Eastry in Kent, near his purchased lands in Worth,
he leased 224 acres of land from Canterbury Cathedral Priory.[127] At Enfield, next
to his great house at Elsings, he took lands from anyone he could find, leasing the
demesnes of the duchy of Lancaster manor for more than £39 a year, eight and a
half acres of marsh from Holywell Priory, and the herbage of a park from Henry
Frowyk to pasture his oxen and geldings.[128]

[119] Alnwick Castle, Syon MS X.II.I, box 16b; PRO, C54/390, m. 16; Petworth House, 5728.
[120] PRO, SC6/Henry VII/1241; C54/392, mm. 30d–31d.
[121] BL, Addl. MS 12463 (*LP* IV, i. 367); PRO, E36/95, fos. 2v, 7v, 10v, 13r, 40v; C54/419, m. 37d.
[122] PRO, SC6/Henry VIII/1684.
[123] *CFR*, 33, 311; *The Victoria History of the County of Essex*, ed. H. A. Doubleday et al., 11 vols
(London, 1903–), vi. 256, 258; BL, Addl. MS 21480, fos. 193v, 195r.
[124] PRO, SC6/Henry VII/414–19; *LP* II, i. 2625, IV, i. 546 (15).
[125] *HMC Rutland*, iv. 262.   [126] *HMC Rutland*, iv. 262; PRO, C1/632/50.
[127] Mate, *Trade and Economic Developments*, 208.
[128] BL, Harley Roll Y28; *HMC Rutland*, iv. 262.

He contrived to make extra profit from several of these farms by the simple expedient of not paying the rent. At Castle Rising, he was £50 in arrears by 1508, the sum was still unpaid in 1516 and in 1517 the auditors made a note to have a word with him about it.[129] At Cheshunt, he declined to pay tithes, and since he was a 'great man' the vicar sued the prioress rather than him.[130] In Docking, he occupied additional lands lately held by John, Lord Fitzwalter, but paid neither the king nor Lady Fitzwalter any rent for them, leaving her to meet the crown's demands for £40. When challenged about the matter, he 'deferred and delayed, saying he would examine the matter further by his servants' and then pay back 'such money as of right he ought to do', but he never got round to it.[131] The fellows of Merton College, Oxford found him equally evasive over a small rent owed to them.[132] At Enfield he again fell behind with his rent, saved money as keeper of the park by allowing the fences to fall into decay, and helped himself to 1,500 loads of timber and five oaks from the park.[133]

Others used leases, as Lovell did, to complement their own concentrated purchases or inheritances of lands. Windsor joined Ankerwyke Priory's manor of Stanwell Park to his own manor of Stanwell and a New College, Oxford meadow at High Wycombe to his Buckinghamshire lands.[134] Hussey added Germain Pole's half of the Castle Bytham estate to his own and at Sleaford took over a fifty-year lease of the bishop of Lincoln's marsh, five watermills, and a bakery and rented the manor of Spanby by Sleaford, thought to be worth £20, for £13 6s 8d.[135] By a combination of lease and purchase of reversions he gained control of valuable lands around Chilwell, apparently taking advantage of Sir Robert Sheffield's need to pay a huge star chamber fine and then of the minority of his grandson Edmund.[136] Southwell took a disputed lease on land at Shipdham, near his home at Woodrising, for £5 a year from the prior of Ely when he was managing the see's temporalities in a vacancy in 1500.[137] Brandon leased Odiham, in Hampshire, near his wives' lands, and Southwold, in Suffolk, near his brother's.[138] Wyatt leased Reading Abbey's manor of Windhill, near his own purchased lands in Hoo hundred, and applied his characteristic management techniques. He agreed with the tenants in 1528 at their 'humble suit and request' that all rents were payable on 1 June and 11 November and all those failing to pay on time would share the cost of Wyatt's officers' expenses while they waited for payment. 'Notwithstanding the agreement before rehearsed', Wyatt also reserved the right to be 'at his liberty against them

[129] DCRO, DC Roll 215, fo. 32r; Roll 216, m. 18r.

[130] *LP* IV, i. 368.   [131] PRO, C1/632/50.

[132] *Registrum Annalium Collegii Mertonensis 1483–1521*, ed. H. E. Salter, OHS 76 (Oxford, 1923), 192.

[133] PRO, DL1/4/R5–6.   [134] *VCH Middlesex*, iii. 41; *VE*, ii. 259.

[135] PRO, E315/393, fos. 99v, 100v; *LP* XIV, i. 906 (15).

[136] PRO, E36/95, fos. 6v, 10r, 20r, 45r–45v, 94v, 108r–109r; E326/7196; CP25/2/33/220/37; CP40/1041, m. 439r; *Derbyshire Feet of Fines 1323–1546*, ed. H. J. H. Garratt and C. Rawcliffe, Derbyshire RS 2 (Chesterfield, 1985), no. 1217; P. Gwyn, *The King's Cardinal: The Rise and Fall of Thomas Wolsey* (London, 1990), 134–7.

[137] PRO, KB27/969, m. 75r.   [138] BL, MS Lansdowne 127, fo. 51v; *CCR 1485–1500*, 1231.

that fail of their payment and take his advantage such as the law shall give him'.[139] Office-holding, too, might be filled out by leases, Wyatt renting the grazing rights in Conisbrough Park, where he was keeper, from 1500, lands in Conisbrough manor, where he was steward, from 1505, and pastures around Carlisle Castle, where he had been captain, from 1506.[140] Others did as Lovell did and piled up profits by neglecting to pay the rent: Guildford farmed Kennington, Surrey from the duchy of Cornwall from 1485, and was already well behind with his payments by 1494–5.[141]

Wyatt was what contemporaries called a leasemonger, buying up valuable leases and selling them on. He took a forty-year reversionary lease of the manor of Letcombe Regis from Westminster Abbey in September 1507 at £60 a year; the reversion fell in fifteen months later, but by around 1530 he had sold out his interest to John Audelet.[142] Hussey profited from sub-letting, paying Vaudey Abbey £18 a year for Hanbeck Grange and sub-letting it for £37 and charging his subtenant in the bishop's mills and bakehouse at Sleaford a rent in money and wheat sufficient to make a profit of about £10 a year.[143] Cutt, too, was a dealer in leases and an improver of the land he leased. He took a ninety-eight-year lease of a large mansion and wharf in Lower Thames Street, London, from Holy Trinity Priory, Aldgate, but then sold it on.[144] He took a lease of the manor of Holmes in Shenley from St Bartholomew's Priory, West Smithfield, and then sub-let it to a local yeoman for twenty-one years. His tenant was to pay him the same rent he paid the priory, but was to clear the land of trees and brambles, hedge and ditch it, so it was fit for ploughing and sowing, within the first seven years. He did not, so Cutt sued him and won £2 10s damages.[145] As a duchy of Lancaster insider, Cutt went on collecting duchy and crown leases to the end of his life.[146]

Leases were a means to establish a hold over land that might be purchased in due course. Empson leased the manor of Towcester from the earl of Kent a few months after buying the reversion to it; a few months later he secured the earl's renunciation of the annual rent of £50 due under the lease.[147] Windsor bought Stanwell Park when Ankerwyke Priory was dissolved.[148] Impermanent grants from one king might be made permanent by another. Brandon and his brother Sir Robert held the manors of Thorndon and Wattisfield on a temporary basis by 1504, and within months of Thomas's death Robert was granted possession for life with reversion to

---

[139] PRO, SC2/181/88, mm. 6–7.

[140] *CPR 1494–1509*, 219; YAS, DD5/41, m. 1v; *CFR*, 837.

[141] DCRO, DC Roll 212, m. 7; PRO, SC6/Henry VII/1081, mm. 2r, 6r.

[142] WAM, Lease Book II, fo. 222v; PRO, C1/628/44.

[143] PRO, E315/393, fo. 98v; E36/95, fos. 35r, 64r, 100r.

[144] W. Foster, 'Nicholas Gibson and his Free School at Ratcliff', *London Topographical Record* 17 (1936), 4.

[145] *Year Book of Henry VIII: 12–14 Henry VIII 1520–1523*, ed. J. H. Baker, SS 119 (London, 2002), 29–32; E. A. Webb, *The Records of St Bartholomew's Priory and of the Church and Parish of St Bartholomew the Great West Smithfield*, 2 vols (Oxford, 1921), i. 364.

[146] BL, Harley Roll Y28; PRO, SP2/M, fo. 167r (*LP* V, 1714).

[147] Northamptonshire RO, MTD/D18/8, 27/4, 27/5.

[148] *VCH Middlesex*, iii. 41.

their nephew Charles.[149] Hussey made faster progress with the manors of Holywell and Stretton, leased to him by the king in 1494 and then granted outright in 1495, and with Lord Audley's forfeited manor of Sapperton.[150]

Leases were the best way to obtain London houses and the amenities necessary for comfortable metropolitan living. In 1507 Empson took ninety-nine-year leases both on a mansion and gardens in St Bride's parish from Westminster Abbey and on an adjoining orchard and gardens running down to the Thames from the Order of St John, all for only £3 2s 8d.[151] Dudley leased a large house with gardens in Candlewick Street.[152] Lovell bought from Sir Thomas Thwaytes the remainder of a ninety-eight-year crown lease on a house in the parish of St Thomas the Apostle in Vintry Ward, though he may no longer have needed it once he built at Holywell.[153] Wyatt rented two tenements and gardens within the Dominican friary from 1505 for £4 7s 4d, and sometimes stayed there.[154] Guildford rented a suite of rooms from the same friary, with running water and a window looking into the church, for £5 6s 8d.[155] Marney had, perhaps on lease, a house in the parish of St Swithin by London stone, where, as he put it in his will, 'I am sometime abiding'.[156]

Such leases were equally desirable in the suburbs and just beyond. In 1504 Wyatt leased the manor of Barnes for ninety-six years from the dean and chapter of St Paul's at £16 6s 8d, a lease he kept until about 1530 and then sold on.[157] From Westminster Abbey he leased a tenement in Westminster for fifty years and four shops for thirty years in 1513, then sold his title to the crown in 1531 for £25 to enable the expansion of Whitehall Palace.[158] On the other side of the city he rented thirty acres of Stepney Marsh from the bishop of London and part of Porter's Fee in Dagenham from the Husseys.[159] The most impressive and practical assemblage was Brandon's in Southwark. He inherited from his father the house on the High Street that facilitated the family's keepership of the king's bench prison opposite, but he added to it from 1502 the lease of 48 acres of adjoining meadow from the bishop of Winchester, a lease he secured for ninety years in 1508 to create a valuable suburban park, including fishponds to supply his house.[160]

However they gained control of their lands, the new men made them work for their profit, power and pleasure. Their techniques were by no means unique.

[149] NRO, Bishop's Register 13B, fos. 36r, 57r, Register 14, fo. 87r; SROB, Ac613/142/2, 4; *LP* I, i. 682 (40).
[150] *CPR 1485–94*, 497; *CPR 1494–509*, 58; PRO, SC11/828.
[151] WAM, Lease Book II, fo. 73r; E. G. O'Donohue, *Bridewell Hospital, Palace, Prison, Schools* (London, 1923), 26.
[152] *LP* III, ii. 3586(28).   [153] PRO, PROB11/23/27.
[154] SHC, LM/344/17; *LP* Addenda, i. 493.   [155] ESRO, SAS/G21/18.
[156] 'Ancient Wills', ed. H. W. King, *TEAS* 4 (1869), 148.
[157] *The Victoria History of the County of Surrey*, ed. H. E. Malden, 4 vols (London, 1902–14), iv. 5; *LP* IV, ii. 4088, iii. 6430, 6726.
[158] WAM, Lease Book II, fos 50v–52r; *The Survey of London*, ed. C. R. Asbee et al., 50 vols (London, 1900–), xiv. 5.
[159] PRO, C54/397, mm. 11d–12d; *The Politics of Fifteenth-Century England: John Vale's Book*, ed. M. L. Kekewich et al. (Stroud, 1995), 102–3, 267.
[160] Carlin, *Medieval Southwark*, 51, 64; Hampshire RO, 21M65/A1/20, fos. 59r–60r.

Contemporary gentlemen made the best they could of demesne farms, new rentals and leases, of pastures rural and suburban, of enclosures and mills, of timber, rabbits, sheep, and cattle, though some missed out and many struggled to manage estates as widely dispersed as those some of the new men assembled.[161] Successful lawyers like Thomas Kebell or Roger Townshend turned to enclosure, sheep, and cattle with particular vigour but also made the best of short leases and strict terms for repairs.[162] Even a great lord like Buckingham strove, albeit with questionable success, to maximize his estate income by pressure on his tenants and local officers, by precise record-keeping and an evaluation of the relative merits of leasing and direct administration, higher rents and higher fines, selling and preserving woods, manumission, and the pursuit of servile dues.[163] Yet the new men applied the estate management wisdom of their day with characteristic thoroughness, all the more impressively as they had so much else on their minds.

[161] C. Carpenter, *Locality and Polity: A Study of Warwickshire Landed Society, 1401–1499* (Cambridge, 1992), 153–95; S. M. Wright, *Derbyshire Gentry in the Fifteenth Century*, Derbyshire RS 8 (Chesterfield, 1983), 12–28.

[162] E. W. Ives, *The Common Lawyers Lawyers of Pre-Reformation England. Thomas Kebell: A Case Study* (Cambridge, 1983), 348–52; Moreton, *Townshends*, 138–90.

[163] B. J. Harris, *Edward Stafford, Third Duke of Buckingham, 1478–1521* (Stanford CA, 1986), 104–35.

15

Expenditure and status

Like their master, who built impressively at Richmond and Greenwich, filled his houses with tapestries and plate, and celebrated the wedding of Arthur to Katherine in lavish style, the new men knew that money had to be spent to convert aspiration into status and influence. But the line between the fitting magnificence that built their power and equipped them to serve the king and the overweening pride that might give licence to destroy them was a fine one.

BUILDING

Money made power visible most conspicuously through building and Lovell created a palace large enough to contain the court on progress at Elsings in Enfield, Middlesex. Surrounded by a moat crossed by a great bridge, it had two courtyards, a three-storey gatehouse, battlemented towers, high, chimneys, a gallery, hall and library, gardens and orchards, a chapel sixty feet high and full suites of rooms for the king and queen alongside the garden, with an oriel window in the king's great chamber and services provided by further 'servants' chambers without the moat'. The arrangement of its lodgings seems to have been based on that at Richmond Palace, and excavations have shown that, like Richmond and the palaces of the Burgundian Netherlands it imitated, it was built in brick, with a string-course of moulded brick, vaulted brick drains, and square towers projecting from its facades. Lovell was still at work on it between 1522 and 1524, buying forty loads of timber, 70,500 roof tiles, 920 paving tiles, and thousands of bricks. His carpenter was one of his best-paid servants, at £3 6s 8d a year, and was perhaps directing work.[1] He built a second substantial house at East Harling in Norfolk, this time with a five-storey battlemented gatehouse with polygonal corner-towers, a chapel, great parlour, great chamber, and other rooms.[2] Lastly, needing a home nearer London, he built elaborate lodgings, what he called in his will a 'mansion place', at Holywell Nunnery in Shoreditch. There he had a hall, a parlour, a chamber with a 'bay window of freestone', and six other chambers, one next to the garden; at least one

---

[1] D. Pam, *A Parish Near London* (Enfield, 1990), 48, 51–4; PRO, PROB2/199; PROB11/23/27; *HKW*, IV, ii. 87–8; S. Thurley, *The Royal Palaces of Tudor England* (New Haven CT and London, 1993), 43; D. G. Hurst, 'Post-Medieval Britain in 1966', *Post-Medieval Archaeology* 1 (1967), 113–14; Belvoir Castle, MS a/c no. 4; *LP* IV, i. 366.

[2] PRO, PROB2/199, mm. 5–8; G. L. Harrison, 'A Few Notes on the Lovells of East Harling', *NA* 18 (1912), plate opposite 52; BL, Addl. MS 12463, fo. 67r.

room had a stone chimney-piece bearing his arms.[3] To keep things in trim he kept full-time gardeners at Holywell and Elsings.[4]

Bray spent at least £1,800 on a new house at Eaton in Bedfordshire, and also built at Newbottle and Edgcote in Northamptonshire, where he had timber, stone, lead, and tile worth £436 4s 8d stockpiled ready to build at the time of his death.[5] Empson built so grandiosely at Easton Neston between 1499 and 1509 that his neighbours complained that his north and east gatehouses obstructed the king's highways.[6] Hobart built Hales Hall in Loddon, Norfolk, in brick with blue diaper-work decoration, octagonal towers, a vast barn, which still survives, and a chapel where he was licensed to marry his wife in 1496.[7] At Hanwell, Cope built himself what Leland reckoned, by the time his son had finished it, 'a very pleasant and gallant house'. Drawings, inventories, and what survives show its resemblance to the houses of his colleagues, brick-built with stone dressings, of three wings around a courtyard, with a gatehouse featuring an oriel window, corner towers with octagonal turrets, a gallery, parlour, chambers, kitchens, and an armoury.[8] Cutt, too, was a builder, at Childerley in Cambridgeshire and Salisbury Park in Hertfordshire, and most grandly at Horham Hall, 'a very sumptuous house in Essex' with 'a goodly pond or lake by it and fair parks there about'. Developed from an earlier timber-framed house on a moated site, it had two-storey brick ranges with a gatehouse, a four-storey tower, a chapel, and a surviving hall with an impressive full-height oriel window.[9] It was sufficiently impressive that Lucas sent his carpenter and glazier to look at it for inspiration when building his own house at Little Saxham in 1506–9.[10] Belknap built a new house in the centre of his estates at Weston under Wetherley.[11] Southwell bought the fine house built by William Worsley, dean of St Paul's, at Hackney, and towards the end of his life was also finishing a new house at Kelvedon Easterford, buying up lead, iron, plaster, glass, red and yellow ochre, hinges, locks, nails, hooks, and curtain rings, and sending them out to Essex, sometimes by boat.[12]

---

[3] PRO, PROB2/199, mm. 8–9; PROB11/23/27; H. Ellis, *The History and Antiquities of the Parish of St Leonard Shoreditch, and Liberty of Norton Folgate, in the Suburbs of London* (London, 1798), 195.

[4] *HMC Rutland*, iv. 261–2.

[5] M. M. Condon, 'From Caitiff and Villain to *Pater Patriae*: Reynold Bray and the Profits of Office', in M. A. Hicks (ed.), *Profit, Piety and the Professions in later Medieval England* (Gloucester, 1990), 144, 154, 158; PRO, E154/2/10, fo. 10r.

[6] Northamptonshire RO, MTD/U/35/5; PRO, KB9/452/127–8.

[7] N. Pevsner, *North-West and South-West Norfolk* (Harmondsworth, 1962), 183–4; NNRO, Register 12, fo. 188v.

[8] J. Leland, *The Itinerary of John Leland in or about the Years 1535–1543*, ed. L. T. Smith, 5 vols (London, 1906–10), ii. 40; *The Victoria History of the County of Oxford*, ed. W. Page et al., 17 vols (London, 1907–), ix. 113–14.

[9] M. Howard, *The Early Tudor Country House: Architecture and Politics 1490–1550* (London, 1987), 201, 204; Leland, *Itinerary*, ii. 30–1; A. Emery, *Greater Medieval Houses of England and Wales 1300–1550*, 3 vols (Cambridge, 1996–2006), ii. 114–16.

[10] Howard, *Country House*, 15.

[11] C. Carpenter, *Locality and Polity: A Study of Warwickshire Landed Society, 1401–1499* (Cambridge, 1992), 199.

[12] *The Survey of London*, ed. C. R. Asbee et al., 50 vols (London, 1900–), xxviii. 54–73; PRO, SP1/230, fos. 109r, 110v, 111r, 114r, 116r, 118r–118v, 119v, 121r (*LP* I, ii. 2765).

Figure 2. Westenhanger Castle, Kent. Photograph by the author.

Poynings at Westenhanger and Wyatt at Allington, both in Kent, bought thir-teenth- or fourteenth-century castles and built new apartments inside them. This was presumably cheaper than building from scratch, but may also have served to simulate ancient, inherited authority.[13] At Westenhanger, as Figures 2 and 3 show, Poynings kept the fourteenth-century curtain walls, gatehouse, towers, and moat, but added brick ranges two or three storeys high. The chambers were generously lit with dressed-stone or brick windows and comfortably heated with brick fireplaces, the hall combined new with re-used windows, and the kitchen was equipped for hospitality with two great fireplaces, a bakehouse, and a drain. The death of a mason from syphilis in 1519 would suggest that work was still underway in Sir Edward's last years, perhaps on the chapel, which was dated 1520 and apparently had a screen of Caen stone.[14] The site at Allington, shown in Figure 4, was more complex: a compact thirteenth-century castle with a gatehouse and corner towers had been created out of a later twelfth-century manor house and the remnants of an earlier castle. Henry and his son Thomas—probably mostly Henry, as Thomas outlived his father by only five years and had money problems—added a new kitchen building, long gallery, hall porch, and privy garden wall, and, calcu-lating on comfort like Poynings, new larger windows and fireplaces inside older ranges.[15]

[13] Howard, *Country House*, 207–8.
[14] D. Martin and B. Martin, 'Westenhanger Castle—A Revised Interpretation', *AC* 121 (2001), 207–29; PRO, KB9/479/105.
[15] W. M. Conway, 'Allington Castle', *AC* 28 (1909), 337–62.

Figure 3. New range at Westenhanger Castle. Photograph by the author.

Figure 4. Allington Castle, Kent. Photograph by Sir Robert Worcester.

Hussey and Marney were more innovative. Hussey had inherited a solid house on the edge of Boston, with a three-storey brick tower, gatehouse, hall, parlour, chapel, chambers, buttery, pantry, kitchen, larder, brewhouse, and stables, with tile and lead roofs and some large glazed windows.[16] At Sleaford he made a statement with a grander 'house or manor place...southward without the town', graced with a garden and orchard, which Leland found 'lately almost new built of stone and timber'.[17] Almost certainly he was also the author of a more fashionable project, a three-storey brick hunting lodge with two rooms on each floor at Kneesall in Nottinghamshire, where he had a deer park. It was one of the first brick buildings in the county, and the window frames and newel stairway to the top floor were made of high-quality dark-red terracotta, the courtier's material of choice in the 1520s.[18] Terracotta was even more prominent in the most spectacular survivor of all these projects, Layer Marney. The Marney family home with its chamber, parlour, hall with a 'bay window', and 'summer hall' was already there in the 1480s and 1490s, but towards the end of his life Marney began to rebuild on an impressive scale, aiming to create a house of two courtyards, one roughly a hundred feet square, the other longer but narrower. Only three ranges were completed, mostly of two storeys in brick with diapered decoration, moulded brick string courses, and twisted brick chimneys, though the grand towers of the gatehouse are eight storeys high and look out to sea. Plaster was used to simulate stone dressings on the lower windows, but the upper windows and parapet were made of terracotta with moulded motifs taken from the classicizing decorative vocabulary of the Italian renaissance, winged cherubs, dolphins, scrolls, urns, and Corinthian capitals.[19]

These houses came into their own when they hosted royal visits. Henry VII stayed once each with Guildford, at Halden in August 1504, with Empson, at Easton Neston in August 1507, with Poynings, at Westenhanger in August 1504, with Windsor, at Stanwell in October 1506, and with Hussey at Dagenhams in Romford, in August 1508. Bray welcomed him to Freefolk in November 1497 and September 1499, and to Edgcote in September 1498. Lovell, at Elsings, he visited again and again, in May 1498, December 1499, July 1507, and August 1508, and Henry VIII followed his lead, visiting in eight years between 1509 and 1522, arriving in seven different months of the year, and using it for his sister Margaret, dowager queen of Scots in 1516.[20] In 1522 Henry visited Lovell at Holywell,

---

[16] Leland, *Itinerary*, v. 34; PRO, E315/393, fos. 67v–68r; Emery, *Greater Medieval Houses*, ii. 223–24.

[17] Leland,*Itinerary*, i. 27; PRO, E315/393, fo. 4r.

[18] N. Summers, 'Old Hall Farm, Kneesall', *Transactions of the Thoroton Society* 76 (1972), 17–25.

[19] PRO, SC6/Henry VII/160, mm. 1–2, 4, 6–7; SC6/Henry VII/161; Howard, *Country House*, 131–5; RCHM *Essex*, iii. 157–9; C. F. Hayward, 'Architectural Notes on Layer Marney Hall, Essex, and on the Parish Church Adjoining', *TEAS* 3 (1865), 20–8; D. Andrews et al., 'Plaster or Stone? Some Observations on Layer Marney Church and Tower', *Essex Archaeology and History* 17 (1986), 172–6.

[20] L. L. Ford, 'Conciliar Politics and Administration in the Reign of Henry VII', University of St Andrews Ph.D. Thesis (2001), 243, 245, 251, 249, 251–2, 268, 277, 279, 281; *Memorials*, 128; Condon, 'Profits of Office', 138; N. Samman, 'The Progresses of Henry VIII, 1509–1529', in D. N. J. MacCulloch (ed.), *The Reign of Henry VIII: Politics, Policy and Piety* (Basingstoke, 1995), 66–7; PRO, OBS1/1418, 1, 9, 39, 46, 51, 72; *LP* II, i. 1861; Pam, *Parish Near London*, 54–5.

Marney at Layer Marney, and Cutt at Horham, and in 1536 he joined Wyatt at Allington.[21] Henry VIII was a more alarming guest than his father. He demanded Stanwell and Westenhanger after enjoyable visits—he did at least stay in them occasionally once he owned them—and executed Hussey four years before lodging at Sleaford in 1541.[22]

INTERIORS

Such grand houses were not left empty. Lovell used wainscot, wooden panelling, for a cupboard and a hall screen with doors at Holywell and for a chapel screen at Elsings, but apparently not for lining walls.[23] Southwell, in contrast, was buying wainscot with sufficient regularity in 1511–14 that he must have been using it in the new fashion to keep rooms warm at Easterford.[24] Layer Marney and Allington also had rooms panelled in wood, and the hall at Horham Hall had wood panelling and a panelled oak screen.[25] The more traditional practice was to cover walls with hangings of various qualities. At the lower end came plain or painted cloth or canvas, above that tapestries, the value largely dependent on the quality of materials, as silk thread was more expensive than woollen and precious-metal thread more costly still.[26] Many of Lovell's servants' rooms contained some kind of hanging and the hall at Enfield and great parlour at East Harling were hanged with say cloth, but the rooms for his family and guests were decorated with tapestry, albeit some of it old or 'sore worn'. Foliage designs or 'verdures' were most common, often with wild beasts, but there was also 'imagery', and some of an improving sort: he had the Nine Worthies in the green chamber at Elsings and the four cardinal virtues on the wall of his chamber at Holywell.[27] Bray likewise had many verdures, and Southwell's accounts show his servants carrying tapestries, perhaps borrowed, to the London houses of the earls of Oxford and Shrewsbury.[28] Dudley, too, had painted cloths and other hangings in many rooms, seven pieces of embroidered imagery 'for the months of the year to set upon a cloth' and seven panes of 'coarse tapestry work', but also better-quality tapestry, counterfeit arras and rich arras, some kept in a press, some hanging. One little altar cloth of arras he hanged 'strained in a frame with a little curtain of white and black paly afore it', like a panel painting.[29]

[21] PRO, OBS1/1418, 43, 47, 53.

[22] W. Dugdale, *The Baronage of England*, 2 vols (London, 1675), ii. 307–8; PRO, OBS1/1418, 50, 56, 63, OBS1/1419, fo. 77v; *HKW*, iv. 283–4; *Chapter Acts of the Cathedral Church of St Mary of Lincoln, AD 1520–1536*, ed. R. E. G. Cole, Lincoln RS 12 (Lincoln, 1915), xxii.

[23] PRO, PROB2/199, mm. 4, 5, 8.

[24] PRO, SP1/230, fos. 109r, 115r, 121r (*LP* I, ii. 2765); Howard, *Country House*, 109–11.

[25] Hayward, 'Layer Marney', 24–5; RCHM *Essex*, iii. 159; Conway, 'Allington Castle', 355–7; Emery, *Greater Medieval Houses*, ii. 115.

[26] T. Campbell, *Henry VIII and the Art of Majesty: Tapestries at the Tudor Court* (New Haven CT and London, 2007), 92–100; S. Foister, 'Paintings and Other Works of Art in Sixteenth-Century English Inventories', *Burlington Magazine* 123 (1981), 274–5, 279.

[27] PRO, PROB2/199.

[28] PRO, E154/2/10, fo. 4; PRO, SP1/230, fo. 118r–118v (*LP* I, ii. 2765).

[29] PRO, E154/2/17.

Rich textiles were also used as hangings and coverings for beds and as cushions and carpets to place on chairs and tables. Lovell's houses were full of sparvers, testers, celures, curtains, and counterpanes, many of them in checked or other multi-coloured designs, blue and yellow, black and yellow, green and red, red and tawney, red and white, red and blue, or red and black, the best in silk fabrics, like the white and green Bruges satin hangings round the bed in the earl of Oxford's chamber at Elsings, the red sarcenet counterpane on the king's bed there and the celure and tester of sendal above it, or the counterpane of cloth of gold and black and crimson velvet on the queen's bed. No wonder he kept an embroiderer and a carpet-maker on his staff.[30] Poynings had sparvers and curtains of satin, velvet, and silk; Dudley had sparvers of cloth of gold and satin, counterpanes of verdure, a tester of embroidered baudekin, and a counterpane of tapestry with 'divers kings' arms upon it'; but visually the most interesting beds were Bray's: they included a celure and tester with red and black lions and fishes and a celure, tester, and counterpane 'with imagery of the story of Sibyl and Solomon'.[31]

Cushions, too, could be luxurious: Lovell's made of violet, tawney, or red Bruges satin, of red and black sarcenet, of verdures or other tapestry, or 'embroidered in Venice gold'; Dudley's of purple velvet or crimson damask. Carpets might come from England, Genoa, Ghent, or, most valuable, Turkey: Lovell's Turkey carpets were concentrated in high-status rooms like the green chamber, queen's privy chamber, and king's dining chamber.[32] Such fabrics might come as gifts, like the seven ells of damask cloth the town of Bruges presented to Poynings in 1492.[33] In use, many of them also carried their owner's identity in the shape of arms or badges. Dudley had two verdures with his arms and his wife's Lisle arms 'matched together', and a sumpter-cloth with the Dudley arms to cover a pack horse.[34] Lovell's falcon's wings appeared on carpets, cushions, and the borders of green say hangings, his arms on English carpets and on the twelve verdure tapestries he bequeathed to Lord Roos's younger brothers, Oliver and Richard.[35] Heraldry was also to the fore in the stained glass windows of the principal rooms, like the hall at Layer Marney with its display of Marney's arms and those of his ancestors and relations by marriage.[36] Much furniture was rather functional, trestle tables or plank tables for servants to eat, joined stools or forms, bedsteads, chests, presses, or cupboards, but some was more elegant or exotic. Dudley had a 'table of Spanish making' and several French chairs. Lovell had a number of Flanders chairs, five covered with leather, four of them red, and an admittedly decrepit-sounding 'French old chair old'.[37]

---

[30] PRO, PROB2/199; *HMC Rutland*, iv. 261.

[31] PRO, PROB11/20/21; E154/2/17; E154/2/10, fos. 7–8.

[32] PRO, PROB2/199; E154/2/17.

[33] *Inventaire des archives de la ville de Bruges*, ed. L. Gilliodts-Van Severen, 9 vols (Bruges, 1871–85), vi. 360.

[34] PRO, E154/2/17.   [35] PRO, PROB2/199, mm. 2, 3, 9; PROB11/23/27.

[36] P. Morant, *The History and Antiquities of the County of Essex*, 2 vols (East Ardsley, 1978 edn), i. 408n.

[37] PRO, PRO, E154/2/17; PROB2/199.

Chapels, too, had forms and altar boards, but they were the spaces where glass, fabrics, plate, books, and music came together in the most comprehensive way. At Elsings, where he employed three household chaplains and an organist, Lovell had two candlesticks and a crucifix with other 'divers tablets gilt', plate for the altar, a pair of small organs, six altar hangings, three corporal cases and corporal cloths, and an array of books for priests and choir: two massbooks, printed and written; two large old antiphoners written on parchment; four graduals, one on parchment; four processionals printed on paper; and a copy of the *Golden Legend*. More impressive still was his collection of vestments. He had eight surplices 'great and small', presumably for singing men and boys, ten chasubles of satin, damask, fustian, and bustian, white, red, green and blue, and two velvet copes, one crimson, one violet, each embroidered with falcon's wings.[38] The chapel at East Harling was more low-key, but did feature four 'cloths painted of damask work'.[39] In 1513 Southwell was buying expensive glass for a chapel window, while Poynings's chapel at Westenhanger had statues of St Anthony and St Christopher.[40] Even amidst the financial chaos of his last months, Guildford was concerned that the chapel at Halden should be properly equipped with his great psalter and a volume combining texts for matins and dirge with the seven penitential psalms.[41] Meanwhile, provision for more private devotion was made by the altar with its red sarcenet hangings, candlesticks, and aumbry in Lovell's chamber at Elsings, or the altar with older hangings in Oxford's closet there, or by Dudley's personal psalter.[42]

PLATE AND JEWELS

Gold and silver plate was a prime ingredient of social display, set out on cupboards as well as used for dining, and has even been called 'the essential indicator of status' in early Tudor society.[43] It was expensive, but those close to the king could build up a collection through the practice of New Year gift-giving. Dudley, for example, had a 'Rhenish cruse gilt with a cover graven with rose fleur-de-lis and portcullis', which sounds as though it came from the king.[44] Brandon regularly exchanged New Year's gifts with Henry, but no records survive of what the king gave.[45] The fuller accounts of the next reign allow us to track a hierarchy of gifts. One goldsmith's delivery in 1513 included gilt cups with covers weighing 23 oz and 22¼ oz

---

[38] *HMC Rutland*, iv. 260–1; PRO, PROB2/199, m. 4; PRO11/23/27.

[39] PRO, PROB2/199, m. 5.

[40] PRO, SP1/230, fo. 118r (*LP* I, ii. 2765); E. Hasted, *The History and Topographical Survey of the County of Kent*, 12 vols (Wakefield, 1972 edn), viii. 65.

[41] PRO, PROB11/17/28.

[42] PRO, PROB2/199, m. 3; A. B. Emden, *A Biographical Register of the University of Oxford to AD 1500*, 3 vols (Oxford, 1957–9), i. 598.

[43] P. Glanville, 'Cardinal Wolsey and the Goldsmiths', in S. Gunn and P. G. Lindley (eds), *Cardinal Wolsey: Church, State and Art* (Cambridge, 1991), 131–40.

[44] PRO, E154/2/17.   [45] PRO, E36/214, fos. 9v, 59v, 112r, 156r.

for Marney and Poynings, smaller than Archbishop Warham's, but larger than those for lesser courtiers; around the same time Wyatt got a gilt goblet worth £11 1s 3d.[46] In two years around 1520, Lovell, with a gilt cup and cover of 28½ oz one year and over 32 oz the other, was ahead of Marney and Wyatt, with similar but smaller cups, and well ahead of Hussey, who received a gilt pot and cover weighing only 11¾ oz and a laver of similar weight.[47] In 1528 Lovell and Marney were gone, and Wyatt and Hussey now got salts, but the hierarchy was preserved, Wyatt's weighing 20¼ oz and Hussey's 13¾ oz.[48] By 1532–4, Hussey had come up in the world, but Wyatt was still ahead. Over three years Wyatt got two gilt cups with covers, a gilt bowl with a cover and a gilt cruse with a cover, each year totalling between 34 and 38 oz of plate. Hussey had two gilt covered cups and a cruse, weighing between 18 and 21 oz, and Windsor two cruses and a salt, each between 15 and 21 oz.[49] By 1539, only Windsor was left, his 14¼ oz covered gilt cup one of the smallest gifts given to the barons.[50] When such plate came into use and display in the recipient's home, it marked out not just their social rank but also their proximity to the king: Hussey and Windsor were peers and Wyatt was not, but it was clear who stood higher in royal esteem.

Foreign rulers also rewarded those who visited them with plate. William Cope was given a great gilt standing cup with branches by James IV of Scots, probably when he took the last instalment of Queen Margaret's dowry north in 1505.[51] Poynings's repeated campaigns and embassies in the Netherlands brought him a rich haul of plate fashioned by the luxury goldsmiths of Bruges and Brussels. In 1515–16 alone he brought home eighteen trenchers, twelve covered goblets, six covered cups, four flagons, two pots, two ewers, and one basin, to a total value of around £300.[52] Bequests from patrons and friends, too, might top up the plate cupboard. Lady Margaret Beaufort left sumptuous items to her executors. Lovell's gold cup was engraved, perhaps like the surviving cup densely patterned with roses, portcullises, and marguerites she gave to Christ's College, Cambridge, with a blue enamelled gil-lyflower in the bottom and a pearl on the pommel; Marney's gold pot had a red rose on the cover and the crowned royal arms surrounded by the garter.[53] Sir Robert Sheffield reckoned the gold cup and cover he left Lovell was worth £40.[54] The earl of Oxford's bequests did not run to gold plate, only silver-gilt, but the 25 oz salt topped

[46] *LP* I, i. 1549, II, ii. 1463.

[47] PRO, SP1/73, fos. 70r, 71v, 80r (*LP* V, 1711); *LP* Addenda, i. 367.

[48] PRO, E101/420/4 (*LP* IV, ii. 3748).

[49] PRO, E101/420/15, mm. 2r, 4r; SP2/N, fos. 3r, 4r, 5r; SP2/P, fos. 1r, 3r (*LP* V. 686, VI. 32, VII. 10).

[50] Folger Shakespeare Library, Zd11.

[51] *Testamenta Vetusta*, ed. N. H. Nicolas, 2 vols (London, 1826), ii. 748; *Foedera, Conventiones, Literae et cujuscunque generis Acta Publica*, ed. T. Rymer, 20 vols (London, 1704–35), xiii. 119.

[52] ADN, B2144, fo. 176v; B2229, fos. 230v–231r; B2259/78376; *Inventaire-sommaire des archives départementales. Nord*, ed. C. Dehaisnes et al., 10 vols (Lille, 1877–1906), viii. 205.

[53] R. Marks and P. Williamson (eds), *Gothic: Art for England 1400–1547* (London, 2003), 250–1; C. H. Cooper, *Memoir of Margaret, Countess of Richmond and Derby* (Cambridge, 1874), 134.

[54] PRO, PROB11/19/15.

with a pearl he left to Lovell must still have been handsome.[55] Sir Henry Heydon, more modestly, left Lovell a cup and cover.[56] Alice, dowager Lady Morley, distributed jewellery rather than plate, leaving Lovell as her executor a gold St Anthony's cross with pendant beads and a gold ring with a flat diamond.[57] Jewellery, similarly, seems to have been the mainstay of Prince Henry's New Year gift-giving before he became king. In 1508 he gave Marney a ring with a little pointed diamond, and in 1509 a gold tablet depicting St John the Baptist and the Three Kings of Cologne.[58]

Such gifts, bolstered by purchases, built the very considerable stocks of plate and jewels evident in wills and inventories. Lovell left his garter collar and 'a ring with a capon's stone of a great virtue', a polished stone from the gizzard of a capon thought to have powerful medicinal properties, to the king; Wolsey got a standing cup of gold; his great-nephew Lord Roos a gold salt. Thereafter, there remained to distribute among less eminent legatees two cups with covers, one of them fully gilt, five basins and five ewers partly-gilt, a complete silver dining service, several sets of chapel plate, £200 worth of silver plate to be shared among old servants, and a cup, a goblet, or a gold ring to each of his 'good lovers and friends'.[59] Poynings's will mentioned eighteen covered bowls, six goblets, two pots, one little drinking pot, one flagon, and one salt of silver, plus two great pots and a goblet partly gilt, two gilt pots, one flat gilt cup, and one gilt salt.[60] Windsor divided among his sons a gold spoon and two dozen silver spoons, a silver-gilt cup 'called the helmet', a great chafing dish, basin, and ewer of silver, two great pots, two basins and two ewers partly gilt, three silver-gilt bowls, two silver-gilt cups with garlands around them, and four silver-gilt salts bearing the Windsor arms.[61] Brandon bequeathed plate worth £533 6s 8d.[62] Dudley, too, had impressive plate, an engraved silver-gilt standing cup partly enamelled with pictures of kings, a standing cup with the Dudley arms in the bottom, a silver-gilt goblet with fleurs-de-lis on the cover, four gilt pots with the Dudley arms, a basin and ewer partly-gilt bearing the arms of his wife Lady Lisle, and six gilt spoons with 'woodwose', wild men, on the ends.[63] Plate was also useful to the financially adventurous or embarrassed as an asset that could easily be sold or mortgaged. In 1527 Hussey borrowed £100 from Thomas Cromwell on the security of a salt, six bowls, and two flagons.[64] Glass was an attractive alternative to plate for drinking vessels. Lovell had four glasses and two standing cups of 'beryl', high-quality glass, and Dudley had various 'glasses and bottles of beyond sea making', perhaps Venetian glassware.[65]

---

[55] 'The Last Testament and Inventory of John de Veer, thirteenth earl of Oxford', ed. W. H. StJ. Hope, *Archaeologia* 66 (1915), 313.

[56] *The Visitation of Norfolk in the Year 1563*, ed. G. H. Dashwood and E. Bulwer Lytton, 2 vols (Norwich, 1878–95), ii. 221.

[57] PRO, PROB11/19/15.

[58] *The Antient Kalendars and Inventories of the Treasury of His Majesty's Exchequer*, ed. F. Palgrave, 3 vols (London, 1836), iii. 397–8.

[59] PRO, PROB11/23/27; C. J. Duffin, 'Alectorius: The Cock's Stone', *Folklore* 118 (2007), 325–41.

[60] PRO, PROB11/20/21. [61] PRO, PROB11/29/23. [62] PRO, PROB11/16/29.

[63] PRO, E154/2/17. [64] PRO, SP1/42, fos. 184–6 (*LP* IV, ii. 3250).

[65] PRO, PROB2/199, m. 6; E154/2/17.

CLOTHES AND HORSES

Clothes were a more everyday index of status than plate, and one sharply defined by the stipulations of the sumptuary statutes that certain fabrics were appropriate only for persons of high rank.[66] Expensive imported silk cloths were the sign of wealth and standing, and gowns made of them were lined with imported furs such as martens, or cheaper fur such as lamb. Lovell had eight velvet gowns and six of cloth, some of the latter lined with satin or sarcenet, three velvet jackets, two satin doublets, and a satin coat. Bray, too, had equal numbers of gowns made of woollen cloth and made of velvet, satin, and damask; he had a taste for tinsel satin, incorporating precious metal threads, in which he had a gown and a doublet. When he did wear cloth, much of it was French, and his gowns, too, were often lined with satin or velvet or furred with marten. Dudley barely bothered with woollen cloth at all, having ten satin and velvet doublets and jackets and nine velvet, satin, and damask gowns. He did own thirteen cloth gowns, but eight of those, five of them explicitly 'old', were relegated to the little wardrobe alongside offcuts of cloth.

Black seems to have been the colour of choice for Lovell in particular. All but two of his gowns, jackets, doublets, and coats were black, and to top off his outfits he had two furred black velvet tippets and five old black hats, though he must have stood out on cold days in his scarlet cloak. Bray was a little more adventurous, with nine black gowns, four tawny, and three crimson, three tawny jackets (to one black), a crimson doublet, and one crimson riding gown (to three black). Fourteen of Dudley's seventeen gowns of identifiable colour were black, but he had two in crimson and one in russet, and his doublets included green, crimson, and purple. In 1505–6 his eye for colour led him to buy up some spare carnation coloured satin from the king's great wardrobe.[67] Wyatt wore a black fur-lined doublet and gown and a close-fitting black hat to be painted by Holbein. Black was a fashionable colour and was the most common shade for the valuable garments bequeathed in wills, but it also had overtones of seriousness, much worn by lawyers and clergy; just right for a Lovell, stately without frivolity. Crimson was expensive but quite widely used. Dudley's purple was the controversial choice, a colour normally reserved for royalty, which can have done nothing for his reputation for overreaching himself.[68] Then again Brandon had not only a gown of russet tinsel satin furred with genet, but also two gowns of cloth of gold, which should have been restricted to use by peers. Presumably, he was expected to look good when riding with the king on court occasions, like Henry VIII's coronation procession when he wore cloth of tissue—like cloth of gold, but with more gold—embroidered with gold roses.[69]

Black gowns set off well the heavy gold chains fashionable at court. At Arthur's wedding, Brandon's and Guildford's particularly struck observers, and at Henry

---

[66] M. Hayward, *Rich Apparel: Clothing and the Law in Henry VIII's England* (Farnham, 2009).

[67] PRO, E101/416/3, fo. 36v.

[68] PRO, PROB2/199, m. 8; E154/2/10, fos. 1–2; E154/2/17; Hayward, *Rich Apparel*, 97–101, 344–5.

[69] PRO, PROB11/16/29; Hall, *Chronicle*, 508; Hayward, *Rich Apparel*, 89, 345–6.

VIII's coronation Brandon's was once again 'great and massy'.[70] Wyatt's sits heavily on his shoulders in his Holbein portrait as he grips the cross suspended from it, late in life.[71] Windsor left his son a chain much like Wyatt's, bearing a cross with diamonds and pearls.[72] The style was sufficiently conspicuous for Erasmus to satirize it in his *Praise of Folly* of 1515: courtiers' self-esteem, he argued, 'rests on the weight of the chain their necks have to carry, as if they have to show off their physical strength as well as their riches'.[73] The new men aimed to cut a dash on the battlefield, too. Bray's 'complete harness for his own body' had 'the headpiece garnished with silver and gilt' and he also possessed 'a coat set with plate covered with cloth of gold and black velvet' and a 'bonnet of black velvet lined with plate'.[74] Dudley had 'ii pair of briganders for himself, one of black velvet with gilt nail and gilt buckle, the other of crimson velvet set with rose nail and crowns gilt about it'. Even his charger would have been well protected with a horse-armour of 'beyond sea making'.[75]

Horses were another valuable item for investment, use, and display, especially for the more militarily or courtly inclined. Philip the Fair gave Poynings a valuable horse in 1500, in 1516 the earl of Northumberland gave him another, and his building works at Westenhanger included a large stable block.[76] Brandon must have had many horses and much horse furniture, for he ordered all his great horses and geldings to be distributed among his servants with a saddle, bridle, and harness for each.[77] At the end of his life Lovell rode a bay gelding, or even a mule like a cleric, but the animals were still of some quality: his gelding was worth £3, whereas the other ten horses for riding, seven cart horses, and a pack horse in his stables were worth £1 each at most.[78] Keeping them in tack ran up a bill of over £5 a year with his saddler, William Baynebryg of Lombard Street, and straw for their stables cost nearly £3. He had six horse-keepers and an ostler to look after them, and shoeing them kept the Enfield blacksmith Andrew Wistow busy: in 1523 he put 1,036 new horseshoes and 709 re-used ones on Lovell's horses, while running repairs at London by William Garnet of Shoreditch added another 52 and 28 of each type. Baldwin Shirley, one of his gentleman servants, took overall responsibility for the stables, taking up 'young colts to be broken' and seeing some horses sent out to farriers 'for to be holpen of diverse diseases and mallenders' with 'leechcraft'.[79]

[70] *The Great Chronicle of London*, ed. A. H. Thomas and I. D. Thornley (London, 1938), 311; *Receyt*, 65; E. Hall, *Hall's Chronicle*, ed. H. Ellis (London, 1809), 508.
[71] S. Foister, *Holbein and England* (New Haven CT and London, 2004), 240.
[72] PRO, PROB11/29/23.
[73] D. Erasmus, *Praise of Folly and Letter to Martin Dorp, 1515* (London, 1971 edn), 176.
[74] PRO, E154/2/10, fo. 6.   [75] PRO, E154/2/17.
[76] J. Molinet, *Chroniques de Jean Molinet*, ed. G. Doutrepont and O. Jodogne, 3 vols (Brussels, 1935–7), ii. 475; *LP* IV, ii. 3380 (2, ii); Martin and Martin, 'Westenhanger Castle', 232–3.
[77] PRO, PROB11/16/29.   [78] PRO, PROB2/199, m. 7.
[79] Belvoir Castle, MS a/c no. 4 (*HMC Rutland*, iv. 261–2).

FOOD AND DRINK

Hospitality built power and demanded a well-supplied household. Gifts in kind helped the new men to keep their standards up. The London vintners' company, for example, litigating in the Star Chamber in winter 1516–17, produced a hogshead of wine each, some 200 litres, for Windsor and Cutt and an extra barrel of muscadel for Windsor.[80] The great gifts with which Poynings returned from the campaign of 1511 included wine from the town of 's Hertogenbosch.[81] Venison was another characteristic gift from aristocrats with parks. Thomas, earl of Ormond ordered the dispatch of a buck from his park at Rochford to his 'singular good friend' Thomas Lucas in May 1503.[82] It could backfire. One doe sent by Bergavenny to Lovell was so scrawny that Lovell's cook thought the lord 'mocked his master to send so lean a thing to his house'.[83] The hind baked in a pasty sent to Lovell by the earl of Northumberland in 1522–3 seems to have gone down better, in a year when Northumberland, eager to please, also sent him a bay ambling nag and twelve cygnets.[84] Lesser gentlemen sent lesser foodstuffs, swans, geese, pheasants, cranes, capons, goats, pigs, rabbits, fish, and fruit to Hussey in 1534–5, for example.[85] Seagulls might be sent by those with coastal estates: Sir Robert Constable sent Hussey two dozen in 1535–6.[86] More varied but just as tasty, as we have seen, were the gifts that flowed into Westenhanger from the ports under Poynings's protection.

Courtiers could buy up surplus stocks of royal wine for their own use and wine flowed freely in their homes. In 1522–3 Lovell had at least five tuns—over a thousand gallons—of Gascon wine, three vats of Rhine wine, and a butt—more than a hundred gallons—of malmsey.[87] Dudley had four hogsheads of red and two of claret, more than three hundred gallons in total, stored at his London home when he fell.[88] Southwell, as chief butler, was even better placed and in seven months in 1511 alone, at a cost of £21 17s 11d, he laid in for general drinking around 950 gallons of white, red, and claret, some 50 gallons of Rhine wine for variety, and for the sweeter palate 19½ gallons of malmsey, 5 gallons of rumney, and 39 gallons of sack.[89] When he, in turn, was chief butler, Hussey shipped in wine for his house at Sleaford through Boston, six tuns in 1533–4.[90] For ale and beer, in contrast, home brewing seems to have outweighed purchases. Lovell bought ale in some quantity from brewers in Enfield and Cheshunt, over 2,500 gallons for £11 10s 10d in 1522–3.[91] But far more, 10,000 gallons at least, must have been produced by the brewer, under-brewer, and expert beer brewer he employed, as they worked with his 'great mashing tun' and

[80] BL, MS Egerton 1143, fos. 54v, 55r.
[81] *Inventaris der archieven van de stad 's Hertogenbosch … Stads Rekeningen van het jaar 1399–1800*, ed. R. A. Van Zuijlen, 3 vols ('s Hertogenbosch, 1863–70), i. 216.
[82] PRO, SC1/52/71.   [83] PRO, SP1/237 fo. 66 (*LP* Addenda, i. 745).
[84] *HMC Rutland*, iv. 265.   [85] PRO, E36/95, fos. 52v–53v.
[86] PRO, E36/95, fo. 99v.
[87] *LP* IV, i. 966; Belvoir Castle, MS a/c no. 4 (*HMC Rutland*, iv. 262).
[88] PRO, E154/2/17.   [89] PRO, SP1/230, fos. 109r–110r (*LP* I, ii. 2765).
[90] PRO, E36/95, fo. 26v.   [91] Belvoir Castle, MS a/c no. 4.

'great brewing lead' on the 200 quarters of malt and over 2,800 lb of hops he bought that year. The figures sound large, but they are credible when we remember that Lovell was catering for more than eighty people, at a rate of several pints a day because ale was so much healthier than water.[92] Southwell bought imported beer when he wanted a top quality beverage, but in 1512 he spent £6 12s 1d on a copper brewing vessel weighing some 317 lb, and like Lovell he bought large quantities of hops so his servants could brew not just ale, but hopped beer.[93]

Outlying estates generated supplies for the household. In 1520–1 Wyatt had twenty ewes and two cows driven to Allington, perhaps to maintain stock there, or perhaps for slaughter.[94] Hussey had sheep and oxen driven south from his Lincolnshire estates to provision his household when he was staying in London, just as at Christmas 1534 he had 102 sheep, sixteen cattle, and six pigs brought in and butchered at Sleaford.[95] In 1522–3 Lovell's bailiff at Holt in Norfolk was ordered to buy up 500 ling at Cley next the Sea and John Dedyk, the farmer at Beachamwell, told to buy 200 fat muttons and send them to Enfield, where they added to the 800 wethers bred on the Norfolk estates and driven south by Lovell's shepherd, Thomas Parre. More exotic meats than mutton also came from Lovell's lands. Fourteen swans, fattened up on oats at East Harling by Adam Flower the keeper of the swans there, were sent the 66 miles to Enfield by cart to grace Sir Thomas's table, together with six cygnets from Beachamwell and nine cranes from the Norfolk marshes.[96] Windsor, similarly, kept swans and peacocks at Bentworth Hall in Hampshire and Baylham in Suffolk and had them sent to his house at Stanwell.[97] Hussey's stewardship of Epworth, in the marshy Isle of Axholme, came with a lease of the mark of swans there.[98] More prosaically, Lovell's lands also provided wood and charcoal for fuel and hay for livestock, just as Hussey had a home farm at Sleaford producing hay, barley, and peas, or Poynings had hay sent the 20 miles or so from his manor of Fawkham to his house in Southwark.[99] Around his house at Elsings, meanwhile, Lovell kept the livestock for immediate needs: fifteen milking cows, a few pigs and goats, capons and geese, six pairs of breeding swans, and three pairs of breeding rabbits, like the ones in Hussey's warren at Sleaford.[100] Most likely he had a dovecote, too, like Hussey's, cleaned out for 6d in January 1535.[101]

Most food was not home-grown, but bought from neighbouring farmers or on the open market. Wheat, used to make the finest bread, was one of Lovell's

[92] PRO, PROB2/199, m. 7; Belvoir Castle, MS a/c no. 4; C. Dyer, *Standards of Living in the Later Middle Ages: Social Change in England c.1200–1520* (Cambridge, 1989), 58, 64, 153.

[93] PRO, SP1/230, fos. 111v, 113r (*LP* I, ii. 2765).

[94] PRO, SC6/Henry VIII/1684, m. 3r.   [95] PRO, E36/95, fos. 59r–59v, 99v.

[96] Belvoir Castle, MS a/c no. 4; BL, Addl. MS 12463, fos. 54v, 65v–67r; C. M. Woolgar, *The Great Household in Late Medieval England* (New Haven CT and London, 1999), 114, 133–5.

[97] Hampshire RO, 25M75/M2, mm. 16–18 and unnumbered; SROI, HB8/1/254, m. 3d.

[98] PRO, E326/12389.

[99] Belvoir Castle, MS a/c no. 4; BL, Addl. MS 12463, fo. 39v (*LP* IV, i. 367); PRO, E36/95, fos 7r, 12v, 22r, 79v–80r, 99v, 119r; SC6/Henry VIII/1937; Alnwick Castle, Syon MS X.II.I, box 16b.

[100] PRO, PROB2/199, m. 7; E315/393, fo. 4v.

[101] PRO, E315/393, fo. 4v; E36/95, fo. 55r.

largest expenses. In 1522–3 he bought 307 quarters of it at a cost of £112 2s 8d. Barley he bought only to feed his poultry, oats presumably to feed horses. On beef, the meaty mainstay of aristocratic diets, he spent a fraction more than on wheat, £113 9s 10d for eighty-six oxen, eight steers, and twelve cows; thirty-one of the oxen were bought at Coventry fair and driven south to Enfield, while twelve others were 'large oxen fat', stall-fed ready for the end of Lent. Goats were bought from a Welsh drover, but there were only twenty of them. Fish, in contrast, was the third great area of food purchase. William Holleston, the king's fishmonger, supplied £92 4s 8d worth of salt fish: 700 ling, 600 cod, ten barrels of salmon the largest items; 300 stockfish, thirteen cades of red herrings, thirteen barrels of white herrings, four cades of sprats the more basic fare; half a barrel of sturgeon and one barrel of eels the specialities. To it he added at least £26 13s 4d worth of fresh fish and half a barrel of salmon from another supplier. Then came the specialist Richard Coward of Cambridge, pikemonger, supplier of the highest-status fresh fish. For £20 13s 8d, including carriage, he delivered sixty small pikes, 120 large pikes and, a little more expensive still, sixty 'large pikes and fat'. Salt and sugar were the last bulk buys, forty bushels of the first and seventy-nine loaves, totalling 649 lb, of the second. Further fresh food purchases, finally, must have been wrapped up in the £122 7s 4d spent on general costs and diets of the household by the clerk of the kitchen, about a third of it in the run-up to Christmas.[102]

Southwell's household was much smaller, costing perhaps a quarter as much as Lovell's, but his accounts survive in more detail and show better the variety of the food he bought. The selection of fish was similar: salmon, sturgeon, herring, stockfish, sprats, pike, lampreys, flounders, halibut, and haddock. Fish, meat, and baked goods were flavoured and coloured with a range of spices, another marker of status: cinnamon, cloves, dragon's blood, galingale, ginger, grains of paradise, mace, nutmeg, pepper, saffron, turnsole. Mediterranean products added further allure: olives, oranges, capers, rice. But what really sticks out is the sweet tooth. There were pounds and pounds of sugar, raisins, currants, dates, prunes, figs, almonds, and liquorice, and various sugary sweetmeats, biscuits, comfits, caraways, succades, and possets. All that auditing must have driven him to suck on something sweet.[103] Wyatt's household accounts do not survive, but his estate accounts show the range of wildfowl available to him in Kent. In 1520–1 he bought not only wheat and cheese, capons, and hens, but also teals, stints, and heron.[104] The fare bought for Hussey's household, similarly, drew on the Lincolnshire marshlands for curlews, plovers, lapwings, sandpipers, mallards, teals, bitterns, and cranes, but added in sugar, figs, prunes, almonds, currants, oranges, comfits, and a range of fish.[105]

Lovell's houses and staff were well designed to collect, store, prepare, and serve all this food. Under the steward of the household and clerk of the kitchen, two of

[102] Belvoir Castle, MS a/c no. 4; Dyer, *Standards of Living*, 60, 62.
[103] PRO, SP1/230, fos. 109–25 (*LP* I, ii. 2765); Dyer, *Standards of Living*, 62–3.
[104] PRO, SC6/Henry VIII/1684, m. 3r.   [105] PRO, E36/95, fos. 35v, 57r–61r.

his best-paid servants, operated three cooks, one of them foreign by the sound of
his name, a caterer to buy fresh supplies, yeomen of the buttery, cellar, and larder,
a keeper of the granary, three bakers, and a maker of wafers. At the bottom of the
hierarchy came John, who turned the spits in the kitchen for 13s 4d a year. The
kitchens at Enfield were full of pots, pans, and cauldrons, frying pans, dripping
pans, colanders, ladles, knives, pestles, mortars, baskets, and tubs, while the bake-
house had a kneading trough and a moulding board. A cooper provided for storage,
a miller for flour, a warrener, shepherd, keeper of the dairy grounds, slaughterman,
and female keepers of the dairy and poultry, for livestock. A widow, Agnes Petche,
specialized in the care of wine, just as Anne Fostalf exercised a responsible but less
well-defined role in Marney's household, perhaps close to his wife: the widow of
one of his tenants left Fostalf 'a fine kercher that was Mistress Marney's'.[106] Even
the washing-up had to be done on a large scale, and Lovell's scullery was equipped
with a four-gallon brass pan set in a furnace where John Petwyn his scullion could
really get things clean. For feeding his servants and lowlier guests, Lovell had a
good stock of leather pots and pewter tableware: five garnishes in total, probably
five dozen plates, dishes and saucers, topped up with a fresh garnish of pewter ware
from the king's pewterer in 1522–3 for £1 9s 1d.[107] Dudley's household was
smaller, but he had pewter for two or three dozen and a good stock of linen.[108]
Extra tableware could always be hired in for big occasions, as Hussey did for a
wedding and for Christmas 1534.[109] For the final touch in dining, tables and cup-
boards were covered with table cloths, for which Lovell bought over 300 feet of
linen in 1522–3.[110]

ENTERTAINMENT

Entertainment was also part of hospitality. Hunting was the supreme pastime for
the elite, and parks with hunting and fishing rights, like that of 430 acres devel-
oped by Empson at Easton Neston, were the places to pursue it.[111] Hussey's park
at Castle Bytham had 120 deer and that at Kneesall 60, Wyatt had a charter of free
warren, with exclusive rights to hunt pheasants, partridges, hares, and rabbits, for
Allington and his surrounding manors, and Lovell had a huntsman and two fal-
coners to provide his visitors with field sports.[112] For indoor entertainment, mean-
while, Dudley had a 'closh board' covered with green cloth, for playing a kind of

---

[106] PRO, SC6/Henry VII/160, mm. 2, 4–6, 9; ERO, D/ACR2, fos 119v–120r.
[107] PROB2/199, mm. 4, 5, 7; Belvoir Castle, MS a/c no. 4.
[108] PRO, E154/2/17.   [109] PRO, E36/95, fos. 50r, 59v.
[110] Belvoir Castle, MS a/c no. 4.   [111] Northamptonshire RO, MTD/U/35/5.
[112] PRO, E315/393, fos. 59v, 83v; *LP* II, ii. 4391; R. B. Manning, *Hunters and Poachers: A Cultural
and Social History of Unlawful Hunting in England 1485–1640* (Oxford, 1993), 80; *HMC Rutland*,
iv. 261.

table-top skittles or croquet.[113] Lovell's goods included 'certain divers playing coats', presumably for household drama, and Hussey bought paper gowns, a satin kirtle, straw hats, cotton caps, and 'hoary beards' for 'players' gear' in 1534–5.[114] Though the great patrons of travelling players and other entertainers in Henry VII's time, as later, were the king, queen, princes, and great lords, the new men played their part. Hobart's minstrel visited Thetford Priory in 1507–8 and Belknap's four players were in Worcester in 1519.[115] Poynings's minstrel toured the Cinque Ports from at least 1502 and entertained at Battle Abbey in 1521, while his bearward visited Rye in 1502–6.[116] When there were jousts at court before the French, Spanish, and Flemish ambassadors in March 1508, Brandon's harper sang elegantly in praise of the jousters' exploits, while a month earlier two boys of Brandon's had played to entertain the duke of Buckingham.[117] The Marney household was well equipped for music, with a great pair and two little pairs of virginals, a great lute, and a portable organ in the great chamber at Layer Marney.[118] Visiting players and the patronage of local festivities added to household jollity, nine troupes performing in Hussey's household over the twelve days of Christmas 1534 after a warm-up visit by the St Nicholas clerks of Old and New Sleaford, a boy bishop and his retinue.[119]

Book-reading might seem a more private activity, but books were lent, shared, and given as gifts and the new men had them in quantity and variety. Lovell had forty-three large and small French printed books, which may well have been law reports rather than light reading, but his 'large boke written in parchment in French well bound with boards' valued at £4, twice the price of the other forty-three put together, must have been very special, perhaps an illustrated history or romance. This may have been the illuminated French book he paid 3s 4d to have rebound in 1522–3, when he also spent 4s 8d on two leather coffers with locks to keep books in.[120] His taste apparently ran to classic Middle English literature, too, with an early-fifteenth-century manuscript of *Piers Plowman*.[121] Dudley, ever the lawyer, had a manuscript volume of statutes, but also other books including 'a little book in French printed'.[122] Sutton followed Henry VII's taste for hand-illuminated printed books with the missal he gave to Brasenose College.[123] Books played an important role in Windsor's family circle. His sister Margaret, prioress of Syon, had printed

[113] PRO, E154/2/17.   [114] PRO, PROB2/199, m. 4; E36/95, fo. 55r–55v.

[115] *Records of Plays and Players in Norfolk and Suffolk, 1330–1642*, ed. D. Galloway and J. Wasson, Malone Society Collections 11 (Oxford, 1981), 218; *REED Herefordshire and Worcestershire*, ed. D. N. Klausner (Toronto, 1990), 460.

[116] *Records of Plays and Players in Kent 1450–1642*, ed. G. E. Dawson, Malone Society Collections 7 (Oxford, 1965), 176; HL, MS BA278; ESRO, Rye 60/4, fos. 120r, 140v, 182v.

[117] *Memorials*, 112; *LP* III. 1285 (1).

[118] 'Ancient Wills', ed. H. W. King, *TEAS* 4 (1869), 160.

[119] PRO, E36/95, fos. 51r, 53r–53v.

[120] PRO, PROB2/199, mm. 5, 9; *HMC Rutland*, iv. 264.

[121] *Western Illuminated Manuscripts: A Catalogue of the Collection in Cambridge University Library*, ed. P. Binski and P. Zutshi (Cambridge, 2011), 183.

[122] PRO, E154/2/17.   [123] E. Auerbach, *Tudor Artists* (London, 1954), 29.

editions of Boccaccio on the fall of great men in French and a mid-fifteenth-century pious treatise in English, but her most interesting volume was a manuscript psalter including the Syon sisters' liturgy and decorated with her brother's arms and a request to pray for him.[124] His wife Lady Elizabeth owned a manuscript of Lydgate's poems and a mid-fifteenth-century book of hours decorated with twenty-nine large illuminated miniatures, tantalizingly inscribed with a poem sending it as a New Year gift to a 'Mistress Anne' and signed 'A.W.'; the hand could be Windsor's, but who the recipient was and why the signature includes the Percy motto 'En dieu esperaunce' is hard to guess, unless it testifies obliquely to the doomed courtship of Henry Percy and Anne Boleyn.[125]

Marney was the patron of William Walter, an author who described himself as his servant in the three books he published, all printed by Wynkyn de Worde. Two were verse translations, made from Latin intermediaries, of stories from Boccaccio's *Decameron*. The third was a poem of his own, *The Spectacle of Lovers*, in which he is at pains to talk some sense about the fickleness of the fair sex into a young man whom he encounters expanding at tiresome length on the theme

> … alas for sorrow I shall die
> Venus' dart hath wounded me so cruelly.[126]

Sadly, what role Walter played in Marney's service is otherwise undocumented, but one might imagine a place for him in household revels at Layer Marney. Wyatt of course had a poet for a son. His thoughts on the subject are not recorded, though we do know he thought Thomas's life was in need of rather more self-discipline.[127]

The gifts the new men gave were also an opportunity to display wealth and taste. The New Year presents they gave the king were, disappointingly, often merely of cash, and, at £6 13s 4d or £13 6s 8d, roughly equal to the value of the plate he gave them, albeit presented in a red or black purse and made up of gold coins rather than everyday silver. Windsor, as we might expect from his role at the great wardrobe, was more imaginative, producing a tablet of gold in 1532 and again in 1534, one with a small chain and the other weighing $1\frac{7}{8}$ oz.[128] Presumably they had some kind of engraved or embossed decoration on them, like that on surviving panels from girdle book covers or the pictures of saints on the tablets given to

---

[124] S. Powell, 'Margaret Pole and Syon Abbey', *HR* 79 (2005), 566–7.

[125] C. M. Meale and J. Boffey, 'Gentlewomen's Reading', in L. Hellinga and J. B. Trapp (eds), *The Cambridge History of the Book in Britain, volume iii 1400–1557* (Cambridge, 1999), 527–9; HL, MS HM 1087; *Guide to Medieval and Renaissance Manuscripts in the Huntington Library*, ed. C. W. Dutschke et al., 2 vols (San Marino, CA, 1989), ii. 393–6.

[126] A. S. G. Edwards, 'Walter, William', *ODNB*; *Early English versions of the tales of Guiscardo and Ghismonda and Titus and Gisippus from 'The Decameron'*, ed. H. G. Wright, EETS o.s. 205 (London, 1937); William Walter, *The spectacle of louers: here after foloweth a lytell contrauers dyalogue bytwene loue and councell, with many goodly argumentes of good women and bad, very compendyous to all estates, newly compyled by wyllyam walter seruaunt vnto syr Henry Marnaye knyght Chauncelour of the Duchye of Lancastre* (London, 1533), A2r.

[127] S. Brigden, *Thomas Wyatt; The Heart's Forest* (London, 2012), 281, 290–1.

[128] PRO, E101/420/15, mm. 3v, 5v; E101/421/13, mm. 2r, 4r (*LP* V. 686, VII. 9); *Calendar of the Manuscripts of the Marquis of Bath*, 5 vols, HMC 58 (London, 1904–80), ii. 7.

Prince Henry in the last years of his father's reign.[129] Rings were also an option, Dudley giving the prince a gold ring, enamelled in red and black, with a pointed diamond.[130] So were exotic coins: Southwell gave the courtier John Sharp a 'portygyse', probably a gold Portuguese coin, as a New Year gift in 1513 at a cost of £2 5s.[131] For less elevated recipients simpler gifts were in order, like the knives Wyatt bought to give away in 1520–1.[132]

Food and drink were also part of the currency of gift exchange. Southwell bought wine to send to his colleagues, most generously to Wyatt who got a hogshead most years, but also to Englefield, the judges Fyneux and Rede, the dean of Windsor, Nicholas West, Wolsey, and his East Anglian neighbours John Daniel, Sir Robert Drury, Sir William Waldegrave, and the abbot of Bury.[133] Windsor sent swans to his sister Alice and her husband George Puttenham and other friends.[134] In 1507 alone Marney sent eight pheasants, four young herons, and two bucks from his park at Gibcracks to the earl of Oxford.[135] Horses, too, might be given as gifts, as Hussey gave Lord Lisle a gelding in 1534.[136]

DEATH AND COMMEMORATION

Medical care was also an item of luxury consumption. Especially as they aged, the new men consulted the best physicians they could find. Thomas Linacre, translator of Galen, and Dr Robert Yaxley attended Bray and Brandon on their deathbeds; in 1518 both would be founding fellows of the Royal College of Physicians.[137] When Lovell fell fatally ill, one of his servants rode to Cambridge to fetch Dr William Butts, later one of Henry VIII's leading doctors.[138] Expert midwifery was just as important, and Lady Hussey had a special midwife rushed from London to Hecklington in August 1530.[139] Medical supplies were regularly needed, and in 1535 Hussey was buying in pints of borage and bugloss and three urinals.[140]

Careful preparations were made for burial and remembrance. Cope built himself a black marble tomb at Banbury which Leland thought the only 'notable tomb' in the church there.[141] Lovell made his white alabaster tomb in a chapel he had built on the south side of the choir at Holywell Priory, the lead roof of which was

[129] D. R. Starkey (ed.), *Henry VIII: A European Court in England* (London, 1991), 114–15; *Antient Kalendars*, iii. 394, 396–7.
[130] *Antient Kalendars*, iii. 398.   [131] PRO, SP1/230, fo. 112v (*LP* I, ii. 2765).
[132] PRO, SC6/Henry VIII/1684, m. 3r.
[133] PRO, SP1/230, fos. 109v, 114r–115r, 118v, 120v, 121r–122r (*LP* I, ii. 2765).
[134] Hampshire RO, 25M75/M2, m. 18 and following unnumbered membranes.
[135] Longleat House, Misc. Vol. 11, fos. 9v, 33r, 40v, 46r.   [136] *LP* VII. 652, 1665.
[137] Condon, 'Profits of Office', 159; PRO, PROB11/16/29; Emden, *Oxford to 1500*, ii. 1157–9; A. B. Emden, *A Biographical Register of the University of Cambridge to AD 1500* (Cambridge, 1963), 664–5.
[138] *LP* IV, i. 366; C. T. Martin, rev. R. E. Davies, 'Butts, Sir William', *ODNB*.
[139] PRO, C1/624/44.   [140] PRO, E36/95, fo. 56v.   [141] Leland, *Itinerary*, ii. 39.

being put on in 1522–3.[142] Windsor asked for a stone tomb with appropriate
arms, images, and inscriptions in Holy Trinity Church, Hounslow, the church of
the dissolved Trinitarian Friary where he had already buried his wife and his son
George. Tombs for him and George were in place by 1571, and although a plaque
with his arms was lost when the church burned down in 1943, a pair of figures
from a wall monument, perhaps of Andrew and his wife, perhaps of George and
his, survive today.[143] Hussey requested burial at Sempringham Priory, where he
had buried his father and paid regularly for his obits.[144] Marney wished to be bur-
ied at Layer Marney among his ancestors, but was still building his chapel there
when he made his will. The tomb, effigy, and windows he ended up with must have
been the product of his son's executors' choices rather than his own, for his son's
will spoke of his father's tomb as not yet made and the heraldry of the glass post-
dates 1524. But what resulted was an impressive mausoleum, arranged more like a
saint's shrine than a conventional burial chapel, with effigies in black Cornish
Catacleuse stone and canopies of high-quality terracotta.[145] Apart from those exe-
cuted for treason, Brandon's monument was probably the plainest. Though he had
buried his first wife in the priory of St Mary Overies in Southwark, he requested
interment under a plain stone in the London Dominican house.[146]

Funerals provided striking opportunities to proclaim the deceased's honour,
prowess, piety, and connections. Marney's will set out an elaborate scheme for his
funeral, much concerned as a newly created peer that everything be done accord-
ing to his degree. His coffin was to be escorted out of London by the four orders
of friars, rest overnight at a series of churches on the way to Layer Marney and be
greeted with their crosses in procession by other parishes along the way. At his
burying twenty-four poor men gowned in black were to hold torches while thirty
priests said mass for his soul and 'some Doctor or cunning man make a sermon'.
At least 2,400 and perhaps 4,800 paupers were to share in a charitable dole.[147] The
instructions were thoroughly carried out. Marney died in his London house
between 11 and 12 at night on Sunday 24 May 1523. Friars watched around his
embalmed and coffined corpse and said mass every day for a week, his house
hanged with black cloth and escutcheons of his arms. Then the procession set out
for Layer Marney, the journey taking four days by way of Walbrook, Cornhill,
Whitechapel, Brentwood, and Chelmsford. The bishop of St Asaph's, abbots of St

[142] PRO, PROB11/23/27; *HMC Rutland*, iv. 265; W. Robinson, *The History and Antiquities of Enfield, in the County of Middlesex*, 2 vols (London, 1823), i. 136.
[143] PRO, PROB11/29/23; *An Inventory of the Historical Monuments in Middlesex*, RCHM (London, 1937), 74; *The Victoria History of the County of Middlesex*, ed. W. Page et al., 13 vols (London, 1911–), iii. 127–8.
[144] PRO, SP1/122, fo. 159r (*LP* XII, ii. 187(3)); PRO, E36/95, fos. 29r, 99r.
[145] 'Ancient Wills', 155; F. C. Eeles, 'The Black Effigies at Layer Marney Re-examined', *TEAS* n.s. 22 (1936–40), 272–5; RCHM *Essex*, iii. 156–7; A. P. Baggs, 'Sixteenth Century Terracotta Tombs in East Anglia', *Archaeological Journal*, 125 (1968), 296–301.
[146] PRO, PROB11/16/29; J. Stow, *A Survey of London*, ed. C. L. Kingsford, 2nd edn, 2 vols (Oxford, 1971), ii. 58.
[147] 'Ancient Wills', 149.

Osith's and Coggeshall, and priors of St Botolph Colchester and the Chelmsford Blackfriars played their parts, and two kings of arms, a herald, and a pursuivant saw that everything went to plan. His son John followed the coffin as chief mourner, accompanied by his sons-in-law Edmund Bedingfield and Thomas Bonham, while a third son-in-law, William Latham, carried a banner. Four Essex and Suffolk knights associated with him as feoffees and sureties acted as mourners, and lesser local gentlemen were banner-bearers.[148]

The culminating mass on the feast of Corpus Christi tied his commemoration to the rhythms of the sacred year and the saints represented on the processional banners were noteworthy, too, not just the Trinity and Our Lady, but St George for his knighthood of the garter and King Henry VI for both his name and his loyalty to the Lancastrian cause. The funeral sermon, by Dr John Watson, theologian, master of Christ's College, Cambridge, and friend of Erasmus, took the theme 'Blessed are the dead who die in the Lord'.[149] Marney's heraldry was everywhere, on banners, bannerols, and pennons, on candlesticks, on escutcheons handed out to every church on the route, on the six black-trapped horses that drew the chariot bearing the coffin, showing the distinction of his ancestry and the status of his wives. In Layer Marney church his entire genealogy was laid out heraldically on a valance, or hanging drape, eleven yards long, which also bore his crest and his motto.[150] The mass of black was relieved by a pall of cloth of gold draped over the coffin, on which rested his sword, shield, and coat of arms, which were presented by the mourners at the final requiem mass together with his helm, crest, and banner. On the journey, through half of the city of London and most of the breadth of Essex, the sides of the wagon were kept open so that people could see 'the representation of the body', presumably an effigy like those used for kings and queens, and the cloth of gold pall.[151] To make sure no-one missed his passing, great torches were carried by poor men alongside the cortege in built-up areas, twenty-four in London and at Layer Marney and twelve in other towns. No expense was spared. The painters' bill alone came to more than £28, the heralds were given £10 in gold in addition to their costs and clothing, and their account noted appreciatively the inns at which they had been put up en route, the Hart at Brentwood and the Bell at Chelmsford.[152]

No wonder it was Marney's son to whom Lovell's executors turned twelve months later for the details of his father's funeral as a model for Lovell's own. Geographically, Lovell's funeral was the opposite of Marney's, proceeding from Enfield towards London via Tottenham, Edmonton, Hackney, and Shoreditch for his burial at Holywell. In other respects, it was the same, but bigger, the costs running to some £1,250. He made provision for £200, ten times as much as

---

[148] CA, MS I 7, fos. 50r–52v.   [149] Emden, *Cambridge*, 622–3.

[150] 'Ancient Wills', 150; BL, Addl. MS 45131, fo. 93v.

[151] A. P. Harvey and R. Mortimer (eds), *The Funeral Effigies of Westminster Abbey* (Woodbridge, 1994).

[152] BL, Addl. MS 45131, fo. 93v; CA, MS I 7, fos 51v–52v.

Marney, to be distributed to the poor, so many of them that a warden of the beggars and two assistants had to be hired for three days to keep order.[153] He lay in state in his chapel at Elsings for eleven days before his cortege set out and had fifty gowned poor men with torches to see him to his grave and a hundred priests to sing for his soul. His painter's bill was £33 3s. He had four banners where Marney had two. The role of the kings of arms and friars, the profusion of heraldry with its emphasis on his aristocratic marriage connections, the valance with his badge, arms, and motto were similar to Marney's, but other elements were subtly superior.

The bishop of London, Cuthbert Tunstall, sang his requiem mass and the abbot of Waltham and prior of St Mary Spital assisted. The valance was accompanied by a 'majestic hanging' showing the Last Judgment and the four evangelists. The mayor and aldermen of London, the gentlemen of the inns of court, and the freemen of several livery companies stood by as he reached Holywell and were entertained to wine, beer, ale, hippocras, comfits, and spiced bread. The food was set out on 246 feet of wooden tables in the cloisters, plus extra tables hired from the London Guildhall, all draped with more than 930 feet of linen table cloths. The drink was served in 600 white ashwood cups. Superior service for the lords and aldermen was assured by the presence of the mayor's butler and carver and their staffs. Lord Roos was his chief mourner, but the earls of Shrewsbury and Devon, the Prior of St John's, and Lord Sandys were in attendance, too. So were a knot of the new men and their associates and subordinates: Sir Henry Wyatt, Sir Thomas Nevile, Sir John Daunce, Sir Richard Wingfield, Thomas Lucas, Brian Tuke, and Guildford's sons, Sir Edward and Sir Henry.[154] His relations by blood and marriage were there, various Lovells and Manners and the husbands of his nieces. His senior household officers were there, Robert Leech and Martin Cotton bearing banners, William Kyrkeby, the steward of the household, and Richard Tuppyn, the clerk of the kitchen.[155] His estate officers and farmers were there, Thomas Netlam from Ryhall and John Dedyk from Beachamwell.[156] His colleagues in central and local offices were there, too, John Shirley, cofferer of the household, Thomas Roberts, Richard Hawkes, and William Young from the wards office, the porter from the Tower of London.[157]

While Lovell's and Marney's funerals are the best documented of the group, others clearly followed similar patterns, albeit on a more modest scale. Wyatt asked for 'no pomp nor vainglory' and Hussey ordered no more than £66 13s 4d be spent on his funeral—a funeral he never got, as an executed traitor—but such directions should be read alongside Lovell's request to be buried 'in honest manner and not pompously'.[158] Drawings survive of the heraldic banner and shields

[153] PRO, PROB11/23/27.   [154] Robinson, *Enfield*, i. 130–7; *LP* IV, i. 366.
[155] PRO, PROB11/23/17.   [156] BL, Addl. MS 12463, fos. 2v, 54v, 73v.
[157] Richardson, *Tudor Chamber Administration*, 284–5, 484.
[158] PRO, PROB11/23/27; SP1/122, fo. 159r (*LP* XII, ii. 187(3)); PROB11/26/7.

of arms used at Southwell's funeral.[159] Windsor's wife, Elizabeth, was accompanied to her burial in the friary at Hounslow in 1531 by five chaplains, twenty-four torchbearers, thirty-eight yeomen, and forty-seven gentlewomen.[160] Brandon's funeral at the London Blackfriars on 30 January 1510, lastly, shows the roles the other new men took in bidding him farewell. Much of the ceremonial was familiar, though restrained: at £6 12s 3d his painter's bill was a quarter Marney's. There were masses and a sermon, staff torches, long torches and hearse lights, black cloths draping the church, twenty-four poor men, offerings of sword, shield, coat of arms, helm, and crest. There was a 'sumptuous dinner' and other refreshments, including red and white wine, malmsey, hippocras, ale, beer, bread, wafers, dates, currants, and prunes. His arms were everywhere, on banner, pencels, and escutcheons. The Blackfriars and Austin Friars, the bishop of Carlisle and abbot of Reading, Garter king-of-arms and Rougecroix pursuivant played their parts. His kin were prominent: Sir Robert Brandon, his brother, chief mourner; his nephew Charles Brandon and cousins, Anthony and Humphrey Wingfield and John Brews, mourners; his nephew, William Sidney, banner-bearer. But the timing of his death, at the very point of the new men's triumphant survival into the reign of their master's son, brought an impressive attendance of courtier lords: Bergavenny, Mountjoy, Willoughby de Broke, and two of the younger brothers of the marquess of Dorset. And at the heart of the obsequies and the chivalric ceremonial stood two of his executors, Poynings and Lovell.[161]

The new men died as they had lived, calculating their consumption to mark the status they had won and build the connections they needed to exercise power. They used the common currencies of social display and networking: building, clothing, plate, gifts, hospitality, funeral commemoration. Of course, the greatest lords and bishops—Warham and Wolsey, Buckingham, Northumberland, and Norfolk—built greater homes, gave larger banquets, had more extravagant funerals than they did.[162] But it took skill to judge how close they should come to matching such magnificence. The incomes they won by their service to the king and their influence among his subjects equalled those of middling peers and prelates and the richest county gentry.[163] They kept such incomes flowing freely by their careful management of money and land and they bade fair to settle their wealth on their descendants by their success in buying estates. If their expenditure worked, it might convince those around them, given time, that it was natural for them to be

---

[159] BL, Addl. MS 45131, fo. 74v.   [160] CA, MS I 15, for. 145r.

[161] BL, Addl. MS 45131, fos. 153v–154v; WAM 5477; PRO, PROB11/16/29.

[162] Howard, *Country House*, 25–6, 57–8, 78, 85–90, 207, 211, 214–15; B. J. Harris, *Edward Stafford, Third Duke of Buckingham, 1478–1521* (Stanford CA, 1986), 76–103; F. Heal, *Hospitality in Early Modern England* (Oxford, 1990), 24–90, 223–56; K. Claiden-Yardley, 'Tudor Noble Funerals' in P. Lindley (ed.), *The Howards and the Tudors: Studies in Science and Heritage* (Donington, 2015), 34–42.

[163] J. Cornwall, *Wealth and Society in Early Sixteenth-Century England* (London, 1988), 140–7; F. Heal, *Of Prelates and Princes: A Study of the Economic and Social Position of the Tudor Episcopate* (Cambridge, 1980), 50–73.

wealthy and that their use of their wealth displayed a magnificence of spirit appropriate to their rank. If it did not work, it might all too easily raise hackles about their pride and convince those around them of the need to cut them down to size: if Lovell's black gowns and mule looked like those of a man who 'through his great wisdom and virtuous behaviour…ruled the common weal to his great honour', did Dudley's purple velvet doublet help create the fatal impression that he was 'so proud that the best duke in this land was more easy to sue and to speak to, than he was'?[164]

---

[164] *The Plays of Henry Medwall*, ed. A. H. Nelson (Cambridge, 1980), 34; *Great Chronicle*, 348.

SURVIVAL

16

The new reign

Life in government posed various challenges to the survival of Henry VII's new men. Waves of political change might submerge them: in Henry's troubled later years, at the accession of his son, in the rise of Cardinal Wolsey, or, for those who lived so long, in the tumultuous 1530s. Personal survival was not enough: success had somehow to be transmitted to the next generation, to sons, daughters, sons-in-law, nephews or nieces. And after a life spent in worldly accumulation and aggrandizement and the cutting of moral corners, serious steps might be needed to save their eternal souls.

POLITICAL TURBULENCE

Henry VII's entire reign was troubled by plots and rumours of plots which could not leave even his closest supporters untouched. Reports from agents, double-agents, and trouble-makers, confessions, and intercepted correspondence occasionally suggested that the new men or their relatives knew more about Yorkist plans than they should, or at least that they featured in the hopes of Yorkist plotters: Brandon, Hussey, and Hussey's uncle Peter, archdeacon of Northampton, in the mid-1490s; Guildford and Poynings in the early 1500s.[1] Yet Henry was known for the careful way he sifted such accusations, and none of the new men lost power as a result. The last years of the reign, from the death of Prince Arthur in 1502, leaving the Tudor line hanging on the life of his ten-year-old brother Henry, were marked by deeper dynastic uncertainty and the fiscal oppression born of the king's urge for control. These bore more heavily on aristocrats than on the king's low-born ministers. By 1509, the earl of Suffolk, the marquess of Dorset, and Lord William Courtenay, heir to the earldom of Devon, had each spent several years in prison. The duke of Buckingham, the earl of Northumberland, and George, Lord Bergavenny, paid heavily for pardons from the king and saw their local power constrained.[2]

Yet new men suffered, too. Bergavenny's rival in Kent, Sir Richard Guildford, had persistent financial problems and never managed to establish a sound landed base. His sons and followers tussled riotously with Bergavenny's retainers in a

---

[1] I. Arthurson, *The Perkin Warbeck Conspiracy 1491–1499* (Stroud, 1994), 77, 91, 137; *LPRH*, i. 237.

[2] S. J. Gunn, 'The Courtiers of Henry VII', *EHR* 108 (1993), 47–8; B. J. Harris, *Edward Stafford, Third Duke of Buckingham, 1478–1521* (Stanford CA, 1986), 151–65.

struggle for local supremacy that called for repeated interventions by king and council, and saw Bergavenny, himself no backwoodsman but an active courtier and councillor, steadily gain in influence among the lesser gentry. By July 1505, the king had had enough. Guildford was arrested and spent five months in the Fleet prison, charged with failing to account for the money he had spent as master of the ordnance between 1486 and 1494, while his lands were taken over by his creditors. Having settled his affairs as best he could and secured a royal pardon on 4 April 1506, he set off on pilgrimage to Jerusalem, where he died that summer. Henry had acted in a 'ruthless but realistic' fashion, the analyst of this episode concluded, to secure political stability.[3] He had sacrificed his servant in the process, a lesson his son would follow with other and greater new men.

Sir James Hobart's fate is less well documented, but he too left office suddenly after a long career and a controversial episode. As attorney-general, he had sponsored attacks on the jurisdiction of the church courts that infuriated Bishop Nykke of Norwich, who urged Archbishop Warham as chancellor, apparently in 1504, to stop Hobart, 'the enemy of God and his church'. By 1505 Hobart was retaliating by encouraging Norfolk and Suffolk suits that challenged the bishop's enforcement of tithes and probate fees and charged him with lax prison-keeping. Nykke called chancery's jurisdiction into play and Hobart countered with that of king's bench. In April 1506 Nykke had to sue the king for pardon. But in July 1507 Hobart, with ten years still to live and no compensating promotion, was replaced as attorney-general and in November he paid Dudley £533 6s 8d in cash for a pardon of his own.[4] It cannot be proved he was dismissed, but it might be suspected. For a king whose life was slipping away and a realm whose future looked fragile, keeping the peace between the common lawyers and the churchmen was just as important as keeping the peace in Kent.

Henry's death threatened more thorough-going change. Those trusted by the old king might not be trusted by the new; those excluded by the old king or those close to the new king might see their chance to take power; those who had served the old king and thereby offended his subjects might find themselves cast as scapegoats. Englishmen in 1509 had help in imagining these scenarios. The Bible gave them the story of Solomon's son Rehoboam and his rejection of his father's councillors in favour of younger, rasher men. In the Burgundian Netherlands in 1477 and France in 1483–4, the closest servants of Charles the Bold and Louis XI had been thrown to the wolves to expiate their masters' oppressions. In England itself in 1483, within the memory of anyone aged much over thirty in 1509, Lord Hastings, Earl Rivers and the duke of Buckingham had gone to the block in quick succession. No wonder John de Vere, earl of Oxford, stalwart of Henry's regime, made his will on 10 April 1509 as the king lay dying, 'being in good health and perfect mind, not grieved vexed troubled nor diseased with any bodily sickness', but 'knowing and considering well the uncertainty and unstableness of this wretched life'.[5]

[3] S. Cunningham, *Henry VII* (London, 2007), 174–80.
[4] P. R. Cavill, '"The Enemy of God and his Church": James Hobart, Praemunire and the Clergy of Norwich Diocese', *Journal of Legal History* 32 (2011), 127–50.
[5] 'The Last Testament and Inventory of John de Veer, thirteenth earl of Oxford', ed. W. H. StJ. Hope, *Archaeologia* 66 (1915), 311.

The new men faced particular concerns because of their difficult relationships with leading noblemen. Contemporaries expected competition, envy, and resentment between men like Publius Cornelius and Manhode on one side and men like Gaius Flaminius, Covetous, and Folly on the other. Henry's use of the new men as his agents in managing the nobility sharpened the issue. It was Dudley, for example, who negotiated the terms on which harsh fines were imposed on the earls of Derby and Northumberland and Lords Bergavenny and Clifford for retaining and other offences.[6] It was Bray, 'in whom my special trust is in', that the earl of Shrewsbury asked for guidance over how soon he should come to see the king to secure a grant he desired.[7] It was Wyatt who told Henry frankly from the northern borders in 1496 that Lord Clifford was 'not where he should be when we have need' and indeed was 'led and guided by simple and indiscreet persons, and to his great hurt.'[8]

In the most extreme cases Henry was heavily dependent on the new men in dealing with his noble subjects. When Edmund de la Pole, earl of Suffolk, was involved in a murderous affray in Whitechapel in 1498, it was Bray who personally delivered the indictment against him from the Middlesex sessions into king's bench.[9] When the earl then fled to Guînes in the Calais Pale and needed to be recalled before he became an international nuisance, Henry sent Guildford and a clerical colleague after him. They were to coax the earl back, making him offers as though 'they so did without the king's knowledge' because of 'the favour they specially bear unto him'. But if he proved truculent, the carrot was to be replaced by the stick. Guildford was to warn him, again as though doing him a private favour, that if the earl pressed on into exile Henry would turn all his allies against him, to his 'utter clear destruction'. The combination worked and Suffolk came home, at least for a time.[10]

The new men's propensity to quarrel with noblemen in advancing their own power might advantage the king. Brandon seems to have been unafraid to tangle with Robert, second Lord Willoughby de Broke, who never commanded Henry's confidence as his father, a veteran of 1485, had done. In 1504 the young lord was bound in £100 for his servants to keep the peace against Brandon and his men, presumably in disputes related to Brandon's new-found role in the South-West as husband of the dowager Lady Fitzwarin; two years later Brandon was bound over in £500 for his men to keep the peace against Willoughby de Broke's. It was such constraints that kept the young lord dependent on the king and on ministers such as Bray who handled negotiations with him.[11]

---

[6] 'The Petition of Edmund Dudley', ed. C. J. Harrison, *EHR* 87 (1972), 82–99.

[7] *HMC Rutland*, i. 16.

[8] A. E. Conway, *Henry VII's Relations with Scotland and Ireland, 1485–1498* (Cambridge, 1932), 238.

[9] PRO, KB9/417/50.

[10] A. Hanham, 'Edmund de la Pole, Defector', *Renaissance Studies* 2 (1988), 240–1; *LPRH*, i. 129–34.

[11] *CCR 1500–9*, 304, 559; D. A. Luckett, 'The Rise and Fall of a Noble Dynasty: Henry VII and the Lords Willoughby de Broke', *HR* 69 (1996), 260–5.

Buckingham showed a particular penchant for falling out with the new men. His nastiest feud was with Thomas Lucas, whom he first accused of depriving him of rights and income by finding a false inquisition in 1499. In 1506–7 there was more trouble over an exchange of lands in Suffolk. At that stage, Lucas seemed to be in propitiatory mood towards 'the right excellent prince the duke of Buckingham', producing documentary proof of his landed title in the hope that 'my lord's grace more instructed of the very truth will be my good and gracious lord, and give less credence unto that untrue and simple body that gave his highness that wrong and sinister information'. But when Buckingham fought libel suits against Lucas after 1509, in star chamber and elsewhere, the lawyer admitted he had been rather less diplomatic, saying of an earlier lawsuit 'by the duke's feigned action I set not two pence' and, of his seizures of property in Suffolk, 'the said duke has small conscience so to deal with me'. This was not quite the wording with which he was charged—'the said duke hath no more conscience than a dog'—but it was still not how people expected esquires to speak of dukes, and it cost Lucas £40 in damages. In a second suit, Lucas was accused of saying that it was 'the true service' that he had done to Henry VII that caused the duke's 'inward grudge' against him.[12] The duke also nurtured a deep resentment of Lovell, telling his intimates that if he became king he would behead him together with Wolsey. No doubt he blamed Lovell for the fact that, as he allegedly put it, 'all that' Henry VII 'had done, he had done wrongfully', but it must also have been painful to have to borrow money from him.[13] Buckingham's execution in 1521 must have come as a relief to a number of the new men. In the context it was unusually heart-warming of Wyatt to recommend that Henry VIII send letters of consolation to the duke's wife and son.[14]

Even noblemen close to the heart of the regime might feel challenged by the new men. George Talbot, earl of Shrewsbury, lord steward of the king's household from 1505, was a major local office-holder in the duchy of Lancaster, steward and master forester of the duchy manors in Derbyshire and Staffordshire and constable of Tutbury Castle.[15] He was assertive in the distribution of duchy patronage in his sphere of influence, and his followers flaunted their allegiance to him with his talbot or hunting dog badge: in 1515 three men from Wirksworth summoned to appear before the duchy council 'had the talbot upon their caps seen openly in the court'.[16] By 1513, a first clash with Marney as chancellor of the duchy, in which one of Marney's servants killed one of Shrewsbury's, was calming down, and the Derbyshire officers of the duchy were 'right glad' to hear that the earl and the chancellor were agreed, 'for now…every man may occupy his office in peace'.[17]

---

[12] Harris, *Buckingham*, 147–8; SROB, Ac449/6/5; J. H. Baker, *The Men of Court 1440 to 1550: A Prosopography of the Inns of Court and Chancery and the Courts of Law*, 2 vols, SS supplementary series 18 (London, 2012), ii. 1036.

[13] *LP* III, i. 1070, 1284, 1285(5).   [14] *LP* III, i. 1292.

[15] R. Somerville, *A History of the Duchy of Lancaster, I, 1265–1603* (London, 1953), 286n, 541–2, 546, 549–50, 557.

[16] PRO, DL12/12, undated note to the duchy attorney John Fitzjames; DL 5/5, fo. 34v.

[17] *HMC Various Collections*, ii. 318 (*LP* I, i. 392); PRO, STAC2/20/26.

Then, at the death of Sir Henry Vernon in 1515, Shrewsbury staked a claim to the stewardship and barmastership of the High Peak, a lucrative office regulating the local lead industry. Marney contested it and the matter had to be settled by Wolsey in star chamber in summer 1516. In the process, the cardinal sharply rebuked Marney, telling him 'that the same Sir Henry had done more displeasure unto the king's grace, by the reason of his cruelness against the great estates of this realm, than any man living'. Yet for all Marney's aggression there were other new men ready to smooth things over. In the midst of the row Poynings assured Shrewsbury that Wolsey bore him 'marvellous great favour' and there was no need for him to come to court.[18]

By that time the new men had seen what happened to those who made too many enemies. When Henry breathed his last at 11 p.m. on 21 April 1509 those around him kept his death secret long enough to establish political stability and place his son securely on the throne. The news was announced at court late on 23 April, and next morning Empson and Dudley were arrested and cast as scape-goats for their master's 'tyrannies'. Quite where the initiative lay in this decision it is hard to say, as it is in many of the political crises of Henry VIII's reign: the new king acted, or at least consented, but on whose advice? Dudley was certainly unpopular with the wrong people: with the Londoners who clamoured against him and his agents; with the great lords who expected to take greater part in the new regime than the old; perhaps with Lady Margaret Beaufort who stepped in to make sure her grandson was safe. He and Empson were closer to each other than to the other leading councillors, and while their patrons had died some years ear-lier, their closest associate at court, Hugh Denis, had lost his place in the king's last months. The policies they had implemented—Empson at the council learned, Dudley with his bonds and fines and customs prosecutions—matched too well those aspects of the old king's rule that it seemed expedient, at least for the moment, to disown.[19]

Others stayed out of gaol and kept their heads but not their jobs. Lucas, Buckingham's bugbear, lost his post as king's solicitor in June.[20] Hussey, so often troubled for corruption or criticized for pomp or violence and associated as master of the wards with another set of policies painful to the landed elite, attended Henry's funeral as comptroller of the household, breaking his staff of office and throwing the fragments into Henry's grave to symbolize that his authority ended with his master's death. The gesture was unusually powerful, for it was not Hussey but Poynings who became comptroller of the new king's household. Worse, Hussey

[18] Somerville, *Duchy of Lancaster*, 552; S. M. Wright, *The Derbyshire Gentry in the Fifteenth Century*, Derbyshire RS 8 (Chesterfield, 1983), 86; HL, MS El 2652, fo. 5r; *LP* II, i. 1815; *Illustrations of British History*, ed. E. Lodge, 3 vols (London, 1838), i. 18–20, 22–5 (*LP* II, i. 1959, 2018).

[19] S. J. Gunn, 'The Accession of Henry VIII', *HR* 64 (1991), 278–88; D. R. Starkey, *Henry: Virtuous Prince* (London, 2008), 251–68; T. Penn, *Winter King: The Dawn of Tudor England* (London, 2011), 337–74; M. K. Jones and M. G. Underwood, *The King's Mother: Lady Margaret Beaufort, Countess of Richmond and Derby* (Cambridge, 1992), 92.

[20] E. W. Ives, *The Common Lawyers of Pre-Reformation England. Thomas Kebell: A Case Study* (Cambridge, 1983), 504.

had to wait an agonizing month before the new king signed two bills allowing him to sue out the general pardon proclaimed at his accession, a pardon from which he had apparently, like Empson and Dudley and their notorious agents, been excluded. Not until 20 August was he released from his debts to the crown, and on 25 August he was deliberately taken off the commission set up to hear complaints about misgovernment in Lincolnshire. His position still looked shaky, but he did manage to retain his mastership of the wards.[21]

HENRY AND WOLSEY

Most of Empson's and Dudley's erstwhile colleagues fared much better, as the councillors of the young king established a system of constraints on his actions, not just witnessing his more formal charters as those about the king had always done, but counter-signing many of his warrants and letters as though he were a minor or even an incompetent like Henry VI. No doubt the aim was the political education of an adolescent who had never, unlike Prince Arthur or Edward V, been sent away to the Welsh borders to learn how to rule. In many instances, too, the lines were blurred between what the councillors did as Henry's mentors and what they did as his father's executors. But the effect was to consolidate the power of the most active councillors. These were not only churchmen like Warham, Fox, and Ruthal, or office-holding lords like the earls of Surrey and Shrewsbury and Lord Herbert, but also many of the new men.

Polydore Vergil picked out Lovell, Poynings, and Wyatt among the leading councillors of the new reign and what survives of the council registers shows that they, together with Marney, Cutt, Hussey, Englefield, and Southwell, were indeed busy in these early years.[22] Warrants, letters, and charters add more names— Thomas Brandon, John Heron—and allow finer-tuned measurement. Surrey, Fox, Ruthal, Lovell, and Marney were the most constant attenders in council throughout the king's first three years; Shrewsbury and Oxford rather faded after 1509, whereas Cutt grew in importance.[23] Henry remembered this period well when he answered the complaint of the rebels of 1536 that noblemen no longer bore sway in his council. 'As touching the beginning of our reign, where ye say so many noble men were counsellors', he told them, 'who were then counsellors, I well remember'. Besides Surrey and Shrewsbury, the lords of his council were 'but scant well born gentlemen; and yet of no great lands, till they were promoted by us, and so

---

[21] *LP* I, i. 20(1, 4), 54(63, 66), 158(56, 76), 289(29), 438(3 m. 8), II, ii. 1446.

[22] *PVAH*, 149; W. H. Dunham, 'The Members of Henry VIII's Whole Council, 1509–1527', *EHR* 59 (1944), 209; PRO, STAC10/4/2/356.

[23] *LP* I, i. 11(12), 54 (33, 48–50), 94(43–4), 132(65), 153, 158(90), 168, 190(19, 25, 34–5, 41), 218(4, 33, 53–4, 57–8, 55–6), 257(4–5, 12, 26, 37, 62, 85), 265, 289, 313, 414(48, 52), 448(1, 4, 8), 555, 596, 602, 604(18, 25, 44), 632(35), 651(13), 784(14, 16, 36, 56), 804(8, 49), 820, 833(5), 845, 857(18), 1003(15, 17), 1083(41), 1123(45); *HMC Various Collections*, ii. 306; *Reading Records: Diary of the Corporation*, ed. J. M. Guilding, 4 vols (London, 1892–6), 117–18; PML, Rulers of England box 2/4, 8; BL, Addl. Ch. 22621; PRO, E101/417/3/82.

made knights, and lords: the rest were lawyers and priests, save two bishops, which were Canterbury and Winchester'.[24]

The young king at length escaped these leading-strings through his partnership with Wolsey, whom he used first to process warrants without the usual signatures and then to handle an ever wider range of business. Finding him to be, as the cardinal's servant and biographer George Cavendish put it, 'a meet instrument for the accomplishment of his devised will and pleasure', Henry 'esteemed him so highly that his estimation and favour put all other ancient counsellors out of their accustomed favour that they were in before'.[25] The effect on Surrey, Fox, and Warham is open to debate—were they annoyed at being pushed aside, happy to retire, or content to work with Wolsey to serve the king?—but that on the new men was far from harmful.[26] Lovell, Marney, Poynings, Wyatt, and Cutt remained among the most active councillors, with Hussey not far behind, and they were joined by Windsor and Belknap.[27] Lovell, 'a very sage counsellor and witty', had combined with Fox to promote Wolsey in Henry VII's service, as the cardinal himself reminisced to Cavendish after his fall.[28] Sir Thomas corresponded jokily with the two prelates in 1514, telling them the English captains at Calais were 'not most gladdest nor best content' at the latest orders to refrain from attacking the French, but that 'if I have done ill ye must repute in me but folly'.[29] Like Fox he relinquished office as Wolsey rose, giving up the treasurership of the household in 1519. Like Fox he may, if Polydore Vergil is to be believed, have acted to restrain Wolsey's adventurous instincts in foreign policy in 1515–16.[30] But the cardinal's dominance did not cloud the end of his career. The same Venetian ambassador who described him as an old servant who interfered but little in June 1516 noted him among the half-dozen leading councillors in October, and he was still at court on many occasions in the next four years, signing and witnessing international treaties, discussing confidential business with the king, and passing on instructions to his colleagues.[31] As late as 1523 Fox could refer Wolsey to him for information on Henry VII's plans for war in Scotland.[32]

Others went from strength to strength under Wolsey's leadership. Poynings advanced from the comptrollership to the treasurership of the household in 1519,

---

[24] *StP*, i. 507 (*LP* XI. 957).
[25] D. R. Starkey, 'Court, Council and Nobility in Tudor England', in R. G. Asch and A. M. Birke (eds), *Princes, Patronage and Nobility: The Court at the beginning of the Modern Age, c.1450–1650* (Oxford, 1991), 176–9; George Cavendish, *The Life and Death of Cardinal Wolsey*, ed. R. S. Sylvester, EETS 243 (Oxford, 1959), 12.
[26] D. R. Starkey, *The Reign of Henry VIII: Personalities and Politics* (London, 1985), 54–64; P. Gwyn, *The King's Cardinal: The Rise and Fall of Thomas Wolsey* (London, 1990), 4–32, 289–93, 565–70.
[27] Dunham, 'Members', 209; J. A. Guy, *The Cardinal's Court: The Impact of Thomas Wolsey in Star Chamber* (Hassocks, 1977), 28.
[28] G. Cavendish, *The Life and Death of Cardinal Wolsey*, ed. R. S. Sylvester, EETS 243 (Oxford, 1959), 7, 9–10.
[29] PRO, SP1/8, f. 126v (*LP* I, ii. 2974).   [30] *AHPV*, 235.
[31] Belvoir Castle, MS a/c no. 4; *LP* II, i. 2183, 2464, ii. 3437(6), 4124–5, 4469, 4475, III, i. 223, 739(2), ii. App. 12, Addenda, i. 286.
[32] *LP* III, ii. 2859.

and Hussey became chief butler in 1521.[33] Marney had been marked out for greatness with painful clarity from the first weeks of the reign, when every knight present at the spring 1509 garter chapter nominated him for election and the king entrusted to him—and subsequently gave him—all the goods confiscated from Dudley's London house.[34] Now he attended closely on the king at court, where his offices secured him permanent lodging. He passed letters to Henry, discussing policy and acting as a messenger between him and Wolsey. He took part in many of the diplomatic meetings of 1516–22, and became the first ever lay keeper of the privy seal just months before his death in 1523.[35] When he was granted some of the duke of Buckingham's lands in 1522, Wolsey himself counter-signed the petition approved by the king.[36] Wyatt took over as treasurer of the chamber in January 1524 and served a little over four years as the prime coordinator of government finances.[37] One of Henry VII's surviving councillors—it is not clear which— offered Wolsey detailed advice on how to investigate the duke of Buckingham's treason with the same circumspection Henry had used against Sir William Stanley.[38]

A certain obsequiousness was sometimes necessary in dealing with the cardinal's self-conscious greatness. Marney, like many others, tagged along in the grandiose procession to celebrate the arrival of Wolsey's cardinal's hat.[39] Belknap had to pay careful attention to Wolsey's instructions for his lodgings at the Field of Cloth of Gold so that the cardinal should not be disappointed when he arrived.[40] Windsor, signing himself Wolsey's 'assured servant', made a point of telling his son, setting out with horses from Henry for Francis I, to call on Wolsey on the way and ask if there was anything he could do for the cardinal in France.[41] 'I am most bounden to pray to God for preservation of Your Grace', Wyatt assured Wolsey.[42] Poynings signed himself 'your own to the best of my little power', wished 'Jesus send Your Grace long and prosperous life', and pledged that 'if there be any thing that I can do to your pleasure I am at your commandment, as knoweth Our Lord, whom I beseech long to preserve Your Grace'.[43] Posthumous provision might also be necessary to keep the great man sweet. Lovell told his executors to give Wolsey, in addition to a gold standing cup set with pearls and stones, at least £66 13s 4d and, if his estate would run to it, £100 in gold, the same sum he left the king, to be

[33] *LP* III, i. 223, 1379(1), ii. 1712.

[34] *The Register of the Most Noble Order of the Garter*, ed. J. Anstis, 2 vols (London, 1724), i. 270–1; PRO, E154/2/17; *LP* I, ii. 2055(72).

[35] *LP* I, ii. 3614(169), II, i. 2464, ii. 3437(6), 4124, 4469, 4475, 4504, 4673, p. 1476, III, i. 491, 528, 702(3), 739(2), 906, 1266, ii. 1387, 1440, 2288(2), 2333(24), 2830; *HMC Rutland*, i. 21.

[36] *LP* III, ii. 2145(18).

[37] W. C. Richardson, *Tudor Chamber Administration, 1485–1547* (Baton Rouge LA, 1952), 96, 238–9; G. R. Elton, *The Tudor Revolution in Government: Administrative Changes in the reign of Henry VIII* (Cambridge, 1953), 169–70.

[38] PRO, SP1/22, fo. 57 (*LP* III, i, p. 490).   [39] *LP* II, i. 1153.

[40] J. G. Russell, *The Field of Cloth of Gold: Men and Manners in 1520* (London, 1969), 64–5.

[41] PRO, SP1/21, fo. 138 (*LP* III, i. 1096).

[42] PRO, SP1/17, fo. 38 (*LP* II, ii. 4400).

[43] PRO, SP1/10, fo. 52, SP1/15, fo. 121, SP1/18, fo. 38 (*LP* II, i. 149, ii. 3244, III, i. 82).

'good and gracious lord' to them in the performance of his will; they found the £100 and added to the cup a gold salt with a cover.[44] But Wolsey was more than happy to work with the new men; indeed, he needed them to make his ministry effective. In spring 1518 the cardinal did not trust all the councillors at court with the king to discuss the secret negotiations he was conducting at London with the French, but Lovell and Marney were clearly in his confidence.[45]

THE NEXT GENERATION

Meanwhile, the new men were smoothing the way for the next generation of their families. A first step was to secure an education for their heirs. After basic schooling—Hussey bought primers for both his son Gilbert and his daughter Mary in 1533–4—many of them turned naturally to the inns of court.[46] Empson's, Englefield's, Hussey's, Mordaunt's, and Windsor's sons, Bray's nephews, and Windsor's grandson, Reginald Corbet, all joined the Middle Temple, while Hobart's and Marney's sons and Southwell's younger brother went to Lincoln's Inn.[47] These young men did not always study with the assiduity that had built their forerunners' fortunes. Francis Southwell was regularly in trouble with the Lincoln's Inn authorities for gambling on dice and cards and refused to serve as butler at Christmas 1502.[48] William Hussey followed in his family's footsteps at Gray's Inn, but his main distinction was to take part in an armed assault on members of Strand Inn.[49] John Marney was equally high-spirited, though he had perhaps learnt his lesson by the time he joined Lincoln's Inn in 1499. While studying in the 1490s at Furnival's Inn, one of the inns of chancery that prepared students for the inns of court, he doubled up as his father's London agent, delivering letters, buying weapons, and passing on news about a Scottish plot to capture Berwick. But a letter to his 'most reverent and worshipful father' enclosed a bill of young John's expenses and of what remained of the money his parents had sent him, 'that ye may see what I need'. What he had been spending it on we might well wonder, as in July 1496 he had given security to the inn's principal that he and another student would conform themselves 'to the good rule and statutes' of the inn and avoid conduct 'in the night or by day' which might 'be to the slander' of the institution.[50] Another option was university, still not a common course for laymen, but becoming more

---

[44] PRO, PROB11/23/27; *LP* IV, i. 366.   [45] *LP* II, ii. 4124.

[46] PRO, E36/95, fo. 28r.

[47] *Register of Admissions to the Honourable Society of the Middle Temple*, ed. H. A. C. Sturgess, 3 vols (London, 1949), i. 4–6, 8, 14, 16; *Minutes of Parliament of the Middle Temple*, ed. C. T. Martin, 4 vols (London, 1904), i. 13; *The Records of the Honourable Society of Lincoln's Inn: Admissions from AD 1420 to AD 1799* (London, 1896), 25.

[48] *The Records of the Honourable Society of Lincoln's Inn: The Black Books*, ed. W. P. Baildon and R. Roxburgh, 5 vols (London, 1897–1968), i. 93, 97, 103–4, 108, 128, 187, 191, 196, 199, 200.

[49] *The Pension Book of Gray's Inn*, ed. R. J. Fletcher, 2 vols (London, 1901–10), i. pp. xvii, xxv–vi.

[50] PRO, SC1/52/33; *Lincoln's Inn Admissions*, 29; *Early Records of Furnival's Inn*, ed. D. S. Bland (Newcastle, 1957), 35–6.

so. Dudley himself may have studied at Oxford; of all the new men he was most likely to have done so, his uncle, a bishop who had served as chancellor of the university, his cousin a fellow of Oriel.[51] In the next generation, Wyatt's son Thomas accumulated learning with the same brio his father applied to money: at the Middle Temple, among the more intellectually ambitious court families, and, apparently, at Cambridge.[52]

Placing sons in the households of great men was another way to secure their advancement. One of Guildford's sons, for example, was a gentleman of Cardinal Morton's household in 1496–7, and two of them waited at table at Archbishop Warham's enthronement feast in 1505, while Brandon's nephew Charles was master of the horse to the earl of Essex.[53] The king's court was the greatest household in the land, and many served there. John Marney was an esquire for the king's body by 1509 and went on to attend the diplomatic meetings of 1520–2.[54] Charles Brandon was a sewer for the board's end by about 1503, waiting on the king at table, and mixed freely in court circles from his home in his uncle's house in Southwark.[55] Henry Guildford was a servant to Prince Henry by 1503 and his brother Edward an esquire for the body by 1509.[56] Mordaunt's son was knighted at Prince Henry's creation as Prince of Wales in 1503.[57] In the 1520s Wyatt's son Thomas made his way at court, in feats of arms, in hunting, on embassy, at Calais, at Paris, in Italy, training himself for a life of service that would in the end exhaust him.[58] By Wyatt's last years his grandson Thomas was one of the king's henchmen, boys educated at court, mixing with those who would rise high in the decades to come.[59] Military careers could be fostered, John Marney leading a hundred men in 1513 and winning knighthood at Tournai.[60] Sons could also be found places in parliament. John Marney sat, probably for Essex, in 1523, Windsor's son William for Chipping Wycombe and Hussey's son William for Grantham in 1529.[61] The records of who sat for which constituency are thin before the 1530s, so many others may have passed a similar apprenticeship.

Another common precaution was to secure the tenure of offices in survivorship with the next generation. Hussey's father had done this for him, and he in turn gained joint grants with his son William of some of his crown stewardships in

---

[51] A. B. Emden, *A Biographical Register of the University of Oxford to AD 1500*, 3 vols (Oxford, 1957–9), i. 597–600; T. A. R. Evans, 'The Numbers, Origins and Careers of Students', in J. I. Catto and T. A. R. Evans (eds), *History of the University of Oxford*, ii: *Late Medieval Oxford* (Oxford, 1992), 521–2.

[52] S. Brigden, *Thomas Wyatt; The Heart's Forest* (London, 2012), 84–90.

[53] KHLC, Sa/FAc 11, m. 6; *Joannis Lelandi Collectanea*, ed. T. Hearne, 6 vols (Oxford, 1774), vi. 18; S. J. Gunn, *Charles Brandon, Duke of Suffolk, c.1484–1545* (Oxford, 1988), 5–6.

[54] *LP* I, i. 20, III, i. 702–4, 906, ii. 2288, App. 35.

[55] Gunn, *Charles Brandon*, 5; PRO, C24/28.

[56] S. T. Bindoff, *History of Parliament: The House of Commons 1509–1558*, 3 vols (London, 1982), ii. 262; PRO, LC2/1, fo. 73v.

[57] C. S. Knighton, 'Mordaunt, John, First Baron Mordaunt', *ODNB*.

[58] Brigden, *Wyatt*, 39–172.

[59] *The Great Wardrobe Accounts of Henry VII and Henry VIII*, ed. M. Hayward, London RS 47 (Woodbridge, 2012), 276.

[60] *LP* I, ii. 2053, 2301.   [61] Bindoff, *Commons*, ii. 427–8, 573, iii. 637–8.

1510 and the stewardship of Sleaford in 1516.[62] In 1523 he purchased the feodaryship of the Honour of Bolingbroke from Sir Edward Guildford for £26 13s 4d and had his second son Sir Giles named to the position, and in 1524 William replaced him in his duchy of Lancaster stewardships.[63] Wyatt set up his son in stewardships and castle constableships jointly with himself or other courtiers and Windsor even asked the abbot and convent of Westminster to appoint him and his son George in survivorship to the reversion of a stewardship.[64] Guildford's precaution in having his son Edward appointed jointly with him to the mastership of the armoury in 1493 proved wise, for Edward succeeded to the office in 1506 amid the ruin of his father's career.[65] Marney's efforts were less successful. In 1514 he secured joint grants or reversions for his son John of half a dozen duchy of Lancaster posts. But when his father died John was unable or unwilling to keep hold of these offices, and they were taken by Sir Richard Wingfield, the new chancellor of the duchy, and more influential courtiers.[66]

Windsor, more subtly, used whatever influence his local offices gave him to secure minor posts or lands for his sons. During his brief supervision of the earl of Derby's estates, his son William was appointed joint steward of the earl's manor of Streatley in a document signed by Andrew and sealed with his stag's head seal.[67] On the St George's College, Windsor manor of Iver, where he held the stewardship, copyhold tenements and offices between 1505 and 1549 went to himself, his sons George and William, and his grandsons Thomas and Edward, while on the queen's manor of Wraysbury and the Westminster Abbey manor of Denham he granted himself tenements and passed them on to his younger son Edmund, pausing only to enclose the Wraysbury common fields.[68] Edmund was also blessed with a sixty-year lease of a Westminster Abbey manor in Surrey, where his father was steward, in 1529, and a perpetual grant of lands in Middlesex from Holy Trinity Friary, Hounslow, site of the family mausoleum, in 1536.[69] Such habits were hereditary: Sir William Windsor became the duchy of Lancaster feodary in Bedfordshire and Berkshire in 1535 and duly passed the post on to his son Thomas in 1544, a year after succeeding his father as Lord Windsor.[70]

MARRIAGE STRATEGIES

Good marriages were also essential. Lovell was a master marriage-broker. In July 1503 he paid Hussey £666 13s 4d for the match between one of his nieces or second cousins— in the end it was his brother Sir Robert's daughter Ursula—and Hussey's eldest

---

[62] PRO, LR14/916; *LP* I, i. 604(31); LA, Bishop's Register 25, fo. 87r.
[63] Somerville, *Duchy of Lancaster*, 574, 577, 582.
[64] Somerville, *Duchy of Lancaster*, 529–30; *LP* XI. 519(4); WAM, Lease Book II, fo. 11v.
[65] Bindoff, *Commons*, ii. 262.
[66] Somerville, *Duchy of Lancaster*, 430, 606; *LP* I, ii. 2863 (12), III, ii. 3146 (6).
[67] PRO, E210/5562.
[68] CBS, D/BASM/45/14, pp. 11, 16, 20, (ii), p. 2; D/BASM/86/1; PR61/28/1, p. 65.
[69] WAM, Lease Book II, fo. 256; LMA, Acc/0928/13/4.
[70] Somerville, *Duchy of Lancaster*, 592.

son William. The deal gave Lovell responsibility for the young couple's upbringing, but also control of their lands until they came of age, and carefully indemnified him lest any of the parties die before he had taken his dues from the estate.[71] More impressively still, he paired Ursula's sister Elizabeth in 1513 with his great-nephew Thomas Manners. Manners was the son of Sir George, who became Lord Roos on the death of Lovell's brother-in-law Edmund, Lord Roos, in 1508, and who died later in 1513, naming Lovell one of his executors. When Elizabeth died, Lovell presumably also had a hand in Roos's marriage to Eleanor, the daughter of Sir William Paston, for Paston was one of the executors of Lovell's will, and Lovell left bequests to his children. Manners's and Lovell's influence perhaps combined in the marriages between three of Eleanor Paston's sisters and members of the Derbyshire and Nottinghamshire gentry.[72] How many more of his younger relatives' marriages Lovell arranged we cannot tell, but he was certainly generous towards them and their children. He left £100 each to the husbands of Sir Robert's four surviving daughters towards the schooling and marriage of their children; £40 to his cousin Chamberlain's daughter; and, recognizing her superior status and perhaps the generous profits he had taken from her family's lands, £400 towards the marriage of Thomas Manners' sister.[73]

Windsor had four sons and four daughters to provide for and did well by them. He left some land in Buckinghamshire and Middlesex to his younger sons Edmund and Thomas.[74] Edmund apparently died unmarried, but Thomas married a local heiress and left issue. His daughters married into knightly families or better: Elizabeth to Sir Peter Vavasour of Spaldington in Yorkshire, Anne to Roger Corbet of Moreton Corbet, Shropshire, whose father had been a knight, Edith to George Ludlow of Hill Deverill, Wiltshire, whose son would be a knight, and Eleanor to Ralph, Lord Scrope of Upsall, who died in 1515, and then to the courtier Sir Edward Neville. As Windsor pointed out in his will, these marriages had cost him 'such great charges' that they should expect no further legacies. He singled out how expensive the Corbet match had been—quite believably when Roger Corbet's wardship had been priced at £666 13s 4d—but did relent to the extent of promising the widowed Anne and her son Andrew £40 towards their building plans.[75] His family network had been constructed at some cost, but it seems to have stuck together. He, his sons, and his sons-in-law regularly served as feoffees together, whether on his daughters' jointures or his sons' land purchases.[76]

[71] *CCR 1500–9*, 338.

[72] *CP*, xi. 106–8, 254; PRO, PROB11/17/24; PROB11/23/27; Bindoff, *Commons*, ii. 518–21; P. W. Hasler, *The House of Commons 1558–1603*, 3 vols (London, 1981), i. 596; *The Visitacion of Norffolk, made and taken by William Hervey, Clarencieux King of Arms, anno 1563, enlarged with another Visitacion made by Clarenceux Cooke, with many other Descents; and also the Vissitation made by John Raven, Richmond, anno 1613*, ed. W. Rye, HS 32 (London, 1891), 216.

[73] PRO, PROB11/23/27.

[74] PRO, PROB11/29/23; CP25/2/3/14/41, 55, 69.

[75] PRO, PROB11/29/23; A. Collins, *Historical Collections of the Noble Family of Windsor* (London, 1754), 47–8; Bindoff, *Commons*, i. 701–2, iii. 7; Hasler, *Commons*, ii. 497–8; Gunn, *Charles Brandon*, 21.

[76] *Testamenta Eboracensia*, ed. J. Raine and J. W. Clay, 6 vols, Surtees Soc. 4, 30, 45, 53, 79, 106 (London, 1836–1902), v. 64; *LP* V. 166 (43); PRO, CP25/2/48/336/3, CP25/2/49/339/21; C54/396, m. 3d.

Guildford, too, tried to make good provision for his children, but was hampered by his financial difficulties. He contracted in 1502 for his daughter Philippa to marry John Gage, a Surrey gentleman. The contract specified that he would pay the costs of his daughter's clothing on her wedding day and for dinner and supper, while Gage would set her up with a jointure worth £40 a year, which he duly did. But Guildford could not pay the marriage portion of £200 in cash and it had to be secured on a rent charge of £66 13s 4d a year on his marshland property. At least the marriage worked in the sense that Gage and his brothers-in-law George and Henry Guildford seem to have stuck together in the next reign.[77] Wyatt's plans went more painfully wrong as Thomas married Elizabeth Brooke, daughter of the Kent peer Lord Cobham, but then abandoned her for her adultery.[78]

Hussey had substantial families by each of his two wives, but did his best to provide for the resulting five sons, one of whom died young, and four daughters. His sons by his first marriage, William and Giles, were entering middle age by the time his second family came along. William, due to inherit his father's lands and well connected through his marriage to Lovell's niece, joined the Holland commission of the peace in 1514 and built a career slowly, gaining knighthood in 1529.[79] Giles perhaps needed to move faster. In a deal settled by his father in 1508, he married Jane, daughter and co-heir of Thomas Pigot of Clotherham, Yorkshire, and settled at Caythorpe.[80] He gained his knighthood at Morlaix in Brittany in 1522 and served on local commissions from 1523, but died soon afterwards.[81] Hussey aimed to provide for his sons by his second wife with lands he had bought or farmed on lease, the farm of Vaudey Abbey's Hanbeck Grange and lands in Ingoldsby for Thomas, the manor of Sapperton and the lands he controlled under the wardship of Roland Sherrard for Gilbert.[82]

When it came to his daughters, all of them born to his second wife, he was prepared to spend heavily to secure good matches. The eldest, Elizabeth, was married in 1532 to Walter, Lord Hungerford, scion of an old-established family about to regain its place in the peerage, perhaps for around the £400 Lord Sandys had paid for his daughter to marry Hungerford just five years earlier. Sadly Elizabeth's marriage was unhappy, indeed she claimed that her husband imprisoned her and tried either to poison or to starve her to death. At least she survived his execution in 1540 to make a second match.[83] For her sister, Mary, born in about 1519, Hussey snapped up in 1522 the one-year old Edmund Sheffield, whose lands would prove extensive enough to merit a peerage in 1547. That cost him £666 13s 4d, £600 of it paid in cash, though as part of the deal he gained control of dower lands worth £66 13s 4d a year. Unfortunately the premature death of Edmund's father in 1531

[77] ESRO, Firle Place MSS Box 21/3–4 and *passim* (NRA report).
[78] Brigden, *Wyatt*, 92–100.   [79] Bindoff, *Commons*, ii. 427–8.
[80] *CCR 1500–9*, 875; *Lincolnshire Pedigrees*, ed. A. R. Maddison, 4 vols, HS 50–2, 55 (London, 1902–6), ii. 527.
[81] W. A. Shaw, *The Knights of England*, 2 vols (London, 1906), i. 45; *LP* III, ii. 3282, IV, i. 213 (2), p. 237.
[82] PRO, E326/9079.   [83] *CP*, vi. 624–5.

and the grant of his wardship to Anne Boleyn's brother broke the match and in 1533–4 Mary came home from Butterwick to Sleaford.[84] For Dorothy, born about 1520, Hussey bought the wardship of Thomas Wymbish of Nocton. They were betrothed by 1537, though it is unclear if they ever married.[85] That left Bridget, born about 1522, and the jilted Mary still to marry when Hussey made his will in 1535, so he provided £333 6s 8d to pay for each of their marriages.[86] In the end, disaster overtook their father before they were old enough to wed.

ENDOWMENTS AND CAREERS

The landed bases and political contacts built up by the new men were often sufficient to propel their heirs into the peerage as the king cast around for dependable and well-endowed men to add to the lords from the opening of the reformation parliament in 1529 onwards.[87] Mordaunt's son, his father's lands amplified by his own marriage to a Northamptonshire heiress in 1499, served through the 1510s and 1520s as an occasional councillor and courtier and a willing local governor, and was made a baron in 1532.[88] Bray had no children, but he did handsomely by his nephews. The eldest, Edmund, was willed most of Sir Reynold's lands, sufficient for him to be made a peer in 1529. Sir Reynold planned that Edmund's younger brothers should be married to the heirs general of his wife, thus keeping her lands in the family, though the plan was partly stymied by his death. Sir William Sandys, the husband of his niece, contested these settlements, but in practice there was so much land to go round that what Sandys gained from the dispute helped support his own dignity as a peer after his elevation in 1523.[89] Lovell, too, managed to endow more than one family. He bolstered the position of his great-nephew Thomas, Lord Roos, by leaving him the great house at Elsings in Enfield and estates in Hampshire, Wiltshire, and Suffolk, which he had obtained from Roos's great-grandmother Philippa, Lady Roos. He also fostered Roos's political career, for example, by nominating him several times for election to the garter.[90] His extensive East Anglian lands he left to Francis Lovell, second son of his cousin Sir Gregory. Perhaps pondering his own descent from a cadet line, he also found scraps of land sufficient to preserve the gentility of Roos's younger brothers Oliver and Richard and Francis's younger brothers John and Edward, and left tapestries

[84] *Abstracts of the Inquisitiones Post Mortem relating to Nottinghamshire*, i, ed. W. Phillimore, Thoroton Society Record Series 3 (Nottingham, 1905), i. 207–10; *CP*, xi. 661–2; PRO, E36/95, fo. 28r.

[85] *LP* XII, ii. 2; *Lincolnshire Pedigrees*, iii. 1118.

[86] PRO, SP1/122, fo. 167 (*LP* XII, ii. 187(3)).

[87] H. Miller, *Henry VIII and the English Nobility* (Oxford, 1986), 22–37.

[88] Knighton, 'Mordaunt'.

[89] M. M. Condon, 'From Caitiff and Villain to *Pater Patriae*: Reynold Bray and the Profits of Office', in M. A. Hicks (ed.), *Profit, Piety and the Professions in later Medieval England* (Gloucester, 1990), 156–62.

[90] *Register of the Garter*, i. 288, 358.

and other household goods to all three Manners brothers and to Sir Thomas Lovell junior, Sir Gregory's eldest son.[91]

Poynings faced particular problems. His only legitimate son, John, was dead by 1504, forcing him to agree that after his death most of his lands would revert to the earls of Northumberland against whom his father had fought so hard for them.[92] He had, however, three illegitimate sons, and wished to make what provision he could for them. In his will he left his purchased lands in Kent in the hands of his trusted servant Edward Thwaites to provide for the boys for twelve years, until the eldest reached the age of 21. All he could manage for his younger sons was an annuity of £5 a year each.[93] Though he did not live to see them, he would surely have been delighted by their careers as leading figures in the Calais and Boulogne garrisons of the 1540s. Edward became captain of the guard at Boulogne and was killed in action in 1546. Adrian was captain of the citadel at Boulogne and went on to be lieutenant of Calais Castle, marshal of Le Havre during the English occupation of 1562–4 and captain of Portsmouth. But it was their elder brother Thomas who went furthest, rising by daring and effective generalship to the command of Boulogne and a peerage in 1545, only to die of plague in August.[94] Sir Edward himself would have been flattered by the chronicler Wriothesley's verdict on Thomas, 'the valiant captain…which had done many great feats of arms against the Frenchmen, for whose death great moan was made'.[95] He would also have been proud of his grandson, namesake and ward, Edward Lord Clinton. Edward lent support to his uncles, Poynings's illegitimate sons, in the 1530s and went on to serve as lord admiral under Edward, Mary, and Elizabeth and win promotion to the earldom of Lincoln.[96]

Brandon similarly had very little land to pass on to his nephew Charles, but the youngster found his own way round that problem. Between about 1506 and 1510—the details are understandably hazy—he contracted marriages with two women, abandoning Anne Browne for her aunt, Dame Margaret Mortimer, then returning to her and having the Mortimer marriage annulled. In the process, he fathered two daughters by Anne, only one indisputably legitimate. But he also gained possession of Margaret Mortimer's lands, and rapidly sold nine or ten of her manors for well over £1,000, a stunning profit when set against the £40 he had paid Dudley for a royal licence to marry her.[97] His uncle had set him the example

[91] PRO, PROB11/23/27.

[92] R. Jeffs, 'The Poynings–Percy Dispute: An Example of the Interplay of Open Strife and Legal Action in the Fifteenth Century', *BIHR* 34 (1961), 162.

[93] PRO, PROB11/20/21.

[94] D. Grummitt, *The Calais Garrison: War and Military Service in England, 1436–1558* (Woodbridge, 2008), 110–11; Miller, *Nobility*, 34; Hasler, *Commons*, iii. 241–2.

[95] Charles Wriothesley, *A Chronicle of England during the Reigns of the Tudors*, ed. W. D. Hamilton, 2 vols, CS 2nd ser. 11, 20 (London, 1875–7), i. 160.

[96] PRO, C54/402, mm. 9d, 13d, C54/403, mm. 26d, 27d, C54/404, m. 26d; A. Duffin, 'Clinton, Edward Fiennes de, First Earl of Lincoln', *ODNB*; *CP*, iii. 317.

[97] Gunn, *Charles Brandon*, 4, 28; *CCR 1500–9*, 841; PRO, CP25/1/30/101/48, CP25/1/46/93/47, CP25/1/170/197/121, CP25/1/202/42/58, CP25/2/28/188/3; *Feet of Fines for Cambridgeshire Henry VIII to Elizabeth*, ed. W. M. Palmer (Norwich, 1909), 25–6; *A Calendar of the Feet of Fines relating to the County of Huntingdon*, ed. G. J. Turner, Cambridge Antiquarian Society 37 (Cambridge, 1913), 117; BL, MS Lansdowne 127, fo. 24r.

of marrying richly landed widows, but the refinement of ridding himself of them once he had stripped their assets was peculiarly and unpleasantly his own.

There are signs that the families of the new men stuck together as one generation succeeded the next. From the last years of Henry VII's reign, Charles Brandon was close to Edward and Henry Guildford, who lived near him in Southwark, perhaps indeed in his uncle's household, attended his wedding in 1508, stood godfathers to his daughters, and joined him in the revels around the young Henry VIII.[98] Cutt's sons John and Henry were among the young gentlemen of Lovell's household in 1524.[99] Thomas Wyatt borrowed money from Henry Guildford and stayed close to Thomas Poynings and his brothers.[100] In 1519, when widowed by the death of Thomas, Lord Clinton, Poynings's daughter Jane married Brandon's cousin Sir Robert Wingfield.[101] In 1526 Mordaunt's grandson John married Lovell's great-niece Ela Fitzlewis.[102]

However carefully the new men planned for the future, they could not guard against drastic political change. Empson was careful to have many of his pensions from religious houses granted jointly to himself and his son Thomas, but after his father's fall Thomas had great difficulty in collecting them.[103] Thomas also shared his father's recordership of Coventry, but lost the succession to Anthony Fitzherbert.[104] All Dudley could hope for by the time he made his will was that the earl of Shrewsbury might see his eldest son John 'married in a honest stock'.[105] Nor could the best planning guard against the failure of sons and heirs to inherit their father's skills. John Leland mused on the fact when he visited Rycote in Oxfordshire. Thomas Fowler, 'a toward fellow', rose from clerk to the customer of London to be Edward IV's chancellor of the duchy of Lancaster, a forerunner of Bray and his ilk. The childless customer bequeathed Rycote to Fowler's son Richard, his godson. But Richard was 'a very unthrift', and sold up to Sir John Heron. Heron's son Giles, in turn, was 'wise in words, but foolish in deeds, as Sir Richard Fowler was'. He sold the manor to John Williams, treasurer of the court of augmentations, one of the next wave of upwardly mobile royal servants.[106]

Most cruelly of all, nothing could guard against premature death. Windsor had married his eldest son George to a sister and co-heiress of the fourteenth earl of Oxford, and had begun to train him up in public affairs, for example as a subsidy commissioner in 1512–15, but George died in 1520 without issue.[107] That left

---

[98]   Gunn, *Charles Brandon*, 6–7; PRO, KB9/449/3; PROB11/16/29.

[99]   *LP* IV, i. 366; H. W. King, 'The Descent of the Manor of Horham, and of the Family of Cutts', *TEAS* 4 (1869), 30.

[100]   PRO, PROB2/484, m. 8; Brigden, *Wyatt*, 71, 215, 317–18, 495–6.

[101]   Bindoff, *Commons*, iii. 642.

[102]   Bindoff, *Commons*, ii. 614; PRO, C1/848/37–8, 850/29–30.

[103]   PRO, C1/360/66, 462/43, 783/57, 786/12; *Reports from the Lost Notebooks of Sir James Dyer*, ed. J. H. Baker, 2 vols, SS 109, 110 (London, 1994), ii. 150.

[104]   *The Coventry Leet Book, 1420–1555*, ed. M. D. Harris, 4 vols, EETS 134–5, 138, 146 (London, 1907–13), iii. 622, 625.

[105]   PRO, SP1/2, fo. 6r (*LP* I, i. 559).

[106]   J. Leland, *The Itinerary of John Leland in or about the Years 1535–1543*, ed. L. T. Smith, 5 vols (London, 1906–10), i. 115–16.

[107]   4 Henry VIII c. 19; 5 Henry VIII c. 17; 6 Henry VIII c. 26.

George's younger brother William as the heir, rather less impressively married to Margaret Sambourne. She was heiress to a handful of manors in Berkshire, Wiltshire, and Somerset, but most of them did not fall in until her mother's death in 1535. William and Margaret litigated hard through the 1520s and 1530s, but without much success, to get their hands on her grandfather's lands, while William slowly established himself at court and in Buckinghamshire.[108] Mortality hit the Marneys harder still. John was married in 1510–11 to Christina Newburgh, the daughter and heiress of a Dorset knight who left them half a dozen manors worth upwards of £60 a year and several thousand sheep when he died in September 1516. They had two daughters but no son, and she outlived her father by less than a year.[109] John married again in autumn 1518, to Bridget, daughter of a Suffolk knight and widow of an Essex gentleman, but they had no children. All this was a sound basis for John's position in local society, as a Dorset JP and a busy Essex commissioner, several times considered for the shrievalty of each county.[110] But when he fell ill and died in April 1525, it left the fruits of his father's career to those who bought the wardships of his daughters, the duke of Norfolk and Lord Fitzwalter. At least the £1,000 each paid to the king was some testimony to what Sir Henry had achieved; and in the end a little of his booty did endow one of his colleagues' sons, for Katherine Marney was left a widow by the death of Fitzwalter's son in the early 1530s and married Thomas Poynings.[111] By political skill, dutiful service, and family strategy most of the new men survived the advent of Henry VIII with considerable success, but sterner challenges lay ahead.

[108] CP, XII, ii. 794–7; Bindoff, *Commons*, iii. 637–8; CIPM, iii. 503–5; PRO, C1/453/36, 590/62–9, 690/2, 920/43, 926/48; CP25/2/46/320/10.
[109] J. Hutchins, *The History and Antiquities of the County of Dorset*, 3rd edn, 4 vols (Westminster, 1861–74), i. 368–9.
[110] Bindoff, *Commons*, ii. 573; LP I, ii. 632 (26), 1462 (14), II, i. 1596, ii. 2787, 4562, III, i. 1081 (14), ii. 1451 (15), 2020, 2667, 2892, 3504; PRO, KB9/458/16, 477/49, 485/27, 487/13; E137/11/4, mm. 7v, 11r, 12r, 13r, 14r, 16v.
[111] LP IV, i. 1241, 1292, 2203–4, iii. 5508 (2); CP, XII, i. 520.

17

Faith and fortune

Twenty years on from the death of their master Henry VII, the surviving new men faced a new set of political earthquakes. Wolsey's fall, the king's divorce and marriage to Anne Boleyn, and the break with Rome posed much more severe challenges than any previous episodes. They brought to the fore a fresh generation of new men, Thomas Cromwell, Thomas Audley, Richard Rich, and others, those whom the rebels of 1536 would denounce as Perkin Warbeck had once denounced Bray, Lovell, and the rest. They also put old loyalties and ingrained pieties to the test.

THOMAS CROMWELL AND ANNE BOLEYN

As the king divorced Katherine of Aragon and sought a male heir through marriage to Anne Boleyn, matters were hardest for Hussey, because of his relationship with the now bastardized and disinherited Princess Mary. Hussey became Mary's chamberlain at some point between 1527 and 1530, sharing the leadership of her household of some 160 servants with her governess, Margaret, countess of Salisbury. At first, Hussey had merely some financial responsibilities, a role in regulating the princess's daily routine, an opportunity to welcome his friends and relations to visit the household as it perambulated around Kent, Surrey, and Essex, and an obligation to petition Cromwell on behalf of his subordinates.[1] The position does not seem to have been hard to combine with on-going involvement in the king's council.[2] In 1533, however, things became awkward, as Henry began to press Mary to accept the invalidity of her parents' marriage, her own illegitimacy, and, from September, her inferiority to the new princess, Elizabeth.

Hussey's first test was the king's order in July 1533 to have Mary's jewels and plate inventoried, probably to facilitate their confiscation. 'I shall not fail to follow' the king's pleasure 'to the best of my power', Hussey told Cromwell, but in late August the countess, stiffened by her long service to the princess and her powerful royal blood as niece of the Yorkist kings, was still stalling Hussey, Cromwell, and the king. 'Would to God that the king and you did know and see what I have had to do here of late', wrote Hussey. A week later he had been checkmated by the countess with the argument that the plate, which Cromwell had now asked for

---

[1] *LP* V, pp. 321–2, VI. 1540, VII. 817, VIII. 440, IX. 900 (probably of 1532).
[2] *LP* IV, iii. 1023, VI. 197.

directly, was being used by Mary, so could be spared only if new plate were bought to replace it.[3] Cromwell made himself a note to summon Hussey and the countess, and from then on Henry bypassed them, sending other councillors to confront Mary and then deciding to dissolve her household and place her, humiliatingly, in Elizabeth's.[4] Hussey was left to tell an astonished Mary the news—humiliatingly, she refused to take it from him and demanded a letter from the king—and then to help her other servants find new jobs.[5]

Henry blamed those around Mary for encouraging her intransigence, but even if Hussey had done so behind the scenes, he had been much less heroic in his opposition to the king than the countess, who responded to the dissolution of the household by offering to continue to serve Mary at her own cost.[6] In June 1536, when Henry resumed browbeating Mary and her friends over her refusal to accept his ecclesiastical supremacy and divorce from her mother, it was not Hussey but his wife who was put in the Tower. There she stayed until August, charged with deliberately calling Mary princess when she visited her on the way south with her husband for parliament. She claimed that she had done so inadvertently: it was old habit, formed when she was one of the princess's ladies, that made her ask for a drink for the princess and tell someone the princess had gone for a walk. She admitted keeping up contact with Mary, sending and receiving gifts and asking her 'how she did'; but she firmly denied that she had maintained the validity of Henry's marriage to Katherine or discussed the sensitive issue of *bona fides parentum*, the strong, but for Henry inconvenient, argument that Mary was legitimate because her parents believed themselves to be legitimately married at the time of her birth. Sick and desperate for fresh air, she declared her penitence and begged the king's mercy. She was released, but the episode cannot have improved Hussey's opinion of the king's proceedings.[7]

Superficially, Hussey found Cromwell's increasing importance easier to deal with than the divorce. He had already seen the advantages in keeping Cromwell sweet when the clever man of business was rising in Wolsey's service, paying him a pension of £4 a year from February 1526.[8] In the early 1530s he wrote to him often asking favours, over his debts to the king, the appointment of sheriffs, exemptions from fines for knighthood, and posts for his kinsmen and friends in the new minister's service. He thanked him 'heartily' for his 'manifold kindness showed to me in all my suits' and for his 'kindness for my friends', and assured him that in complying with each request 'ye shall bind me to do you such pleasure as shall lie in my power'; but perhaps he protested too much, signing one letter 'by me your old friend'.[9] Certainly, where office-holding was concerned, all this

[3] D. M. Loades, *Mary Tudor: A Life* (Oxford, 1989), 72–4, 348; PRO, SP1/78, fos. 11, 141, 169 (*LP* VI. 849, 1009, 1041).
[4] Loades, *Mary Tudor*, 74–80; *LP* VI. 1186, 1249, 1382, 1486, 1528.
[5] *LP* VI. 1139, 1207, VII. 38.
[6] *LP* VI. 1392, VII. 1206; H. Pierce, *Margaret Pole, Countess of Salisbury, 1473–1541: Loyalty, Lineage and Leadership* (Cardiff, 2003), 97–102.
[7] Loades, *Mary Tudor*, 98–105; *LP* VI. 1199, XI. 7, 10, 222.
[8] *LP* V. 1285(vi), XI. App. 16; PRO, E315/237, p. 108.
[9] PRO, SP1/72, fo. 41, SP1/86, fo. 41, SP1/237, fo. 239 (*LP* V. 1556, VII. 1259, Addenda, i. 795); *LP* V. 1238, VII. 516, 1258, 1305, 1566, X. 206.

cultivation of Cromwell did him little good: in 1535 the reversions of two of his posts were granted not to his sons, but to Cromwell's nephew Richard and the courtier Sir Francis Bryan.[10]

Windsor, in contrast, took Anne's rise in his stride. At the great wardrobe it was mainly a matter of processing warrants like that of May 1530, for saddles 'of the French fashion' for 'our dear and right well-beloved the lady Anne Rocheford', including one 'with a head of copper and gilt graven with antique works', and eventually of providing soft furnishings and the like to her household as queen.[11] His son William may have found it harder. He was reported to have said in 1534 that Sir Francis Bryan's 'service to the king'—perhaps on his embassies to France in the attempt to secure the divorce—was 'to the charge of all the realm and to the repentance of all the same'.[12] Nonetheless, William made the best of Anne's coronation, accepting a knighthood of the bath and serving the new queen at dinner, and he was active in the enforcement of government policy in the 1530s, assessing taxation on the church, serving as sheriff of Buckinghamshire in 1537–8, reporting troublesome friars and those speaking treason.[13] Through the 1530s and beyond, his father played his part at court dutifully, greeting Anne of Cleves at her arrival as he had greeted Anne Boleyn at her coronation, helping with the creation of Lord Russell and the obsequies for the king's sister Mary, queen of France and for the Empress Isabella.[14]

Windsor also seems to have found it reasonably easy to cope with Cromwell's dominance. Like Hussey, he paid him a fee, £6 13s 4d a year by 1537.[15] His letters to Cromwell were brisker than Hussey's, but that may have been precisely because they worked together well: one about a man Windsor had arrested at Cromwell's request asserted confidently that the man's offence was 'but negligence', but concluded that 'I doubt not ye will further order him as the matter requireth'.[16] They cooperated profitably in matters of patronage, Windsor offering £40 a year and a rich collar worth £116 13s 4d for Cromwell's assistance in accelerating the grant of an office to one of his clients.[17] Windsor made friends with other rising men too, naming among his executors Lord Chancellor Audley and Sir John Baker, chancellor of first fruits and tenths.[18] He was active on the council in 1532–3 and 1541, though not one of the inner ring that crystallized around this time into the formal privy council.[19] His parliamentary attendance rates were also quite high, certainly in the more active half of the lay peerage. He appeared on between 65 per cent and

---

[10] *LP* VIII. 481 (22), IX. 729 (15).   [11] *LP* IV, iii, App. 256, VI. 602.

[12] *The Household Book (1510–1551) of Sir Edward Don: An Anglo-Welsh Knight and his Circle*, ed. R. A. Griffiths, Buckinghamshire RS 33 (Aylesbury, 2004), 222.

[13] *LP* VI. 562, VIII. 149 (55), X. 850, XI. 1217 (23), XII, ii. 1150 (18), XIII, i. 333.

[14] *LP* VI. 563, XIV, i. 477, XV. 14; PRO, LC2/1, fo. 175v; C. Wriothesley, *A Chronicle of England during the Reigns of the Tudors*, ed. W. D. Hamilton, 2 vols, CS 2nd ser., 11, 20 (London, 1875–7), i. 98.

[15] *LP* XIV, ii. 782.   [16] PRO, SP1/163, fo. 168 (*LP* XV. 1029 (68)).

[17] PRO, SP1/93, fo. 186 (*LP* VIII. 978).   [18] PRO, PROB11/29/23.

[19] *LP* V. 1421, XVI. 978, 1028, 1047, 1261; PRO, STAC2/19/205.

77 per cent of the days the lords sat between 1534 and 1542, though by his last parliament it may have been his age that made him sometimes attend in the morning but slip away—perhaps to doze?—in the afternoon. He never made it to the session of early 1543 and died on 30 March, but by 10 April his son had taken up his seat.[20] Windsor not only lived longer than any of the new men, he also stayed longer at the heart of Tudor government.

Wyatt's position was more complicated. Events in 1533 were unsettling, as one of his servants wrote to Anne Boleyn about the angels who kept visiting him with messages for her, and he decided his son should replace him as chief ewerer at her coronation.[21] What followed in 1536 was very much worse. Early in May his son was sent to the Tower, one of the later arrests in the sweep for Queen Anne's alleged lovers, presumably on account of his pursuit of her before her marriage to the king. Though Thomas's life was thought to be in the balance and he saw his friends executed, he was never put on trial; but was this because there was less evidence against him than against them, or because Cromwell intervened to save him?[22] Certainly, Sir Henry was grateful to Cromwell for his role in Thomas's escape, signing himself as Cromwell's 'assured servant'. But he was also quick to thank Henry for not punishing his son, protesting that if Thomas were unfaithful to the king he would wish 'to see him perish afore my face'; and it is hard to judge the nature of the investigations into Thomas's conduct without the 'comfortable articles' Cromwell sent Sir Henry on 10 May, when it was apparently already clear Thomas would be released.[23]

If Cromwell did lend a helping hand in Thomas's escape, it is also unclear how far it was out of affection or respect for Thomas himself and how far for his father. Sir Henry already trusted Cromwell enough in March 1535 to name him a feoffee for the performance of his will, and then, or soon afterwards, he made him his executor, bequeathing him a cup 'for a small and a poor remembrance'.[24] Sir Henry was also a more dependable agent of the new regime than some of his colleagues, investigating carefully within days of his son's release whether the vicar of Loose, on the far side of Maidstone from his home at Allington, had referred to Urban IV as pope rather than bishop of Rome.[25] Matters were made more complex still by Sir Henry's disapproval of his son's riotous and adulterous style of life. Even before Thomas was out of the Tower, Sir Henry was asking Cromwell to tell him to take his imprisonment as punishment for 'the displeasure that he hath done to God otherwise' and to urge him to 'fly vice and serve God better than he hath done'.[26]

[20] *LJ*, i. 58–221; H. Miller, 'Attendance in the House of Lords during the Reign of Henry VIII', *Historical Journal* 10 (1967), 337.

[21] *LP* VI. 1599; E. Hall, *Hall's Chronicle*, ed. H. Ellis (London, 1809), 798, 804.

[22] *LP* X. 855, 865, 919, 920; G. W. Bernard, *Anne Boleyn: Fatal Attractions* (New Haven CT and London, 2010), 15–18, 175–82, 190–1; E. W. Ives, *Anne Boleyn* (Oxford, 1986), 373, 416; S. Brigden, *Thomas Wyatt; The Heart's Forest* (London, 2012), 274–92.

[23] PRO, SP1/103, fo. 266, SP1/113, fo. 195 (*LP* X. 840, XI. 1492).

[24] PRO, E210/9917; PROB11/26/7.   [25] PRO, SP1/104, fos. 158–9 (*LP* X. 1125).

[26] PRO, SP1/103, fo. 266 (*LP* X. 840).

Once Thomas had been sent home to Allington, his father lectured him on the need to abandon the bad ways that had earned him God's disfavour and the king's and to obey Cromwell's commands like those of a father.[27] Was this the submission of a family of grateful political dependants, or an agreement between two older and staider men to restrain the excesses of Thomas Wyatt's prolonged adolescence?

Alongside all these political troubles came advancing age and declining health. Poynings had asked for his recall from Tournai in 1515 because while there he was 'ever sickly', and now the years were catching up even with the younger new men.[28] Hussey could hardly ride in August 1525, kept his sickbed for fourteen weeks in spring 1534, and in October 1535 again felt 'somewhat sick in my body', sick enough to update his will. By January 1536, he counted himself 'a wretch and a man not able to ride, go, nor yet well stand, but as I am borne', such that 'I look not to come to London alive'.[29] It must indeed have been an indignity for a knight to travel around in a horse-litter covered in yellow cotton.[30] In May 1536, signing his letters in a quavering hand, Wyatt assured his son that 'I cannot go nor ride but to the danger of my life'.[31] Six months later he was dead. Windsor lasted best, but one winter in the late 1530s even he spent five weeks shut in his bedroom at Stanwell, suffering from an ague.[32] For such aged men the pressures of political life must have had a cost. Dugdale speculated that the king's enforced exchange of lands with Windsor was 'no little trouble to his mind: and perhaps might conduce to the shortening of his days'.[33]

RELIGIOUS CHANGE

The religious changes of the 1530s were still more unsettling than those in politics. The new men's piety had been formed at Henry VII's court, and they were not about to give it up in their declining years: as Hussey and his friends agreed, they would be 'none heretic' but would 'die Christian men'.[34] Emphases within the circle varied. Southwell, for example, expressed with particular force the despite for the body, 'my most vile body . . . my wretched carcass and body', as he put it in his will, which characterized some late medieval piety.[35] Hussey founded a hermitage at his manor of Branston.[36] Guildford ended his days in the Holy Land, amidst all the sites of the Passion, at the culmination of a pilgrimage which had taken in the many relics at St Denis, Venice, and Ragusa, the tombs of St Anne, St Matthew,

---

[27] PRO, SP1/104, fo. 165 (*LP* X. 1131).   [28] Hall, *Chronicle*, 583.

[29] *LP* VII, 714, 1665, XII, i. 186(33); PRO, SP1/122, fo. 159 (*LP* XII, ii. 187(3)); SP1/101, fo 172 (*LP* X. 206).

[30] PRO, E36/95, fo. 119r.   [31] PRO, SP1/103, fo. 251 (*LP* X. 819).

[32] PRO, SP1/128, fo. 124 (*LP* XIII, i. 25).

[33] W. Dugdale, *The Baronage of England*, 2 vols (London, 1675), ii. 308.

[34] PRO, SP1/118, fo. 123r–123v (LP XII, i. 899).

[35] PRO, PROB11/18/5.   [36] PRO, E315/393, fo. 27v.

and St Simeon, the emerald cup from which Christ had drunk at the Last Supper, and two paintings of the Virgin by the hand of Saint Luke; admittedly, his party took a less excitable attitude to relics and indulgences than many other pilgrims, as befitted his apparent acquaintance with Erasmus.[37] Poynings regarded his projected delegation to the Lateran Council in 1515 as 'my pilgrimage to Rome'.[38] Others again, such as Mordaunt and Empson, attached sufficient weight to confession and the mass that they applied for special papal powers for their confessors or the right to a portable altar, while Lovell had a private altar in his chamber at Elsings.[39] In their provision for the fate of their souls, however, they came together to follow the old king's lead. The three keynotes of Henry's own elaborate postmortem provisions were friars, especially his trusted Franciscan Observants, almshouses, and masses for the dead, and all were close to the hearts of his new men.[40]

The friars featured heavily in their religion in life and in death. Lovell commissioned prayers from the Norwich Carmelites for the souls of departed brethren in the order of the garter.[41] Guildford left books and other goods with the London Dominicans when he set out on his pilgrimage.[42] Hussey was promised a 'fair bible' by the warden of the Franciscans of Ware.[43] Southwell sent barrels of herring to the Ware Franciscans and the London Dominicans, a butt of malmsey to the prior of the Dominicans, and, most generously, but perhaps a little inappropriately for a famously ascetic order, a hogshead of claret to the Observants of Richmond.[44] This affection carried on into their testamentary provision. Lovell left £2 each to the five friaries in London, the four in Norwich, Lynn, Cambridge, and Oxford, and the two in Thetford; but to Henry VII's favourites, the Observants of Richmond and Greenwich, he left twice that.[45] Southwell and Belknap requested burial in the London Dominican house and the sub-prior of the London Carmelites witnessed Southwell's will.[46] Brandon, whose confessor was the provincial of the Austin friars, left their convent £60 towards their new building in return for their keeping a perpetual memory of his late wife the marchioness of Berkeley and her first husband the marquess; the prior of the Dominicans, where he was himself to be buried, attended his deathbed and came away with £13 6s 8d for repairs to his

[37] *Pylgrymage of Sir Richard Guylforde to the Holy Land, A.D. 1506*, ed. H. Ellis, CS o.s. 51 (London, 1851), 1–40; R. Lutton, 'Richard Guldeford's Pilgrimage: Piety and Cultural Change in late fifteenth- and early sixteenth-century England', *History* 98 (2013), 62–6, 70–1.

[38] PRO, SP1/10, fo. 52 (*LP* II, i. 149).

[39] R. Halstead, *Succinct Genealogies of the Noble and Ancient Houses of Alno or de Alneto etc* (London, 1685), 514–16; *CEPR*, xv. 797; PRO, PROB2/199, m. 3.

[40] M. M. Condon, 'The Last Will of Henry VII: Document and Text', in T. Tatton-Brown and R. Mortimer (eds), *Westminster Abbey: The Lady Chapel of Henry VII* (Woodbridge, 2003), 105, 119, 130–1; M. M. Condon, 'God Save the King! Piety, Propaganda and the Perpetual Memorial', in Tatton-Brown and Mortimer (eds), *Westminster Abbey: The Lady Chapel*, 59–97.

[41] *HMC Rutland*, iv. 264.

[42] S. Cunningham, 'Guildford, Sir Richard', *ODNB*.

[43] PRO, SP1/122, fo. 157r (*LP* XII, ii. 187(2)).

[44] PRO, SP1/230, fos. 113r, 114r, 119r (*LP* I, ii. 2765).

[45] PRO, PROB11/23/27.   [46] PRO, PROB11/18/5; HL, MS STT Personal box 1 (7).

church.[47] Empson was buried in the London Carmelite house and Dudley with the Dominicans.[48] Marney chose the Richmond and Greenwich Observants, together with the friars of London, Chelmsford, Colchester, and Maldon, to celebrate masses for his soul.[49]

Relief of the poor was another pious work much practised, in life but much more so in death. Wyatt was paying £2 8s to maintain poor people at Milton by Gravesend in 1521, Hussey's household was supporting thirteen poor men in 1533–4, and in December 1534 he gave 7s 4d in alms to twenty-one named residents of Sleaford.[50] Lovell left £50 to provide dowries for the marriage of fifteen poor maidens and Poynings left money to care for and marry 'Jane, a maid child which was found unchristened in the parish of Nettlestead', and Mary, a child who was given to his wife.[51] Southwell wanted a poor person hired for a penny each day to attend services in the Blackfriars where he was buried and say Our Lady's Psalter for his soul.[52] Brandon left a hundred nobles to be given within three days after his burial to a hundred poor householders and the bedridden.[53] Windsor wanted a shilling each given to his poor tenants in Stanwell and Horton after his death, and at his annual obit the poor of Stanwell were to share a quarter of wheat and a cheerful 288 pints of beer.[54]

Almshouses were an increasingly popular way to combine a remedy for social need with the provision of prayer for the dead.[55] Cutt founded one in Thaxted and Marney set out exhaustive plans for his at Layer Marney.[56] Brick-built with a tiled roof, it was to house five poor men 'not being able to get their living by labour or other occupations', who would be paid 10d a week and given a russet frieze gown each Michaelmas. They were to say five Paternosters and one Credo, in Latin, every morning in aid of Marney's soul and those of his ancestors, wives, and children, before attending mass in his new chapel in the parish church. While there, they were to kneel before the sacrament with one Paternoster and an Ave Maria, kneel by his tomb for three Paternosters, three Aves, and a Credo, and end in the chancel with Our Lady's Psalter. In the afternoon they were left to their own devices, except on Wednesdays and Fridays when they were to return to his tomb for Our Lady's Psalter or, if they could manage it, the Dirige; but at bedtime they were back on duty with five Paternosters, five Aves, and the choice of a Credo or a De Profundis. Marney's two chantry priests were to live in a chamber by the almshouse, so that the poor men might be 'the better guided and ordered'. Though the sick might be

[47] PRO, PROB11/16/29.
[48] M. M. Condon, 'Empson, Sir Richard', *ODNB*; S. J. Gunn, 'Dudley, Edmund', *ODNB*.
[49] 'Ancient Wills', ed. H. W. King, *TEAS* 4 (1869), 149.
[50] PRO, SC6/Henry VIII/1684, m. 3r; E36/95, fos. 28v, 52v.
[51] PRO, PROB11/23/27; PROB11/20/21.   [52] PRO, PROB11/18/5.
[53] PRO, PROB11/16/29.   [54] PRO, PROB11/29/23.
[55] W. K. Jordan, *The Charities of London 1480–1660: The Aspirations and the Achievements of the Urban Society* (London, 1960), 136–9; W. K. Jordan, *The Charities of Rural England 1480–1660: The Aspirations and the Achievements of the Rural Society* (London, 1961), 254–6.
[56] H. W. King, 'The Descent of the Manor of Horham, and of the Family of Cutts', *TEAS* 4 (1869), 34.

permitted to say their prayers in their rooms rather than in church and other members of the team might be allowed to make up the numbers of prayers due from those so ill that they could not even pray from their beds, the priests were to report any delinquents to Marney's executors so they might be removed. Here were the principles of order and accountability that marked Henry VII's regime applied to the economy of salvation. Marney's priests, of course, had more to do than keep an eye on his almsmen, and were almost equally regimented. They were to say mass for his and his family's souls in his chapel every day in a cycle that rotated each week through the church's major devotions: masses of the Annunciation, Nativity, Five Wounds, Cross, Resurrection, and Corpus Christi; masses of the Virgin and of her Conception, Nativity, Purification, and Assumption; masses of the Holy Trinity, Holy Ghost, and All Saints. They, too, had special duties on Wednesdays and Fridays, with a Placebo and Dirige.[57]

Lovell's preparations for intercessory prayer were less minutely detailed, but he spread his net wide. Under the terms of his gift to the grocers' company, two chantry priests, initially his own unbeneficed chaplains Henry Smyth and Thomas Sperke, were to be maintained at Holywell Nunnery to pray for his soul at the generous rate of £8 a year.[58] The nuns there were to gather at his tomb every day for a year after his decease to say the De Profundis for him; and just in case they were inclined to forget, the windows of his burial chapel were inscribed

All the nuns in Holywell
Pray for the soul of Sir Thomas Lovell.

Further reminders stood in the extensive building work he had done at the convent and the lands to the annual value of £40 he had been licensed to give them in 1511.[59] He left £10 to the dean and chapter of St George's Windsor to pray for him, £10 to the staff of the king's chapel, £10 to the officers of the king's household. Bequests totalling £55 to other nunneries and £42 to the parish churches where he had worshipped at different stages of his life—Beachamwell, East Harling, Enfield, and Shoreditch—must also have been freighted with hopes for intercession.[60] Even his gift of plate to the city of London had a spiritual quid pro quo, for every time the mayor dined or supped off the silver donated by Lovell his chaplain was to ask in the grace for God's mercy on Lovell's soul, and he was also to be prayed for at the corporation's sermons.[61] It was a brilliant idea, but its time was soon past: in 1548, when prayer for the dead was no longer on the menu, the plate was sold off 'for certain good and reasonable considerations'.[62]

[57] 'Ancient Wills', 150–3.
[58] LMA, Rep. 6, fo. 61r; PRO, PROB11/23/27; *VE*, i. 434.
[59] J. Stow, *A Survey of London*, ed. C. L. Kingsford, 2nd edn, 2 vols (Oxford, 1971), ii. 73; *LP* I, i. 804(31); W. Dugdale, *Monasticon Anglicanum*, ed. J. Caley et al., 6 vols in 8 (London, 1817–30), iv. 391.
[60] PRO, PROB11/23/27.   [61] LMA, Rep. 4, fo. 150v.
[62] L. Jewitt and W. H. StJ. Hope, *The Corporation Plate and Insignia of Office, of the Cities and Corporate Towns of England and Wales*, 2 vols (London, 1985), ii. 124–5.

This intense concern for intercession was not unique. Risley gave lands to maintain a perpetual chaplain at St Mary's chapel, Barking, Bray founded a free chapel at Standen Hussey in Berkshire, and Hussey endowed anniversary masses at Tattershall College.[63] Southwell provided for prayers for his parents at Woodrising and for himself and his wives for twenty years at the London Dominicans, but added the ingenious provision that the first friar ordained as a priest who should wash his hands each day at the lavatory in the cloister, near which he was buried, should say the De Profundis, Credo, and Paternoster for him and have a penny reward.[64] Poynings provided for two priests to sing masses for his soul and his parents' souls for twelve years after an initial burst of a hundred masses at his burial and month's mind.[65] Brandon, too, made a quick start on his way through purgatory, with five hundred masses in four London friaries and the Charterhouse and £35 to St George's, Windsor, for prayers.[66] Marney had collected grants of confraternity from religious houses and left 3s 4d to each place 'where I am made a brother under their seal' to be included in their prayers. He also wanted masses soon after his death, this time trentals, sung at friaries and at the Scala Coeli chapel in Westminster, another devotional site favoured by Henry VII and his mother, and one with special power for the relief of souls.[67]

Wyatt was already paying a chantry chaplain at Milton by Gravesend in 1520–1 and steadily put together plans for a permanent foundation. In 1521 he secured a royal grant of the patronage of Milton church and in August 1524 a grant of the endowment of a hospital or chantry there which had been declared defunct at the death of its master in March. In the background of these demure moves lay riotous disputes over the hospital's lands between his men and those of the previous master. Meanwhile, he obtained the licence necessary to endow his own chantry, with two priests, in the chapel and other buildings of the old hospital, and negotiated away the objections of Bishop Fisher, who claimed jurisdiction over parish church and hospital alike. Thus all was prepared for his chantry, as he put it in his will, to 'continue, stand and abide according to such statutes ordinances and rules, the which I have ordained and made, contained and specified in the book of the foundation of the same chantry'.[68] In the event it did not even last until the dissolution of the chantries. By early 1547, the buildings of 'the late chantry called Wyatt's chantry' with their pleasant 'prospect' of the Thames were being squabbled over by his step-son William Wilde and Thomas Mountayne, the hot reformist cleric put into the rectory of Milton by Bishop Holbeach.[69]

[63] *London and Middlesex Chantry Certificate 1548*, ed. C. J. Kitching, London RS 16 (London, 1980), 29; *VE*, ii. 158; LA, 1ANC3/25/55; H1/10–12.
[64] PRO, PROB11/18/5.   [65] PRO, PROB11/20/21.
[66] PRO, PROB11/16/29.
[67] 'Ancient Wills', 148–9; N. Morgan, 'The *Scala Coeli* Indulgence and the Royal Chapels', in B. Thompson (ed.), *The Reign of Henry VII* (Stamford, 1995), 82–103.
[68] *LP* III, i. 1215(4), IV, i. 297(1), 612(1); P. Morant, *The History and Antiquities of the County of Essex*, 2 vols (East Ardsley, 1978 edn), i. 252; Medway Archives, DRc/L9; PRO, SC6/Henry VIII/1684, m. 3r; PROB11/26/7; STAC 2/19/198.
[69] PRO, C1/1144/37; *Narratives of the Days of the Reformation*, ed. J. G. Nichols, CS o.s. 77 (London, 1859), 176–217.

Windsor came last, and he knew it. He wanted a trental of requiems, and an annual obit for forty years, with malmsey and comfits for the choir; he wanted chantries in the churches of Stanwell and Dorney; but only 'if the laws of the realm will it permit and suffer'. It may have been with a sense of the impermanence of institutional intercessory provision that he ended his will by asking for the prayers of each of his four executors and two supervisors. The chantry he was maintaining at Dorney in 1535 must have been swept away together with whatever formal provision his executors made, but some sign of his intentions lasted longer than he feared, for an inscription recording the foundation of an intercessory chapel in 1542 was later recorded at Bradenham.[70]

SUPREMACY, DISSOLUTION, AND REVOLT

In the 1530s other elements of the new men's religious world were disappearing faster than prayer for the dead. The Observants, for example, spoke out against the king's divorce from Easter 1532, and after 1534 many died under arrest or went into exile. The Carthusians, patronized by Brandon and Belknap, also provided prominent victims for the king's campaign to impose his supremacy on the church.[71] Windsor may have been politically adaptable—he had done his bit for the divorce campaign by providing twelve featherbeds for Cardinal Campeggio—but his religious affinities were with the leaders of the church under assault.[72] In May 1532 he was chief mourner at the funeral of Abbot Islip of Westminster, supervisor of Henry VII's grand intercessory foundation, where Wyatt was also to the fore. The preacher was Rowland Phillips, vicar of Croydon, recently browbeaten for his opposition to the royal supremacy and due for arrest again in the following year.[73] In December of that year, Windsor took responsibility as an executor of Archbishop Warham. In his will, written two years earlier, Warham had noted that Windsor had always been a friend to him and his kin. The archbishop had stood up to Henry, at least for a time, and so had at least one of Windsor's fellow-executors, Peter Ligham, dean of the arches. Another executor was Warham's chancellor Dr John Cockys, presented to Windsor's valuable rectory at Midley in 1529 in succession to Dr John Fayter, Katherine of Aragon's proctor at the divorce hearings of that year.[74]

[70] PRO, PROB11/29/23; *VE*, iv. 225; A. Collins, *Historical Collections of the Noble Family of Windsor* (London, 1754), 50.

[71] G. W. Bernard, *The King's Reformation: Henry VIII and the Remaking of the English Church* (New Haven CT and London, 2005), 151–67; PRO, PROB11/16/29; HL, MS STT Personal box 1(7).

[72] PRO, E101/420/1/72.

[73] Dugdale, *Monasticon Anglicanum*, i. 278–9; Bernard, *King's Reformation*, 194–5; B. F. Harvey and H. Summerson, 'Islip, John', *ODNB*.

[74] *Wills from Doctors' Commons: A Selection from the Wills of Eminent Persons proved in the Prerogative Court of Canterbury, 1495–1695*, ed. J. G. Nicholas and J. Bruce, CS o.s. 83 (London, 1863), 26–7; *LP* VI. 300 (18); Bernard, *King's Reformation*, 176–8, 194; A. B. Emden, *A Biographical Register of the University of Oxford to AD 1500*, 3 vols (Oxford, 1957–9), i. 452; A. B. Emden, *A Biographical Register of the University of Oxford 1500–40* (Oxford, 1974), 200–1; *VE*, i. 50; LPL, Canterbury Register Warham II, fos. 395v, 401v.

Such affinities continued to the end of Windsor's life. In the 1539 parliament, Sir William Weston, prior of the order of St John in England, another conservative figure, entrusted him with his proxy.[75] Yet at a time of rapid change even Windsor must have found it hard to judge the spiritual trajectories of those around him. William Rowell, presented to a rectory by his son and son-in-law in 1532, died in 1550 asking his 'especial good lord' the new Lord Windsor to dispose of his goods to satisfyingly conservative ends, 'for his soule helth and myne'.[76] In contrast, Edmund Pierson, presented to a rectory by Windsor himself in 1533, died in 1567 leaving his goods to Jesus Commons in London provided it remained under the administration of 'sincere preachers of God's word'; the bequest was to be revoked if 'any papist' took charge.[77]

By 1518, Windsor's sister Margaret was prioress of Syon, where Sutton had been so involved. It was another centre of opposition to Henry's measures and the veterans of Henry VII's court rallied around it.[78] Windsor was drawn into the king's campaign to secure the nuns' conformity and visited the house to talk to his sister and other kinswomen to that end in December 1535; but he cared for his sister long after her house was dissolved, leaving her a very generous annuity of £83 6s 8d a year with a request to pray for his soul and those of their parents.[79] Hussey, who had called one of his daughters Bridget, after St Bridget of Sweden to whose order Syon belonged, also had connections there. His friend Darcy had tried to help the house when Wolsey abused his powers over it.[80] In 1533 John Fewterer, a Syon monk, translated Ulrich Pinder's Latin treatise on the Passion at Hussey's request for publication in English.[81] It doubtless went with the taste for 'exhortations of holy and divine stories of scripture', for 'virtuous advices, wholesome doctrine and ghostly sayings of divers and many proper stories in scripture, sounding all godly and holy', with which Hussey and Darcy were said to have ingratiated themselves with the dying Lord Monteagle ten years earlier, 'pretending great amity and love . . . to his soul'.[82] More dangerously, Syon was a nerve centre for those impressed by the prophecies of Elizabeth Barton, the Nun of Kent, who dared to convey divine warnings to Henry about his fate should he persist with his divorce and was executed with some of her supporters in April 1534. It was one of the Canterbury Observants who confessed to sharing the Nun's revelations with Lord and Lady Hussey, but they could have come across them at Syon too, while it is intriguing that Poynings's confidant Edward Thwaites served as the nun's publicist in print, escaped with a large fine, and went on to plot against Archbishop Cranmer in 1543.[83]

---

[75] G. J. O'Malley, 'Weston, Sir William', *ODNB*.

[76] LAO, Register 27, fo. 216v; PRO, PROB11/34/21.

[77] GLRO, MS 9531/11, fo. 24v; PRO, PROB11/49/255.

[78] S. Powell, 'Margaret Pole and Syon Abbey', *HR* 79 (2005), 566–7; Bernard, *King's Reformation*, 167–2.

[79] *LP* IX. 986; PRO, PROB11/29/23.   [80] *LP* IV, iii. 5749.

[81] A. Da Costa, 'John Fewterer's *Myrrour or Glasse of Christes Passion* and Ulrich Pinder's *Speculum Passionis Domini Nostri*', *Notes and Queries* 56 (2009), 27–9.

[82] PRO, SP2/J, fo. 1r–1v (*LP* IV, ii. 5105(1)).

[83] Bernard, *King's Reformation*, 87–101, 155; E. Shagan, *Popular Politics and the English Reformation* (Cambridge, 2003), 78, 85–6, 199–202.

That Hussey was deeply alienated by Henry's actions was evident from the interview with him reported by Eustace Chapuys, the imperial ambassador, in September 1534. Hussey, whose prudence and experience as a councillor of Henry VII Chapuys rated highly, told him how much he and those who were of his mind—Chapuys was hearing the same views independently from Lord Darcy, Lord Bray, and the Pole family—desired Chapuys's master Charles V to take action against Henry to preserve the lives of Queen Katherine and Princess Mary and the latter's claim to the throne. He seems to have envisaged that a military initiative by Charles would enable Henry's subjects to rebel and thus, in some not quite defined way, set things to rights. In any case he referred discussion of any strategic detail to Darcy, who knew much more about such things. Darcy continued to discuss the possibilities with Chapuys for some time, but Charles was preoccupied elsewhere, not least with the conquest of Tunis, and nothing came of Hussey's hopes.[84] He may have hoped for change by another route when Anne Boleyn fell. He had stayed away from parliament in 1534 and was too ill to come in January 1536, but in summer 1536 he attended on nineteen of the twenty-four days, including 1 July when the succession bill was debated. We do not know if he spoke up for Mary's claim or against changes in religion. If he did, he was not successful, unless the possibility that Henry might leave the crown to Mary by will, left open by the act, was some comfort.[85] The airing of heretical teaching consequent on Henry's changes in the church worried him too. In summer 1534 he had shared Darcy's disgust at the radical views of a 'naughty priest' patronized by the Yorkshire knight Sir Francis Bigod and in spring 1535 he questioned a Yorkshire gentleman about the spread of heresy there and pledged himself to help stop it.[86]

In the end, Hussey's disaffection did not for Henry, but for Hussey himself. On Monday 2 October 1536 he was at home in Sleaford at about 9 p.m. when he heard news of a riotous assembly in the north of the county, a reaction to the presence of commissioners dissolving the lesser monasteries, assessing taxation, and implementing royal injunctions on clerical conduct. The events of the next few days are hard to reconstruct and harder still to interpret, for almost all the evidence comes either from Hussey himself, his servants or his enemies. He apparently hesitated as the rebellion spread; perhaps he was complacent, perhaps he panicked; conceivably, he waited to see if this was the sort of insurrection that might bring Henry to his senses.

On his own account, he wrote to various neighbouring gentlemen over the following days offering to help stay the revolt, by force if needs be, and wrote to the rioters offering to intervene if the commissioners had exceeded their powers. He got no response except from those gentlemen already captured by the rebels, who asked him to join them and intercede with the king for the rebel demands. He refused—saying he was not ready to lose his head and his lands as the rebels looked

---

[84] *LP* VII, 1206, 1368; Bernard, *King's Reformation*, 202–6.

[85] *LJ*, i. 58–102; *LP* X, 206; Miller, *Nobility*, 124–5; S. E. Lehmberg, *The Later Parliaments of Henry VIII 1536–1547* (Cambridge, 1977), 20–5.

[86] PRO, SP1/118, fo. 123r (*LP* XIII, i. 899); *LP* XII, i. 576, 852.

set to do—and was making plans to leave for Lincoln when events overtook him. Even the servants he had sent to the rebels had been sworn to the rebel cause and on Wednesday 4 October a hundred Sleaford men, including his own tenants, arrived at his house and told him they would protect him, but would not fight the rebels and would not let him leave. Three days later he heard the rebels were approaching, so he disguised himself as a priest and fled to Nottingham to join the earl of Shrewsbury, who had mustered forces for the king and had encouraged Hussey to use his 'policy and wisdom' like 'an honourable and true gentleman' to stay the rebel forces and extricate the gentlemen from among them, which he had singularly failed to do. The final humiliation came when his wife, who had placated the rebels with bread, beer, and salt fish when they failed to find her husband, followed him to Nottingham and begged Shrewsbury to let him go home for fear the rebels would burn their house and kill their children.[87]

Away to the south there had been rumours he had joined the rebels and his conduct was clearly under suspicion. On 17 October, eight days after he reached Nottingham, Henry told Shrewsbury to despatch him to court and keep him isolated from the servants he had sent to talk to the rebels so they might be questioned separately.[88] Hussey claimed to be 'very glad' to go the king, 'not doubting but he should try himself' a 'true subject in every behalf', but his confidence was misplaced.[89] Vital aspects of his conduct had been ambiguous. He had told his senior bailiff John Welshman or Williams, 'a very simple fellow and oft drunken' as Hussey's hostile neighbour Robert Carr of Sleaford put it, to hide harness for 300 men in a hay barn, but Welshman claimed not to know whether this was for use by the king's forces or the rebels.[90] Rather than take a firm lead against the rebels he seemed, at least to Carr, to ask the townsmen's advice how he should respond to events and then decline unnervingly to engage with their concerns. He even told one armed man who offered to 'live and die' with him that he was 'a naughty busy knave'.[91] The servants he sent to the rebels told people that their master had promised the rebels that 'he would and must needs yield to them', even that 'he and all his servants and his house' were at the command of the rebel commons 'whensoever they will come to him'.[92] In his frustration he told various people that he dare not leave his house, that his tenants would not rise for him, that there seemed no remedy but to do as the commons did, that 'he would not be false to his prince nor would be against them, for he said if he should be against them, he thought not one of his tenants would take his part'.[93]

---

[87] R.W. Hoyle, *The Pilgrimage of Grace and the Politics of the 1530s* (Oxford, 2001), 102–34, 159–66; PRO, SP1/107, fo. 69 (*LP* XI. 589); SP1/109, fos. 70v–74r (*LP* XI. 852); *LP* XI. 531, 620, 853, 854, 971, 973, XII, i. 380.

[88] *LP* XI. 625, 747, 851.   [89] PRO, SP1/108, fo. 167 (*LP* XI. 772).

[90] PRO, E315/393, fo. 101r; SP1/109, fo. 73r; SP1/110, fo. 138r (*LP* XI. 852, 969); *LP* XII, i. 1213.

[91] SP1/110, fos. 138r–140r (*LP* XI. 969).

[92] PRO, SP1/107, fo. 66 (*LP* XI. 587(2)); E36/118, fo. 55v (*LP* XI. 853).

[93] *LP* XI. 547, 561, 567, 578, 587(3), 590, 975; PRO, E36/119, fo. 6r (*LP* XII, i. 70(iii)).

At Windsor in November he seemed to be clearing his name, declaring his 'true demeanour' with the backing of the duke of Norfolk, who had returned to court from his confrontation with Darcy and the much larger rebel force in Yorkshire. But there was a price. Norfolk required him to write to Darcy, in a letter approved by the king's council, and ask him to hand over the leader of the Yorkshire movement, Robert Aske, 'quick or dead'. Darcy refused to stain his honour by betraying Aske. He told Hussey's servant who took the letter that he 'was sorry for' Hussey's 'trouble', but that Hussey 'knoweth well enough what a nobleman's promise is'; he suspected rightly that the letter had not been Hussey's idea.[94] Henry and Norfolk were forced to compromise with the rebels and a tense Christmas and New Year ensued. In April, as Lady Hussey spread stories of angry confrontations between Darcy and Cromwell, Hussey found himself in the Tower under renewed interrogation about his role in the origins and unfolding of the revolt.[95] Carr's evidence of his dilatoriness now played a vital role, suggesting as it did 'negligence in Lord Hussey', 'that he little regarded his duty', indeed that 'it appeareth he favoured the traitors'.[96] On 12 May at Sleaford he was indicted for conspiring with various rebels, many of them already executed, to overthrow the king's ecclesiastical supremacy and salutary laws and to depose the king, and then of aiding and abetting the rebel forces, though, contrary to the government's hopes, the jurors declined to indict his bailiff Welshman alongside him. At his trial in Westminster on 15 May, before twenty-one peers including Shrewsbury and Windsor, Hussey pleaded not guilty but was convicted and sentenced to die.[97] After an agonizing wait he left the Tower on 28 June, sent for execution at Lincoln. There he was beheaded early in July before the duke of Suffolk, in an exhibition of the king's power and of his clemency in commuting the usual horrendous penalties of treason.[98] His wife, implicated in every stage of his decline and fall, spent her remaining years trying to protect the interests of their daughters.[99]

PERSEVERANCE

Empson and Dudley met the most spectacular nemesis at one end of Henry VIII's reign, Hussey at the other, but despite the tainted blood and forfeiture formally attached to a treason conviction, their families were not entirely ruined. Their colleagues, meanwhile, faced a slower kind of failure, passing the torch more or less confidently on to their descendants, only for it to be extinguished amid the religious and political conflicts of mid-Tudor England, or to sputter out in a failure to reproduce. Empson's sons were restored to his lands, but never escaped financial difficulties

[94] PRO, SP1/111, fo. 9 (*LP* XI. 1007); *LP* XI. 1245; E36/119, fos. 78–81 (*LP* XII, i. 1013).
[95] *LP* XII, i. 899, 900, 905, 947, 973, 976, 981, 1120.
[96] *LP* XII, i. 1012(4), 1087.
[97] *LP* XII, i. 1187, 1193, 1199(2), 1207, 1213, 1239, 1240.
[98] *LP* XII, i. 1266, 1285, ii. 156, 166, 181, 204, 228, App. 31.
[99] *LP* XIV, i. 1030, XVIII, i. 474(16); *CP*, vii. 18.

and died childless.[100] The Dudleys, in contrast, bounced back twice. Edmund's son John became chief minister in the second half of Edward VI's reign and was then executed at the start of Mary's. His sons Robert, earl of Leicester and Ambrose, earl of Warwick, were among the brightest lights of Elizabeth's court, but neither was able to father a surviving legitimate son to continue the line. Hussey's sons carried on his male line into the Elizabethan age, but it was his brother's heirs who were to take the Hussey name on in Lincolnshire through the seventeenth century.[101]

Belknap avoided political shipwreck but not genetic: he had no children, and his estates were soon dispersed among nephews and other co-heirs.[102] Among those who lasted longer, the Brandons rose fastest of all. Thomas's nephew Charles became duke of Suffolk in 1514 and married Henry VIII's sister Mary the next year. His sons were the playmates of Edward VI, his granddaughter Jane Grey briefly queen; but the sons died unmarried, Jane met her end on the block and those who carried the blood of Brandon and Tudor into the reign of Elizabeth learnt to keep their heads down. Other families were more deeply marked by religious division. Wyatt's grandson Sir Thomas was an executed protestant rebel, Southwell's great-great-nephew Robert a martyred Jesuit poet, though each family bred others who conformed and survived; one of Wyatt's great-great-grandsons was twice governor of Virginia.[103] Cope's great-grandson was a notable agitator for further reformation of the church in Elizabeth's parliaments, though his other descendants lived more quietly amongst the Oxfordshire and Northamptonshire gentry.[104] Sometimes families split down the middle. Hussey's grandson Thomas Hussey of Caythorpe was an imprisoned Catholic rebel, while Thomas's aunt, Hussey's daughter Bridget, married in succession two leading protestant exiles, Sir Richard Morison and Francis Russell, second earl of Bedford, and his uncle, another Thomas Hussey, sat in parliament under Bedford's patronage and made violent speeches against Mary Queen of Scots and the pope.[105]

Predictably, perhaps, Lovell's kin had a smoother ride than most. The Manners, Lords Roos, served the Tudors, Stuarts, and Hanoverians with distinction in war and politics, becoming earls of Rutland in 1525 and dukes of Rutland in 1703, living at Belvoir to this day. Along the way, they survived involvement in Essex's rebellion, introduced the first blast furnace into northern England, and produced that general immortalized in so many pub signs, the marquess of Granby.[106] The

---

[100] *The Victoria History of the County of Northampton*, ed. W. Adkins et al., 7 vols (London, 1902–), v. 109.

[101] *Lincolnshire Pedigrees*, ed. A. R. Maddison, 4 vols, HS 50–2, 55 (London, 1902–6), ii. 527–32; C. Holmes, *Seventeenth-Century Lincolnshire* (Lincoln, 1980), 64–75, 131–3, 219, 244, 248, 257–8.

[102] *The Victoria History of the County of Warwick*, ed. H. A. Doubleday et al., 8 vols (London, 1904–69), vi. 252.

[103] S. T. Bindoff, *History of Parliament: The House of Commons 1509–1558*, 3 vols (London, 1982), iii. 351–7, 670–2; P. W. Hasler, *The House of Commons 1558–1603*, 3 vols (London, 1981), iii. 422; D. Loades, 'Wyatt, George', *ODNB*; V. Bernhard, 'Wyatt, Sir Francis', *ODNB*; N. P. Brown, 'Southwell, Robert [St Robert Southwell]', *ODNB*.

[104] Bindoff, *Commons*, i. 693–4; Hasler, *Commons*, i. 648–50.

[105] Hasler, *Commons*, ii. 357–8.

[106] *CP*, xi. 253–74; L. Stone, *Family and Fortune: Studies in Aristocratic Finance in the Sixteenth and Seventeenth Centuries* (Oxford, 1973), 190; A. W. Massie, 'Manners, John, Marquess of Granby', *ODNB*.

Lovells settled down among the Norfolk gentry and lasted till the eighteenth century, though their lives were not always quiet in that disputatious county.[107] Though Sir Richard Guildford's courtier sons Edward and Henry left no male offspring, the family lived on as county gentry in Kent through the descendants of their stay-at-home brother George, while the Elizabethan earls of Leicester and Warwick were his great-grandsons in the female line.[108] The Cutts likewise lasted out the sixteenth and seventeenth centuries as Cambridgeshire and Essex gentry, culminating in a general who led the southern flank at Blenheim and won an Irish peerage, but left no issue.[109]

The sons of Poynings's sons died young and his male line died out, but his daughter's descendants made recurrent impacts on the politics of the seventeenth, eighteenth, and nineteenth centuries as earls of Lincoln and eventually dukes of Newcastle; the Lincoln title survives today, having passed, much to the excitement of the popular press, to an Australian relative.[110] The lords Bray lasted to 1557, through two generations, the lords Windsor to 1641 through four generations of courtly and military service and local power in Buckinghamshire and Worcestershire; after the Restoration their titles were granted to a female line which rose to the earldom of Plymouth.[111] Sheffield's grandson was made a baron in 1547 and killed in Kett's rebellion two years later, but his descendants lasted until 1735 as earls of Mulgrave and eventually dukes of Buckingham.[112] The lords Mordaunt did better still, surviving a period of eclipse caused by their catholic loyalties, even involvement in Gunpowder Plot, to gain the earldom of Peterborough in 1628. The second earl was a councillor of James II and diehard Jacobite, his nephew, the third earl, a trenchant Whig general and diplomat, a patron of John Locke, Jonathan Swift, and Alexander Pope, and apparently the first English peer to marry an actress. The title lasted in the male line until 1814.[113]

Even they were outdone by the Hobarts. Sir James's great-grandson reached his ancestor's position of attorney-general and then surpassed it, as chief justice of common pleas. He gained a baronetcy, which his own great-great-grandson, brother of a mistress of George II, converted first to a barony and then, in 1746, to the earldom of Buckinghamshire; from him the male line and title continued,

[107] Bindoff, *Commons*, ii. 549–50; G. L. Harrison, 'A Few Notes on the Lovells of East Harling', *NA* 18 (1912), 56–72; F. Blomefield, *An Essay towards a Topographical History of the County of Norfolk*, 11 vols (London, 1805–10), i. 323; A. H. Smith, *County and Court: Government and Politics in Norfolk, 1558–1603* (Oxford, 1974), 52, 58, 166–67, 181–92.
[108] Bindoff, *Commons*, ii. 262–7; S. Adams, 'Dudley, Ambrose, Earl of Warwick', *ODNB*; 'Dudley, Robert, Earl of Leicester', *ODNB*.
[109] King, 'Descent of the Manor of Horham', 30–42; H. M. Chichester and J. B. Hattendorf, 'Cutts, John, Baron Cutts of Gowran', *ODNB*.
[110] D. Grummitt, 'Poynings, Thomas, First Baron Poynings', *ODNB*; Hasler, *Commons*, iii. 241–2; *CP*, vii. 690–700, ix. 532–37; C. Mosley (ed.), *Burke's Peerage, Baronetage & Knightage: Clan Chiefs, Scottish Feudal Barons*, 107th edn, 3 vols (Wilmington DE, 2003), ii. 2341.
[111] *CP*, ii. 287–9, xii-2. 794–800.   [112] *CP*, ix. 388–92, xi. 661–63.
[113] *CP*, ix. 193–99, x. 496–505; V. Stater, 'Mordaunt, Henry, Second Earl of Peterborough', *ODNB*; J. B. Hattendorf, 'Mordaunt, Charles, Third Earl of Peterborough and First Earl of Monmouth', *ODNB*.

sometimes passing to brothers, nephews or cousins, to the present day, the fourth earl notably lending his name to Hobart, Tasmania.[114] Henry VII's new men had not put such a dramatic mark on the composition of England's hereditary ruling elite as would the new men of the next two generations, the Cecils, Pagets, and Paulets, the Riches, Sackvilles, and Wriothesleys. But given where they had started, they would surely have been pleased with what their descendants achieved. Their careers, however, had always been a matter of serving the king and the crown as well as advancing themselves. So was the England of their sons and grandsons the England they had worked to build?

[114] S. Handley, 'Hobart, Sir Henry, First Baronet', *ODNB*; R. Thorne, 'Hobart, Robert, Fourth Earl of Buckinghamshire', *ODNB*; *CP*, ii. 401–6; Mosley (ed.), *Burke's Peerage*, i. 576.

18

The making of Tudor England

Henry VII could not have achieved what he did solely with the aid of his new men. He needed great noblemen to command armies, take the lead in court ceremonial, and preside over regional society: not just early in the reign, when the duke of Bedford and the earls of Oxford and Derby were mainstays of his regime, but also later, when younger magnates such as the earls of Surrey and Shrewsbury came to the fore. Even more active at court, in war, and on important embassies were courtier-peers such as Lords Cheyney, Daubeney, Herbert, and Willoughby de Broke, men who also had their part to play in the rule of the counties where they held land and office. Princes of the church were vital, too, holding the great offices of chancellor and lord privy seal and the presidencies of the regional councils, and helping to govern the provinces through their episcopal authority and their weighty landholdings: John Morton and William Warham at Canterbury, Thomas Savage at London and York, Richard Fox at Durham and Winchester, and so on. Bishops on their way to the top and those who stayed in the middling ranks of the clergy—Christopher Urswick, Henry Ainsworth, and others—did vital duty as diplomats and everyday councillors. Courtiers without much role in the machinery of government kept the king company, advertised his magnificence, fought his wars, and on occasion represented him to his brother monarchs: Matthew Baker, Roland de Veleville, Hugh Denis, and Richard Weston come to mind. Lawyers who had not veered off into administration and politics but followed the straight path of promotion through the courts made sure justice was done in the king's name, from Chief Justice Hussey to Chief Justice Fyneux and beyond.

Yet what Henry achieved would not have been the same without the new men. Their work was essential to the vigour of his council, the lustre of his court, and the efficiency of his parliaments. His drives to make justice more effective and crown finances more powerful would not have succeeded without them. They were centrally involved in his diplomatic and military initiatives and even, on occasion, in his rule over the outlying parts of his realm. The relationships they built with towns, with churchmen, with gentry, with retainers fastened his grasp on local society as much as the fiscal intimidation they organized. Their centrality in his regime was evident in the close bonds they forged with the king's other leading ministers, Lovell, for example, with Daubeney, Fox, and Oxford. For all that their religious affinities were those of Henry's generation and sat ill with the changes underway as the last of them died, the strengths of the regime they helped to build enabled his son's yet more ambitious undertakings and in some ways shaped their direction, in his assault on the church's wealth and jurisdiction, his on-going centralization of power and elaboration of administrative machinery. Their work built both the institutions and the political style of Tudor government, not only in Henry's reign but beyond.

It is hard to divide responsibility for governmental action between the king and his ministers, especially given that the records of central government and politics are far thinner for Henry's reign than for that of his son, over which historians have found it notoriously hard to determine whether Henry VIII, Wolsey, Cromwell, or the play of court faction shaped policy more decisively. In a sense it does not matter, since Henry worked so closely with his councillors. It seems also that individually the new men reflected different aspects of the royal personality. Dudley, with his readings on the statutes and his brisk way with the uncooperative, understood, as the king did, the range and force of royal power. Marney, with his willingness to challenge the mightiest peers, understood that that power could make even the greatest subject bow. Hobart, with his exhausting attendance at sessions, understood the centrality of justice to good governance and political control. Wyatt, with his relentless accumulation of land, understood the power of money and the patience needed to make it work. Lovell, with his great house, his luxury textiles, and his fine but understated clothing, understood the uses of measured magnificence. Poynings, with his rapport with Burgundian courtiers and his willingness to learn from German captains, understood what was needed for England to make its mark in Europe and assert its dominance in the British Isles. Dudley, with his ability to 'speak pleasantly and do overthwartly', echoed the calculated inscrutability of the king who could not let his subjects presume on his favour, the king who took Sir John Pennington by the hand when he left court and then fined him for leaving without permission.[1] Corporately they formed such an active and coordinated emanation of the royal will that at times they obscured the king's own individuality, making it open to question whether it was really the king or his council who ruled.[2]

The new men's disruptive social mobility as the agents of an ambitious royal power was not unparalleled in the English past. Under Henry I and again under the Angevins there had been complaints at the rise of men 'raised . . . from the dust', low-born, versatile, dedicated to the king and the enforcement of his rights, ambitious for their families and able to acquire landholdings equal to barons.[3] Under Richard II and, to a lesser extent, Henry IV, the knights and esquires of the king's chamber did the king's bidding as diplomats, soldiers, and local officers and rose fast, occasionally to peerages, though their rewards were often more temporary.[4] In Henry VI's reign, though royal leadership faltered, talented, and sometimes

---

[1] *The Great Chronicle of London*, ed. A. H. Thomas and I. D. Thornley (London, 1938), 325–6; 'The Petition of Edmund Dudley', ed. C. J. Harrison, *EHR* 87 (1972), 90.

[2] J. L. Watts, '"A New Ffundacion of is Crowne": Monarchy in the Age of Henry VII', in B. Thompson (ed.), *The Reign of Henry VII* (Stamford, 1995), 48–53.

[3] J. A. Green, *The Government of England under Henry I* (Cambridge, 1996), 134–93; R. V. Turner, *Men Raised from the Dust: Administrative Service and Upward Mobility in Angevin England* (Philadelphia PA, 1988), 143–50.

[4] C. Given-Wilson, *The Royal Household and the King's Affinity: Service, Politics and Finance in England, 1360–1413* (New Haven CT and London, 1986), 162–74, 188–97; J. S. Roskell et al., *History of Parliament: The House of Commons 1386–1421*, 4 vols (Stroud, 1992), ii. 99–103, 449–54, iii. 225–8, 843–6, iv. 39–44, 306–10, 620–8.

ruthless men rose from the gentry to peerages and senior offices through service in war, administration, and the royal household. They exercised a sway in local politics made visible in ambitious buildings, like Ralph Boteler, Lord Sudeley's Sudeley Castle, or John, Lord Stourton's Stourton House and in James Fiennes, Lord Saye and Sele's bloody nemesis at the hands of the rebels of 1450.[5] Nor was the combination of skills and responsibilities the new men brought to Henry's regime wholly new in English politics. The trusted financial officials and lawyers of Edward IV and Richard III, men like Sir Richard Fowler and William Catesby, played an important part in their efforts to strengthen royal government in the wake of civil war. In some cases, they directly anticipated Henry's new men in the offices they held, Fowler as chancellor of the exchequer like Lovell and chancellor of the duchy of Lancaster like Bray, Catesby as speaker of the commons like Dudley and steward of St Albans Abbey like Lovell.[6] Equally, Henry's new men had connections of different sorts with such forerunners—Empson as a colleague of Fowler and Catesby—or with the household knights who had borne Edward's authority out from his court to the regions: Guildford as the son of Sir John Guildford, Poynings as the step-son of Sir George Browne and son-in-law of Sir John Scott, Brandon as the nephew of Sir Robert Wingfield and husband of the widow of Sir John Sapcotes.[7] The new men did not come out of nowhere.

Yet Henry's new men were new. Their social origins were generally lower than those of the chamber knights or new peers of preceding centuries and the heights they reached were greater than those of a Fowler or a Catesby. More broadly, the new men combined with a new versatility functions performed by different types of royal servants in the past, the regional authority and political counsel of favoured and often newly promoted peers, the diplomatic, courtly, and military service of household knights, and the technical skills and relentless work-rate of bureaucrats, who had often in the past been clerics.[8] In so doing they helped reconstruct the English royal bureaucracy on a new basis after the breakdown of the established and effective, if conservative, cadres and methods of the chancery, exchequer, and privy seal under Henry VI.[9] They were more politically powerful at the centre and in the localities than earlier generations of bureaucrats, more engaged in the details of justice and finance than earlier generations of lords or courtiers. In their means

[5] A. C. Reeves, 'Boteler, Ralph, first Baron Sudeley', *ODNB*; J. A. Nigota, 'Fiennes, James, first Baron Saye and Sele', *ODNB*; G. L. Harriss, 'Stourton Family', *ODNB*.

[6] R. Somerville, *A History of the Duchy of Lancaster, I, 1265–1603* (London, 1953), i. 391; R. Horrox, 'Catesby, William', *ODNB*; *Registra Johannis Whethamstede, Willelmi Albon, et Willelmi Walingforde, Abbatum Monanasterii Sancti Albani*, ed. H. T. Riley, Rolls Series 28 (London, 1873), 265–7.

[7] M. R. Horowitz, 'Richard Empson, Minister of Henry VII', *BIHR* 55 (1982), 37–8; R. E. Horrox, *Richard III: A Study of Service* (Cambridge, 1989), 104, 142, 171, 237, 252; D. A. L. Morgan, 'The King's Affinity in the Polity of Yorkist England', *TRHS* 5th ser. 23 (1973), 6–7, 24–5.

[8] R. A. Griffiths, 'Public and Private Bureaucracies in England and Wales in the Fifteenth Century', *TRHS* 5th ser. 30 (1980), 109–30; R. L. Storey, 'Gentlemen-bureaucrats', in C. L. Clough (ed.), *Profession, Vocation and Culture in later medieval England: Essays dedicated to the memory of A. R. Myers* (Liverpool, 1982), 97–119.

[9] C. Carpenter, 'Henry VI and the Deskilling of the Royal Bureaucracy', in L. Clark (ed.), *English and Continental Perspectives*, The Fifteenth Century 9 (Woodbridge, 2010), 1–37.

of exercising power and in their career trajectories they anticipated future waves of upwardly mobile Tudor ministers, first Cromwell, Audley, Rich, Paget, Paulet, and Wriothesley, then Cecil, Bacon, Mildmay, Sackville, and Walsingham. As Wilhelm Busch put it, 'Henry set the example for his successors, for the leading statesmen of the Tudors were men of low origin.'[10]

Scholars of Busch's generation saw clear parallels between the rise of Henry's new men and the increasing importance of similar agents of royal power in other European monarchies.[11] Everywhere the increasingly ambitious governments of the later fifteenth and early sixteenth centuries drew heavily on the skills of lawyers and financial officials, who became correspondingly more influential in the councils and courts of the princes they served, and at a time of demographic recovery and cultural innovation found ready opportunities to turn power into money, land, and fashionable displays of status.[12]

The similarities between the careers of Henry's new men and their contemporaries could be close both in general terms and in detail. In the Netherlands, a sequence of officials paid with their lives as Empson and Dudley did for the zeal with which they had imposed princely authority and advanced their own careers in the tense years between the death of Charles the Bold in 1477 and the imprisonment of his son-in-law Maximilian of Habsburg at Bruges in 1488, most notably the lawyer Guillaume Hugonet and the receiver-general Pieter Lanchals.[13] Yet their younger contemporaries built careers like Bray's or Lovell's: Lieven van Pottelsberghe rose from low birth to landed wealth through financial and conciliar office, brokered patronage to advance his dependants and manage the relations between central power and urban elites, and served the common good by his patronage of education.[14] In Bavaria, lay jurists and lesser nobles came to dominate the ducal councils from around 1500 and some would look very familiar to a Lovell or a Hobart: Peter Paumgartner, chancellor to the duke of Bavaria-Landshut from 1503, was the great-grandson of a Tyrolean weaver, had been law professor at Ingolstadt and married his three children into the higher nobility.[15] In the Franche-Comté, Mercurino de Gattinara was forced out of his position as president of the parlement of Dole after a confrontation with the leading nobles of the province featuring his campaign 'for the commonweal' against their manipulation of the local judicial system, his controversial land purchases and even satirical poems

[10] W. Busch, *England under the Tudors*, i: *King Henry VII (1485–1509)* (London, 1895), 295.

[11] S. J. Gunn, 'Politic History, New Monarchy and State Formation: Henry VII in European Perspective', *HR* 82 (2009), 382–5.

[12] R. Schnur (ed.), *Die Rolle der Juristen bei der Entstehung des modernen Staates* (Berlin, 1986); R. Stein (ed.), *Powerbrokers in the Late Middle Ages* (Turnhout, 2001); C. Michon (ed.), *Conseils et conseillers dans l'Europe de la Renaissance v.1450–v.1550* (Tours/Rennes, 2012).

[13] M. Boone, 'La justice en spectacle. La justice urbaine en Flandre et la crise du pouvoir "bourguignon" (1477–1488)', *Revue Historique* 308 (2003), 43–65.

[14] P. P. J. L. van Peteghem, *De Raad van Vlaanderen en staatsvorming onder Karel V (1515–1555): Een publiekrechtelijk onderzoek naar contralisatiestreven in de XVII Provinciën* (Nijmegen, 1990), 266–74.

[15] H. Lieberich, *Landherren und Landleute: Zur politischen Führungsschicht Baierns im Spätmittelalter* (Munich, 1964), 79, 100–1, 136–7.

like those directed at Empson.[16] In France, low-born financial officers made a habit of doing as Wyatt and Poynings did, buying old castles and preserving them as shells for their new residences in the attempt to co-opt the traditional social authority they incarnated.[17] Even in Florence, more used to social mobility and more attuned to classical meritocracy than these northern European societies, the political, social, and sartorial pretensions and sheer rudeness of the secretaries, financial officials, and lawyers promoted by Lorenzo de' Medici, sons of artisans, millers, and notaries, aroused outrage that led to the execution, exile, imprisonment, or dismissal of several of them after his death.[18]

The continuities between the new men's generation and that of the successors who took forward their management of the governmental system under Henry VIII and manned the new institutions of the 1530s and 1540s were often personal. Admittedly, Wolsey, who stood in a different tradition of clerical minister-favourites, was an intermediary, advanced by Lovell, working with Windsor, Wyatt, and others, patron to Cromwell.[19] But there were more direct connections, too. The father of Cromwell's protégé Ralph Sadler worked for Belknap and Brian Tuke, treasurer of the court of general surveyors, was bailiff of the honour of Wallingford under Lovell's stewardship, and eventually bought Layer Marney from Marney's heirs.[20] Richard Whalley, receiver of the court of augmentations and adviser to Protector Somerset, had served as a young gentleman in Lovell's household.[21] Southwell's widow and his friend and executor William Wootton bought the wardship of his nephew and heir Richard and set him on his way to a powerful career in mid-Tudor politics and government: study at Lincoln's Inn, service to the duke of Norfolk, friendship with Thomas Cromwell, seats in parliament, posts in augmentations and general surveyors, treasurer of war, master of the ordnance, and a privy councillor to Edward and Mary. His younger brothers made similar headway, one an augmentations lawyer and frequent MP who served as master of the rolls in the 1540s, the other an auditor for the exchequer and the general surveyors, both establishing prosperous county families.[22]

Like the generations that followed, Henry's new men made very sure to build their own wealth and power while serving the king. Their public actions were largely consistent with the principles of good government they enunciated, though of course the king's and their definition of good government in matters of financial exaction and political control might not be the same as that of his subjects. But

[16] J. M. Headley, 'The Conflict between Nobles and Magistrates in Franche-Comté, 1508–1518', *Journal of Medieval and Renaissance Studies* 9 (1979), 49–80.

[17] P. Hamon, 'Jean Breton (v. 1490–1542)', in C. Michon (ed.), *Les Conseillers de François Ier* (Rennes, 2011), 341.

[18] A. Brown, 'Lorenzo de' Medici's New Men and their Mores: The Changing Lifestyle of Quattrocento Florence', *Renaissance Studies* 16 (2002), 113–42.

[19] G. Cavendish, *The Life and Death of Cardinal Wolsey*, ed. R. S. Sylvester, EETS 243 (Oxford, 1959), 7, 9–10.

[20] *LP* V. 279; PRO, SC6/Henry VIII/1091, m. 4v; P. R. N. Carter, 'Tuke, Sir Brian', *ODNB*.

[21] S. T. Bindoff, *History of Parliament: The House of Commons 1509–1558*, 3 vols (London, 1982), iii. 594–6.

[22] *LP* II, i. 96; Bindoff, *Commons*, 351–6.

they clearly took advantage of their power to assemble and exploit large landed inheritances and local influence to match, and the king's reluctance to reward them with land drove them to particular ingenuity in doing so. If they were less distracted from doing the king's will than some previous generations of royal ministers by notions of clerical duty to ecclesiastical liberties or aristocratic duty to caste privilege or personal honour, there were times when self-aggrandizement clashed with duty to the common weal. The same men who sat on enclosure commissions were vigorous enclosers, the same men who sat in Star Chamber to rebuke judicial malpractice made sure the law ran in their favour, the same men who audited accounts with rigour left rents to the king unpaid. But the systems they manned collectively were capable of calling them individually to account, whether in the everyday give and take of Hussey's debts and Windsor's riots or the cataclysm of Empson and Dudley's fall, and this put their power more clearly at the crown's disposal than that of earlier great men.

They played a central role not only in Henry's exercise of English government but in his and his children's fashioning of English history. Thereby, though how consciously it is hard to say, they helped forge the historical and cultural identity of Tudor England and ensured their own commemoration as part of that story. Henry had less sense of dynastic identity or dynastic mission than the familiar notion of 'Tudor propaganda' suggests, and indeed there were parts of his ancestry and of the history of his accession that he seemed eager to leave obscure.[23] Nonetheless he was deeply concerned with his personal commemoration. Henry entrusted his legacy to his executors, Lovell, Cutt, Empson, and Dudley among them. Empson and Dudley, of course, could not act, but Lovell and Cutt were among those who commissioned from Pietro Torrigiani Henry's splendid tomb with its gilt-bronze effigies of king and queen and the accompanying high altar with its white marble canopy, classical columns, and terracotta angels.[24] Lovell, Mordaunt, Hobart, Empson, and Lucas had already been active in the assembly and conveyancing of the landed endowment designed to support Henry's perpetual commemoration at Westminster Abbey, Bray, Lovell, and Hobart in the financial arrangements between abbey and king for the building of his new chapel.[25] Lovell and Guildford presided over the construction of Henry's almshouses at Westminster, one of the two great charitable projects with which he commemorated himself, in 1500–2, and after his death his executors organized the completion of the second, the Savoy hospital.[26] In 1519 Lovell was also involved, with

---

[23] C. S. L. Davies, 'Tudor: What's in a Name', *History* 97 (2012), 24–42; C. S. L. Davies, 'Information, Disinformation and Political Knowledge under Henry VII and early Henry VIII', *HR* 85 (2012), 228–53.

[24] M. M. Condon, 'The Last Will of Henry VII: Document and Text', in T. Tatton-Brown and R. Mortimer (eds), *Westminster Abbey: The Lady Chapel of Henry VII* (Woodbridge, 2003), 137; P. Lindley, '"The Singuler Mediacions and Praiers of al the Holie Companie of Heven": Sculptural Functions and Forms in Henry VII's Chapel', in Tatton Brown and Mortimer (eds), *Westminster Abbey: The Lady Chapel*, 266–76; J. Britton, *The Architectural Antiquities of Great Britain*, 5 vols (London, 1805–26), ii. 23–5.

[25] WAM 6839***, 14705–8.   [26] *HKW*, iii. 202, 207.

Wolsey, in the plan for Henry VIII to be commemorated by a spectacular tomb carved by Florentine artists.[27] Away from the metropolis, Lovell and Bray glorified Henry and his children in glass as patrons of the Magnificat window at Malvern Priory and pinned down his enemy in alabaster and brass in commissioning the tomb of Richard III, with its dignified inscription, in the Greyfriars at Leciester.[28] All this work directly focused on the promotion of the king's legacy went with their own wide use of the royal badges. And in the making of a written account of the recent past, Bray and perhaps others seem to have been important sources of information for Polydore Vergil, whom Henry commissioned in about 1506 to write a history of England culminating in his reign.[29]

The novelty of the new men's power and their importance in Henry's regime were evident to those reflecting on his rule in the decades after his death. Henry VIII cited Marney as one of the new peers and lawyers prominent among the councillors he had inherited from his father and the duchess of Norfolk, daughter of the duke of Buckingham, gave vent to a more sarcastic version of the same view in disparaging her husband's mistress Bess Holland: she admitted the Hollands were related to Lord Hussey, but then he was only a 'late made' peer.[30] Elizabethan elder statesmen knew their importance. William Paulet, marquess of Winchester, told Elizabeth in 1571 that her grandfather 'had no more counsellors but Cardinal Morton, Fox, Lovell, and Bray, and Sir Giles Daubeney, whom he made baron and lord chamberlain'.[31] Lord Lumley had a portrait of 'old Sir Thomas Lovell, treasurer of the household to K. H. 7' in his gallery of English and foreign notables, in amongst kings and queens, Cromwell and Rich and Burghley and Walsingham, the dukes of Bourbon and Alba and Sebastian Cabot 'the great Navigator'.[32]

The new men were famous for wisdom and valour in Polydore Vergil's printed Latin chronicle of 1534 and Edward Hall's English Chronicle of 1548, which drew heavily on Polydore for events before 1509. In these histories Bray and Lovell came to the fore in the plots of 1483, Bray 'a man sober, secret, and well witted . . . whose prudent policy' was 'known to have compassed things of great importance'.[33] Soon Bray, Lovell, Guildford, Poynings, and Risley were enumerated among Henry's 'wise and grave counsellors', Lovell 'a sage knight', Bray 'a very father of his country, a sage and a grave person and a fervent lover of justice' who, if any injustice were done, would 'plainly reprehend the king, and give him good

[27] C. M. Sicca, 'Pawns of International Finance and Politics: Florentine Sculptors at the Court of Henry VIII', *Renaissance Studies* 20 (2006), 15n.

[28] G. McN. Rushforth, *Medieval Christian Imagery as Illustrated by the Painted Windows of Great Malvern Priory Church Worcestershire* (Oxford, 1936), 369–75; R. Edwards, 'King Richard's Tomb at Leicester', in J. Petre (ed.), *Richard III: Crown and People* (London, 1985), 29–30; J. Ashdown-Hill, *The Last Days of Richard III* (Stroud, 2010), 97–104, 135–6; HL, MS El 1129.

[29] D. Hay, *Polydore Vergil: Renaissance Historian and Man of Letters* (Oxford, 1952), 79, 93.

[30] *StP*, i. 506; B. J. Harris, *Edward Stafford, Third Duke of Buckingham, 1478–1521* (Stanford CA, 1986), 63.

[31] *Original Letters illustrative of English History*, 3rd ser., ed. H. Ellis, 4 vols (London, 1846), iii. 370.

[32] L. Cust, 'The Lumley Inventories', *The Walpole Society* 6 (1918), 22–6.

[33] E. Hall, *Hall's Chronicle*, ed. H. Ellis (London, 1809), 390, 393; *Polydori Vergilii Urbinatis anglicae historiae libri xxvi* (Basel, 1534), 544–5 and subsequent editions misprint his name as Rouell.

advertisement how to reform that offence, and to be more circumspect in another like case'.[34] Poynings was consistently noted for martial skills, 'a politic captain' and 'valiant esquire', 'a valiant knight and hardy captain', 'a valiant knight', a 'valiant captain', and 'a valiant captain and a noble warrior'.[35] It was not only Hall who thought this. Nearly thirty years after Poynings's death, when John Coke, secretary to the English Merchant Adventurers at Antwerp, needed a contemporary English martial icon to counter those so vaunted by the French, he turned to 'the valiant and adventurous knight Syr Edwarde Ponynges'. Poynings, he asserted, 'had in his days been in xxvi fought battles, in England, France, Scotland, Ireland, Flanders, and Gelderland, besides many assaults, tourneys, skirmishes, and sieges'. Thus 'for his high prowess and worthiness' he 'ought not to be put in oblivion'. 'And one thing I dare say', Coke ended, 'that if the . . . Frenchmen, had ever had of their nation such a noble knight they would have made of his acts a great book'.[36] Others' military achievements paled beside those of Poynings, but Polydore and Hall mentioned their presence on campaign—Polydore sometimes in more numbing detail than even Hall could face—and picked out Guildford's role in the defence of Kent in 1495 and 1497.[37]

For Hall, the new men's self-interested rapacity was conveniently epitomized by Empson and Dudley, 'these covetous persons' who 'filled the king's coffers, and enriched themselves'.[38] When he wrote in the early 1540s, the exactions of Dudley were still being chewed over in lawsuits in which foreign merchants in London argued that their case could 'plainly and sufficiently be proved by the confession of the said Edmund Dudley written with his own hand'.[39] John Leland, touring round England in the 1540s, could not help but notice the landed acquisitions and building projects of Cope, Cutt, Hussey, Marney, Poynings, Windsor, and Wyatt and the foiled ambition of Belknap, and noted Henry VII's endowment of 'gentlemen' such as Lovell with forfeited lands.[40] Vergil and Hall also used the new men to illustrate wider political lessons. The blame placed on Bray and Morton for the taxes that provoked the 1497 rising typified the rewards of those great about princes, for rulers were given the credit for anything liked by the commons, but 'if anything be done . . . that soundeth not well in their ears, or is contrary to their opinion or fantasy, they will lay it straight to the council'.[41] The exactions of Empson and Dudley showed the dangers of over-enthusiastic service to the royal will: for 'these two persons contended, which of them by most bringing in might most please and satisfy his master's desire and appetite'.[42] Yet Hall could also canvass the view that their arrest was either prompted 'by malice of them, that with

Hall, *Chronicle*, 424, 497, 539; *AHPV*, 5–6, 128–9, 132–5.
[35]   Hall, *Chronicle*, 394, 404, 452, 465, 523.
[36]   J. Coke, *The Debate Betwene the Heraldes of Englande and Fraunce* (London, 1550), G7r.
[37]   Hall, *Chronicle*, 472–3, 478, 538, 569; *AHPV*, 23, 52, 83, 94–5.
[38]   Hall, *Chronicle*, 503.   [39]   PRO, C1/1022/57.
[40]   J. Leland, *The Itinerary of John Leland in or about the Years 1535–1543*, ed. L. T. Smith, 5 vols (London, 1906–10), i. 27, ii. 23, 30, 39, 40, iv. 34, 47, 74, 90, 111, 132, v. 155, 219.
[41]   Hall, *Chronicle*, 477; *AHPV*, 92.   [42]   Hall, *Chronicle*, 499; *AHPV*, 135.

their authority, in the late king's days were offended, or else to shift the noise, of the straight execution of penal statutes in the late king's days . . . for to satisfy and appease the people.'[43] And Vergil, in his final edition of 1555, safe from the constraints of Henry VIII's reign, even put into the mouth of Empson an unavailing defence speech explaining that they had followed Henry VII's instructions to enforce his laws with maximum severity to the benefit of the commonweal.[44]

Holinshed's dependence on Hall and Vergil ensured that most of these pen-portraits and reports, including Empson's defence speech, were carried over into the most influential Elizabethan treatment of national history.[45] In some instances, additional details, such as some of the charges levelled at Empson, were included.[46] The Holinshed compilers also introduced a reference to Dudley's *Tree of Commonwealth*, although it was known only in manuscript: Dudley 'studied the laws of this land, and profited highly in knowledge of the same, he wrote a book intituled *Arbor Reipublicae*'.[47] John Stow, as he repeatedly pointed out in print, had presented a copy of the *Tree* to Dudley's grandson Leicester in 1562; it was a work 'though rudely written, worthy (for the excellency thereof) to be written with letters of gold'.[48] Stow's printing of material from the London chronicle tradition and Cavendish's manuscript life of Wolsey brought other mentions of the new men's activity to light for the Elizabethan reader. He showed the role of Lovell, Wyatt, and Poynings among the 'grave counsellors' who persuaded the young and potentially devil-may-care Henry VIII 'to be present with them when they sat in council, so to acquaint him with matters pertaining to the politic government of the realm', and the contribution of Lovell 'a very sage counsellor, a witty man' to the rise of Wolsey.[49] He also showed how the 'sudden rising and falling' of Empson and Dudley, 'the which suddenly rose from poverty . . . unto inestimable authority and riches' might serve as a warning to the wise, 'to be well wary how they guide them, when they be put in great authority'.[50]

Here were the materials with which Bacon could build his picture of the new men's centrality in Henry's regime. And it was not only through Bacon that their reputation went on into the seventeenth century. In the popular drama of the early Stuart age, Lovell featured as a trusted counsellor, an agent of state security, and a bugbear of Buckingham in Shakespeare's *Henry VIII*, and Poynings and Guildford as loyal opponents of the rebels of 1497 in John Ford's *Perkin Warbeck*.[51] David Lloyd, in his sweeping evaluation of sixteenth and seventeenth-century English

---

[43] Hall, *Chronicle*, 505.   [44] *AHPV*, 151.

[45] R. Holinshed, *The Chronicles of England, Scotlande, and Irelande*, 4 vols (London, 1577), iv. 1466–7.

[46] Holinshed, *Chronicles*, iv. 1467–8.   [47] Holinshed, *Chronicles*, iv. 1463.

[48] J. Stow, *A Summarie of Englyshe chronicles* (London, 1565), fo. 172r; J. Stow, *The Chronicles of England* (London, 1580), 895; J. Stow, *The Annales of England* (London, 1592), 815.

[49] Stow, *Annales*, 809, 812, 832–3; Stow, *Chronicles*, 906.

[50] Stow, *Annales*, 814.

[51] W. Shakespeare, *Henry VIII*, act 1 scenes 2–4, act 2 scene 1, act 3 scene 2, act 5 scene 1; J. Ford, *The Chronicle History of Perkin Warbeck*, ed. P. Ure (London, 1968), act 3 scene 1.

statesmen, valued Poynings's resolution and vigilance and praised Marney's 'searching Judgement': his 'Judgment was much valued, his Integrity more; ever offering what was solidly safe, rather than what was superficially plausible'.[52]

While many of the new men's buildings and other commissions are lost, the remains show how their taste for sophisticated display made them significant patrons of cultural innovation: Torrigiani's portrait of Lovell, Holbein's of Wyatt, Marney's terracotta towers. While the dissolutions of the monasteries and chantries erased many of the monuments they had created, others survived either in physical form or at least in antiquarian memory. Lovell's bulwark at Calais survived as long as the English held the town.[53] His arms on the gatehouse at Lincoln's Inn lasted much longer. Lovell was hero-worshipped by the grocers' company, who commissioned a portrait of him for their hall in the 1560s and put his sword, collar, arms, crest, and will on display.[54] Stow immortalized Lovell's generosity to Holywell, 'unto the which house he had been a great benefactor, not only in building of a beautiful chapel wherein his body was interred, but in many other goodly buildings, and endowing the same with lands'.[55] Poynings's role in Ireland kept his name in currency. In the 1530s, those in government spoke regularly of 'Ponynges Act', an act of the Irish parliament in 1557 defined 'how Poynings's act shall be expounded and taken' and in James I's reign the judges were still debating the act by name.[56] Families naturally remembered their founders with pride. In the early seventeenth century, George Wyatt celebrated, and perhaps exaggerated, Henry VII's trust in his great-grandfather, so great that 'never willingly he managed affairs of importance without him', while another relative claimed that Henry told his nobles that without the efforts of his 'constant friend' Wyatt, he would not have enjoyed the crown, nor the nobles 'that peace and prosperity and honour which you now possess'.[57]

No doubt, institutional and family pieties might exaggerate the new men's importance. So might the affection of historians for serious-minded meritocrats apparently bent on efficient promotion of the public good. Yet it does seem clear that Henry VII's reign and what his successors built upon its achievements would have been very different without them. The style of governance they helped to shape was in some respects oppressive, though in others participatory, reflecting the common law studied and practised by so many of the new men. While building on existing institutions, it reconstructed royal power on a firmer basis in the wake of civil war, inspired not only by common law but also by chivalry and

[52] D. Lloyd, *State-worthies, or, The states-men and favourites of England since the reformation their prudence and policies, successes and miscarriages, advancements and falls, during the reigns of King Henry VIII, King Edward VI, Queen Mary, Queen Elizabeth, King James, King Charles I* (London, 1670 edn), 147–9.

[53] *HKW*, iii. 342, 345.

[54] R. Tittler, *The Face of the City: Civic Portraiture and Civic Identity in Early Modern England* (Manchester, 2007), 55, 66, 156.

[55] Stow, *Annales*, 875.

[56] *LP* VII. 1122 (7, 12), IX, 65, 90, 125, X, 1030, XII, ii. 1288; *The Reports of Sir Edward Coke, Knt. In Thirteen Parts*, ed. J. H. Thomas and J. F. Fraser, 6 vols (London, 1826), vi. 350–3.

[57] BL, Addl. MS 62135, fos. 245r, 467v–468r.

Ciceronianism, and distributed power across a wider social elite as part of an accelerating phase of state formation. It licensed self-help among those who served the crown, but it also restrained it: the system they had helped to make cost Guildford and Hobart their jobs, Windsor his home, and Empson, Dudley, and Hussey their lives. In many spheres of government activity it met Lovell's and Dudley's desire for 'good governance and rule' informed by 'great study, wisdom and policy'. Many forces shaped Tudor England: population growth and cloth-making, grammar schools and the English Bible, relations with the Irish, Scots, and Welsh, wars with France and Spain. Many men and women shaped it too. But politically, socially, culturally, and historically the new men were central, as instigators, executives, or exemplars of change, at the start and at the heart of the making of Tudor England.

Bibliography

MANUSCRIPT SOURCES

England
Alnwick: Alnwick Castle
Syon MSS

Aylesbury: Centre for Buckinghamshire Studies (CBS)
D/BASM Buckinghamshire Archaeological Society Manorial records
D/P Pigott of Doddershall, Quainton collection
PR61 Denham parish records

Bedford: Bedfordshire and Luton Archives and Records Service (BLARS)
L Lucas collection

Belvoir: Belvoir Castle
Additional MSS
MS accounts

Birmingham: Library of Birmingham
MS 3279 Lyttelton family (Viscount Cobham) of Frankley, later of Hagley Hall
Hampton (Packington) collection
Wingfield Digby collection

Bury St Edmunds: Suffolk Record Office (SROB)
Ac449 Hengrave Hall MSS
Ac613 Barnardiston family archives

Cambridge: Cambridgeshire Archives
P11 Bassingbourne parish records
PB Cambridge borough records
VC Diocese of Ely consistory court records

Cambridge: Cambridge University Library (CUL)
Additonal MSS
Hengrave MSS

Canterbury: Cathedral Archives (CCA)
Dean and Chapter Registers
FA Canterbury borough records
U4 Fordwich borough records

Chelmsford: Essex Record Office (ERO)
D/ACR Registers of wills
D/DFa Luther, Dawtrey and Fane families of Myles and Doddinghust Place estates
D/DFc Deeds and records of Debden and district
D/DWd Deeds of Maldon

Chester: Cheshire Record Office
DCH Cholmondeley of Cholmondeley estate records

Chichester: West Sussex Record Office (WSRO)
Additional MSS
Chichester City Records
EPI/1 Bishops' Registers
MP23 Brewhurst Estate

Chippenham: Wiltshire and Swindon History Centre (WSHC)
Bishops' Registers
G25 Wilton borough records

Durham: Durham University Library
CCB Bishopric of Durham records
Durham Priory Registers

Exeter: Devon Record Office
Chanter Records of the diocese of Exeter
346M Drake of Buckland abbey collection
Z17 Devon manorial and estate records

Hereford: Hereford Cathedral Library and Archives
Hereford Cathedral Muniments (NRA report)

Hertford: Hertfordshire Archives
2AR Will registers
Miscellaneous volumes

Hull: Hull History Centre
U DDEV Constable Maxwell collection (NRA report)

Huntingdon: Huntingdonshire Archives
Archdeaconry wills

Ipswich: Suffolk Record Office (SROI)
HB8 Cobbold, Meneer and Armitage Solicitors
HB26 Stradbroke manuscripts
T4373 Iveagh papers

Keele: Keele University Library (KUL)
Marquess of Anglesey papers
SP10 Purchased Sneyd Papers

Kew: The National Archives (Public Record Office) (PRO)
C 1 Chancery: Early Chancery Proceedings
C 24 Chancery: Examiners' Office: Town Depositions
C 42 Chancery: Awards and Agreements
C 54 Chancery and Supreme Court of Judicature: Close Rolls
C 67 Chancery: Supplementary Patent Rolls
C 142 Chancery: Inquisitions Post Mortem, Series II, and other Inquisitions, Henry VII to Charles I
C 146 Chancery: Ancient Deeds, Series C
CP 25/1 Court of Common Pleas, General Eyres and Court of King's Bench: Feet of Fines Files, Richard I—Henry VII
CP 25/2 Court of Common Pleas: Feet of Fines Files, Henry VIII—Victoria
CP 40 Court of Common Pleas: Plea Rolls
DL 1 Duchy of Lancaster: Court of Duchy Chamber: Pleadings
DL 3 Duchy of Lancaster: Court of Duchy Chamber: Pleadings, Depositions and Examinations, Series I
DL 5 Duchy of Lancaster: Court of Duchy Chamber: Entry Books of Decrees and Orders
DL 10 Duchy of Lancaster: Royal Charters
DL 12 Duchy of Lancaster: Warrants
DL 28 Duchy of Lancaster: Various Accounts
DL 30 Duchy of Lancaster: Court Rolls
DL 34 Duchy of Lancaster: Letters and Diplomatic Documents
E 13 Exchequer of Pleas: Plea Rolls
E 36 Exchequer: Treasury of Receipt: Miscellaneous Books
E 40 Exchequer: Treasury of Receipt: Ancient Deeds, Series A
E 41 Exchequer: Treasury of Receipt: Ancient Deeds, Series AA
E 42 Exchequer: Treasury of Receipt: Ancient Deeds, Series AS
E 101 Exchequer: King's Remembrancer: Various Accounts
E 111 Exchequer, Council and Other Courts: Miscellaneous Equity Proceedings and Special Commissions
E 118 Exchequer: King's Remembrancer: Conventual Leases
E 137 Exchequer: Lord Treasurer's Remembrancer and King's Remembrancer: Estreats
E 154 Exchequer: King's Remembrancer and Treasury of the Receipt: Inventories of Goods and Chattels
E 159 Exchequer: King's Remembrancer: Memoranda Rolls and Enrolment Books
E 179 Exchequer: King's Remembrancer: Particulars of Account and other records relating to Lay and Clerical Taxation
E 210 Exchequer: King's Remembrancer: Ancient Deeds, Series D
E 211 Exchequer: King's Remembrancer: Ancient Deeds, Series DD
E 314 Court of Augmentations and Court of General Surveyors: Miscellanea.
E 315 Court of Augmentations and Predecessors and Successors: Miscellaneous Books
E 323 Court of Augmentations: Treasurers' Accounts
E 326 Exchequer: Augmentation Office: Ancient Deeds, Series B
E 327 Exchequer: Augmentation Office: Ancient Deeds, Series BX

E 328 Exchequer: Augmentation Office: Ancient Deeds, Series BB

E 329 Exchequer: Augmentation Office: Ancient Deeds, Series BS

E 404 Exchequer of Receipt: Warrants for Issue

E 405 Exchequer of Receipt: Jornalia Rolls, Tellers' Rolls, Certificate Books, Declaration Books and Accounts of Receipts and Issues

KB 9 Court of King's Bench: Crown Side: Indictments Files, Oyer and Terminer Files and Informations Files

KB 27 Court of King's Bench: Plea and Crown Sides: Coram Rege Rolls

LC 2 Lord Chamberlain's Department: Records of Special Events

LR 1 Office of the Auditors of Land Revenue and Predecessors: Enrolment Books

LR 2 Office of the Auditors of Land Revenue and Predecessors: Miscellaneous Books

LR 14 Office of the Auditors of Land Revenue: Ancient Deeds, Series E

OBS Obsolete Lists, Indexes and Miscellaneous Summaries and Reports associated with Public Record Office Holdings

PROB 2 Prerogative Court of Canterbury and Other Probate Jurisdictions: Inventories compiled before 1661

PROB 11 Prerogative Court of Canterbury and related Probate Jurisdictions: Will Registers

REQ 1 Court of Requests: Books

SC 1 Special Collections: Ancient Correspondence of the Chancery and the Exchequer

SC 2 Special Collections: Court Rolls

SC 6 Special Collections: Ministers' and Receivers' Accounts

SC 11 Special Collections: Rentals and Surveys, Rolls

SP 1 State Papers Henry VIII: General Series

SP 2 State Papers, Henry VIII: Folios

STAC 2 Court of Star Chamber: Proceedings, Henry VIII

STAC 10 Star Chamber Miscellanea

WARD 9 Court of Wards and Liveries: Miscellaneous Books

Kingston-upon-Thames: Kingston Museum and Heritage Service
Kingston-upon-Thames borough records

Lambeth: Lambeth Palace Library (LPL)
Canterbury Registers

Leeds: Yorkshire Archaeological Society (YAS)
DD5 Osborne, Duke of Leeds collection
MD218 Anne of Burghwallis collection
MD225 Records of the manor of Wakefield

Leicester: Leicestershire Record Office
1D50 Records of Wyggeston Hospital

Lewes: East Sussex Record Office (ESRO)
Firle Place MSS
GLY Glynde Place archives

Rye borough records
SAS/G21 Gage family of Firle archives

Lichfield: Lichfield Joint Record Office (LJRO)
B/A/1 Bishops' Registers
Wills

Lincoln: Lincolnshire Archives (LA)
ANC Ancaster collection
Bishops' Registers
BP Bishopric of Lincoln records
FL Foster Library collection
H Birch-Reynardson family of Adwell, Oxon
LCC Lincoln Consistory Court Wills
L1 Lincoln borough records
Misc. Dep. 511 Court Rolls of the Manor of Uffington with Tallington and Deeping
    1518–1552
Mon Monson collection

London: The British Library (BL)
Additional Charters
Additional MSS
Althorp Papers
Cotton MSS
Egerton Charters
Egerton MSS
Egerton Rolls
Harley Charters
Harley MSS
Harley Rolls
Lansdowne MSS
Lord Frederick Campbell Charters
Stowe MSS

London: College of Arms (CA)
MSS series I, M
Norfolk and Suffolk Deeds (NRA report)

London: Duchy of Cornwall Record Office (DCRO)
DC Duchy of Cornwall rolls

London: London Metropolitan Archives (LMA)
Acc/0530 Berkeley family and estates
Acc/0928 Wood family
A/CSC Corporation of the Sons of the Clergy
MSS 9531 Bishops' Registers
Rep. London Repertories

Longleat: Longleat House
Miscellaneous volumes
NMR North Muniment Room

Maidstone: Kent History and Library Centre (KHLC)
DRb Bishopric of Rochester
Fa Faversham borough records
NR New Romney borough records
PRC Probate records
Sa Sandwich borough records
U301 Patterson family papers
U908 Streatfeild Manuscripts
U947 Kettell and Walter of Fawkham and Selby of Ightham Manuscripts
U1115 Scott of Scotts Hall Manuscripts
U1515 Romney Manuscripts

Manchester: John Rylands Library (JRL)
Latin MSS
Newark Parish Church
Magnus Charity Deeds (NRA report)

Northampton: Northamptonshire Record Office
Archdeaconry Court wills
Bru Brudenell of Deene collection
D Daventry collection
J(D) Jackson of Duddington collection
MTD Fermor-Hesketh collection
SS Stopford-Sackville collection

Norwich: Norfolk Record Office (NRO)
Bishops' Registers
FLT Flitcham estate documents
FOS Documents from Fosters, solicitors
Hare collection
MC 49 Documents of unknown origin. Probably once owned by Henry Harrod
NCAR Norwich chamberlains' account rolls
Phi Manuscripts of Sir Thomas Phillips
Rye MSS

Nottingham: Nottinghamshire Archives
DD/P, DD/2P Portland of Welbeck
DD/SR Savile of Rufford

Nottingham: Nottingham University Library (NUL)
Mi Middleton collection

Oxford: Bodleian Library (Bodl.)
MSS Ashmole
MSS dd Barrett
MSS dd Bertie
MSS dd Ewelme
MSS Kent charters
MSS Norfolk charters
MSS Oxon. charters
MSS Rawlinson
MSS Rolls Oxon.
MSS Tanner
MSS Top. Oxon.
MSS Yorkshire charters

Oxford: Brasenose College
Muniments Cropredy, Faringdon, Shelswell, Wheatley (NRA report)

Oxford: Merton College
MCR muniments

Oxford: Oriel College
SII Dudley papers
Shadwell muniments

Oxford: Oxfordshire History Centre (OHC)
DD Par Great Haseley Great Haseley parish records
M/112 Manor of Holton
MS Wills Oxon. Oxfordshire wills
Wi Willoughby Family of Marsh Baldon

Petworth House (Consulted at WSRO)
Petworth House Archives

Reading: Berkshire Record Office
D/ESK Skrine family of Warleigh
W Wallingford borough records

Shrewsbury: Shropshire Archives
327 Corbet of Adderley
946 Shavington (Needham family, Earls of Kilmorey)

Southampton: Southampton Archives Office
SC5/3 Southampton mayors' accounts

Stafford: Staffordshire Record Office
D260 Littleton family of Teddesley and Hatherton
D593 Sutherland-Leveson-Gower family
D(W)1734 Paget family
D(W)1790 Vernon collection (NRA report)

Stratford upon Avon: Shakespeare Birthplace Trust Record Office
DR3 Ferrers of Baddesley Clinton collection

Strood: Medway Archives
DRc Rochester Priory and other religious houses

Taunton: Somerset Heritage Centre
DD/HI Hippisley family of Ston Easton collection
DD/WHb Walker-Heneage and Button family and estate papers

Truro: Cornwall Record Office
DDME Edgcumbe of Mount Edgcumbe collection

Walsall: Walsall Local History Centre
MSS 277 Walsall borough records

Warwick: Warwickshire Record Office
H2 Coleshill School
Weasenham Hall, Norfolk
Weasenham Hall Muniments (NRA report)

Westminster: Westminster Abbey
WAM Westminster Abbey Muniments

Winchester: Hampshire Record Office
21M65 Winchester diocese records
25M75 Manors of Bentworth and Broxhead
Wills
WR Will Registers

Windsor: Windsor Castle
The Aerary Records of St George's Chapel

Woking: Surrey History Centre (SHC)
212 Properties and families in Surrey: deeds
281 Carew collection
LM Loseley collection

Worcester: Worcestershire Archives
BA1146 Cookes, Jefferys and allied families in Bentley Pauncefoot, Tardebigge,
    Bromsgrove, Feckenham, Claines and elsewhere
BA2648 Bishops' Registers
BA3964 Papers relating to land and property in Hanbury, Feckenham, Droitwich,
    Bromsgrove, and elsewhere
BA7335 Vernon family of Hanbury Hall

York: Borthwick Institute of Historical Research (BI)
Bishops' Registers
Probate Registers

France
Lille: *Archives Départementales du Nord (ADN)*
Série B Archives of the *Chambre des Comptes* of Lille and Letters of Margaret of Austria

USA
New York: *Pierpoint Morgan Library*
Rulers of England series

San Marino, CA: Huntington Library
MSS BA Battle Abbey collection
MSS El Ellesmere collection
MSS HA Hastings collection
MSS HM Huntington collection
MSS STT Temple of Stowe collection

Washington DC: Folger Shakespeare Library
Folger MSS

SIXTEENTH-CENTURY PRINTED WORKS

Anon, *Here Begynneth A Propre Newe Interlude of the Worlde and the Chylde, otherwise called Mundus & Infans* (London, 1522).
Anon, *The Traduction and Mariage of the Princesse* (London, 1500).
Coke, John, *The Debate Betwene the Heraldes of Englande and Fraunce* (London, 1550).
Holinshed, Raphael, *The Chronicles of England, Scotlande, and Irelande*, 4 vols (London, 1577).
Stow, John, *The Annales of England* (London, 1592).
Stow, John, *The Chronicles of England* (London, 1580).
Stow, John, *A Summarie of Englyshe chronicles* (London, 1565).
Vergil, Polydore, *Polydori Vergilii Urbinatis anglicae historiae libri xxvi* (Basel, 1534).
Walter, William, *The spectacle of louers: here after foloweth a lytell contrauers dyalogue bytwene loue and councell, with many goodly argumentes of good women and bad, very compendyous to all estates, newly compyled by wyllyam walter seruaunt vnto syr Henry Marnaye knyght Chauncelour of the Duchye of Lancastre* (London, 1533).

PRINTED PRIMARY SOURCES

Abstracts of Feet of Fines relating to Wiltshire 1377–1509, ed. J. L. Kirby, Wiltshire RS 41 (Devizes, 1986).

Abstracts of Inquisitiones Post Mortem relating to the City of London, Tudor Period, ed. G. Fry et al., 3 vols (London, 1896–1908).

Abstracts of the Inquisitiones Post Mortem relating to Nottinghamshire, i, ed. W. Phillimore, Thoroton Society Record Series 3 (Nottingham, 1905).

Abstracts of Surrey Feet of Fines 1509–1558, ed. C. A. F. Meekings, 2 vols, Surrey RS 45–6 (Frome, 1946).

Account Rolls of the Obedientiaries of Peterborough, ed. J. Greatrex, Northamptonshire RS 33 (Northampton, 1984).

Acts of Court of the Mercers' Company 1453–1527, ed. L. Lyell and F. D. Watney (Cambridge, 1936).

'Ancient Wills', ed. H. W. King, *TEAS* 4 (1869), 147–82.

The Annals of Gonville and Caius College by John Caius MD, ed. J. Venn, Cambridge Antiquarian Society 8o ser. 40 (Cambridge, 1904).

The Antient Kalendars and Inventories of the Treasury of His Majesty's Exchequer, ed. F. Palgrave, 3 vols (London, 1836).

The Antiquarian Repertory, ed. F. Grose et al., 4 vols (London, 1809).

Bacon, Francis, *The History of the Reign of King Henry VII and Selected Works*, ed. B. Vickers (Cambridge, 1998).

Bacon, Francis, *Essays* (Oxford, 1937).

'Banners, Standards and Badges, temp. Hen VIII', *Collectanea Topographica et Genealogica* 3 (1836), 49–76.

Banners, Standards and Badges from a Tudor Manuscript in the College of Arms, ed. [T.] Lord Howard de Walden (London, 1904).

The Bede Roll of the Fraternity of St Nicholas, ed. N. W. James and V. A. James, 2 vols, London RS 39 (London, 2004).

Bedfordshire Wills proved in the Prerogative Court of Canterbury 1383–1548, ed. M. McGregor, Bedfordshire Historical RS 58 (Bedford, 1979).

'Bridge House Collection, Document No. 36: "1417–1570. An Abstract of the Earls of Derby, Govrs & Officers of this Island, for Sevll Years 1417–1570"', *Journal of the Manx Museum* 2/32 (1932), 71.

British Library Harleian MS 433, ed. R. Horrox, P. W. Hammond, 4 vols (Gloucester, 1979–83).

Calendar of the Close Rolls, Edward IV–Henry VII, 4 vols (London, 1953–63).

Calendar of the Deeds and Documents belonging to the Corporation of Walsall, ed. R. Sims (Walsall, 1882).

Calendar of Entries in the Papal Registers relating to Great Britain and Ireland, ed. W. H. Bliss et al., 19 vols (London and Dublin, 1893–).

A Calendar of the Feet of Fines relating to the County of Huntingdon, ed. G. J. Turner, Cambridge Antiquarian Society 37 (Cambridge, 1913).

A Calendar to the Feet of Fines for London and Middlesex, ed. W. J. Hardy and W. Page, 2 vols (London, 1892–3).

Calendar of the Fine Rolls preserved in the Public Record Office, Henry VII (London, 1962).

Calendar of Inquisitions Post Mortem, Henry VII, 3 vols (London, 1898–1955).

Calendar of Institutions by the Chapter of Canterbury Sede Vacante, ed. C. E. Woodruff and I. A. Churchill, Kent Archaeological Society Records Branch 8 (Canterbury, 1924).

Calendar of Letters, Despatches, and State Papers, relating to the Negotiations between England and Spain, Preserved in the Archives at Simancas and Elsewhere, ed. G. Bergenroth et al., 13 vols (London, 1862–1954).

Calendar of the Manuscripts of the Dean and Chapter of Wells, 2 vols, HMC 12 (London, 1907–14).

Calendar of the Manuscripts of the Marquis of Bath, 5 vols, HMC 58 (London, 1904–80).

Calendar of Nottinghamshire Coroners' Inquests 1485–1558, ed. R. F. Hunnisett, Thoroton Society Record Series 25 (Nottingham, 1966).

Calendar of the Patent Rolls, Edward IV–Henry VII, 4 vols (London, 1899–1916).

Calendar of State Papers and Manuscripts in the Archives and Collections of Milan 1385–1618, ed. A. B. Hinds (London, 1912).

Calendar of State Papers and Manuscripts, Relating to English Affairs, Existing in the Archives and Collections of Venice and other Libraries of Northern Italy, 1534–1554, ed. R. Brown (London, 1873).

A Calendar of the White and Black Books of the Cinque Ports, ed. F. Hull, Kent Records 19 (London, 1967).

Calendar of Wills proved and enrolled in the Court of Husting, London, A.D. 1258–A.D. 1688, ed. R. R. Sharpe, 2 vols (London, 1889–90).

Calendarium Inquisitionum Post Mortem sive Escaetarum, ed. J. Caley and J. Bayley, 4 vols (London, 1806–28).

Canterbury College Oxford, iii, ed. W. A. Pantin, OHS n.s. 8 (Oxford, 1950).

A Catalogue of Manuscripts in the College of Arms: Collections, i, ed. L. Campbell and F. Steer (London, 1988).

A Catalogue of the Medieval Muniments at Berkeley Castle, ed. B. Wells-Firby, 2 vols, Gloucestershire Record Series 17–18 (Bristol, 2004).

Cavendish, George, *The Life and Death of Cardinal Wolsey*, ed. R. S. Sylvester, EETS 243 (Oxford, 1959).

The Certificate of Musters for Buckinghamshire in 1522, ed. A. C. Chibnall, Buckinghamshire RS 17 (London, 1973).

Chapter Acts of the Cathedral Church of St Mary of Lincoln, AD 1520–1536, ed. R. E. G. Cole, Lincoln RS 12 (Lincoln, 1915).

The Charters of Quarr Abbey, ed. S. F. Hockey, Isle of Wight Records Series 3 (Newport, 1991).

Christ Church Letters, ed. J. B. Sheppard, CS n.s. 19 (London, 1877).

The Chronicle of Calais, ed. J. G. Nichols, CS o.s. 35 (London, 1846).

'Church-wardens' Accounts All Saints' Church Walsall 1462–1531', ed. G. P. Mander, *Collections for a History of Staffordshire*, 3rd ser. for 1928 (1930), 173–267.

A Collection of Ordinances and Regulations for the Government of the Royal Household (London, 1790).

Complete Works of St Thomas More, iii-2: *Latin Poems*, ed. C. H. Miller et al. (New Haven CT and London, 1984).

Constable, Robert, *Prerogativa Regis, Tertia Lectura Roberti Constable de Lyncolnis Inne Anno 11 H 7*, ed. S. E. Thorne (New Haven CT, 1949).

Cornish Wills 1342–1540, ed. N. Orme, Devon and Cornwall RS n.s. 50 (Exeter, 2007).

Correspondance de l'Empereur Maximilien Ier et de Marguerite d'Autriche, ed. A. J. G. Le Glay, Société de l'histoire de France, 2 vols (Paris, 1839).

Correspondencia de Gutierre Gomez de Fuensalida, ed. Duque de Berwick y de Alba (Madrid, 1907).

The County Community under Henry VIII, ed. J. Cornwall, Rutland Record Series 1 (Oakham, 1980).

The Court Rolls of the Manor of Bromsgrove and King's Norton 1494–1504, ed. A. F. C. Baber, Worcestershire Historical Society n.s. 3 (Kineton, 1963).

The Courts of the Archdeaconry of Buckingham, 1483–1523, ed. E. M. Elvey, Buckinghamshire RS 19 (Aylesbury, 1975).

The Coventry Leet Book, 1420–1555, ed. M. D. Harris, 4 vols, EETS 134–5, 138, 146 (London, 1907–13).

The Customs of London, otherwise called Arnold's Chronicle, ed. F. Douce (London, 1811).

Derbyshire Feet of Fines 1323–1546, ed. H. J. H. Garratt and C. Rawcliffe, Derbyshire RS 2 (Chesterfield, 1985).

A Descriptive Catalogue of Ancient Deeds in the Public Record Office, 6 vols (London, 1890–1915).

Descriptive Catalogue of the Charters and Muniments in the Possession of the Rt Hon Lord Fitzhardinge at Berkeley Castle, ed. I. H. Jeayes (Bristol, 1892).

A Descriptive Catalogue of the Western Manuscripts in the Library of Queens' College, Cambridge, ed. M. R. James (Cambridge, 1905).

The Domesday of Inclosures, 1517–1518, ed. I. S. Leadam, 2 vols (London, 1897).

Dudley, Edmund, *The Tree of Commonwealth*, ed. D. M. Brodie (Cambridge, 1948).

'Early Berkshire Wills from the PCC, ante 1558', ed. G. F. T. Sherwood, *Quarterly Journal of the Berks Archaeological and Architectural Society* 3 (1893–5), 148–52.

Early English versions of the tales of Guiscardo and Ghismonda and Titus and Gisippus from 'The Decameron', ed. H. G. Wright, EETS o.s. 205 (London, 1937).

Early Northampton Wills, ed. D. Edwards et al., Northamptonshire RS 42 (Northampton, 2005).

Early Records of Furnival's Inn, ed. D. S. Bland (Newcastle, 1957).

Early Tudor Craven: Subsidies and Assessments 1510–1547, ed. R. W. Hoyle, YASRS 145 (Leeds, 1987).

'Ely Episcopal Registers', ed. J. H. Crosby, in *Ely Diocesan Remembrancer* (1908–11), 280–312.

An Episcopal Court Book for the Diocese of Lincoln 1514–1520, ed. M. Bowker, Lincoln RS 61 (Lincoln, 1967).

Epistolae Academicae Oxon, ii, ed. F. Anstey, OHS 36 (Oxford, 1898).

Epistolae Academicae 1508–1596, ed. W. T. Mitchell, OHS, n.s. 26 (Oxford, 1980).

Erasmus, Desiderius, *Praise of Folly and Letter to Martin Dorp, 1515* (London, 1971 edn).

The Estate and Household Accounts of William Worsley, Dean of St Paul's Cathedral 1479–1497, ed. H. Kleineke and S. R. Hovland, London RS 40 (London, 2004).

'Expenses of the Corporation of Faversham, temp. Hen. VIII', ed. F. F. Giraud, *AC* 10 (1876), 233–41.

Extracts from the Account Rolls of the Abbey of Durham, ed. J. T. Fowler, 3 vols, Surtees Society 99, 100, 103 (Durham, 1898–1901).

Feet of Fines for Cambridgeshire Henry VIII to Elizabeth, ed. W. M. Palmer (Norwich, 1909).

Feet of Fines for the County of Sussex, iii, ed. L. F. Salzmann, Sussex RS 23 (London, 1916).

Feet of Fines, Divers Counties, ed. E. F. Kirk (London, 1913–24).

Feet of Fines for Essex, ed. R. E. G. Kirk et al., 6 vols (Colchester, 1899–1993).

Feet of Fines of the Tudor Period, ed. F. Collins, 4 vols, YASRS 2, 5, 7, 8 (Wakefield, 1887–90).

Final Concords of the County of Lancaster…part III…AD 1377–1509, ed. W. Farrer, Record Society of Lancashire and Cheshire 50 (Manchester, 1905).

'Fines of Mixed Counties', ed. G. Wrottesley, *Collections for a History of Staffordshire* 12/1 (London, 1891), 175–325.

Foedera, Conventiones, Literae et cujuscunque generis Acta Publica, ed. T. Rymer, 20 vols (London, 1704–35).

Ford, John, *The Chronicle History of Perkin Warbeck*, ed. P. Ure (London, 1968).

The Great Chronicle of London, ed. A. H. Thomas and I. D. Thornley (London, 1938).

The Great Wardrobe Accounts of Henry VII and Henry VIII, ed. M. Hayward, London R S 47 (Woodbridge, 2012).

Grace Book B, ed. M. Bateson, 2 vols, Cambridge Antiquarian Society Luard Memorial Series 2–3 (Cambridge, 1903–5).

Guide to Medieval and Renaissance Manuscripts in the Huntington Library, ed. C. W. Dutschke et al., 2 vols (San Marino, CA, 1989).

Hall, Edward, *Hall's Chronicle*, ed. H. Ellis (London, 1809).

Halifax Wills, ed. J. W. Clay and E. W. Crossley (Halifax, 1904).

Henley Borough Records: Assembly Books i–iv, 1395–1543, ed. P. M. Briers, ORS 41 (Oxford, 1960).

The Herald's Memoir 1486–1490: Court Ceremony, Royal Progress and Rebellion, ed. E. Cavell (Donington, 2009).

Herts Genealogist and Antiquary, ed. W. Brigg, 3 vols (St Albans, 1896–8).

HMC First Report (London, 1874).

HMC Third Report (London, 1872).

HMC Fifth Report (London, 1876).

HMC Seventh Report (London, 1879).

HMC Eighth Report (London, 1881).

HMC Ninth Report (London, 1883).

Historiae Dunelmensis Scriptores Tres, ed. J. Raine, Surtees Soc. 9 (London, 1839).

History from Marble, Compiled in the Reign of Charles II by Thomas Dingley, Gent., ii, ed. J. G. Nichols, CS o.s. 97 (London, 1868).

The History of Methley, ed. H. S. Darbysire and G. D. Lumb, Thoresby Soc. 35 (Leeds, 1937).

The Honour and Forest of Pickering, ed. R. B. Turton, 4 vols, North Riding Records, n.s. 1–4 (London, 1894–7).

The Household Book (1510–1551) of Sir Edward Don: An Anglo-Welsh Knight and his Circle, ed. R. A. Griffiths, Buckinghamshire RS 33 (Aylesbury, 2004).

The Household Books of John Howard, Duke of Norfolk, 1462–1471, 1481–1483, ed. A. Crawford (Stroud, 1992).

Illustrations of British History, ed. E. Lodge, 3 vols (London, 1838).

Illustrations of the Manners and Expenses of Antient Times in England, ed. J. Nichols (London, 1791).

'Income Tax Assessments of Norwich, 1472 and 1489', ed. M. Jurkowski, in *Poverty and Wealth: Sheep, Taxation and Charity in Late Medieval Norfolk*, ed. M. Bailey, M. Jurkowski, and C. Rawcliffe, Norfolk RS 71 (Norwich, 2007), 99–156.

Inventaire des archives de la ville de Bruges, ed. L. Gilliodts-Van Severen, 9 vols (Bruges, 1871–85).

Inventaire-sommaire des archives départementales. Nord, ed. C. Dehaisnes et al., 10 vols (Lille, 1877–1906).

Inventaris der archieven van de stad 's Hertogenbosch... Stads Rekeningen van het jaar 1399–1800, ed. R. A. Van Zuijlen, 3 vols ('s Hertogenbosch, 1863–70).

Inventaris van de Nassause domeinraad. Tweede deel: het archief van de raad en rekenkamer te Breda tot 1581: stukken betreffende de rechten en goederen van Anna van Buren, ed. S. W. A. Drossaers, 5 vols (The Hague, 1955).

Joannis Lelandi Collectanea, ed. T. Hearne, 6 vols (Oxford, 1774).

John Spelman's Reading on Quo Warranto, ed. J. H. Baker, SS 113 (London, 1997).

Journals of the House of Lords, 10 vols (London, 1846 edn).

Kentish Visitations of Archbishop Warham and his Deputies, 1511–1512, ed. K. L. Wood-Legh, Kent Records, 24 (Maidstone, 1984).

Kingsford's Stonor Letters and Papers 1290–1483, ed. C. Carpenter (Cambridge, 1996).

'The Last Testament and Inventory of John de Veer, thirteenth earl of Oxford', ed. W. H. StJ. Hope, *Archaeologia* 66 (1915), 275–348.

Leland, John, *The Itinerary of John Leland in or about the Years 1535–1543*, ed. L. T. Smith, 5 vols (London, 1906–10).

Letters and Papers, Foreign and Domestic, of the Reign of Henry VIII, ed. J. S. Brewer et al., 23 vols in 38 (London, 1862–1932).

Letters and Papers illustrative of the Reigns of Richard III and Henry VII, ed. J. Gairdner, 2 vols, Rolls Series 24 (London, 1861–3).

Lincoln Wills, ed. C. W. Foster, 3 vols, Lincoln RS 5, 10, 24 (Lincoln, 1914–30).

Lincoln Wills, 1532–1534, ed. D. Hickman, Lincoln RS 89 (Lincoln, 2001).

Lincolnshire Church Notes, ed. R. E. G. Cole, Lincoln RS 1 (Lincoln, 1911).

The Lisle Letters, ed. M. St C. Byrne, 6 vols (Chicago, 1981).

'List of the Gentry of Kent in the Time of Henry VII', ed. J. Greenstreet, *AC* 11 (1877), 394–97.

'List of Members of the Fourth Parliament of Henry VII', ed. W. Jay, *BIHR* 3 (1925–6), 168–75.

London and Middlesex Chantry Certificate 1548, ed. C. J. Kitching, London RS 16 (London, 1980).

Lost Glass from Kent Churches, ed. C. R. Councer, Kent Records 22 (Maidstone, 1950).

Luffield Priory Charters, part ii, ed. G. R. Elvey, Buckinghamshire RS 18 (n.p., 1975).

Lusy, Antoine de, *Le journal d'un bourgeois de Mons, 1505–1536*, ed. A. Louant, Commission royale d'histoire (Brussels, 1969).

Macquéreau, Robert, *Traicté et recueil de la maison de Bourgogne*, ed. J. A. C. Buchon, Choix de chroniques et mémoires sur l'histoire de France (Paris, 1838).

Manship, Henry, *The History of Great Yarmouth*, ed. C. J. Palmer (Great Yarmouth, 1854).

The Manuscripts of the Duke of Leeds, the Bridgewater Trust, Reading Corporation, the Inner Temple, HMC 11th report 7 (London, 1888).

The Manuscripts of His Grace, the Duke of Rutland, G.C.B., preserved at Belvoir Castle, 4 vols, HMC 24 (London, 1888–1908).

The Manuscripts of Lincoln, Bury St Edmunds, and Great Grimsby Corporations, HMC 37 (London, 1895).

The Manuscripts of Lord Middleton, preserved at Wollaton Hall, HMC 69 (London, 1911).

The Manuscripts of the Marquess of Abergavenny, Lord Braye, G. F. Luttrell, Esq., &c, HMC 10th Report 6 (London, 1887).

The Manuscripts of St George's Chapel, Windsor Castle, ed. J. N. Dalton (Windsor, 1937).

Materials for a History of the Reign of Henry VII, ed. W. Campbell, 2 vols, Rolls Series 60 (London, 1873–7).

Medieval Archives of the University of Oxford, ii, ed. H. E. Salter, OHS 73 (Oxford, 1921).

Memorials of King Henry VII, ed. J. Gairdner, Rolls Series 10 (London, 1858).

The Merchant Taylors' Company of London: Court Minutes 1486–1493, ed. M. Davies (Stamford, 2000).

The Military Survey of 1522 for Babergh Hundred, ed. J. F. Pound, Suffolk RS 28 (Woodbridge, 1986).

The Military Survey of Gloucestershire, 1522, ed. R. W. Hoyle, Gloucestershire Record Series 6 (Stroud, 1993).

Minutes of Parliament of the Middle Temple, ed. C. T. Martin, 4 vols (London, 1904).

Miscellaneous State Papers. From 1501–1726, ed. P. Yorke, Earl of Hardwicke, 2 vols (London, 1778).

Molinet, Jean, *Chroniques de Jean Molinet*, ed. G. Doutrepont and O. Jodogne, 3 vols (Brussels, 1935–7).

Muniments of Hon Mrs Trollope Bellew at Casewick (NRA report, 1958).

'A Muster Roll and Clergy List in the Hundred of Holt, circa 1523', ed. B. Cozens-Hardy, *NA* 22 (1923–5), 46–58.

Muster Roll for the Hundred of North Greenhoe (circa 1523), ed. H. L. Bradfer-Lawrence, Norfolk RS 1 (Norwich, 1930).

Narratives of the Days of the Reformation, ed. J. G. Nichols, CS o.s. 77 (London, 1859).

Naval Accounts and Inventories in the reign of Henry VII 1485–8, 1494–7, ed. M. Oppenheim, Navy Records Society 8 (London, 1896).

'Norfolk Subsidy Roll, 15 Hen VIII', *Norfolk Antiquarian Miscellany* 2 (1883), 399–410.

The Notebook of Sir John Port, ed. J. H. Baker, SS 102 (London, 1986).

Original Letters illustrative of English History, 3rd ser., ed. H. Ellis, 4 vols (London, 1846).

The Parliament Rolls of Medieval England, 1275–1504, ed. C. Given-Wilson (Woodbridge and London, 2005).

The Paston Letters 1422–1509, ed. J. Gairdner, 3 vols (London, 1872–5).

Paston Letters and Papers of the Fifteenth Century, ed. N. Davis, 2 vols (Oxford, 1971–6).

The Pension Book of Gray's Inn, ed. R. J. Fletcher, 2 vols (London, 1901–10).

Peterborough Local Administration: The Last Days of Peterborough Monastery, ed. W. T. Mellows, Northamptonshire RS 12 (1947).

'The Petition of Edmund Dudley', ed. C. J. Harrison, *EHR* 87 (1972), 82–99.

The Plays of Henry Medwall, ed. A. H. Nelson (Cambridge, 1980).

Plumpton Letters and Papers, ed. J. Kirby, CS 5th ser. 8 (London, 1996).

The Politics of Fifteenth-Century England: John Vale's Book, ed. M. L. Kekewich et al. (Stroud, 1995).

Privy Purse Expenses of Elizabeth of York: Wardrobe Accounts of Edward the Fourth, ed. N.H. Nicolas (London, 1830).

The Pylgrymage of Sir Richard Guylforde to the Holy Land, A.D. 1506, ed. H. Ellis, CS o.s. 51 (London, 1851).

Reading Records: Diary of the Corporation, ed. J. M. Guilding, 4 vols (London, 1892–6).

Readings and Moots at the Inns of Court, ed. S. E. Thorne, J. H. Baker, 2 vols, SS 71, 105 (London, 1952, 1989).

The Receyt of the Ladie Kateryne, ed. G. Kipling, EETS 296 (Oxford, 1990).

Records of the Borough of Leicester, ed. M. Bateson et al., 7 vols (London, 1899–1974).

Records of the Borough of Nottingham, ed. W. H. Stevenson, 3 vols (Nottingham, 1885).

Records of the City of Norwich, ed. W. Hudson, J. C. Tingey, 2 vols (Norwich, 1906–10).

Records of Convocation, ed. G. Bray, 20 vols (Woodbridge, 2005–6).

The Records of the Honourable Society of Lincoln's Inn: Admissions from AD 1420 to AD 1799 (London, 1896).

The Records of the Honourable Society of Lincoln's Inn: The Black Books, ed. W. P. Baildon and R. Roxburgh, 5 vols (London, 1897–1968).

Records of Lydd, ed. A. Finn (Ashford, 1911).

Records of Plays and Players in Kent 1450–1642, ed. G. E. Dawson, Malone Society Collections, 7 (Oxford, 1965).

Records of Plays and Players in Norfolk and Suffolk, 1330–1642, ed. D. Galloway and J. Wasson, Malone Society Collections 11 (Oxford, 1981).

The Red Paper Book of Colchester, ed. W. G. Benham (Colchester, 1902).

REED Herefordshire and Worcestershire, ed. D. N. Klausner (Toronto, 1990).

REED Lincolnshire, ed. J. Stokes, 2 vols (Toronto, 2009).

Register of Admissions to the Honourable Society of the Middle Temple, ed. H. A. C. Sturgess, 3 vols (London, 1949).

The Register of the Fraternity or Guild of the Holy and Undivided Trinity and Blessed Virgin Mary in the Parish Church of Luton, in the county of Bedford, from AD MCCCCLXXV to MVCXLVI, ed. H. Gough (London, 1906).

The Register of the Gild of the Holy Cross, the Blessed Mary and St John the Baptist, of Stratford-upon-Avon, ed. J. H. Bloom (London, 1907).

The Register of the Guild of Knowle in the County of Warwick, ed. W. B. Blickley (Walsall, 1894).

The Register of John Morton, Archbishop of Canterbury 1486–1500, ed. C. Harper-Bill, 3 vols, CYS 75, 78, 89 (Leeds and Woodbridge, 1987–2000).

The Register of the Most Noble Order of the Garter, ed. J. Anstis, 2 vols (London, 1724).

The Register of Thetford Priory, ed. D. Dymond, 2 vols, Norfolk Record Society, 59–60 (Oxford, 1995–6).

The Register of Thomas Langton, Bishop of Salisbury, 1485–93, ed. D. P. Wright, CYS 74 (Oxford, 1985).

The Register of Thomas Rotherham, Archbishop of York 1480–1500, ed. E. E. Barker, CYS 69 (Torquay, 1976).

The Registers of Oliver King, Bishop of Bath and Wells, 1496–1503, and Hadrian de Castello, Bishop of Bath and Wells, 1503–1518, ed. H. C. Maxwell Lyte, Somerset RS 54 (London, 1939).

Registra Johannis Whethamstede, Willelmi Albon, et Willelmi Walingforde, Abbatum Monanasterii Sancti Albani, ed. H. T. Riley, Rolls Series 28 (London, 1873).

Registra Stephani Gardiner et Johannis Poynet Episcoporum Wintoniensium, ed. H. Chitty and H. E. Malden, CYS 37 (Oxford, 1930).

Registrum Annalium Collegii Mertonensis 1483–1521, ed. H. E. Salter, OHS 76 (Oxford, 1923).

Registrum Cancellarii 1498–1506, ed. W. T. Mitchell, OHS n.s. 27 (Oxford, 1980).

Registrum Caroli Bothe, Episcopi Herefordensis, ed. A. T. Bannister, CYS 28 (London, 1921).

Registrum Thome Bourgchier, Cantuariensis Archiepiscopi, A.D. 1454–1486, CYS 54 (Oxford, 1957).

The Reign of Henry VII from Original Sources, ed. A. F. Pollard, 3 vols (London, 1913–14).

Remains of the Early Popular Poetry of England, ed. W. C. Hazlitt, 4 vols (London, 1864–6).

Report on Manuscripts in Various Collections, 8 vols, HMC 55 (London, 1901–13).

Report on the Manuscripts of Lord de L'Isle & Dudley, 6 vols, HMC 77 (London, 1925–66).

Report on the Manuscripts of the late Reginald Rawdon Hastings, Esq., 4 vols, HMC 78 (London, 1928–47).

Reports of Cases by John Caryll, ed. J. H. Baker, 2 vols, SS 115–16 (London, 1999–2000).

Reports of Cases from the Time of King Henry VIII, ed. J. H. Baker, 2 vols, SS 120–1 (London, 2003–4).

Reports from the Lost Notebooks of Sir James Dyer, ed. J. H. Baker, 2 vols, SS 109–10 (London, 1994).

The Reports of Sir Edward Coke, Knt. In Thirteen Parts, ed. J. H. Thomas, J. F. Fraser, 6 vols (London, 1826).

The Reports of Sir John Spelman, ed. J. H. Baker, 2 vols, SS 93–4 (London, 1976–7).

The Reports of William Dalison 1552–1558, ed. J. H. Baker, SS 124 (London, 2007).

Rotuli Parliamentorum, ed. J. Strachey et al., 6 vols (London, 1767–77).

Rutland Papers, ed. W. Jerdan, CS o.s. 21 (London, 1842).

Schaumburg, Wilwolt von, *Die Geschichten und Taten Wilwolts von Schaumburg*, ed. A. Von Keller, Bibliothek des Litterarischen Vereins in Stuttgart, 50 (Stuttgart, 1859).

Sede Vacante Wills, ed. C. E Woodruff, Kent Archaeological Society records branch 3 (Canterbury, 1914).

Select Cases in the Council of Henry VII, ed. C. G. Bayne, W. H. Dunham, SS 75 (London, 1958).

Select Cases before the King's Council in the Star Chamber, ii, ed. I. S. Leadam, SS 25 (London, 1911).

Selections from the Records of the City of Oxford, ed. W. H. Turner (Oxford, 1880).

Shakespeare, William, *Henry VIII*.

Six Town Chronicles of England, ed. R. Flenley (Oxford, 1911).

Some Oxfordshire Wills proved in the Prerogative Court of Canterbury, 1393–1510, ed. J. R. H. Weaver and A. Beardwood, ORS 39 (Oxford, 1958).

'The "Spouselles" of the Princess Mary', ed. J. Gairdner, *The Camden Miscellany*, ix, CS n.s. 53 (London, 1853).

State Papers, King Henry the Eighth, 5 vols in 11 (London, 1830–52).

Statutes of the Realm, ed. A. Luders et al., 11 vols (London, 1810–28).

Stow, John, *A Survey of London*, ed. C. L. Kingsford, 2nd edn, 2 vols (Oxford, 1971).

A Subsidy Collected in the Diocese of Lincoln in 1526, ed. H. Salter, OHS 63 (Oxford, 1913).

Subsidy Roll for the County of Buckingham Anno 1524, ed. A. C. Chibnall and A. V. Woodman, Buckinghamshire RS 8 (Bedford, 1950).

'A Subsidy Roll for the Wapentake of Agbrigg and Morley of the 15th Henry VIII', ed. J. J. Cartwright, *Yorkshire Archaeological Journal* 2 (1873), 43–60.

Suffolk in 1524, ed. S. H. A. Hervey, Suffolk Green Books 10 (Woodbridge, 1910).

Sussex Chantry Records, ed. J. E. Ray, Sussex RS 36 (Cambridge, 1930).

Sussex Manors, Advowsons etc recorded in the Feet of Fines, Henry VIII to William IV (1509–1833), ed. E. H. W. Dunkin, Sussex RS 19–20 (London, 1914–15).

Testamenta Eboracensia, ed. J Raine and J. W. Clay, 6 vols, Surtees Society 4, 30, 45, 53, 79, 106 (London, 1836–1902).

Testamenta Vetusta, ed. N. H. Nicolas, 2 vols (London, 1826).

Third Report of the Deputy Keeper of the Public Records (London, 1842).

Thirty-First Annual Report of the Deputy Keeper of the Public Records (London, 1870).

'Thomas Wall's Book of Crests', *The Ancestor* 11 (1904), 178–90.

Transcripts of Sussex Wills, ed. W. H. Godfrey, 4 vols, Sussex RS 41–3, 45 (Lewes, 1935–41).

Trevelyan Papers Prior to AD 1558, ed. J. P. Collier, CS o.s. 67 (London, 1857).

Tudor Royal Proclamations, ed. P. L. Hughes, J. F. Larkin, 3 vols (New Haven CT and London, 1964).

Valor Ecclesiasticus, ed. H. Caley, 6 vols (London, 1810–33).

Vergil, Polydore, *Three Books of Polydore Vergil's English History, Comprising the Reigns of Henry VI, Edward IV, and Richard III*, ed. H. Ellis, CS o.s. 29 (London, 1844).

Vergil, Polydore, *The Anglica Historia of Polydore Vergil A.D. 1485–1537*, ed. D. Hay, CS 3rd ser. 74 (London, 1950).

'View of the Castles of Tickhill and Conisbro' made by Special Commissioners 29 Henry VIII', ed. W. Brown, *Yorkshire Archaeological Journal* 9 (1885–6), 221–22.

The Visitacion of Norffolk, made and taken by William Hervey, Clarencieux King of Arms, anno 1563, enlarged with another Visitacion made by Clarenceux Cooke, with many other Descents; and also the Vissitation made by John Raven, Richmond, anno 1613, ed. W. Rye, HS 32 (London, 1891).

The Visitation of Norfolk in the Year 1563, ed. G. H. Dashwood and E. Bulwer Lytton, 2 vols (Norwich, 1878–95).

A Visitation of the North of England circa 1480–1500, ed. C. H. Hunter-Blair, Surtees Soc. 144 (Durham, 1930).

The Visitation of Suffolk, 1561, ed. J. Corder, 2 vols, HS n.s. 2–3 (London, 1981–4).

Visitations in the Diocese of Lincoln 1517–1531, ed. A. H. Thompson, 3 vols, Lincoln RS 33, 35, 37 (Lincoln, 1940–7).

The Visitations of Essex by Hawley, 1552; Hervey, 1558; Cooke, 1570; Raven, 1612; and Owen and Lilly, 1634, ed. W. C. Metcalfe, 2 vols, HS 13–14 (London, 1878–9).

Visitations and Memorials of Southwell Minster, ed. A.F. Leach, CS n.s. 48 (London, 1891).

Western Illuminated Manuscripts: A Catalogue of the Collection in Cambridge University Library, ed. P. Binski and P. Zutshi (Cambridge, 2011).

'Will of Sir Roger le Strange, Knt', ed. H. Le Strange, *NA 9* (1880–4), 226–39.

William Browne's Town: Stamford Hall Book 1465–1492, ed. A. Rogers (Stamford, 2005).

Wills from Doctors' Commons, ed. J. G. Nichols and J. Bruce, CS o.s. 83 (London, 1863).

The Wiston Archives: A Catalogue, ed. J. M. L. Booker (Chichester, 1975).

Wriothesley, Charles, *A Chronicle of England during the Reigns of the Tudors*, ed. W. D. Hamilton, 2 vols, CS 2nd ser., 11, 20 (London, 1875–7).

Year Book of Henry VIII: 12–14 Henry VIII 1520–1523, ed. J. H. Baker, SS 119 (London, 2002).

York Civic Records, ed. A. Raine, 8 vols, YASRS, 98, 103, 106, 108, 110, 112, 115, 119 (Wakefield, 1939–53).

Yorkshire Deeds, v, ed. C. T. Clay, YASRS 69 (Wakefield, 1926).

Yorkshire Deeds, vii, ed. C. T. Clay, YASRS 73 (Wakefield, 1932).

Yorkshire Star Chamber Proceedings, ed. W. Brown et al., 4 vols, YASRS 41, 45, 51, 70 (Wakefield, 1909–27).

SECONDARY SOURCES

Adams, S., 'Baronial Contexts?: Continuity and Change in the Noble Affinity, 1400–1600', in J. L. Watts (ed.), *The End of the Middle Ages? England in the Fifteenth and Sixteenth Centuries* (Stroud, 1998), 155–97.

Alsop, J. D., 'The Exchequer in late medieval Government, c1485–1530', in J. G. Rowe (ed.), *Aspects of Late Medieval Government and Society: Essays presented to J. R. Lander* (Toronto, 1986), 179–212.

Alsop, J. D., 'The Structure of early Tudor Finance, c.1509–1558', in C. Coleman and D. Starkey (eds), *Revolution Reassessed: Revisions in the History of Tudor Government and Administration* (Oxford, 1986), 135–62.

Andrews, D. et al., 'Plaster or Stone? Some Observations on Layer Marney Church and Tower', *Essex Archaeology and History* 17 (1986), 172–6.

Alford, S., *Burghley: William Cecil at the Court of Elizabeth I* (New Haven CT and London, 2008).

Anglo, S., 'The Court Festivals of Henry VII: A Study Based on the Account Books of John Heron, Treasurer of the Chamber', *Bulletin of the John Rylands Library* 43 (1960–1), 46–69.

Anglo, S., 'Ill of the Dead. The Posthumous Reputation of Henry VII', *Renaissance Studies*, 1 (1987), 27–47.

Anglo, S., *Images of Tudor Kingship* (London, 1992).

Anglo, S., 'William Cornish in a Play, Pageants, Prison and Politics', *Review of English Studies*, n.s. 10 (1959), 347–60.

Anstis, J., *Observations Introductory to an Historical Essay upon the Knighthood of the Bath* (London, 1725).

Arthurson, I., 'The King's Voyage into Scotland: the War the Never Was', in D. T. Williams (ed.), *England in the Fifteenth Century* (Woodbridge, 1987), 1–22.

Arthurson, I., *The Perkin Warbeck Conspiracy 1491–1499* (Stroud, 1994).

Ashdown-Hill, J., *The Last Days of Richard III* (Stroud, 2010).

Ashdown-Hill, J., 'A Pyramidal Seal Matrix of Sir John Marney (1402–c1471)', *Essex Archaeology and History* 38 (2007), 120–25.

Auerbach, E., *Tudor Artists* (London, 1954).

Baggs, A. P., 'Sixteenth Century Terracotta Tombs in East Anglia', *Archaeological Journal* 125 (1968), 296–301.

Bainbridge, V., *Gilds in the Medieval Countryside: Social and Religious Change in Cambridgeshire c.1350–1558* (Woodbridge, 1996).

Baker, J. H., *The Men of Court 1440 to 1550: A Prosopography of the Inns of Court and Chancery and the Courts of Law*, 2 vols, SS supplementary series 18 (London, 2012).

Baker, J. H., *The Oxford History of the Laws of England*, vi: *1483–1558* (Oxford, 2003).

Barnett, R. C., *Place, Profit, and Power: a Study of the Servants of William Cecil, Elizabethan Statesman* (Chapel Hill NC, 1969).

Barron, C. M., *London in the Later Middle Ages: Government and People 1200–1500* (Oxford, 2004).

Barron, O., 'The Brays of Shere', *The Ancestor* 6 (1903), 1–11.

Bateson, E. et al. (eds), *A History of Northumberland*, 15 vols (Newcastle, 1893–1940).

Bean, J. M. W., *The Estates of the Percy Family, 1416–1537* (London, 1958).

Bean, J. M. W., 'Landlords', in E. Miller (ed.), *The Agrarian History of England and Wales*, iii: *1348–1500* (Cambridge, 1991), 568–86.

Beaven, A. P., *The Aldermen of the City of London temp. Henry III-1908*, 2 vols (London, 1908).

Bell, H. E., *An Introduction to the History and Records of the Court of Wards and Liveries* (Cambridge, 1953).

Bennett, M., *The Battle of Bosworth* (Stroud, 1985).

Bennett, M., *Lambert Simnel and the Battle of Stoke* (Gloucester, 1987).

Bernard, G. W., *Anne Boleyn: Fatal Attractions* (New Haven CT and London, 2010).

Bernard, G. W., 'The Fortunes of the Greys, Earls of Kent, in the Early Sixteenth Century', *HJ* 25 (1982), 671–85.

Bernard, G. W., *The King's Reformation: Henry VIII and the Remaking of the English Church* (New Haven CT and London, 2005).

Bernard, G. W. (ed.), *The Tudor Nobility* (Manchester, 1992).

Bietenholz, P. G. and Deutscher, T. B. (eds), *Contemporaries of Erasmus*, 3 vols (Toronto, 1985–7).

Bindoff, S. T., *History of Parliament: The House of Commons 1509–1558*, 3 vols (London, 1982).

Bindoff, S. T., *Tudor England* (Harmondsworth, 1950).

Blanchard, J., *Commynes l'européen. L'invention du politique* (Geneva, 1996).

Blomefield, F., *An Essay towards a Topographical History of the County of Norfolk*, 11 vols (London, 1805–10).

Boone, M., 'La justice en spectacle. La justice urbaine en Flandre et la crise du pouvoir "bourguignon" (1477–1488)', *Revue Historique* 308 (2003), 43–65.

Bowden, P. J., *The Wool Trade in Tudor and Stuart England* (London, 1962).

Brigden, S., *Thomas Wyatt: The Heart's Forest* (London, 2012).

Britnell, R., *Britain and Ireland, 1050–1530: Economy and Society* (Oxford, 2004).

Britton, J., *The Architectural Antiquities of Great Britain*, 5 vols (London, 1805–26).

Brodie, D. M., 'Edmund Dudley: Minister of Henry VII', *TRHS* 4th ser. 15 (1932), 133–61.

Brooke, C. N. L., *A History of Gonville and Caius College* (Woodbridge, 1985).

Brookes, C. C., *History of Steeple Aston and Middle Aston* (Shipston-on-Stour, 1929).

Brown, A., 'London and North-West Kent in the Later Middle Ages: The Development of a Land Market', *AC* 92 (1976), 145–55.

Brown, A., 'Lorenzo de' Medici's New Men and their Mores: The Changing Lifestyle of Quattrocento Florence', *Renaissance Studies* 16 (2002), 113–42.

Brown, C., *A History of Newark-on-Trent*, 2 vols (Newark, 1904–7).

Busch, W., *England under The Tudors*, i: *King Henry VII (1485–1509)* (London, 1895).

Cameron, A., 'Complaint and Reform in Henry VII's Reign: The Origins of the Statue of 3 Henry VII, c.2?', *BIHR* 51 (1978), 83–89.

Cameron, A., 'A Nottinghamshire Quarrel in the Reign of Henry VII', *BIHR* 45 (1972), 27–37.

Cameron, A., 'Sir Henry Willoughby of Wollaton', *Transactions of the Thoroton Society* 74 (1970), 10–21.

Campbell, B. M. S., 'The Land', in R. Horrox and W. M. Ormrod (eds), *A Social History of England 1200–1500* (Cambridge, 2006), 179–237.

Campbell, T., *Henry VIII and the Art of Majesty: Tapestries at the Tudor Court* (New Haven CT and London, 2007).

Carlin, M., *Medieval Southwark* (London, 1996).

Carpenter, C., 'Henry VI and the Deskilling of the Royal Bureaucracy', in L. Clark (ed.), *English and Continental Perspectives*, The Fifteenth Century 9 (Woodbridge, 2010), 1–37.

Carpenter, C., *Locality and Polity: A Study of Warwickshire Landed Society, 1401–1499* (Cambridge, 1992).

Carpenter, C., *The Wars of the Roses: Politics and the Constitution in England, c.1437–1509* (Cambridge, 1997).

Catto, J. I., 'Theology after Wycliffism', in J. I. Catto and T. A. R. Evans (eds), *History of the University of Oxford*. Volume ii: *Late Medieval Oxford* (Oxford, 1992), 263–80.

Catto, J. I. and Evans, T. A. R. (eds), *History of the University of Oxford*. Volume ii: *Late Medieval Oxford* (Oxford, 1992).

Cave, C. J. P. and London, H. S., 'The Roof-Bosses in St George's Chapel, Windsor', *Archaeologia* 95 (1953), 107–21.

Cavill, P. R., '"The Enemy of God and his Church": James Hobart, Praemunire and the Clergy of Norwich Diocese', *Journal of Legal History* 32 (2011), 127–43.

Cavill, P. R., *The English Parliaments of Henry VII, 1485–1504* (Oxford, 2009).

Challis, C. E., 'Lord Hastings to the Great Silver Recoinage, 1464–1699', in C. E. Challis (ed.), *A New History of the Royal Mint* (Cambridge, 1992), 179–397.

Challis, C. E., *The Tudor Coinage* (Manchester, 1978).

Chauncy, H., *The Historical Antiquities of Hertfordshire*, 2 vols (Dorking, 1975 edn).

Chope, R. P., 'The Last of the Dynhams', *Transactions of the Devonshire Association* 50 (1918), 431–92.

Chrimes, S. B., *Henry VII* (London, 1972).

Claiden-Yardley, K., 'Tudor Noble Funerals' in P. Lindley (ed.), *The Howards and the Tudors: Studies in Science and Heritage* (Donington, 2015), 34–42.

Clark, J. G., 'Monastic Confraternity in Medieval England: the Evidence from the St Albans Abbey *Liber Benefactorum*', in E. Jamroziak and J. Burton (eds), *Religious and Laity in Western Europe 1000–1400: Interaction, Negotiation and Power* (Turnhout, 2006).

Clark, P. and Hoskins, J., *Population Estimates of English Small Towns 1550–1851*, 2nd edn (Leicester, 1993).

Clinch, G., 'Notes on the Remains of Westenhanger House, Kent', *AC* 31 (1915), 76–81.

Cobb, H. S., '"Books of Rates" and the London Customs, 1507–1558', *Guildhall Miscellany* 4 (1971–3), 1–13.

Cobban, A. B., 'Colleges and Halls 1430–1500', in J. I. Catto and T. A. R. Evans (eds), *History of the University of Oxford.* Volume ii: *Late Medieval Oxford* (Oxford, 1992), 581–634.

Cokayne, G. E., *The Complete Peerage*, ed. V. Gibbs et al., 13 vols (London, 1910–59).

Coleman, C. and Starkey, D. (eds), *Revolution Reassessed: Revisions in the History of Tudor Government and Administration* (Oxford, 1986).

Collins, A., *Historical Collections of the Noble Family of Windsor* (London, 1754).

Collinson, J., *The History and Antiquities of the County of Somerset*, 3 vols (Bath, 1792).

Colvin H. M. (ed.), *The History of the King's Works*, 6 vols (London, 1963–82).

Condon, M. M., 'An Anachronism with Intent? Henry VII's Council Ordinance of 1491/2', in R. A. Griffiths and J. Sherborne (eds), *Kings and Nobles in the Later Middle Ages* (Gloucester, 1986), 228–53.

Condon, M. M., 'From Caitiff and Villain to *Pater Patriae*: Reynold Bray and the Profits of Office', in M. A. Hicks (ed.), *Profit, Piety and the Professions in later Medieval England* (Gloucester, 1990), 136–68.

Condon, M. M., 'God Save the King! Piety, Propaganda and the Perpetual Memorial', in T. Tatton-Brown and R. Mortimer (eds), *Westminster Abbey: The Lady Chapel of Henry VII* (Woodbridge, 2003), 59–97.

Condon, M. M., 'The Last Will of Henry VII: Document and Text', in T. Tatton-Brown and R. Mortimer (eds), *Westminster Abbey: The Lady Chapel of Henry VII* (Woodbridge, 2003), 99–140.

Condon, M. M., 'Ruling Elites in the Reign of Henry VII', in C. D. Ross (ed.), *Patronage, Pedigree and Power in Later Medieval England* (Gloucester, 1979), 109–42.

Conway, A. E., *Henry VII's Relations with Scotland and Ireland, 1485–1498* (Cambridge, 1932).

Conway, A. E., 'The Maidstone Sector of Buckingham's Rebellion, Oct. 18, 1483', *AC* 37 (1925), 97–120.

Conway, W. M., 'Allington Castle', *AC* 28 (1909), 337–62.

Cooper, C. H., *Annals of Cambridge*, 5 vols (Cambridge, 1842–1908).

Cooper, C. H., *Memoir of Margaret, Countess of Richmond and Derby* (Cambridge, 1874).

Cooper, C. H., and Cooper, T., *Athenae Cantabrigienses*, 3 vols (Cambridge, 1858–1913).

Cooper, J. P., 'Henry VII's Last Years Reconsidered', *HJ* 2 (1959), 103–29.

Cooper, J. P. D., *Propaganda and the Tudor State: Political Culture in the Westcountry* (Oxford, 2003).

Copinger, W. A., *The Manors of Suffolk*, 7 vols (London and Manchester, 1905–11).

Cornwall, J., *Wealth and Society in Early Sixteenth-Century England* (London, 1988).

Councer, C. R., 'The Medieval Painted Glass of Chilham', *AC* 58 (1945), 8–13.

Cripps-Day, F. H., *The History of the Tournament in England and France* (London, 1918).

Cross, C. et al. (eds), *Law and Government under the Tudors: Essays Presented to Sir Geoffrey Elton on his Retirement* (Cambridge, 1988).

Crouch, D. J. F., *Piety, Fraternity and Power: Religious Guilds in Late Medieval Yorkshire 1389–1547* (Woodbridge, 2000).

Cruickshank C. G., *The English Occupation of Tournai 1513–1519* (Oxford, 1971).

Cunningham, S., *Henry VII* (London, 2007).

Cunningham, S., 'Loyalty and the Usurper: Recognizances, the Council and Allegiance under Henry VII', *HR* 82 (2009), 459–81.

Currin, J. M., 'England's International Relations 1485–1509: Continuities amidst Change', in S. Doran and G. Richardson (eds), *Tudor England and its Neighbours* (Basingstoke, 2005), 14–43.

Currin, J. M., 'Henry VII and the Treaty of Redon (1489): Plantagenet Ambitions and Early Tudor Foreign Policy', *History* 81 (1996), 343–58.

Currin, J. M., '"The King's Army into the Parts of Bretaigne": Henry VII and the Breton Wars, 1489–1491', *War in History* 7 (2000), 379–412.

Currin, J. M., 'Persuasions to Peace: The Luxembourg-Marigny-Gaguin Embassy and the State of Anglo-French Relations, 1489–90', *EHR* 113 (1998), 882–904.

Currin, J. M., '"Pro Expensis Ambassatorum": Diplomacy and Financial Administration in the Reign of Henry VII', *EHR* 108 (1993), 589–609.

Currin, J. M., 'To Traffic with War'? Henry VII and the French Campaign of 1492' in D. Grummitt (ed.), *The English Experience in France: War, Diplomacy and Cultural Exchange, c.1450–1558* (Aldershot, 2002), 106–31.

Cust, L., 'The Lumley Inventories', *The Walpole Society* 6 (1918), 15–35.

Da Costa, A., 'John Fewterer's *Myrrour or Glasse of Christes Passion* and Ulrich Pinder's *Speculum Passionis Domini Nostri*', *Notes and Queries* 56 (2009), 27–9.

Davies, C. S. L., 'The Crofts: Creation and Defence of a Family Enterprise under the Yorkists and Henry VII', *HR* 68 (1995), 241–65.

Davies, C. S. L., 'Information, Disinformation and Political Knowledge under Henry VII and early Henry VIII', *HR* 85 (2012), 228–53.

Davies, C. S. L., 'Tudor: What's in a Name', *History* 97 (2012), 24–42.

Davies, M., 'Lobbying Parliament: the London Companies in the Fifteenth Century', *Parliamentary History* 23 (2004), 136–48.

Davies, M. and Saunders, A., *The History of the Merchant Taylors' Company* (Leeds, 2004).

Davis, W. G., 'Whetehill, of Calais', *New England Historical and Genealogical Register* 102 (1948), 241–54; 103 (1949), 5–19.

Duffin, C. J., 'Alectorius: The Cock's Stone', *Folklore* 118 (2007), 325–41.

Dugdale, W., *The Baronage of England*, 2 vols (London, 1675).

Dugdale, W., *Monasticon Anglicanum*, ed. J. Caley et al., 6 vols in 8 (London, 1817–30).

Dunham, W. H., 'The Members of Henry VIII's Whole Council, 1509–1527', *EHR* 59 (1944), 187–210.

Dyer, A., 'Appendix: Ranking Lists of English Medieval Towns', in D. M. Palliser (ed.), *The Cambridge Urban History of Britain*, i: *600–1540* (Cambridge, 2000), 747–70.

Dyer, C., *Standards of Living in the Later Middle Ages: Social Change in England c.1200–1520* (Cambridge, 1989).

Eagleston, A. J., *The Channel Islands under Tudor Government, 1485–1642* (Cambridge, 1949).

Edwards, R., 'King Richard's Tomb at Leicester', in J. Petre (ed.), *Richard III: Crown and People* (London, 1985), 29–30.

Eeles, F. C., 'The Black Effigies at Layer Marney Re-examined', *TEAS* n.s. 22 (1936–40), 272–5.

Ellis, H., *The History and Antiquities of the Parish of St Leonard Shoreditch, and Liberty of Norton Folgate, in the Suburbs of London* (London, 1798).

Ellis, S. G., 'Henry VII and Ireland, 1491–1496', in J. F. Lydon (ed.), *England and Ireland in the Later Middle Ages* (Blackrock, 1981), 237–54.

Ellis, S. G., *Tudor Frontiers and Noble Power: The Making of the British State* (Oxford, 1995).

Elton, G. R., 'Henry VII: A Restatement', in G. R. Elton, *Studies in Tudor and Stuart Politics and Government*, 4 vols (Cambridge, 1984–92), i. 66–99.

Elton, G. R., 'Henry VII: Rapacity and Remorse', in G. R. Elton, *Studies in Tudor and Stuart Politics and Government*, 4 vols (Cambridge, 1984–92), i. 45–65.

Elton, G. R., *Studies in Tudor and Stuart Politics and Government*, 4 vols (Cambridge, 1984–92).

Elton, G. R., *The Tudor Revolution in Government: Administrative Changes in the reign of Henry VIII* (Cambridge, 1953).

Emden, A. B., *A Biographical Register of the University of Cambridge to AD 1500* (Cambridge, 1963).

Emden, A. B., *A Biographical Register of the University of Oxford 1500–40* (Oxford, 1974).

Emden, A. B., *A Biographical Register of the University of Oxford to AD 1500*, 3 vols (Oxford, 1957–9).

Emery, A., *Greater Medieval Houses of England and Wales 1300–1550*, 3 vols (Cambridge, 1996–2006).

Evans, T. A. R., 'The Numbers, Origins and Careers of Students', in J. I. Catto and T. A. R. Evans (eds), *History of the University of Oxford*, ii: *Late Medieval Oxford* (Oxford, 1992), 485–538.

Farnham, G. F., *Leicestershire Medieval Village Notes*, 6 vols (Leicester, 1929–33).

Farnham, G. F. and Thompson, A. H., 'The Castle and Manor of Castle Donington', *Transactions of the Leicestershire Archaeological Society* 14 (1925), 31–86.

Farnhill, K., *Guilds and the Parish Community in Late Medieval East Anglia c.1470–1550* (Woodbridge, 2001).

Finch, M. E., *The Wealth of Five Northamptonshire Families, 1540–1640*, Northamptonshire RS 19 (Oxford, 1956).

Fleming, R., 'The Hautes and their "Circle": Culture and the English Gentry', in D. T. Williams (ed.), *England in the Fifteenth Century* (Woodbridge, 1987), 85–102.

Fletcher, A. D., and MacCulloch, D. N. J., *Tudor Rebellions*, 4th edn (London, 1997).

Ford, E., *A History of Enfield* (Enfield, 1873).

Foister, S., *Holbein and England* (New Haven CT and London, 2004).

Foister, S., 'Paintings and Other Works of Art in Sixteenth-Century English Inventories', *Burlington Magazine* 123 (1981), 273–82.

Foster, W., 'Nicholas Gibson and his Free School at Ratcliff', *London Topographical Record* 17 (1936), 1–18.

Frampton, T. S., 'St Mary's, Westenhanger (church destroyed). Rectors and Patrons', *AC* 31 (1915), 82–91.

Garrett-Goodyear, H. 'The Tudor Revival of Quo Warranto and Local Contributions to State Building', in M. S. Arnold et al. (eds), *On the Laws and Customs of England: Essays in honor of Samuel E. Thorne* (Chapel Hill NC, 1981), 231–95.

Giry-Deloison, C., 'Le personnel diplomatique au début du xvie siècle. L'exemple des relations franco-anglaises de l'avènement de Henry VII au Camp du Drap d'Or', *Journal des Savants* (July–Sept 1987), 205–53.

Given-Wilson, C., *The Royal Household and the King's Affinity: Service, Politics and Finance in England, 1360–1413* (New Haven CT and London, 1986).

Glanville, P., 'Cardinal Wolsey and the Goldsmiths', in S. Gunn and P. G. Lindley (eds), *Cardinal Wolsey: Church, State and Art* (Cambridge, 1991), 131–48.

Glass, K., *Bradenham Manor, Past and Present* (n.p., 1985).

Goring, J. J., 'The General Proscription of 1522', *EHR* 86 (1971), 681–705.

Gray A., and Brittain, F., *A History of Jesus College Cambridge* (London, 1979).

Grazebrook, H. S., *The Barons of Dudley*, Collections for a History of Staffordshire 9/2 (London, 1888).

Green, J. A., *The Government of England under Henry I* (Cambridge, 1996).

Greenslade. S. L., 'The Faculty of Theology', in J. McConica (ed.), *History of the University of Oxford*, iii: *The Collegiate University* (Oxford, 1986), 295–334.

Griffin, R., 'An Inscription in Little Chart Church', *AC* 36 (1923), 131–42.

Griffiths, R. A., 'Public and Private Bureaucracies in England and Wales in the Fifteenth Century', *TRHS* 5th ser. 30 (1980), 109–30.

Grummitt, D., *The Calais Garrison: War and Military Service in England, 1436–1558* (Woodbridge, 2008).

Grummitt, D. (ed.), *The English Experience in France: War, Diplomacy and Cultural Exchange, c.1450–1558* (Aldershot, 2002).

Grummitt, D., 'Henry VII, Chamber Finance and the "New Monarchy": Some New Evidence', *HR* 72 (1999), 229–43.

Gunn, S. J., 'The Accession of Henry VIII', *HR* 64 (1991), 278–88.

Gunn, S. J., 'The Act of Resumption of 1515', in D. T. Williams (ed.), *Early Tudor England: Proceedings of the Fourth Harlaxton Symposium* (Woodbridge, 1989), 87–106.

Gunn, S. J., *Charles Brandon, Duke of Suffolk, c.1484–1545* (Oxford, 1988).

Gunn, S. J., 'Chivalry and Politics at the Early Tudor Court', in S. Anglo (ed.), *Chivalry in the Renaissance* (Woodbridge, 1990), 107–28.

Gunn, S. J., 'The Court of Henry VII' in S. J. Gunn and A. Janse (eds), *The Court as a Stage: England and the Low Countries in the Later Middle Ages* (Woodbridge, 2006), 132–44.

Gunn, S. J., 'The Courtiers of Henry VII', *EHR* 108 (1993), 23–49.

Gunn, S. J., 'The Duke of Suffolk's March on Paris in 1523', *EHR* 101 (1986), 596–634.

Gunn, S. J., *Early Tudor Government 1485–1558* (Basingstoke, 1995).

Gunn, S. J., 'Edmund Dudley and the Church', *Journal of Ecclesiastical History* 51 (2000), 509–26.

Gunn, S. J., 'Henry Bourchier, earl of Essex, (1472–1540)', in G. W. Bernard (ed.), *The Tudor Nobility* (Manchester, 1992), 134–79.

Gunn, S. J., 'Politic History, New Monarchy and State Formation: Henry VII in European Perspective' *HR* 82 (2009), 380–92.

Gunn, S. J., 'Prince Arthur's Preparation for Kingship', in S. Gunn and L. Monckton (eds), *Arthur Tudor, Prince of Wales: Life, Death and Commemoration* (Woodbridge, 2009), 7–19.

Gunn, S. J., 'The Rise of the Burgh Family, c.1431–1550', in P. Lindley (ed.), *Gainsborough Old Hall*, Society for Lincolnshire History and Archaeology Occasional Papers 8 (Lincoln, 1991), 8–12.

Gunn, S. J., 'Sir Thomas Lovell (c.1449–1524): A New Man in a New Monarchy?', in J. L. Watts (ed.), *The End of the Middle Ages? England in the Fifteenth and Sixteenth Centuries* (Stroud, 1998), 117–53.

Gunn, S., Grummitt, D., and Cools, H., *War, State and Society in England and the Netherlands, 1477–1559* (Oxford, 2007).

Gunn, S. and Lindley, P. G. (eds), *Cardinal Wolsey: Church, State and Art* (Cambridge, 1991).

Gunn, S. and Monckton L. (eds), *Arthur Tudor, Prince of Wales: Life, Death and Commemoration* (Woodbridge, 2009).

Guy, J. A., *The Cardinal's Court: The Impact of Thomas Wolsey in Star Chamber* (Hassocks, 1977).

Guy, J. A., 'A Conciliar Court of Audit at work in the last months of the reign of Henry VII', *BIHR* 49 (1976), 289–95.

Guy, J. A., 'The Privy Council: Revolution or Evolution?', in C. Coleman and D. Starkey (eds), *Revolution Reassessed: Revisions in the History of Tudor Government and Administration* (Oxford, 1986), 68–85.

Guy, J. A., *The Public Career of Sir Thomas More* (New Haven CT and London, 1980).

Gwyn, P., *The King's Cardinal: The Rise and Fall of Thomas Wolsey* (London, 1990).

Halstead, R., *Succinct Genealogies of the Noble and Ancient Houses of Alno or de Alneto etc* (London, 1685).

Hammond, P. W. and Horrox, R. (eds), *Richard III: Crown and People* (London, 1985).

Hamon, P., 'Jean Breton (v. 1490–1542)', in C. Michon (ed.), *Les Conseillers de François Ier* (Rennes, 2011), 335–42.

Hampton, W. E., 'John Nesfield', in J. Petre (ed.), *Richard III: Crown and People* (London, 1985), 176–83.

Hanham, A., 'Edmund de la Pole, Defector', *Renaissance Studies* 2 (1988), 239–50.

Harcourt, L. W. V., *His Grace the Steward and the Trial of Peers* (London, 1907).

Harris, B. J., *Edward Stafford, Third Duke of Buckingham, 1478–1521* (Stanford CA, 1986).

Harris, B. J., *English Aristocratic Women, 1450–1550* (New York, 2002).

Harrison, G. L., 'A Few Notes on the Lovells of East Harling', *NA* 18 (1912), 46–77.

Harvey, A. P. and Mortimer, R. (eds), *The Funeral Effigies of Westminster Abbey* (Woodbridge, 1994).

Hasler, P. W., *The House of Commons 1558–1603*, 3 vols (London, 1981).

Hasted, E., *The History and Topographical Survey of the County of Kent*, 12 vols (Wakefield, 1972 edn).

Havinden, M. A., 'The Resident Gentry of Somerset, 1502', *Somerset Archaeology and Natural History* 139 (1996), 1–15.

Hay, D., *Polydore Vergil: Renaissance Historian and Man of Letters* (Oxford, 1952).

Hayward, C. F., 'Architectural Notes on Layer Marney Hall, Essex, and on the Parish Church Adjoining', *TEAS* 3 (1865), 16–32.

Hayward, M., *Dress at the Court of King Henry VIII* (Leeds, 2007).

Hayward, M., *Rich Apparel: Clothing and the Law in Henry VIII's England* (Farnham, 2009).

Head, D. M., *The Ebbs and Flows of Fortune: the Life of Thomas Howard, Third Duke of Norfolk* (Athens GA, 1995).

Headley, J. M., 'The Conflict between Nobles and Magistrates in Franche-Comté, 1508–1518', *Journal of Medieval and Renaissance Studies* 9 (1979), 49–80.

Heal, F., *Hospitality in Early Modern England* (Oxford, 1990).

Heal, F., *Of Prelates and Princes: A Study of the Economic and Social Position of the Tudor Episcopate* (Cambridge, 1980).

Hepburn, F., 'The Portraiture of Prince Arthur and Katherine of Aragon', in S. Gunn and L. Monckton (eds), *Arthur Tudor, Prince of Wales: Life, Death and Commemoration* (Woodbridge, 2009), 31–49.

Hewerdine, A., *The Yeomen of the Guard and the Early Tudors: The Formation of a Royal Bodyguard* (London, 2012).

Hicks, M. A., *Bastard Feudalism* (London, 1995).

Hicks, M. A. (ed.), *The Fifteenth-Century Inquisitions Post Mortem: A Companion* (Woodbridge, 2012).

Hoak, D., 'The Iconography of the Crown Imperial', in D. Hoak (ed.), *Tudor Political Culture* (Cambridge, 1995), 54–103.

Hodgett, G. A. J., *Tudor Lincolnshire* (Lincoln, 1975).

Holford, M., '"Notoriously Unreliable": The Valuations and Extents', in M. A. Hicks (ed.), *The Fifteenth-Century Inquisitions Post Mortem: A Companion* (Woodbridge, 2012), 117–44.

Holmes, C., *Seventeenth-Century Lincolnshire* (Lincoln, 1980).

Holmes, P., 'The Great Council in the reign of Henry VII', *EHR* 101 (1986), 840–62.

Hooker, J. R., 'Some Cautionary Notes on Henry VII's Household and Chamber "System"', *Speculum* 33 (1958), 69–75.

Hope, W. H. StJ., *Cowdray and Easebourne Priory* (London, 1919).

Horowitz, M. R., '"Agree with the King": Henry VII, Edmund Dudley and the Strange Case of Thomas Sunnyff', *HR* 79 (2005), 325–66.

Horowitz, M. R., '"Contrary to the Liberties of this City": Henry VII, English Towns and the Economics of Law and Order', *HR* 85 (2012), 32–56.

Horowitz, M. R., 'Henry Tudor's Treasure', *HR* 82 (2009), 560–79.

Horowitz, M. R., 'Policy and Prosecution in the reign of Henry VII', *HR* 82 (2009), 412–58.

Horowitz, M. R., 'Richard Empson, Minister of Henry VII', *BIHR* 55 (1982), 35–49.

Horrox, R. E., *Richard III: A Study of Service* (Cambridge, 1989).

Horrox, R. E., 'Urban Patronage and Patrons in the Fifteenth Century', in R. A. Griffiths (ed.), *Patronage, the Crown and the Provinces in Later Medieval England* (Gloucester, 1986), 145–66.

Howard, M., *The Early Tudor Country House: Architecture and Politics 1490–1550* (London, 1987).

Hoyle, R. W., *The Pilgrimage of Grace and the Politics of the 1530s* (Oxford, 2001).

Hoyle, R. W., 'The fortunes of the Tempest Family of Bracewell and Bowling in the Sixteenth Century', *Yorkshire Archaeological Journal* 74 (2002), 169–89.

Hurst, D. G., 'Post-medieval Britain in 1966', *Post-Medieval Archaeology* 1 (1967), 107–21.

An Inventory of the Historical Monuments in Essex, 4 vols, RCHM (London, 1916–23).

An Inventory of the Historical Monuments in London, 5 vols, RCHM (London, 1924–30).

An Inventory of the Historical Monuments in Middlesex, RCHM (London, 1937).

Ives, E. W., '"Against Taking Away of Women": The Inception and Operation of the Abduction Act of 1487', in E. W. Ives et al. (eds), *Wealth and Power in Tudor England: Essays Presented to S. T. Bindoff* (London, 1978), 21–44.

Ives, E. W., *Anne Boleyn* (Oxford, 1986).

Ives, E. W., *The Common Lawyers of Pre-Reformation England. Thomas Kebell: A Case Study* (Cambridge, 1983).

Ives, E. W., 'Crime, Sanctuary and Royal Authority under Henry VIII: The Exemplary Sufferings of the Savage Family', in M. S. Arnold et al. (eds), *On the Laws and Customs of England: Essays in Honor of Samuel E. Thorne* (Chapel Hill NC, 1981), 296–320.

Ives, E. W. et al. (eds), *Wealth and Power in Tudor England: Essays Presented to S. T. Bindoff* (London, 1978).

Jeffs, R., 'The Poynings–Percy Dispute: An Example of the Interplay of Open Strife and Legal Action in the Fifteenth Century', *BIHR* 34 (1961), 148–64.

Jewitt, L. and Hope, W. H. St J., *The Corporation Plate and Insignia of Office, of the Cities and Corporate Towns of England and Wales*, 2 vols (London, 1985).

Johnson, A. H., *The History of the Worshipful Company of the Drapers of London*, 5 vols (Oxford, 1914–22).

Jones, M., '"For My Lord of Richmond, a *pourpoint*... and a palfrey": Brief Remarks on the Financial Evidence for Henry Tudor's Exile in Brittany 1471–1484', *The Ricardian* 13 (2003), 283–93.

Jones, M. K., 'Lady Margaret Beaufort, the Royal Council and an early Fenland Drainage Scheme', *Lincolnshire History and Archaeology* 21 (1986), 11–18.

Jones, M. K., and Underwood, M. G., *The King's Mother: Lady Margaret Beaufort, Countess of Richmond and Derby* (Cambridge, 1992).

Jordan, W. K., *The Charities of London 1480–1660: The Aspirations and the Achievements of the Urban Society* (London, 1960).

Jordan, W. K., *The Charities of Rural England 1480–1660: The Aspirations and the Achievements of the Rural Society* (London, 1961).

Keene, D. and Harding, V., *Historical Gazeteer of London before the Great Fire, I, Cheapside* (Cambridge, 1987).

King, H. W., 'The Descent of the Manor of Horham, and of the Family of Cutts', *TEAS* 4 (1869), 25–42.

King, W. L., 'Pedigree of the Family of De Fynes', *AC* 28 (1909), 22–7.

Kingdon, J. A., *List of Wardens of the Grocers' Company from 1345 to 1907* (London, 1907).

Kleineke, H., 'Lobbying and Access: The Canons of Windsor and the Matter of the Poor Knights in the Parliament of 1485', *Parliamentary History* 25 (2006), 145–59.

Kleineke, H., '"Morton's Fork"—Henry VII's "Forced Loan" of 1496', *The Ricardian* 13 (2003), 315–27.

Lancashire, I., 'The Auspices of *The World and the Child*', *Renaissance and Reformation* 12 (1976), 96–105.

Lander, J. R., 'Bonds, Coercion and Fear: Henry VII and the Peerage' in his *Crown and Nobility, 1450–1509* (London, 1976), 267–300.

Lander, J. R., *English Justices of the Peace, 1461–1509* (Gloucester, 1989).

Langdon, J., *Mills in the Medieval Economy: England 1300–1540* (Oxford, 2004).

Leadam, I. S., 'The Early Years of the College', in *Brasenose College Quartercenenary Monographs*, Volume ii Part i, OHS 53 (Oxford, 1909), 3–212.

Lee, F. G., *The History, Description and Antiquities of the Prebendal Church of the Blessed Virgin Mary of Thame* (London, 1883).

Lee, J., 'Urban Policy and Urban Political Culture: Henry VII and his Towns', *HR* 82 (2009), 493–510.

Lee, J., 'Urban Recorders and the Crown in Late Medieval England', in L. Clark (ed.), *Authority and Subversion*, The Fifteenth Century 3 (Woodbridge, 2003), 163–79.

Lehmberg, S. E., *The Later Parliaments of Henry VIII 1536–1547* (Cambridge, 1977).

Le Neve, J., *Fasti ecclesiae anglicanae 1300–1541: Bath and Wells*, ed. B. Jones (London, 1964).

Le Neve, J., *Fasti ecclesiae anglicanae 1300–1541: Hereford*, ed. J. M. Horn (London, 1962).

Le Neve, J., *Fasti ecclesiae anglicanae 1300–1541: Salisbury*, ed. J. M. Horn (London, 1962).

Le Neve, J., *Fasti ecclesiae anglicanae 1300–1541: St Paul's London*, ed. J. M. Horn (London, 1963).

Lewis, G. R., *The Stannaries: a Study of the English Tin Miner* (Boston MA and New York, 1908).

Lexton, R., 'Henry Medwall's *Fulgens and Lucrece* and the Question of Nobility under Henry VII', in L. Clark (ed.), *Rule, Redemption and Representations in Late Medieval England and France* (Woodbridge, 2008), 163–82.

Lieberich, H., *Landherren und Landleute: Zur politischen Führungsschicht Baierns im Spätmittelalter* (Munich, 1964).

Lindley, P., '"The Singuler Mediacions and Praiers of al the Holie Companie of Heven": Sculptural Functions and Forms in Henry VII's Chapel', in T. Tatton-Brown and R. Mortimer (eds), *Westminster Abbey: The Lady Chapel of Henry VII* (Woodbridge, 2003), 259–93.

List of Escheators for England and Wales, List and Index Society 72 (London, 1971).

List of Sheriffs for England and Wales, PRO Lists and Indexes 9 (London, 1898).

Lloyd, D., *State-worthies, or, The states-men and favourites of England since the reformation their prudence and policies, successes and miscarriages, advancements and falls, during the reigns of King Henry VIII, King Edward VI, Queen Mary, Queen Elizabeth, King James, King Charles I* (London, 1670 edn).

Loades, D. M., *John Dudley, Duke of Northumberland 1504–1553* (Oxford, 1996).

Loades, D. M., *Mary Tudor: A Life* (Oxford, 1989).

Loades, D. M., *The Tudor Court* (Bangor, 1992 edn).

Loades, D. M., *The Tudor Navy: An Administrative, Political and Military History* (Aldershot, 1992).

Luckett, D. A., 'Crown Office and Licensed Retinues in the Reign of Henry VII', in R. Archer and S. Walker (eds), *Rulers and Ruled in Late Medieval England: Essays presented to Gerald Harriss* (London, 1995), 223–38.

Luckett, D. A., 'Henry VII and the South-Western Escheators', in B. Thompson (ed.), *The Reign of Henry VII* (Stamford, 1995), 54–64.

Luckett, D. A., 'The Rise and Fall of a Noble Dynasty: Henry VII and the Lords Willoughby de Broke', *HR* 69 (1996), 254–65.

Lutton, R., 'Richard Guldeford's Pilgrimage: Piety and Cultural Change in Late Fifteenth- and Early Sixteenth-Century England', *History* 98 (2013), 41–78.

McConica, J. (ed.), *History of the University of Oxford, iii: The Collegiate University* (Oxford, 1986).

McConica, J., 'The Rise of the Undergraduate College' in J. McConica (ed.), *History of the University of Oxford, iii: The Collegiate University* (Oxford, 1986), 1–68.

MacCulloch, D. N. J., 'Bondmen under the Tudors', in C. Cross et al. (eds), *Law and Government under the Tudors: Essays Presented to Sir Geoffrey Elton on his Retirement* (Cambridge, 1988), 91–109.

MacCulloch, D. N. J., *Suffolk and the Tudors: Politics and Religion in an English County 1500–1600* (Oxford, 1986).

MacCulloch, D. N. J., *Thomas Cranmer: A Life* (New Haven CT and London, 1996).

McGlynn, M., *The Royal Prerogative and the Learning of the Inns of Court* (Cambridge, 2003).

McGlynn, M., '"Of Good Name and Fame in the Countrey": Standards of Conduct for Henry VII's Chamber Officials', *HR* 82 (2009), 547–59.

McIntosh, M.K., *Autonomy and Community: The Royal Manor of Havering, 1200–1500* (Cambridge, 1986).

McIntosh, M.K., *Controlling Misbehaviour in England, 1370–1600* (Cambridge, 1998).

Manning, R. B., *Hunters and Poachers: A Cultural and Social History of Unlawful Hunting in England 1485–1640* (Oxford, 1993).

Markham, F., *A History of Milton Keynes and District*, 2 vols (Luton, 1973–5).

Marks, R. and Williamson, P. (eds), *Gothic: Art for England 1400–1547* (London, 2003).

Marsh, C., *Popular Religion in Sixteenth-Century England* (Basingstoke, 1998).

Marshall, P., *The Catholic Priesthood and the English Reformation* (Oxford, 1994).

Martin, D. and Martin, B., 'Westenhanger Castle—A Revised Interpretation', *AC* 121 (2001), 207–29.

Mate, M., *Trade and Economic Developments, 1450–1550: The Experience of Kent, Surrey and Sussex* (Woodbridge, 2006).

Matthew, H. C. G. and Harrison, B. (eds), *Oxford Dictionary of National Biography*, 60 vols (Oxford, 2004).

Mattingly, G., *Renaissance Diplomacy* (London, 1955).

Mayhew, G., *Tudor Rye* (Falmer, 1987).

Meale, C. M. and Boffey, J., 'Gentlewomen's Reading', in L. Hellinga and J. B. Trapp (eds), *The Cambridge History of the Book in Britain*, iii: *1400–1557* (Cambridge, 1999), 526–40.

Meek, E. L., 'The Career of Sir Thomas Everingham, "Knight of the North"', in the Service of Maximillian, Duke of Austria, 1477–81', *HR* 74 (2001), 238–48.

Michon, C. (ed.), *Conseils et conseillers dans l'Europe de la Renaissance v.1450–v.1550* (Tours/Rennes, 2012).

Miller, H., 'Attendance in the House of Lords during the Reign of Henry VIII', *Historical Journal* 10 (1967), 325–51.

Miller, H., 'London and Parliament in the Reign of Henry VIII', *BIHR* 35 (1962), 128–49.

Miller, H., *Henry VIII and the English Nobility* (Oxford, 1986).

Minet, W., 'The Capells at Rayne, 1486–1622', *TEAS* n.s. 9 (1906), 243–72.

Morant, P., *The History and Antiquities of the County of Essex*, 2 vols (East Ardsley, 1978 edn).

Moreton, C. E., *The Townshends and their World: Gentry, Law and Land in Norfolk c.1450–1551* (Oxford, 1992).

Morgan, D. A. L., 'The King's Affinity in the Polity of Yorkist England', *TRHS* 5th ser. 23 (1973), 1–25.

Morgan, N., 'The *Scala Coeli* Indulgence and the Royal Chapels', in B. Thompson (ed.), *The Reign of Henry VII* (Stamford, 1995), 82–103.

Mosley, C. (ed.), *Burke's Peerage, Baronetage & Knightage: Clan Chiefs, Scottish Feudal Barons*, 107th edn, 3 vols (Wilmington DE, 2003).

Murray, K. M. E., *The Constitutional History of the Cinque Ports* (Manchester, 1935).

Myers, A. R., *The Household of Edward IV* (Manchester, 1959).

Newcourt, R., *Repertorium ecclesiasticum parochiale Londinense*, 2 vols (London, 1708–10).

Nichols, J., *The History and Antiquities of the County of Leicester*, 4 vols in 8 (Wakefield, 1971 edn).

O'Donohue, E. G., *Bridewell Hospital, Palace, Prison, Schools* (London, 1923).

Ollard, S. L., *Fasti Wyndesorienses* (Windsor, 1950).

O'Malley, G., *The Knights Hospitaller of the English Langue 1460–1565* (Oxford, 2005).

Owen, H., and Blakeway, J. B., *A History of Shrewsbury*, 2 vols (London, 1825).

Palliser, D. M. (ed.), *The Cambridge Urban History of Britain*, i: *600–1540* (Cambridge, 2000).

Palmer, A. N., 'Isycoed, County Denbigh', *Archaeologia Cambrensis*, 6th ser. 10 (1910), 229–70.

Pam, D., *A Parish Near London* (Enfield, 1990).

Payne, E. J. 'The Montforts, the Wellesbournes and the Hughenden effigies', *Records of Buckinghamshire* 7 (1896), 362–402.

Penn, T., *Winter King: The Dawn of Tudor England* (London, 2011).

Petre, J. (ed.), *Richard III: Crown and People* (London, 1985).

Pevsner, N., *North-West and South-West Norfolk* (Harmondsworth, 1962).

Pierce, H., *Margaret Pole, Countess of Salisbury, 1473–1541: Loyalty, Lineage and Leadership* (Cardiff, 2003).

Pollard, A. F., *Wolsey* (London, 1953 edn).

Polsue, J., *Lake's Parochial History of the County of Cornwall*, 4 vols (Wakefield, 1974).

Polwhele, R., *The History of Devonshire*, 3 vols (London, 1793–1806).

Poulson, G., *The History and Antiquities of the Seignory of Holderness*, 2 vols (London, 1840–1).

Powell, E., 'Arbitration and the Law in England in the Late Midde Ages', *TRHS* 5th ser. 33 (1983), 49–67.

Powell, S., 'Margaret Pole and Syon Abbey', *HR* 79 (2005), 563–7.

Power, G., *A European Frontier Elite: The Nobility of the English Pale in Ireland, 1496–1566* (Hanover, 2012).

Preston, A. E., *The Church and Parish of St Nicholas Abingdon*, OHS 99 (Oxford, 1935).

Pugh, R. B., *Imprisonment in Medieval England* (Cambridge, 1968).

Pugh, T. B., 'Henry VII and the English Nobility', in G. W. Bernard (ed.), *The Tudor Nobility* (Manchester, 1992), 49–110.

Ramsay, G. D., *The City of London in International Politcs at the accession of Elizabeth Tudor* (Manchester, 1975).

Reddaway, T. F. and Walker, L. E. M., *The Early History of the Goldsmiths' Company, 1327–1509* (London, 1975).

Richards, G. C. and Shadwell, C. L., *The Provosts and Fellows of Oriel College, Oxford* (Oxford, 1922).

Richardson, W. C., *Mary Tudor, the White Queen* (London, 1970).

Richardson, W. C., 'The Surveyor of the King's Prerogative', *EHR* 56 (1941), 63–75.

Richardson, W. C., *Tudor Chamber Administration, 1485–1547* (Baton Rouge LA, 1952).

Richmond, C., *The Paston Family in the Fifteenth Century: Fastolf's Will* (Cambridge, 1996).

Richmond, C., *The Paston Family in the Fifteenth Century: The First Phase* (Cambridge, 1990).

Rigby, S. H. and Ewan, E., 'Government, Power and Authority 1300–1540', in D. M. Palliser (ed.), *The Cambridge Urban History of Britain*, i: *600–1540* (Cambridge, 2000), 291–312.

Robertson, M. L., 'The Art of the Possible: Thomas Cromwell's Management of West Country Government', *HJ* 32 (1989), 793–816.

Robertson, W. A. S., 'The Passion Play and Interludes at New Romney', *AC* 13 (1879), 216–26.

Robertson, W. A. S., 'Peche of Lullingstone', *AC* 16 (1886), 227–40.

Robinson, W., *The History and Antiquities of Enfield, in the County of Middlesex*, 2 vols (London, 1823).

Robinson, W. R. B., 'The Administration of the Lordship of Monmouth under Henry VII', *The Monmouthshire Antiquary* 18 (2002), 23–40.

Robinson, W. R. B., 'Family and Fortune: The Domestic Affairs of Edward Sutton (d. 1532), Lord Dudley', *Staffordshire Studies* 10 (1998), 29–48.

Rosenfield, M. C., 'Holy Trinity, Aldgate, on the eve of the Dissolution', *Guildhall Miscellany* 3 (1969–71), 159–73.

Roskell, J. S. et al., *History of Parliament: The House of Commons 1386–1421*, 4 vols (Stroud, 1992).

Ross, J., *John de Vere, Thirteenth Earl of Oxford (1442–1513):'The Foremost Man of the Kingdom'* (Woodbridge, 2011).

Rowse, A. L., *Tudor Cornwall* (London, 1941).

Rushforth, G. McN., *Medieval Christian Imagery as Illustrated by the Painted Windows of Great Malvern Priory Church Worcestershire* (Oxford, 1936).

Russell, J. G., *The Field of Cloth of Gold: Men and Manners in 1520* (London, 1969).

Sainty, J. C., *Officers of the Exchequer*, List and Index Society Special Series 18 (London, 1983).

Samman, N., 'The Progresses of Henry VIII, 1509–1529', in D. N. J. MacCulloch (ed.), *The Reign of Henry VIII: Politics, Policy and Piety* (Basingstoke, 1995), 59–73.

Saul, N., 'The Cuckoo in the Nest: A Dallingridge Tomb in the Fitzalan Chapel at Arundel', *Sussex Archaeological Collections* 147 (2009), 125–33.

Scarisbrick, J. J., 'Cardinal Wolsey and the Common Weal', in E. W. Ives et al. (eds), *Wealth and Power in Tudor England: Essays Presented to S. T. Bindoff* (London, 1978), 45–67.

Schnur, R. (ed.), *Die Rolle der Juristen bei der Entstehung des modernen Staates* (Berlin, 1986).

Schofield, P. R., *Peasant and Community in Medieval England, 1200–1500* (Basingstoke, 2003).

Schofield, R., 'Taxation and the Political Limits of the Tudor State' in C. Cross et al. (eds), *Law and Government under the Tudors: Essays Presented to Sir Geoffrey Elton on his Retirement* (Cambridge, 1988), 227–55.

Scott, J. R., *Memorials of the Family of Scott of Scot's-Hall* (London, 1876).

Shagan, E., *Popular Politics and the English Reformation* (Cambridge, 2003).

Sicca, C. M., 'Consumption and Trade of Art between Italy and England in the First Half of the Sixteenth Century: the London House of the Bardi and Cavalcanti Company', *Renaissance Studies* 16 (2002), 163–201.

Sicca, C. M., 'Pawns of International Finance and Politics: Florentine Sculptors at the Court of Henry VIII', *Renaissance Studies* 20 (2006), 1–34.

Shaw, W. A., *The Knights of England*, 2 vols (London, 1906).

Slack, P. A., *Poverty and Policy in Tudor and Stuart England* (London, 1988).

Slavin, A. J., *Politics and Profit: a Study of Sir Ralph Sadler, 1507–1547* (Cambridge, 1966).

Smith, A., '"The Greatest Man of that Age": The Acquisition of Sir John Fastolf's East Anglian Estates', in R. Archer and S. Walker (eds), *Rulers and Ruled in Late Medieval England: Essays presented to Gerald Harriss* (London, 1995), 137–53.

Smith, A. G. R., *Servant of the Cecils: the Life of Sir Michael Hickes, 1543–1612* (London, 1977).

Smith, A. H., *County and Court: Government and Politics in Norfolk, 1558–1603* (Oxford, 1974).

Smith, J. B., 'Crown and Community in the Principality of North Wales in the Reign of Henry Tudor', *Welsh History Review* 3 (1966), 145–71.

Smith, R. B., *Land and Politics in the England of Henry VIII: The West Riding of Yorkshire, 1530–1546* (Oxford, 1970).

Smyth, J., *The Berkeley Manuscripts: The Lives of the Berkeleys, Lords of the Honour, Castle and Manor of Berkeley in the County of Gloucester from 1066 to 1618, with a Description of the Hundred of Berkeley and of its Inhabitants*, ed. J. Maclean, 3 vols (Gloucester, 1883–5).

Somerville, R., 'Henry VII's "Council Learned in the Law"', *EHR* 54 (1939), 427–42.

Somerville, R., *A History of the Duchy of Lancaster, I, 1265–1603* (London, 1953).

Squibb, G. D., *Doctors' Commons: A History of the College of Advocates and Doctors of Law* (Oxford, 1977).

Starkey, D. R., 'Court, Council and Nobility in Tudor England', in R. G. Asch and A. M. Birke (eds), *Princes, Patronage and Nobility: The Court at the beginning of the Modern Age, c.1450–1650* (Oxford, 1991), 175–203.

Starkey, D. R., 'England', in R. Porter and M. Teich (eds), *The Renaissance in National Context* (Cambridge, 1992), 146–63.

Starkey, D. R., *Henry: Virtuous Prince* (London, 2008).

Starkey, D. R., 'Intimacy and Innovation: The Rise of the Privy Chamber, 1485–1547', in D. R. Starkey (ed.), *The English Court from the Wars of the Roses to the Civil War* (London, 1987), 71–118.

Starkey, D. R., *The Reign of Henry VIII: Personalities and Politics* (London, 1985).

Starkey, D. R. (ed.), *Henry VIII: A European Court in England* (London, 1991).

Stein, R. (ed.), *Powerbrokers in the Late Middle Ages* (Turnhout, 2001).

Stewart-Brown, R., 'The Cheshire Writs of Quo Warranto in 1499', *EHR* 49 (1934), 676–84.

Stone, L., *Family and Fortune: Studies in Aristocratic Finance in the Sixteenth and Seventeenth Centuries* (Oxford, 1973).

Storey, R. L., 'Gentlemen-bureaucrats', in C. L. Clough (ed.), *Profession, Vocation and Culture in Later Medieval England: Essays Dedicated to the Memory of A.R. Myers* (Liverpool, 1982), 97–119.

Storey, R. L., 'University and Government 1430–1500', in J. I. Catto and T. A. R. Evans (eds), *History of the University of Oxford*, ii: *Late Medieval Oxford* (Oxford, 1992), 709–46.

Streitberger, W. R., *Court Revels, 1485–1559* (Toronto, 1994).

Summers, N., 'Old Hall Farm, Kneesall', *Transactions of the Thoroton Society* 76 (1972), 17–25.

Summerson, H., *Medieval Carlisle: The City and the Borders from the Late Eleventh to the mid-Sixteenth Century*, 2 vols, Cumberland and Westmorland Antiquarian and Archaeological Society, extra ser. 25 (Kendal, 1993).

The Survey of London, ed. C. R. Asbee et al., 50 vols (London, 1900–).

Sutton, A. F., *The Mercery of London: Trade, Goods and People, 1130–1578* (Aldershot, 2005).

Tatton-Brown, T., 'Church Building on Romney Marsh in the Later Middle Ages', *AC* 107 (1989), 253–65.

Tatton-Brown, T., 'The Constructional Sequence and Topography of the Chapel and College Buildings at St George's', in C. Richmond and E. Scarff (eds), *St George's Chapel, Windsor, in the Late Middle Ages* (Windsor, 2001), 3–38.

Tatton-Brown, T. and Mortimer, R. (eds), *Westminster Abbey: The Lady Chapel of Henry VII* (Woodbridge, 2003).

Temperley, G., *Henry VII* (London, 1917).

Thiry, S., 'De constructie van een vorstelijk imago: Perkin Warbeck in de Nederlanden en het Heilige Roomse Rijk', *Tijdschrift voor Geschiedenis* 124 (2011), 156–73.

Thompson, B. (ed.), *The Reign of Henry VII* (Stamford, 1995).

Thompson, P., *The History and Antiquities of Boston* (Sleaford, 1997).

Thomson, J. A. F., *The Early Tudor Church and Society, 1485–1529* (London, 1993).

Thornton, T., *Cheshire and the Tudor State, 1480–1560* (Woodbridge, 2000).

Thoroton, R., *The Antiquities of Nottinghamshire*, 3 vols (Wakefield, 1972).

Thurley, S., 'The Domestic Building Works of Cardinal Wolsey', in S. Gunn and P. G. Lindley (eds), *Cardinal Wolsey: Church, State and Art* (Cambridge, 1991), 76–102.

Thurley, S., *The Royal Palaces of Tudor England* (New Haven CT and London, 1993).

Tittler, R., *The Face of the City: Civic Portraiture and Civic Identity in Early Modern England* (Manchester, 2007).

Trollope, E., *Sleaford and the Wapentakes of Flaxwell and Aswardhurn in the County of Lincoln* (London, 1872).

Turner, R. V., *Men Raised from the Dust: Administrative Service and Upward Mobility in Angevin England* (Philadelphia PA, 1988).

Underwood, M., 'The Impact of St John's College as Landowner in the West Fields of Cambridge in the early Sixteenth Century', in P. Zutshi (ed.), *Medieval Cambridge: Essays on the Pre-Reformation University* (Woodbridge, 1993), 167–88.

Van Peteghem, P. P. J. L., *De Raad van Vlaanderen en staatsvorming onder Karel V (1515–1555): Een publiekechtelijk onderzoek naar contralisatiestreven in de XVII Provinciën* (Nijmegen, 1990).

Venn, J. and Venn, J. A., *Alumni Cantabrigienses*, 10 vols (Cambridge, 1922–54).

The Victoria History of the County of Berkshire, ed. P. Ditchfield et al., 4 vols (London, 1906–27).

The Victoria History of the County of Buckingham, ed. W. Page, 5 vols (London, 1905–28).

The Victoria History of the County of Cambridge and the Isle of Ely, ed. L. F. Salzman et al., 10 vols (London, 1938–2002).

The Victoria History of the County of Essex, ed. H. A. Doubleday et al., 11 vols (London, 1903–).

The Victoria History of the County of Hertford, ed. W. Page, 5 vols (London, 1902–23).

The Victoria History of the County of Kent, ed. W. Page, 3 vols (London, 1908–32).

The Victoria History of the County of Lancaster, ed. W. Farrer and J. Brownbill, 8 vols (London, 1906–14).

The Victoria History of the County of Middlesex, ed. W. Page et al., 13 vols (London, 1911–).

The Victoria History of the County of Northampton, ed. W. Adkins et al., 7 vols (London, 1902–).

The Victoria History of the County of Oxford, ed. W. Page et al., 17 vols (London, 1907–).

The Victoria History of the County of Rutland, ed. W. Page, 2 vols (London, 1908–36).

The Victoria History of the County of Stafford, ed. W. Page et al., 14 vols (London, 1908–).

The Victoria History of the County of Surrey, ed. H. E. Malden, 4 vols (London, 1902–14).

The Victoria History of the County of Sussex, ed. W. Page et al., 9 vols in 11 (London, 1905–).

The Victoria History of the County of Warwick, ed. H. A. Doubleday et al., 8 vols (London, 1904–69).

The Victoria History of the County of York: North Riding ed. W. Page, 2 vols (London, 1914–25).

The Victoria History of Hampshire and the Isle of Wight, ed. H. A. Doubleday and W. Page, 6 vols (London, 1900–14).

The Victoria History of Wiltshire, ed. R. B. Pugh et al., 18 vols (London, 1953–).

Virgoe, R., 'Sir John Risley (1443–1512), Courtier and Councillor', *NA* 38 (1981–3), 140–8.

Wakelin, D., *Humanism, Reading, and English Literature 1430–1530* (Oxford, 2007).

Wall, A., 'Patterns of politics in England, 1558–1625', *HJ* 31 (1988), 947–63.

Watts, J. L., '"A New Ffundacion of is Crowne": Monarchy in the Age of Henry VII', in B. Thompson (ed.), *The Reign of Henry VII* (Stamford, 1995), 31–53.

Watts, J. L. (ed.), *The End of the Middle Ages? England in the Fifteenth and Sixteenth Centuries* (Stroud, 1998).

Webb, E. A., *The Records of St Bartholomew's Priory and of the Church and Parish of St Bartholomew the Great West Smithfield*, 2 vols (Oxford, 1921).

Wedgwood, J. C., *History of Parliament: Biographies of the Members of the Commons House, 1439–1509* (London, 1936).

Welch, C., *History of the Worshipful Company of Pewterers*, 2 vols (London, 1902).

Westervelt, T., 'The Changing Nature of Politics in the Localities in the later Fifteenth Century: William Lord Hastings and his Indentured Retainers', *Midland History* 26 (2001) 96–106.

Whittle, J., *The Development of Agrarian Capitalism: Land and Labour in Norfolk, 1440–1580* (Oxford, 2000).

Williams, D. T. (ed.), *England in the Fifteenth Century* (Woodbridge, 1987).

Willmore, F. W., *A History of Walsall and its Neighbourhood* (Walsall, 1887).

Wolffe, B. P., *The Crown Lands, 1461–1536* (London, 1970).

Wolffe, B. P., *The Royal Demesne in English History: The Crown Estate in the Governance of the Realm from the Conquest to 1509* (London, 1971).

Woolgar, C. M., *The Great Household in Late Medieval England* (New Haven CT and London, 1999).

Wright, S. M., *The Derbyshire Gentry in the Fifteenth Century*, Derbyshire RS 8 (Chesterfield, 1983).

Wrightson, K., *Earthy Necessities: Economic Lives in Early Modern Britain, 1470–1750* (London, 2002 edn).

Yates, M., *Town and Countryside in Western Berkshire c.1327–c.1600: Social and Economic Change* (Woodbridge, 2007).

Zell, M. L., 'Early Tudor JPs at Work', *AC* 93 (1977), 125–43.

UNPUBLISHED THESES

Ford, L. L., 'Conciliar Politics and Administration in the Reign of Henry VII', University of St Andrews Ph.D. Thesis (2001).

Peberdy, R., 'The Economy, Society and Government of a Small Town in late medieval England: a study of Henley-on-Thames from c1300 to c1540', University of Leicester Ph.D. Thesis (1994).

Index

Places in England and Wales are given in their early sixteenth-century counties.